Volume 3 — Eι

M000305183

1999
Edition

Dow Jones

Guide to the

Global

Stock

Market

By the Editors of Dow Jones & Company, Inc.

In association with  Worldscope/Disclosure

Contents: Volume 3

Europe/Africa

Introduction to Europe/Africa

Harold H. Seneker
Publications Editor, Dow Jones Indexes

The year ended June 30, 1998, was nothing short of spectacular for this region of the world. As well as the U.S. stock markets performed (see The Americas volume), Europe's performed better.

In general, the world's expectations for the EC economies was rising along with the performance of the economies themselves, and it showed in their stock markets. Buzz about the much-awaited common currency unit, the euro, and the advantages of closer economic union that are supposed to follow on, no doubt also helped. Furthermore, western Europe largely escaped the debt-and-currency crises shaking other parts of the world. It probably did not hurt that for a few years now, the prospective economic union has pressed many of the EC countries to follow deficit-reducing, interest-rate-moderating policies to meet the guideline requirements for inclusion.

Consider Europe's Big Three: Britain, Germany, and France. In The City, U.K. shares were bid up 31.6% (in terms of total return in U.S. dollars, as are all other comparisons on this page), the only one of these that didn't beat the United States. The Paris Bourse roared ahead 45.6% for the 12 months. And in Frankfurt, German shares ran up 44.9%.

Both were well ahead of the strong performance of the U.S. markets (up 31.0%) and all three closed close to their 52-week highs. Together, they accounted for 56% of this region's total market cap. But drill down deeper, and Europe's performance gets even more impressive.

Switzerland, number four (9.94% of the region's market cap), ran ahead 32.6%; and little Holland (number five at 8.29%) rose 33.5%. Beyond those, it turns out that five out of the five top-performing stock markets

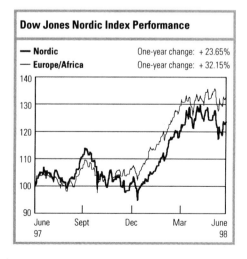

Dow Jones Europe/Africa Index Performance

— Europe (ex. U.K. and S. Africa) One-year change: + 35.07%
— Europe/Africa One-year change: + 32.15%

Dow Jones Nordic Index Performance

— Nordic One-year change: + 23.65%
— Europe/Africa One-year change: + 32.15%

of the 34 we tracked worldwide were European markets: Belgium (up 50.1%), Finland (up 55.5%), Ireland (56.2%), Portugal (57.2%), and the world champ, Italy, up 61.5% for the 52 weeks.

Weren't there any losers? Well, yes. There was a bear market in South Africa (down 34.0%), exacerbated by a bear market in precious metals stocks generally (the Dow Jones Index for this industrial category was down 32.4% worldwide). And there was a weak performance in Norway, where falling prices for the North Sea oil that heavily affects its economy evidently hurt.

But even with those figured in, the Dow Jones Index for this region closed out June, 1998, up 35.2% for the 52-week period (these last two countries accounted for only 2.04% and 0.78%, respectively, of the region's total market cap).

Altogether, of 17 countries included here, 11 outperformed the world's de facto benchmark, the U.S. markets.

If anything, this performance is all the more striking because the United States is noticeably more heavily weighted toward technology stocks, which on balance did well, than is Europe. The Europeans are noticeably heavier in financial stocks — yet U.S. bank stocks dramatically outperformed bank stocks elsewhere during this year. For Europe to outperform the United States anyway indicates that a very broad-based bull market prevailed in Europe, and that

should bode well for this region's relative performance compared to the rest of the World Index which, by the way, managed only a 14.5% gain.

Dow Jones STOXX

Dow Jones, Deutsche Börse, SBF-Bourse de Pari,s and Schweizer Börse have together founded a new company, named STOXX Limited, and created a new family of indexes. They consist of 4 major indexes and 19 sector indexes calculated for western Europe and the EURO Zone. The four major indexes are:
- Dow Jones STOXX
- Dow Jones STOXX 50
- Dow Jones EURO STOXX
- Dow Jones EURO STOXX 50

Securities are selected for Dow Jones STOXX so as to represent the largest and most liquid securities in the market and to reflect the economic sector breakdown of the market. The goal is to represent 80% of the investable universe of each market. There are about 650 stocks in this index.

Dow Jones EURO STOXX is a subset of Dow Jones STOXX. Only companies from countries that are part of the European Monetary Union are included in Dow Jones EURO STOXX. There are about 325 stocks in this index.

The European and EURO sector indexes comprise the same components as the respective broad indexes.

Dow Jones STOXX 50 is a subset of 50 companies in the European broad index with the intent of reflecting the leading blue-chip companies in each sector. Dow Jones EURO STOXX 50 is a subset of 50 companies of Dow Jones EURO STOXX with the intent of reflecting the sector leaders.

The purpose of these indexes is to provide a definitive standard for measuring stock market performance on a European and EUROwide basis, and to provide a liquid base for derivative products. Dow Jones STOXX and Dow Jones EURO STOXX and their respective sector indexes provide the standard for measuring stock market performance, while the European and the EURO blue-chip indexes are designed for derivative products.

The methodology used to construct and maintain the indexes aims to produce an investable index in which all constituent stocks are readily accessible and are well-traded. The indexes offer a historical perspective dating back to 1991.

The indexes are capitalization-weighed and are calculated on both a price- and a total-return basis. All price indexes (in ECU initially and in Euro from 1999 forward) are calculated in real-time and are disseminated every 15 seconds. The total return indexes and indexes in U.S. dollars are calculated and disseminated at the end of each trading day.

Calculation of the indexes is based on Laspeyres' Formula.

The Dow Jones STOXX family of indexes is available from major data vendors and appears daily in *The Wall Street Journal Europe* and in U.S. editions of *The Wall Street Journal* and *Barron's*.

Greenwich Mean Time (GMT): Originating on the Greenwich Meridian, this is the basis for estimating Standard Time.

Standard Time: Legal time of a region or country that is a fixed number of hours differing from the Greenwich Mean Time.

Daylight Saving Time (DST): A period of time, usually during the summer months, that is one hour ahead of Standard Time.

Europe/Africa: DST is observed in most European countries from the last Sunday in March until the last Sunday in October. However, South Africa does not observe DST.

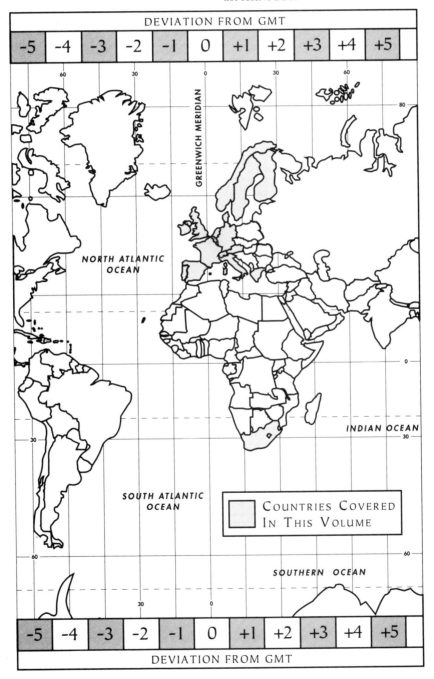

Regional Statistical Overview

Dow Jones Global Indexes Regional Performance Evaluation Table

In U.S. Dollars

Region/Country	6/30/98 Closing Index	% Chg from 12/31/97	12 Mo. Chg %	12 Mo. High	12 Mo. Low	P/E Ratio	P/B Ratio
Europe/Africa	**235.01**	**24.48**	**32.14**	**241.61**	**173.48**	**25.61**	**3.18**
Austria	126.98	16.95	16.09	141.18	102.77	19.08	2.09
Belgium	254.99	43.38	46.49	254.99	162.85	20.37	2.89
Denmark	196.16	6.54	25.50	209.62	156.77	20.83	2.81
Finland	490.73	57.99	52.34	494.22	297.78	18.11	2.82
France	217.58	38.08	42.58	222.03	143.85	31.36	2.91
Germany	260.79	34.99	41.84	263.69	170.33	28.81	3.63
Greece	231.99	53.22	44.27	260.01	137.69	27.33	5.24
Ireland	320.07	31.64	53.10	337.00	209.41	18.22	3.33
Italy	206.22	32.46	58.86	230.56	130.91	44.27	2.52
Netherlands	335.90	26.14	30.58	348.09	249.02	21.26	3.65
Norway	160.35	-5.92	-4.74	198.66	150.24	15.46	1.95
Portugal	304.92	34.00	55.32	361.91	192.71	30.44	4.91
South Africa	87.33	-15.31	-35.69	136.74	87.33	10.77	1.75
Spain	256.87	40.56	44.31	268.00	157.09	27.64	3.27
Sweden	297.91	24.85	21.19	312.17	223.96	22.25	3.49
Switzerland	392.70	20.14	30.81	400.81	275.25	54.47	2.51
United Kingdom	200.53	14.51	27.80	208.94	158.36	21.96	3.74
Europe/Africa (ex. S. Africa)	243.39	25.68	35.08	249.00	176.77	26.32	3.23
Europe/Africa (ex.U.K. & S.A.)	270.15	30.94	38.14	276.89	187.71	28.70	3.06

Indexes based on 6/30/82=100 for U.S., 12/31/91=100 for World.

Best Performing Countries in Europe/Africa in Local Currency
Year Ending 06/30/98

Country	Return
Italy	66.84%
Portugal	63.37%
Finland	61.07%
Greece	60.12%
Ireland	52.87%

Worst Performing Countries in Europe/Africa in Local Currency
Year Ending 06/30/98

Country	Return
South Africa	-15.45%
Norway	-0.41%
Austria	20.00%
Sweden	25.30%
UK	27.61%

Best Performing Countries in Europe/Africa in U.S. Dollars
Year Ending 06/30/98

Country	Return
Italy	58.86%
Portugal	55.32%
Ireland	53.10%
Finland	52.34%
Belgium	46.49%

Worst Performing Countries in Europe/Africa in U.S. Dollars
Year Ending 06/30/98

Country	Return
South Africa	-35.69%
Norway	-4.74%
Austria	16.09%
Sweden	21.19%
Denmark	25.50%

Regional Company Rankings for Europe/Africa

Largest Companies – Market Capitalization

as of 06/30/98

Company	Country	Industry	Market Cap (U.S. mil)	P/E	P/B	Dividend Yield %
Royal Dutch/Shell Group	Netherlands/UK	OIL	187,763	26.99	3.27	2.75
Glaxo Wellcome	United Kingdom	DRG	107,944	34.60	35.07	1.95
Novartis	Switzerland	DRG	102,698	33.21	6.45	0.99
Unilever Group	Netherlands/UK	OFD	85,502	16.57	7.40	1.38
British Petroleum	United Kingdom	OIL	84,896	20.18	3.62	2.57
Nestlé	Switzerland	OFD	84,074	31.89	5.23	1.08
Allianz	Germany	INF	80,191	53.23	7.90	0.31
BT	United Kingdom	TLS	79,172	27.72	4.40	2.57
UBS Group	Switzerland	BAN	76,916	NMF	0.66	9.16
Lloyds TSB	United Kingdom	BAN	75,931	19.19	7.38	2.05
Deutsche Telekom	Germany	TLS	75,270	42.61	2.91	2.42
France Telecom	France	TLS	68,800	28.06	4.45	1.56
Roche Holding AG	Switzerland	DRG	68,757	NMF	7.04	0.56
SmithKline Beecham	United Kingdom	DRG	67,964	36.94	23.75	1.39
ING	Netherlands	FIS	60,078	21.63	2.36	1.73
CS Holding	Switzerland	FIS	59,164	NMF	4.77	1.48
Daimler-Benz	Germany	AUT	55,442	11.47	2.63	0.90
ENI	Italy	OIS	52,280	20.03	3.66	2.40
Ericsson	Sweden	CMT	52,131	36.93	8.63	0.75
Aegon	Netherlands	INF	50,385	41.11	6.94	1.05
Telefónica de España	Spain	TLS	47,471	35.12	3.44	1.40
Deutsche Bank	Germany	BAN	44,945	72.13	2.52	1.18
Barclays Bank	United Kingdom	BAN	43,531	23.23	3.49	2.14
Diageo	United Kingdom	DST	42,326	30.21	2.83	3.80
Munich Reinsurance	Germany	INP	40,929	45.32	13.73	0.20
Zeneca	United Kingdom	DRG	40,743	33.40	11.30	1.50
Telecom Italia Mobile	Italy	TLS	40,486	57.37	29.77	0.78
Vodafone	United Kingdom	TLS	39,154	55.92	22.91	0.72
Telecom Italia	Italy	TLS	38,576	37.21	3.25	1.45
Elf Aquitaine	France	OIL	38,491	38.92	2.58	1.76
Bayer	Germany	CHC	37,609	21.26	2.90	2.04
L'Oréal	France	COS	37,503	57.04	7.91	0.48
AXA-UAP	France	INF	37,384	27.94	2.89	1.32
Mannesmann	Germany	IDD	37,234	137.83	9.74	0.55
Swiss Reinsurance	Switzerland	INF	36,846	26.44	4.94	1.15
SAP	Germany	SOF	36,607	114.62	37.13	0.26
Siemens	Germany	DTC	35,444	23.55	2.35	1.37
Banco Bilbao Vizcaya	Spain	BAN	34,785	38.77	6.85	1.19
Vivendi	France	WAT	33,740	30.89	3.85	1.16
Generali	Italy	INF	33,265	52.97	4.87	0.62
Alcatel Alsthom	France	CMT	33,146	41.41	4.24	0.93
Nokia	Finland	CMT	33,108	35.15	10.64	0.93
ABN-Amro	Netherlands	BAN	32,936	18.03	2.79	2.52
VEBA	Germany	CGL	32,856	18.33	2.67	1.77
Total	France	OIL	31,687	25.35	2.90	1.65
B.A.T. Industries	United Kingdom	TOB	31,353	18.75	3.92	4.33
NatWest	United Kingdom	BAN	30,649	29.34	2.55	2.44
Zurich Insurance	Switzerland	INF	29,829	29.53	2.21	0.93
Volkswagen	Germany	AUT	29,749	48.28	5.63	0.67
BASF	Germany	CHC	29,283	15.83	2.30	2.35

Austria

http://www.dowjones.com/indexes/Htmls01/austria.html

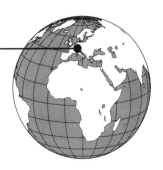

Exchanges:

Vienna Stock Exchange

Austria

Geoff Smith
Vienna

A year ago, the emergence of cross-border stock market alliances was threatening to leave Vienna the remotest of backwaters in a monetarily unified Europe.

Twelve months later, thanks in part to an activist and far-sighted new management team at the Vienna stock exchange, the future looks much brighter.

Faced with the choice of keeping liquidity by pooling resources with another exchange, or watching it migrate to deeper, broader, more modern markets while Vienna withered on the vine, Christian Imo and Wolfram Littich, joint chief executives, opted for the former. By common consent, they got the best deal they could hope for.

As of the second half of 1999, the Vienna exchange will adopt the screen-based Xetra trading system developed and used by the Frankfurt-based Deutsche Boerse. All its major stocks will be listed under the same conditions as those in Germany, and members of either bourse will have equal access to trading in the other's listings. Xetra will replace the overstretched EQOS electronic system through which the bulk of trade in Vienna is currently executed.

At the same time, the two bourses wil found a new "Eastern Exchange", using as its base the 80 or so central and eastern European (CEE) stocks listed in Frankfurt and Vienna's family of CEE indices and derivatives on individual stocks from the region.

In making an ally out of a rival, the deal greatly strengthened Vienna's attempts to establish itself as the leading market in Europe for CEE equities, especially since it was struck before Deutsche Boerse announced its plans to link up with the London Stock Exchange.

However, it also effectively means that the market for Austrian stocks gets swallowed by the German one, even if the clearing of trades in Austrian stocks will stay in the control of Oesterreichische Kontrollbank for the present.

The authorities may protest otherwise to soothe national sensitivities, but a map distributed by Deutsche Boerse when it announced the link-up said it all. The map showed the various countries of Europe shaded so as to reflect their degree of cooperation with Germany. Austria was the same solid black as its northern neighbor.

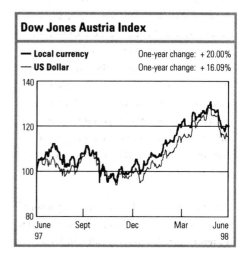

Dow Jones Austria Index

— Local currency   One-year change: + 20.00%
— US Dollar   One-year change: + 16.09%

The effect was strikingly reminiscent of a 1938 map of Europe after the Anschluss.

In another decision symbolic of the move to electronic trading, the bourse announced in January that it would leave its 19th-century headquarters on Schottenring, home of the old trading floor, for more economic premises on Strauchgasse.

If the country's leading market-makers were upset at losing their prestigious positions in the domestic market, they hid it well. In reality, they knew it had to happen. The concentration of the country's banking sector in 1997, which saw Bank Austria's takeover of Creditanstalt and Erste Bank's takeover of Girocredit, had left the exchange in the untenable position of having only three main market-makers (Raiffeisen Zentralbank being the other).

To combat the poor liquidity that the shortage of market-makers helped to create, the bourse introduced an incentive and penalty system (MIPS) at the start of June 1998 for market-makers who don't consistently fulfill their obligations toward ATX stocks and ATX derivatives products. The bourse can now levy fines of up to ATS100,000 per day on errant market-makers and redistribute the money to those market-makers with the best price-quoting performance.

Another novelty is the auction of "specialist" status to market-makers in individual stocks. In return for pledging to maintain for a

Country Information

Trading Hours:
   Local: 9:00 am - 3:00 pm

   EST: 3:00 am - 9:00 am

   GMT: 0800 - 1400

Population (6/98):
8,133,611

Unemployment (97):
4.4%

Main Industries:
Food, iron and steel, machines, textiles, chemicals, electrical, paper and pulp, tourism, mining, and automobiles

Gross Domestic Product (97):
US$206.24 billion

GDP per Capita (97):
US$25,541.83

Three-Year Average GDP Growth (94-97):
1.5%

Average Annual CPI Growth (96-97):
+ 1.31%

Monetary Unit:
Austrian Schilling

Exchange Rate (6/98):
ATS12.69 to US$1.00

year the narrowest bid/offer spread over the largest order size, a market-maker can win exemption from transaction fees in a given stock.

While MIPS aims to improve liquidity among existing participants, the bourse also has tried to attract new liquidity by abolishing signing-on fees for both the cash and futures markets. It also halved its fees for derivatives- clearing membership, to ATS600,000 for General Clearers and ATS400,000 for Direct Clearers. Both measures took effect July 1, 1998.

In addition to a new trading system and lower fees, Vienna also has restructured its official and regulated markets into four segments: A-, B- and C-, which list mature stocks, and the Austrian Growth Market (AGM), which had floundered after its launch under the name of the "fit" market in 1997.

The A-market consists of the 22 stocks in the benchmark ATX index, representing the most liquid stocks with the largest market capitalization. The ATX added Austria Tabakwerke and Erste Bank common stock after IPOs in late 1997 that were the largest ever seen in Austria. Erste Bank in particular attracted first-time domestic retail buyers in large numbers with an innovative and high-profile ad campaign.

Also, Best Water Technology and Semperit AG Holding have replaced paper group Leykam Muerztaler and insurer Wiener

Ten Largest Capitalized Companies In The Dow Jones Austria Index
as of 6/30/98

Stock	Market Cap. US$ Thousands
Bank Austria	5,867,275
ÖMV	3,620,563
Erste Bank der Osterreichischen	2,692,775
Wienerberger Baustoff Industrie	2,102,563
EA Generali	2,058,330
VA Technologie	1,868,342
Verbund	1,809,615
Evn Energie	1,707,837
Voest Alpine Stahl (VA Stahl)	1,324,158
Austria Tabak	1,226,168

Staedtische Allgemeine Versicherung in the ATX.

More changes in the near future will be the delisting of Creditanstalt shares, which Bank Austria will replace with its own. Bank Austria will also merge its preferred and common shares, creating by far the most liquid and heavily-weighted stock in the ATX.

The ATX had a respectable but comparatively unspectacular first half of 1998, rising 15% to 1490.35.

Whereas one "specialist" and at least two other market-makers are required for the A-market, the B- market requires only a "specialist". The C-market consists mainly of stocks in the official and regulated market that aren't continuously traded.

The three-way segmentation augments, but doesn't replace, the original division of the

Austrian stock market into an official, a regulated and an unregulated market.

The strictest admission criteria are set for companies seeking a listing on the official market. Generally, these companies must have high trading volumes, nominal share value of at least ATS40 million and a minimum value of other securities of ATS10 million as well as having existed and filed annual reports for at least three years.

Companies listed on the regulated market must have existed for at least a year and have a nominal share value of at least ATS10 million. Admittance to the unregulated market requires only that the company's shares be printed properly.

The new-look AGM has been revamped to be virtually identical with Frankfurt's Neuer Markt segment, in the hope of inspiring the same kind of stock performance. Despite a pickup in activity since the German link-up was announced, the segment still only numbers four stocks — environmental services groups Hirsch Servo and SW Umwelttechnik, ice-cream box maker Austria Haustechnik and catering company Do & Co.

Only banks, official brokers and non-official brokers can trade on the Vienna Stock Exchange's three markets: the officia market, the regulated market and the unregulated market. There are no significant restrictions that apply specifically to foreign brokers.

Market Sector Performance In The Dow Jones Austria Index
1 Year Change Through 6/30/98

Market Sector	Change % (US$)
Financial	41.54
Utilities	38.98
Consumer, Cyclical	29.82
Industrial	7.93
Energy	4.75
Consumer, Non-Cyclical	1.18
Basic Materials	-0.67

The Vienna Stock Exchange tracks turnover using the double-count method, recording both sales and purchases on the market.

Austria Tabak

DJGI Industry: **Tobacco**
Stoxx Sector: **Consumer Non-Cyclical**

Austria Tabakwerke AG (Austria Tabak) is a group of industrial and trading companies involved primarily in the processing and wholesaling of tobacco. It produces and markets tobacco products, operating as wholesaler through its subsidiary Tobaccoland, as well as licensing its products. Among the 10 biggest selling brands are Memphis Classic, Marlboro, Milde Sorte, and Marlboro Lights. In 1997, Austria Tabak sold nearly 20 billion cigarettes. Another 0.882 billion cigarettes were produced by foreign licensees. Wholesale tobacco accounted for 93% of 1997 revenues.

	ATS mil 12/95	12/96	12/97	US$mil 12/97				
Sales	41,530.8	43,162.6	51,507.9	4,078.5	P/E Ratio	10.4	Price (6/30/98)	707.00
Net Income	-1,179.3	1,199.8	1,492.4	118.2	P/B Ratio	3.8	52 Wk Hi-Low	818.00-512.00
Book Value	2,021.7	2,908.0	4,100.5	324.7	Yield %	3.7	Market Cap	US$1,226.2mil

| Address | Porzellangasse 51 | Tel 1-313-420 | ADR | -- | Chmn Supv Bd | K. Hollweger |
| | 1091 Vienna | Fax 1-313-421251 | SEDOL | 5355921 | Chmn Mgt Bd | H. Schiendl |

Austrian Airlines

DJGI Industry: **Airlines**
Stoxx Sector: **Consumer Cyclical**

Austrian Airlines AG, Austria's flagship passenger airline, is majority-owned by the state. With an emphasis on flights to eastern Europe and Africa, it provides charter and cargo services and flies to more than 70 destinations in 40 countries. Its subsidiaries include Touropa Austria and 43%-owned regional Austrian airline Tyrolean. In March 1997, the company took a 36% controlling stake in domestic archrival Lauda Air Luftfahrt AG. In April 1998, the group said it planned to issue 8 million new shares in a capital increase in the fall, which would dilute the government's stake to 39.7%.

	ATS mil 12/95	12/96	12/97	US$mil 12/97				
Sales	12,449.0	13,125.7	18,248.3	1,444.9	P/E Ratio	17.5	Price (6/30/98)	418.00
Net Income	58.8	168.7	622.8	49.3	P/B Ratio	1.7	52 Wk Hi-Low	480.00-198.00
Book Value	5,493.5	5,658.1	6,384.0	505.5	Yield %	0.0	Market Cap	US$856.8mil

| Address | Fontanastr. 1 | Tel 1-17660 | ADR | -- | Memb Mgt Bd | M. Rehulka |
| | 1107 Vienna | Fax 1-688-5505 | SEDOL | 5288726 | Memb Mgt Bd | H. Bammer |

Bank Austria

DJGI Industry: **Banks - Regional (All)**
Stoxx Sector: **Bank**

Bank Austria AG is the country's largest commercial bank, providing retail banking, investment advice, asset management, and life insurance. It operates 517 domestic branch offices and 148 international branches, with Central and Eastern Europe being its most important markets. Bank Austria offers electronic-banking and bank-by-phone services. In January 1997, the group acquired the state's 70% stake in its rival, Creditanstalt Bankverein AG. In March 1997, Bank Austria agreed to sell its 56% stake in GiroCredit Bank to Die Erste Österreichische Spar-Casse Bank AG.

	ATS mil 12/95	12/96	12/97	US$mil 12/97				
Revenues	47,540.0	47,034.2	104,517.0	8,276.0	P/E Ratio	15.8	Price (6/30/98)	1,032.90
Net Income	2,446.6	1,407.7	5,127.9	406.0	P/B Ratio	2.0	52 Wk Hi-Low	1,165.0-580.0
Book Value	28,869.3	34,630.4	50,648.4	4,010.5	Yield %	1.4	Market Cap	US$5,867.3mil

| Address | Zollamtstr. 13 | Tel 1-711910 | ADR | BAAGY | V Chmn Mgt Bd | K. Samstag |
| | 1030 Vienna | Fax 1-711916155 | SEDOL | 4999621 | Chmn Mgt Bd | G. Randa |

BBAG

DJGI Industry: **Distillers & Brewers**
Stoxx Sector: **Food & Beverage**

Österreichische Brau Beteiligungs AG (BBAG) is a holding company for beverage producers that distribute beer and non-alcoholic beverages such as soft drinks, mineral water, and fruit juices. The company also runs specialty restaurants and staff canteens. Its brand-name beverages include Kaiser beer, Gössinger mineral water, and Pago fruit juice. Principal operations are in Austria, where it holds about two-thirds of the beer market. Beer accounted for 80% of 1997 revenues; non-alcoholic beverages, 14%; real estate, 2%; merchandise, 2%; and other 2%.

	ATS mil 12/95	12/96	12/97	US$mil 12/97				
Sales	9,419.1	8,628.1	8,914.9	705.9	P/E Ratio	23.8	Price (6/30/98)	750.00
Net Income	380.7	849.7	326.0	25.8	P/B Ratio	1.5	52 Wk Hi-Low	840.00-590.00
Book Value	3,553.1	4,216.0	4,394.6	348.0	Yield %	2.5	Market Cap	US$510.8mil

| Address | Poschacherstr. 35 | Tel 732-69510 | ADR | -- | Memb Mgt Bd | W. Sachs |
| | 4020 Linz | Fax 732-695-1150 | SEDOL | 4621731 | Chmn Mgt Bd | J. Brandl |

Boehler Uddeholm

DJGI Industry: **Steel**
Stoxx Sector: **Basic Resources**

Boehler Uddeholm AG is one of the world's leading producers of specialty steel. The company's primary focuses are high- grade steel, welding technology, strip steel products, and forging technology. Boehler also is involved in the distribution of steel. It has subsidiaries worldwide. In November 1997, Boehler announced it will set up a joint venture with Thyssen AG of Germany in the area of forging technology. Trading of steel accounted for 54% of 1997 revenues; high-grade steel products, 26%; strip steel products, 10%; welding technology, 7%; and forging technology, 3%.

	ATS mil 12/95	12/96	12/97	US$mil 12/97				
Sales	18,272.1	17,085.7	18,321.0	1,450.7	P/E Ratio	13.0	Price (6/30/98)	839.00
Net Income	1,044.5	979.0	711.9	56.4	P/B Ratio	1.4	52 Wk Hi-Low	1,030.0-628.0
Book Value	5,661.8	6,321.9	6,659.6	527.3	Yield %	3.1	Market Cap	US$727.5mil

| Address | Modecenterstrasse 14/A/3 | Tel 1-798-69010 | ADR | BDHHY | President | -- |
| | 1030 Vienna | Fax -- | SEDOL | 4121305 | Chmn Mgt Bd | C. J. Raidl |

Brau-Union

DJGI Industry: **Distillers & Brewers**
Stoxx Sector: **Food & Beverage**

Brau-Union AG, which shortened its name from Brau-Union Göess-Reininghaus Österreichische Brau AG in June 1997, is Austria's largest beer brewery and one of the 10 leading beer producers in Europe. Principal operations are in Austria, but it also has substantial sales in Hungary, Romania, and the Czech Republic. Its principal shareholder is Österreichische Brau Beteiligungs AG with a 61% stake. Brand-name beers include Kaiser Bier, Gösser, Starobrno, and Puntigamer. In March 1997, the company merged its units Steirerbrau AG and Brau AG into Brau Union Österreich AG.

	ATS mil 12/95	12/96	12/97	US$mil 12/97					
Sales	61.2	7,850.0	7,976.6	631.6	P/E Ratio	14.3	Price (6/30/98)		750.00
Net Income	226.3	523.5	423.2	33.5	P/B Ratio	1.3	52 Wk Hi-Low		907.00-590.00
Book Value	5,175.1	5,937.7	6,104.1	483.3	Yield %	3.1	Market Cap		US$591.2mil

Address	Poschacherstr. 35	Tel 732-69510	ADR	--	Memb Mgt Bd	W. Sachs
	4020 Linz	Fax 732-695-1150	SEDOL	4378383	Chmn Mgt Bd	Dr. J. Brandl

EA Generali

DJGI Industry: **Insurance - Full Line**
Stoxx Sector: **Insurance**

EA Generali AG is Austria's largest provider of insurance services. The company has operations throughout Europe, including Germany, Switzerland, Slovenia, Hungary, Poland, the Czech Republic, and Slovakia. The company offers a range of insurance policies, including automobile, life, property-damage, health, general-liability, legal, fire, and accident insurance. Premium income accounted for 73% of 1997 revenues; investment income accounted for 22%, gain and loss on disposal of securities made up 3%, and income from other operations was 2%.

	ATS mil 12/95	12/96	12/97	US$mil 12/97					
Revenues	39,114.5	45,601.4	44,311.8	3,508.7	P/E Ratio	44.1	Price (6/30/98)		3,730.00
Net Income	289.6	546.1	417.6	33.1	P/B Ratio	3.6	52 Wk Hi-Low		4,540.0-2,750.0
Book Value	7,280.8	7,549.4	7,632.2	604.3	Yield %	0.5	Market Cap		US$2,058.3mil

Address	Landskrongasse 1-3	Tel 1-534010	ADR	--	CFO	G. Neumann
	1101 Vienna	Fax 1-53401226	SEDOL	4373645	Chmn Mgt Bd	D. Karner

Erste Bank

DJGI Industry: **Banks - Regional (All)**
Stoxx Sector: **Bank**

Erste Bank AG is Austria's second-largest financial institution. The company was formed as a result of the 1997 merger of Die Erste, Österreichische Spar-Casse-Bank AG, and Austrian GiroCredit. At the end of 1997, the company operated 458 branch offices. Erste Bank's services include retail banking, lending, automobile and real estate leasing, and working capital financing, as well as real estate development, fund management, and securities trading. The bank has subsidiaries and representative offices worldwide. Interest and fees on loans accounted for 71% of 1997 revenues.

	ATS mil 12/95	12/96	12/97	US$mil 12/97					
Revenues	20,081.0	18,507.0	44,545.3	3,527.2	P/E Ratio	149.1	Price (6/30/98)		770.00
Net Income	618.4	670.0	229.4	18.2	P/B Ratio	1.8	52 Wk Hi-Low		865.00-610.00
Book Value	7,997.8	8,879.2	18,679.5	1,479.1	Yield %	2.1	Market Cap		US$2,692.8mil

Address	Graben 21	Tel 1-531-000	ADR	ERTBYP	President	--
	1010 Vienna	Fax 1-531-002272	SEDOL	5289837	Chairman	Mag A. Treichl

EVN

DJGI Industry: **Electrical Utilities (All)**
Stoxx Sector: **Utility**

Energie-Versorgung Niederöesterreich AG (EVN) produces and distributes electricity and natural gas. It operates 63 power stations, 52 of which are hydroelectric. The company supplies energy to 800,000 individual and industrial customers in lower Austria. In fiscal 1996, EVN and Bayernwerk AG, through a joint venture, acquired KOEGAZ, a Hungarian gas supply company. The company has subsidiaries in Austria and Hungary. Generation and distribution of electricity accounted for 65% of fiscal 1997 revenues; distribution of natural gas, 32%; and district heating and other, 3%.

	ATS mil 08/95	08/96	08/97	US$mil 08/97					
Sales	10,978.6	11,907.4	11,842.3	935.1	P/E Ratio	17.0	Price (6/30/98)		1,900.35
Net Income	880.4	1,117.6	1,184.0	93.5	P/B Ratio	1.6	52 Wk Hi-Low		1,994.0-1,254.0
Book Value	6,273.9	7,173.0	13,179.8	1,040.7	Yield %	1.6	Market Cap		US$1,707.8mil

Address	Johann-Steinböck-Str. 1	Tel 223-620-00	ADR	EVNVY	Memb Mgt Bd	A. Scheicher
	2344 Maria Enzerdorf	Fax 223-620-02600	SEDOL	4295374	Chmn Mgt Bd	S. Ludwig

Flughafen Wien

DJGI Industry: **Other Industrial & Commercial Services**
Stoxx Sector: **Industrials**

Flughafen Wien AG (VIA), is responsible for the construction, management, and operation of the Vienna International Airport and the Vöslau Airfield. It provides aviation-related services, such as terminal services, airside and landside handling, cargo handling, and runway operations. The company also manages airport buildings, leasing much of the space to companies that provide various services. VIA itself manages a business center, 12 executive lounges, an emergency medical unit, and parking areas at the airport. Aviation-related services accounted for 72% of 1997 revenues.

	ATS mil 12/95	12/96	12/97	US$mil 12/97					
Sales	3,791.4	3,971.6	4,071.7	322.4	P/E Ratio	20.4	Price (6/30/98)		609.00
Net Income	789.3	601.5	618.2	49.0	P/B Ratio	1.8	52 Wk Hi-Low		676.00-480.00
Book Value	5,464.4	6,892.3	7,174.6	568.1	Yield %	2.6	Market Cap		US$745.3mil

Address	Postfach 1	Tel 222-70070	ADR	--	Memb Mgt Bd	F. Kotrba
	1300 Vienna	Fax 222-7007-3001	SEDOL	4359690	Memb Mgt Bd	G. Kastelic

Lenzing

DJGI Industry: **Chemicals - Commodity**
Stoxx Sector: **Chemical**

Lenzing AG is the world's largest manufacturer of viscous fibers. The company also produces plastics, synthetic fibers, and paper. Other products include plastics machinery, high-performance products, and synthetic films. Operations are divided into four main areas: cellulose products, plastics, paper, and machinery and equipment. It supplies its products to the garment, textile, tire, and printing industries. Its subsidiaries include wholly owned U.S. companies Lenzing USA and Lenzing Fibers, and Indonesian company P.T. South Pacific Viscose.

	ATS mil 12/95	12/96	12/97	US$mil 12/97					
Sales	8,700.5	7,786.2	7,176.4	568.2	P/E Ratio	NMF	Price (6/30/98)		970.00
Net Income	406.7	-79.6	-514.8	-40.8	P/B Ratio	2.2	52 Wk Hi-Low		970.00-610.00
Book Value	2,148.2	2,193.1	1,624.5	128.6	Yield %	0.0	Market Cap		US$281.0mil

Address	Lenzing Aktiengesellschaft	Tel 7672-7010	ADR	LNZNY	V Chmn Mgt Bd	J. Zauner
	4860 Lenzing	Fax 7672-96301	SEDOL	4512330	Chmn Mgt Bd	H.E. Stepniczka

Mayr-Melnhof Karton

DJGI Industry: **Paper Products**
Stoxx Sector: **Basic Resources**

Mayr-Melnhof Karton AG is a forest products and paper company. The company is Europe's largest manufacturer of cardboard production and packaging. It also manufactures folding boxes and has waste-paper salvaging and trading interests. The company's subsidiaries include folding-box manufacturer Walmsley of the United Kingdom; and German recycling companies Holz and Loerch, which collect 34,000 tons of waste paper annually. Production and sale of paperboard accounted for 52% of 1997 revenues; packaging paperboard, 36%; and paper recycling, 12%.

	ATS mil 12/95	12/96	12/97	US$mil 12/97					
Sales	12,252.6	10,496.9	11,524.9	912.6	P/E Ratio	14.1	Price (6/30/98)		830.00
Net Income	318.9	439.0	637.5	50.5	P/B Ratio	2.1	52 Wk Hi-Low		964.00-615.00
Book Value	4,192.8	4,712.2	4,843.7	383.5	Yield %	2.0	Market Cap		US$785.2mil

Address	Brahmsplatz 6	Tel 222-501360	ADR	MMKAY	V Chmn Mgt Bd	A. Fogarassy
	1040 Vienna	Fax 222-501-3667	SEDOL	4563640	Chmn Mgt Bd	M. Groeller

Oberbank

DJGI Industry: **Banks - Regional (All)**
Stoxx Sector: **Bank**

Oberbank AG, formerly Bank für Oberösterreich und Salzburg, one of Austria's largest commercial banks, offers asset management, foreign-exchange services, money-market trading, and investment advice to corporate clients and private customers. It has 92 branches throughout Austria and offices in Munich and Prague. Oberbank has subsidiaries in Austria, Germany, and the Czech Republic. Interest and fees on loans accounted for 64% of 1997 revenues; interest on securities, 18%; commissions and fees, 15%; trading account income, 2%; and other interest and dividend income, 1%.

	ATS mil 12/95	12/96	12/97	US$mil 12/97					
Revenues	5,531.2	5,603.1	5,651.3	447.5	P/E Ratio	17.5	Price (6/30/98)		840.00
Net Income	226.9	341.7	386.6	30.6	P/B Ratio	1.4	52 Wk Hi-Low		951.00-672.00
Book Value	4,155.6	4,395.9	4,694.8	371.7	Yield %	1.5	Market Cap		US$463.5mil

Address	Hauptplatz 10-11	Tel 732-78020	ADR	--	V Chmn Mgt Bd	J. Kneidinger
	4010 Linz	Fax 732-785810	SEDOL	4081294	Chmn Mgt Bd	H. Bell

ÖMV

DJGI Industry: **Oil Companies - Secondary**
Stoxx Sector: **Energy**

ÖMV AG, Austria's largest industrial concern, operates mainly in Austria, but it also has production sites in the United Kingdom, Libya, and Pakistan. It focuses on three segments: energy, chemicals, and plastics. ÖMV is involved in crude-oil exploration, production, transit, and storage. In 1997, the company extended its exploration activities in Sudan, Pakistan, and Turkmenistan, and its filling station network consisted of 983 stations. Oil refining and marketing accounted for 65% of 1997 revenues; gas, 14%; plastics, 13%; chemicals, 6%; and exploration and production and other, 2%.

	ATS mil 12/95	12/96	12/97	US$mil 12/97					
Sales	73,299.1	78,269.0	83,031.4	6,574.7	P/E Ratio	15.8	Price (6/30/98)		1,701.00
Net Income	2,157.0	2,095.4	2,485.4	196.8	P/B Ratio	2.5	52 Wk Hi-Low		1,948.0-1,449.0
Book Value	14,536.7	16,177.8	18,116.5	1,434.5	Yield %	1.5	Market Cap		US$3,620.6mil

Address	Otto-Wagner-Platz 5	Tel 222-40440	ADR	OMVAY	CFO	H.G. Stahl
	1091 Vienna	Fax 222-4044-0909	SEDOL	4651459	Chmn Mgt Bd	R. Schenz

RHI

DJGI Industry: **Industrial - Diversified**
Stoxx Sector: **Industrials**

RHI AG, formerly Radex-Heraklith Industriebeteiligungs AG, focuses on the manufacture of fireproof materials, building materials, and insulation. Its refractories/engineering division produces materials used in high-temperature processes, mainly in the iron and steel, cement and lime, glass, and nonferrous metals industries. The insulating-materials division manufactures materials for insulation against heat, sound, fire, and dampness. Other products include polystyrene board, refractories, and roofing shingles. Its brand names include Thor, Penta, Radex, Coriglas, Heralan, and Villas.

	ATS mil 12/95	12/96	12/97	US$mil 12/97					
Sales	21,691.3	21,004.9	21,455.4	1,698.9	P/E Ratio	13.3	Price (6/30/98)		615.00
Net Income	418.3	508.0	682.4	54.0	P/B Ratio	3.3	52 Wk Hi-Low		690.00-428.00
Book Value	2,263.7	2,503.3	2,567.7	203.3	Yield %	2.6	Market Cap		US$674.9mil

Address	Opernring 1	Tel 222-587-7671	ADR	--	Memb Mgt Bd	R. Kanzi
	1010 Vienna	Fax 222-587-3380	SEDOL	4719915	Chmn Mgt Bd	W. Ressler

Steyr-Daimler-Puch

DJGI Industry: **Land Transportation**
Stoxx Sector: **Industrials**

Steyr-Daimler-Puch AG is a manufacturer of automotive components. Its main products include components for commercial vehicles, agricultural machinery, military technology, and weapons. It also distributes, services, and repairs passenger vehicles and small trucks with the Fiat, Lancia, and Alfa Romeo brand names in Austria. Steyr-Daimler-Puch products include Steyr trucks, Puch Pinzgauer all-terrain motor vehicles, and Steyr Mannlicher hunting rifles. In March 1998, Creditanstalt-Bankverein sold its controlling 66.8% stake in Steyr to Canadian automotive group Magna Inc.

	ATS mil 12/95	12/96	12/97	US$mil 12/97				
Sales	10,695.6	11,401.7	14,216.5	1,125.7	P/E Ratio	14.3	Price (6/30/98)	348.00
Net Income	70.9	14.1	243.5	19.3	P/B Ratio	1.5	52 Wk Hi-Low	487.00-260.00
Book Value	2,054.9	2,069.0	2,252.5	178.4	Yield %	2.3	Market Cap	US$274.3mil

Address	Franz-Josefs-Kai 51	Tel 222-531440	ADR	--	Memb Mgt Bd	A.G. Koch
	1010 Vienna	Fax 222-535638	SEDOL	4846608	Chmn Mgt Bd	R. Streicher

VA Stahl

DJGI Industry: **Steel**
Stoxx Sector: **Basic Resources**

Vöst Alpine Stahl AG (VA Stahl) is an integrated European steel producer. Its flat-steel products division makes hot- and cold-rolled products and forging and casting products for the automotive, steel, mechanical-engineering, and construction industries. The long-steel products division supplies rails, rolled wire, and seamless tubes to the railroad and oil industries. All production centers are in Austria, but some processing and sales centers are located throughout Europe. Flat-steel products accounted for 75% of 1998 revenues, and long-steel products contributed 25%.

	ATS mil 12/96	03/97 *	03/98	US$mil 03/98				
Sales	31,519.1	31,547.6	34,649.1	2,665.9	P/E Ratio	9.8	Price (6/30/98)	509.00
Net Income	1,683.6	1,904.4	1,941.4	149.4	P/B Ratio	1.1	52 Wk Hi-Low	635.50-425.10
Book Value	14,027.1	14,672.3	16,100.3	1,238.8	Yield %	2.9	Market Cap	US$1,324.2mil

Address	Voest Alpine Str. 1	Tel 1-732-65850	ADR	--	Memb Mgt Bd	W. Haidenthaler
	4020 Linz	Fax 1-732-69800	SEDOL	4943402	Chmn Mgt Bd	P. Strahammer

*Irregular period due to fiscal year change.

VA Technologie

DJGI Industry: **Industrial - Diversified**
Stoxx Sector: **Industrials**

VA Technologie AG, Austria's largest technology group, provides engineering and construction services in three areas: energy and environmental engineering, which generated 42% of 1997 revenues; metallurgical engineering, which generated 29% of revenues; and construction and engineering services, which generated 29% of revenues. It provides mechanical and electrical engineering, maintenance services, and system solutions to its customers. It also builds thermal and hydroelectric power plants. Nearly half of the company's orders originate in non-European countries.

	ATS mil 12/95	12/96	12/97	US$mil 12/97				
Sales	26,085.5	33,536.5	38,413.8	3,041.7	P/E Ratio	19.4	Price (6/30/98)	1,580.00
Net Income	1,300.7	1,317.6	1,480.4	117.2	P/B Ratio	3.1	52 Wk Hi-Low	2,721.0-1,545.0
Book Value	6,487.0	7,089.5	7,712.6	610.7	Yield %	2.0	Market Cap	US$1,868.3mil

Address	Lunzerstr. 64	Tel 732-698-69222	ADR	VATXY	CFO	H. Hamminger
	4031 Linz	Fax 732-698-03416	SEDOL	4921635	Chmn Mgt Bd	O. Puehringer

Verbund

DJGI Industry: **Electrical Utilities (All)**
Stoxx Sector: **Utility**

Österreichische Elektrizitaetswirtschafts-AG Verbundgesellschaft, known as Verbund, is the leading generator of electricity in Austria, providing more than half of the country's supply. Verbund runs the national power grid and is the country's sole importer-exporter of electricity. Verbund also manages water and waste materials, and is involved in energy conservation and the tourist industry. Its principle operations are in Austria, but exports account for about 8% of sales. Electricity accounted for 97% of 1997 revenues; planning and consulting services, 2%; and user and management fees, 1%.

	ATS mil 12/95	12/96	12/97	US$mil 12/97				
Sales	19,635.1	20,037.1	20,489.8	1,622.4	P/E Ratio	32.0	Price (6/30/98)	1,520.00
Net Income	1,206.3	1,146.8	557.6	44.2	P/B Ratio	2.6	52 Wk Hi-Low	1,591.1-854.0
Book Value	16,387.3	17,167.3	16,558.1	1,311.1	Yield %	1.1	Market Cap	US$1,809.6mil

Address	Am Hof 6	Tel 222-53-1130	ADR	OEZVY	Dpty Spkmn Mgt Bd	H. Schroefelbauer
	1010 Vienna	Fax 222-531134191	SEDOL	4661607	Spkmn Mgt Bd	H. Haider

Wienerberger

DJGI Industry: **Building Materials**
Stoxx Sector: **Construction**

Wienerberger Baustoffindustrie AG, the world's largest brick producer, is a building-materials company that operates 127 production sites in 21 countries. Its operations are divided into the following areas: metals and chemicals; wall, ceiling, and roofing systems; Austrian fittings distribution; pipes and environmental technology; and real estate development and management. Wall, ceiling, and roofing systems accounted for 56% of 1997 revenues; pipe systems and sewage technology, 24%; alloy metals, powder metals, and other chemicals, 19%; and real estate, 1%.

	ATS mil 12/95	12/96	12/97	US$mil 12/97				
Sales	12,855.0	15,061.2	15,323.2	1,213.3	P/E Ratio	26.2	Price (6/30/98)	3,072.00
Net Income	1,105.4	777.4	1,198.5	94.9	P/B Ratio	2.6	52 Wk Hi-Low	3,255.0-2,285.0
Book Value	7,862.0	9,638.5	10,379.6	821.9	Yield %	1.5	Market Cap	US$2,102.6mil

Address	Wienerbergerstr. 7	Tel 1-60192419	ADR	WBRBY	V Chmn Mgt Bd	W. Reithofer
	1100 Vienna	Fax 1-60192412	SEDOL	4969602	Chmn Mgt Bd	E. Schaschl

Wolford

DJGI Industry: Clothing & Fabrics
Stoxx Sector: Consumer Cyclical

Wolford AG manufacturers, distributes, and trades in textiles of all types, mainly knitwear and hosiery as well as legwear and bodywear that is sold under the Wolford brand name. Wolford has subsidiaries in Germany, Switzerland, France, Great Britain, Italy, Spain, and Denmark. In 1996, the company operated 280 shops worldwide. In 1995, Wolford was launched in the Japanese market and the group embarked on a program to open a chain of Wolford Boutiques, with plans to build a network of 200 retail franchisees throughout the United States within two years.

	ATS mil 04/96	04/97	04/98	US$mil 04/98				
Sales	1,475.4	1,651.7	1,664.3	131.7	P/E Ratio	21.2	Price (6/30/98)	805.00
Net Income	166.3	190.6	126.6	10.0	P/B Ratio	4.6	52 Wk Hi-Low	1,290.0-712.0
Book Value	726.7	882.2	961.0	76.1	Yield %	1.2	Market Cap	US$317.3mil

Address	Wolfordstrasse. 1			ADR	WLFDY	Dpty Chmn Mgt Bd	J. Metzler
	6901 Bregenz	Tel	557-469-00	SEDOL	4940685	Chmn Mgt Bd	F. Humer
		Fax	557-479-44				

Belgium

http://www.dowjones.com/indexes/Htmls01/belgium.html

Exchanges:

Brussels Stock Exchange

Antwerp Stock Exchange

Belgium

Jennifer M. Freedman
Brussels

The Brussels bourse reflects trends that are changing the face of equities markets around Europe.

It is gearing up for the launch of the euro in January 1999. The bourse has said it will be ready for the transition by mid-November 1998, and will — like other exchanges — begin to list stocks and their derivatives in euros from January 4.

The introduction of the single currency is widely expected to boost cooperation among European markets, as it becomes easier for investors to compare stocks of different countries. The Brussels bourse has already taken steps to form alliances with others, amidst concerns that acquisitions of Belgian companies by foreigners could leave the bourse too weak to continue on its own.

There are plans to link the bourse's forward market — containing Belgium's blue-chips — with those of Amsterdam and Luxembourg. Data among the three bourses are to be shared beginning in September 1998, and cross-membership is to be established by the end of the year. A member of one market will be free to trade in all shares listed on the other markets, without paying an additional membership fee. A Benelux stock index is to be created in 1999, although this is considered a strategic alliance, not a merger.

Brussels bourse officials also have said they wouldn't rule out accepting an invitation to join Frankfurt and London in their planned trading alliance, though that decision wouldn't be made without consulting their Benelux neighbors.

Cross-membership on the Euro.NM, the exchange linking growth exchanges in Amsterdam, Paris, Frankfurt, and Brussels, was to begin in the second half of 1998. The screen-based Euro.NM markets operate alongside each city's traditional bourse. Easdaq, the European Association of Securities Dealers Automated Quotation market, makes its home in Brussels. Since its November 1996 start, 34 companies have joined this pan-European exchange for small, rapid-growth stocks.

Meanwhile, with low interest rates and mild inflation, healthy and apparently sustainable economic growth, and the coming currency union, the Brussels bourse enjoyed a bull run in 1997 and the first half of 1998. The Bel-20 index rose 27.6% in 1997, to end the year at

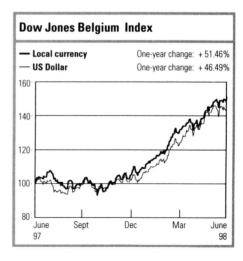

Dow Jones Belgium Index

— **Local currency**   One-year change: + 51.46%
— **US Dollar**   One-year change: + 46.49%

2418.42. By the end of June 1998, it had topped the 3,500 mark, a whopping 46% rise, making Belgium one of the best-performing stock markets in Europe.

Mergers and acquisitions in Belgium's important financial sector in late 1997 and early 1998— including a number of cross-border transactions — reshaped the the Bel-20 index. The late 1997 takeover of Banque Bruxelles Lambert by the Netherlands' ING Groep ended with BBL's removal from the Bel-20. It was replaced by municipal lender Dexia, which came into existence in November 1996, when Belgium's Crédit Communal de Belgique and France's Crédit Local de France merged.

In the first six months of 1998, the Bel-20 lost two other financial stocks — insurer Royale Belge, which was bought by French insurance giant AXA-UAP, and Générale de Banque, which was acquired in June by the Belgian-Dutch financial-services group Fortis.

The "new" Fortis, represented on the Bel-20 by Fortis AG, will become the largest company on the Brussels bourse. Its market capitalization was BEF795 billion as of July 1, 1998, not including the shares of Fortis Amev in the Netherlands which, with Fortis AG, controls the Fortis group.

The second largest company on the bourse is also a banking group: KBC Bancassurance Holding, whose market capitalization stood at BEF926 billion on July 1, 1998. KBC replaced Kredietbank, which merged with its

Country Information

Trading Hours:
  Local: 10:00 am - 4:30 pm

  EST: 4:00 am - 10:30 am

  GMT: 0900 - 1530

Population (6/98):
10,174,922

Unemployment (97):
9.5%

Main Industries:
Engineering and metal products, automobile assembly, food and beverages, chemicals, basic metals, textiles, glass, petroleum, and coal

Gross Domestic Product (97):
US$242.50 billion

GDP per Capita (97):
US$23,833.42

Three-Year Average GDP Growth (94-97):
1.7%

Average Annual CPI Growth (96-97):
+ 1.59%

Monetary Unit:
Belgian Franc

Exchange Rate (6/98):
BEF37.19 to US$1.00

parent holding company Almanij, CERA Bank of Leuven, and insurer ABB to create a new entity.

Almanij also joined the Bel-20 in 1998, along with chemicals group Tessenderlo and auto distributor D'Ieteren. Société Générale de Belgique, which had been Belgium's largest listed concern, was dropped from the index when it was delisted following its acquisition by France's Suez Lyonnaise des Eaux.

These changes are straining some of the rules governing the workings of the Bel-20. For example, no single stock in the index is to account for more than 10% of the market cap of the entire index. But Fortis AG alone accounted for more than 9% before the merger and Générale de Banque's was more than 6%. As of early July, the bourse hadn't yet decided how to deal with the problem, but one option was for the new Fortis to retain the excess capitalization until the end of the year, when all Bel-20 stocks are to be reweighted.

The 197-year-old bourse had already taken some steps to ensure that it doesn't get left behind or forgotten once the currency union begins. For instance, it announced a merger with the Belgian Futures and Options Exchange and the national deposit bank Caisse Interprofessionnel de Dépôts et de Virement de Titres in 1997. That move, designed to give the stock exchange more transparency and coherence, also ensures that the means of clearing transactions in Belgium are as modern as anywhere else in the world.

Ten Largest Capitalized Companies In The Dow Jones Belgium Index
as of 6/30/98

Stock	Market Cap. US$ Thousands
Almanij (Algem Maatsch Voor Nijv)	17,739,736
Electrabel	15,452,843
KBC Bancassurance	13,586,319
Tractebel Investment	12,378,660
Société Générale de Belgique	12,054,778
Fortis	10,717,982
PetroFina	9,619,284
UCB	7,573,554
Solvay et Cie	6,657,145
Credit Communal Holding Dexia	5,528,335

Even before that, the bourse switched to the New Trading System from its former screen-based quotation system as a major step toward complete computerization. The new system split the so-called forward market, which is based on a two-week payment period, into two categories. In the continuous market, shares are traded throughout the session from 0800 GMT until 1445 GMT; in the semicontinuous market, which is designed for less liquid major stocks, prices are fixed twice a day, at 0915 GMT and again at 1315 GMT.

The switch to the New Trading System contributed in part to record volume on the bourse in 1997, when BEF1.23 trillion were traded, compared with some BEF808 billion in 1996. The market's capitalization at the end of 1997 was a record BEF5.1 trillion, compared with BEF3.8 trillion in 1996, compared with a 21.5% the year before.

Halfway through 1998, the bourse was on the way to breaking the records set in 1997. Overall trading volume in the first six months of the year amounted to BEF1.178 trillion, and market capitalization at end of June totaled BEF8.32 trillion.

At the end of 1997, a total of 287 companies were listed on the Brussels bourse, up from 278 in 1996. Nearly half of those, 140, were foreign listings. The bourse's 1997 net profit amounted to BEF146.5 million, more than double the BEF57.6 million of 1996.

The Brussels bourse admitted 11 new Belgian companies and 6 foreign companies on the first market — the official regulated market — in 1997, and two Belgian companies joined the Euro.NM Brussels.

The most actively traded stock in 1997 was petrochemicals giant PetroFina, with 78,717,294,195 shares traded. Along with financials, metals and chemicals companies were the most common sectors represented in the Bel-20 index in 1997.

The Belgian government levies a 25% withholding tax on most company dividends for ordinary shares and a 15% withholding tax on so-called VVPR shares. Withholding taxes on fixed-income interest is the same as for VVPR shares. There is no tax exemption in Belgium on dividend income.

Market Sector Performance In The Dow Jones Belgium Index
1 Year Change Through 6/30/98

Market Sector	Change % (US$)
Financial	63.27
Independent	54.55
Utilities	48.34
Basic Materials	34.35
Consumer, Non-Cyclical	34.12
Industrial	19.93
Energy	14.19

Almanij

DJGI Industry: **Diversified Financial Services**
Stoxx Sector: **Financial Services**

Almanij NV (Algem Maatschappij Voor Nijverheidskrediet) is Belgium's largest financial services company, by market capitalization. It offers services in banking, finances, insurance, and asset management. Almanij derives the lion's share of its income from its primary holding, Kredietbank, which is Belgium's third-largest bank, by assets, and from KB Luxembourg and its financial services arm. In May 1997, Almanij agreed to split industrial holding company Gevaert NV with financial holding company Cobepa SA. Almanij will be the majority shareholder of the new company.

	BEF mil 12/95	12/96	12/97	US$mil 12/97					
Revenues	4,952.4	6,327.3	4,912.5	132.6	P/E Ratio		26.9	Price (6/30/98)	3,410.00
Net Income	6,257.9	7,083.3	8,592.5	231.9	P/B Ratio		4.0	52 Wk Hi-Low	3,740.0-1,486.0
Book Value	50,718.6	56,101.4	84,841.2	2,289.3	Yield %		1.0	Market Cap	US$17,740mil

Address	Schoenmarkt, 33	Tel 3-234-27-95	ADR	--	V Chairman	F. Collin
	2000 Antwerp	Fax 3-231-44-09	SEDOL	4021104	Chairman	J. Huyghebaert

Barco

DJGI Industry: **Industrial Technology**
Stoxx Sector: **Technology**

Barco NV (Belgian American Radio Corp.) manufactures visualization equipment, including projectors, video monitors, display systems, and cable and satellite equipment. The company also produces graphics systems for use in the printing industry and equipment for the textiles and plastics industries. It also performs subcontracting services. Barco provides services and products in approximately 95 countries. Visualization equipment accounted for 49% of 1997 revenues; graphic systems, 20%; automation, 14%; communication systems, 10%; and inspection systems, 4%.

	BEF mil 12/95	12/96	12/97	US$mil 12/97					
Sales	15,076.1	18,919.5	22,998.4	620.6	P/E Ratio		41.6	Price (6/30/98)	10,400
Net Income	1,802.0	2,365.6	3,057.0	82.5	P/B Ratio		7.7	52 Wk Hi-Low	10,800.0-7,070.0
Book Value	8,089.7	14,193.4	16,635.7	448.9	Yield %		0.7	Market Cap	US$3,436.6mil

Address	President Kennedypark 35	Tel 5-626-26-11	ADR	--	President & CEO	H. Vandamme
	8500 Kortrijk	Fax 5-626-22-62	SEDOL	4089049	Sr. V Pres & COO	E. Dejonghe

Bekaert

DJGI Industry: **Steel**
Stoxx Sector: **Basic Resources**

Bekaert SA is a worldwide manufacturer of wire, wire products, and steel cord. Its products include steel wire and cables for rubber reinforcement, steel and metal fibers, and high-carbon steel wires. The company supplies customers in the automotive, tire, chemical, and computer industries. The group operates 60 manufacturing facilities in 28 countries and has subsidiaries in the United States and Europe. Wire, wire products, and cables accounted for 60% of 1997 revenues and rubber and plastic reinforcement for 34%.

	BEF mil 12/95	12/96	12/97	US$mil 12/97					
Sales	60,668.9	61,816.4	70,148.7	1,892.8	P/E Ratio		25.0	Price (6/30/98)	30,900
Net Income	3,010.2	2,278.2	2,780.1	75.0	P/B Ratio		1.8	52 Wk Hi-Low	31,075.0-20,900.0
Book Value	32,873.3	34,417.5	37,577.7	1,014.0	Yield %		1.9	Market Cap	US$1,571.2mil

Address	President Kennedypark 18	Tel 5-623-05-11	ADR	--	Executive Director	E. DeBruyne
	8500 Kortrijk	Fax 5-623-05-43	SEDOL	4089481	Chairman	R. Decaluwé

CBR

DJGI Industry: **Building Materials**
Stoxx Sector: **Construction**

CBR Cement Works SA (Cimenteries CBR Cementbedrijven SA) produces cement, ready-mix concrete, and aggregates. The company's products have a significant market share in Belgium, the Netherlands, and Germany. CBR also operates in Germany, western Canada, the United States, especially on the West Coast, the Czech Republic, Poland, and Turkey. The group's supporting businesses include construction services, the production of concrete pipes for sewer and water works, concrete blocks, asphaltic concrete, and the sale of fly ash.

	BEF mil 12/95	12/96	12/97	US$mil 12/97					
Sales	49,795.3	56,352.4	68,131.7	1,838.4	P/E Ratio		21.7	Price (6/30/98)	4,170.00
Net Income	3,866.2	4,335.0	4,426.1	119.4	P/B Ratio		2.7	52 Wk Hi-Low	4,255.0-2,900.0
Book Value	29,716.4	32,705.4	35,946.2	969.9	Yield %		2.4	Market Cap	US$2,579.5mil

Address	Chaussée de la Hulpe 185	Tel 2-678-33-53	ADR	--	CFO	Donald Fallon
	1170 Brussels	Fax 2-678-33-55	SEDOL	4161408	Chairman & CEO	Donald Fallon

CMB

DJGI Industry: **Marine Transportation**
Stoxx Sector: **Industrials**

Compagnie Maritime Belge SA (CMB) is a diversified company that transports oil, gas, and dry cargo; operates liner and port services in Antwerp and Zeebrugge; and provides insurance and financial services. The company's BOCIMAR subsidiary conducts its bulk and crude-oil operations, while liner services are provided by two majority-owned subsidiaries. Liner services accounted for 30% of 1997 revenues; bulk and crude oil transportation, 27%; port activities 25%; gas transportation, 14%; and insurance and other, 4%.

	BEF mil 12/95	12/96	12/97	US$mil 12/97					
Sales	40,645.0	37,894.0	46,335.0	1,250.3	P/E Ratio		12.0	Price (6/30/98)	2,810.00
Net Income	1,734.0	4,360.0	2,083.0	56.2	P/B Ratio		1.2	52 Wk Hi-Low	3,020.0-2,370.0
Book Value	16,627.0	18,378.0	19,597.0	528.8	Yield %		5.7	Market Cap	US$680.0mil

Address	De Gerlachekaai 20	Tel 3-247-59-11	ADR	--	President	N. Saverys
	2000 Antwerp	Fax 3-248-09-06	SEDOL	4221948	Chairman	M. Saverys

Cobepa

DJGI Industry: **Diversified Financial Services**
Stoxx Sector: **Financial Services**

Compagnie Benelux Paribas SA (COBEPA) is a holding company that invests in companies involved in the insurance, banking, distribution, textile, and other sectors. It provides assistance in the areas of stock-exchange listings, mergers and acquisitions, and capital increases. French holding company Paribas owns two-thirds of the company. Cobepa's holdings include stakes in four financial holding and investment companies: IBEL, Texaf, Companie Générale Mosane, and Luxembourg's CPI. Investment income accounted for 90% of 1997 revenues; interest income, 8%; and other income, 2%.

	BEF mil 12/95	12/96	12/97	US$mil 12/97				
Revenues	2,286.8	3,512.3	7,839.9	211.5	P/E Ratio	14.3	Price (6/30/98)	2,590.00
Net Income	3,361.1	3,209.2	23,410.2	631.7	P/B Ratio	3.0	52 Wk Hi-Low	2,720.0-1,450.0
Book Value	44,052.7	47,040.3	54,793.6	1,478.5	Yield %	3.3	Market Cap	US$2,680.3mil

Address	Blvd. Emile Jacqmain 162	Tel 2-204-32-10	ADR	--	CFO	C. Evers
	1000 Brussels	Fax 2-203-15-20	SEDOL	4207205	CEO	C. Varin

Colruyt

DJGI Industry: **Food Retailers & Wholesalers**
Stoxx Sector: **Consumer Non-Cyclical**

Colruyt Etn. Fr. NV is a major Belgian retailer that distributes grocery products, clothing, wines, and gardening supplies through its retail distribution chain, catalog sales, and other distribution channels. The company is also involved in computer applications and graphic design. Colruyt has testing laboratories to ensure that only fresh meat reaches supermarket shelves and is involved in the recycling of bottles and packaging. The company operates primarily in Belgium, with 140 stores, but also has investments in Spain and France.

	BEF mil 03/96	03/97	03/98	US$mil 03/98				
Sales	59,453.0	68,446.0	76,300.0	2,002.1	P/E Ratio	48.1	Price (6/30/98)	29,200
Net Income	1,931.9	2,162.5	2,620.0	68.7	P/B Ratio	10.5	52 Wk Hi-Low	29,700.0-16,500.0
Book Value	8,984.1	10,579.2	N/A	N/A	Yield %	0.6	Market Cap	US$3,058.2mil

Address	Edingensesteenweg, 196	Tel 2-360-10-40	ADR	--	President	--
	1500 Halle	Fax 2-360-02-07	SEDOL	4211853	Chairman	J. Colruyt

Delhaize

DJGI Industry: **Food Retailers & Wholesalers**
Stoxx Sector: **Consumer Non-Cyclical**

Delhaize Frères & Cie SA (Le Lion) is a food retailer with more than 1,816 outlets under 7 trade names in 5 countries. Its majority-owned U.S. subsidiary, Food Lion, has more than 1,000 Food Lion supermarkets in 14 states, generating 65% of the group's revenues. In December 1997, Delhaize sold 50% of its P.G. unit to France's Comptoirs Modernes SA. Other activities include pet-food chain Tom & Co. and mail-order house Caddy-Home. Retail sales in the United States accounted for 74% of 1997 revenues; in Belgium, 20%; and in Greece, 3%.

	BEF mil 12/95	12/96	12/97	US$mil 12/97				
Sales	368,477.9	412,345.8	508,591.8	13,723.5	P/E Ratio	25.9	Price (6/30/98)	2,600.00
Net Income	3,766.7	4,354.0	4,931.7	133.1	P/B Ratio	4.0	52 Wk Hi-Low	2,710.0-1,555.0
Book Value	23,980.3	28,200.8	33,853.1	913.5	Yield %	1.5	Market Cap	US$3,615.6mil

Address	Rue Osseghem 53	Tel 2-412-21-11	ADR	--	Jnt V Chairman	P.O. Beckers
	1080 Brussels	Fax 2-412-21-94	SEDOL	4262118	Chairman	G. de Vaucleroy

Dexia Belgium

DJGI Industry: **Banks - Regional (All)**
Stoxx Sector: **Bank**

Dexia Belgium (Credit Communal Holding) is a leading commercial bank in Belgium with a network of 950 branches throughout the country. It is the leading provider of banking and asset-management services to the public and industrial sectors. Dexia Belgium is the second largest general bank in Belgium whose clients represent one in every five of the population. It is has subsidiaries in Luxembourg and in New York City. In 1996, the company merged with Dexia France to form the Dexia Groupñthe result of the alliance of Credit Communal de Belgique and Credit Local de France.

	BEF mil 12/95	12/96	12/97	US$mil 12/97				
Revenues	33,833.0	38,130.0	44,584.0	1,203.0	P/E Ratio	19.0	Price (6/30/98)	5,600.00
Net Income	8,573.0	9,686.0	10,801.0	291.4	P/B Ratio	2.3	52 Wk Hi-Low	5,800.0-3,535.0
Book Value	71,500.0	77,529.0	88,763.0	2,395.1	Yield %	2.3	Market Cap	US$5,528.3mil

Address	44 Blvd Pacheco	Tel 2-222-11-11	ADR	--	V Chairman	F.X. De Donnea
	1000 Brussels	Fax 2-222-40-32	SEDOL	5150290	Chairman	T. Van Parys

Electrabel

DJGI Industry: **Electrical Utilities (All)**
Stoxx Sector: **Utility**

Electrabel SA generates and supplies electricity, distributes natural gas, and provides cable-television services. It provides 94% of Belgium's electricity requirements, 92% of its natural-gas distribution, and 53% of its cable-television subscriptions. The company is also involved in several new power-generating research projects and in building several combined-cycle steam and gas turbines. Electricity generation and distribution accounted for 76% of 1997 revenues; distribution of natural gas, 20%; cable television, 2%; and heat, steam, and other, 2%.

	BEF mil 12/95	12/96	12/97	US$mil 12/97				
Sales	215,956.1	221,485.2	238,501.5	6,435.5	P/E Ratio	17.4	Price (6/30/98)	10,550
Net Income	28,812.0	30,397.8	32,994.5	890.3	P/B Ratio	2.6	52 Wk Hi-Low	11,025.0-7,220.0
Book Value	214,858.7	216,701.7	223,800.0	6,038.9	Yield %	4.6	Market Cap	US$15,453mil

Address	Blvd. du Regent 8	Tel 2-518-61-11	ADR	--	Managing Director	J. Hansen
	1000 Brussels	Fax 2-518-64-00	SEDOL	4294791	Chairman	P. Bodson

In EuroStoxx 50.

Electrafina

DJGI Industry: **Oil Companies - Secondary**
Stoxx Sector: **Energy**

Electrafina SA is the holding company for a group of oil and natural-gas businesses. Oil-industry subsidiaries include Cometra of Canada and 66%-controlled Nimex Resources. The group also has interests in multimedia, primarily through multimedia holding company CLMM, in which Electrafina has a 25% stake. Electrafina is 45%-controlled by the Belgian holding company Groupe Bruxelles Lambert (GBL). Investment income accounted for 75% of 1997 revenues; interest income accounted for 21%, and other income for 4%.

	BEF mil 12/95	12/96	12/97	US$mil 12/97				
Sales	1,261.0	1,289.0	3,909.0	105.5	P/E Ratio	17.0	Price (6/30/98)	4,800.00
Net Income	5,294.0	24,269.0	10,538.0	284.3	P/B Ratio	1.5	52 Wk Hi-Low	5,420.0-3,140.0
Book Value	77,159.0	121,024.0	127,769.0	3,447.6	Yield %	3.0	Market Cap	US$4,849.4mil

Address	Ave. Marnix 24	Tel 2-547-21-11	ADR	--	Managing Director	Thierry de Rudder
	1050 Brussels	Fax 2-547-22-73	SEDOL	4213075	Chairman	Albert Frère

Fortis

DJGI Industry: **Diversified Financial Services**
Stoxx Sector: **Financial Services**

Fortis AG, formerly Fortis Groupe AG, provides financial and insurance services in Europe, the United States, Australia, and Southeast Asia. A partnership agreement signed with Fortis AMEV in 1990 led to the creation of Fortis, a leading international group in the areas of banking, insurance, and financial services. Fortis AG holds 50% of Fortis. It offers life, annuity, and pension policies as well as retail banking, mortgages, and fund-management services. Interest income accounted for 64% of 1997 revenues, investment and other income for 36%.

	BEF mil 12/95	12/96	12/97	US$mil 12/97				
Revenues	135.4	205.5	142.0	3.8	P/E Ratio	21.7	Price (6/30/98)	9,500.00
Net Income	11,170.1	13,452.2	18,032.0	486.6	P/B Ratio	2.7	52 Wk Hi-Low	11,325.0-6,570.0
Book Value	81,440.5	102,913.2	145,399.0	3,923.3	Yield %	1.6	Market Cap	US$10,718mil

Address	Blvd. Emile Jacqmain 53	Tel 2-220-81-11	ADR	--	V Chairman	Viscoun E. Davignon
	1000 Brussels	Fax 2-220-81-50	SEDOL	4001526	Chairman & CEO	Maurice Lippens

In EuroStoxx 50.

GBL

DJGI Industry: **Conglomerates**
Stoxx Sector: **Conglomerate**

Groupe Bruxelles Lambert (GBL) SA is an investment holding company with a broad portfolio that includes investments in the energy, multimedia, finance, and property sectors. The company aims to influence strategic planning and managerial selection in the companies in which it invests. Its holdings include 48% of Electrafina, 23% of Petrofina, 51% of Royale Belge, 12% of BBL, 41% of Parfinance, 51% of Audiofina, and 40% of Bernheim-Comofi. Investment income accounted for 86% of 1997 revenues; interest income, 9%; and other operating income, 5%.

	BEF mil 12/95	12/96	12/97	US$mil 12/97				
Sales	3,360.0	23,423.0	29,598.0	798.7	P/E Ratio	5.6	Price (6/30/98)	7,510.00
Net Income	6,602.0	16,891.0	31,726.0	856.1	P/B Ratio	1.7	52 Wk Hi-Low	8,630.0-5,090.0
Book Value	75,597.0	88,676.0	117,319.0	3,165.7	Yield %	2.8	Market Cap	US$4,906.7mil

Address	Ave. Marnix 24	Tel 2-547-23-52	ADR	--	CFO	P. de Vos
	1000 Brussels	Fax 2-547-22-85	SEDOL	4391551	Chairman	G. Frere

Gevaert

DJGI Industry: **Conglomerates**
Stoxx Sector: **Conglomerate**

Gevaert NV, formerly Gevaert-Photo Produits SA, is a holding company with interests in financial institutions, transport, real estate, publishing, and chemicals in Belgium, the Netherlands, and Germany. Its major holdings are Bayer (Germany), Aegon (the Netherlands), Almanij (Belgium), and Compagnie de Navigation Mixte (France). These four companies generate nearly 60% of Gevaert's dividend income. It also holds a stake in Kredietbank SA Luxembourgeoise. Investment income accounted for 64% of 1997 revenues; interest income, 34%; and other operating income, 2%.

	BEF mil 12/95	12/96	06/97 *	US$mil 06/97				
Sales	3,635.3	4,713.1	7,155.3	198.9	P/E Ratio	8.1	Price (6/30/98)	2,460.00
Net Income	2,939.6	4,225.8	6,780.2	188.5	P/B Ratio	2.0	52 Wk Hi-Low	2,610.0-1,360.0
Book Value	29,115.4	31,456.1	32,203.3	895.3	Yield %	6.1	Market Cap	US$1,705.3mil

Address	Septestraat 27	Tel 3-443-02-11	ADR	GEVAY	V Chairman	F. Vreys
	2640 Mortsel	Fax 3-440-04-78	SEDOL	5318883	Chairman	André Leysen

*Irregular period due to fiscal year change.

GIB

DJGI Industry: **Food Retailers & Wholesalers**
Stoxx Sector: **Consumer Non-Cyclical**

GIB SA is a major Belgian retail group. It operates supermarkets, hypermarkets, department stores, home-improvement stores, fast-food restaurants, and specialized retail outlets. The company's food-retail division, which accounts for approximately 60% of revenues, consists of more than 600 stores. GIB also operates about 149 specialty retailers, including Pearle Vision Center and Inno. Supermarkets and hypermarkets accounted for 66% of fiscal 1998 revenues; D.I.Y. stores, 19%; fast-food restaurants, 8%; and speciality retailing and other, 7%.

	BEF mil 01/96	01/97	01/98	US$mil 01/98				
Sales	227,779.9	216,556.7	217,878.0	5,773.1	P/E Ratio	24.7	Price (6/30/98)	2,100.00
Net Income	-4,385.0	3,385.4	2,902.6	76.9	P/B Ratio	4.1	52 Wk Hi-Low	2,100.0-1,550.0
Book Value	13,372.4	15,555.2	17,592.7	466.2	Yield %	2.2	Market Cap	US$1,715.8mil

Address	Ave. des Olympiades 20	Tel 2-729-21-11	ADR	--	President	B. Albrecht
	1140 Brussels	Fax 2-729-20-96	SEDOL	4357735	Chairman	D. du Monceau

Kredietbank

DJGI Industry: **Banks - Major International**
Stoxx Sector: **Bank**

Kredietbank NV, Belgium's fourth-largest bank, offers banking, insurance, and other financial services. Its shareholders include the Antwerp-based Almanij NV, which holds 41% of the bank's shares, as well as HSA NV, KB Securities NV, Credit General SA de Banque, Kredietbank-Petercam Derivatives NV, Arfina NV, and Spaarkrediet NV. Kredietbank operates mainly in Belgium but also has subsidiaries in the United States, Africa, Asia, and the rest of Europe. Interest and fees on loans and interest income on bank deposits accounted for 61% of 1997 revenues.

	BEF mil 12/95	12/96	12/97	US$mil 12/97					
Revenues	227,432.4	239,050.7	278,592.9	7,517.3	P/E Ratio	34.1	Price (6/30/98)	3,330.00
Net Income	11,551.1	13,111.6	14,717.2	397.1	P/B Ratio	4.6	52 Wk Hi-Low	3,330.0-1,355.0
Book Value	86,879.1	95,580.7	108,414.4	2,925.4	Yield %	1.2	Market Cap	US$13,586mil

Address	Arenbergstraat 7	Tel 2-546-411-11	ADR	--	Jnt Mng Dir	R. Vermeiren
	1000 Brussels	Fax 2-546-41-09	SEDOL	4497749	Chairman	M. Cockaerts

Petrofina

DJGI Industry: **Oil Companies - Major**
Stoxx Sector: **Energy**

Petrofina SA is a petroleum company that explores for and produces oil and natural gas; manufactures feedstocks, plastics, and paints; and operates the Fina chain of gas stations in Europe and the southern United States. Its exploration centers on the North Sea, the United States, and Africa. The company also has operations in Asia and the former Soviet Union. During 1997 the group made discoveries in Vietnam, Angola, and the North Sea. Petroleum products accounted for 83% of 1997 revenues; chemicals, 12%; paints, 4%; and other products, 1%.

	BEF mil 12/95	12/96	12/97	US$mil 12/97					
Sales	551,810.0	612,872.0	492,961.0	13,301.7	P/E Ratio	16.2	Price (6/30/98)	15,275
Net Income	11,608.0	16,048.0	22,060.0	595.3	P/B Ratio	2.3	52 Wk Hi-Low	15,525.0-12,575.0
Book Value	121,690.0	132,575.0	155,915.0	4,207.1	Yield %	3.0	Market Cap	US$9,619.3mil

Address	52 rue de l'Industrie	Tel 2-288-91-11	ADR	FIN	CFO	François Cornelis
	1040 Brussels	Fax 2-288-34-45	SEDOL	4684002	Chairman	Albert Frère

In EuroStoxx 50.

Société Générale de Belgique

DJGI Industry: **Conglomerates**
Stoxx Sector: **Conglomerate**

Société Générale de Belgique SA (SGB) is Belguim's largest holding company, maintaining interests in eight large companies in the industrial and service sectors. It is controlled by French holding company Cie de Suez. The company holds an 18% share of Coficem, the majority shareholder in French company Sagem, which specializes in electronics and advanced telecommunications technology. SGB also invests in the following companies: Générale Bank, Fortis Group, Union Minière, Recticel, and Arbed.

	BEF mil 12/95	12/96	12/97	US$mil 12/97					
Sales	160,598.0	159,198.0	500,615.0	13,508.2	P/E Ratio	23.2	Price (6/30/98)	6,350.00
Net Income	9,205.0	11,220.0	19,326.0	521.5	P/B Ratio	2.5	52 Wk Hi-Low	6,840.0-3,070.0
Book Value	166,470.0	166,335.0	178,079.0	4,805.2	Yield %	1.9	Market Cap	US$12,055mil

Address	Rue Royale 30	Tel 2-507-02-11	ADR	--	CFO	A. Chaigneau
	1000 Brussels	Fax 2-513-43-27	SEDOL	4819677	Chmn & Mng Dir	C. Morin-Postel

Solvay

DJGI Industry: **Chemicals - Commodity**
Stoxx Sector: **Chemical**

Solvay SA is the parent company of a chemical group that specializes in five major areas: alkalis, peroxygens, plastics, processing, and health. Its alkalis sector supplies products to the glass, metal, textile, and paper industries. It produces high-density polyethylene, polypropylene, and polyvinyl chloride. Plastics processing includes coating, extrusion, blow molding, and thermoforming. The health sector makes pharmaceuticals and enzymes. Chemicals accounted for 35% of 1997 revenues; plastics, 30% ; processing, 19%; and health products, 16%.

	BEF mil 12/95	12/96	12/97	US$mil 12/97					
Sales	273,353.0	281,967.0	310,979.0	8,391.2	P/E Ratio	18.6	Price (6/30/98)	2,950.00
Net Income	12,291.0	13,301.0	13,332.0	359.7	P/B Ratio	2.1	52 Wk Hi-Low	3,060.0-1,975.0
Book Value	94,694.0	107,170.0	118,772.0	3,204.9	Yield %	2.7	Market Cap	US$6,657.1mil

Address	Rue du Prince Albert 33	Tel 2-509-61-11	ADR	SLVYY	V Chairman	A. Michielsen
	1050 Brussels	Fax 2-509-66-17	SEDOL	4821100	Chairman & CEO	B.D. Janssen

Tessenderlo Chemie

DJGI Industry: **Chemicals - Specialty**
Stoxx Sector: **Chemical**

Tessenderlo Chemie SA is one of the leading chemical companies in the world. Its business divisions produce plastics (PVC and VCM); mineral products (potash sulphate, soda sulphate, and phosphates); synthetic organic products (phenylchloroform, benzyl chloride, benzyl alcohol, and glycine); natural organic products (gelatin, animal fats, and protein); organic chemical synthesized products, alkalis, and derivatives (caustic soda and caustic potash). The company has operations in France, Italy, Luxembourg, the Netherlands, the United Kingdom, Hungary, and the United States.

	BEF mil 12/95	12/96	12/97	US$mil 12/97					
Sales	47,810.9	51,412.7	61,519.4	1,660.0	P/E Ratio	23.6	Price (6/30/98)	2,700.00
Net Income	3,102.2	2,566.9	3,285.4	88.7	P/B Ratio	3.4	52 Wk Hi-Low	3,010.0-1,720.0
Book Value	20,266.3	22,133.4	24,933.8	672.8	Yield %	1.3	Market Cap	US$2,099.7mil

Address	Stationstraat	Tel 1-361-22-11	ADR	TSDOY	President	--
	3980 Tessenderlo	Fax 1-366-81-40	SEDOL	4884006	Chairman & CEO	G. Marchand

Tractebel

DJGI Industry: **Electrical Utilities (All)**
Stoxx Sector: **Utility**

Tractebel SA, through its subsidiary Electrabel, generates 93% of Belgium's electricity. It is a utilities and industrial services group with interests in electricity, natural gas, communications, water distribution, environment, real estate, infrastructure, and industry. Communications services include cable television, mobile telephones, and computers. The company has investments in Europe, the United States, Canada, Argentina, and Hong Kong. Electricity and gas accounted for 78% of 1997 revenues; technical services, 17%; engineering, 3%; and communications and other, 2%.

	BEF mil 12/95	12/96	12/97	US$mil 12/97				
Sales	321,699.1	344,326.1	384,017.8	10,362.1	P/E Ratio	28.1	Price (6/30/98)	5,450.00
Net Income	11,335.6	12,094.3	16,403.0	442.6	P/B Ratio	3.3	52 Wk Hi-Low	5,630.0-2,925.0
Book Value	96,231.1	105,797.3	140,396.5	3,788.4	Yield %	2.0	Market Cap	US$12,379mil

Address	Pl. du Trône 1		Tel 2-510-73-37	ADR	--	CFO	E. Van Innis
	1000 Brussels		Fax 2-510-73-88	SEDOL	4900300	Chmn Mgt Bd	B. Bodson

UCB

DJGI Industry: **Chemicals - Specialty**
Stoxx Sector: **Chemical**

UCB SA is a diversified pharmaceutical and chemical company. Its activities are divided into three areas: the pharmaceutical sector is involved in the research, production, and marketing of prescription pharmaceuticals; the chemical sector manufactures intermediate, fine, and specialty chemicals; and the films and packaging sector is involved in the production and conversion of flexible materials for the food and medical industries. Prescription medicines and other pharmaceuticals accounted for 44% of 1997 revenues; chemicals, 36%; and transparent packaging and other films, 20%.

	BEF mil 12/95	12/96	12/97	US$mil 12/97				
Sales	54,111.0	50,825.0	60,537.0	1,633.5	P/E Ratio	44.9	Price (6/30/98)	193,050
Net Income	3,264.0	5,710.0	6,272.0	169.2	P/B Ratio	9.1	52 Wk Hi-Low	199,000-113,350
Book Value	21,128.0	26,072.0	30,958.0	835.3	Yield %	0.7	Market Cap	US$7,573.6mil

Address	Ave. Louise 326		Tel 2-641-14-11	ADR	--	V Chairman	D. Janssen
	1050 Brussels		Fax 2-641-16-49	SEDOL	4910622	Chairman	G. Jacobs

Union Minière

DJGI Industry: **Other Non-Ferrous Metals**
Stoxx Sector: **Basic Resources**

Union Minière (UM) SA is involved in the refining, primary transformation, and recycling of nonferrous metals, and in mining, smelting, and related services. These metals are used in basic and advanced technological industries and in the construction and research sectors. UM has operations in France, Germany, Morocco, the Netherlands, the United Kingdom, Mexico, Canada, and the United States. Technology and services accounted for 26% of 1997 revenues; zinc, 23%; copper, 21%; precious metals, 16%; diamonds, 7%; advanced materials, 6%; and other activities, 1%.

	BEF mil 12/95	12/96	12/97	US$mil 12/97				
Sales	127,351.0	131,027.0	156,912.0	4,234.0	P/E Ratio	16.0	Price (6/30/98)	2,300.00
Net Income	-954.0	391.0	3,680.0	99.3	P/B Ratio	1.4	52 Wk Hi-Low	3,840.0-2,255.0
Book Value	34,389.0	35,149.0	41,230.0	1,112.5	Yield %	1.9	Market Cap	US$1,449.1mil

Address	Rue Du Marais 31		Tel 2-27-71-11	ADR	--	Director	F. Blanc
	1000 Brussels		Fax 2-227-79-00	SEDOL	4005001	Chairman & CEO	K. Vinck

Denmark

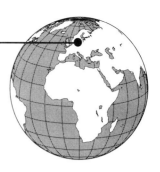

Exchange:

The Copenhagen Stock Exchange

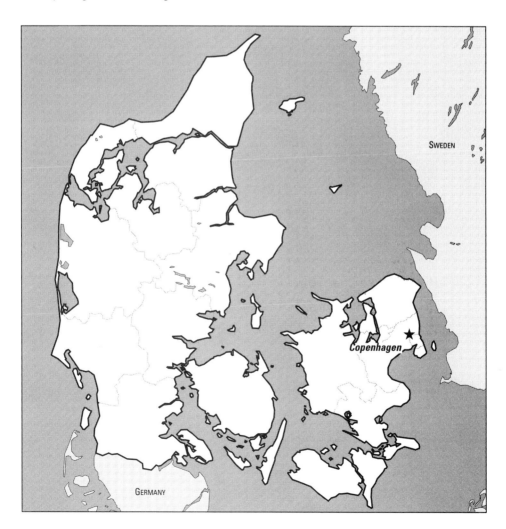

Denmark

Lauren Madsen
Copenhagen

As stock exchange mergers and alliances were sweeping through Europe in 1998, the modest-sized Copenhagen Stock Exchange made a bid for survival by formalizing plans to link its own share trading with the much larger operations in neighboring Sweden.

The plan, called the NOREX alliance, becomes reality in the second quarter of 1999. The Copenhagen and Stockholm bourses, which together account for about 75% of the equity trading in the Nordic region by both volume and market value, will integrate their share dealings via a common trading system and joint trading rules.

The two bourses have formed a joint company, called Nordic Exchanges A/S, to market and develop the common trading system and services. The bourses will, however, continue to exist as separate entities with individual relationships with member companies and issuers.

Eventually, the bourses plan to expand the cooperation to include trade in interest-bearing securities and derivatives. In addition, they hope to expand the operation geographically to Nordic neighbors Norway, Finland, and Iceland.

The venture aims at creating a larger, less expensive, more easily accessible exchange to lure foreign investors. Gaining attention abroad is of particular importance following decisions by both Denmark and Sweden to abstain, at least at the start, from participation in the single European currency.

On the practical side, the combined equity market will boast not only a common trading system, but also a harmonized set of regulations governing share dealings. It will offer joint membership in both exchanges to brokerages at a discounted price.

The 300-year-old Copenhagen Stock Exchange will be thrust into the 21st century by the adoption of Stockholm's state-of-the-art SAX2000 electronic trading system, scheduled to go live in Copenhagen on April 1, 1999. The SAX2000 system will replace Copenhagen's ELECTRA trading system, which dates back to 1988, when floor dealings were abolished.

The alliance with the Stockholm bourse is just one of several initiatives taken in recent years to boost Copenhagen's appeal abroad. Others include the extension of trading hours to 5 p.m. local time to overlap with equity trading in New York, the establishing

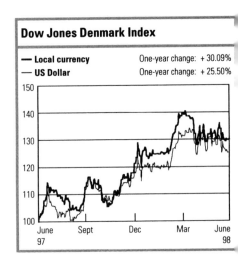

Dow Jones Denmark Index

— Local currency   One-year change: + 30.09%
— US Dollar   One-year change: + 25.50%

of an Internet web site *(www.xcse.dk)*, and the launch of a specialized submarket devoted exclusively to high-growth, small-cap shares.

The latest of the Exchange's initiatives, the New Market planned for the second half of 1998, is aimed not only at attracting investors to small-cap stocks but also at encouraging small companies to publicly list shares. The stocks will be included in the Exchange's all-share index as well as in respective industry lists.

Shares listed on the New Market must meet certain criteria, such as an annual growth rate above the 10% to 15% of the general market, and companies are required to plow most of the proceeds generated by listing back into the company, rather than into the pockets of owners. In return, companies initially listing shares on the New Market will benefit from a more relaxed set of listing rules.

Five new companies listed shares on the Exchange in 1997 and six listed in the first half of 1998. In total, there were 249 stocks listed in the Copenhagen market at the end of 1997 and 254 stocks by mid-1998.

Low foreign interest has historically been a problem for the Exchange, caused to a large extent by the relatively small size of most listed Danish companies. In mid-1998, analysts estimated that only about 20% of the shares in Danish listed companies were held by foreign investors,

Country Information

Trading Hours:
  Local: 8:30 am - 5:00 pm

  EST: 2:30 am - 11:00 am

  GMT: 0800 - 1600

Population (6/98):
5,333,617

Unemployment (97):
8.0%

Main Industries:
Food processing, machinery and equipment, textiles and clothing, chemical products, electronics, construction, furniture, and other wood products, and shipbuilding

Gross Domestic Product (97):
US$161.11 billion

GDP per Capita (97):
US$30,541.83

Three-Year Average GDP Growth (94-97):
2.8%

Average Annual CPI Growth (96-97):
+ 2.19%

Monetary Unit:
Danish Krone

Exchange Rate (6/98):
DKK6.88 to US$1.00

well below estimates of more than 30% foreign ownership in Sweden.

Whether or not recent initiatives have lured foreign investors to Copenhagen, they have helped to pick up the pace of trading on the Exchange. Equity turnover soared to a record 310 billion kroner in 1997, up from 217 billion in 1996 and nearly double the Exchange's volume of 157 billion in 1995. Average daily volume jumped 42% in 1997, to 1.2 billion kroner.

The trend continued in 1998, with turnover in equities rising 51% to 231 billion kroner just in the first half, pushing the average daily volume up to 1.9 billion kroner.

The class B stock of pharmaceutical giant Novo Nordisk A/S was the most actively traded share in the first half of 1998, with turnover of 26.3 billion kroner. It was followed by Danish telecommunications concern Tele Danmark A/S, the former state-owned telephone monopoly, with turnover of 25.7 billion kroner.

Investors tend to focus their attention on the blue-chip stocks included in Copenhagen's benchmark KFX index. Turnover of KFX shares represented 60% of the volume traded on the Exchange in 1997, even though the market capitalization of the companies listed on the index represented only 46% of the market's value.

Launched in 1989, the KFX index is composed of the 20 shares with the

Ten Largest Capitalized Companies In The Dow Jones Denmark Index
as of 6/30/98

Stock	Market Cap. US$ Thousands
Tele Danmark	10,374,969
D/S 1912	9,254,884
D/S Svendborg	8,938,980
Novo-Nordisk	8,850,737
Den Danske Bank	6,341,763
Ratin	5,591,623
Carlsberg	4,640,950
Unidanmark	4,194,044
Danisco	4,033,517
BG Bank	1,811,235

highest market capitalization in a portfolio of the 25 most actively traded shares during the previous 12 months. The member stocks are selected once a year in November and the index is reconfigured in December.

The KFX index had a banner year in 1997, rising to 56 separate record highs and increasing a total of 55%. That topped the performance of Copenhagen's broad index, the All-Share index, which climbed 43%.

In June 1998, the KFX included Denmark's four largest commercial banks, one of the world's largest shipping companies, two telecommunications companies, three industrial services and cleaning concerns, a pair of food and drink companies, an airline holding company and one airport operator, a pharmaceuticals manufacturer and a medical supplies maker, two industrial companies, a security and emergency services company, and a high-end consumer electronics manufacturer.

Companies listed on the Exchange can have two classes of shares, both A and B. An A share entitles the holder to ten votes, while a B share carries only one vote. However, there is no restriction on foreign ownership of either class of stock.

Meanwhile, all foreign investors are exempt from Danish turnover tax. The capital transfer tax was abolished in 1993 and there are no currency restrictions.

The recent year was marked by the resignation of the Exchange's president and chief executive, Lars Johansen. He was succeeded by Hans-Ole Jochumsen on June 1, 1998.

Mr. Johansen was credited with transforming the Exchange into a modern European bourse. Apart from the ground-breaking alliance with the Stockholm Exchange and other initiatives taken to boost equity turnover, he is also responsible for leading the Exchange's transformation into a public limited company.

On January 1, 1996, the Copenhagen Stock Exchange was converted from an independent nonprofit institution into a limited company with a share capital of 40 million kroner and an equity capital of 80 million kroner. Subsequently, FUTOP, the Danish Futures and Options clearing

Market Sector Performance In The Dow Jones Denmark Index
1 Year Change Through 6/30/98

Market Sector	Change % (US$)
Utilities	84.57
Consumer, Cyclical	40.30
Technology	35.65
Financial	28.70
Consumer, Non-Cyclical	22.17
Industrial	18.66

center, was merged with the Copenhagen Stock Exchange, becoming a subsidiary of the publicly listed bourse as of January 1, 1997.

The Copenhagen Stock Exchange, which had 28 members in mid-1998, falls under the supervision of the Danish Securities Council and the Danish Financial Supervisory Authority.

Aalborg Portland

DJGI Industry: **Building Materials**
Stoxx Sector: **Construction**

Aalborg Portland Holding A/S, a subsidiary of FLS Industries A/S, produces and markets cement, lime, chalk, sand, gravel, other cement-related materials, cable products, and products used in the security industry, including industrial flooring and support structures. The company and its subsidiaries operate in Denmark, the rest of Scandinavia, Africa, North and South America, and Europe. In 1997, pretax profit jumped 71% to DKK221 million, while net profit rose 78% to DKK146 million. Cement accounted for 56% of 1997 revenues, and other building materials made up 38%.

	DKK mil 12/95	12/96	12/97	US$mil 12/97					
Sales	2,636.0	1,979.8	2,300.9	336.1	P/E Ratio	12.4	Price (6/30/98)		700.00
Net Income	29.1	222.0	211.4	30.9	P/B Ratio	1.0	52 Wk Hi-Low		863.00-698.25
Book Value	2,133.0	2,510.4	2,682.3	391.8	Yield %	2.1	Market Cap		US$227.8mil

Address	Rordalsvej 44	Tel 36-18-28-00	ADR	--	V Chairman	J.F. Nissen
	9100 Aalborg	Fax 36-44-11-46	SEDOL	4001979	Chairman	C. Kjær

Bang & Olufsen

DJGI Industry: **Consumer Electronics**
Stoxx Sector: **Consumer Cyclical**

Bang & Olufsen Holding A/S develops, manufactures, and markets audio, video, telecommunications, and medical equipment. The company's products include conventional and cordless telephones, stereos, televisions, and plastic units for medical use. Audio and video equipment accounted for 86% of 1997 revenues. The company is also involved in developing noninvasive measuring methods and advance software packages. In May 1997, the company repurchased, for DKK540 million, its 25% audio-visual unit stake from Philips, which had acquired the shares in the early 1990's.

	DKK mil 05/96	05/97	05/98	US$mil 05/98					
Sales	2,717.4	3,008.2	3,117.2	458.0	P/E Ratio	21.5	Price (6/30/98)		495.00
Net Income	142.9	179.4	308.0	45.3	P/B Ratio	5.7	52 Wk Hi-Low		500.00-365.00
Book Value	896.5	1,034.4	1,162.8	170.9	Yield %	0.5	Market Cap		US$876.3mil

Address	Peter Bangs Vej 15	Tel 96-84-11-22	ADR	--	President & CEO	H. Peterson
	7600 Struer	Fax 97-85-18-88	SEDOL	4161293	Chairman	P. Skak Olufsen

Bikuben

DJGI Industry: **Banks - Regional (All)**
Stoxx Sector: **Bank**

Bikuben Girobank (BG Bank) is Denmark's third-largest banking group. It was created in 1995 by the merger of Sparekassen Bikuben and Denmark's fifth-largest bank, Girobank. The bank provides commercial and investment banking, house financing and consultancy, stockbroking, securities trading and management, and general insurance. BG Bank's three-way alliance with Nykredit A/S and Topdanmark A/S was dissolved in June 1997 after full merger efforts failed. In April 1998, BG Bank will launch a joint venture mortgage credit unit, BG Kredit, with Realkredit Danmark.

	DKK mil 12/95	12/96	12/97	US$mil 12/97					
Revenues	13,293.0	11,433.2	11,071.6	1,617.4	P/E Ratio	7.3	Price (6/30/98)		425.93
Net Income	1,688.4	1,406.9	979.5	143.1	P/B Ratio	1.5	52 Wk Hi-Low		500.00-364.57
Book Value	6,009.2	8,160.8	8,226.9	1,201.8	Yield %	4.7	Market Cap		US$1,811.2mil

Address	Hokbro Plads 10	Tel 43-30-30-30	ADR	--	V Chairman	E. Vinum
	1200 Copenhagen K	Fax 33-15-90-33	SEDOL	4833194	Chairman	P. Hojland

Carlsberg

DJGI Industry: **Distillers & Brewers**
Stoxx Sector: **Food & Beverage**

Carlsberg A/S is a brewing company that generates most of its beer revenues outside Europe and has brewing operations in several countries. Its best-selling alcohol products are Carlsberg and Tuborg beers. The company, Denmark's largest beer brewer, holds 51% of a new company, Coca-Cola Nordic Beverages A/S, set up in March of 1997 with Coca-Cola Co. for bottling and distribution. In August of 1997, Carlsburg bought the remaining 50% stake in the Carlsburg-Tetley joint venture for GBP110 million.

	DKK mil 09/95	09/96	09/97	US$mil 09/97					
Sales	13,351.0	13,931.0	14,918.0	2,226.2	P/E Ratio M	21.6	Price (6/30/98) M		500.00
Net Income	1,003.0	1,063.0	1,242.0	185.3	P/B Ratio M	3.3	52 Wk Hi-Low M		500.00-328.00
Book Value	7,808.0	8,406.0	9,644.0	1,439.2	Yield % M	0.7	Market Cap M		US$2,560.4mil

Address	Vesterfælledvej 100	Tel 33-27-33-27	ADR	--	Executive Bd	M.C. Luul
	1799 Copenhagen V	Fax 33-27-47-11	SEDOL	4169208	President & CEO	F. Lindelov

M=Multiple issues in index; reflects most active.

Christian Hansen

DJGI Industry: **Other Food**
Stoxx Sector: **Food & Beverage**

Christian Hansen Holdings A/S manufactures and distributes special products and natural ingredients for the food industry, particularly natural food additives, biological products for agriculture, and allergy treatment and testing. Sales to the food industry of products such as enzymes, bacteria cultures, colors, and natural flavors generated 72% of the company's 1997 revenues. The diagnosis and treatment of allergies accounted for 23% of 1997 revenues. The company markets its products in Scandinavia, the rest of Europe, North America, South America, and Australia.

	DKK mil 08/95	08/96	08/97	US$mil 08/97					
Sales	1,760.0	2,199.6	2,757.7	400.7	P/E Ratio	24.3	Price (6/30/98)		901.00
Net Income	146.0	162.8	186.4	27.1	P/B Ratio	3.1	52 Wk Hi-Low		942.66-720.00
Book Value	1,248.8	1,315.4	1,454.1	211.3	Yield %	0.4	Market Cap		US$602.5mil

Address	Boge Allé 10-12	Tel 45-76-76-76	ADR	--	V Chairman	J. Nordin
	2970 Horsholm	Fax 45-76-55-76	SEDOL	4173179	Chairman	S. Dyrlov Madsen

Codan

DJGI Industry: **Insurance - Full Line**
Stoxx Sector: **Insurance**

A/S Forsikringsselskabet Codan is a leading Danish insurance group that became the largest in the Danish nonlife sector after its 1993 acquisition of Hafnia Holding, a rival insurance company almost double its size. Codan provides insurance, reinsurance, securities trading and management, commercial banking, real estate, pension schemes, and other financial services in Denmark, Sweden, Norway, the United States, Singapore, and Bermuda. Nonlife and life insurance premiums accounted for 57% of 1997 fiscal revenues, and investment income accounted for 41%.

	DKK mil 12/95	12/96	12/97	US$mil 12/97					
Revenues	9,998.0	10,498.0	10,651.0	1,555.9	P/E Ratio	8.3	Price (6/30/98)		960.00
Net Income	561.0	1,071.0	782.0	114.2	P/B Ratio	1.0	52 Wk Hi-Low		1,298.7-870.0
Book Value	5,023.0	5,941.0	6,570.0	959.8	Yield %	2.3	Market Cap		US$945.6mil

Address	Codanhus, Gl. Kongevej 60	Tel 31-21-21-21	ADR	--	Managing Director	Peter Zobel
	1790 Copenhagen V	Fax 31-21-21-22	SEDOL	4324858	Chairman	Henrik Christrup

Coloplast

DJGI Industry: **Advanced Medical Devices**
Stoxx Sector: **Technology**

Coloplast A/S develops, manufactures, and markets ostomy and incontinence appliances, wound dressings, mastectomy appliances, skin-care products, and other health-care products in Scandinavia, Europe, the United States, Canada, and Japan. The company's trademarks include Assura, Alterna, Conveen, Comfeel, Sween, Amoena, Discrene, and Compeed. Ostomy appliances accounted for 39% of fiscal 1997 revenues; incontinence appliances, 20%; wound dressings, 17%; mastectomy appliances, 14%; skin-care products, 7%; and consumer products, 3%.

	DKK mil 09/95	09/96	09/97	US$mil 09/97					
Sales	1,683.7	1,974.5	2,398.5	357.9	P/E Ratio	32.5	Price (6/30/98)		675.00
Net Income	150.5	184.8	237.4	35.4	P/B Ratio	8.0	52 Wk Hi-Low		700.00-443.00
Book Value	738.1	895.0	1,015.7	151.6	Yield %	0.6	Market Cap		US$1,088.2mil

Address	Holtedam 1	Tel 49-11-11-11	ADR	--	V Chairman	N.P. Louis-Hansen
	3050 Humlebaek	Fax 4-9-11-15-55	SEDOL	4209580	Chairman	P. Marcus

Copenhagen Airports

DJGI Industry: **Other Industrial & Commercial Services**
Stoxx Sector: **Industrials**

Copenhagen Airports A/S (Kobenhavns Lufthavne) operates Denmark's largest airport, the Copenhagen International Airport, and Roskilde Airport, a small domestic airport just outside Copenhagen. It is a hub airport for the regional flag carrier Scandinavian Airlines System (SAS). Copenhagen Airports provides passenger, cargo, and security services, as well as bus transportation. In addition, it operates a shopping center and parking lots. Traffic income accounted for 51% of 1997 revenues; concession income, 39%; rental income, 7%; and sale of services, 3%.

	DKK mil 12/95	12/96	12/97	US$mil 12/97					
Sales	1,200.6	1,395.3	1,499.1	219.0	P/E Ratio	23.4	Price (6/30/98)		834.25
Net Income	247.4	279.5	323.3	47.3	P/B Ratio	4.0	52 Wk Hi-Low		860.00-702.00
Book Value	1,411.7	1,628.3	1,879.4	274.5	Yield %	1.0	Market Cap		US$1,096.6mil

Address	Box 74, Lufthavnsboulevarden 6	Tel 32-31-32-31	ADR	--	V Chairman	O. Rendbaek
	2770 Kastrup	Fax 32-31-31-32	SEDOL	4155285	Chairman	V. Anderson

Danisco

DJGI Industry: **Other Food**
Stoxx Sector: **Food & Beverage**

Danisco A/S is the largest sugar producer in northern Europe. and it has substantial interests in spirits, snacks, frozen foods, food ingredients, and packaging. The company consists of 11 divisions and more than 100 units. Dansico operates four sectors including Food & Beverage, Sugar, Ingredients, and Packaging. Sugar generated 37% of Danisco's 1997 revenues; packaging, 31%; foods and beverages, 16%; and food ingredients, 16%. The group is based in Denmark but has large production units in Sweden, Germany, the United Kingdom, Spain, the United States, and Mexico.

	DKK mil 04/96	04/97	04/98	US$mil 04/98					
Sales	16,186.4	17,002.0	18,802.0	2,746.8	P/E Ratio	22.6	Price (6/30/98)		462.00
Net Income	1,215.2	1,390.0	1,220.0	178.2	P/B Ratio	2.3	52 Wk Hi-Low		466.00-343.00
Book Value	7,739.8	9,954.0	12,173.0	1,778.4	Yield %	1.3	Market Cap		US$4,033.5mil

Address	Box 17, Langebrogade 1	Tel 32-66-20-00	ADR	--	Jnt V Chairman	E.B. Rasmussen
	1001 Copenhagen K	Fax 32-66-21-75	SEDOL	4155586	Chairman	H. Schroder

Den Danske Bank

DJGI Industry: **Banks - Major International**
Stoxx Sector: **Bank**

Den Danske Bank A/S is Denmark's largest banking group, with 425 branch offices in 1997. The company provides domestic and international banking, securities trading and management, leasing, insurance, residential-mortgage financing, and other financial services. Interest and fees on loans accounted for 53% of 1997 revenues; interest on government securities, 21%; interest on bank deposits, 11%; other interest income, 3%; and non-interest income, 12%. Den Danske Bank bought a Swedish regional bank, Oestgoeta Enskilda Bank AB, in March 1997.

	DKK mil 12/95	12/96	12/97	US$mil 12/97					
Revenues	28,591.3	29,061.2	33,450.0	4,886.4	P/E Ratio	10.4	Price (6/30/98)		825.00
Net Income	3,628.8	3,649.6	4,201.0	613.7	P/B Ratio	1.6	52 Wk Hi-Low		965.00-638.00
Book Value	22,800.3	25,622.7	27,023.0	3,947.6	Yield %	2.2	Market Cap		US$6,341.8mil

Address	Holmens Kanal 2-12	Tel 33-44-00-00	ADR	DEAFY	V Chairman	P. Marcus
	1092 Copenhagen K	Fax 31-18-58-73	SEDOL	4262925	Chairman	P. Svanholm

D/S 1912

DJGI Industry: **Marine Transportation**
Stoxx Sector: **Industrials**

Dampskibsselskabet af 1912 A/S (D/S 1912) operates a shipping, oil, and natural-gas partnership with Dampskibsselskabet Svendborg A/S under the Maersk name. The partnership involves shipping with self-owned and chartered vessels, container shipping services, and tank- and gas-transport. The company is involved in offshore drilling activities that include supply rigs and drilling rigs in the North Sea, and Qatar, and it is part of a consortium in Algeria. D/S 1912 also carries out test drillings in locations such as China and Indonesia.

	DKK mil 12/95	12/96	12/97	US$mil 12/97				
Sales	116.0	276.0	422.0	61.6	P/E Ratio M	126.9	Price (6/30/98) M	59,000
Net Income	200.0	384.0	502.0	73.3	P/B Ratio M	29.4	52 Wk Hi-Low M	69,800.0-47,000.0
Book Value	1,629.0	1,851.0	2,169.0	316.9	Yield % M	0.3	Market Cap M	US$4,627.4mil

Address	**Esplanaden 50**		Tel **33-63-33-63**		ADR	--	Managing Owner	**A.P. Moller**
	1098 Copenhagen K		Fax --		SEDOL	4248765	Chairman	**M. M. Moller**

M=Multiple issues in index; reflects most active.

D/S Svendborg

DJGI Industry: **Marine Transportation**
Stoxx Sector: **Industrials**

Dampskibsselskabet Svendborg A/S (D/S Svendborg) is engaged in international shipping, container services, and oil and natural gas production. The company operates a fleet of tankers and liners under the name Maersk through a 50/50 partnership with Dampskibsselskabet af 1912 A/S. The partnership operates container and supply vessels, tankers, and gas carriers, as well as drilling rigs. Other activities the company participates in include: air transport, medicine, information technology, shipbuilding, and retail trade through the ownership of Dansk Supermarked A/S.

	DKK mil 12/95	12/96	12/97	US$mil 12/97				
Sales	116.0	276.0	422.0	61.6	P/E Ratio M	115.2	Price (6/30/98) M	81,000
Net Income	232.0	410.0	524.0	76.5	P/B Ratio M	23.1	52 Wk Hi-Low M	100,000.0-68,500.0
Book Value	2,042.0	2,281.0	2,611.0	381.4	Yield % M	0.3	Market Cap M	US$4,388.2mil

Address	**Esplanaden 50**		Tel **33-63-33-63**		ADR	--	Managing Owner	**A.P. Moller**
	1098 Copenhagen K		Fax --		SEDOL	4253059	Chairman	**M. M. Moller**

M=Multiple issues in index; reflects most active.

FLS Industries

DJGI Industry: **Industrial - Diversified**
Stoxx Sector: **Industrials**

FLS Industries A/S operates as a holding company with engineering, building materials, packaging, and aerospace subsidiaries. The company operates in Denmark, the rest of Europe, North and South America, Africa, and Asia. FLS Industries' subsidiaries produce cement, provide international transport and forwarding services, manufacture industrial packaging and perforated metal products for the building industry, and provide aircraft maintenance services. In May 1997, the group sold parts of its packaging interests and plans to sell the remaining units in the division.

	DKK mil 12/95	12/96	12/97	US$mil 12/97				
Sales	18,024.0	19,484.0	21,890.0	3,197.7	P/E Ratio	14.2	Price (6/30/98)	175.00
Net Income	309.0	510.0	567.0	82.8	P/B Ratio	2.1	52 Wk Hi-Low	265.00-155.00
Book Value	2,943.0	3,433.0	3,815.0	557.3	Yield %	2.3	Market Cap	US$988.7mil

Address	**Vigerslev Allé 77**		Tel **36-18-18-00**		ADR	--	V Chairman	**M. Fiorini**
	2500 Valby		Fax **36-30-44-41**		SEDOL	5263574	Chairman	**J. Munter**

GN Great Nordic

DJGI Industry: **Communications Technology**
Stoxx Sector: **Technology**

GN Great Nordic Ltd. (GN Store Nord A/S) is a worldwide group involved in the research, development, production, and marketing of telecommunications equipment. It operates international telecommunications networks, manufactures pay phones, headsets, and hearing aids, and makes electronic measuring instruments for data-communication and telecommunications applications. The company owns 53.5% of Sonofon, a Danish mobile-telephone network. In August 1997, shareholders approved dropping a holding company structure that has existed since 1928.

	DKK mil 12/95	12/96	12/97	US$mil 12/97				
Sales	2,133.7	2,722.2	3,543.0	517.6	P/E Ratio	34.0	Price (6/30/98)	210.00
Net Income	127.5	143.8	195.0	28.5	P/B Ratio	4.1	52 Wk Hi-Low	218.00-95.00
Book Value	1,863.5	1,071.1	1,808.0	264.1	Yield %	1.1	Market Cap	US$1,110.8mil

Address	**Kongens Nytorv 26**		Tel **33-95-08-88**		ADR	--	V Chairman	**C.F. Sverdrup**
	1016 Copenhagen K		Fax **33-95-08-89**		SEDOL	5323274	Chairman	**E.B. Rasmussen**

ISS

DJGI Industry: **Other Industrial & Commercial Services**
Stoxx Sector: **Industrials**

ISS (International System Service A/S) specializes in cleaning and maintenance services for commercial, retail, and industrial clients worldwide. It offers services to health-care institutions, food processing companies, and the transport industry and provides airport and aircraft cleaning services. Other operations include the distribution of cleaning products and machinery. The company operates in Scandinavia, Europe, Brazil, and Asia. The company divested its American subsidiary, ISS Inc., in 1996. In 1997, the company acquired 13 small companies in Asia and Scandinavia.

	DKK mil 12/95	12/96	12/97	US$mil 12/97				
Sales	14,391.1	15,396.2	11,782.0	1,721.1	P/E Ratio	26.4	Price (6/30/98)	400.00
Net Income	162.1	-1,855.5	451.1	65.9	P/B Ratio	9.2	52 Wk Hi-Low	412.00-184.00
Book Value	1,232.4	876.2	1,293.9	189.0	Yield %	0.5	Market Cap	US$1,506.1mil

Address	**Bedgade 30**		Tel **38-17-00-00**		ADR	ISS	V Chairman	**K. Vagner**
	1260 Copenhagen K		Fax **38-17-00-11**		SEDOL	4442620	Chairman	**A. Madsen**

Jyske Bank

DJGI Industry: **Banks - Regional (All)**
Stoxx Sector: **Bank**

Jyske Bank A/S is the fourth-largest banking group in Denmark. The bank distinguishes itself from the top three banks through its strong provincial customer base. It offers retail, investment, and corporate banking, real estate, leasing, factoring, stockbroking, securities management, mortgage lending, insurance products, and other financial services. It also offers currency exchange. Jyske Bank operates in Denmark, Germany, Switzerland, Gibraltar, Spain, and the United States. Interest and fees on loans accounted for 57% of 1997 revenues.

	DKK mil 12/95	12/96	12/97	US$mil 12/97				
Revenues	4,951.3	4,466.4	4,473.1	653.4	P/E Ratio	16.8	Price (6/30/98)	811.21
Net Income	723.6	640.1	435.7	63.6	P/B Ratio	1.5	52 Wk Hi-Low	865.00-572.00
Book Value	3,675.8	4,236.3	4,710.7	688.1	Yield %	1.5	Market Cap	US$1,060.4mil

Address	**Vestergade 8-16**	Tel **89-22-22-22**	ADR	--	V Chmn Supv Bd	**N. Vagn Jessen**
	8600 Silkeborg	Fax **89-22-24-96**	SEDOL	4479963	Chairman	**Leon Rasmussen**

NKT Holding

DJGI Industry: **Electrical Components & Equipment**
Stoxx Sector: **Industrials**

NKT Holding A/S is a leading Danish industrial group that specializes in high-voltage industrial cables, domestic electrical wiring, vacuum cleaners, and fiber-optic telecommunications cables. Its wholly owned subsidiary in the United Kingdom makes electrical-installation equipment and electricity meters. The company's Nilfisk unit manufactures vacuum cleaners. Vacuum cleaners accounted for 35% of 1997 revenues; cables, 26%; electrical installation equipment, 26%; bolts, screws, axles, pins, and rivets, 7%; steel products, 3%; electronic and optical components, 2%; and other, 1%.

	DKK mil 12/95	12/96	12/97	US$mil 12/97				
Sales	4,612.1	4,770.8	5,580.8	815.3	P/E Ratio	19.8	Price (6/30/98)	535.00
Net Income	40.6	108.0	202.9	29.6	P/B Ratio	1.5	52 Wk Hi-Low	590.00-448.30
Book Value	2,439.6	2,454.6	2,645.3	386.4	Yield %	2.6	Market Cap	US$582.0mil

Address	**NKT Allé 1**	Tel **43-48-20-00**	ADR	--	V Chairman	**H. Lavesen**
	2605 Brondby	Fax **43-96-18-20**	SEDOL	4642464	Chairman	**C. Kjær**

Novo Nordisk

DJGI Industry: **Pharmaceuticals**
Stoxx Sector: **Pharmaceutical**

Novo Nordisk AS manufactures pharmaceuticals and bioindustrial products. It is a leading global producer of insulin and insulin delivery systems used in the treatment of diabetes, and it manufactures hormone replacement therapy products. The company also produces and distributes industrial, technical, and animal-feed enzymes for the detergent, starch, and textile industries. Novo Nordisk is headquartered in Copenhagen, with manufacturing facilities in seven countries and major production plants in Denmark and the United States.

	DKK mil 12/95	12/96	12/97	US$mil 12/97				
Sales	14,003.0	15,337.0	17,608.0	2,572.2	P/E Ratio	29.6	Price (6/30/98)	948.00
Net Income	1,563.0	1,799.0	2,212.0	323.1	P/B Ratio	3.9	52 Wk Hi-Low	1,200.0-652.0
Book Value	14,310.0	15,872.0	17,953.0	2,622.6	Yield %	0.6	Market Cap	US$8,850.7mil

Address	**Novo Allé**	Tel **44-44-88-88**	ADR	NVO	V Chairman	**A. Philip**
	2880 Bagsvaerd	Fax **44-49-05-55**	SEDOL	5154656	Chairman	**V. Andersen**

Potagua

DJGI Industry: **Building Materials**
Stoxx Sector: **Construction**

Potagua A/S is a holding company with interests in the construction, engineering, packaging, aerospace, and service industries in Europe, North and South America, Africa, and Asia. It provides engineering, transportation, computer, and other services and produces and markets cement, lime, chalk, sand, gravel, calcium carbonate products, and building materials. The engineering division consists of 75 subsidiaries located in northern Europe and the United States. Engineering accounts for about 43% of the company's revenues, and building materials account for about 22%.

	DKK mil 12/95	12/96	12/97	US$mil 12/97				
Sales	18,044.0	19,502.0	21,913.0	3,201.1	P/E Ratio	13.8	Price (6/30/98)	190.00
Net Income	182.0	277.0	309.0	45.1	P/B Ratio	1.7	52 Wk Hi-Low	260.00-175.00
Book Value	2,055.0	2,277.0	2,466.0	360.2	Yield %	3.2	Market Cap	US$380.2mil

Address	**Kalvebod Brygge 20**	Tel **33-91-58-00**	ADR	--	CEO	**N. Bro-Rasmussen**
	1560 Copenhagen V	Fax **33-91-17-50**	SEDOL	5298792	Chairman	**K. Arnstedt**

Radiometer

DJGI Industry: **Advanced Medical Devices**
Stoxx Sector: **Technology**

Radiometer A/S researches, manufactures, develops, and sells measuring and monitoring instruments used primarily in medical and industrial applications. The company's products include blood-analyzing instruments, patient-monitoring equipment, pH meters, instruments for metallographic sample preparation, and measuring instruments for chemical analysis. Sales of the company's medical instruments generate more than 71% of its revenues. The company restructured its operations in 1997.

	DKK mil 04/96	04/97	04/98	US$mil 04/98				
Sales	1,682.8	1,690.0	1,639.3	239.5	P/E Ratio	29.5	Price (6/30/98)	274.75
Net Income	230.6	80.6	304.8	44.5	P/B Ratio	3.1	52 Wk Hi-Low	355.00-260.00
Book Value	1,370.8	923.4	1,098.9	160.5	Yield %	18.2	Market Cap	US$359.9mil

Address	**Alandevej 21**	Tel **38-27-38-27**	ADR	--	V Chairman	**J. Meldgaard**
	2700 Bronshoj	Fax **38-27-27-27**	SEDOL	4720092	Chairman	**S. Rasborg**

Ratin

DJGI Industry: **Other Industrial & Commercial Services**
Stoxx Sector: **Industrials**

Ratin A/S is a holding company that owns shares in Rentokil Initial PLC, an international service company which provides electronic security, manned guarding, hygiene and cleaning services, distribution and plant services, personnel services, and conference and training center facilities. The company also provides a range of property services, and is the world's leading supplier and maintainer of indoor tropical plants. Rentokil Initial operates in over 40 countries in Europe, North America, Asia Pacific, and Africa, and its two major brands, Rentokil and Initial, enjoy wide recognition internationally.

	DKK mil 12/95	12/96	12/97	US$mil 12/97				
Sales	N/A	N/A	N/A	N/A	P/E Ratio M	37.2	Price (6/30/98) M	1,450.00
Net Income	N/A	730.9	1,032.9	150.9	P/B Ratio M	NMF	52 Wk Hi-Low M	1,465.0-1,131.3
Book Value	N/A	42.0	57.3	8.4	Yield % M	0.8	Market Cap M	US$1,386.2mil

Address **Klausdalsbrovej 1**   Tel **39-69-99-41**   ADR   --   President & CEO   **H. Werdelin**
      2860 Soborg   Fax **39-69-99-78**   SEDOL   **5402377**   Chairman   **R. Koch-Nielsen**
M=Multiple issues in index; reflects most active.

SAS Danmark

DJGI Industry: **Airlines**
Stoxx Sector: **Consumer Cyclical**

SAS Danmark A/S is the joint national air carrier of Sweden, Norway, and Denmark. It conducts passenger air transport operations, freight operations, inflight and airport sales, and hotel operations. Scandinavian Airlines System (SAS) is jointly owned by Sweden's SAS Sverige, Norway's SAS Norge, and SAS Danmark. Each parent company is 50%-owned by its respective state government. The company conducts air transport activities through three consortia: SAS, Scanair, and SAS Commuter. In 1997, SAS joined Star Alliance, a global cooperation by a group of airlines.

	DKK mil 12/95	12/96	12/97	US$mil 12/97				
Sales	N/A	N/A	N/A	N/A	P/E Ratio	11.6	Price (6/30/98)	138.00
Net Income	281.0	299.7	379.6	55.5	P/B Ratio	2.2	52 Wk Hi-Low	138.00-77.50
Book Value	2,024.1	2,772.1	2,983.7	435.9	Yield %	2.5	Market Cap	US$942.0mil

Address **Box 150, Hedegardsvej 88**   Tel **32-32-00-00**   ADR   --   V Chairman   **A. Eldrup**
      2770 Kastrup   Fax --   SEDOL   **5065811**   Chairman   **H. Schroder**

Sophus Berendsen

DJGI Industry: **Other Industrial & Commercial Services**
Stoxx Sector: **Industrials**

Sophus Berendsen A/S provides business services and manufactures industrial equipment. It has three main business areas: textile services, electronics, and industrial components. The company has a 35.8% interest in Rentokil Group PLC, of the United Kingdom, a company that provides environmental, security, personnel, and delivery services. Sophus Berendsen also makes hydraulics, workwear, and mats, and it operates laundry services. In 1997, Sophus announced plans to split itself into two new companies, Sophus Berendsen A/S and Ratin A/S.

	DKK mil 12/95	12/96	12/97	US$mil 12/97				
Sales	13,765.6	6,718.9	7,492.9	1,094.6	P/E Ratio M	35.7	Price (6/30/98) M	285.00
Net Income	958.8	910.5	211.6	30.9	P/B Ratio M	2.4	52 Wk Hi-Low M	289.00-161.49
Book Value	2,288.7	1,326.1	3,172.6	463.5	Yield % M	0.5	Market Cap M	US$823.7mil

Address **Klausdalsbrovej 1**   Tel **39-69-85-00**   ADR   --   V Chairman   **E. Somonsen**
      2860 Soborg   Fax **39-69-73-00**   SEDOL   **5402667**   Chairman   **R. Koch-Nielsen**
M=Multiple issues in index; reflects most active.

Superfos

DJGI Industry: **Heavy Construction**
Stoxx Sector: **Construction**

Superfos A/S operates through three main divisions: road construction, packaging, and chemicals. The company's road contruction division produces asphalt and broken granite and also surfaces roads. Its wholly owned subsidiary, Jeppsson Pac, manufactures plastic and cardboard containers in Sweden and France. Superfos doubled its chemical division by acquiring Swedish chemical trade and distribution company Chematex. Road construction, including asphalt production and surfacing, accounted for 55% of 1997 revenues; packaging, 23%; and trading of chemicals, 22%.

	DKK mil 12/95	12/96	12/97	US$mil 12/97				
Sales	4,860.6	5,417.1	6,884.6	1,005.7	P/E Ratio	18.4	Price (6/30/98)	185.00
Net Income	258.2	300.4	307.8	45.0	P/B Ratio	3.3	52 Wk Hi-Low	204.00-155.00
Book Value	1,608.0	1,693.9	1,697.5	248.0	Yield %	2.2	Market Cap	US$830.0mil

Address **Frydenlundsvej 30**   Tel **45-67-00-00**   ADR   --   V Chairman   **J.E. Karlskov**
      2950 Vedbæk   Fax **45-66-04-05**   SEDOL   **5211926**   Chairman   **J. Tandrup**

Tele Danmark

DJGI Industry: **Telephone Utilities (All)**
Stoxx Sector: **Telecom**

Tele Danmark A/S is Denmark's largest telecommunications operator. Domestic telephone services are its core business activity, with more than 3 million lines and nearly 1 million mobile phone subscribers. It supplies and services business telecommunications and data networks, operates a cable television network with more than half a million subscribers, publishes telephone directories, and provides public telephone services. The company operates in Denmark, Sweden, Norway, the rest of Europe, and the United States.

	DKK mil 12/95	12/96	12/97	US$mil 12/97				
Sales	18,846.0	23,304.0	28,996.0	4,235.8	P/E Ratio	56.2	Price (6/30/98)	660.00
Net Income	3,494.0	3,104.0	1,539.0	224.8	P/B Ratio	3.1	52 Wk Hi-Low	703.00-339.00
Book Value	25,939.0	27,879.0	28,338.0	4,139.7	Yield %	2.7	Market Cap	US$10,375mil

Address **Kannikegade 16**   Tel **89-33-77-77**   ADR   **TLD**   V Chairman   **T.J. Cawley**
      8000 Aarhus C   Fax **89-33-77-19**   SEDOL   **4889874**   Chairman   **K. Heinesen**

Topdanmark

DJGI Industry: **Insurance - Full Line**
Stoxx Sector: **Insurance**

Topdanmark A/S is the parent company of a financial services group that offers life and general insurance, reinsurance, and personal and corporate financial services. It derives 78% of its general insurance income from auto, personal, and agricultural insurance products. Its nonlife insurance unit is the second-largest in Denmark. Nonlife insurance premiums accounted for 54% of 1997 revenues; life insurance premiums, 20%; investment income, 14%; and gains and losses on sale of securities and other income, 12%.

DKK mil	12/95	12/96	12/97	US$mil 12/97					
Revenues	4,707.6	5,163.0	6,268.0	915.6	P/E Ratio	11.0	Price (6/30/98)	1,150.00
Net Income	152.3	272.0	411.0	60.0	P/B Ratio	1.4	52 Wk Hi-Low	1,363.4-839.0
Book Value	2,639.8	2,917.0	3,338.0	487.6	Yield %	2.6	Market Cap	US$661.8mil

Address	Borupvang 4	Tel 44-68-33-11	ADR	--	V Chairman	H.C. Nielsen
	2750 Ballerup	Fax 44-68-26-68	SEDOL	4897747	Chairman	K. Bonde Larsen

Tryg-Baltica Forsikring

DJGI Industry: **Insurance - Full Line**
Stoxx Sector: **Insurance**

Tryg-Baltica Forsikring A/S became Denmark's largest nonlife insurance group following a merger between Tryg and Baltica's non-life insurance interests in 1995. Tryg-Baltica smba the holding cooperative behind Tryg-Baltica Forsikring, sold 4 million shares in Tryg-Baltica Forsikring in May 1996. Since the offer, Tryg-Baltica smba now holds 74.6% of the share capital of Tryg-Baltica Forsikring and 76.9% of voting rights. The company is in a joint venture with an insurance company to give pension customers lower hospital insurance.

DKK mil	12/95	12/96	12/97	US$mil 12/97					
Revenues	N/A	16,009.0	12,946.0	1,891.2	P/E Ratio	7.2	Price (6/30/98)	187.00
Net Income	N/A	1,068.0	1,330.0	194.3	P/B Ratio	1.2	52 Wk Hi-Low	232.40-139.60
Book Value	N/A	6,814.0	7,907.0	1,155.1	Yield %	2.6	Market Cap	US$1,358.0mil

Address	Klausdalsbrovej 601	Tel 44-20-20-20	ADR	--	V Chairman	C. Hoeg Madsen
	2750 Ballerup	Fax 44-20-66-00	SEDOL	5058714	Chairman	P. Heegaard

Unidanmark

DJGI Industry: **Banks - Major International**
Stoxx Sector: **Bank**

Unidanmark A/S provides commercial and investment banking to retail and corporate customers, including mortgage loans, pension insurance, home contents and motor insurance, securities brokerage and trading, real estate, leasing, factoring, foreign exchange trading, and other financial services. The bank is one of the largest in Denmark, with 376 branches in 1997. Much of Unidanmark's business is conducted through its wholly owned subsidiary Unibank. Unidanmark has overseas offices in major cities such as London, Frankfurt, Geneva, New York, and Hong Kong.

DKK mil	12/95	12/96	12/97	US$mil 12/97					
Revenues	21,389.2	21,779.8	24,463.0	3,573.6	P/E Ratio	11.3	Price (6/30/98)	618.00
Net Income	2,102.1	2,024.7	2,878.6	420.5	P/B Ratio	1.8	52 Wk Hi-Low	618.00-373.00
Book Value	14,751.0	16,060.3	17,998.3	2,629.2	Yield %	2.4	Market Cap	US$4,194.0mil

Address	Torvegade 2	Tel 33-33-33-33	ADR	UDNGAY	V Chmn Supv Bd	N. Orgaard
	1786 Copenhagen	Fax 33-33-63-63	SEDOL	4914185	Chmn Supv Bd	J. Pedersen

William Demant

DJGI Industry: **Advanced Medical Devices**
Stoxx Sector: **Technology**

William Demant Hldg. A/S (formerly Oticon Holding A/S) develops, manufactures and markets non-linear, multi-channel, fully automatic, and modular hearing aids and related software. Trademarks include DigiFocus, MultiFocus, PrimoFocus and MicroFocus. Among the worlds largest in the hearing aid industry, Demant has operations throughout Europe and in the United States, New Zealand, Australia, and Japan. In 1997, it acquired Phonic Ear Holdings Inc. of the United States. Hearing aids accounted for 88% of 1997 revenues; sound systems, 9% and diagnostic equipment, 3%.

DKK mil	12/95	12/96	12/97	US$mil 12/97					
Sales	940.2	1,087.3	1,413.4	206.5	P/E Ratio	37.2	Price (6/30/98)	356.00
Net Income	99.2	120.3	148.3	21.7	P/B Ratio	10.5	52 Wk Hi-Low	439.00-258.35
Book Value	448.9	539.8	524.3	76.6	Yield %	0.5	Market Cap	US$801.2mil

Address	Strandvejen 58	Tel 39-17-71-00	ADR	--	President	--
	2900 Hellerup	Fax 39-27-79-00	SEDOL	5217117	Chairman	S. Folmer Thomsen

Finland

http://www.dowjones.com/indexes/Htmls01/finland.html

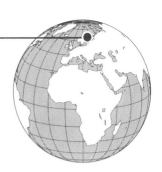

Exchanges:

Helsinki Stock Exchange

Finland

Anette Jonsson
Stockholm

Finland's stock market is soaring as the nation prepares to be the only Nordic country to join the euro-zone in 1999. In the first six months of 1998 the all-share index soared an impressive 53%, to 5,055.61, following gains of 32% in 1997 and 46% in 1996.

But heightened investor interest has been a gradual development since the beginning of the 1990s. In 1991, trading volume on the main list at the Helsinki Stock Exchange was just six billion markkaa (FIM), a figure that escalated to 101 billion in 1996 and 189 billion in 1997. At the end of June 1998, trading volume had already reached FIM134 billion, suggesting another turnover record in 1998.

Still, the Helsinki bourse is the third smallest in the single-currency zone. The managing director of the Helsinki Exchange has said that an international partnership will be needed in the future, although so far, the Helsinki Stock Exchange has declined to join Stockholm and Copenhagen in their efforts to create a Nordic market.

The fact that neither Sweden nor Denmark will be members of the economic and monetary union from the start is one reason the Helsinki bourse prefers to look to the rest of Europe for a potential partner.

But the Exchange recognizes the difficulties of being a small market on the physical outskirts of the single-currency zone, and in December 1997, the Helsinki Stock Exchange merged with Finland's futures and options

exchange under the name HEX Ltd., Helsinki Stock and Derivatives Exchange, Clearing House.

The aim of the merger was to create a single strong national marketplace for both cash and derivatives that would leave Helsinki in a better position to face increasing international competition and the changing structures of domestic capital markets.

Shares on the Helsinki Exchange will be quoted in euros from January 1, 1999, and derivatives prices will follow relatively quickly, according to bourse management.

The abolition of the markka in favor of the much broader euro could help attract more foreign investors, providing a spur similar to the one that occurred when Finland joined the European Union exchange-rate mechanism in October 1996, proving its commitment to financial integration.

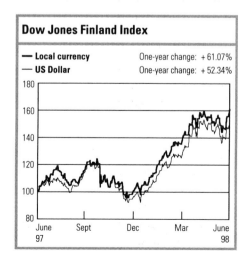

Dow Jones Finland Index

— **Local currency** One-year change: + 61.07%
— **US Dollar** One-year change: + 52.34%

By the end of June 1998, nonresident investors held 50% of the total equity market value, up from 43% at the end of 1997 and from 14% in 1993, when restrictions on foreign ownership were lifted. Nonresidents can now buy both Finnish equities and Finnish real estate without restrictions.

During 1997, the market value on the main "official list" increased by almost FIM100 billion to FIM389 billion. By the end of June 1998 it had jumped farther, to 613 billion.

A favorable economic backdrop, with growth of 6.4% in the first quarter of 1998, amid a low-inflation environment underscores the potential for profit growth. In addition, a collective labor settlement at the end of 1997 that keeps wage increases at a modest level in the coming two years is expected to put a lid on inflation, despite expectations of a pickup in consumption.

Helsinki's efforts to ensure continued strong development of the markets include a new Australian-made trading system that will increase order-handling capacity some 50 times and reduce costs. The new system will replace the ten-year-old automated HETI trading and information system currently in use.

The new trading system was first launched in March 1998, but had to be withdrawn after only a few hours as it couldn't cope with the increased data flow. After changes, the Helsinki Exchange planned to make a new try at the end of August or early in September,

Country Information

Trading Hours:
  Local: 9:30 am - 5:30 pm

  EST: 2:30 am - 10:30 am

  GMT: 0730 - 1530

Population (6/98):
5,149,242

Unemployment (97):
15.0%

Main Industries:
Metal products, shipbuilding, pulp and paper, copper refining, foodstuffs, chemicals, textiles, and clothing

Gross Domestic Product (97):
US$116.17 billion

GDP per Capita (97):
US$22,601.17

Three-Year Average GDP Growth (94-97):
4.0%

Average Annual CPI Growth (96-97):
+ 1.20%

Monetary Unit:
Finnish Markka

Exchange Rate (6/98):
FIM5.48 to US$1.00

pending the results of tests that were
continuing in the middle of July.

Following extensive changes to the
Companies Act in September 1997, Finland
will revise its securities legislation in 1998 and
1999, taking into account new instruments
such as securities lending and repurchase
agreements. Reforms to the Companies Act in
1997 made it possible for a company to buy
back its own shares and allowed preference
shares without voting rights alongside the
current ordinary shares with voting rights.

Ten Largest Capitalized Companies In The Dow Jones Finland Index as of 6/30/98	
Stock	Market Cap. US$ Thousands
Nokia	44,278,427
UPM-Kymmene	7,645,539
Merita	5,050,275
Enso	3,358,988
Sampo	2,872,438
Raision Group	2,296,015
Orion Yhtyma	2,143,753
Outokumpu	1,590,243
Valmet	1,347,825
Kemira	1,332,264

In 1997, nine new companies began trading
on the official list, bringing the total to 80
companies (101 shares) at the end of that
year. In coming years, the Finnish state is
expected to be the main provider of new
companies for the Helsinki bourse as it
continues its extensive privatization program.

Next in line is the giant energy holding
company Fortnum, created in early 1998
when the state combined oil company Neste,
in which it held a majority stake, with its
electricity producer IVO. A 25% stake in
Fortnum was expected to be sold in autumn
1998. Another state company with a similar
stake up for sale is telecom operator Sonora,
formerly Telecom Finland. Each of these
offerings will have an approximate size of
FIM5 billion.

In 1997, the state reduced its holdings in four
state-owned companies. The merger of
Finnish forestry products company Enso with
Sweden's Stora, announced in spring 1998,
will mean a lowering of the state's stake in
Enso to less than 20%

Still, the Finnish state is the majority or
controlling shareholder in several large
companies, including chemicals group
Kemira and mining and metals groups
Rautaruukki and Outokumpo. But partial
or full privatization initiatives are in the
pipeline, and have in many cases already
been authorized by Parliament.

Investors, both Finnish and international,
have welcomed the reduction in the state's
influence because it introduces new large
companies into a market that has been
criticized as being dominated by only a
handful of shares.

The true giant in the Helsinki market is
telecommunications company Nokia, which
accounted for almost 42% of total trading
volume in 1997. Given its heavy weighting,
Nokia's 108% gain in the first six months of

1998 was an important reason for the jump in the all-share benchmark HEX index.

Nokia was transformed from a diverse conglomerate in the early 1990s into a high-tech global player in the telecommunications field. However, the most frequently traded shares are still those of companies in the forestry, metals, mining, building materials, and heavy machinery sectors.

In autumn 1998, the Helsinki Exchange was to tighten the criteria for listing on the official list. At the same time, the Over-the-Counter (OTC) and Brokers' lists were to be combined into an Investors' list with less stringent capital requirements. A New Market list will be introduced for growth companies, and for companies still considering a listing there will be a Pre-List.

As an incentive to foreign investment in Finland, remote brokering has been allowed on the Helsinki Exchange since August 1996. By the end of 1997, the Exchange had 27 members, of which 4 were remote.

The official index is the HEX index, which includes all shares listed and is updated every two minutes.

Foreign investors don't have to pay tax on either capital gains or interest income obtained in Finland, and there is no stamp duty. Nonresidents do, however, have to pay withholding tax on dividends at a rate specified in the tax treaty between Finland and their home country.

Market Sector Performance In The Dow Jones Finland Index
1 Year Change Through 6/30/98

Market Sector	Change % (US$)
Financial	98.12
Technology	96.24
Consumer, Cyclical	30.63
Consumer, Non-Cyclical	24.94
Industrial	3.84
Basic Materials	-3.80

The Helsinki Stock Exchange is a limited company with approximately 130 owners, including issuers, banks, brokerage houses, and certain business organizations, the biggest of which are Nordic banking group MeritaNordbanken PLC with a 28% stake, and Sweden's OM Gruppen AB, which also owns and operates the Stockholm Stock Exchange, with just over 20% of the equity.

Amer Group

DJGI Industry: **Other Recreational Products & Services**
Stoxx Sector: **Consumer Cyclical**

Amer Group Oyj (Amer-Yhtyma Oyj) manufactures and trades a variety of consumer products, including Wilson racquets and golf and team sports equipment. Amer Group manufactures Marlboro, L&M, and Belmont cigarettes under a licensing agreement with U.S.-based Philip Morris and makes its own brands of cigarettes and tobacco products. Its Austrian sports-equipment subsidiary, Atomic, manufactures downhill and crosscountry skis, snowboards, in-line skates, hiking boots, and clothing. Sporting goods accounted for 86% of fiscal 1997 revenues.

	FIM mil 12/95	12/96	12/97	US$mil 12/97				
Sales	6,166.0	4,958.0	4,694.0	862.6	P/E Ratio	NMF	Price (6/30/98)	106.00
Net Income	2.0	-326.0	3.0	0.6	P/B Ratio	1.3	52 Wk Hi-Low	119.00-86.50
Book Value	2,513.0	2,118.0	2,050.0	376.7	Yield %	0.0	Market Cap	US$470.4mil

Address	Box 130, Mäkelänkatu 91	Tel 972-57800	ADR	AGPDY	V Chairman	T. Huhtala
	00601 Helsinki	Fax 972-578200	SEDOL	4024006	Chairman	P. Kainulainen

Asko

DJGI Industry: **Building Materials**
Stoxx Sector: **Construction**

Asko Oyj manufactures and markets plastic piping systems, household appliances, yarns and textiles, furniture, floor coverings, cast-iron forgings for vehicles, and is involved in real estate operations. In 1997, the company sold the business of Asko Components Ltd. to Santasalo-JOT Ltd.. Also, Uponor bought three heating and sanitary engineering companies in the U.S., Germany and Denmark. Plastic piping systems accounted for 57% of 1997 revenues; household appliances, 15%; textile yarns and textiles, 11%; furniture, 8%; floor coverings, 5%; and other, 4%.

	FIM mil 12/95	12/96	12/97	US$mil 12/97				
Sales	7,065.5	7,428.9	7,315.0	1,344.2	P/E Ratio	10.1	Price (6/30/98)	116.50
Net Income	210.5	241.6	450.0	82.7	P/B Ratio	1.9	52 Wk Hi-Low	122.00-79.99
Book Value	1,818.4	2,026.5	2,430.2	446.6	Yield %	2.3	Market Cap	US$825.2mil

Address	Box 45, Askonkatu 3	Tel 381-511	ADR	--	President & CEO	J. Rytilahti
	15101 Lahti	Fax 381-52600	SEDOL	5232671	Chairman	J. Ihamuotila

Cultor

DJGI Industry: **Other Food**
Stoxx Sector: **Food & Beverage**

Cultor Oyj is a food-processing company that manufactures animal feed, health-care products, sweeteners, bakery products, and related enzymes and additives. It generates almost half of its revenues from its animal-feed business. Cultor's subsidiaries include sweetener producers Finnsugar and Xyrofin and industrial enzyme manufacturer Genencor. Cultor also operates the Vaasa chain of bakeries and has a majority stake in the Estonian bakery company Leibur. The group employs some 7,200 people, approximately 50% of whom are based outside Finland.

	FIM mil 12/95	12/96	12/97	US$mil 12/97				
Sales	5,767.3	8,361.8	8,437.4	1,550.5	P/E Ratio	19.4	Price (6/30/98)	89.00
Net Income	334.7	283.4	365.5	67.2	P/B Ratio	2.1	52 Wk Hi-Low	123.33-84.00
Book Value	2,501.2	2,697.9	2,959.1	543.8	Yield %	2.1	Market Cap	US$739.4mil

Address	Box 105, Kyllikinportti 2	Tel 134-411	ADR	CULTY	President	Björn Mattsson
	Helsinki 00241	Fax 1344-1344	SEDOL	5451249	Chairman	J.K. Leskinen

Enso

DJGI Industry: **Paper Products**
Stoxx Sector: **Basic Resources**

Enso Oyj, founded in 1872, is one of Europe's leading manufacturers of publication paper, fine paper, packaging board, and sawn goods. Enso has production plants in Finland and eight other countries and employs about 20,000. A 1996 merger with state-owned Veitsiluoto Oy made the company Finland's second-largest forest products company. The Finnish state owns about a 44% stake in the company. Publication paper accounted for 27% of 1997 revenues; fine paper, 24%; packaging board, 24%; pulp and sawn goods, 20%; and marketing and transport companies, 5%.

	FIM mil 12/95	12/96	12/97	US$mil 12/97				
Sales	21,063.4	25,660.2	29,263.9	5,377.6	P/E Ratio M	9.2	Price (6/30/98) M	59.30
Net Income	1,823.8	1,033.3	578.9	106.4	P/B Ratio M	1.0	52 Wk Hi-Low M	69.00-40.20
Book Value	8,338.3	9,897.5	9,889.7	1,817.4	Yield % M	3.7	Market Cap M	US$2,102.6mil

Address	Box 309 Kanavaranta 1	Tel 204-6131	ADR	--	President & CEO	J. Harmala
	Helsinki 00160	Fax 204-621471	SEDOL	5072673	Chairman	J. Harmala

M=Multiple issues in index; reflects most active.

Finnair

DJGI Industry: **Airlines**
Stoxx Sector: **Consumer Cyclical**

Finnair Oyj is the national airline of Finland. It operates scheduled and charter flights, tours, travel agencies, and restaurants in Scandinavia, Europe, Canada, and Estonia. Finnair's additional services include a catering company, a company involved in the development and updating of travel information and distribution systems, and real estate companies. Flight operations accounted for 80% of fiscal 1997 revenues; tour operations accounted for 13%; travel agencies for 4%; and other for 3%. Finnair sold its hotel operations in fiscal 1997.

	FIM mil 03/96	03/97	03/98	US$mil 03/98				
Sales	7,181.9	7,403.2	8,057.6	1,436.3	P/E Ratio	8.1	Price (6/30/98)	49.50
Net Income	372.2	322.8	509.7	90.9	P/B Ratio	1.3	52 Wk Hi-Low	59.00-36.50
Book Value	2,589.9	2,751.7	3,205.7	571.5	Yield %	3.5	Market Cap	US$747.7mil

Address	Box 15, Tietiell A	Tel 981-881	ADR	--	Exec. V Pres	M. Annala
	Finnair 01053	Fax 981-84401	SEDOL	4336392	Chairman	A. Potila

Finnlines

DJGI Industry: **Marine Transportation**
Stoxx Sector: **Industrials**

Finnlines Oyj provides a wide range of freight and passenger transportation, stevedoring, logistics, port operations, and related services. The company operates mainly among Finland, Sweden, Great Britain, and Continental Europe and had an average of 80 vessels in service during 1997. Shipping and sea transportation services accounted for 87% of 1997 revenues and port operations for 13%. In 1998 Finnlines sold a controlling interest in Swedish transport company BTL AB to Stinnes AG. Finnlines received Poseiden AG from Stinnes as part of the transaction.

	FIM mil 12/95	12/96	12/97	US$mil 12/97					
Sales	2,554.4	2,007.1	2,242.3	412.1	P/E Ratio		9.2	Price (6/30/98)	340.00
Net Income	215.6	278.6	346.7	63.7	P/B Ratio		4.2	52 Wk Hi-Low	353.00-150.00
Book Value	1,055.5	1,285.4	1,570.2	288.5	Yield %		1.5	Market Cap	US$1,220.6mil

Address	Lonnrotinkatu 21	Tel 105-5440	ADR	--	President & CEO	A. Lagerroos
	Helsinki 00121	Fax 105-544425	SEDOL	4402743	Chairman	L.J. Jouhki

Huhtamäki

DJGI Industry: **Other Food**
Stoxx Sector: **Food & Beverage**

Huhtamäki Oyj manufactures and markets confectionery under the trade name Leaf and single-use tableware under the trade name Polarcup. Leaf, which makes Jolly Rancher, PayDay, and Heath confectionery products, is one of the world's top confectionery groups trading branded consumer products; Polarcup is a leader in food packaging. In February 1997, Huhtamäki brought the Pacific World Packaging Group, a major food packaging manufacturer in the Asia-Pacific region. Food containers, food and beverage service products accounted for 51% of 1997 revenues.

	FIM mil 12/95	12/96	12/97	US$mil 12/97					
Sales	7,835.6	7,505.5	6,387.4	1,173.8	P/E Ratio		19.6	Price (6/30/98)	314.00
Net Income	191.1	553.0	412.2	75.7	P/B Ratio		2.3	52 Wk Hi-Low	350.00-191.00
Book Value	3,702.3	3,719.8	4,080.1	749.8	Yield %		1.9	Market Cap	US$991.2mil

Address	Lansituulentie 7	Tel 968-6881	ADR	HUHTYP	V Chairman	K. Tanhuanpaa
	Espoo 02100	Fax 966-0622	SEDOL	4447476	Chmn Pres & CEO	T. Peltola

Instrumentarium

DJGI Industry: **Advanced Medical Devices**
Stoxx Sector: **Technology**

Instrumentarium Oyj operates in three main sectors: health-care equipment, optical services, and consumer and commercial products. The health-care sector manufactures and markets patient-monitoring equipment and special X-ray imaging equipment. The optical division sells ophthalmic products and provides related optical services. The division of consumer and commercial products supplies information systems and sells equipment, hardware, and related services. It also imports, manufactures, and sells cosmetics and related products. The company has 2,600 employees.

	FIM mil 12/95	12/96	12/97	US$mil 12/97					
Sales	2,147.9	2,335.5	2,720.2	499.9	P/E Ratio		26.0	Price (6/30/98)	346.00
Net Income	139.6	275.4	246.1	45.2	P/B Ratio		3.7	52 Wk Hi-Low	390.00-165.00
Book Value	1,507.6	1,732.3	1,910.6	351.1	Yield %		1.2	Market Cap	US$965.9mil

Address	Box 100, Kuortaneenkatu 2	Tel 394-11	ADR	INMRY	President & CEO	O. Riikkala
	Helsinki 00031	Fax 146-4172	SEDOL	4434155	Chairman	G. Wendt

Kemira

DJGI Industry: **Chemicals - Specialty**
Stoxx Sector: **Chemical**

Kemira Oyj is a Helsinki-based chemicals producer with sales and production all over the world. The company operates through eight divisions: Kemira Chemicals, Kemira Pigments, Kemira Agro, Kemira Fibres, Tikkurila, Kemira Metalkat, Kemira Safety, and Vihtavuori. In June 1997, Kemira sold all shares in Kemira Fibres oy to Indonesian paper, pulp, and chemicals company PT Inti Indorayon Utama. Fertilizers accounted for 43% of 1997 revenues; industrial chemicals, 23%; titanium dioxide pigments, 16%; and decorative and industrial paints, 14%.

	FIM mil 12/95	12/96	12/97	US$mil 12/97					
Sales	12,352.0	13,471.2	14,386.3	2,643.7	P/E Ratio		11.3	Price (6/30/98)	56.70
Net Income	552.3	616.6	619.0	113.7	P/B Ratio		1.3	52 Wk Hi-Low	63.00-45.80
Book Value	4,146.1	4,997.1	5,489.5	1,008.8	Yield %		3.0	Market Cap	US$1,332.3mil

Address	Box 330, Porkkalankatu 3	Tel 108-611	ADR	KERPP	V Chairman	T. Mattila
	Helsinki 00101	Fax 108-621119	SEDOL	4513612	Chairman & CEO	H. Karinen

Kesko

DJGI Industry: **Food Retailers & Wholesalers**
Stoxx Sector: **Consumer Non-Cyclical**

Kesko Oyj, one of Finland's largest diversified retail companies, supplies a network of nearly 2,500 stores. Its commercial operations are organized into three divisions: foodstuffs, specialty and home goods, and an international division. Groceries and fresh food accounted for 50% of 1997 revenues; agricultural and builders' supplies, 22%; home and specialty goods, 15%; and international division, 13%. Kesko's products include household goods, building supplies, clothing, and shoes. It imports and retails Volkswagen and Seat cars and operates more than 700 grocery stores in Finland.

	FIM mil 12/95	12/96	12/97	US$mil 12/97					
Sales	26,438.5	29,278.6	34,824.1	6,399.4	P/E Ratio		14.8	Price (6/30/98)	86.50
Net Income	644.5	481.3	526.1	96.7	P/B Ratio		1.0	52 Wk Hi-Low	96.00-69.10
Book Value	5,354.8	7,601.5	7,954.9	1,461.8	Yield %		3.5	Market Cap	US$914.8mil

Address	Box 135, Satamakatu 3	Tel 105-311	ADR	--	President	T. Karake
	Helsinki 00016	Fax 657-465	SEDOL	4490005	Chairman & CEO	M. Honkala

Kone

DJGI Industry: **Industrial - Diversified**
Stoxx Sector: **Industrials**

Kone Oyj is a leader in the manufacture, installation, modernization, and maintenance of elevators and escalators. The company has production units in several countries in Europe, North and South America, and Asia. In 1994, Kone acquired U.S.-based Montgomery Elevator Company, significantly increasing its presence in North America. The company sold its instruments and steel foundry divisions in 1995. Modernization and maintenance of elevators accounted for 59% of 1997 revenues and manufacture of elevators and escalators for 41%.

	FIM mil 12/95	12/96	12/97	US$mil 12/97				
Sales	9,523.2	10,618.6	12,255.2	2,252.0	P/E Ratio	47.9	Price (6/30/98)	770.00
Net Income	66.9	17.8	46.2	8.5	P/B Ratio	1.7	52 Wk Hi-Low	860.00-600.00
Book Value	2,313.0	2,927.2	3,002.2	551.7	Yield %	1.3	Market Cap	US$780.6mil

Address	Box 8, Kartanontie 1	Tel 204-751	ADR	--	Dep Chmn & CEO	A. Herlin
	Helsinki 00331	Fax 204-754496	SEDOL	4496672	Chairman	Pekka Herlin

Merita

DJGI Industry: **Banks - Regional (All)**
Stoxx Sector: **Bank**

Merita Oyj provides retail and corporate banking, investment management, securities trading, life insurance, real estate and other financial services at home and abroad. It also provides portfolio management, foreign-exchange services, and other financial services to both retail and corporate clients. The company merged with Kansallis-Osake-Pankki in 1995 and is one of the largest financial services groups in the Nordic region. Interest income accounted for 66% of 1997 revenues; commissions and fees, 13%; trading income, 11%: and dividend, foreign exchange, and other, 10%.

	FIM mil 12/95	12/96	12/97	US$mil 12/97				
Revenues	19,025.0	18,020.0	18,168.0	3,338.6	P/E Ratio	14.9	Price (6/30/98)	36.20
Net Income	59.0	1,720.0	3,303.0	607.0	P/B Ratio	2.2	52 Wk Hi-Low	39.10-17.30
Book Value	8,816.0	10,668.0	13,587.0	2,496.8	Yield %	2.8	Market Cap	US$5,050.3mil

Address	Aleksanterinkatu 30	Tel 912-341	ADR	--	V Chairman	J. Palmstierna
	Helsinki 00101	Fax 165-42211	SEDOL	4827175	Chairman	T. Peltola

Metra

DJGI Industry: **Industrial - Diversified**
Stoxx Sector: **Industrials**

Metra Oyj Abp, an international industrial corporation, manufactures diesel engines, steel, and ceramic bathroom products. The company is a world leader in the manufacture of medium-speed diesel engines and it is Europe's largest producer of bathroom ceramics. The company's other divisions manufacture special steels and factory automation systems. Wartsila Diesel marine engines and engines for the generation of electricity by power plants accounted for 74% of 1997 revenues; Sanitec baths and bathroom accessories, 19%; and Imatra Steel special steels, 7%.

	FIM mil 12/95	12/96	12/97	US$mil 12/97				
Sales	10,616.9	11,660.4	15,297.0	2,811.0	P/E Ratio	56.1	Price (6/30/98)	180.00
Net Income	479.4	724.4	244.4	44.9	P/B Ratio	2.5	52 Wk Hi-Low	197.00-120.00
Book Value	3,135.9	3,641.8	3,892.5	715.3	Yield %	1.5	Market Cap	US$1,312.4mil

Address	Box 230 Ranta 2	Tel 970-951	ADR	--	V Chairman	V. Vainio
	Helsinki 00101	Fax 762-278	SEDOL	4525189	Chairman	R.G. Ehrnrooth

Metsä-Serla

DJGI Industry: **Paper Products**
Stoxx Sector: **Basic Resources**

Metsä-Serla Oyj develops and manufactures paper and paperboard, pulp, corrugated board, and tissue. In March 1995, it sold its sawmilling and building supplies businesses to Metsaliitto, and in 1996, it sold its chemical division and is now focusing exclusively on paper, board, and pulp. Metsä-Serla has production operations in Sweden, Denmark, the Netherlands, the United Kingdom, Greece, and the Canary Islands. Magazine and fine paper accounted for 33% of 1997 revenues; packaging paper, 27%; chemical pulp, 21%; marketing, 10%; and tissue paper, 9%.

	FIM mil 12/95	12/96	12/97	US$mil 12/97				
Sales	13,122.6	14,670.5	19,182.0	3,524.9	P/E Ratio	8.2	Price (6/30/98)	53.00
Net Income	1,109.4	471.7	1,289.8	237.0	P/B Ratio	0.9	52 Wk Hi-Low	61.00-38.60
Book Value	6,817.4	7,098.1	8,243.7	1,514.9	Yield %	3.4	Market Cap	US$992.6mil

Address	Revontulentie 6	Tel 104-611	ADR	--	V Chairman	A. Uusitalo
	Espoo 02100	Fax 104-694353	SEDOL	5071432	Chairman	A. Oksanen

Nokia

DJGI Industry: **Communications Technology**
Stoxx Sector: **Technology**

Nokia Oyj is a telecommunications and cable company. It supplies telecommunications systems and equipment for fixed- and mobile-phone networks and is the world's second largest manufacturer of all mobile phones. It makes satellite receivers, computer monitors, car-audio systems, and other industrial and consumer electronics. The company divested its tires and cable machinery businesses in 1995 and its color television division in 1996. Mobile phones accounted for 51% of 1997 revenues, general communication products, 35% and telecommunication systems and other, 14%.

	FIM mil 12/95	12/96	12/97	US$mil 12/97				
Sales	36,810.0	39,321.0	52,612.0	9,668.1	P/E Ratio M	35.1	Price (6/30/98) M	403.50
Net Income	1,971.0	3,470.0	6,499.0	1,194.3	P/B Ratio M	10.6	52 Wk Hi-Low M	404.00-181.00
Book Value	12,075.0	14,409.0	20,245.0	3,720.3	Yield % M	0.9	Market Cap M	US$33,108mil

Address	Eteläesplanadi 12	Tel 180-71	ADR	NOKA	President & CEO	Jorma Ollila
	Helsinki 00101	Fax 656-388	SEDOL	5444498	Chairman	Casimir Ehrnrooth

M=Multiple issues in index; reflects most active; In DJ Stoxx 50; In EuroStoxx 50.

Orion Group

DJGI Industry: **Pharmaceuticals**
Stoxx Sector: **Pharmaceutical**

The Orion Group (Orion Yhtyma Oyj) manufactures and markets pharmaceuticals, veterinary preparations, tests and test systems for clinical laboratories, cosmetics and personal care products, underground vehicles for mining, and equipment for timber handling. Pharmaceutical trademarks include Eldepryl, Beclomet, Divina, Cardi, Bonyl, Deprakine, and Aciloc. Pharmaceutical products accounted for 48% of 1997 revenues; wholesale and distribution of health care products, 32%; and cosmetics, hairdressing, personal, home-care, and hospital-hygiene products, 12%;

	FIM mil 12/95	12/96	12/97	US$mil 12/97				
Sales	4,058.5	4,282.8	4,695.0	862.8	P/E Ratio M	21.7	Price (6/30/98) M	167.00
Net Income	544.2	611.4	699.3	128.5	P/B Ratio M	2.5	52 Wk Hi-Low M	189.00-121.43
Book Value	2,523.8	2,937.3	3,409.3	626.5	Yield % M	4.5	Market Cap M	US$1,127.8mil

Address	Orionintie 1	Tel 9-4291	ADR	--	V Chairman	A. Prihti
	Espoo 02200	Fax 9-4292801	SEDOL	4622198	Chairman	J. Leikola

M=Multiple issues in index; reflects most active.

Outokumpu

DJGI Industry: **Other Non-Ferrous Metals**
Stoxx Sector: **Basic Resources**

Outokumpu Oyj, 40%-owned by the Finnish government, is an integrated metals and engineering company. It mines, smelts, and refines copper, zinc, nickel, and stainless steel, and produces a wide range of metal tubes, strips, and rolls. The company manufactures stainless steel products and equipment for industries ranging from mining to power generation. Its operations are located in Europe, North America, and Australia. Copper products accounted for 36% of 1997 revenues; base metals, 26%; stainless steel, 22%; technology services, 7%; and other, 9%.

	FIM mil 12/95	12/96	12/97	US$mil 12/97				
Sales	16,952.0	16,549.0	19,055.0	3,501.6	P/E Ratio	22.1	Price (6/30/98)	70.00
Net Income	1,037.0	188.0	703.0	129.2	P/B Ratio	1.1	52 Wk Hi-Low	106.30-62.00
Book Value	7,077.0	7,099.0	7,714.0	1,417.5	Yield %	2.9	Market Cap	US$1,590.2mil

Address	Box 140, Riihitontuntie 7b	Tel 421-1	ADR	--	V Chairman	M. Puhakka
	Espoo 02201	Fax 421-3888	SEDOL	4665148	Chairman	G. Wendt

Partek

DJGI Industry: **Building Materials**
Stoxx Sector: **Construction**

Partek Oyj Abp, established in 1898, manufactures building products, mines and processes minerals, and makes cargo-handling equipment. The company is the world's principal producer of cargo-handling equipment and the leading producer of rock-wool-based insulation products. Its wholly owned subsidiary Nordkalk mines and processes limestone. Through its Cargotec division, Partek manufactures knuckleboom cranes and Loglift forestry cranes. The company has operations in about 30 countries. In January 1997, Partek acquired Sisu Oy.

	FIM mil 12/95	12/96	12/97	US$mil 12/97				
Sales	6,556.4	6,159.9	10,743.5	1,974.3	P/E Ratio	10.8	Price (6/30/98)	95.00
Net Income	149.4	515.0	350.8	64.5	P/B Ratio	1.4	52 Wk Hi-Low	111.00-78.00
Book Value	1,747.4	2,221.7	3,206.1	589.2	Yield %	4.2	Market Cap	US$844.0mil

Address	Sornaisten Rantatie 23	Tel 204-5511	ADR	--	V Chairman	R. Virrankoski
	Helsinki 00501	Fax 204-554844	SEDOL	4672632	Chairman	B. Mattsson

Pohjola-Yhtymä

DJGI Industry: **Insurance - Property & Casualty**
Stoxx Sector: **Insurance**

Pohjola-Yhtymä Vakuutus Oyj (Pohjola Insurance Co. Ltd.) is the largest Finnish insurance group. It covers the entire spectrum of insurance services including nonlife, life, pension, travel, corporate, and private insurance and is involved in investment activities. In 1997, Pohjola purchased Salama Life Assurance and began to offer life insurance and other, related forms of private insurance policies. Income derived from insurance premiums accounted for 61% of 1997 revenues; investment income, 21%; gain/loss on disposal of securities, 14%; and other, 4%.

	FIM mil 12/95	12/96	12/97	US$mil 12/97				
Revenues	3,953.5	3,822.3	5,652.5	1,038.7	P/E Ratio	20.0	Price (6/30/98)	273.00
Net Income	114.4	280.8	555.0	102.0	P/B Ratio	5.2	52 Wk Hi-Low	348.00-148.50
Book Value	1,440.5	1,657.0	2,126.2	390.7	Yield %	1.1	Market Cap	US$1,036.5mil

Address	Lapinmaentie 1	Tel 105-5911	ADR	--	CEO	I. Viinanen
	Helsinki 00300	Fax 955-0923	SEDOL	4691949	Chairman	T. Matomaki

Raisio Group

DJGI Industry: **Other Food**
Stoxx Sector: **Food & Beverage**

Raisio Group PLC (Raisio Yhtymä Oyj) manufactures and markets margarines and edible vegetable oils, flour, flakes, starch, malts, dry bread, preserves, processed potatoes, and animal feeds. The company also produces chemicals for the paper industry. Its long- term research and development program has recently produced Benecol margarine, which contains a plant sterol effective in bringing down cholesterol levels. Margarines and edible vegetable oils accounted for 34% of 1997 revenues; flour, cereals, and animal feeds, 31%; chemicals, 31%; and other, 4%.

	FIM mil 12/95	12/96	12/97	US$mil 12/97				
Sales	3,224.4	3,927.9	4,947.2	909.1	P/E Ratio M	N/A	Price (6/30/98) M	99.00
Net Income	103.8	94.6	84.3	15.5	P/B Ratio M	N/A	52 Wk Hi-Low M	107.50-35.70
Book Value	813.5	1,098.5	1,610.8	296.0	Yield % M	N/A	Market Cap M	US$2,296.0mil

Address	Box 101, Raisonkaari 55	Tel 2434-2711	ADR	--	CEO	M. Salminen
	Raiso 21201	Fax 2434-2147	SEDOL	5020973	Chairman	H. Haavisto

M=Multiple issues in index; reflects most active.

Rauma

DJGI Industry: **Heavy Machinery**
Stoxx Sector: **Industrials**

Rauma Oyj is an international metal and engineering company that consists of four divisions. Sunds Defibrator supplies fiber- processing plants and systems and produces equipment for the pulp, paper, and panelboard industries. Timberjack is the world's leading manufacture of timber-harvesting machines, which include feller bunches, skidders, log loaders, and harvesters. Nordberg is the world's leading supplier of rock-crushing systems and related services. Neles-Jamesbury offers a full range of industrial valves and accessories.

	FIM mil 12/95	12/96	12/97	US$mil 12/97						
Sales	9,837.0	10,220.0	10,866.0	1,996.8	P/E Ratio		11.2	Price (6/30/98)		112.50
Net Income	448.0	460.0	519.0	95.4	P/B Ratio		2.0	52 Wk Hi-Low		123.80-79.00
Book Value	2,414.0	2,722.0	3,020.0	555.0	Yield %		2.9	Market Cap		US$1,087.7mil

Address	Box 1220, Fabianinkatu 9A	Tel 204-80100	ADR	RMA	V Chairman	J. Rantala
	Helsinki 00101	Fax 204-80101	SEDOL	4723381	Chairman	P. Voutilaninen

Rautaruukki

DJGI Industry: **Steel**
Stoxx Sector: **Basic Resources**

Rautaruukki Oy, the largest steel company in the Nordic countries, manufactures steel and processes it into plate, sheets, tubes, pipes, and sections. The company has production plants in several European countries and sales outlets worldwide. The products include welded steel pipes, hollow sections and cold-formed sections, cold-rolled, galvanized, and coil-coated sheet products, hot-rolled plate and sheet, profiled sheet, facade elements, and rolling stock. Steel wire and bars accounted for 30% of 1997 revenues.

	FIM mil 12/95	12/96	12/97	US$mil 12/97						
Sales	9,213.0	12,834.0	13,650.0	2,508.4	P/E Ratio		5.9	Price (6/30/98)		42.00
Net Income	786.0	199.0	461.0	84.7	P/B Ratio		1.0	52 Wk Hi-Low		59.00-39.00
Book Value	2,958.0	2,880.0	3,705.0	680.8	Yield %		4.8	Market Cap		US$1,020.8mil

Address	Box 217 Kiilakiventie 1	Tel 888-360	ADR	--	President & CEO	M. Kivimaki
	Oulu 90101	Fax 888-36450	SEDOL	4727662	Chairman	M. Kivimaki

Sampo

DJGI Industry: **Insurance - Property & Casualty**
Stoxx Sector: **Insurance**

Sampo Insurance Co. Ltd. (Vakuutusosakeyhtio Sampo Oyj) is the leading non-life insurance group in Finland and is the parent company of the Sampo Non-Life Group. Its insurance activities include fire, property, workers' compensation, personal accident, and motor insurance. Its Kaleva Mutual Insurance subsidiary provides life and pension services for individuals and companies, and its wholly owned Industrial Insurance subsidiary insures companies. Premium income accounted for 74% of 1997 revenues; investment income, 16%; and gain/loss on disposal of securities and other, 10%.

	FIM mil 12/95	12/96	12/97	US$mil 12/97						
Revenues	5,218.2	5,351.6	7,012.3	1,288.6	P/E Ratio		31.2	Price (6/30/98)		260.00
Net Income	139.8	254.6	487.3	89.5	P/B Ratio		3.9	52 Wk Hi-Low		273.00-126.25
Book Value	3,375.3	3,570.7	4,003.2	735.6	Yield %		1.2	Market Cap		US$2,872.4mil

Address	Yliopistonkatu 27	Tel 10-515300	ADR	--	V Chairman	K.O. Sohlberg
	Turku 20100	Fax 10-5141811	SEDOL	5226038	Chairman	J. Harmala

Stockmann

DJGI Industry: **Retailers - Broadline**
Stoxx Sector: **Retail**

Stockmann Oyj Abp, founded in 1862, is a broadly diversified retail company. Its department store division owns five department stores in Finland and also has operations in Russia and Estonia. It also operates an automotive sales division, grocery stores, and hypermarkets. Its Academic Bookstores are located in Finland's university cities. In May 1997, Helkama Auto and Stockmann signed an agreement on the purchase of two auto dealerships selling Mitsubishi and Skoda. Stockmann also owns Hobby Hall, a household and leisure products mail-order company.

	FIM mil 12/95	12/96	12/97	US$mil 12/97						
Revenues	5,162.6	6,164.5	6,900.0	1,268.0	P/E Ratio		29.9	Price (6/30/98)		164.00
Net Income	192.5	217.6	300.5	55.2	P/B Ratio		3.5	52 Wk Hi-Low		180.00-91.28
Book Value	1,394.6	1,522.4	1,717.8	315.7	Yield %		1.6	Market Cap		US$744.0mil

Address	Aleksanterinkatu 52	Tel 121-1	ADR	--	Managing Director	Ari Heiniö
	Helsinki 00101	Fax 121-3101	SEDOL	5462371	Chairman	Lasse Koivu

Tamro Yhtyma

DJGI Industry: **Medical Supplies**
Stoxx Sector: **Consumer Non-Cyclical**

Tamro Yhtyma Oy (Oy Tamro AB) is a health-care company made up of four main divisions: Pharmaceutical Distributing; Hospital and Laboratory; Kolmi-Set, which manufactures disposable sterile products; and Oy Tamba Ab, which markets pharmaceuticals and health-care products. Tamro is a leading pharmaceutical distributor in western Europe and one of the major producers of disposable hospital textiles in Europe. Distribution of pharmaceuticals accounts for more than 90% of its revenues. The company has sales offices in Scandinavia and the Baltic countries.

	FIM mil 12/95	12/96	12/97	US$mil 12/97						
Sales	10,735.0	13,219.7	12,893.0	2,369.3	P/E Ratio		20.5	Price (6/30/98)		35.50
Net Income	119.6	149.7	149.6	27.5	P/B Ratio		1.8	52 Wk Hi-Low		42.60-29.00
Book Value	1,557.0	1,658.1	1,739.3	319.6	Yield %		2.5	Market Cap		US$571.0mil

Address	PL 11 Rajatorpantie 41 B	Tel 204-4511	ADR	--	President	M. Elovaara
	Vantaa 01641	Fax 204-454010	SEDOL	4834443	Chairman	E.J. Toivanen

UPM-Kymmene

DJGI Industry: **Paper Products**
Stoxx Sector: **Basic Resources**

UPM-Kymmene Oyj, created through the merger of Kymmene Oy, Repola Oy, and its subsidiary United Paper Mills Ltd. in 1995, is Europe's largest forest products company. In 1997, UPM-Kymmene bought the Release Paper and Consumer Products business of Daubert Coated Products Inc. of the United States. Magazine papers accounted for 26% of 1997 revenues; fine papers, 15%; newsprint, 13%; packaging materials, 10%; special products, 9%; sawn timber, 9%; plywood, 7%; chemical pulp, 2%; and other, 9%.

	FIM mil 12/95	12/96	12/97	US$mil 12/97					
Sales	54,738.0	51,757.0	50,406.0	9,262.7	P/E Ratio		9.1	Price (6/30/98)	151.00
Net Income	1,883.0	994.0	4,182.0	768.5	P/B Ratio		1.5	52 Wk Hi-Low	174.00-98.30
Book Value	14,706.0	14,123.0	26,380.0	4,847.7	Yield %		3.6	Market Cap	US$7,645.5mil

Address	Box 203 Snellmaninkatu 13	Tel 204-15111	ADR	UPMKY	President	--
	Helsinki 00171	Fax 204-15110	SEDOL	5051252	Chairman	T. Matomaki

Valmet

DJGI Industry: **Factory Equipment**
Stoxx Sector: **Industrials**

Valmet Oyj is an engineering company involved in the paper technology industry. The company operates printing paper machines, pulp-drying machines, board and tissue machines, stock preparation, service, and paper-finishing systems, air systems, and automation units. Valmet also operates materials-handling equipment and is involved with power transmissions, factory automation, logging, tractor operations, and automobiles. Paper and board machinery accounted for 81% of 1997 revenues; automation systems, 12%; cars, 5%; and power transmission, 2%.

	FIM mil 12/95	12/96	12/97	US$mil 12/97					
Sales	8,573.6	11,764.0	12,313.0	2,262.7	P/E Ratio		8.6	Price (6/30/98)	94.60
Net Income	655.5	806.0	863.0	158.6	P/B Ratio		1.9	52 Wk Hi-Low	100.00-68.80
Book Value	3,066.0	3,247.0	3,893.0	715.4	Yield %		4.4	Market Cap	US$1,347.8mil

Address	Box 27, Panuntie 6	Tel 777-051	ADR	VA	V Chairman	J. Rauramo
	Helsinki 00621	Fax 777-05580	SEDOL	5031588	Chairman	P. Rantanen

France

http://www.dowjones.com/indexes/Htmls01/france.html

Exchanges:

SBF - Bourse de Paris

France

John Carreyrou
Paris

Its former trading floor may be mostly idle, but the French stock market has been anything but. Stocks are hot again in France as the country's long sluggish economy picks up the pace, improved corporate results restore confidence, and new legislation makes investing in shares more attractive.

The CAC 40, which is made up of France's 40 most actively traded stocks, racked up a 41% gain in the first half of 1998 to close at 4,203.45 on June 30, adding to strong performances in 1996 and 1997.

On June 23, the Paris Bourse set a new single-day volume record of FRF29.5 billion, eclipsing the previous record by some FRF8.5 billion. Average daily volume has nearly tripled in the past two years to around FRF15 billion. This surge in activity has enabled Paris to hold its position as the world's fifth-largest exchange, behind New York, Tokyo, London and Frankfurt.

Foreign investors have done more than their share to foster the current mood of euphoria on the Bourse. Today, they represent 35% of total stock market capitalization and 40% of trading volume. The French state has worked hard to stimulate their interest by eliminating stamp duties on securities transactions for nonresidents.

Nonresidents are taxed only on their income from French sources and are not taxed on capital gains or other types of income. All dividends are subject to a 25% withholding

tax, although if the investor resides in a country that has signed a tax treaty with France, this tax is usually either waived or reduced.

The Paris Bourse is divided into four sub-markets: one for big companies, one for small and medium-sized companies that have published financial statements for at least two years, one for over-the-counter transactions, and one for high-growth companies. The latter, which was launched in 1996 and goes by the name Nouveau Marché, boasts 58 companies.

The Bourse has gone through drastic transformations in its drive to become Europe's most technology-savvy exchange. Ten years ago, it introduced an electronic trading system akin to the one used by the U.S. Nasdaq, driving stock brokers from its headquarters in the Palais Brongniart. The early 19th-century building in Paris's

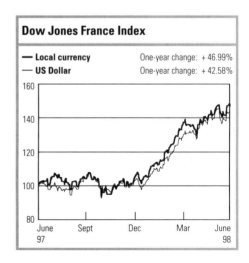

Dow Jones France Index

— Local currency   One-year change: + 46.99%
— US Dollar   One-year change: + 42.58%

June 97	Sept	Dec	Mar	June 98

business district on the right bank continued to serve a purpose thereafter, housing the Monep, the market for stock futures and options, and the Matif, the market for French treasury futures, which both still relied on open-outcry trading.

In April 1998, the Bourse sounded the death knell for open-outcry trading on the Monep and the Matif by introducing a dual trading system that offered investors the option of placing orders electronically, as they had long done on the cash market for stocks. Finding it more convenient and cheaper than going through a broker, investors flocked to electronic trading. Within two months, traders had vanished from the Palais Brongniart.

Now, the Bourse's operator, La Société des Bourses Françaises (SBF), has to figure out what to do with the 600 square meters of open space the traders vacated on the building's ground floor. The SBF converted the second and third floors to other uses. It transformed one room into a members-only restaurant, another into an auditorium, and yet another into a museum of France's financial markets.

The SBF reckons it has a good idea of how to use the Parquet Room, as it is formally known. It is considering subleasing it by the day to companies listed on the Bourse for use as a conference hall. Companies headquartered in Paris often need large rooms when they hold big events such as annual shareholder meetings.

Country Information

Trading Hours:
  Local: 10:00 am - 5:00 pm

  EST: 4:00 am - 11:00 am

  GMT: 0900 - 1600

Population (6/98):
58,804,944

Unemployment (97):
12.5%

Main Industries:
Steel, machinery, chemicals, automobiles, metallurgy, aircraft, electronics, mining, textiles, food processing, and tourism

Gross Domestic Product (97):
US$1,396.54 billion

GDP per Capita (97):
US$23,840.29

Three-Year Average GDP Growth (94-97):
1.9%

Average Annual CPI Growth (96-97):
+ 1.20%

Monetary Unit:
French Franc

Exchange Rate (6/98):
FRF6.06 to US$1.00

But first the SBF will have to get a green light from the city of Paris, the building's owner. The SBF leases the Palais Brongniart from the city for FRF15 million a year. The lease expires in December 1998, and to obtain an extension, the SBF must convince the city that the building will be used for a worthy cause.

In the meantime, the SBF has decided to capitalize on this prime piece of real estate. For a fee of FRF75,000, it agreed to let the Japanese designer Yohji Yamamoto stage a men's fashion show there in early July 1998. Fashion shows are probably not what the city has in mind for the 1827 neoclassical building, a designated historical landmark. But the SBF promises this was a one-time event and, once it gets the city's approval, the building will revert to a role more in keeping with its history.

Contrary to what many observers feared, the Socialist government of Prime Minister Lionel Jospin, which came to power in April 1997, has been kind to the Bourse. Even as it placated the public with some populist measures, such as a bill reducing the official work week from 39 hours to 35 hours, it has pushed on with the previous right-wing government's privatization program.

In October 1997, state-controlled national telecom operator France Telecom was allowed to sell 20% of its capital to the public through an initial public offering that met with resounding success. In early July 1998, France Telecom shares were trading at

Ten Largest Capitalized Companies In The Dow Jones France Index as of 6/30/98	
Stock	Market Cap. US$ Thousands
France Telecom	68,800,413
Elf Aquitaine	38,491,430
L'Oréal	37,503,408
AXA	37,384,118
Vivendi	33,739,966
Alcatel Alsthom	33,145,955
Total	31,686,861
Carrefour	24,280,916
Société Générale	21,170,906
Rhône-Poulenc	20,924,571

around FRF400, or 42% higher than their initial listing price. The company has by far the biggest market capitalization of any listed company.

Other high-profile privatizations have included Crédit Industriel et Commercial and its parent, Groupement des Assurances Nationales. The government sold CIC to Crédit Mutuel, a French mutualist bank, and GAN to Groupama, a rival French insurer. The Jospin government has also pledged to privatize troubled bank Crédit Lyonnais by October 1999, and has tentative plans to list 20% of flag-carrier Air France on the stock market.

Privatization isn't the only means the Socialist government has used to signal its pro-investment stance. In May 1998, parliament passed a law giving tax breaks to life insurance funds that are 50% invested in the stock market and 5% invested in non-quoted or high-tech companies. Analysts say the law could steer hundreds of billions of francs into the stock market.

In April 1998, parliament passed a law reducing the tax shareholders pay on income from share buybacks. The move was widely seen as an effort to promote shareholder value, as buybacks enable companies to boost earnings per share.

The government also plans to present a draft bill to parliament in the autumn of 1998 that will allow the creation of U.S.-style private pension funds. The government hopes to meet two goals with the initiative: It aims to put to work the large sums of cash the French are known to hoard in low-yielding savings accounts and to boost the market capitalizations of French companies so that they can better defend themselves against takeovers.

The new pension funds are expected to raise demand for stocks, triggering an influx of capital into the French stock market similar to that witnessed in the United States a decade ago. Morgan Stanley has estimated that in the long run, pension reform could inject up to US$16 billion into French equities, while Société Générale predicts that the mere passage of the bill will boost the CAC 40 by 10% to 15%.

Industry Group Performance In The Dow Jones France Index
1 Year Change Through 6/30/98

Industry	Change % (US$)
Best Performing	
Software	202.63
Auto Manufacturers	123.29
Banks, Money Centers	95.90
Banks (All)	89.41
Lodging	86.50
Worst Performing	
Home Furnishings & Appliances (All)	-17.09
Other Furnishings	-17.09
Distillers & Brewers	-19.12
Beverages (All)	-19.12
Non-Ferrous Metals (All)	-37.40

Accor

DJGI Industry: **Lodging**
Stoxx Sector: **Consumer Cyclical**

Accor SA, the world's largest hotel group, owns and operates hotels, restaurants, and leisure facilities. Its business-services division also provides service vouchers and institutional catering, and it operates travel agencies. Accor owns more than 2,378 luxury and budget hotels, including those in the Novotel, Ibis, Sofitel, and Motel 6 chains. Traditional hotels accounted for 33% of 1997 revenues; economy hotels, 25%; company restaurants and canteens, 12%; railway restaurants and catering, 6%; service vouchers, 5%; and other activities, 7%.

	FRF mil 12/95	12/96	12/97	US$mil 12/97				
Sales	30,212.0	27,888.0	31,365.0	5,214.5	P/E Ratio	39.9	Price (6/30/98)	1,692.00
Net Income	923.0	1,058.0	1,508.0	250.7	P/B Ratio	3.3	52 Wk Hi-Low	1,747.0-880.0
Book Value	13,284.0	16,135.0	18,654.0	3,101.0	Yield %	1.4	Market Cap	US$10,011mil

Address	33 ave. du Maine	Tel 1-45-38-87-55	ADR	ACRFY	Director	S. Boinet
	75755 Paris Cedex 15	Fax 1-45-38-85-67	SEDOL	4112321	Chairman	M. Espalioux

AGF

DJGI Industry: **Insurance - Full Line**
Stoxx Sector: **Insurance**

Recently privatized Assurances Générales de France (AGF) SA is among the largest insurance companies in France. Its products include life, health, auto, transport, and fire insurance. In 1995, the group generated more than 43% of its premium income outside France. The company owns 27.5% of the German insurer Aachener und Münchener Beteiligungs and 38.9% of real estate company Groupement pour le Financement de la Construction. AGF was privatized in May 1996 for 128 francs a share, with the government reducing its stake in the company to less than 10%.

	FRF mil 12/95	12/96	12/97	US$mil 12/97				
Revenues	103,851.0	90,716.0	95,076.0	15,806.5	P/E Ratio	25.2	Price (6/30/98)	342.10
Net Income	1,082.0	1,536.0	1,925.0	320.0	P/B Ratio	1.9	52 Wk Hi-Low	389.90-187.50
Book Value	22,788.0	24,420.0	32,120.0	5,340.0	Yield %	1.5	Market Cap	US$10,367mil

Address	87 rue de Richelieu	Tel 1-42-44-04-44	ADR	AGF144	V Chairman	J.D. le Franc
	75113 Paris	Fax 1-42-44-19-56	SEDOL	4034737	Chairman	A. Jeancourt-Galignani

Alcatel Alsthom

DJGI Industry: **Communications Technology**
Stoxx Sector: **Technology**

Alcatel Alsthom Cie. Générale d'Electricité SA provides telecommunications equipment and transportation services and generates power on a global basis. Its cable subsidiary is the largest producer of power transmission cables in the world. The company also engages in electrical engineering activities. Telecommunications accounted for 44% of 1997 revenues; telecommunication cables, 23%; energy and transportation, 18%; and electrical systems, 14%. Alcatel's biggest single shareholder is the Fidelity group of mutual funds, which built up a 10% shareholding in July 1997.

	FRF mil 12/95	12/96	12/97	US$mil 12/97				
Sales	160,416.0	162,102.0	185,868.0	30,900.7	P/E Ratio	41.4	Price (6/30/98)	1,231.00
Net Income	-25,583.0	2,725.0	4,665.0	775.6	P/B Ratio	4.2	52 Wk Hi-Low	1,302.0-653.0
Book Value	32,993.0	39,170.0	45,858.0	7,623.9	Yield %	0.9	Market Cap	US$33,146mil

Address	54 rue La Boétie	Tel 1-40-76-10-10	ADR	ACAAY	V President	J.P. Halbron
	75382 Paris Cedex 08	Fax 1-40-76-14-00	SEDOL	4216825	Chairman & CEO	S. Tchuruk

In DJ Stoxx 50; In EuroStoxx 50.

AXA-UAP

DJGI Industry: **Insurance - Full Line**
Stoxx Sector: **Insurance**

AXA-UAP SA, the world's largest insurer, provides a full range of insurance and reinsurance services in Europe, North America, and Asia, and it offers banking and real estate services in France and the United States. Brokerage and investment banker Donaldson, Lufkin & Jenrette is a wholly owned subsidiary. Axa has a 49% stake in U.S. insurance company The Equitable and a 51% stake in National Mutual, Australia's second-largest life insurance company. Accident, life, and fire insurance premiums accounted for 68% of 1997 revenues.

	FRF mil 12/95	12/96	12/97	US$mil 12/97				
Revenues	156,998.0	200,888.0	445,145.0	74,005.8	P/E Ratio	27.9	Price (6/30/98)	680.00
Net Income	2,730.0	3,809.0	7,920.0	1,316.7	P/B Ratio	2.9	52 Wk Hi-Low	736.00-365.50
Book Value	33,391.0	44,837.0	76,572.0	12,730.2	Yield %	1.3	Market Cap	US$37,384mil

Address	16 ave. Matignon	Tel 1-40-75-57-06	ADR	AXA	President	G. de la Martiniere
	75008 Paris	Fax 1-40-75-57-50	SEDOL	4026927	Chairman & CEO	C. Bébéar

In DJ Stoxx 50; In EuroStoxx 50.

Bail Investissement

DJGI Industry: **Real Estate**
Stoxx Sector: **Financial Services**

Bail Investissement SA owns and manages real estate throughout France and the United Kingdom. It leases and rents warehouses, commercial and professional space, and parking lots. Its property portfolio is concentrated in Paris and London. Rental income accounts for almost all its revenue. Two of the company's main properties are an office and retail center in London and an apartment building in France. Bail Investissement also has some holding activities. Rental income accounted for 95% of 1997 revenues and interest and other operating income accounted for 5%.

	FRF mil 12/95	12/96	12/97	US$mil 12/97				
Sales	883.7	988.3	915.0	152.1	P/E Ratio	46.2	Price (6/30/98)	964.00
Net Income	267.8	242.2	63.8	10.6	P/B Ratio	2.0	52 Wk Hi-Low	993.00-711.00
Book Value	1,566.7	1,590.5	1,457.6	242.3	Yield %	6.7	Market Cap	US$485.7mil

Address	Grand Ecran, 30 pl. d'Italie	Tel 1-40-78-52-52	ADR	--	President	J.P. Fournie
	75628 Paris	Fax 1-40-78-53-53	SEDOL	4070708	Chairman	A. Marcheteau

Banque Nationale de Paris

DJGI Industry: **Banks - Major International**
Stoxx Sector: **Bank**

Banque Nationale de Paris SA (BNP), a money-center bank in France, offers retail banking, foreign exchange, commercial banking, and investment banking services to customers in Europe, North America, and Asia. The company also provides securities-trading facilities, brokerage services, and international financing. BNP operates branches in approximately 80 countries, and it has two agencies in India and a subsidiary in Mexico. In 1996, the company opened five new subsidiaries, including two in Australia, one in Italy, one in Hong Kong, and another in France.

	FRF mil 12/95	12/96	12/97	US$mil 12/97				
Revenues	129,486.0	132,106.0	150,747.0	25,061.8	P/E Ratio	17.5	Price (6/30/98)	494.00
Net Income	1,784.0	3,856.0	5,962.0	991.2	P/B Ratio	1.7	52 Wk Hi-Low	552.00-242.20
Book Value	48,642.0	55,202.0	60,522.0	10,061.8	Yield %	1.4	Market Cap	US$17,381mil

Address	16 blvd. des Italiens	Tel 1-40-14-45-46	ADR	BNPPYP	Director General	B. Prot
	75009 Paris	Fax 1-40-14-75-46	SEDOL	4133667	Chairman & CEO	M. Pebereau

BIC

DJGI Industry: **Household Products (Non-Durable)**
Stoxx Sector: **Consumer Non-Cyclical**

Société Bic (BIC) SA is one of the world's leading manufacturers of writing instruments, correction fluids, lighters, and razors. It also manufactures sailboards and, through its subsidiaries Guy Laroche and Conte, is engaged in the sale of women's and men's apparel and perfumes. Bic has manufacturing facilities in Europe, North and South America, South Africa, Australia, and Malaysia. The group acquired Sheaffer and Tipp-Ex Group in 1997. Writing instruments, correction fluids, lighters, and razors accounted for 98% of 1997 revenues, and apparel and perfumes for 2%.

	FRF mil 12/95	12/96	12/97	US$mil 12/97				
Sales	5,993.0	6,351.9	7,506.0	1,247.9	P/E Ratio	29.7	Price (6/30/98)	430.00
Net Income	597.7	683.6	800.2	133.0	P/B Ratio	3.9	52 Wk Hi-Low	543.00-326.80
Book Value	4,663.1	5,235.4	6,040.7	1,004.3	Yield %	1.4	Market Cap	US$3,923.0mil

Address	8 impasse des Cailloux	Tel 1-45-19-52-00	ADR	--	President	--
	92110 Clichy	Fax 1-45-19-52-99	SEDOL	5298781	Chairman	B. Bich

Bongrain

DJGI Industry: **Other Food**
Stoxx Sector: **Food & Beverage**

Bongrain SA produces dairy products and gourmet foods. The company's cheeses, which accounted for 67% of 1997 revenues, are sold under such brand names as Caprice des Dieux, Geramont, and St. Moret. Bongrain has activities in Europe, North America, South America, Australia, and Japan, and it is expanding into central and eastern Europe, most notably in the former Soviet Union, the Czech Republic, and Hungary. France is Bongrain's largest European market, accounting for nearly one-half of sales, while Germany accounts for about 13% of sales.

	FRF mil 12/95	12/96	12/97	US$mil 12/97				
Sales	9,922.4	10,402.6	11,530.2	1,916.9	P/E Ratio	20.5	Price (6/30/98)	3,036.00
Net Income	356.8	300.5	313.7	52.2	P/B Ratio	1.7	52 Wk Hi-Low	3,250.0-2,033.0
Book Value	3,495.9	3,683.8	3,871.1	643.6	Yield %	2.1	Market Cap	US$1,059.9mil

Address	42 rue Rieussec	Tel 3-86-54-63-00	ADR	--	CFO	J.H. Vadot
	78223 Viroflay	Fax 3-86-75-41-22	SEDOL	4110444	Chairman	B. Lacan

Bouygues

DJGI Industry: **Heavy Construction**
Stoxx Sector: **Construction**

Bouygues SA is a construction, public-works, and real estate company that also holds interests in media and mobile communications. Its operations include infrastructure projects, maritime construction, waterproofing, public utilities, and gas exploration. A partner in the Channel Tunnel project, Bouygues also controls 39% of the French television station TF1. The company has operations in 80 countries. Construction of buildings and public works accounted for 38% of 1997 revenues; construction of roads, 29%; public services management, 14%; and television activities (TF1), 11%.

	FRF mil 12/95	12/96	12/97	US$mil 12/97				
Sales	73,842.0	73,372.0	91,073.0	15,141.0	P/E Ratio	37.3	Price (6/30/98)	1,098.00
Net Income	-2,912.0	654.0	755.0	125.5	P/B Ratio	3.4	52 Wk Hi-Low	1,150.0-473.2
Book Value	6,332.0	7,063.0	8,262.0	1,373.6	Yield %	1.5	Market Cap	US$4,633.5mil

Address	1 ave. Eugène-Freyssinet	Tel 1-30-60-23-11	ADR	BWG	Director General	M. Derbesse
	78061 St.-Quentin-Yvelines	Fax 1-30-60-31-40	SEDOL	4115159	Chairman & CEO	M. Bouygues

Canal Plus

DJGI Industry: **Cable & Broadcasting**
Stoxx Sector: **Media**

Canal Plus SA operates a pay-television station, manufactures reception equipment, and produces and distributes films and television programs. Canal Plus is the leading pay-television company in the world, boasting 8.2 million subscribers in France, Belgium, Spain, Germany, and West Africa. It owns and operates foreign-language and thematic channels, including the European Sports Network and the MCM music channel. Subscriptions to television channels accounted for 77% of 1997 revenues; advertising and sponsorship, 4%; and other, 19%.

	FRF mil 12/95	12/96	12/97	US$mil 12/97				
Sales	10,156.9	11,628.0	10,430.0	1,734.0	P/E Ratio	21.8	Price (6/30/98)	1,130.00
Net Income	665.8	741.0	1,530.0	254.4	P/B Ratio	3.3	52 Wk Hi-Low	1,377.0-958.0
Book Value	7,661.7	9,467.0	10,880.0	1,808.8	Yield %	1.8	Market Cap	US$5,846.7mil

Address	85/89 quai André Citroën	Tel 1-44-25-10-00	ADR	CNPLY	V Chairman	M.A. Feffer
	75711 Paris Cedex 15	Fax 1-44-25-12-34	SEDOL	4171720	Chairman & CEO	P. Lescure

Cap Gemini

DJGI Industry: **Software**
Stoxx Sector: **Technology**

Cap Gemini SA (formerly known as Cap Gemini Sogeti SA) is the largest computer-services group in Europe providing custom-designed information-technology services. Specialized services are provided to the oil and gas, financial, and telecommunications sectors. The company's markets include France, the Benelux countries, Germany, Scandinavia, the United Kingdom, Ireland, and the United States. In June 1997, Daimler-Benz AG (DAI) gave up an attempt to take control of the company. Daimler-Benz InterServices AG, or Debis, sold its 24.4% Cap Gemini stake.

	FRF mil 12/95	12/96	12/97	US$mil 12/97				
Sales	11,328.9	14,819.8	20,177.0	3,354.4	P/E Ratio	78.7	Price (6/30/98)	950.00
Net Income	52.3	281.9	762.0	126.7	P/B Ratio	6.5	52 Wk Hi-Low	978.00-300.67
Book Value	5,840.9	7,962.8	9,228.0	1,534.2	Yield %	0.4	Market Cap	US$10,729mil

Address	11 rue de Tilsitt	Tel 1-47-54-50-00	ADR	--	COO	G. Unwin
	75017 Paris	Fax --	SEDOL	4163437	Chairman & CEO	S. Kampf

Carrefour

DJGI Industry: **Retailers - Broadline**
Stoxx Sector: **Retail**

Carrefour SA, a large-scale retailer, sells food, housewares, electronics, clothing, and hardware; some of its stores also sell insurance products and vacation packages. It operates 308 Carrefour hypermarkets and supermarkets in 14 countries, including France, Spain, Portugal, Brazil, Argentina, Taiwan, the United States, and Asia. The company operates 117 hypermarkets in France and 191 that are located in other countries. The group is also involved in the distribution of gasoline and heating oil and in the provision of credit services to its customers.

	FRF mil 12/95	12/96	12/97	US$mil 12/97				
Revenues	144,612.0	154,905.0	169,269.0	28,141.1	P/E Ratio	39.3	Price (6/30/98)	3,825.00
Net Income	3,536.0	3,123.0	3,583.0	595.7	P/B Ratio	6.6	52 Wk Hi-Low	4,392.0-2,802.0
Book Value	15,434.0	19,052.0	21,746.0	3,615.3	Yield %	0.8	Market Cap	US$24,281mil

Address	6 ave. Raymond Poincaré	Tel 1-53-70-19-00	ADR	--	CFO	H. Deffore
	75116 Paris	Fax 1-53-70-86-16	SEDOL	4177546	Chairman	D. Bernard

In DJ Stoxx 50; In EuroStoxx 50.

Casino Guichard

DJGI Industry: **Food Retailers & Wholesalers**
Stoxx Sector: **Consumer Non-Cyclical**

Groupe Casino Guichard Perrachon SA (Casino) owns retail, restaurant, food-processing, wine-bottling, and real estate businesses in France and the United States. It operates convenience stores, warehouse stores, supermarkets, and hypermarkets as well as Casino Cafeteria restaurants. Casino manages the majority-owned Smart and Final retailer, with stores in the United States and in Mexico. The company also provides short-term customer credit, carries out advertising and sponsorship activities, and has real estate investments.

	FRF mil 12/95	12/96	12/97	US$mil 12/97				
Sales	64,130.0	66,842.0	76,257.0	12,677.8	P/E Ratio	35.0	Price (6/30/98)	482.80
Net Income	633.0	838.0	1,114.0	185.2	P/B Ratio	4.2	52 Wk Hi-Low	482.80-276.13
Book Value	7,572.0	7,757.0	9,090.0	1,511.2	Yield %	1.6	Market Cap	US$5,811.0mil

Address	24 rue de la Montat	Tel 4-77-45-31-31	ADR	--	CEO	Georges Plassat
	42100 Saint-Etienne	Fax 4-77-21-85-15	SEDOL	4178419	Chairman	Antoine Guichard

Castorama Dubois Investissement

DJGI Industry: **Retailers - Other Specialty**
Stoxx Sector: **Retail**

Castorama Dubois Investissements SCA, known as Castorama, distributes do-it-yourself products for home and garden through its 134 shops in France. The company also has six shops in Germany, two in Belgium, and five in Italy. Castorama opened its first shop in Warsaw, Poland, and Sao Paulo, Brazil in 1997. Castorama also sells building materials through its six Dubois Materiaux shops and pet-care products. Do-it-yourself hardware products accounted for 94% of 1997 revenues; building materials, 5%; and pet care, 1%.

	FRF mil 12/95	12/96	12/97	US$mil 12/97				
Revenues	13,788.1	14,922.3	17,659.0	2,935.8	P/E Ratio	48.8	Price (6/30/98)	1,064.00
Net Income	522.2	546.4	348.9	58.0	P/B Ratio	4.0	52 Wk Hi-Low	1,068.0-525.0
Book Value	3,445.0	3,986.5	4,245.1	705.7	Yield %	1.0	Market Cap	US$2,813.3mil

Address	Zone Industrielle	Tel 3-20-16-75	ADR	--	President	--
	59175 Templemars	Fax 3-20-16-75	SEDOL	4179144	Chairman	C. Dubois

CGIP

DJGI Industry: **Diversified Financial Services**
Stoxx Sector: **Financial Services**

Compagnie Générale d'Industrie et de Participations SA (CGIP) is an industrial holding company with interests in diversified companies that operate in various sectors, including packaging for food, aerosols, and special products; abrasives production; computer services; management services; biological research; real estate; and other activities. In 1997, CGIP aquired 20.25% of car-components maker Valeo SA, and in 1998, it disposed of its 20% stake in Crown Cork & Seal Co. of the United States. The Wendel family is the majority shareholder with more than 26% of CGIP's share capital.

	FRF mil 12/95	12/96	12/97	US$mil 12/97				
Revenues	25,877.4	1,343.1	1,554.6	258.5	P/E Ratio	18.3	Price (6/30/98)	3,195.00
Net Income	591.4	1,298.6	1,208.3	200.9	P/B Ratio	1.8	52 Wk Hi-Low	3,350.0-1,670.0
Book Value	9,209.6	10,616.4	12,440.4	2,068.2	Yield %	1.3	Market Cap	US$3,652.6mil

Address	89 rue Taitbout	Tel 1-42-85-30-00	ADR	--	CFO	G. Moulin
	75009 Paris	Fax 1-42-80-68-67	SEDOL	4162616	Chairman & CEO	E. A. Seillière

Chargeurs International

DJGI Industry: **Clothing & Fabrics**
Stoxx Sector: **Consumer Cyclical**

Chargeurs International SA was created in July 1996 when Chargeurs SA decided to split its business activities into two separate, publicly traded companies, Chargeurs International and Pathé Cinéma SA. Chargeurs International is a textiles, surfacing, and transportation company. Its activities include the processing and distribution of wool, woolen garments, clothes interlining, and car fabric, and the production of coated protective adhesive films for industry. Woolen products accounted for 48% of 1997 revenues; clothes interlining, 24%; car fabric, 21%; and adhesive films, 7%.

	FRF mil 12/95	12/96	12/97	US$mil 12/97					
Sales	8,819.0	8,671.0	9,045.0	1,503.7	P/E Ratio		12.6	Price (6/30/98)	499.50
Net Income	87.0	136.0	302.0	50.2	P/B Ratio		1.0	52 Wk Hi-Low	529.00-325.00
Book Value	3,389.0	3,705.0	3,825.0	635.9	Yield %		1.9	Market Cap	US$632.4mil

Address	5 blvd. Malesherbes	Tel 1-49-24-42-64	ADR	--	CFO	R. Bellande
	75008 Paris	Fax 1-49-24-42-64	SEDOL	5021318	Chairman & CEO	E. Malone

Club Méditerranée

DJGI Industry: **Other Recreational Products & Services**
Stoxx Sector: **Consumer Cyclical**

Club Méditerranée SA manages 139 resort villages in 38 countries, runs cruises, and provides all-season package tour holidays. Its resorts operate under the Club Med, Valtur, Club Med Affaires, and Club Aquarius names. It owns two cruise ships: Club Med 1, which sails the Mediterranean and Caribbean, and Club Med 2, which cruises the Pacific. The company has operations in Europe, Africa, and South America. Holiday resort chain operations accounted for 79% of fiscal 1997 and revenues and transportation accounted for 21%.

	FRF mil 10/95	10/96	10/97	US$mil 10/97					
Sales	8,467.3	8,004.6	8,225.6	1,424.1	P/E Ratio		NMF	Price (6/30/98)	522.00
Net Income	168.6	-742.7	-1,294.3	-224.1	P/B Ratio		3.1	52 Wk Hi-Low	613.00-375.68
Book Value	4,139.9	3,480.8	2,371.6	410.6	Yield %		0.0	Market Cap	US$1,287.7mil

Address	11 rue de Cambrai	Tel 1-53-35-35-53	ADR	CLMDY	CFO	C. Ravilly
	75019 Paris	Fax 1-53-35-36-16	SEDOL	4204370	Chairman & CEO	S. Trigano

Colas

DJGI Industry: **Heavy Construction**
Stoxx Sector: **Construction**

Colas SA is a major company that specializes in road construction and bridge building and is involved in civil engineering, pipeline projects, building construction, and the production of asphalt paving mixtures. A partially owned subsidiary of construction and real estate company Bouygues, Colas is active in Asia, Africa, and most European countries where it builds distribution systems for utilities and public services, moves earth, and builds dams. Road construction and related activities accounted for 73% of 1997 revenues.

	FRF mil 12/95	12/96	12/97	US$mil 12/97					
Sales	18,778.0	18,883.0	26,206.0	4,356.8	P/E Ratio		20.0	Price (6/30/98)	1,181.00
Net Income	390.0	400.0	433.0	72.0	P/B Ratio		2.1	52 Wk Hi-Low	1,255.0-742.0
Book Value	3,406.0	3,745.0	4,113.0	683.8	Yield %		2.4	Market Cap	US$1,427.5mil

Address	7 pl. René Clair	Tel 1-47-61-75-00	ADR	--	Director	M. Cote
	92100 Boulogne-Billancourt	Fax 1-47-61-76-00	SEDOL	4208918	Chairman & CEO	A. Dupont

Comptoirs Modernes

DJGI Industry: **Food Retailers & Wholesalers**
Stoxx Sector: **Consumer Non-Cyclical**

Comptoirs Modernes SA is a holding company with subsidiaries in the food-retailing industry. Its supermarket chains include 368 Stoc supermarkets and 312 Comod local shops and supermarkets. In addition, Comptoirs Modernes operates 11 Merca Plus supermarkets in northeastern Spain. The French retailer Carrefour runs 16 Carrefour hypermarkets in a joint venture with Comptoirs Modernes. Stoc supermarkets accounted for 79% of fiscal 1997 revenues; Carrefour hypermarkets, 13%; and local shops, supermarkets, and franchises, 8%.

	FRF mil 12/95	12/96	12/97	US$mil 12/97					
Sales	27,038.9	30,243.6	32,746.0	5,444.1	P/E Ratio		31.5	Price (6/30/98)	3,150.00
Net Income	450.1	500.5	551.7	91.7	P/B Ratio		4.9	52 Wk Hi-Low	3,250.0-2,136.4
Book Value	2,881.3	3,283.8	3,701.4	615.4	Yield %		0.8	Market Cap	US$2,976.9mil

Address	1 pl. de Gué de Maulny	Tel 2-43-86-28-20	ADR	--	Jnt Mng Dir	B. Gautier
	72019 Le Mans	Fax 2-43-72-32-75	SEDOL	4215167	Chairman & CEO	J.C. Plassart

CPR

DJGI Industry: **Diversified Financial Services**
Stoxx Sector: **Financial Services**

Compagnie Parisienne de Réescompte SA (CPR) offers banking, proprietary-trading, asset-management, and brokerage services. The company also has financing and capital-markets operations. Its main subsidiaries include Banque CGM, CPR Gestion, Schelcher-Prince, Paresco Gestion & Cie., CPR Maubeuge, and CPR Holding. Through its interest in CGM, CPR controls BBT-Dagues-Bie, France's third-largest money broker, by revenues. Interest income on bank deposits accounted for 41% of 1997 revenues.

	FRF mil 12/95	12/96	12/97	US$mil 12/97					
Revenues	13,257.9	12,764.9	12,214.2	2,030.6	P/E Ratio		15.4	Price (6/30/98)	487.00
Net Income	282.6	361.0	325.2	54.1	P/B Ratio		1.5	52 Wk Hi-Low	529.00-426.10
Book Value	2,840.3	3,220.7	3,538.5	588.3	Yield %		4.5	Market Cap	US$894.8mil

Address	30 rue St. Georges	Tel 1-45-96-20-00	ADR	--	Jnt Director Gen	Jean-Néel Barthélémy
	75312 Paris	Fax 1-45-96-25-55	SEDOL	4671888	Chairman	Henri Cukierman

Crédit Commercial

DJGI Industry: **Banks - Regional (All)**
Stoxx Sector: **Bank**

Crédit Commercial de France SA (CCF) operates in four broad business segments: retail banking, investment banking, asset management, and international private banking. It is also involved in insurance and equipment-leasing businesses and in airport money-exchanging offices. CCF is represented in several countries in Europe and abroad. Interest income on bank deposits accounted for 32% of 1997 revenues; interest and fees on loans, 32%; other interest or dividend income, 18%; commissions & fees, 11%; and noninterest income, 7%.

	FRF mil 12/95	12/96	12/97	US$mil 12/97					
Revenues	35,496.7	35,956.1	43,742.5	7,272.2	P/E Ratio	22.8	Price (6/30/98)	509.00
Net Income	1,231.1	1,373.6	1,603.1	266.5	P/B Ratio	2.1	52 Wk Hi-Low	544.00-249.00
Book Value	15,032.4	16,139.9	17,480.6	2,906.2	Yield %	1.3	Market Cap	US$6,113.5mil

Address	103 ave. des Champs-Elysées	Tel 1-40-70-70-40	ADR	--	V Chairman	R. de la Serre
	75419 Paris Cedex 08	Fax 1-40-70-70-09	SEDOL	4230870	Chairman & CEO	C. de Croisset

Danone

DJGI Industry: **Other Food**
Stoxx Sector: **Food & Beverage**

Groupe Danone SA is the largest producer of fresh dairy products in the world. The company also makes packaging materials. Its products include Evian and Volvic mineral waters, Danone and Dannon yogurt, and Kanterbrau and Kronenbourg beers. Danone also owns Irish cookie maker W&R Jacob, U.S.-based sauce producer Lea & Perrins, and 80% of Italian cheese producer Galbani. Dairy products accounted for 42% of 1997 revenues; beverages, 22%; biscuits, 21%; other food businesses, 8%; and containers, 7%.

	FRF mil 12/95	12/96	12/97	US$mil 12/97					
Sales	79,450.0	83,940.0	88,476.0	14,709.2	P/E Ratio	33.2	Price (6/30/98)	1,667.00
Net Income	2,133.0	3,382.0	3,664.0	609.1	P/B Ratio	2.9	52 Wk Hi-Low	1,735.0-809.0
Book Value	36,254.0	40,383.0	42,717.0	7,101.7	Yield %	1.1	Market Cap	US$20,112mil

Address	7 rue de Téhéran	Tel 1-44-35-20-20	ADR	GPDNY	V Chmn & COO	P. Lenain
	75381 Paris Cedex 08	Fax 1-42-25-67-16	SEDOL	4070236	Chairman & CEO	F. Riboud

Dassault Systemès

DJGI Industry: **Software**
Stoxx Sector: **Technology**

Dassault Systemès SA develops and sells software products for computer-aided design, computer-aided manufacturing, and computer-aided engineering. All the products are sold to the private sector. They are marketed, distributed, and supported in nearly all world markets by IBM. The company also provides services and support to IBM in its marketing and distribution efforts, provides customer support, technological consulting services, and has interests in hardware resale. In 1998, the company formed a partnership with Edsa Micro Corp.

	FRF mil 12/95	12/96	12/97	US$mil 12/97					
Sales	1,135.8	1,394.6	1,886.2	313.6	P/E Ratio	NMF	Price (6/30/98)	285.00
Net Income	221.3	342.5	-111.3	-18.5	P/B Ratio	25.3	52 Wk Hi-Low	297.50-151.00
Book Value	1,490.5	1,377.9	1,250.2	207.8	Yield %	0.4	Market Cap	US$5,310.6mil

Address	9 quai Marcel Dassault	Tel 1-40-99-40	ADR	DASTY	CFO	T. De Tersant
	92150 Suresnes	Fax 1-42-04-45	SEDOL	5330047	Chairman & CEO	C. Elstenne

Dexia France

DJGI Industry: **Banks - Regional (All)**
Stoxx Sector: **Financial Services**

Dexia France SA, formerly known as Crédit Local de France, provides banking services. It specializes in offering loans and services to local authorities to promote regional development. Dexia is the main source of financing for the French local-development sector; the company acts as a partner to the municipal authorities, who help promote local development through their investments. The company is also active in the United States and the rest of Europe through its subsidiaries. The company was privatized in 1993.

	FRF mil 12/95	12/96	12/97	US$mil 12/97					
Revenues	29,737.0	6,265.0	7,259.0	1,206.8	P/E Ratio	16.7	Price (6/30/98)	814.00
Net Income	1,480.0	1,550.0	1,752.0	291.3	P/B Ratio	2.1	52 Wk Hi-Low	859.00-524.00
Book Value	12,408.0	13,123.0	14,161.0	2,354.3	Yield %	2.1	Market Cap	US$4,937.6mil

Address	Quai André Citroën	Tel 1-43-92-77-77	ADR	--	Joint Dirs Gen	J. Guerber / G. Oucliz
	75901 Paris Cedex 15	Fax 1-43-92-70-00	SEDOL	4228518	Chairman	P. Richard

Elf Aquitaine

DJGI Industry: **Oil Companies - Major**
Stoxx Sector: **Energy**

Elf Aquitaine SA, privatized in 1994, is is the largest publicly traded oil and natural-gas company in Europe. Elf operates in 80 countries through 819 subsidiaries. It explores in 28 countries, with production mainly in West Africa and the North Sea. Elf is involved in refining oil, producing chemicals, and manufacturing health-care products, including pharmaceuticals, perfumes, and beauty products. Oil refining, marketing, and trading accounted for 59% of 1997 revenues; chemicals, 23%; healthcare, 10%; and oil and gas exploration and production, 8%.

	FRF mil 12/95	12/96	12/97	US$mil 12/97					
Sales	208,290.0	232,707.0	254,306.0	42,278.6	P/E Ratio	38.9	Price (6/30/98)	850.00
Net Income	5,035.0	6,977.0	5,602.0	931.3	P/B Ratio	2.6	52 Wk Hi-Low	890.00-613.00
Book Value	78,672.0	80,062.0	83,985.0	13,962.6	Yield %	1.8	Market Cap	US$38,491mil

Address	Tour Elf, pl. de la Coupole	Tel 1-47-44-45-46	ADR	ELF	President	J.I. Vermeulen
	92400 Courbevoie	Fax 1-47-44-40-24	SEDOL	4824080	Chairman & CEO	P. Jaffré

In DJ Stoxx 50; In EuroStoxx 50.

Eridania Béghin-Say

DJGI Industry: **Other Food**
Stoxx Sector: **Food & Beverage**

Eridania Béghin-Say SA processes sugar, starch, oil, and animal feed. The company also produces its own brands of consumer products, such as salad dressings, sauces, pastry ingredients, herbs, and spices. In early 1998, the Franco-Italian group acquired Unilever's FRF500 million French seed oil business, and under a separate deal, Eridania Beghin-Say sold its Vegetaline cooking oil business to Unilever. Oil-crushing and refining accounted for 37% of 1997 revenues; sugar and derivatives, 21%; starch, 17%; consumer goods, 14%; animal feed, 10%; and other, 1%.

	FRF mil 12/95	12/96	12/97	US$mil 12/97				
Sales	50,806.0	54,978.0	63,650.0	10,581.9	P/E Ratio	18.2	Price (6/30/98)	1,335.00
Net Income	1,526.0	1,660.0	1,904.0	316.5	P/B Ratio	1.7	52 Wk Hi-Low	1,375.0-770.0
Book Value	17,802.0	18,773.0	19,887.0	3,306.2	Yield %	2.6	Market Cap	US$5,714.4mil

Address	Rue Joseph Beghin	Tel 3-20-62-44-00	ADR	--	CFO	E. Vigano
	59239 Thumeries	Fax 3-20-62-43-92	SEDOL	4089403	Chairman & CEO	S. Meloni

Essilor

DJGI Industry: **Medical Supplies**
Stoxx Sector: **Consumer Non-Cyclical**

Essilor International SA is the world's leading ophthalmic goods company. Its range of activities includes the design, manufacture, and marketing of vision-correction products. Essilor manufactures contact lenses, metal and plastic lenses and frames, protective glasses, and eye-examination equipment. It has subsidiaries in Europe, North and South America, and Asian-Pacific countries. Recent acquisitions include U.S.-based Omega, Southern Optical, Wisconsin Optical Services Inc., and Duffens Optical. Essilor also established a four-year supplier agreement with Oakley.

	FRF mil 12/95	12/96	12/97	US$mil 12/97				
Sales	6,538.0	7,845.3	9,353.3	1,555.0	P/E Ratio	39.9	Price (6/30/98)	2,557.00
Net Income	498.5	520.2	616.3	102.5	P/B Ratio	4.8	52 Wk Hi-Low	2,680.0-1,444.0
Book Value	3,438.0	4,109.9	5,254.5	873.6	Yield %	0.7	Market Cap	US$4,126.4mil

Address	147 rue de Paris	Tel 1-49-77-42-24	ADR	--	Managing Director	P. Alfroid
	94227 Charenton	Fax 1-49-77-43-24	SEDOL	4303761	Chairman	X. Fontanet

Eurafrance

DJGI Industry: **Diversified Financial Services**
Stoxx Sector: **Financial Services**

Eurafrance SA is a holding company for investment and insurance concerns, including companies involved in real estate, asset trading, money brokering, corporate finance, and mergers-and-acquisitions consulting. It holds investments in La France, Compagnie Francaise de Participations et d'Assurances, and Société de Participations. The company also has significant holdings in other companies. Investment income accounted for 69% of 1997 revenues; interest income accounted for 30%, and other income made up only 1%.

	FRF mil 12/95	12/96	12/97	US$mil 12/97				
Revenues	1,466.8	1,678.1	1,616.9	268.8	P/E Ratio	21.0	Price (6/30/98)	3,800.00
Net Income	735.1	930.0	682.0	113.4	P/B Ratio	1.2	52 Wk Hi-Low	3,900.0-2,277.0
Book Value	10,568.3	11,263.8	11,890.7	1,976.8	Yield %	1.4	Market Cap	US$2,363.0mil

Address	12 ave. Percier	Tel 1-44-13-01-11	ADR	--	V Chmn & Mng Dir	Antoine Bernheim
	75008 Paris	Fax 1-47-66-87-57	SEDOL	4321547	Chairman	Michel David-Weill

Euro Disney

DJGI Industry: **Other Recreational Products & Services**
Stoxx Sector: **Consumer Cyclical**

Euro Disney SCA was formed to develop and operate the Euro Disney Resort recreational park, which contains a theme park, a golf course, six hotels, a conference center, a ranch, and an entertainment center. It is situated near Paris. The company also operates tours through its Euro Disney Vacances subsidiary. EDL Holding Company, a subsidiary of U.S.-based Walt Disney Co., owns 39% of Euro Disney. Theme-park operations and hotels accounted for 53% of fiscal 1997 revenues, hotels, 39%, construction and related services, 2%, and other, 6%.

	FRF mil 09/95	09/96	09/97	US$mil 09/97				
Sales	4,667.0	5,009.0	5,582.0	944.3	P/E Ratio	42.2	Price (6/30/98)	12.10
Net Income	114.0	202.0	217.0	36.7	P/B Ratio	1.5	52 Wk Hi-Low	12.85-6.90
Book Value	5,610.0	5,813.0	6,038.0	1,021.4	Yield %	0.0	Market Cap	US$1,530.3mil

Address	Route Nationale 34	Tel 1-64-74-58-55	ADR	--	CFO	P. Misteli
	77700 Chessy	Fax 1-64-74-56-36	SEDOL	4320878	Chairman & CEO	G. Pelisson

Foncière Lyonnaise

DJGI Industry: **Real Estate**
Stoxx Sector: **Financial Services**

Société Foncière Lyonnaise SA is a real estate company that manages and rents residential and commercial properties. Most of its holdings are in the exclusive districts of Paris and the surrounding western suburbs, primarily Neuilly. The company increased its holdings in 1997 with the acquisition of 23,000 square meters of residential and commercial real estate and 676 parking lots. In June 1997, Société Foncière purchased several buildings from Crédit Foncier de France. Rental income accounted for 98% of 1997 revenues, and service income accounted for 2%.

	FRF mil 12/95	12/96	12/97	US$mil 12/97				
Sales	184.4	263.5	300.3	49.9	P/E Ratio	75.0	Price (6/30/98)	955.00
Net Income	69.4	104.9	85.3	14.2	P/B Ratio	2.2	52 Wk Hi-Low	1,020.0-690.0
Book Value	2,115.1	2,182.6	2,869.0	477.0	Yield %	2.0	Market Cap	US$1,050.6mil

Address	1 rue Marengo	Tel 1-42-97-27-00	ADR	--	Dir General	Y. Defline
	75001 Paris	Fax 1-42-97-00-65	SEDOL	4344157	Chairman & CEO	T. Wyand

France Telecom

DJGI Industry: **Telephone Utilities (All)**
Stoxx Sector: **Telecom**

France Telecom is a state-owned provider of basic telephone services, mobile telephony, and data services. It is also responsible for the construction and maintenance of telephone lines and telecommunications networks. France Telecom is active in the visual and audio communications sectors, through the production, transmission, and broadcasting of programs. Telephone products, telematics, and fax machines accounted for 69% of 1997 revenues; mobile phones,11%; dedicated lines and networks, 8%; information services, 5%; cable, broadcast, and video, 5%; and other 2%.

	FRF mil 12/95	12/96	12/97	US$mil 12/97				
Sales	147,820.0	151,259.0	156,731.0	26,056.7	P/E Ratio	28.1	Price (6/30/98)	417.00
Net Income	9,193.0	2,107.0	14,863.0	2,471.0	P/B Ratio	4.4	52 Wk Hi-Low	429.80-187.00
Book Value	140,296.0	78,493.0	93,711.0	15,579.6	Yield %	1.6	Market Cap	US$68,800mil

Address **Pl. d'Alleray 6**   Tel **1-44-44-22-22**   ADR   **FTE**   President   **--**
        75505 Paris   Fax **1-42-50-02-17**   SEDOL **5176177**   Chairman   **M. Bon**
In DJ Stoxx 50; In EuroStoxx 50.

Gaz et Eaux

DJGI Industry: **Conglomerates**
Stoxx Sector: **Conglomerate**

Société Financière et Industrielle Gaz et Eaux SA is a diversified holding company that has business investments in Luxembourg, France, the United States, and the United Kingdom. Its investments are spread across the financial, food, industrial, distribution, publishing, and communication sectors. In 1997, the company acquired a 5% stake in Francois-Charles Oberthur Fiduciaire. Its main holdings include Pearson PLC and Saint Gobain. Investment income accounted for 70% of 1997 revenues; interest income, 29% and other income, 1%.

	FRF mil 12/95	12/96	12/97	US$mil 12/97				
Sales	925.2	524.1	1,001.6	166.5	P/E Ratio	14.2	Price (6/30/98)	331.40
Net Income	696.5	395.1	756.3	125.7	P/B Ratio	1.5	52 Wk Hi-Low	348.90-214.29
Book Value	6,237.0	6,466.1	7,055.7	1,173.0	Yield %	1.6	Market Cap	US$1,771.7mil

Address **3 rue Jacques Bingen**   Tel **1-47-66-02-64**   ADR   **--**   Managing Director **G.F. Brandford Griffith**
        75017 Paris   Fax **1-47-66-84-41**   SEDOL **5481406**   Chairman & CEO   **B. Roger**

GFC

DJGI Industry: **Real Estate**
Stoxx Sector: **Financial Services**

Groupement pour le Financement de la Construction SA (GFC) develops and manages real estate. Its activities also include property rental and leasing, land acquisition, and real estate financing. Its property holdings are 80% residential and 20% commercial and professional. The company's properties are located in Paris and in the provinces. Residential buildings accounted for 72% of 1996 revenues, nonresidential buildings for 28%. All revenues were derived from rental and leasing income.

	FRF mil 12/95	12/96	12/97	US$mil 12/97				
Sales	357.0	367.9	461.5	76.7	P/E Ratio	30.8	Price (6/30/98)	660.00
Net Income	177.5	193.6	184.2	30.6	P/B Ratio	2.8	52 Wk Hi-Low	705.00-493.00
Book Value	1,860.6	2,046.9	2,061.0	342.7	Yield %	3.0	Market Cap	US$954.1mil

Address **Tour Franklin**   Tel **1-49-01-02-88**   ADR   **--**   CFO   **H. Guillemin**
        92042 Paris-La Défense   Fax **1-49-01-13-73**   SEDOL **4391807**   Chairman & CEO **E. Sermondadaz**

GTM-Entrepose

DJGI Industry: **Heavy Construction**
Stoxx Sector: **Construction**

GTM-Entrepose SA is an international construction and public-works company. Most of its services are in civil engineering and road and building construction, and secondary activities include industrial and electrical installations, offshore oil facilities, public-service concessions, design engineering, and property development. In 1995, GTM-Entrepose increased its stake in Jean Lefebvre to 96% from 52% through a public exchange offer and Dumez-GTM merged into the company. GTM-Entrepose has operations in more than 70 countries.

	FRF mil 12/95	12/96	12/97	US$mil 12/97				
Sales	36,863.0	43,041.0	44,582.0	7,411.8	P/E Ratio	37.3	Price (6/30/98)	628.00
Net Income	198.0	-45.0	254.0	42.2	P/B Ratio	2.0	52 Wk Hi-Low	640.00-294.10
Book Value	4,637.0	4,586.0	4,837.0	804.2	Yield %	1.4	Market Cap	US$1,562.3mil

Address **61 ave. Jules-Quentin**   Tel **1-46-95-76-93**   ADR   **--**   Dir General & Sec **J. Tolot**
        92003 Nanterre   Fax **1-46-95-77-95**   SEDOL **4358794**   Chairman & CEO   **Jean-Louis Brault**

Guilbert

DJGI Industry: **Retailers - Other Specialty**
Stoxx Sector: **Retail**

Guilbert SA is a business-to-business office-supplies retailer. Its products, numbering over 10,000, include papers, industrial adhesives, writing instruments, furniture, and equipment. The group's operations are based primarily in France with subsidiaries in the United Kingdom, Belgium, Spain, and Germany. Guilbert acquired JM Bruneau, an office supply distributor, in a 50/50 partnership with the mail-order company, 3 Suisses International, in 1997. Since 1996, Guilbert has been entering new mail order and retail outlet businesses through distribution ventures and partnerships.

	FRF mil 12/95	12/96	12/97	US$mil 12/97				
Revenues	2,596.9	4,173.7	5,643.9	938.3	P/E Ratio	25.2	Price (6/30/98)	956.00
Net Income	218.2	203.9	257.8	42.9	P/B Ratio	4.4	52 Wk Hi-Low	1,125.0-735.0
Book Value	1,352.3	1,632.3	1,929.6	320.8	Yield %	1.4	Market Cap	US$1,436.0mil

Address **126 ave. du Poteau**   Tel **3-44-54-54-54**   ADR   **--**   CEO   **B. Bernard**
        60451 Senlis   Fax **3-44-54-55-99**   SEDOL **4395779**   Chairman   **P. Cuvelier**

Havas Advertising

DJGI Industry: **Advertising**
Stoxx Sector: **Media**

Havas Advertising SA is the leading communications company in France and the eighth-largest ad agency in the world. The company has 200 agencies operating in 61 countries. Its divisions include Euro RSCG, Mediapolis, Campus, and Diversified Agencies. The company provides direct mail advertising, sales promotion, design, public relations, sponsoring, recruitment, communications, and marketing research services. In May 1997, Havas acquired 51% of the marketing agency Lifestyle Marketing Group which specializes in sports marketing.

	FRF mil 12/95	12/96	12/97	US$mil 12/97					
Sales	12,238.3	14,340.8	17,222.4	2,863.2	P/E Ratio		36.2	Price (6/30/98)	1,222.00
Net Income	68.5	104.8	162.8	27.1	P/B Ratio		3.2	52 Wk Hi-Low	1,327.0-631.9
Book Value	1,741.0	1,833.5	1,987.0	330.3	Yield %		1.2	Market Cap	US$1,138.9mil

Address	84 rue de Villiers	Tel 1-41-34-30-00	ADR	HAVSY	Jnt V Chairman	J. Seguela
	92300 Levallois-Perret	Fax 1-41-34-45-67	SEDOL	4301594	Chairman & CEO	A. de Pouzilhac

Hermes International

DJGI Industry: **Clothing & Fabrics**
Stoxx Sector: **Consumer Cyclical**

Hermes International SCA manufactures and distributes luxury goods. Its products include leather goods, silk scarves, women's clothing, ties, perfumes, men's clothing, accessories, enamel, gloves, and other products. The company distributes its products through Europe, Asia, Australia, and North America. Leather goods accounted for 23% of 1997 revenues; silk, 26%; women's ready to wear, 15%; watches and clocks, 10%; perfumes, 6%; "art de la table," 4%; other sectors (including jewelry, gloves, enamel, and silk goods, 10%; other products, 6%.

	FRF mil 12/95	12/96	12/97	US$mil 12/97					
Sales	3,826.0	4,182.8	4,858.4	807.7	P/E Ratio		32.8	Price (6/30/98)	475.00
Net Income	404.0	457.0	530.9	88.3	P/B Ratio		6.0	52 Wk Hi-Low	583.00-332.00
Book Value	2,028.5	2,407.0	2,891.5	480.7	Yield %		0.8	Market Cap	US$2,879.7mil

Address	24 rue du Faubourg St.Honore	Tel 1-40-17-49-20	ADR	--	President	--
	75008 Paris	Fax 1-40-17-49-21	SEDOL	5253973	Chairman	J.L. Dumas

Imétal

DJGI Industry: **Building Materials**
Stoxx Sector: **Construction**

Imétal SA produces building materials, is involved in metal processing, and manufactures industrial minerals. The company's products include clay and ceramic tiles, bricks, mechanical and structural tubing, refractory technical ceramics, bimetallic wires, kaolin and crushed calcium carbonate, fillers for plastics, ceramic fibers, high-purity synthetic and natural graphite, and technical lubricants. Industrial minerals accounted for 39% of the company's 1997 revenues; metal processing, 35%; and building materials, 26%.

	FRF mil 12/95	12/96	12/97	US$mil 12/97					
Sales	7,737.5	8,100.5	11,050.5	1,837.2	P/E Ratio		20.0	Price (6/30/98)	831.00
Net Income	595.8	613.7	620.3	103.1	P/B Ratio		1.9	52 Wk Hi-Low	887.00-601.00
Book Value	5,328.7	5,848.9	6,573.1	1,092.8	Yield %		3.4	Market Cap	US$2,046.7mil

Address	33 ave. du Maine	Tel 1-45-38-48-48	ADR	--	Jnt Asst CEO	M. Sindzingre
	75755 Paris	Fax 1-45-38-74-78	SEDOL	4457765	Chairman & CEO	R. Mitieus

Immeubles de France

DJGI Industry: **Real Estate**
Stoxx Sector: **Financial Services**

Société des Immeubles de France SA manages, rents, and leases over 110,000 square meters of residential, commercial, and parking space in Paris and it invests in other leasing and renting companies. The company also has property interests in suburban Paris, Lyon, and London that add up to more than 35,000 square meters. Office and commercial property make up the majority of the company's assets. The remainder is residential property. Rental income accounted for 97% of 1997 revenues; interest income accounted for 3%.

	FRF mil 12/95	12/96	12/97	US$mil 12/97					
Sales	162.1	184.9	205.6	34.2	P/E Ratio		37.0	Price (6/30/98)	496.00
Net Income	1.5	71.4	94.3	15.7	P/B Ratio		1.5	52 Wk Hi-Low	511.00-317.10
Book Value	2,142.0	2,214.2	2,288.3	380.4	Yield %		1.3	Market Cap	US$576.3mil

Address	18-20 pl. de la Madeleine	Tel 1-44-71-34-00	ADR	--	CEO	C. Tron
	75008 Paris	Fax 1-40-17-05-82	SEDOL	4801533	Chairman	J. Meyssonier

Labinal

DJGI Industry: **Other Auto Parts**
Stoxx Sector: **Automobile**

Labinal SA manufactures gas turbines, connectors, and other equipment for the aeronautics, space, defense, electronics, and automobile industries. Labinal's aerospace division supplies filters, electrical wiring, and electrical motors. Its automotive products include filters, valves, cables, and switches for cars and commercial vehicles. The group includes 11 French subsidiaries and 45 foreign subsidiaries and has 18 production plants in France and 22 abroad. Automotive equipment accounted for 62% of 1997 revenues, gas turbines for 21%, and aerospace equipment for 10%.

	FRF mil 12/95	12/96	12/97	US$mil 12/97					
Sales	10,361.6	11,653.2	12,801.1	2,128.2	P/E Ratio		20.5	Price (6/30/98)	2,062.00
Net Income	152.3	201.2	412.7	68.6	P/B Ratio		2.4	52 Wk Hi-Low	2,350.0-1,430.0
Book Value	2,697.9	2,946.2	3,467.2	576.4	Yield %		1.3	Market Cap	US$1,397.6mil

Address	Pas du Lac, 5 ave. Newton	Tel 1-30-85-30-85	ADR	--	Director Bd of Dir	Monique Antiglio
	78051 Montigny-le-Bretonneux	Fax 1-30-43-41-71	SEDOL	4699404	Chairman & CEO	Amaury Halna du Fretay

Lafarge

DJGI Industry: **Building Materials**
Stoxx Sector: **Construction**

Lafarge SA, formerly known as Lafarge Coppée SA, produces and sells cement, lime, concrete, gypsum, and specialty products (including calcium aluminates and ready-to-use premixed products) in 45 countries. The company has 57 cement plants in 15 countries. It sold its stake in U.S.-based National Gypsum in May 1995. In 1997, Lafarge took over United Kingdom-based materials group Redland. Cement accounted for 46% of 1997 revenues; concrete and aggregates, 28%; specialty products, 15%; gypsum, 10%; and other, 1%.

	FRF mil 12/95	12/96	12/97	US$mil 12/97				
Sales	33,218.0	35,262.0	42,066.0	6,993.5	P/E Ratio	23.5	Price (6/30/98)	625.00
Net Income	2,350.0	1,846.0	2,432.0	404.3	P/B Ratio	2.3	52 Wk Hi-Low	657.00-333.21
Book Value	23,204.0	24,160.0	26,121.0	4,342.6	Yield %	1.7	Market Cap	US$10,577mil

Address	61 rue des Belles Feuilles	Tel 1-44-34-11-11	ADR	LFGEY	CEO	B. Kasriel
	75782 Paris Cedex 16	Fax 1-44-34-12-00	SEDOL	4502706	Chairman	B. Collomb

Lagardère

DJGI Industry: **Publishing**
Stoxx Sector: **Media**

Lagardère Groupe SCA is a diversified company with interests in the publishing, distribution, communication, technology, and media industries. It has a 93% holding in Matra-Hachette SA, which has operations in the following sectors: book and periodical distribution; publishing; defense and aerospace; telecommunications; automobile and electronic components; and transport operations. Distribution services contribute 25% of revenues; print media, 16%; aerospace, 13%; book publishing, 12%; telecommunications, 10%; automobiles, 10%; and defense electronic systems, 7%.

	FRF mil 12/95	12/96	12/97	US$mil 12/97				
Sales	52,579.2	56,401.4	65,903.2	10,956.5	P/E Ratio	21.8	Price (6/30/98)	251.70
Net Income	630.3	1,038.0	1,380.1	229.4	P/B Ratio	2.5	52 Wk Hi-Low	275.60-156.10
Book Value	5,205.5	7,215.8	11,899.1	1,978.2	Yield %	1.7	Market Cap	US$4,976.5mil

Address	4 rue de Presbourg	Tel 1-40-69-16-00	ADR	LGDDY	CFO	P. Camus
	75116 Paris	Fax 1-46-22-22-11	SEDOL	4547213	CEO	J.I. Lagardere

L'Air Liquide

DJGI Industry: **Chemicals - Specialty**
Stoxx Sector: **Chemical**

L'Air Liquide SA produces gases and chemicals and has welding, engineering, and construction operations. It also manufactures medical products such as anesthesiology equipment, operating tables, and surgical lighting systems. It produces industrial gases used by the healthcare, chemical, paper, and space industries. It also manufactures welding and cutting equipment and related products, including electrodes and wires. Industrial gases accounted for 67% of 1997 revenues; medical instruments, 13%; welding equipment, 11%; engineering, 4%; chemicals, 3%; and other, 2%.

	FRF mil 12/95	12/96	12/97	US$mil 12/97				
Sales	32,188.7	34,382.0	38,382.0	6,381.0	P/E Ratio	26.6	Price (6/30/98)	1,000.00
Net Income	2,660.8	2,773.0	3,090.0	513.7	P/B Ratio	3.0	52 Wk Hi-Low	1,080.9-756.4
Book Value	22,293.1	24,658.0	27,363.0	4,549.1	Yield %	1.4	Market Cap	US$13,584mil

Address	75 quai d'Orsay	Tel 1-40-62-55-55	ADR	AIQUY	Asst Director Gen	G. Levy
	75321 Paris	Fax 1-45-51-33-44	SEDOL	4011406	Chairman & CEO	A. Joly

In EuroStoxx 50.

Legrand

DJGI Industry: **Electrical Components & Equipment**
Stoxx Sector: **Industrials**

Legrand SA makes electrical fittings and accessories for household, commercial, and industrial uses. Its home electrical products include switches, dimmers, intercoms, alarm systems, detectors, sockets, circuit breakers, information signs, and remote controls. The company also supplies programmable thermostats, broadcast-music systems, and theft-protection equipment for industrial use. Legrand has subsidiaries and offices in 29 countries. During 1997, sales outside of France represented 58% of the company's total revenues.

	FRF mil 12/95	12/96	12/97	US$mil 12/97				
Sales	10,886.0	11,339.0	12,842.0	2,135.0	P/E Ratio	41.0	Price (6/30/98)	1,600.00
Net Income	923.0	927.0	1,065.0	177.1	P/B Ratio	6.3	52 Wk Hi-Low	1,749.0-1,035.0
Book Value	4,974.0	5,934.0	6,821.0	1,134.0	Yield %	0.6	Market Cap	US$5,651.1mil

Address	128 ave. de Lattre de Tassigny	Tel 5-55-06-87-87	ADR	--	President	P. Puy
	87000 Limoges	Fax 5-55-06-88-88	SEDOL	4558583	Chairman	F. Grappotte

L'Oréal

DJGI Industry: **Cosmetics & Personal Care**
Stoxx Sector: **Consumer Non-Cyclical**

L'Oréal SA is one of the world's largest producers of cosmetics, perfumes, and hair-care products, most of which it markets under the L'Oréal name. It also makes and markets Lancôme, Vichy, Helena Rubenstein, Maybelline cosmetics, Lanvin luxury goods, and Plenitude beauty products. The company also produces pharmaceutical products, publishes the magazine Marie-Claire, and operates an art gallery. Cosmetics, toiletries, and perfumes accounted for 81% of 1997 revenues; pharmaceuticals, 17%; and other activities, 2%

	FRF mil 12/95	12/96	12/97	US$mil 12/97				
Sales	53,370.7	60,346.6	69,120.5	11,491.4	P/E Ratio	57.0	Price (6/30/98)	3,363.00
Net Income	3,148.6	3,497.6	3,985.8	662.6	P/B Ratio	7.9	52 Wk Hi-Low	3,401.0-1,992.0
Book Value	22,721.3	25,608.9	28,735.1	4,777.2	Yield %	0.5	Market Cap	US$37,503mil

Address	14 rue Royale	Tel 1-40-20-60-00	ADR	LORLY	Jnt V Chairman	G. Chouraqui
	75008 Paris	Fax 1-40-20-64-74	SEDOL	4534787	Chairman & CEO	L. Owen-Jones

In DJ Stoxx 50; In EuroStoxx 50.

LVMH

DJGI Industry: **Distillers & Brewers**
Stoxx Sector: **Food & Beverage**

LVMH-Moët Hennessy Louis Vuitton SA manufactures alcoholic beverages, beauty products and perfumes, luggage and leather goods, and apparel. It also holds 20% of the Guinness-Grand Met partnership. Its products include Moët & Chandon, Veuve Clicquot, and Canard Duchene & Pommery champagnes; Hennessy and Hines cognacs; Givenchy, Dior, and Kenzo perfumes and cosmetics; Givenchy, Christian Lacroix, and Kenzo couture; and Louis Vuitton luggage and leather goods. Each of LVMH's four luxury divisions contributes roughly one-fourth of sales.

	FRF mil 12/95	12/96	12/97	US$mil 12/97				
Sales	29,775.0	31,142.0	48,035.0	7,985.9	P/E Ratio	23.2	Price (6/30/98)	1,210.00
Net Income	4,047.0	3,683.0	4,166.0	692.6	P/B Ratio	2.8	52 Wk Hi-Low	1,638.0-894.0
Book Value	29,846.0	33,318.0	36,678.0	6,097.8	Yield %	1.8	Market Cap	US$17,491mil

Address	30 ave. Hoche	Tel	1-44-13-22-22	ADR	LVMHY	Jnt V Chairman	A. Bernheim
	75008 Paris	Fax	1-44-13-21-19	SEDOL	4535649	Chairman & CEO	B. Arnault

In EuroStoxx 50.

Michelin

DJGI Industry: **Tires & Rubber**
Stoxx Sector: **Automobile**

Compagnie Générale des Etablissements Michelin, is the world's largest tire manufacturer, with 18% of the worldwide tire market. It has 74 industrial facilities in Europe, Asia, Africa, and North and South America. Michelin produces a wide variety of tires and wheels for passenger and commercial vehicles. Its secondary products include bicycle and aircraft tires, tubes, steel cables, and maps. In 1997, the company purchased a 51% controlling interest in German wheel manufacturing group Mannesman Kronprinz AG. Tires and wheels accounted for 98% of 1997 revenues.

	FRF mil 12/95	12/96	12/97	US$mil 12/97				
Sales	66,110.3	71,245.8	79,691.9	13,248.9	P/E Ratio	10.8	Price (6/30/98)	349.00
Net Income	2,795.9	2,891.4	3,882.9	645.5	P/B Ratio	2.0	52 Wk Hi-Low	408.90-273.80
Book Value	11,824.9	16,020.9	24,040.1	3,996.7	Yield %	1.1	Market Cap	US$7,839.3mil

Address	12 cours Sablon	Tel	4-73-30-42-21	ADR	--	Managing Partner	E. Michelin
	63000 Clermont-Ferrand	Fax	4-73-23-52-92	SEDOL	4588364	Managing Partner	F. Michelin

Moulinex

DJGI Industry: **Other Home Furnishings**
Stoxx Sector: **Consumer Cyclical**

Moulinex SA manufactures and distributes household appliances and industrial equipment. About 80% of its products are sold in Europe under the Moulinex and Krups brand names. It has more than 20 factories worldwide, making food processors, microwave ovens, toasters, coffee makers, irons, and pressure cookers. Other products include coffee-makers, vacuum cleaners, and irons. Its products are sold in more than 120 countries. Sales by foreign subsidiaries accounted for 80% of 1997 revenues.

	FRF mil 03/96	03/97	03/98	US$mil 03/98				
Sales	7,787.9	7,745.7	8,027.6	1,297.4	P/E Ratio	26.2	Price (6/30/98)	156.90
Net Income	-702.0	28.9	202.9	32.8	P/B Ratio	4.2	52 Wk Hi-Low	194.00-120.00
Book Value	695.5	1,272.4	1,447.2	233.9	Yield %	0.0	Market Cap	US$879.1mil

Address	76-78 ave. des Champs-Elysées	Tel	1-49-20-71-00	ADR	--	Jnt Asst CEO	A. Grimm-Hecker
	75008 Paris	Fax	1-48-97-30-04	SEDOL	4608121	Chairman	P. Blayau

Natexis

DJGI Industry: **Banks - Regional (All)**
Stoxx Sector: **Bank**

Natexis SA, formerly known as Credit National SA, is one of the leading financial institutions in France. Through its subsidiaries, the group operates in corporate lending, equity financing, capital markets, real estate, and general banking activities. It also has international and commercial banking operations. In 1998 Groupe Banques Populaires increased its holding in Natexis to 71.4%. Interest and fees on loans accounted for 50% of 1997 revenues; interest income on bank deposits, 24%; other interest and dividend income, 15%; and noninterest income, 11%.

	FRF mil 12/95	12/96	12/97	US$mil 12/97				
Revenues	14,117.0	21,547.0	25,136.0	4,178.9	P/E Ratio	19.5	Price (6/30/98)	380.00
Net Income	463.0	98.0	289.0	48.0	P/B Ratio	0.6	52 Wk Hi-Low	455.00-314.00
Book Value	8,258.0	8,387.0	8,905.0	1,480.5	Yield %	2.6	Market Cap	US$935.4mil

Address	45 rue Saint-Dominique	Tel	1-45-50-90-00	ADR	--	V Chairman	E. Rodocanachi
	75700 Paris	Fax	1-45-55-68-96	SEDOL	4242455	Chairman	J. Delmas-Marsalet

Paribas

DJGI Industry: **Diversified Financial Services**
Stoxx Sector: **Financial Services**

Paribas is a multibank holding company with corporate banking, asset management, security, brokerage, corporate advisory, and real estate financing activities. The bank has offices in France and in other countries and also has representative offices abroad. In 1998, the bank absorbed Compagnie Financière de Paribas as part of a restructuring plan involving the merger of Compagnie Bancaire, Compagnie Mixte de Navigation, and three other finance companies. Interest income on bank deposits accounted for 37% of 1997 revenues, and interest on fees and loans accounted for 22%.

	FRF mil 12/95	12/96	12/97	US$mil 12/97				
Revenues	57,083.0	58,989.0	54,528.0	9,065.3	P/E Ratio	41.7	Price (6/30/98)	647.00
Net Income	-2,872.0	1,824.0	1,480.0	246.1	P/B Ratio	1.7	52 Wk Hi-Low	661.00-582.00
Book Value	15,207.0	20,752.0	21,847.0	3,632.1	Yield %	2.1	Market Cap	US$17,093mil

Address	B.P. 141, 3 rue D'Antin	Tel	1-42-98-12-34	ADR	--	President	--
	75078 Paris	Fax	1-42-98-11-42	SEDOL	5471731	Chairman	A. Levy-Lang

In EuroStoxx 50.

Pathé Cinéma

DJGI Industry: **Entertainment**
Stoxx Sector: **Consumer Cyclical**

Pathé Cinéma SA was formed in 1996 when Chargeurs SA split its business activities into two separate, publicly traded companies, Chargeurs International and Pathé Cinéma. Pathé produces and distributes films in Europe and coproduces films in the United States. The company has partnerships with News Corp., Twentieth Century Fox, and Canal Plus for the distribution of recorded videotapes. Film production and distribution accounted for 38% of 1997 revenues; movie theatre operations, 38%; television, 4%; and other, 20%.

	FRF mil 12/95	12/96	12/97	US$mil 12/97				
Sales	1,093.0	1,841.0	2,265.0	376.6	P/E Ratio	42.3	Price (6/30/98)	1,185.00
Net Income	-509.0	186.0	210.0	34.9	P/B Ratio	2.8	52 Wk Hi-Low	1,315.0-970.0
Book Value	3,047.0	3,354.0	3,033.0	504.2	Yield %	0.8	Market Cap	US$1,500.6mil

Address	5 blvd. Malesherbes	Tel 1-49-24-40-83	ADR	--	V Chmn & Jnt CEO	Eduardo Malone
	75008 Paris	Fax 1-49-24-40-89	SEDOL	5021341	Chmn & Jnt CEO	Jerome Seydoux

Pechiney

DJGI Industry: **Aluminum**
Stoxx Sector: **Basic Resources**

Pechiney SA is an international aluminum and packaging group. Its packaging products include beverage cans and glass bottles, plastic and aluminium food containers, plastic packaging such as plastic bags, rigid containers for industrial and medical products, airless pump packaging and tubes for personal care products, and packaging for deluxe perfume and cosmetics. Pechiney is the world's leading producer of packaging materials. It also produces aluminium metal and milled products that are used in the transportation, construction, domestic equipment, and engineering industries.

	FRF mil 12/95	12/96	12/97	US$mil 12/97				
Sales	77,040.0	64,372.0	69,745.0	11,595.2	P/E Ratio	10.8	Price (6/30/98)	243.50
Net Income	1,465.0	-2,977.0	1,814.0	301.6	P/B Ratio	1.2	52 Wk Hi-Low	308.90-213.00
Book Value	13,460.0	13,734.0	16,321.0	2,713.4	Yield %	1.6	Market Cap	US$3,232.8mil

Address	10 Place Des Vosges	Tel 1-46-91-46-91	ADR	PY	President	J.D. Senard
	La Defense 5, 92400 Courbevoie	Fax 1-46-91-46-46	SEDOL	4943792	Chairman	J.P. Rodier

Pernod Ricard

DJGI Industry: **Distillers & Brewers**
Stoxx Sector: **Food & Beverage**

Pernod Ricard SA manufactures and distributes alcoholic and nonalcoholic beverages. The company's products include Pernod, Ricard, and Dubonnet aperitifs, Aberlour Single Malt and Clan Campbell Scotch whiskies, and Wild Turkey bourbon. Pernod Ricard also produces Crus et Domaines de France table wines and Carlton and Blancs de Fruits flavored wines. In December 1997, Pernod Ricard sold its Orangina softdrink brand to Coca-Cola Co. for FRF5 billion. Nonalcoholic beverages accounted for 53% of 1997 revenues and wines and spirits accounted for the remaining 47% of revenues.

	FRF mil 12/95	12/96	12/97	US$mil 12/97				
Sales	15,934.0	16,814.0	19,049.0	3,166.9	P/E Ratio	17.4	Price (6/30/98)	419.00
Net Income	1,103.0	1,190.0	1,354.0	225.1	P/B Ratio	2.0	52 Wk Hi-Low	457.50-257.10
Book Value	9,261.0	10,470.0	11,585.0	1,926.0	Yield %	2.3	Market Cap	US$3,898.1mil

Address	142 blvd. Haussmann	Tel 1-40-76-77-78	ADR	PDRDY	Exec Dir	Thierry Jacquillat
	75359 Paris Cedex	Fax 1-42-25-95-66	SEDOL	4682329	Chairman & CEO	Patrick Ricard

Peugeot

DJGI Industry: **Automobile Manufacturers**
Stoxx Sector: **Automobile**

Peugeot SA, which includes Automobiles Peugeot and Automobiles Citroën, makes automobiles and auto components, including diesel engines, exhaust systems, and seats. The company is also involved in aerospace and defense technology, and it makes wheeled, light-armored vehicles. It controls about 30% of the French passenger-car market and 12% of the European market. Car manufacturing and sales by Peugeot and Citroen accounted for 92% of 1997 revenues, mechanical activities and services, 5%; and financial services, 3%.

	FRF mil 12/95	12/96	12/97	US$mil 12/97				
Sales	164,248.0	172,668.0	186,785.0	31,053.2	P/E Ratio	NMF	Price (6/30/98)	1,300.00
Net Income	1,703.0	734.0	-2,768.0	-460.2	P/B Ratio	1.2	52 Wk Hi-Low	1,410.0-568.0
Book Value	54,630.0	55,501.0	52,999.0	8,811.1	Yield %	0.2	Market Cap	US$10,749mil

Address	75 ave. de la Grande-Armée	Tel 1-40-66-55-11	ADR	PEUGY	Jnt Director Gen	Pierre Peugeot
	75116 Paris	Fax 1-40-66-54-14	SEDOL	4683827	Chairman	Jacques Calvet

Pinault-Printemps-Redoute

DJGI Industry: **Retailers - Broadline**
Stoxx Sector: **Retail**

Pinault-Printemps-Redoute SA is the result of a merger between consumer-goods retailer Pinault-Printemps and catalog retailer La Redoute. The company is France's leading consumer goods and specialized distribution group, and it also provides international trade operations and credit and financial services. It operates the Au Printemps department stores, Prisunic convenience shops, Conforama furniture stores, and La Redoute and Cyrillus electronics and appliance stores. In September 1998, it announced it will start a mail-order company, selling office supplies and furniture.

	FRF mil 12/95	12/96	12/97	US$mil 12/97				
Revenues	77,799.0	80,394.0	89,179.0	14,826.1	P/E Ratio	39.8	Price (6/30/98)	5,060.00
Net Income	1,516.0	2,065.0	2,853.0	474.3	P/B Ratio	7.0	52 Wk Hi-Low	5,330.0-2,500.0
Book Value	13,072.0	15,161.0	17,589.0	2,924.2	Yield %	0.8	Market Cap	US$19,603mil

Address	18 pl. Henri-Bergson	Tel 1-44-90-61-00	ADR	--	Chmn Exec Bd	Pierre Blayau
	75008 Paris	Fax 1-44-11-20-18	SEDOL	4703844	Chmn Supv Bd	Ambroise Roux

Primagaz

DJGI Industry: **Oil Companies - Secondary**
Stoxx Sector: **Energy**

Compagnie des Gaz de Pétrole Primagaz SA distributes fuel for heating, automotive, industrial, agricultural, and domestic uses. The company is a major distributor of liquefied petroleum gas (LPG). Primagaz also manufactures containers, bottles, and tanks for LPG storage and transportation. Primagaz's products include Viff motor fuel, Freon refrigerator gas, and Suva coolants. Primagaz also holds real estate interests and operations in 14 countries. Industrial and domestic LPG distribution accounted for 97% of 1997 revenues.

	FRF mil 12/95	12/96	12/97	US$mil 12/97				
Sales	7,376.4	9,270.8	9,945.2	1,653.4	P/E Ratio	30.9	Price (6/30/98)	531.00
Net Income	333.8	370.9	348.0	57.9	P/B Ratio	2.6	52 Wk Hi-Low	572.00-408.10
Book Value	3,807.4	4,057.4	4,199.8	698.2	Yield %	1.6	Market Cap	US$1,770.0mil

Address	64 ave. Hoche	Tel 1-40-55-25-00	ADR	--	Jnt Mng Dir	F. Bruneau
	75008 Paris	Fax 1-40-55-26-90	SEDOL	4678771	Chairman & CEO	Jean-Charles Inglessi

Promodès

DJGI Industry: **Food Retailers & Wholesalers**
Stoxx Sector: **Consumer Non-Cyclical**

Promodès SA is a food retailer that operates 614 hypermarkets and supermarkets and 987 convenience stores in France. These include Continent hypermarkets, Champion and Dia supermarkets, and convenience stores trading under the names Shopi, 8 à Huit, and Codec. It also operates in Spain, Germany, Portugal, Italy, and Greece. Its cash-and-carry and wholesale chains operate under the Promocash, Negoce, Puntocash, and Prodirest names. Hypermarkets accounted for 43% of 1997 revenues; logistics and holdings, 32%; discount stores, 11%; wholesale, 9%; and supermarkets, 5%.

	FRF mil 12/95	12/96	12/97	US$mil 12/97				
Sales	100,576.0	103,535.0	110,666.0	18,398.3	P/E Ratio	38.7	Price (6/30/98)	3,350.00
Net Income	1,022.0	1,247.0	1,619.0	269.2	P/B Ratio	6.6	52 Wk Hi-Low	3,450.0-1,800.0
Book Value	5,992.0	8,148.0	9,549.0	1,587.5	Yield %	0.5	Market Cap	US$10,423mil

Address	Z.I. - Route de Paris	Tel 2-31-70-60-00	ADR	--	V Chairman	R. Halley
	14127 Mondeville	Fax 2-31-83-56-19	SEDOL	4706672	Chairman & CEO	P. L. Halley

Renault

DJGI Industry: **Automobile Manufacturers**
Stoxx Sector: **Automobile**

Renault SA, privatized by France in 1996, manufactures passenger cars, light commercial vehicles, trucks, coaches, buses, and industrial equipment. It is also involved in providing credit to customers through its finance division. The company also has industrial operations in Spain, Belgium and Turkey. In 1997, Renault announced that it would build a car assembly plant in Brazil which the state of Parana would own 40%. Automobile sales accounted for 79% of 1997 revenues; commercial vehicles, 16%; and finance leases, 5%.

	FRF mil 12/95	12/96	12/97	US$mil 12/97				
Sales	184,065.0	184,078.0	207,912.0	34,565.6	P/E Ratio	15.1	Price (6/30/98)	343.90
Net Income	2,139.0	-5,248.0	5,427.0	902.2	P/B Ratio	1.9	52 Wk Hi-Low	354.00-140.60
Book Value	43,796.0	37,770.0	43,917.0	7,301.2	Yield %	1.0	Market Cap	US$13,606mil

Address	34 quai du Point-du-Jour	Tel 1-41-04-50-50	ADR	RNAUYP	Jnt CEO	P. Faure
	92109 Boulogne-Billancourt	Fax 1-46-09-33-23	SEDOL	4712798	Chmn & Jnt CEO	L. Schweitzer

Rexel

DJGI Industry: **Electrical Components & Equipment**
Stoxx Sector: **Industrials**

Rexel SA, formerly known as CDME or Compagnie de Distribution de Matériel Electrique, is a leading distributor of electrical-installation materials, including wires and cables as well as heating, ventilation, and lighting equipment. The company has subsidiaries in 14 countries, representing more than 700 distribution outlets throughout Europe and North America. In 1995, Rexel sold its 30% interest in Guillevin International of Canada and its total interest in SEIG of Gabon. In 1996, the company acquired 100% of Dutch Wolff through a takeover bid.

	FRF mil 12/95	12/96	12/97	US$mil 12/97				
Sales	22,084.0	24,394.6	28,738.0	4,777.7	P/E Ratio	40.4	Price (6/30/98)	2,578.00
Net Income	520.3	610.7	720.8	119.8	P/B Ratio	5.6	52 Wk Hi-Low	2,822.0-1,445.0
Book Value	3,613.3	4,256.9	5,427.9	902.4	Yield %	0.9	Market Cap	US$5,020.7mil

Address	25 rue de Clichy	Tel 1-42-85-85-00	ADR	--	Director General	C. Gelbart
	75009 Paris	Fax 1-45-26-25-83	SEDOL	4169338	Chairman & CEO	S. Wienberg

Rhône-Poulenc

DJGI Industry: **Pharmaceuticals**
Stoxx Sector: **Pharmaceutical**

Rhône-Poulenc SA is an international pharmaceutical and chemical company. It develops, produces, and markets specialty chemicals, polymers, organic- and inorganic-chemical intermediates, and pharmaceuticals. The health-care division sells products that treat cardiovascular illnesses, cancer, and allergies. Rhône-Poulenc also produces animal-nutrition products and veterinary pharmaceuticals. Human health and pharmaceuticals accounted for 37% of 1997 revenues; chemicals, 28%; agrochemicals and veterinary products, 21%; fibers and polymers, 13%; and other, 1%.

	FRF mil 12/95	12/96	12/97	US$mil 12/97				
Sales	84,793.0	85,818.0	89,955.0	14,955.1	P/E Ratio	NMF	Price (6/30/98)	341.00
Net Income	2,871.0	3,420.0	-4,348.0	-722.9	P/B Ratio	2.9	52 Wk Hi-Low	346.90-222.80
Book Value	33,093.0	37,478.0	42,002.0	6,982.9	Yield %	1.1	Market Cap	US$20,925mil

Address	25 quai Paul-Doumer	Tel 1-47-68-12-34	ADR	RP	V Chairman	J.M. Bruel
	92408 Courbevoie	Fax 1-47-68-19-11	SEDOL	4736817	Chairman & CEO	Jean-René Fourtou

In DJ Stoxx 50; In EuroStoxx 50.

SAGEM

DJGI Industry: **Diversified Technology**
Stoxx Sector: **Technology**

SAGEM SA, formerly called Société d'Applications Générales d'Electricité et de Mécanique, manufactures navigation, defense, telecommunications, and electronic equipment. The company's products include cellular and cordless telephones, facsimile and telex machines, navigation systems, automobile electronics, and military-guidance systems.Telecommunications and computer terminals accounted for 53% of 1997 revenues; electronic components and cables, 26%; and navigation, optronic, and defense equipment, 21%.

	FRF mil 12/95	12/96	12/97	US$mil 12/97				
Sales	15,075.9	15,408.7	16,756.9	2,785.9	P/E Ratio	24.4	Price (6/30/98)	4,704.00
Net Income	548.9	638.3	698.2	116.1	P/B Ratio	4.2	52 Wk Hi-Low	4,780.0-2,517.0
Book Value	3,136.3	3,698.3	4,302.3	715.3	Yield %	0.6	Market Cap	US$2,321.3mil

Address	6 ave. d'Iéna	Tel 1-40-70-63-63	ADR	--	Jnt Asst Dir Gen	M. Colaiacovo
	75783 Paris	Fax 1-47-20-39-46	SEDOL	4771410	Chairman & CEO	P. Faure

Saint-Gobain

DJGI Industry: **Building Materials**
Stoxx Sector: **Construction**

Compagnie de Saint-Gobain SA operates glass and building-materials businesses in 38 countries. The company produces flat glass, glass containers, glass and rock-wool insulation products, fiber reinforcements, industrial ceramics, abrasives, pipes, and roofing products. Its building-materials businesses are concentrated in the United States and Brazil. Most of its sales are made outside France. In September 1996, the company acquired management control of construction materials maker Poliet from Paribas and has the option to acquire majority control by the end of 1999.

	FRF mil 12/95	12/96	12/97	US$mil 12/97				
Sales	70,310.0	91,384.0	107,078.0	17,801.8	P/E Ratio	17.3	Price (6/30/98)	1,121.00
Net Income	4,212.0	4,323.0	5,628.0	935.7	P/B Ratio	1.8	52 Wk Hi-Low	1,186.0-781.0
Book Value	41,873.0	47,355.0	55,194.0	9,176.1	Yield %	1.7	Market Cap	US$16,503mil

Address	Les Miroirs, 18 ave. d'Alsace	Tel 1-47-62-30-00	ADR	--	CFO	J.F. Phelizon
	92400 Courbevoie	Fax 1-47-78-45-03	SEDOL	4768371	Chairman & CEO	Jean-Louis Beffa

In EuroStoxx 50.

Sanofi

DJGI Industry: **Pharmaceuticals**
Stoxx Sector: **Pharmaceutical**

Sanofi SA (formerly Elf-Sanofi SA) is a pharmaceutical company that operates primarily in two business sectors: human health-care and perfumes and beauty products. It is also involved in bio-industries and research. Human health-care includes ethical pharmaceuticals and over-the-counter medicines. Beauty product brand names include Yves Rocher, Nina Ricci, Yves Saint Laurent, and Oscar de la Renta. Bioactivities include food additives and agroveterinary products. Human health-care products accounted for 84% of 1997 revenues, perfumes and beauty products for 16%.

	FRF mil 12/95	12/96	12/97	US$mil 12/97				
Sales	23,031.0	23,645.0	25,690.0	4,271.0	P/E Ratio	39.1	Price (6/30/98)	711.00
Net Income	1,575.0	1,743.0	1,920.0	319.2	P/B Ratio	3.3	52 Wk Hi-Low	752.00-479.00
Book Value	18,401.0	20,352.0	22,673.0	3,769.4	Yield %	1.0	Market Cap	US$12,509mil

Address	32-34 rue Marbeuf	Tel 1-53-77-40-00	ADR	--	CFO	J.P. Leon
	75008 Paris	Fax 1-53-77-41-33	SEDOL	4887704	Chairman & CEO	Jean-François Dehecq

Schneider

DJGI Industry: **Electrical Components & Equipment**
Stoxx Sector: **Industrials**

Schneider SA, formerly known as Spie-Batignolles, produces and distributes electrical-distribution equipment, industrial-engineering equipment, automation controls, and environmental controls through its subsidiaries. The company constructs and maintains power stations and produces switchgears. Subsidiaries include Schneider Electric (formerly Merlin Gerlin and Télémécanique) and Spie-Batignolles, a construction company. In 1997, Schneider SA controlled 73 domestic and 105 foreign subsidiaries.

	FRF mil 12/95	12/96	12/97	US$mil 12/97				
Sales	59,420.0	61,637.0	47,398.0	7,880.0	P/E Ratio	32.3	Price (6/30/98)	482.10
Net Income	817.0	1,320.0	2,198.0	365.4	P/B Ratio	3.1	52 Wk Hi-Low	523.00-300.00
Book Value	16,150.0	18,497.0	23,909.0	3,974.9	Yield %	1.3	Market Cap	US$12,104mil

Address	64-70 ave. Jean-Baptiste Clement	Tel 1-46-99-70-00	ADR	--	Jnt Director Gen	R. Jeanteur
	92646 Boulogne-Billancourt	Fax 1-46-99-71-00	SEDOL	4834108	Chairman & CEO	D. Pineau-Valencienne

In EuroStoxx 50.

SEB

DJGI Industry: **Other Home Furnishings**
Stoxx Sector: **Consumer Cyclical**

Groupe SEB SA manufactures and distributes electrical appliances and household goods. Its products include small kitchen appliances, including Rowenta coffee makers and toasters, Tefal cooking equipment, and bathroom appliances, such as Tefal scales and electric toothbrushes. SEB also sells Calor vacuum cleaners and irons. Other products include food processors, steam irons, and pressure cookers. While SEB's business is concentrated in France and Germany, it has expanded into eastern Europe, North America, and Asia.

	FRF mil 12/95	12/96	12/97	US$mil 12/97				
Sales	9,103.9	9,856.6	11,846.9	1,969.6	P/E Ratio	24.7	Price (6/30/98)	838.00
Net Income	450.5	480.3	521.4	86.7	P/B Ratio	3.4	52 Wk Hi-Low	1,125.0-659.0
Book Value	3,108.0	3,571.7	3,812.0	633.7	Yield %	1.5	Market Cap	US$2,131.3mil

Address	Les 4 M-Chemin du Petit-Bois	Tel 4-72-18-18-18	ADR	--	Jnt Mng Dir	B. Dupont
	69132 Ecully	Fax 4-72-18-16-55	SEDOL	4792132	Chairman & CEO	J. Gairard

SEFIMEG

DJGI Industry: **Real Estate**
Stoxx Sector: **Financial Services**

SEFIMEG, also known as Société Française d'Investissements Immobiliers et de Gestion SA, is a real estate investment company that constructs and manages commercial and residential rental space, primarily in and around Paris. Residential property makes up 66% of SEFIMEG's holdings, and commercial properties, 34%. Residential properties accounted for 54% of rental income in 1997, and office, commercial, and parking properties accounted 46%. SEFIMEG is part of the Fimalac group, which holds the largest interest in SEFIMEG.

	FRF mil 12/95	12/96	12/97	US$mil 12/97				
Sales	600.8	692.7	738.7	122.8	P/E Ratio	22.2	Price (6/30/98)	438.00
Net Income	-258.9	383.0	313.3	52.1	P/B Ratio	1.8	52 Wk Hi-Low	530.00-300.00
Book Value	3,660.1	3,767.2	3,810.2	633.4	Yield %	3.4	Market Cap	US$1,146.1mil

Address	157 ave. Charles de Gaulle	Tel	1-40-88-18-18	ADR	--	V Chmn & Dir Gen	A. Gomez
	92200 Neuilly-sur-Seine	Fax	1-40-88-18-20	SEDOL	4764302	Chmn & CEO	M.L. de Lacharrière

Seita

DJGI Industry: **Tobacco**
Stoxx Sector: **Consumer Non-Cyclical**

Seita, also known as Société Nationale des Tabacs SA, is France's biggest producer of tobacco products such as French and foreign cigarettes, cigars, pipe and rolling tobacco, and snuff. The company also produces and distributes Gauloises, Gitanes, Royales, and News cigarettes; Ninas, Havanitos, and Fleur de Savane cigars; Caporal and Amsterdamer loose tobacco; and matches. Distribution of tobacco accounted for 48% of 1997 revenues; production of cigarettes, tobacco, and cigars, 33%; distribution of other products, 18%; production of matches and other products and services, 1%.

	FRF mil 12/95	12/96	12/97	US$mil 12/97				
Sales	16,350.8	17,362.8	18,393.5	3,057.9	P/E Ratio	17.2	Price (6/30/98)	274.00
Net Income	684.0	786.1	826.8	137.5	P/B Ratio	2.5	52 Wk Hi-Low	279.50-170.60
Book Value	4,710.7	5,302.2	5,659.5	940.9	Yield %	2.7	Market Cap	US$2,339.6mil

Address	53 quai D'Orsay	Tel	1-45-56-61-50	ADR	--	V Chmn & CFO	G. Dutreix
	75007 Paris Cedex 07	Fax	1-45-56-65-62	SEDOL	4798839	Chmn & CEO	J.D. Comolli

Sidel

DJGI Industry: **Factory Equipment**
Stoxx Sector: **Industrials**

Sidel SA manufactures blow-molding machines used to produce plastic bottles. The company's main French subsidiaries are Sidel Conditionnement, Ouest Conditionnement, Sidel Machines & Systems, and Kalix. It also has seven foreign subsidiaries in Europe, North and South America, and Asia. Sidel's machines manufacture bottles and containers that are used predominantly in the consumer drinks market and they also produce HDPE and PVC containers for nongaseous liquids, toys, industrial parts, and cosmetics. The group absorbed Gebo in 1997.

	FRF mil 12/95	12/96	12/97	US$mil 12/97				
Sales	3,704.3	3,119.7	4,178.2	694.6	P/E Ratio	43.4	Price (6/30/98)	440.00
Net Income	374.1	263.0	339.0	56.4	P/B Ratio	9.9	52 Wk Hi-Low	497.00-324.00
Book Value	963.9	1,113.3	1,489.3	247.6	Yield %	1.1	Market Cap	US$2,429.8mil

Address	B.P. 204, 55 rue du Pont VI	Tel	2-32-85-86-87	ADR	SIELY	President	B. Roger
	76053 Le Havre	Fax	2-32--85-81-00	SEDOL	5092433	Chairman	F. Oliver

Simco

DJGI Industry: **Real Estate**
Stoxx Sector: **Financial Services**

Simco-Union pour l'Habitation SA, commonly referred to as Simco, develops and manages residential, office, and commercial property. The company also undertakes construction and refurbishment work. More than 90% of its holdings are in the Paris area. Residential properties made up about 76% of Simco's property portfolio. French insurer Union des Assurances de Paris is Simco's major shareholder, owning about a third of its stock. In 1996, 62% of rental income was derived from residential properties, and 38% came from commercial properties.

	FRF mil 12/95	12/96	12/97	US$mil 12/97				
Sales	603.3	596.1	750.1	124.7	P/E Ratio	NMF	Price (6/30/98)	496.00
Net Income	368.3	363.7	-26.3	-4.4	P/B Ratio	1.6	52 Wk Hi-Low	528.00-400.00
Book Value	3,986.3	4,089.2	5,845.8	971.9	Yield %	3.0	Market Cap	US$1,566.7mil

Address	34 rue de la Fédération	Tel	1-40-61-66-20	ADR	--	Jnt CEO	Jean-Paul Sorand
	75015 Paris	Fax	1-40-61-65-06	SEDOL	4809689	Chmn & Jnt CEO	Georges Mazaud

S.I.T.A.

DJGI Industry: **Pollution Control & Waste Management**
Stoxx Sector: **Industrials**

S.I.T.A., also known as Société Industrielle des Transports Automobiles SA, collects, sorts, recycles, treats, and stores industrial and household waste. The company has contracts for collecting domestic refuse and cleaning streets in urban areas. S.I.T.A. also collects industrial toxic waste, operates landfill sites for waste storage, collects paper and cardboard for recycling, and manufactures street-cleaning and garbage-collection vehicles. Waste collection, sanitation, and cleaning services accounted for 99% of 1997 revenues; waste treatment and recycling accounted for 1%.

	FRF mil 12/95	12/96	12/97	US$mil 12/97				
Sales	8,021.9	9,249.5	10,887.5	1,810.1	P/E Ratio	37.8	Price (6/30/98)	1,530.00
Net Income	236.4	260.4	298.4	49.6	P/B Ratio	3.7	52 Wk Hi-Low	1,580.0-985.0
Book Value	2,198.8	2,694.5	3,080.5	512.1	Yield %	0.9	Market Cap	US$1,844.3mil

Address	94 rue de Provence	Tel	1-53-21-20-00	ADR	--	Asst CEO	P. Viterbo
	75425 Paris Cedex 09	Fax	1-53-21-22-00	SEDOL	4808868	Chairman & CEO	J. Petry

Société Générale

DJGI Industry: **Banks - Major International**
Stoxx Sector: **Bank**

Société Générale de France SA, the largest private bank in France, provides its retail and corporate clients with services such as loans, financing, insurance, asset management, lease financing, and capital-market operations at its network of 2,000 branch offices. The bank operates in about 70 countries and oversees more than 250 consolidated subsidiaries. Société Générale also holds significant real estate interests through its wholly owned Genefimmo subsidiary. In February 1997, SGB sold its 9% stake in French hotels group Accor.

	FRF mil 12/95	12/96	12/97	US$mil 12/97				
Revenues	129,183.0	132,741.0	167,616.0	27,866.3	P/E Ratio	20.2	Price (6/30/98)	1,257.00
Net Income	3,817.0	4,544.0	6,111.0	1,016.0	P/B Ratio	1.9	52 Wk Hi-Low	1,390.0-656.0
Book Value	51,231.0	55,688.0	63,375.0	10,536.2	Yield %	1.7	Market Cap	US$21,171mil

Address	29 boulevard Haussman	Tel 1-42-14-20-20	ADR	SCGLY	Jnt CEO	P. Duverger
	75009 Paris	Fax 1-42-14-38-28	SEDOL	4817756	Chairman & CEO	D. Bouton

In EuroStoxx 50.

Sodexho

DJGI Industry: **Other Industrial & Commercial Services**
Stoxx Sector: **Industrials**

Sodexho Alliance SA is the world's largest supplier of remotesite management services and contract food services and the second-largest issuer of service vouchers. It provides contract management services as well as remotesite management services, leisure services, and service vouchers to businesses, health-care establishments, and schools. Sodexho's acquisition of Gardner Merchant in 1995 created the world's largest contract food-services group. The group has activities in over 60 countries. Contract food services accounted for 84% of 1997 revenues.

	FRF mil 08/95	08/96	08/97	US$mil 08/97				
Sales	18,348.0	24,961.0	29,497.0	4,847.5	P/E Ratio	65.0	Price (6/30/98)	1,143.00
Net Income	284.4	684.9	538.2	88.5	P/B Ratio	6.2	52 Wk Hi-Low	1,297.0-643.8
Book Value	3,514.1	4,497.4	5,606.2	921.3	Yield %	0.8	Market Cap	US$6,305.8mil

Address	3 ave. Newton	Tel 1-30-85-75-00	ADR	--	Jnt CEO	P. Douce
	78180 Montigny-le-Bretonneux	Fax 1-30-43-09-58	SEDOL	4818306	Chmn & Jnt CEO	P. Bellon

Sommer Allibert

DJGI Industry: **Other Auto Parts**
Stoxx Sector: **Automobile**

Sommer Allibert SA supplies coverings and plastic products for household, industrial, and medical uses. Its products include tiles and bathroom fixtures, containers and packaging materials for the cosmetics industry, and trolleys and tables for the medical industry. It also produces interior plastic finishing and upholstery for automobiles. Sommer Allibert also produces linoleum and sports surfaces. Automotive products accounted for 65% of 1997 revenues; wall and floor coverings, 27%; furnishings, 5%; other plastic products, 2%; and packaging, 1%.

	FRF mil 12/95	12/96	12/97	US$mil 12/97				
Sales	12,691.1	14,038.6	16,952.9	2,818.4	P/E Ratio	21.4	Price (6/30/98)	314.20
Net Income	177.7	241.8	315.9	52.5	P/B Ratio	2.1	52 Wk Hi-Low	336.00-175.50
Book Value	2,834.7	3,023.6	3,292.4	547.4	Yield %	1.4	Market Cap	US$1,117.5mil

Address	2 rue de l'Egalité	Tel 1-41-20-40-40	ADR	--	CFO	P. Chaubeau
	92748 Nanterre	Fax 1-47-21-49-09	SEDOL	5050806	Chairman	M. Assa

Sophia

DJGI Industry: **Real Estate**
Stoxx Sector: **Financial Services**

Sophia SA is a land and real estate company that operates nonresidential buildings, including offices, warehouses, commercial centers, and hotels. Most of its real estate holdings are located in Paris, Paris suburbs, and in the French provinces. The company also holds a varied investment portfolio, and it has 18 fully consolidated subsidiaries, including Sophia-Bail, Sophia-Mur, Soferbail, Coderbail, and Figemi. Rental income accounted for roughly 98% of the company's 1997 revenues and other operating income accounted for 6%.

	FRF mil 12/95	12/96	12/97	US$mil 12/97				
Sales	3,116.4	2,410.0	2,523.0	419.5	P/E Ratio	23.6	Price (6/30/98)	279.50
Net Income	285.8	253.0	175.0	29.1	P/B Ratio	1.5	52 Wk Hi-Low	296.00-206.00
Book Value	2,721.5	2,721.0	2,647.0	440.1	Yield %	5.3	Market Cap	US$681.2mil

Address	63 ave. des Champs-Elysées	Tel 1-44-35-47-47	ADR	--	Dirs Gen	R. Gancil / P. Thuiller
	75008 Paris	Fax 1-44-35-47-00	SEDOL	4960575	Chairman & CEO	J.C. Wagner

STMicroelectronics

DJGI Industry: **Semiconductors**
Stoxx Sector: **Technology**

STMicroelectronics, formerly SGS-Thomson Microelectronics NV, is a global independent semiconductor company. The Franco-Italian company designs, develops, manufactures, and markets a broad range of semiconductor integrated circuits (ICs) and discrete devices that are used in a variety of microelectronics applications, including telecommunications systems, computer systems, consumer products, automotive products, and industrial automation and control systems. ST's main shareholders include IRI S.p.A., Comitato SIR of Italy, CEA Industrie, and France Telecom.

	FRF mil 12/95	12/96	12/97	US$mil 12/97				
Sales	17,269.2	20,880.9	23,224.6	3,861.1	P/E Ratio	25.1	Price (6/30/98)	428.50
Net Income	2,582.4	3,202.8	2,378.5	395.4	P/B Ratio	3.5	52 Wk Hi-Low	627.00-310.00
Book Value	13,056.0	16,919.3	19,890.8	3,306.9	Yield %	0.0	Market Cap	US$10,049mil

Address	165 rue Edouard Branly	Tel 4-50-40-26-40	ADR	STM	President & CEO	P. Pistorio
	01637 St. Genis Pouilly	Fax --	SEDOL	4776705	CFO	M. Ghirga

Suez Lyonnaise

DJGI Industry: **Water Utilities**
Stoxx Sector: **Utility**

Suez Lyonnaise des Eaux SA is an urban-development and environmental-services group. As one of Europe's largest construction and engineering groups, the company is involved in heavy construction, road construction, and related activities; water distribution; refrigeration and air-conditioning services; and refuse collection. Other activities include cable television and audiovisual. The company also manages private prisons, retirement homes, and realestate investments. Lyonnaise provides waste-management and recycling services and manages construction for civil projects.

	FRF mil 12/95	12/96	12/97	US$mil 12/97					
Sales	98,615.0	91,620.0	190,420.0	31,657.5	P/E Ratio	30.8	Price (6/30/98)		995.00
Net Income	906.0	1,349.0	4,013.0	667.2	P/B Ratio	2.6	52 Wk Hi-Low		1,068.0-567.0
Book Value	16,547.0	18,385.0	49,174.0	8,175.2	Yield %	1.5	Market Cap		US$20,723mil

Address	72 ave. de la Liberté	Tel 1-40-06-67-89	ADR	--	Jnt Director Gen	P. Brongniart
	92022 Nanterre	Fax 1-40-06-66-10	SEDOL	4540438	Chairman	G. Mestrallet

Technip

DJGI Industry: **Heavy Construction**
Stoxx Sector: **Construction**

Compagnie Française d'Etudes et de Construction Technip SA refines and distributes gas and petroleum, produces pharmaceutical preparations, and provides architectural and engineering services. The company also designs and builds industrial facilities for its hydrocarbon and petrochemical activities as well as for diversified industries. It also provides turnkey contracts, engineering, and other services in the fields of chemicals, food processing, and industrial project management. Gas refining accounted for 47% of 1997 revenues; petrochemicals accounted for 29%.

	FRF mil 12/95	12/96	12/97	US$mil 12/97					
Sales	9,205.0	10,140.1	11,868.4	1,973.1	P/E Ratio	20.1	Price (6/30/98)		739.00
Net Income	440.3	534.2	627.1	104.3	P/B Ratio	3.7	52 Wk Hi-Low		875.00-572.00
Book Value	2,256.4	2,745.1	3,269.0	543.5	Yield %	2.0	Market Cap		US$2,024.6mil

Address	170 pl. Henri Regnaul	Tel 1-47-78-21-21	ADR	TECHNY	COO	J. Verdier
	92973 Paris	Fax 1-47-78-33-40	SEDOL	4874160	Chairman & CEO	P. Vaillaud

Télévision Française 1

DJGI Industry: **Cable & Broadcasting**
Stoxx Sector: **Media**

Télévision Française 1 SA (TF1) operates one of the main television stations in France and is funded primarily by advertising. The group produces and broadcasts television programs, including news, documentaries, dramas, sports, and children's productions. The company is also involved in producing and selling videocassettes and publishing books, and it provides teleshopping services. In addition, the group operates the Eurosport sports channel and La Chaine Info, the first French-speaking continuous news channel. Bouygues is the company's major shareholder.

	FRF mil 12/95	12/96	12/97	US$mil 12/97					
Sales	9,140.0	9,685.3	10,309.8	1,714.0	P/E Ratio	40.9	Price (6/30/98)		937.00
Net Income	601.6	575.3	481.5	80.1	P/B Ratio	7.4	52 Wk Hi-Low		1,006.0-487.0
Book Value	2,276.9	2,516.7	2,664.6	443.0	Yield %	1.7	Market Cap		US$3,246.5mil

Address	176/180 rue de l'Université	Tel 1-41-41-12-34	ADR	--	V Chairman	E. Mougeotte
	75007 Paris	Fax 1-41-41-29-10	SEDOL	4881160	Chairman & CEO	P. Le Lay

Thomson-CSF

DJGI Industry: **Aerospace & Defense**
Stoxx Sector: **Technology**

Thomson-CSF SA is a high-tech European leader in defense electronics manufacture and ranks third worldwide in the field of underwater activities. Thomson-CSF provides services in aerospace, avionics, detection and missile systems, communication and command, and information technology. The company's products include radars, automated control system components, naval combat systems, broadcasting equipment, and computer hardware and software. Military defense accounted for the majority of revenues in 1997.

	FRF mil 12/95	12/96	12/97	US$mil 12/97					
Sales	35,497.0	36,271.0	38,531.0	6,405.8	P/E Ratio	13.0	Price (6/30/98)		230.00
Net Income	-791.0	745.0	2,122.0	352.8	P/B Ratio	1.8	52 Wk Hi-Low		257.80-145.90
Book Value	12,504.0	13,715.0	15,539.0	2,583.4	Yield %	1.6	Market Cap		US$4,536.4mil

Address	173 blvd. Haussmann	Tel 1-53-77-89-02	ADR	TCSFY	Jnt Mng Dir	D. Rapenne
	75008 Paris	Fax 1-53-77-86-59	SEDOL	4162791	Chairman & CEO	M. Roulet

Total

DJGI Industry: **Oil Companies - Major**
Stoxx Sector: **Energy**

Total SA, formerly known as Total Compagnie Française des Pétroles SA, is a petroleum company that explores for, produces, refines, ships, distributes, and markets oil and natural gas. The company also produces petrochemicals and coal. It has a solid oil-reserve base in the Middle East and a growing role in gas production, chemicals, and paints. Overseas sales generate roughly half of Total's revenues. In September 1997, Total signed a $2 billion contract with National Iranian Oil Co. to develop the South Pars gas field, which has gas reserves estimated at 300 trillion cubic feet.

	FRF mil 12/95	12/96	12/97	US$mil 12/97					
Sales	135,829.0	176,577.0	191,085.0	31,768.1	P/E Ratio	25.4	Price (6/30/98)		786.00
Net Income	2,305.0	5,698.0	7,671.0	1,275.3	P/B Ratio	2.9	52 Wk Hi-Low		796.00-569.00
Book Value	52,398.0	59,258.0	66,632.0	11,077.6	Yield %	1.7	Market Cap		US$31,687mil

Address	24 cours Michelet	Tel 1-41-35-40-00	ADR	TOT	Executive Dir	A. Madec
	92800 Puteaux	Fax 1-41-35-42-91	SEDOL	4905413	Chairman & CEO	T. Desmarest

UIF

DJGI Industry: **Real Estate**
Stoxx Sector: **Financial Services**

Union Immobilière de France SA (UIF) is one of France's largest real estate investment companies in terms of rental income. The company builds and manages commercial, office, and residential rental space as well as parking lots and warehouses. Of these properties, 76% are residential holdings, 23% commercial properties, and 1% parking areas. Half of its property holdings are in Paris and the surrounding area; other properties are in Provence and Boulogne. The company presented consolidated accounts for the first time in 1997.

	FRF mil 12/95	12/96	12/97	US$mil 12/97				
Sales	309.2	311.8	326.1	54.2	P/E Ratio	44.9	Price (6/30/98)	477.00
Net Income	200.1	190.9	88.3	14.7	P/B Ratio	1.9	52 Wk Hi-Low	515.00-392.00
Book Value	1,959.8	2,029.1	2,117.1	352.0	Yield %	2.7	Market Cap	US$656.4mil

Address	78 rue Lecourbe	Tel 1-44-38-01-23	ADR	--	Managing Director	Henri Pochon
	75015 Paris	Fax 1-49-27-95-63	SEDOL	4913546	Chairman & CEO	Claude Rivé

Unibail

DJGI Industry: **Real Estate**
Stoxx Sector: **Financial Services**

Unibail SA, also known as Union du Crédit-Bail Immobilier, is active in property rental and leasing, finance, and construction. Office buildings and commercial retail space account for most of its property portfolio, with light industrial parks and residential apartment properties representing the remainder. The company's properties are concentrated in Paris and neighboring areas. Other Unibail holdings are located in ten additional French cities and in London. Rental and leasing income accounted for 92% of 1997 revenues; interest income, 2%; and other income, 6%.

	FRF mil 12/95	12/96	12/97	US$mil 12/97				
Sales	2,199.9	1,854.7	1,503.3	249.9	P/E Ratio	36.2	Price (6/30/98)	782.00
Net Income	265.1	275.0	204.0	33.9	P/B Ratio	1.9	52 Wk Hi-Low	908.00-545.00
Book Value	4,192.7	4,216.5	4,112.1	683.6	Yield %	3.8	Market Cap	US$1,217.4mil

Address	108 rue de Richelieu	Tel 1-40-15-21-21	ADR	--	Director Gen	A. Bennon
	75002 Paris	Fax 1-40-15-22-04	SEDOL	4911346	Chairman & CEO	L. Bressler

Usinor Sacilor

DJGI Industry: **Steel**
Stoxx Sector: **Basic Resources**

Usinor Sacilor SA is the foremost steel producer in Europe and the third-biggest steelmaker in the world; it provides 90% of France's raw steel. The company produces hot- and cold-rolled flat-steel products, sheet and strip galvanized products, aluminum tins, and heavy plates as well as long-steel products such as wire rod, rails, beams, sheet piling, and merchant bars and stainless, electric, and leaded sheets. It distributes steel products, processed steel, and industrial supplies. In mid-1995, the French government privatized Usinor Sacilor, selling 70.2% of its 80% stake.

	FRF mil 12/95	12/96	12/97	US$mil 12/97				
Sales	78,423.0	71,059.0	72,001.0	11,970.2	P/E Ratio	11.1	Price (6/30/98)	93.40
Net Income	4,430.0	1,489.0	2,055.0	341.6	P/B Ratio	0.8	52 Wk Hi-Low	125.00-75.40
Book Value	25,113.0	25,703.0	26,959.0	4,482.0	Yield %	3.5	Market Cap	US$3,748.0mil

Address	Immeuble Pacific, La Défense 7	Tel 1-41-255-020	ADR	URSAYP	CFO	R. Hudry
	92800 Puteaux	Fax 1-41-256-048	SEDOL	4894544	Chairman & CEO	F. Mer

Valeo

DJGI Industry: **Other Auto Parts**
Stoxx Sector: **Automobile**

Valeo SA manufactures automotive systems and components for cars and trucks. As Europe's second-largest automotive components group, its products include engine-cooling systems, lighting components, climate-control systems, clutches, clutch facings, and electrical, security, and wiper systems. It also markets replacement parts under the Valeo, Cible, Marchal, and Paul Jounée brand names. Valeo has 92 plants and technical facilities in 19 countries. Mechanical equipment accounted for 47% of 1997 revenues; electrical equipment, 42%; and distribution, 11%.

	FRF mil 12/95	12/96	12/97	US$mil 12/97				
Sales	25,230.0	28,870.0	33,970.0	5,647.5	P/E Ratio	29.3	Price (6/30/98)	618.00
Net Income	1,010.0	1,200.0	1,480.0	246.1	P/B Ratio	3.6	52 Wk Hi-Low	652.00-354.40
Book Value	10,000.0	10,556.0	12,234.0	2,033.9	Yield %	1.1	Market Cap	US$7,196.5mil

Address	43 rue Bayen	Tel 1-40-55-20-20	ADR	VLEEY	Jnt Asst CEO	B. De Monseignant
	75017 Paris	Fax 1-40-55-21-71	SEDOL	4937579	Chairman & CEO	N. Goutard

Vivendi

DJGI Industry: **Water Utilities**
Stoxx Sector: **Utility**

Vivendi SA formerly Compagnie Générale des Eaux SA, is a diversified water distributor with activities in energy, construction, waste management, electrical energy services, and real estate. The group sold off 334 companies in 1997, exiting the health, cable television, laundry, restaurant, and car-parking sectors. During the same period it created or acquired 24 companies in various sectors. The group consists of about 2,500 companies. Construction projects accounted for 31% of 1997 revenues; water distribution, 25%; thermal energy, 12%.

	FRF mil 12/95	12/96	12/97	US$mil 12/97				
Sales	160,588.9	165,479.7	165,037.1	27,437.6	P/E Ratio	30.9	Price (6/30/98)	1,291.00
Net Income	-3,686.3	1,952.7	5,392.5	896.5	P/B Ratio	3.9	52 Wk Hi-Low	1,291.0-646.2
Book Value	30,175.6	33,681.9	44,911.3	7,466.6	Yield %	1.2	Market Cap	US$33,740mil

Address	42 avenue de Friedland	Tel 1-49-24-49-24	ADR	VDIY	Director Gen	P.I. Girardot
	75380 Paris Cedex 08	Fax 1-49-24-69-99	SEDOL	4175926	Chairman & CEO	Jean-Marie Messier

In DJ Stoxx 50; In EuroStoxx 50.

Zodiac

DJGI Industry: **Aerospace & Defense**
Stoxx Sector: **Technology**

Zodiac SA manufactures equipment for air-transport and recreational marine uses. Zodiac designs and manufactures aircraft cabin equipment, marine-leisure equipment, and aerospace equipment. Marine leisure equipment includes inflatable and above-ground swimming pools, inflatable motorboats, and dinghies. Aircraft cabin equipment includes emergency escape chutes and parachutes. Aircraft cabin equipment accounted for 35% of fiscal 1997 revenues; marine equipment, 34%; and other aviation equipment, 31%.

	FRF mil 08/95	08/96	08/97	US$mil 08/97				
Sales	3,032.7	3,413.6	3,858.9	634.2	P/E Ratio	33.6	Price (6/30/98)	1,660.00
Net Income	151.1	174.2	196.4	32.3	P/B Ratio	4.8	52 Wk Hi-Low	1,750.0-1,140.0
Book Value	1,121.0	1,326.1	1,671.7	274.7	Yield %	0.7	Market Cap	US$1,345.6mil

Address	**2 rue Mauricemallet**	Tel **1-41-23-23-23**	ADR	--	Director Gen	**M. Pinault**
	92137 Issy-les-Moulineaux	Fax **1-46-48-83-87**	SEDOL	4994693	Chairman & CEO	**J.I. Gerondeau**

Germany

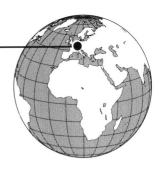

http://www.dowjones.com/indexes/Htmls01/germany.html

Exchanges:

Frankfurt Stock Exchange

Rhineland-Westphalian Stock Exchange in Düsseldorf

Bavarian Stock Exchange in Munich

Hanseatic Stock Exchange in Hamburg

Baden-Württemberg Stock Exchange in Stuttgart

Berlin Stock Exchange

Stock Exchange of Lower Saxony in Hannover

Bremen Stock Exchange

Germany

Sarah Sloat
Frankfurt

Amidst the growing perception that European exchanges effectively constitute a single market, an outlook reinforced by the coming launch of the euro currency in January 1999, Frankfurt's stock exchange in the summer of 1998 announced plans for a partnership with the London bourse.

The proposed partnership, ending a long-standing rivalry among Europe's biggest stock markets, will be based on a common trading platform of top companies, that can be expanded should new members join. Scheduled to take effect January 1,1999, it represents the first step toward a pan-European stock market.

Across the Atlantic, Frankfurt's Exchange also set up a working group to investigate potential business cooperation with the Nasdaq stock market in the United States.

Meanwhile, Germany's stock market began another dynamic year in 1998. By early July, the Xetra DAX index had appreciated about 40% since the end of 1997, reaching 6,001.24 on July 10. In 1997, the DAX index advanced 47%.

Market watchers credited the gains chiefly to low German interest rates, which made other investments less attractive. Also buoying shares were the strong dollar, advances on Wall Street, solid corporate earnings, and speculation about accelerating consolidation in a number of sectors.

Consolidation in Germany's major sectors, such as banks, insurance, and cars, contributed a great deal to increased investor interest in the stock market in the first half of 1998. And observers expect more deals after a number of significant mergers and collaborations were announced in the past year.

Most notably, two big German banks — Bayerische Vereinsbank AG and Bayerische Hypotheken und Wechselbank AG — were to finalize their merger in the fall. Also steel and industrial groups Thyssen AG and Fried.Krupp-Hoesch AG are joining up, and German industrial giant Daimler-Benz AG has announced it will merge with Chrysler Corp. of the United States.

German companies will have to continue on a consolidation course if they hope to remain competitive, analysts say. Among the companies being eyed for potential news on

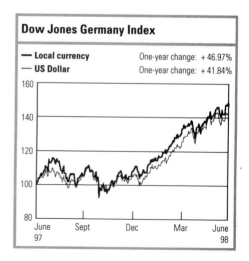

Dow Jones Germany Index

— **Local currency**   One-year change: + 46.97%
— **US Dollar**   One-year change: + 41.84%

that front are automaker Volkswagen AG and Commerzbank AG.

The financial crisis in Asia did put a damper on sentiment during the year, although on the whole, it isn't expected to have more than a minimal effect on Germany's stock market. German companies' exports to Asia have increased in recent years, and some, such as electronics group Siemens AG, were forced to revise sales and profits forecasts downward. The crisis, some observers warn, could also lead to asset price inflation due to outflows of funds from Asia.

Indeed, there seem to be few threats to the bull market. Even a change in Germany's government, which could result from general elections in September, would do little to spoil the party, analysts say. If, as polls indicate, the left-leaning opposition Social Democrats (SPD) succeed in ousting Chancellor Helmut Kohl's conservative Christian Democratic Party/Christian Social Union (CDU/CSU) government, it isn't expected to be more than a temporary restraint on the upward market. Although industry might prefer to see Kohl's coalition reinstalled, SPD policy is more market-friendly than ever.

In the market itself, a focus during the past year has been Germany's burgeoning telecommunications sector. The industry has continued to grow since the market was fully opened in January 1998, when Deutsche Telekom AG — which sold shares to the public for first time in November 1996 — lost its status as official state carrier. Liberalization

Country Information

Trading Hours:

  Local: 8:30 am - 5:00 pm

  EST: 2:30 am - 11:00 am

  GMT: 0730 - 1600

Population (6/98):
82,079,454

Unemployment (97):
11.4%

Main Industries:
Iron, steel, coal, cement, chemicals, machinery, vehicles, machine tools, electronics, food and beverages, metal fabrication, brown coal, shipbuilding, textiles, and petroleum refining

Gross Domestic Product (97):
US$2,100.11 billion

GDP per Capita (97):
US$25,587.28

Three-Year Average GDP Growth (94-97):
1.2%

Average Annual CPI Growth (96-97):
+ 1.76%

Monetary Unit:
German Mark

Exchange Rate (6/98):
DEM1.81 to US$1.00

has spurred a number of partnerships among German companies, as well as across borders, including a joint venture between Viag AG and British Telecom PLC of the United Kingdom. Utility groups, particularly, have been grabbing up market share, touting lower prices and customized services.

The growth of initial public offerings in Germany over the past couple of years has been a boon to the market. According to Deutsche Boerse AG, the group that runs Frankfurt's stock exchange and the Xetra electronic trading system, about 30 IPOs were launched in the first half of 1998 alone, compared with 36 in all of 1997 and 14 in 1996. Many of the IPOs have been for high-growth, technology-oriented companies, which traditionally in Germany have remained in private hands. Researchers credit Deutsche Telekom's IPO in late 1996 with beginning the flood of IPOs, saying its success offered encouragement to other companies.

Telekom's IPO, which was accompanied by a flashy advertising campaign, has also been credited with increasing private stock ownership in Germany. In 1997, the number of private investors rose to 4.1 million from 3.8 million in 1996, according to the DAI German Stock Research Institute.

Foreign ownership is also key to the German market, especially purchases by U.S. and U.K. investors. In 1997, about 12.2% of German shares were in foreign hands, up from 10.6% a year earlier. Germany imposes no tax on transactions.

Ten Largest Capitalized Companies In The Dow Jones Germany Index
as of 6/30/98

Stock	Market Cap. US$ Thousands
Allianz	80,191,065
Deutsche Telecom	75,270,007
SAP	66,466,027
Daimler-Benz	55,441,959
Deutsche Bank	44,945,179
Muenchener Ruckversicherungs-Namen	40,928,849
Bayer	37,608,719
Mannesmann	37,233,783
Siemens	35,443,501
Veba	32,855,884

The most significant recent structural change on the German market is the growing emphasis on electronic trading. At the end of 1997, Deutsche Boerse launched the Xetra electronic trading system, discarding the outmoded IBIS system. Along with a transparent open order book, Xetra offers a wider selection of shares. It was to be expanded to include bonds and other securities in the fall of 1998.

Xetra also brought lower transaction costs, and it allows small retail orders alongside wholesale, which previously was possible in only floor trading. Xetra has the capability of making floor trading obsolete, though Deutsche Boerse says it is up to market participants to decide if that should happen.

Germany's two main indexes are the Xetra DAX, which tracks prices in electronic trading, and the weighted DAX index, which follows floor trading of the same 30 shares. Shares are selected on the basis of high turnover and market capitalization. The indexes are reviewed regularly to ensure that the market and its trends are adequately reflected.

The Frankfurt Exchange also produces the DAX 100 and MDAX indexes. The DAX 100 includes the 100 biggest companies whose stock is traded continuously; the MDAX is a mid-cap index of the 70 shares on the DAX 100 not listed on the blue-chip DAX.

Besides electronic trading, Germany has eight regional bourses. The largest of those is Frankfurt, with over 1,800 listings and the highest turnover.

Frankfurt divides its listings into four segments: the first, second, and third segments and the new market. In the first and second segments, shares undergo a formal listing process. In the first, sometimes called the "official" segment, only companies that have been in operation for at least three years qualify. Shares must have a minimum value of DEM2.5 million and 25% of the total nominal capital has to be widely held. The stock exchange also requires annual and interim reports.

Companies under three years old seeking a listing turn to the second segment of trading. Here, shares must have a nominal value of at least DEM500,000. Companies are not required to submit interim reports but must provide enough information to allow investors to arrive at an informed opinion.

The third segment has few formal requirements. It consists mainly of German shares and traded options and foreign shares that brokers have requested they be allowed to trade.

Introduced in 1997, the Neuer Markt, or New Market, segment has become a hot spot for smaller companies seeking a listing even though they fall short of the capitalization and share requirements demanded in the first and second segments. The Neuer Markt is intended primarily for high-growth shares. As a rule, investors have gobbled up shares in this segment, resulting in oversubscription and high share prices.

Options and futures trading in Germany takes place on the Eurex Deutschland, formerly the Deutsche Termin Boerse (DTB). In the fall of 1998, it was to be linked with its counterpart in Switzerland as part of a merger.

Industry Group Performance In The Dow Jones Germany Index
1 Year Change Through 6/30/98

Industry	Change % (US$)
Best Performing	
Software	210.36
Banks, Regional	102.73
Insurance, Property & Casualty	73.69
Chemicals, Specialty	71.48
Industrial, Diversified	71.02
Worst Performing	
Steel	6.68
Pharmaceuticals	6.04
Diversified Technology	0.68
Heavy Construction	-2.95
Factory Equipment	-26.88

Adidas-Salomon

DJGI Industry: **Footwear**
Stoxx Sector: **Consumer Cyclical**

Adidas-Salomon AG, formerly Adidas AG, is a leading manufacturer of sports shoes, sportswear, and sporting equipment and also collects licensing fees for the use of the Adidas brand name and sponsors sporting events, sports teams, and athletes. The company manufactures its products mainly in China, Indonesia, and Thailand, but it has worldwide subsidiaries. In 1997, Adidas AG acquired Salomon SA, a French manufacturer of ski boots, inline-skates, and golf products, and changed its name to Adidas-Salomon AG.

	DM mil 12/95	12/96	12/97	US$mil 12/97				
Sales	3,500.2	4,709.4	6,698.3	3,722.9	P/E Ratio	**NMF**	Price (6/30/98)	310.05
Net Income	244.9	314.1	465.0	258.4	P/B Ratio	10.9	52 Wk Hi-Low	327.80-192.00
Book Value	576.6	904.3	1,351.9	751.4	Yield %	0.5	Market Cap	US$7,776.8mil

Address	**ADI-Dassier-Str. 2**	Tel **9132-840**	ADR	**ASHUYP**	Memb Mgt Bd	**C. Tourres**
	91074 Herzogenaurach	Fax **9132-842241**	SEDOL	**4031976**	Chmn Mgt Bd	**R. Louis-Dreyfus**

Allianz

DJGI Industry: **Insurance - Full Line**
Stoxx Sector: **Insurance**

Allianz AG Holding, is one of Europe's largest insurers. It sells property, casualty, and life insurance. The company's property and casualty insurance includes auto, fire, storm, property damage, accident, and industrial coverage. Allianz offers property and casualty insurance in Germany through its subsidiary Allianz Versicherung, which forms the core of its operations. It expanded internationally by acquiring U.S.-based insurance company Fireman's Fund Insurance. Allianz has extensive minority interest shareholdings in domestic industrial, banking, and utility companies.

	DM mil 12/95	12/96	12/97	US$mil 12/97				
Revenues	81,888.0	87,448.7	101,122.5	56,203.9	P/E Ratio	53.2	Price (6/30/98)	592.50
Net Income	1,514.4	1,649.9	2,031.1	1,128.9	P/B Ratio	7.9	52 Wk Hi-Low	624.00-358.55
Book Value	14,077.7	15,362.5	17,235.3	9,579.4	Yield %	0.3	Market Cap	US$80,191mil

Address	**Königinstr. 28**	Tel **89-3800-0**	ADR	--	Chmn Supv Bd	**K. Liesen**
	80802 Munich	Fax **89-349941**	SEDOL	**5231485**	Chmn Mgt Bd	**H. Schulte-Noelle**

In DJ Stoxx 50; In EuroStoxx 50.

BASF

DJGI Industry: **Chemicals - Commodity**
Stoxx Sector: **Chemical**

BASF AG is one of Germany's largest chemical manufacturing companies. It has five major divisions. The plastics and fibers division develops synthetic materials. The dyestuffs and finishing products division manufactures dyes and color pigments. The health and nutrition division is involved in phamaceuticals as well as fertilizers and herbicides. The chemicals division creates products for industrial applications. And the oil and gas division explores for, refines, and markets petroleum products, crude oil, and natural gas. Plastics and fibers accounted for 26% of 1997 revenues.

	DM mil 12/95	12/96	12/97	US$mil 12/97				
Sales	46,229.1	48,776.0	55,780.1	31,002.6	P/E Ratio	15.8	Price (6/30/98)	85.11
Net Income	2,470.5	2,790.2	3,235.7	1,798.4	P/B Ratio	2.3	52 Wk Hi-Low	86.80-54.90
Book Value	17,574.3	20,003.6	23,031.2	12,800.7	Yield %	2.3	Market Cap	US$29,283mil

Address	**Carl-Bosch-Str. 38**	Tel **621-60-0**	ADR	**BASFY**	V Chmn Mgt Bd	**H.H. Stechl**
	67056 Ludwigshafen	Fax **621-604-2525**	SEDOL	**5086577**	Chmn Mgt Bd	**J. Strube**

Bayer

DJGI Industry: **Chemicals - Commodity**
Stoxx Sector: **Chemical**

Bayer AG manufactures pharmaceuticals, chemicals, industrial and organic products, polymers, photographic film, and imaging systems for medical diagnosis, materials testing, and micrographics. Its products include Bayer Aspirin and Alka-Seltzer. Bayer's industrial-products and polymers divisions produce pigments, ceramics, polyurethanes, and synthetic products. The company has subsidiaries in countries around the world. Polymers accounted for 30% of 1997 revenues; health-care products accounted for 25%, and chemical products for 20%.

	DM mil 12/95	12/96	12/97	US$mil 12/97				
Sales	44,580.0	48,608.0	55,005.0	30,571.8	P/E Ratio	21.3	Price (6/30/98)	93.10
Net Income	2,394.0	2,725.0	2,941.0	1,634.6	P/B Ratio	2.9	52 Wk Hi-Low	93.35-57.10
Book Value	17,816.0	20,599.0	23,486.0	13,053.5	Yield %	2.0	Market Cap	US$37,609mil

Address	**Bayerwerk**	Tel **214-301**	ADR	**BAYZY**	CFO	**W. Wenning**
	51368 Leverkusen	Fax **214-306-6328**	SEDOL	**5069211**	Chmn Mgt Bd	**M. Schneider**

In DJ Stoxx 50; In EuroStoxx 50.

Bayerische Vereinsbank

DJGI Industry: **Banks - Regional (All)**
Stoxx Sector: **Bank**

Bayerische Vereinsbank AG offers commercial and mortgage banking, retail banking, portfolio management, public sector lending, and other financial services. In July 1997, Vereinsbank and Bayerische Hypotheken-und Wechsel-Bank AG announced they will merge in September of 1998 to form Germany's second-largest bank. The new bank will be called Bayerische Hypo-und Vereinsbank. At the end of 1997, Vereinsbank maintained 823 offices in Germany and 48 operative outlets in other countries.

	DM mil 12/95	12/96	12/97	US$mil 12/97				
Revenues	24,611.4	26,214.7	28,964.8	16,098.6	P/E Ratio	54.8	Price (6/30/98)	152.35
Net Income	600.7	811.4	845.5	469.9	P/B Ratio	3.3	52 Wk Hi-Low	158.80-70.35
Book Value	9,541.1	9,959.1	13,975.8	7,767.8	Yield %	1.1	Market Cap	US$23,257mil

Address	**Kardinal-Faulhaber-Str. 1-14**	Tel **89-378-0**	ADR	**BAVNY**	V Chmn Supv Bd	**H. Betz**
	80333 Munich	Fax **89-378-26415**	SEDOL	**4325419**	Chmn Supv Bd	**M. Hackl**

Beiersdorf

DJGI Industry: **Cosmetics & Personal Care**
Stoxx Sector: **Consumer Non-Cyclical**

Beiersdorf AG is a German specialty chemicals group. It manufactures cosmetics, pharmaceuticals, and medical goods and is best known for its Nivea brand of personal-care products. Its personal-care line also includes a variety of soaps, toothpastes, and deodorants. Additionally, the company produces Tesa adhesive tapes, Hansaplast bandages, and hospital supplies. The company has world wide subsidiaries. Cosmetics accounted for 55% of 1997 revenues; medical products, 23%; and adhesive tapes and films, 22%.

	DM mil 12/95	12/96	12/97	US$mil 12/97					
Sales	5,344.7	5,778.2	6,288.2	3,495.0	P/E Ratio	72.3	Price (6/30/98)	118.00
Net Income	221.3	229.2	137.2	76.2	P/B Ratio	5.9	52 Wk Hi-Low	122.50-71.40
Book Value	1,481.1	1,636.3	1,686.2	937.2	Yield %	0.8	Market Cap	US$5,482.3mil

Address	Unnastr. 48	Tel 40-490-92332	ADR	--	CFO	P. Schaefer
	20245 Hamburg	Fax 40-490-93434	SEDOL	5107401	Chmn Mgt Bd	R. Kunisch

Bilfinger & Berger Bau

DJGI Industry: **Heavy Construction**
Stoxx Sector: **Construction**

Bilfinger & Berger Bau AG is a diversified group of construction companies that specializes in erecting apartment houses, commercial buildings, waste disposal and water treatment plants, oil pipelines, multi story car parks, and civil engineering projects such as bridges and tunnels. As one of Germany's largest construction companies, it manufactures construction materials and machinery worldwide. Building construction accounted for 72% of 1997 work volume; environmental technology and plant construction, 16%; civil engineering, 7%; and construction materials, 5%.

	DM mil 12/95	12/96	12/97	US$mil 12/97					
Sales	7,038.1	7,026.7	8,018.6	4,456.7	P/E Ratio	59.0	Price (6/30/98)	62.00
Net Income	106.6	91.8	39.5	22.0	P/B Ratio	1.6	52 Wk Hi-Low	81.90-47.20
Book Value	1,339.8	1,391.5	1,386.0	770.3	Yield %	1.6	Market Cap	US$1,237.8mil

Address	Carl-Ress Platz 1-5	Tel 621-459-0	ADR	--	Chmn Supv Bd	J. Sarrazin
	68165 Mannheim	Fax 621-459-2366	SEDOL	5117381	Chmn Mgt Bd	C. Roth

BMW

DJGI Industry: **Automobile Manufacturers**
Stoxx Sector: **Automobile**

Bayerische Motoren Werke AG, better known as BMW, is a leading manufacturer of luxury automobiles and motorcycles. The company produces cars under the BMW and Rover names. It also manufactures aircraft engines under its subsidiary's name, BMW Rolls-Royce. BMW has manufacturing operations in Germany, Austria, the United States, Mexico, and South Africa. The company plans to construct a new plant in Egypt. BMW automobiles accounted for 59% of 1997 revenues; Rover automobiles, 27%; vehicle finance leasing, 11%; motorcycles, 2%; and aircraft engines, 1%.

	DM mil 12/95	12/96	12/97	US$mil 12/97					
Sales	46,144.0	52,265.0	60,137.0	33,424.1	P/E Ratio	35.9	Price (6/30/98)	1,818.00
Net Income	687.0	813.0	1,246.0	692.5	P/B Ratio	4.4	52 Wk Hi-Low	1,960.6-905.7
Book Value	8,074.0	8,943.0	10,119.0	5,624.1	Yield %	0.9	Market Cap	US$22,213mil

Address	Petuelring 130	Tel 89-3820	ADR	--	Memb Mgt Bd	V. Doppelfeld
	80788 Muenchen	Fax 89-3822-5858	SEDOL	4085229	Chmn Mgt Bd	B. Pischetsrieder

Commerzbank

DJGI Industry: **Banks - Major International**
Stoxx Sector: **Bank**

Commerzbank AG, one of Germany's three largest banks, provides commercial and investment banking and related financial services. It offers home loans, real estate leasing, life insurance, and asset-management services. Commerzbank operates 19 foreign branches and 26 foreign representative offices. In 1997, the bank disposed of shareholdings in Karadstadt AG and Kolbenschmidt AG and reduced its holdings in Heidelberger Druckmaschinen AG to 9.9% from 13.8%. Interest and fees on loans accounted for 76% of 1997 revenues.

	DM mil 12/95	12/96	12/97	US$mil 12/97					
Revenues	26,891.0	29,532.0	33,353.0	18,537.6	P/E Ratio	23.8	Price (6/30/98)	67.92
Net Income	920.0	1,190.0	1,323.0	735.3	P/B Ratio	2.0	52 Wk Hi-Low	74.80-48.50
Book Value	11,977.0	12,895.0	15,775.0	8,767.7	Yield %	2.2	Market Cap	US$17,849mil

Address	Neue Mainzer Str. 32-36	Tel 69-1-3620	ADR	CRZBY	Chmn Supv Bd	W. Seipp
	60311 Frankfurt	Fax 69-28-5389	SEDOL	4325538	Chmn Mgt Bd	M. Kohlhaussen

Continental

DJGI Industry: **Tires & Rubber**
Stoxx Sector: **Automobile**

Continental AG manufactures tires and automotive and industrial components for commercial and passenger vehicles. The company is diversifying into automotive and industrial technology through its ContiTech division, which manufactures automotive interior design and textiles as well as automotive drive systems. The company makes tires under the Continental, General Tire, and Uniroyal brand names. Tires accounted for 71% of 1997 total revenues, while industrial products accounted for the other 29%.

	DM mil 12/95	12/96	12/97	US$mil 12/97					
Sales	10,252.6	10,430.6	11,186.1	6,217.2	P/E Ratio	19.7	Price (6/30/98)	55.60
Net Income	55.9	156.0	277.3	154.1	P/B Ratio	2.6	52 Wk Hi-Low	58.35-38.80
Book Value	1,483.5	1,591.7	2,410.3	1,339.6	Yield %	1.3	Market Cap	US$3,525.0mil

Address	Vahrenwalder Str. 9	Tel 511-938-01	ADR	CTTAY	CFO	J.P. Howaldt
	30165 Hannover	Fax 511-938-2766	SEDOL	4598589	Chmn Mgt Bd	H. von Gruenberg

Daimler-Benz

DJGI Industry: **Automobile Manufacturers**
Stoxx Sector: **Automobile**

Daimler-Benz AG is Germany's largest automobile manufacturer by sales. It comprises 3 divisions: Mercedes-Benz, which produces motor vehicles; Daimler-Benz Aerospace (DASA), which manufactures aircraft systems; Daimler-Benz InterServices (Debis), which offers financial, insurance, and mobile-communication services; and AEG, which is its electrical engineering company. In May 1998, Daimler announced that it will merge with America's Chrysler Corp. Motor vehicles accounted for 72% of 1997 revenues; aerospace, 12%; services, 11%; and other engineering, 5%.

	DM mil 12/95	12/96	12/97	US$mil 12/97				
Sales	103,549.0	106,339.0	124,050.0	68,947.0	P/E Ratio	11.5	Price (6/30/98)	175.50
Net Income	-5,674.0	2,762.0	8,042.0	4,469.7	P/B Ratio	2.6	52 Wk Hi-Low	178.70-91.92
Book Value	12,965.0	26,393.0	35,085.0	19,500.2	Yield %	0.9	Market Cap	US$55,442mil

Address	**Box 80 02 30**					
	70546 Stuttgart	Tel **711-170**	ADR	**DAI**	Chmn Exec Bd	**E. Reuter**
		Fax **711-179-4022**	SEDOL	**5083998**	Chmn Mgt Bd	**J.E. Schrempp**

In DJ Stoxx 50; In EuroStoxx 50.

Degussa

DJGI Industry: **Precious Metals**
Stoxx Sector: **Basic Resources**

Degussa AG is the world's third-largest producer of precious metals. It refines, purchases, and sells precious metals for the jewelry and electronics markets. Additionally, the company produces inorganic, industrial, and fine chemicals, chemicals for dental use, and pharmaceuticals. The company has subsidiaries in Germany, the United States, Brazil, Singapore, Japan, and South Korea. Precious metals accounted for 45% of fiscal 1997 revenues; special chemicals, 11%; pharmaceuticals, 10%; rubber and pigments, 7%; and silicates and chemical catalysts, 7%.

	DM mil 09/95	09/96	09/97	US$mil 09/97				
Sales	13,861.8	13,792.3	15,343.4	8,712.0	P/E Ratio	24.9	Price (6/30/98)	111.50
Net Income	278.7	291.0	380.3	215.9	P/B Ratio	4.6	52 Wk Hi-Low	118.35-75.00
Book Value	1,959.4	1,987.0	2,209.7	1,254.7	Yield %	1.3	Market Cap	US$5,677.4mil

Address	**Weissfrauenstr. 9**					
	60287 Frankfurt	Tel **69-2183618**	ADR	--	Memb Mgt Bd	**P. Coenen**
		Fax **69-2183849**	SEDOL	**5237223**	Chmn Mgt Bd	**U.E. Bufe**

Deutsche Bank

DJGI Industry: **Banks - Major International**
Stoxx Sector: **Bank**

Deutsche Bank, Germany's largest bank, provides retail, private, and institutional banking and offers mortgage and investment banking, fund management, capital-market exchange, corporate financing, and mergers-and-acquisitions consulting. In 1997, the bank restructured its activities into five divisions: Retail and Private Clients, Corporate and Institutional Banking, Investment Banking, Asset Management, and Transaction Services. Interest and fees on loans accounted for 61% of 1997 revenues.

	DM mil 12/95	12/96	12/97	US$mil 12/97				
Revenues	54,765.0	61,455.0	73,254.0	40,714.6	P/E Ratio	72.1	Price (6/30/98)	152.20
Net Income	2,060.0	2,134.0	956.0	531.3	P/B Ratio	2.5	52 Wk Hi-Low	161.90-101.90
Book Value	28,043.0	29,690.0	32,086.0	17,833.4	Yield %	1.2	Market Cap	US$44,945mil

Address	**Taunusanlage 12**					
	60262 Frankfurt	Tel **69-910-00**	ADR	**DTBKY**	Chmn Supv Bd	**H. Kopper**
		Fax **69-910-34227**	SEDOL	**4326672**	Spkmn Mgt Bd	**R.E. Breuer**

In DJ Stoxx 50; In EuroStoxx 50.

Deutsche Lufthansa

DJGI Industry: **Airlines**
Stoxx Sector: **Consumer Cyclical**

Deutsche Lufthansa AG provides passenger and cargo air services worldwide. More than 300 aircraft make up its fleet which reaches over 250 destinations and provides flights to all continents. Lufthansa's secondary interests are tourism, hotels, catering, and aviation-related insurance. It owns 25% of the DHL International express-delivery service and the Condor and Lufthansa CityLine subsidiaries, which provide passenger service in Europe. In 1997, the company formed a tourism holding company with Karstadt AG. Passenger transportation accounts for over 70% of revenues.

	DM mil 12/95	12/96	12/97	US$mil 12/97				
Sales	19,900.4	20,862.0	23,148.8	12,866.1	P/E Ratio	14.0	Price (6/30/98)	45.00
Net Income	1,466.0	554.0	830.2	461.4	P/B Ratio	2.9	52 Wk Hi-Low	48.25-29.30
Book Value	4,924.1	5,339.3	5,902.8	3,280.8	Yield %	2.0	Market Cap	US$9,497.8mil

Address	**Von-Gablenz-Str. 2-6**					
	50679 Cologne	Tel **221-8260**	ADR	**DLAGY**	V Chmn Mgt Bd	**K.G. Schlede**
		Fax **221-826-3818**	SEDOL	**5287488**	Chmn Mgt Bd	**J. Weber**

In EuroStoxx 50.

Deutsche Telekom

DJGI Industry: **Telephone Utilities (All)**
Stoxx Sector: **Telecom**

Deutsche Telekom AG is a German telecommunications group with fixed-network, mobile-phone, and on-line services. The company is involved in satellite operations, cable television transmission via its wide-frequency network, video conferencing, audiovisual and textual data transmission, and multimedia services. In November 1996, Deutsche Telekom sold shares to the public for the first time in Europe's largest-ever initial public offering. It has subsidiaries in Germany, the United States, Europe, Japan, Singapore, and Canada. Telecommunications accounted for 82% of 1997 revenues.

	DM mil 12/95	12/96	12/97	US$mil 12/97				
Sales	66,135.0	63,075.0	67,552.0	37,545.4	P/E Ratio	42.6	Price (6/30/98)	49.60
Net Income	5,272.0	1,758.0	3,303.0	1,835.8	P/B Ratio	2.9	52 Wk Hi-Low	50.14-29.90
Book Value	24,727.0	45,404.0	46,692.0	25,951.4	Yield %	2.4	Market Cap	US$75,270mil

Address	**Postfach 2000**					
	53105 Bonn	Tel **228-181-4949**	ADR	**DT**	CFO Mgt Bd	**J. Kroeske**
		Fax **228-181-8941**	SEDOL	**5119387**	Chmn Mgt Bd	**R. Sommer**

In DJ Stoxx 50; In EuroStoxx 50.

Dresdner Bank

DJGI Industry: **Banks - Major International**
Stoxx Sector: **Bank**

Dresdner Bank, one of Germany's three largest banks, provides lending services, securities and commodities brokerage, and investment banking services. Dresdner operates 1,553 branch offices in 70 countries worldwide. Its subsidiaries include Deutsch-Suedamerikanische Bank AG, Banque Internationale de Placement SA Bank for Europe Ltd., United Overseas Bank, and RCM Capital Management. Interest and fees on loans accounted for 67% of 1997 revenues; commissions and fees, 15%; interest on government and other securities, 7%.

	DM mil 12/95	12/96	12/97	US$mil 12/97				
Revenues	29,804.1	31,944.0	36,357.3	20,207.4	P/E Ratio	27.6	Price (6/30/98)	96.49
Net Income	1,171.5	1,537.3	1,660.3	922.8	P/B Ratio	2.7	52 Wk Hi-Low	108.75-59.73
Book Value	13,391.8	14,676.0	18,493.0	10,278.4	Yield %	1.6	Market Cap	US$29,181mil

Address	Jürgen-Ponto-Platz 1	Tel 69-26-30	ADR	DBMKYP	Chmn Supv Bd	A. Titzrath
	60329 Frankfurt	Fax 69-263-4831	SEDOL	4355870	Memb Mgt Bd	B. Walter

Ergo Versicherungsgruppe

DJGI Industry: **Insurance - Full Line**
Stoxx Sector: **Insurance**

Ergo Versicherungsgruppe AG was formed in 1997 through the merger of Victoria Holding AG, including its subsidiaries D.A.S. Versicherung and DKV Versicherung, with Hamburg-Mannheimer Versicherungs AG, a holding of insurance companies involved in life, accident, health, property, and nonlife insurance. Hamburg-Mannheimer Versicherungs AG previously had been a privately owned company. Ergo has subsidiaries in Germany, Belgium, the Netherlands, Italy, the Czech Republic, Slovakia, Spain, Greece, Luxembourg, and Austria.

	DM mil 12/95	12/96	12/97	US$mil 12/97				
Revenues	8,528.9	8,771.9	29,329.6	16,301.4	P/E Ratio	7.5	Price (6/30/98)	318.00
Net Income	102.4	114.2	522.2	290.2	P/B Ratio	4.7	52 Wk Hi-Low	380.00-245.50
Book Value	749.0	851.1	4,115.7	2,287.5	Yield %	0.3	Market Cap	US$13,858mil

Address	Victoriaplatz 2	Tel 21-149370	ADR	--	President	--
	40198 Duesseldorf	Fax 21-14937151	SEDOL	5377947	Chmn Mgt Bd	E. Jannot

Fresenius Medical Care

DJGI Industry: **Advanced Medical Devices**
Stoxx Sector: **Technology**

Fresenius Medical Care AG is one of the world's largest developers, manufacturers, and suppliers of renal and dialysis services and products. The company operates its own treatment clinics and provides related care. At the end of 1997, the company was serving more than 68,000 patients in approximately 900 dialysis clinics in 17 countries. The company operates over 20 production sites in 14 countries. FMC has worldwide subsidiaries. Health-care services accounted for 62% of 1997 revenues and dialysis products and supplies for 38%.

	DM mil 12/95	12/96	12/97	US$mil 12/97				
Sales	N/A	2,262.7	5,663.1	3,147.6	P/E Ratio	38.1	Price (6/30/98)	112.50
Net Income	N/A	132.1	156.8	87.1	P/B Ratio	2.6	52 Wk Hi-Low	161.80-110.50
Book Value	N/A	3,320.4	4,276.4	2,376.8	Yield %	0.9	Market Cap	US$4,355.7mil

Address	Borkenberg 14	Tel 617-167-2525	ADR	FMS	President	--
	61440 Oberursel	Fax 617-167-2488	SEDOL	5129074	Chairman	Dr. G. Krick

GEHE

DJGI Industry: **Retailers - Drug-Based**
Stoxx Sector: **Retail**

GEHE AG is a pharmeceuticals company with additional interests in mail-order services for office and warehouse furniture, accessories, and promotional gifts. In 1997, GEHE acquired Lloyds Chemists PLC. Combined with the AAH Group, GEHE now operates the largest chain of pharmacies in the United Kingdom. GEHE has sold all its subsidiaries involved in the production of pharmaceuticals to concentrate on the wholesale and retail sale of pharmaceuticals. Wholesale pharmaceuticals accounted for 85% of 1997 revenues.

	DM mil 12/95	12/96	12/97	US$mil 12/97				
Revenues	19,156.3	21,425.0	25,035.7	13,914.9	P/E Ratio	25.4	Price (6/30/98)	98.00
Net Income	203.8	435.4	280.8	156.1	P/B Ratio	3.1	52 Wk Hi-Low	123.50-87.50
Book Value	1,982.2	2,126.1	2,327.7	1,293.7	Yield %	1.3	Market Cap	US$3,951.5mil

Address	Neckartalstrasse 155	Tel 711-500-100	ADR	--	Memb Mgt Bd	K.G. Eick
	70376 Stuttgart	Fax 711-500-1500	SEDOL	5105182	Chmn Mgt Bd	D. Kaemmerer

Heidelberger Druckmaschinen

DJGI Industry: **Factory Equipment**
Stoxx Sector: **Industrials**

Heidelberger Druckmaschinen AG (Heidelberg) is a world leader in the manufacture of printing machinery. The company is structured into three business units which offer a comprehensive range of machinery for the printing industry. The sheet-fed unit produces machinery using paper sheets; the web unit produces machinery using paper from rolls; and the finishing unit produces machinery for the preparation or finishing of the printing process. Heidelberg has worldwide subsidiaries, but the Nafta region remains its primary market. In 1998, Heidelberg acquired Denmark-based EAC.

	DM mil 03/96	03/97	03/98	US$mil 03/98				
Sales	4,286.1	5,057.5	6,875.6	3,720.4	P/E Ratio	20.4	Price (6/30/98)	149.25
Net Income	268.3	1,142.1	500.1	270.6	P/B Ratio	2.4	52 Wk Hi-Low	173.00-95.80
Book Value	2,147.4	3,321.9	3,135.6	1,696.7	Yield %	1.1	Market Cap	US$5,909.8mil

Address	Kurfürsten-anlage 52-60	Tel 62-21-920	ADR	--	President	--
	69115 Heidelberg	Fax 62-21-926999	SEDOL	5367227	Chmn Mgt Bd	H. Mehdorn

Heidelberger Zement

DJGI Industry: **Building Materials**
Stoxx Sector: **Construction**

Heidelberger Zement AG produces cement and concrete and manufactures construction materials. The company's products include such building materials as plaster, mortar, gypsum, natural building stone, sand-lime brick, and insulation systems. In addition, Heidelberger Zement produces concrete as a liquid ready-mix and in prefabricated forms. Heidelberger Zement has developed a new aluminous cement designed for the lining of pipes in sewage plants. Heidelberger has subsidiaries worldwide. Cement accounted for 50% of gross 1997 revenues.

	DM mil 12/95	12/96	12/97	US$mil 12/97				
Sales	6,038.5	6,473.5	7,256.2	4,033.0	P/E Ratio	23.4	Price (6/30/98)	171.00
Net Income	250.2	338.0	355.7	197.7	P/B Ratio	2.8	52 Wk Hi-Low	178.00-123.00
Book Value	2,277.1	2,641.4	3,009.4	1,672.6	Yield %	1.0	Market Cap	US$4,026.5mil

Address	Berliner Str. 6	Tel 6221-481-0	ADR	--	CFO	H.R. Wolf
	69120 Heidelberg	Fax 6221-481477	SEDOL	5120679	Chmn Mgt Bd	R. Huelstrunk

Henkel

DJGI Industry: **Chemicals - Specialty**
Stoxx Sector: **Chemical**

Henkel KGaA, publicly held since 1985, is a specialty-chemicals manufacturer that produces general chemicals, industrial adhesives, technical consumer products, detergents, and household cleaners. In addition, the company is involved in the production of personal hygiene and bathing products and is the second-largest producer of hair-care products in Europe. It has subsidiaries worldwide, including Hong Kong, China, Turkey, South Africa, and Mexico. In 1997 Henkel acquired the remaining interest in Loctite Corp.

	DM mil 12/95	12/96	12/97	US$mil 12/97				
Sales	14,198.0	16,301.0	20,065.0	11,152.1	P/E Ratio	23.1	Price (6/30/98)	175.90
Net Income	433.0	445.0	1,062.0	590.3	P/B Ratio	5.1	52 Wk Hi-Low	185.50-85.00
Book Value	3,639.0	4,106.0	5,076.0	2,821.2	Yield %	0.8	Market Cap	US$5,777.9mil

Address	Henkelstr. 67	Tel 211-797-0	ADR	HENKY	CFO	U. Lehner
	40589 Dusseldorf	Fax 211-798-4008	SEDOL	5076705	CEO	H.D. Winkhaus

Hochtief

DJGI Industry: **Heavy Construction**
Stoxx Sector: **Construction**

Hochtief AG is Germany's second-largest construction company. It builds industrial plants, commercial buildings, and residential apartments. The company also carries out a wide range of civil engineering infrastructure projects, such as tunnels, dams, bridges, and roadworks. Hochtief has foreign subsidiaries in the United States, Brazil, Argentina, Australia, Austria, and Luxembourg. Commercial building projects accounted for 53% of the total domestic volume of work in 1997, public sector building projects for 27%, and housing for 20%.

	DM mil 12/95	12/96	12/97	US$mil 12/97				
Sales	5,991.2	6,769.5	6,151.8	3,419.2	P/E Ratio	38.4	Price (6/30/98)	86.60
Net Income	136.7	145.6	157.5	87.5	P/B Ratio	2.5	52 Wk Hi-Low	93.00-60.60
Book Value	2,455.8	2,460.7	2,405.2	1,336.8	Yield %	1.4	Market Cap	US$3,352.9mil

Address	Opernplatz 2	Tel 201-8240	ADR	--	Chmn Supv Bd	D. Kuhnt
	45128 Essen	Fax 201-824-2777	SEDOL	5108664	Chmn Mgt Bd	H.P. Keitel

Hoechst

DJGI Industry: **Chemicals - Commodity**
Stoxx Sector: **Chemical**

Hoechst AG is one of Germany's top three chemical groups. The company restructured its business by changing Hoechst AG into a holding company for the other group companies, which operate independently. The company is active in producing pharmaceuticals and biotechnological goods, chemicals, plastics, and paints. Its main products are drugs for humans and animals, crop protectants, and pesticides. Hoechst has worldwide subsidiaries. Biotechnological and pharmaceutical products accounted for 46% of 1997 revenues, industrial chemicals, plastics, and paints for 54%.

	DM mil 12/95	12/96	12/97	US$mil 12/97				
Sales	52,177.0	50,927.0	52,100.0	28,957.2	P/E Ratio	38.2	Price (6/30/98)	89.35
Net Income	1,709.0	2,114.0	1,343.0	746.4	P/B Ratio	3.3	52 Wk Hi-Low	90.45-58.80
Book Value	12,445.0	14,508.0	16,012.0	8,899.5	Yield %	1.7	Market Cap	US$29,056mil

Address	Bruening Str. 50	Tel 69-3050	ADR	HOE	CFO	K.J. Schmieder
	65926 Frankfurt	Fax 69-30-36-65	SEDOL	5070376	Chmn Mgt Bd	J. Dormann

IVG

DJGI Industry: **Other Industrial & Commercial Services**
Stoxx Sector: **Industrials**

Industrieverwaltungsgesellschaft AG (IVG) is a diversified conglomerate. It develops real estate, rents out commercial, industrial, and residential buildings, operates rail transport services, and leases fuel storage space in bulk stations and caverns. IVG also provides facility management services. The company owns extensive real estate, as well as a large fleet of specialized rail wagons. The company has international subsidiaries. Logistics accounted for 55% of 1997 revenues; real estate development and property rental, 23%; and services 22%.

	DM mil 12/95	12/96	12/97	US$mil 12/97				
Sales	475.0	542.9	782.2	434.8	P/E Ratio	34.6	Price (6/30/98)	83.00
Net Income	40.3	44.5	62.5	34.8	P/B Ratio	3.9	52 Wk Hi-Low	83.00-44.10
Book Value	411.8	631.8	649.8	361.2	Yield %	1.9	Market Cap	US$1,423.1mil

Address	Zanderstr. 5	Tel 228-844-0	ADR	--	Memb Mgt Bd	G. Kuehn
	53177 Bonn	Fax 228-844-107	SEDOL	5130065	Chmn Mgt Bd	E.J. von Freyend

Karstadt

DJGI Industry: **Retailers - Broadline**
Stoxx Sector: **Retail**

Karstadt AG is Germany's largest department store chain. The company's principal focus is department and specialty stores operating in Germany under the Karstadt, Hertie, Neckermann names. In 1997, the company had 290 department stores, 175 specialized shops (sports and electronics) and 51 restaurants. Karstadt is also involved in mail order (Neckermann Versand), travel agencies/holiday clubs (Nur Touristic), and insurance services. Additionally, it has subsidiaries that provide electrical repair service, transport and storage service, and banking service.

	DM mil 12/95	12/96	12/97	US$mil 12/97					
Revenues	24,091.6	24,047.0	23,784.0	13,219.1	P/E Ratio		44.7	Price (6/30/98)	873.00
Net Income	108.0	58.4	162.2	90.1	P/B Ratio		2.9	52 Wk Hi-Low	984.90-530.00
Book Value	2,465.2	2,407.8	2,477.9	1,377.2	Yield %		1.1	Market Cap	US$4,056.0mil

Address	Theodor-Althoff-Str. 2	Tel 201-7271	ADR	KARDY	V Chmn Mgt Bd	J. Krueger
	45133 Essen	Fax 201-7275696	SEDOL	4484105	Chmn Mgt Bd	W. Deuss

Lahmeyer

DJGI Industry: **Factory Equipment**
Stoxx Sector: **Industrials**

Lahmeyer AG is a holding group that comprises companies operating in seven core business sectors: the manufacture of printing machinery; power generation and distribution; construction of power lines and plants; the manufacture of electric components and devices; the installation of electrical and communication systems; engineering consultancy; and the production of medical equipment. Printing presses and other machinery accounted for 59% of fiscal 1997 revenues; power line and plant construction, 16%; electrical installation and communications systems, 7%.

	DM mil 06/96	06/97	06/98	US$mil 06/98					
Sales	8,181.8	8,697.3	10,500.0	5,807.5	P/E Ratio		14.8	Price (6/30/98)	82.00
Net Income	221.1	415.4	530.0	293.1	P/B Ratio		2.4	52 Wk Hi-Low	107.00-65.50
Book Value	2,696.5	3,067.1	N/A	N/A	Yield %		1.2	Market Cap	US$4,084.5mil

Address	Guiollettstrasse 48	Tel 69-971-620	ADR	--	President	--
	60325 Frankfurt am Main	Fax 69-971-62100	SEDOL	5237621	Chmn Mgt Bd	F. Heigl

Linde

DJGI Industry: **Industrial - Diversified**
Stoxx Sector: **Industrials**

Linde AG is an engineering and industrial-gases company. The company's gas activities include the development of air-separation processes (mainly into liquid oxygen, nitrogen, and argon) and gas distribution. Its engineering division constructs gas plants and provides wastewater treatment. Linde manufactures forklifts, industrial trucks, earth-moving machinery, and hydraulic components, as well as display cabinets and refrigerated display cases for the retail sector. Materials handling equipment accounted for 44% of 1997 revenues.

	DM mil 12/95	12/96	12/97	US$mil 12/97					
Sales	8,283.8	8,800.9	9,545.9	5,305.6	P/E Ratio		25.0	Price (6/30/98)	1,231.45
Net Income	322.4	360.6	413.3	229.7	P/B Ratio		2.4	52 Wk Hi-Low	1,430.0-990.0
Book Value	3,781.0	4,036.4	4,358.3	2,422.3	Yield %		1.6	Market Cap	US$5,724.8mil

Address	Abraham-Lincoln-Str. 21	Tel 611-770-0	ADR	--	Memb Mgt Bd	H. Brahms
	65189 Wiesbaden	Fax 611-770-269	SEDOL	4517001	Chmn Mgt Bd	G. Full

MAN

DJGI Industry: **Industrial - Diversified**
Stoxx Sector: **Industrials**

MAN AG offers a diversified range of industrial products and services. Its core businesses involve the production of commercial vehicles, diesel engines, printing presses, and other machinery for industrial plants. Its products include trucks, buses, sheet-fed offset presses, rotary web presses, and automotive, industrial, and marine engines. MAN also provides logistics and engineering services to the construction industry. The company has subsidiaries in Germany, Austria, France, Denmark, and the United States. Trucks and components accounted for 37% of fiscal 1997 revenues.

	DM mil 06/96	06/97	06/98	US$mil 06/98					
Sales	20,269.9	21,354.1	24,793.0	13,713.0	P/E Ratio		25.7	Price (6/30/98)	701.25
Net Income	302.4	315.5	612.0	338.5	P/B Ratio		2.8	52 Wk Hi-Low	737.50-475.50
Book Value	3,705.3	3,803.9	N/A	N/A	Yield %		2.0	Market Cap	US$4,277.3mil

Address	Ungererstr. 69	Tel 89-360-98-0	ADR	--	Chmn Supv Bd	K. Götte
	80805 Munich	Fax 89-360-9825-0	SEDOL	4398303	Chmn Mgt Bd	R. Rupprecht

Mannesmann

DJGI Industry: **Industrial - Diversified**
Stoxx Sector: **Industrials**

Mannesmann AG is a diversified industrial company that builds plants for steel companies and manufactures machinery, pipes, process automation technology, and automotive electronics. It is also active in telecommunications and owns a mobile telephone network, D2. In July 1996, Germany's Deutsche Bahn AG chose a Mannesmann-led consortium as a strategic partner for its telecom subsidiary DBKom, which was renamed Mannesmann Arcor in January 1997. The Mannesmann-led consortium holds an option to increase its stake in Arcor to 74.9% in 1999.

	DM mil 12/95	12/96	12/97	US$mil 12/97					
Sales	32,094.0	34,683.0	39,096.0	21,729.6	P/E Ratio		137.8	Price (6/30/98)	182.90
Net Income	533.0	383.0	489.0	271.8	P/B Ratio		9.7	52 Wk Hi-Low	185.80-71.80
Book Value	6,507.0	6,589.0	6,924.0	3,848.4	Yield %		0.5	Market Cap	US$37,234mil

Address	Mannesmannufer 2	Tel 211-820-0	ADR	MNNSY	V Chmn Mgt Bd	K. Esser
	40213 Dusseldorf	Fax 211-820-1846	SEDOL	5460955	Chmn Mgt Bd	J. Funk

In DJ Stoxx 50; In EuroStoxx 50.

Metallgesellschaft

DJGI Industry: **Industrial - Diversified**
Stoxx Sector: **Industrials**

Metallgesellschaft MG is a diversified industrial company that provides trading, financial, and engineering services. The trading division is a wholesaler and broker of nonferrous metals and concentrates, nonferrous and steel waste metal, primary metals, and chemicals. The chemicals division produces explosives, synthetic materials, high-performance ceramics, and specialized and pigment chemicals. The plant construction and engineering division designs and builds production facilities for the metal-producing, chemical, and energy-generating industries.

	DM mil 09/95	09/96	09/97	US$mil 09/97				
Sales	17,643.0	15,825.3	18,166.5	10,315.0	P/E Ratio	25.6	Price (6/30/98)	37.10
Net Income	77.1	189.9	214.0	121.5	P/B Ratio	8.6	52 Wk Hi-Low	43.18-30.85
Book Value	11.1	358.2	578.5	328.5	Yield %	0.5	Market Cap	US$2,753.5mil

Address	Reuterweg 14	Tel 69-711990	ADR	--	President	K. Hornung
	60271 Frankfurt	Fax 69-7119905	SEDOL	4557104	Chmn Mgt Bd	K.J. Neukirchen

Metro

DJGI Industry: **Retailers - Broadline**
Stoxx Sector: **Retail**

Metro AG is Europe's largest retailing conglomerate. Among Metro's most important businesses are department stores, cash-and-carry shops, wholesale outlets, grocery stores, and household electronics and electrical appliances. Other areas include home-improvement stores, computers, furniture, and shoes. Metro operates 2,141 stores throughout Germany and 1,037 stores in Austria, France, Switzerland, the Netherlands, Italy, Belgium, Spain, Poland, Hungary, Luxembourg, Greece, Turkey, Romania, Denmark, China, and the United Kingdom.

	DM mil 12/95	12/96	12/97	US$mil 12/97				
Revenues	N/A	55,033.9	56,840.0	31,591.7	P/E Ratio	47.1	Price (6/30/98)	107.00
Net Income	N/A	610.4	553.9	307.9	P/B Ratio	6.3	52 Wk Hi-Low	122.31-63.55
Book Value	N/A	3,849.7	4,149.7	2,306.4	Yield %	1.9	Market Cap	US$13,125mil

Address	Leonhard-Tietz Str. 1	Tel 221-225-5870	ADR	--	CFO	S. Kaske
	50676 Cologne	Fax 221-225-5871	SEDOL	5041413	Spkmn Mgt Bd	E. Conradi

In EuroStoxx 50.

Munich Reinsurance

DJGI Industry: **Insurance - Property & Casualty**
Stoxx Sector: **Insurance**

Münchener Rückversicherungsgesellschaft AG, better known as Munich Reinsurance, is the world's largest reinsurance company. It specializes in industrial and commercial coverage. Its reinsurance-underwriting services include life, fire, and motor-vehicle insurance and personal-liability, natural-disaster, marine, and aviation coverage. In 1997 the company acquired Europe's biggest health insurer DKV Deutsche Krankenversicherung Ag from Allianz Holding AG, and also U.S.-based reinsurer American Re Corp. Premium income accounted for 75% of fiscal 1997 revenues.

	DM mil 06/96	06/97	06/98	US$mil 06/98				
Revenues	29,000.0	32,200.0	44,400.0	24,557.6	P/E Ratio	45.3	Price (6/30/98)	880.05
Net Income	595.0	699.0	1,149.0	635.5	P/B Ratio	13.7	52 Wk Hi-Low	954.00-480.00
Book Value	4,171.2	6,604.0	9,962.0	5,510.0	Yield %	0.2	Market Cap	US$40,929mil

Address	Königinstr. 107	Tel 89-3891-0	ADR	--	Chmn Supv Bd	U. Hartmann
	80802 Munich	Fax 89-3990-56	SEDOL	5294121	Chmn Mgt Bd	H.J. Schinzler

Philipp Holzmann

DJGI Industry: **Heavy Construction**
Stoxx Sector: **Construction**

Philipp Holzmann AG is Germany's largest construction company. About two-thirds of its construction activity is conducted in Germany. Holzmann constructs housing and industrial buildings, provides structural engineering for the public sector, and offers specialized civil engineering services. Its main divisions are general construction; the mining and processing of construction materials energy/environmental plant construction; and real estate development and management. Commercial building projects make up more than half of its domestic construction output.

	DM mil 12/95	12/96	12/97	US$mil 12/97				
Sales	11,274.7	11,406.3	13,039.9	7,247.6	P/E Ratio	NMF	Price (6/30/98)	439.50
Net Income	-463.2	-1.9	-790.4	-439.3	P/B Ratio	1.3	52 Wk Hi-Low	625.00-377.00
Book Value	1,541.1	1,496.3	643.1	357.4	Yield %	0.0	Market Cap	US$1,066.7mil

Address	Taunusanlage 1	Tel 69-262-1	ADR	--	CFO	R. Klee
	60299 Frankfurt	Fax 69-262-433	SEDOL	4434100	Chmn Mgt Bd	L. Mayer

Preussag

DJGI Industry: **Industrial - Diversified**
Stoxx Sector: **Industrials**

Preussag AG is a large, diversified manufacturing company. It produces steel, lead, zinc, crude oil, and natural gas, and it manufactures tank cars, trucks, container ships, rail vehicles, building materials, automotive-soundproofing equipment, mobile buildings, and fire-extinguishing systems for buildings. Preussag also engages in drilling contracting, construction, and engineering and is one of Germany's leading copper traders. Its steel-producing subsidiaries include Preussag Stahl and 51%-owned Metaleurop. In 1997, the company acquired the transportation group Hapag-Lloyd.

	DM mil 09/95	09/96	09/97	US$mil 09/97				
Sales	26,352.6	25,043.5	26,658.0	15,136.4	P/E Ratio	19.1	Price (6/30/98)	644.00
Net Income	371.4	250.8	361.9	205.5	P/B Ratio	3.4	52 Wk Hi-Low	669.00-447.00
Book Value	3,194.7	3,011.9	2,901.6	1,647.5	Yield %	1.9	Market Cap	US$5,746.2mil

Address	Karl-Wiechert-Allee 4	Tel 511-566-00	ADR	--	Chmn Supv Bd	F. Neuber
	30625 Hannover	Fax 511-566-1901	SEDOL	4701707	Chmn Mgt Bd	M. Frenzel

RWE

DJGI Industry: **Electrical Utilities (All)**
Stoxx Sector: **Utility**

RWE AG produces and distributes electric power, natural gas, and water. The company also provides telecommunications services, processes petroleum products, operates waste-disposal and construction businesses, and manufactures printing machines and medical appliances. Hochtief is RWE's international construction and civil engineering arm. Petroleum products and related chemicals accounted for 40% of fiscal 1997 revenues; energy, 29%; industrial machinery, 12%; construction, 11%; mining, 6%; and waste and refuse systems, 2%.

	DM mil 06/96	06/97	06/98	US$mil 06/98				
Sales	54,781.0	61,197.0	72,200.0	39,933.8	P/E Ratio	41.2	Price (6/30/98)	104.00
Net Income	1,196.0	1,303.0	1,400.0	774.3	P/B Ratio	6.8	52 Wk Hi-Low	110.80-73.00
Book Value	8,137.0	8,454.0	N/A	N/A	Yield %	1.5	Market Cap	US$19,003mil

Address	Opernplatz 1	Tel 201-1200	ADR	RWEPY	Chmn Supv Bd	F. Neuber
	45128 Essen	Fax 201-121-5199	SEDOL	5007307	Chmn Mgt Bd	D. Kuhnt

In DJ Stoxx 50; In EuroStoxx 50.

SAP

DJGI Industry: **Software**
Stoxx Sector: **Technology**

SAP AG is Germany's largest software publisher. It designs, manufactures, and markets standard application computer software. SAP's two main software products, the operating systems R/2 and R/3, are designed for mainframe applications and client/server systems, respectively. The main applications for the operating systems include accounting, financial management, logistics, personnel, specialized programming, and basic functions. SAP is one of the top standard application software producers worldwide. The company also provides software consultancy and training services.

	DM mil 12/95	12/96	12/97	US$mil 12/97				
Sales	2,696.4	3,722.1	6,017.5	3,344.5	P/E Ratio M	114.6	Price (6/30/98) M	1,085.00
Net Income	403.3	566.2	923.0	513.0	P/B Ratio M	37.1	52 Wk Hi-Low M	1,096.0-349.0
Book Value	1,526.5	2,207.1	3,047.8	1,694.0	Yield % M	0.3	Market Cap M	US$36,607mil

Address	Neurottstr. 16	Tel 6227-747474	ADR	SAPYYP	President	H. Kagermann
	69190 Walldorf	Fax 6227-757575	SEDOL	4846288	Chmn Supv Bd	D. Hopp

M=Multiple issues in index; reflects most active.

Schering

DJGI Industry: **Pharmaceuticals**
Stoxx Sector: **Pharmaceutical**

Schering AG develops, manufactures, and distributes pharmaceuticals and diagnostic substances. Schering's products include X-ray, MRI, and ultrasound contrast media, oral contraceptives and hormone replacement medication, drugs to combat disabling diseases, and corticoid creams and other dermatological preparations. In 1997, the company's best selling products were Betaferon, Lopamiron, and Magnevist. Fertility control and hormone therapy accounted for 34% of 1997 revenues; therapeutics, 31%; diagnostics, 25%; dermatology, 6%; and other, 4%.

	DM mil 12/95	12/96	12/97	US$mil 12/97				
Sales	4,647.5	5,272.2	6,245.8	3,471.4	P/E Ratio	32.2	Price (6/30/98)	214.80
Net Income	248.4	361.9	446.4	248.1	P/B Ratio	3.8	52 Wk Hi-Low	222.90-152.00
Book Value	3,209.5	3,495.2	3,821.2	2,123.8	Yield %	1.2	Market Cap	US$8,119.4mil

Address	Müllerstr. 170-178	Tel 30-468-1111	ADR	--	Dpty Chmn Mgt Bd	K. Pohle
	13342 Berlin	Fax 30-468-5305	SEDOL	4845757	Chmn Mgt Bd	G. Vita

Schmalbach-Lubeca

DJGI Industry: **Containers & Packaging**
Stoxx Sector: **Industrials**

Schmalbach-Lubeca AG is one of Europe's largest packaging manufacturers. Its principal operations are in plastic returnable bottles, beverage cans, and glass container tops. In May 1997, the company spun off of its metal packaging activities to a joint venture with Impress Metal-packaging Holding BV in Amsterdam. It also acquired the Plastic Container Division of Johnson Controls Inc.; combined operations will produce 10 billion PET containers a year (15% of the worldwide PET market) in 15 countries. Beverage cans accounted for 36% of 1997 revenues and PET containers for 34%.

	DM mil 12/95	12/96	12/97	US$mil 12/97				
Sales	4,124.2	4,089.1	4,344.2	2,414.5	P/E Ratio	11.0	Price (6/30/98)	461.50
Net Income	0.9	51.5	163.5	90.9	P/B Ratio	2.2	52 Wk Hi-Low	475.00-296.50
Book Value	576.1	668.7	919.1	510.8	Yield %	1.3	Market Cap	US$957.2mil

Address	Kaiserwertherst 115	Tel 2102-130460	ADR	--	Memb Mgt Bd	J.M. Henderson
	40880 Ratingen	Fax 2102-130150	SEDOL	4779577	Chmn Mgt Bd	H. Fiedler

Siemens

DJGI Industry: **Diversified Technology**
Stoxx Sector: **Technology**

Siemens AG is Germany's largest electronics engineering company. Its products include electronic components and telecommunications systems, power plant engineering products (including turbines), automotive electronics, transportation systems, and medical engineering products. Siemens operates through a broad network of subsidiaries located around the world. The company's industrial technology and communications divisions account for nearly half of its 1997 revenues. In 1998, Siemens formed a joint venture with Taiwanese PC manufacturer Acer Group.

	DM mil 09/95	09/96	09/97	US$mil 09/97				
Sales	88,763.0	94,180.0	106,930.0	60,714.9	P/E Ratio	23.6	Price (6/30/98)	109.65
Net Income	1,855.0	2,775.0	2,394.0	1,359.3	P/B Ratio	2.3	52 Wk Hi-Low	130.00-99.50
Book Value	20,960.0	23,560.0	26,683.8	15,151.0	Yield %	1.4	Market Cap	US$35,444mil

Address	Wittelsbacherplatz 2	Tel 89-63632812	ADR	SMAWY	CFO	K.H. Baumann
	80333 Munich	Fax 89-63632825	SEDOL	5047734	Chmn Mgt Bd	H von Pierer

In DJ Stoxx 50; In EuroStoxx 50.

Thyssen

DJGI Industry: **Steel**
Stoxx Sector: **Basic Resources**

Thyssen AG is a diversified steel producer that oversees 310 consolidated companies. Its Thyssen Stahl subsidiary operates the group's steel-manufacturing businesses. Thyssen's products include spare parts, brake components, cement, and machine tools. It also owns a 30.12% stake in the E-Plus mobile phone service. Thyssen has subsidiaries in Germany, France, the Netherlands, Great Britain, Spain, the United States, and Brazil. The company is in negotiations with Preussag AG to merge the two companies' shipyard units.

	DM mil 09/95	09/96	09/97	US$mil 09/97				
Sales	39,122.5	38,672.8	40,753.4	23,139.8	P/E Ratio	7.1	Price (6/30/98)	456.50
Net Income	749.3	297.9	2,127.9	1,208.2	P/B Ratio	2.2	52 Wk Hi-Low	468.50-350.00
Book Value	4,805.1	4,957.3	7,126.6	4,046.5	Yield %	2.2	Market Cap	US$8,675.6mil

Address	August-Thyssen. Str. 1		Tel 211-8241	ADR	THAGY	Supv Bd	H. Kriwet
	40211 Dusseldorf		Fax 211-8243-6000	SEDOL	4891084	Chmn Mgt Bd	D.H. Vogel

VEBA

DJGI Industry: **Conglomerates**
Stoxx Sector: **Conglomerate**

VEBA AG is a diversified holding company with business activities that include the production and distribution of electricity, oil, chemicals, and natural gas. The company also provides paging, mobile-phone, satellite-communication, and cable-television telecommunications services. VEBA is the second-largest competitor in the German telecommunications market and the fourth-largest company in Germany. In 1998, VEBA acquired 64% of the new chemical company Degussa-Huels, which will be formed in 1999.

	DM mil 12/95	12/96	12/97	US$mil 12/97				
Sales	66,323.0	68,095.0	76,067.0	42,278.0	P/E Ratio	18.3	Price (6/30/98)	118.95
Net Income	1,915.0	2,458.0	2,810.0	1,561.8	P/B Ratio	2.7	52 Wk Hi-Low	130.85-88.65
Book Value	17,491.0	19,490.0	22,155.0	12,313.7	Yield %	1.8	Market Cap	US$32,856mil

Address	Bennigsenplatz 1		Tel 211-4579-1	ADR	VEB	Memb Mgt Bd	W. Bonse-Geuking
	40474 Dusseldorf		Fax 211-457-9501	SEDOL	4942904	Chmn an Mgt Bd	U. Hartmann

In DJ Stoxx 50; In EuroStoxx 50.

Viag

DJGI Industry: **Electrical Utilities (All)**
Stoxx Sector: **Utility**

Viag AG is a German industrial group with activities in packaging, logistics, energy, chemicals, and telecommunications. Its principal operations and sales are within Germany. Viag makes a range of glass, plastic, and metal packaging products and offers steel-trading, transport, and chemicals- and energy-distribution services. It also makes chemicals for the pharmaceutical, industrial, agricultural, and building industries. Logistics accounted for 42% of 1997 revenues; packaging, 22%; energy, 21%; chemicals, 14%; and other, 1%.

	DM mil 12/95	12/96	12/97	US$mil 12/97				
Sales	41,932.5	42,452.3	49,545.2	27,537.2	P/E Ratio	35.7	Price (6/30/98)	1,240.00
Net Income	1,157.8	797.9	859.4	477.7	P/B Ratio	4.1	52 Wk Hi-Low	1,240.0-749.5
Book Value	5,634.6	8,215.1	8,064.8	4,482.4	Yield %	1.1	Market Cap	US$22,369mil

Address	Nymphenburger Str. 37		Tel 89-1254-4522	ADR	VGAGY	CFO	E. Schipporeit
	80335 Munich		Fax 89-1254-4520	SEDOL	4929242	Chmn Mgt Bd	G. Obermeier

Volkswagen

DJGI Industry: **Automobile Manufacturers**
Stoxx Sector: **Automobile**

Volkswagen AG is the largest auto maker in Europe and one of the largest in the world. It produces motor vehicles under the names Volkswagen, Audi, Skoda, and SEAT. In 1997, Volkswagen manufactured a total of 4,290,875 motor vehicles, of which 62% were produced or assembled by foreign subsidiaries. In 1997, it launched the new model series of the VW Golf, the VW Passat Variant, and the Audi A3 and A6, and in 1998, the rebirth of the famous Beetle. Vehicle sales accounted for 80% of 1997 revenues; rental and leasing business, 9%; spare parts, 7%; and others, 4%.

	DM mil 12/95	12/96	12/97	US$mil 12/97				
Sales	88,119.0	100,123.0	113,245.0	62,941.6	P/E Ratio	48.3	Price (6/30/98)	1,740.85
Net Income	354.0	659.0	1,339.0	744.2	P/B Ratio	5.6	52 Wk Hi-Low	1,766.0-883.0
Book Value	10,513.0	11,462.0	12,822.0	7,126.5	Yield %	0.7	Market Cap	US$29,749mil

Address	Volkswagenwerk		Tel 536-190	ADR	VLKAY	Chmn Exec Bd	Ferdinand Piëch
	38436 Wolfsburg		Fax 536-192-8282	SEDOL	4930307	Chmn Supv Bd	Klaus Liesen

Greece

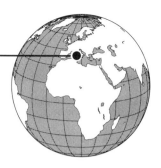

Exchanges:

Athens Stock Exchange

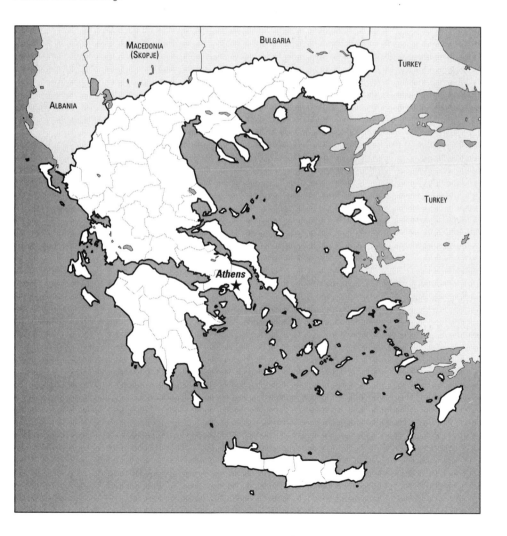

Greece

Jenny Paris
Athens

The drachma's entry in the European Monetary System's exchange rate mechanism (ERM) in March 1998 opened a new era for the Athens Stock Exchange (ASE), which is now aiming for a place among other developed European markets as it attempts to shake off emerging-market status.

Greece's increased chances of joining the European economic and monetary union by 2001 have been reflected in stock prices. Trading volume in 1998 broke through several records previously thought unbeatable.

Since Greece's entry into the exchange rate mechanism, new foreign investors have added US$2 billion to the market's liquidity and average daily trading volume has doubled.

The ASE general share prices index — a composite index representing about 80% of the market's capitalization — gained a stunning 85% in the first half of 1998, or more than 1,000 points. On July 21, a sustained rally led the index to a new all-time record of 2,825.52 points.

Analysts are optimistic that the index could break through the psychological barrier of 3,000 points before year's end, barring any setbacks in the government's economic policy.

International interest prompted the FT/S&P Actuaries World Index to include 32 Greek companies in its world indexes for the first time in May. FT/S&P calculates more 2,000 different indexes daily, from the Americas, Europe, Nordic countries, and the Pacific

Basin. It is owned jointly by FTSE International, Standard and Poor's, and Goldman Sachs.

The Greek market's advance started in 1997, with Greek stocks rallying for most of the year until the market fell victim to the Asian financial crisis in October. Market capitalization almost doubled in 1997 from 1996, amounting to 9.8 trillion drachmas (GRD), while annual trading value jumped to GRD5.8 trillion from just GRD1.9 trillion in 1996. The ASE general index surged 58% from its mark at the end of 1996.

In recent years, bourse officials have been struggling to transform the ASE from a small and illiquid regional market into a sprawling modern exchange that will meet the standards of its European counterparts.

Outgoing stock market president Manolis Xanthakis took steps to improve the market's

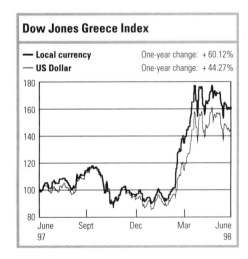

Dow Jones Greece Index

— Local currency   One-year change: + 60.12%
— US Dollar   One-year change: + 44.27%

180	
160	
140	
120	
100	
80	

June Sept Dec Mar June
97   98

transparency and trading practices. He sparked the process of turning paper shares into electronic ones, hired specialized personnel, and set up a stock exchange center in the northern Greek city of Salonika, making it easier for northern Greek companies to be listed.

The bourse's newly appointed president Spyros Kouniakis is expected to continue his predecessor's efforts to modernize the market. The shift to electronic shares is to be completed by the end of 1998, contributing to greater market transparency, and the existing trading system will be upgraded in 1999. The system currently operates with paper shares.

The upgraded electronic trading system will incorporate the trading of bonds and derivatives and will deal with the technical problems involved in the transition to the euro at the start of 1999. Trading currently takes place either on the floor or through remote brokerage operations.

Other steps are planned to upgrade the market, including the introduction of short-selling and securities lending, currently forbidden, and the trading of derivatives. Listing requirements will also be changed to allow local subsidiaries of multinational companies to enter the market.

ASE is also boosting efforts to become a regional capital market center by seeking cooperation with southeastern European

Country Information

Trading Hours:
  Local: 10:45 am - 1:30 pm

  EST: 3:45 am - 6:30 am

  GMT: 0845 - 1130

Population (6/98):
10,662,138

Unemployment (97):
10.1%

Main Industries:
Tourism, food and tobacco processing, textiles, chemicals, metal products, mining, and petroleum

Gross Domestic Product (97):
US$119.11 billion

GDP per Capita (97):
US$11,334.98

Three-Year Average GDP Growth (94-97):
2.7%

Average Annual CPI Growth (96-97):
+ 5.54%

Monetary Unit:
Greek Drachma

Exchange Rate (6/98):
GRD304.80 to US$1.00

bourses and exploiting niche markets such as tourism and shipping.

Cooperation agreements have been signed with the stock exchanges of Bucharest in Romania and Sofia in Bulgaria, and the Greek bourse is looking into similar deals with other Balkan markets. Bourse officials also hope to attract Greece's large number of tourism and shipping companies, most of which have stayed out of the market.

In a bid for greater autonomy from the government, the Exchange floated an offering of 40% of its own stock in 1997, and planned to offer an additional tranche by the end of 1998.

The Greek bourse will have to cope with the effects of the government's ambitious privatization program, as up to 49% of most public-sector companies will be listed by the end of 1999.

Capital market officials, however, do not fear liquidity problems as a result of the increased privatization activity, saying that privatized listings will represent only 5% of the market's capitalization, which at the end of June 1998 amounted to GRD17.6 trillion.

With most listed Greek companies relatively small by international standards, the privatization of large state enterprises and consolidation in the banking sector are expected to create large capitalization stocks that will appeal to foreign investors.

Ten Largest Capitalized Companies In The Dow Greece Index
as of 6/30/98

Stock	Market Cap. US$ Thousands
Hellenic Telecom	12,899,649
Hellenic Bottling	3,881,421
Alpha Credit Bank	3,560,738
National Bank of Greece	3,466,544
Ergo Bank	2,163,776
Commercial Bank of Greece	1,611,005
Ionian Bank	1,318,723
Titan Cement	1,242,882
Intracom	1,191,692
Heracles General Cement	1,174,536

After years of limited presence in Greece's volatile market, foreigners have made a strong showing since last March, focusing on shares in the telecom, banking, and cement industries that represent slightly more than half of the trading volume.

Foreign investors can reclaim a 35% tax withheld from dividends on listed shares. They are also free to import capital for investment in securities and to reexport any capital gains that are not taxed in Greece.

Foreign funds are expected to be drawn to in Hellenic Telecommunications Organization (OTE) this autumn, for what is expected to be the biggest flotation in the Greek market's history. OTE, already the market's largest listing, with a 28% share of total market capitalization, will offer another 15% stake in addition to its already floated 20% stake.

OTE has doubled its share price since it was first listed in spring 1996, to about

GRD8,000 in mid-July 1998 from GRD4,000.

The second largest state company to enter the bourse was Hellenic Petroleum, which made a successful debut June 30, 1998, posting sharp gains in its first week of trading.

But the driving force of the market is the banking industry which, in its bid to consolidate ahead of the euro's introduction in 1999, has come in to the spotlight. The state-run National Bank of Greece, the largest banking group in Greece, and Alpha Credit Bank, the nation's largest private lender, are the leading market players.

The cement sector is dominated by Titan General Cement Co. and Heracles General Cement Co.

The number of listed companies grew to 235 in the first half of 1998 from 227 in 1997.

The Athens bourse has come a long way since it was first established in 1876 as a self-regulated public institution. For almost a century, the market operated as a closed club in which only a handful of shares were traded.

But regulations introduced in 1988, which changed the market's concept and function, led to its rapid expansion over the past decade. A small capital market and a central securities depository were established, and the Exchange's board of directors was enlarged.

Market Sector Performance In The Dow Jones Greece Index
1 Year Change Through 6/30/98

Market Sector	Change % (US$)
Technology	117.93
Consumer, Non-Cyclical	62.16
Financial	40.30
Basic Materials	38.83
Industrial	34.30
Utilities	21.05

Since then, the number of listed companies has doubled, and capitalization and trading volumes have soared. Capitalization was less than GRD1 trillion in 1988. The average value of the daily trading volume was at US$1.2 million in 1988, compared with US$171 million in 1998.

Aktor

DJGI Industry: **Heavy Construction**
Stoxx Sector: **Construction**

Aktor SA is a construction company that builds highways and streets, bridges and tunnels, utility lines, and residential and industrial buildings. The company operates one subsidiary in Greece, Electron SA, in which it holds a 50% share. Aktor closed a deal with Hyatt Regency Hotels & Tourism, the American chain of hotels, involving the construction of a luxurious hotel in Salonica. The project has an estimated cost of GDR7.35 billion and the hotel is expected to be operational by the end of 1998.

	DR mil 12/94	12/95	12/96	US$mil 12/96					
Sales	2,138.6	3,528.3	4,081.5	16.7	P/E Ratio		19.0	Price (6/30/98)	2,650.00
Net Income	2,062.9	2,023.2	1,751.9	7.2	P/B Ratio		2.6	52 Wk Hi-Low	3,560.3-1,900.0
Book Value	11,095.7	12,019.7	13,023.3	53.2	Yield %		2.8	Market Cap	US$119.4mil

Address	18 Filelinon St.	Tel	68-44-312	ADR	--	President	--
	Chalandri, Athens	Fax	68-15-794	SEDOL	4018247	Chairman	D. Koutras

Alpha Credit Bank

DJGI Industry: **Banks - Regional (All)**
Stoxx Sector: **Bank**

Alpha Credit Bank SA is a multibranch commercial bank that provides a range of depository, lending, and related financial services to individuals and companies. The bank offers investment advice and brokerage, insurance, leasing, and other services. It operates 135 branches and sub-branches throughout Greece and has a network of 184 ATM machines, the largest number in that country. Interest on government securities accounted for 36% of 1997 revenues; interest and fees on loans, 30%; commissions and fees, 13%; trading account income, 11%; and other operating income, 10%.

	DR mil 12/95	12/96	12/97	US$mil 12/97					
Revenues	301,697.3	337,272.3	380,856.7	1,342.0	P/E Ratio		18.3	Price (6/30/98)	24,665
Net Income	39,363.8	47,212.2	60,781.9	214.2	P/B Ratio		4.8	52 Wk Hi-Low	24,705.0-13,414.1
Book Value	115,697.7	138,860.8	230,241.1	811.3	Yield %		2.7	Market Cap	US$3,560.7mil

Address	40 Stadiou St.	Tel	32-60-000	ADR	--	President	--
	102 52 Athens	Fax	--	SEDOL	4235864	Chairman	Y.S. Costopoulos

Alpha Finance

DJGI Industry: **Securities Brokers**
Stoxx Sector: **Financial Services**

Alpha Finance SA is an investment bank engaged in the business of underwriting and the distribution of securities. It also offers mercantile financing and bond and equity portfolio management services through its subsidiaries. Alpha Finance is in the process of acquiring Alpha Crimatistiriaki, which will enable the company to continue to develop its strength as an investment organization. Alpha Finance will obtain 100% of Alpha Crimatistiriaki through an exchange of shares. Commissions and fees account for the majority of the company's revenues.

	DR mil 12/94	12/95	12/96	US$mil 12/96					
Sales	7,480.2	2,493.7	10,073.7	41.1	P/E Ratio		1.1	Price (6/30/98)	11,500
Net Income	1,360.9	2,414.5	2,555.4	10.4	P/B Ratio		0.4	52 Wk Hi-Low	14,450.0-7,050.0
Book Value	3,439.2	6,744.7	10,732.2	43.8	Yield %		26.1	Market Cap	US$240.5mil

Address	5 Merlin St.	Tel	36-09-054	ADR	--	President	--
	106 71 Athens	Fax	36-04-040	SEDOL	4036506	Chmn & Mng Dir.	P.A. Vourloumis

Altec

DJGI Industry: **Diversified Technology**
Stoxx Sector: **Technology**

Altec SA distributes a wide range of personal computers, laptops, printers, peripherals, and software and is a leader in the Greek information technology market. It also offers repair and support service to all brands of computers through Service on Line, System Software Support, and BBS Services. Altec sells its products in over 85 outlets and was granted ISO 9001 certification in 1996. In July 1998, Altec purchased a 70% stake in Microland, another top Greek technology company, strengthening its position in the home computing sector.

	DR mil 12/94	12/95	12/96	US$mil 12/96					
Sales	N/A	10,154.8	18,528.6	75.7	P/E Ratio		173.8	Price (6/30/98)	6,360.00
Net Income	N/A	392.1	684.5	2.8	P/B Ratio		51.4	52 Wk Hi-Low	9,460.0-742.2
Book Value	N/A	1,403.1	2,313.8	9.5	Yield %		1.3	Market Cap	US$457.0mil

Address	47 Evelpidon St.	Tel	82-04-000	ADR	--	President	--
	113 62 Athens	Fax	88-16-187	SEDOL	5078682	Chairman & CEO	T. Athanassoulis

Aluminium

DJGI Industry: **Aluminum**
Stoxx Sector: **Basic Resources**

Aluminium Company of Greece SA produces and processes aluminum, trades aluminum, alumina, and bauxite, and manufactures related products such as tubes, cans, cables, and castings. The company operates one production unit in Veotia, Greece, and two subsidiaries -- Epalme SA (35%) and Delphi-Distomon SA (99.98%). Aluminium of Greece SA was awarded the ISO 9002 in 1994 for both the aluminum and the alumina plants. It has both domestic sales and exports, which are mainly to France and Italy. Aluminum accounted for 78% of 1997 revenues; alumina, 21%; and other, 1%.

	DR mil 12/95	12/96	12/97	US$mil 12/97					
Sales	90,141.3	82,135.3	95,962.6	338.1	P/E Ratio		NMF	Price (6/30/98)	18,000
Net Income	5,013.6	-523.5	3,725.6	13.1	P/B Ratio		1.9	52 Wk Hi-Low	24,690.0-12,300.0
Book Value	67,306.0	66,721.9	71,931.5	253.5	Yield %		7.0	Market Cap	US$310.1mil

Address	1 Sekeri St.	Tel	36-93-000	ADR	--	President	--
	106 71 Athens	Fax	36-93-615	SEDOL	4026778	Chairman	B. Legrand

Aspis Pronia

DJGI Industry: **Insurance - Full Line**
Stoxx Sector: **Insurance**

Aspis Pronia General Insurance SA, a subsidiary of Aspis Group, is one of the leading insurance companies in Greece. The company provides primarily general insurance and reinsurance and represents Greek and foreign insurance companies in Greece and abroad. In May 1998, the company signed an agreement with Swiss Life, making it a collaborator with the Swiss company in the group insurances sector. Aspis increased its life insurance production significantly, and its department in Sweden developed rapidly in 1997 by targeting Swedish citizens and Greek immigrants.

	DR mil 12/94	12/95	12/96	US$mil 12/96				
Revenues	2,430.1	1,593.2	1,272.0	5.2	P/E Ratio	NMF	Price (6/30/98)	3,665.00
Net Income	7.6	-261.5	-102.7	-0.4	P/B Ratio	22.1	52 Wk Hi-Low	4,000.0-2,205.0
Book Value	577.4	2,910.1	6,634.0	27.1	Yield %	0.0	Market Cap	US$298.3mil

Address	10 Mavromihali St.	Tel 36-06-411	ADR	--	President	--
	106 79 Athens	Fax 36-01-741	SEDOL	4460257	Chairman	G. Vasilikos

Athens Medical Center

DJGI Industry: **Health Care Providers**
Stoxx Sector: **Consumer Non-Cyclical**

Athens Medical Center SA operates two general medical and surgical hospitals in Greece and one overseas. It also operates five subsidiaries in Greece: Center of Medical Research SA (98.5%), Iatriki Techniki SA (51%), Institute of Isotopic Studies (50%), Electronystagmographic SA (40%), and Aggeiologike Dierevnisi Ltd. (20%). One of the company's goals is to develop and trade software products in the welfare and health sectors. Additionally, the company's investment program includes the operation of a diagnostic medical center in Bulgaria and the former Yugoslavia.

	DR mil 12/94	12/95	12/96	US$mil 12/96				
Sales	8,681.5	10,477.6	12,843.3	52.5	P/E Ratio	60.5	Price (6/30/98)	5,990.00
Net Income	1,229.1	1,677.9	1,966.3	8.0	P/B Ratio	21.9	52 Wk Hi-Low	6,880.0-2,100.0
Book Value	4,293.6	4,860.5	5,439.8	22.2	Yield %	1.4	Market Cap	US$390.6mil

Address	5-7 Distomou St.	Tel 68-62-111	ADR	--	President	--
	151 25 Marousi, Athens	Fax 68-98-555	SEDOL	4056612	Chmn & Mng Dir	G. Apostolopoulos

Attica Enterprises

DJGI Industry: **Marine Transportation**
Stoxx Sector: **Industrials**

Attica Enterprises SA of Greece deals in freight and passenger transportation services. The company operates four high-speed vessels on the Adriatic Sea. In April 1998, Attica doubled its capacity on the Patras-to-Ancona route to four SuperFast ferries, with the delivery of two new craft from Kvaerner Masa of Finland. The company signed a contract with Howaldtswerke Deutsche Werft AG for the construction of four high-speed vessels. In the first quarter of 1998, profit rose to GDR643 million. Attica is expected to make a rights issue in 1998.

	DR mil 12/94	12/95	12/96	US$mil 12/96				
Sales	N/A	9,085.3	14,012.5	57.2	P/E Ratio	45.7	Price (6/30/98)	4,390.00
Net Income	287.8	2,144.3	2,820.5	11.5	P/B Ratio	6.7	52 Wk Hi-Low	5,940.0-2,222.1
Book Value	10,725.7	16,252.5	19,321.7	78.9	Yield %	1.1	Market Cap	US$999.3mil

Address	157 Alkionidon St.	Tel 96-57-777	ADR	--	President	--
	166 73 Voula	Fax 96-57-970	SEDOL	4051446	Chairman	P. Panagopoulos

Commercial Bank Of Greece

DJGI Industry: **Banks - Regional (All)**
Stoxx Sector: **Bank**

Commercial Bank of Greece SA offers depository, lending, and other financial services such as investment advice, life insurance, and brokerage. It has the second-largest banking network in Greece and holds about 20% of the domestic market. The bank is undergoing resructuring and is considering a merger with Ionian Bank. The bank also offers international banking services. Interest and fees on loans accounts for 86% of 1996 revenues; commission and fees, 11%; and trading account income and other operating income, 3%.

	DR mil 12/95	12/96	12/97	US$mil 12/97				
Revenues	585,171.3	614,267.2	602,504.6	2,123.1	P/E Ratio	19.3	Price (6/30/98)	22,570
Net Income	24,278.1	-2,904.6	17,920.7	63.1	P/B Ratio	2.4	52 Wk Hi-Low	24,695.0-8,650.0
Book Value	185,275.3	198,421.1	205,726.0	724.9	Yield %	1.3	Market Cap	US$1,611.0mil

Address	11 Sofokleous St.	Tel 32-84-000	ADR	--	General Manager	G. Mihelis
	102 35 Athens	Fax 32-53-746	SEDOL	4212823	Chairman	K. Georgoutsakos

Delta Dairy

DJGI Industry: **Other Food**
Stoxx Sector: **Food & Beverage**

Delta Dairy SA is the Greek market leader in the production of foods, including milk products, fruit juices, ice cream, yogurts, and frozen foods. The company's products are sold in eight other countries and it is involved in various joint ventures and international alliances. In 1997, Delta launched 18 new products and acquired VIGLA SA. Delta holds a 45% share of the Greek ice cream market and its network includes 25,000 outlets. Delta plays a pivotal role in the development of cattle breeding in Greece; it has its own cattle and collaborates with 1,700 professional breeders.

	DR mil 12/95	12/96	12/97	US$mil 12/97				
Sales	73,727.9	85,128.0	98,092.2	345.7	P/E Ratio	38.3	Price (6/30/98)	3,630.00
Net Income	1,915.5	2,263.8	2,347.7	8.3	P/B Ratio	1.8	52 Wk Hi-Low	4,335.0-2,600.0
Book Value	57,606.4	59,130.1	59,227.4	208.7	Yield %	1.9	Market Cap	US$203.9mil

Address	3 Kerkyras St.	Tel 34-94-000	ADR	--	CEO	A. Daskalopoulos
	177 78 Tavros	Fax 34-94-040	SEDOL	4260190	Chmn Bd of Dir	A. Daskalopoulos

Elais
DJGI Industry: **Other Food**
Stoxx Sector: **Food & Beverage**

Elais Oleaginous Products (Elais) SA is a leading Greek edible oils and fats processor. The company produces, processes, and sells margarine, cooking fats, olive oil, seed oils, and other related products. Products distributed include Unilever brands and Lipton, Zwan, John West, Calve, Linea, Raguletto, and Iglo frozen foods. Cooking oil includes the Friol brand. The group also distributes general industrial products worldwide and is boosting its exports to retail sale chains in Canada and the United States. In 1997, exports increased more than 37% over 1996 exports.

	DR mil 12/95	12/96	12/97	US$mil 12/97				
Sales	60,423.5	63,148.0	54,060.2	190.5	P/E Ratio	23.2	Price (6/30/98)	11,500
Net Income	3,563.4	3,406.9	4,273.3	15.1	P/B Ratio	5.7	52 Wk Hi-Low	15,145.0-7,230.0
Book Value	11,962.1	13,645.5	14,307.4	50.4	Yield %	4.6	Market Cap	US$255.2mil

Address	74 Athinon-Pireos Ave.	Tel 48-96-001	ADR	--	President	--
	185 47 Attiki	Fax 48-32-991	SEDOL	4306254	Chairman	S. Desyllas

Elval
DJGI Industry: **Aluminum**
Stoxx Sector: **Basic Resources**

Elval Aluminium Processing Co. SA, founded in 1981, is a Greek metals products company. It primarily processes and paints aluminum and galvanized steel and laminates aluminum foil with paper. The company specializes in aluminum ducts. Elval exports approximately 80% of its products to more than 65 countries in the European Union, the United States, and the Far East. Elval is a subsidiariy of the Viohalko Group. With the completion of investment programs, the company expects total production of rolled products to reach 150,000 tons by the year 2000.

	DR mil 12/94	12/95	12/96	US$mil 12/96				
Sales	N/A	N/A	47,334.4	193.3	P/E Ratio	61.6	Price (6/30/98)	4,700.00
Net Income	N/A	N/A	2,652.1	10.8	P/B Ratio	10.7	52 Wk Hi-Low	5,220.0-1,629.2
Book Value	N/A	N/A	15,272.7	62.4	Yield %	1.0	Market Cap	US$490.5mil

Address	Moira St.	Tel 53-92-178	ADR	--	Mem Mgt Bd	G. Konstantakopoulos
	196 00 Mandra, Attiki	Fax 55-51-077	SEDOL	5078693	Mem Bd Dir	E. Rabaounis

Ergo Bank
DJGI Industry: **Banks - Regional (All)**
Stoxx Sector: **Bank**

Ergo Bank SA is a multibranch commercial bank providing depository, lending, and related financial services through its network of 70 branches in Greece. The bank is involved in securities trading through its wholly owned subsidiary Ergosecurities, computer-technology services through Ergodata, equipment leasing through 62%-owned Ergoleasing, and portfolio-management services through Ergoinvest and Ergo Mutual Funds. Ergo Bank also holds 14.4% of Allianz Life Insurance Co. Interest and fees on loans accounted for 42% of 1997 revenues.

	DR mil 12/95	12/96	12/97	US$mil 12/97				
Revenues	147,670.5	157,040.4	175,254.5	617.5	P/E Ratio	17.0	Price (6/30/98)	26,005
Net Income	25,665.7	29,061.6	37,139.6	130.9	P/B Ratio	5.6	52 Wk Hi-Low	30,990.0-12,910.0
Book Value	63,546.4	76,091.4	116,813.3	411.6	Yield %	3.1	Market Cap	US$2,163.8mil

Address	3-5 Kolokotroni & Voulis St.	Tel 36-01-011	ADR	--	President	--
	106 79 Athens	Fax 32-28-906	SEDOL	4303073	Chairman Bd Dir	X. Nikitas

Ethniki General Insurance
DJGI Industry: **Insurance - Full Line**
Stoxx Sector: **Insurance**

Ethniki General Insurance SA (EGI) is one of the largest insurance companies in Greece. It has general insurance and reinsurance in Greece and abroad, and represents foreign insurance organizations. EGI offers life, fire, marine, motor, and other insurance coverage to its customers. The company operates 79 branches and 149 life insurance offices throughout Greece. Premiums earned account for 96% of the company's revenues and other operating income accounts for 4%. EGI currently employs 4,200 insurance agents.

	DR mil 12/94	12/95	12/96	US$mil 12/96				
Revenues	74,878.6	81,919.2	5,207.7	21.3	P/E Ratio	46.4	Price (6/30/98)	7,195.00
Net Income	1,410.7	1,078.7	1,275.8	5.2	P/B Ratio	4.6	52 Wk Hi-Low	9,790.0-3,680.0
Book Value	10,078.4	10,466.7	12,877.3	52.6	Yield %	0.0	Market Cap	US$351.6mil

Address	8 Karageorghi Servias St.	Tel 32-22-121	ADR	--	General Manager	M. Nektarios
	102 10 Athens	Fax 32-36-101	SEDOL	4314536	Chairman	K. Stamoulis

Goody's
DJGI Industry: **Food Retailers & Wholesalers**
Stoxx Sector: **Consumer Non-Cyclical**

Goody's SA is the largest operator of fast food and hamburger chains in Greece. The company operates restaurants in all major Greek cities, and is expanding its business in the Balkan states. It operates 130 fast food restaurants and 13 Flocafe espresso bars, and will open 5 more restaurants by the end of fiscal 1998. Goody's is seeking final shareholder approval to merge its operations late in 1998 with Touristiki Ependytiki in a move to improve the efficiency of the two companies and to take advantage of economies of scale. Touristiki is a partner in 34 Goody's and Flocafe outlets.

	DR mil 12/94	12/95	12/96	US$mil 12/96				
Sales	11,366.5	17,836.7	20,214.7	82.6	P/E Ratio	35.8	Price (6/30/98)	7,570.00
Net Income	683.2	1,405.8	2,114.0	8.6	P/B Ratio	9.6	52 Wk Hi-Low	9,500.0-3,760.0
Book Value	5,869.4	6,372.4	7,856.0	32.1	Yield %	0.9	Market Cap	US$248.4mil

Address	27 Ploutonos St.	Tel 42-62- 61	ADR	--	Managing Director	V. Mpogiatzis
	546 55 Thessaloniki	Fax 42-91-24	SEDOL	4366430	Chairman	A. Folias

Halcor

DJGI Industry: **Industrial - Diversified**
Stoxx Sector: **Industrials**

Halcor SA, with over 50 years' experience in manufacturing copper and copper alloy products, enjoys a leading position in the Greek market as well as a strong international presence. The company manufactures copper and brass sheets and strips for architectural use; copper and brass circles for cartridge case cups and disks for artillery shells and coin blanks; and a range of extruded and drawn round, square, hexagonal, and hollow brass rods for industrial and other technical applications. Halcor also makes Talos brand copper tubes for the refrigeration and air conditioning industry.

	DR mil 12/94	12/95	12/96	US$mil 12/96					
Sales	N/A	2,406.1	2,425.5	9.9	P/E Ratio	N/A	Price (6/30/98)	5,095.00
Net Income	N/A	482.5	536.3	2.2	P/B Ratio	N/A	52 Wk Hi-Low	5,095.0-1,231.0
Book Value	N/A	294.9	357.4	1.5	Yield %	N/A	Market Cap	US$467.9mil

Address	252 Pireaus St.	Tel 48-13-651	ADR	--	President	--
	177 78 Athens	Fax 48-98-394	SEDOL	5266142	Chairman	E. Rabaounis

Hellas Can

DJGI Industry: **Containers & Packaging**
Stoxx Sector: **Industrials**

Hellas Can SA is involved in the production, trading, and import of packaging products as well as the raw materials, mainly metal containers and metal cans, used in the food and beverage industries. The company operates two production factories in Greece, one in Thessaloniki and the other in Korinthos. Beer and beverage cans accounted for 67% of 1997 revenues; food cans, 23%; aerosol cans, 5%; and other cans, 5%. French company CarnaudMetalbox aquired 72.79% of Hellas Can's shares in 1998.

	DR mil 12/95	12/96	12/97	US$mil 12/97					
Sales	28,365.3	29,895.6	26,120.4	92.0	P/E Ratio	10.6	Price (6/30/98)	4,900.00
Net Income	3,833.7	4,094.2	3,968.7	14.0	P/B Ratio	2.0	52 Wk Hi-Low	5,150.0-3,580.0
Book Value	20,220.9	23,073.5	25,598.4	90.2	Yield %	3.1	Market Cap	US$154.7mil

Address	Thiseos & Solonos 135	Tel 67-73-461	ADR	--	President	--
	176 75 Athens	Fax 67-73-203	SEDOL	4420682	Chmn & Mng Dir	A.P. Kapoor

Hellenic Bottling

DJGI Industry: **Soft Drinks**
Stoxx Sector: **Food & Beverage**

Hellenic Bottling Co. (HBC) is the leading Greek producer, bottler, and distributor of soft drinks. It produces and sells primarily Coca-Cola Co. soft drinks, but also processes fruit juices and mineral water. Through subsidiaries, the company produces Coca-Cola and other soft drinks in the Republic of Ireland, Northern Ireland, Romania, Moldova, Russia, and Bulgaria. The company controls 65% of Greece's soft drinks market. Hellenic Bottling has established a joint venture with Athenian Breweries SA to produce beer in Bulgaria.

	DR mil 12/95	12/96	12/97	US$mil 12/97					
Sales	143,655.2	143,112.7	273,069.3	962.2	P/E Ratio	40.7	Price (6/30/98)	9,400.00
Net Income	23,764.6	17,249.8	27,068.4	95.4	P/B Ratio	15.8	52 Wk Hi-Low	12,500.0-4,850.0
Book Value	57,453.4	61,239.9	120,079.3	423.1	Yield %	0.8	Market Cap	US$3,881.4mil

Address	58 Kifissias Ave. & Delfon 1	Tel 61-83-100	ADR	--	Managing Director	C. Komninos
	151 25 Maroussi, Athens	Fax 68-95-515	SEDOL	4420723	Chairman	G.A. David

Hellenic Sugar Industry

DJGI Industry: **Other Food**
Stoxx Sector: **Food & Beverage**

Hellenic Sugar Industry SA (HSI) is involved primarily in the refining, production, and distribution of refined and raw sugar, molasses, and beet pulp, which is used for livestock feed. The company operates five industrial units throughout Greece -- in Larissa, Plati, Serres, Xanthe, and in Orestiada. Hellenic Sugar Industry's other activities include the production of potato seed, the conducting of farming research, and the development of educational programs for its staff. The company is the only sugar producer in Greece.

	DR mil 06/95	06/96	06/97	US$mil 06/97					
Sales	81,592.1	84,013.5	75,189.9	264.9	P/E Ratio	26.2	Price (6/30/98)	2,980.00
Net Income	7,973.3	8,156.7	3,506.7	12.4	P/B Ratio	2.5	52 Wk Hi-Low	3,650.0-1,025.0
Book Value	30,069.3	34,867.0	37,027.2	130.5	Yield %	2.2	Market Cap	US$300.4mil

Address	34 Mitropoleos St.	Tel 36-21-315	ADR	--	V President	K. Amanatidis
	541 10 Thessaloniki	Fax 27-39-52	SEDOL	4416614	Chmn Bd of Dir	A. Papagiannis

Hellenic Technodomiki

DJGI Industry: **Heavy Construction**
Stoxx Sector: **Construction**

Hellenic Technodomiki SA is one of the largest general contractors in Greece, specializing in turnkey and phase-to-phase contract services. The company is engaged in heavy construction, including highways, bridges, irrigation projects, flood control projects, hospitals, residential complexes, and other buildings. It holds a 50% interest in Technolit SA and a 24% interest in Violignit SA. Hellenic Technodomiki is participating in a consortium led by the French group GTM for the construction of the Rio-Antirio bridge project, which will link Rio with Antirio in central Greece.

	DR mil 12/94	12/95	12/96	US$mil 12/96					
Sales	16,118.8	16,743.7	17,080.4	69.8	P/E Ratio	9.7	Price (6/30/98)	2,670.00
Net Income	1,721.8	1,637.3	2,299.9	9.4	P/B Ratio	2.4	52 Wk Hi-Low	5,075.0-1,870.0
Book Value	7,535.9	8,219.7	9,471.3	38.7	Yield %	2.4	Market Cap	US$96.4mil

Address	10 Davaki St.	Tel 64-96-821	ADR	HLTQF	President	--
	115 26 Athens	Fax 64-96-850	SEDOL	4205351	Chairman	G. Papadakis

Hellenic Telecom

DJGI Industry: **Telephone Utilities (All)**
Stoxx Sector: **Telecom**

Hellenic Telecommunications Organization SA (OTE) is Greece's state-controlled telecommnications monopoly. It provides telecomunication services throughout Greece by means of its network of 5.5 million lines which cover the entire area. The company also provides Internet and mobile phone services. In March 1998, OTE signed a contract to acquire 90% of ArmenTel, the national telecommunications operator of Armenia, for $142.5 million. In June 1997, the company offered 12% of its stake through a public offering and a rights issue, raising its privatized stake to 20%.

	DR mil 12/95	12/96	12/97	US$mil 12/97				
Sales	593,032.8	679,483.9	810,808.7	2,660.1	P/E Ratio	53.8	Price (6/30/98)	7,800.00
Net Income	122,132.5	147,940.9	180,608.8	592.5	P/B Ratio	4.4	52 Wk Hi-Low	9,450.0-4,419.0
Book Value	433,652.5	640,697.0	909,728.1	2,984.7	Yield %	1.1	Market Cap	US$12,900mil

Address	99 Kifisias Ave.	Tel 61-15-011	ADR	HLTOY	Managing Director	P. Lambrou
	151 81 Marousi, Athens	Fax 32-43-668	SEDOL	5051605	Chairman	D. Papoulias

Heracles General Cement

DJGI Industry: **Building Materials**
Stoxx Sector: **Construction**

Heracles General Cement SA (IHGC) is Greece's leading cement producer and is a major exporter, with exports directed to the United States, Europe, and the Middle East. The company's main subsidiary is Halkis Cement. Heracles was the first company to be privatized when Italy's Calcestruzzi S.p.A. (I.CAL) bought a controlling stake in 1991. In 1996, control was transferred to holding company Concretum, which currently holds a 54% stake, the National Bank of Greece (NBG) has 33%, and the remaining stake is floated on the Athens Stock Exchange.

	DR mil 12/94	12/95	12/96	US$mil 12/96				
Sales	87,678.6	99,597.7	111,683.0	456.1	P/E Ratio	43.6	Price (6/30/98)	7,090.00
Net Income	5,256.0	8,738.3	8,206.4	33.5	P/B Ratio	44.9	52 Wk Hi-Low	9,800.0-4,650.0
Book Value	56,179.3	61,856.9	73,638.1	300.8	Yield %	2.0	Market Cap	US$1,174.5mil

Address	49-51 Sophocli Venizelou St.	Tel 28-98-232	ADR	--	President	--
	141 23 Athens	Fax 28-19-406	SEDOL	4421555	Chairman	M.U. Giudici

Intracom

DJGI Industry: **Communications Technology**
Stoxx Sector: **Technology**

Intracom SA produces and distributes electronic and telecommunications devices. Products include digital and analog systems, telephone sets, modems, pagers, and digital switches. Intracom conducts research on optical communications and digital technologies. The company exports its products to Hungary, Romania, Bulgaria, Albania, and Pakistan. In January 1998, Intracom and Northrop Grumman Corp. signed an agreement to pursue a $450 million contract to supply the Greek Air Force with military surveillance aircraft.

	DR mil 12/94	12/95	12/96	US$mil 12/96				
Sales	160,189.4	152,031.2	143,191.3	584.8	P/E Ratio	32.6	Price (6/30/98)	10,305
Net Income	11,418.5	7,294.1	12,928.3	52.8	P/B Ratio	8.9	52 Wk Hi-Low	13,150.0-3,988.1
Book Value	34,942.6	37,879.3	47,088.6	192.3	Yield %	0.9	Market Cap	US$1,191.7mil

Address	19.5th Klm. Markopoulo Ave.	Tel 66-44-961	ADR	--	V Chmn & Mng Dir	C. Dimitriadis
	190 02 Peania	Fax 66-44-379	SEDOL	5482023	Chmn & Mng Dir	S. Kokkalis

Ionian Bank

DJGI Industry: **Banks - Regional (All)**
Stoxx Sector: **Bank**

Ionian and Popular Bank of Greece SA (Ionian Bank) is a multibranch commercial bank that offers a wide range of commercial banking and related services. The group has the fourth largest commercial banking network in Greece, with 225 branches. In 1997, the bank opened five new branches. Activities include retail banking, credit card services, foreign exchange and investment, state bonds, insurance brokering and underwriting, and lease financing services. Ionian Bank is currently in the process of being privatized.

	DR mil 12/95	12/96	12/97	US$mil 12/97				
Revenues	196,317.7	211,185.0	214,578.9	756.1	P/E Ratio	107.2	Price (6/30/98)	14,353
Net Income	10,250.2	N/A	3,750.8	13.2	P/B Ratio	4.2	52 Wk Hi-Low	14,800.0-4,500.0
Book Value	87,456.7	86,744.5	95,322.7	335.9	Yield %	0.0	Market Cap	US$1,318.7mil

Address	45 Panepistimiou St.	Tel 32-25-501	ADR	--	President	--
	102 43 Athens	Fax 32-22-882	SEDOL	4489337	Chmn & Mng Dir	C. Stamatopoulos

Michaniki

DJGI Industry: **Heavy Construction**
Stoxx Sector: **Construction**

Michaniki SA is one of the largest construction companies in Greece. The company is engaged primarily in the construction of highways, industrial and residential buildings, as well as the consturction of bridges and tunnels. Michaniki also produces construction and building materials such as sand and ores. In 1998, the company won the bid for the construction of the hydroelectric dam for the Public Power Corp. at Temenos as well as the four bridge sections in Mesovounio Krystalopigi in northern Greece. Michaniki holds a 34.52% stake in the Casino of Rhodes SA.

	DR mil 12/94	12/95	12/96	US$mil 12/96				
Sales	17,049.5	17,916.9	18,893.8	77.2	P/E Ratio	9.5	Price (6/30/98)	1,600.00
Net Income	3,511.4	2,772.0	3,634.9	14.8	P/B Ratio	1.2	52 Wk Hi-Low	2,310.0-1,195.0
Book Value	22,441.4	23,323.9	29,669.6	121.2	Yield %	7.5	Market Cap	US$107.2mil

Address	1 Komninon St.	Tel 61-43-340	ADR	--	President	--
	546 24 Thessaloniki	Fax 61-43-356	SEDOL	4588784	Chmn & Gen Mngr	P.S. Emfietzoglou

National Bank of Greece

DJGI Industry: **Banks - Regional (All)**
Stoxx Sector: **Bank**

National Bank of Greece SA is the largest state-run commercial bank in Greece, offering a full range of financial services, including commercial banking, life insurance, investment advice, and security brokerage through its network of over 600 branches, both at home and abroad. The bank dominates the Greek banking sector with 40% of deposits and 25% of lending. Interest on loans accounted for 51% of 1997 revenues; interest on government securities, 31%; commissions and fees, 9%; trading account income, 6%; and sale of securities and other income, 3%.

	DR mil 12/95	12/96	12/97	US$mil 12/97					
Revenues	1,145,058	1,265,919	1,464,390	5,160.1	P/E Ratio	45.4	Price (6/30/98)		38,990
Net Income	45,650.5	19,112.5	45,298.1	159.6	P/B Ratio	4.2	52 Wk Hi-Low		48,300.0-15,916.7
Book Value	225,257.1	198,299.7	260,635.1	918.4	Yield %	2.4	Market Cap		US$3,466.5mil

Address	86 Eolou St.	Tel 32-10-411	ADR	NBGRYP	President	--
	102 32 Athens	Fax 32-28-187	SEDOL	4625959	Chairman & CEO	T. Karatzas

National Mortgage Bank

DJGI Industry: **Diversified Financial Services**
Stoxx Sector: **Financial Services**

National Mortgage Bank of Greece provides lending, depository and related financial services, and specializes in mortgages. It is Greece's leading bank in the housing loans market. National Mortgage is a major subsidiary of the National Bank of Greece, the country's largest state-run commercial bank. In 1997, it merged with the National Housing Bank, another National Bank subsidiary, and together they have a 70% share in the mortgage lending market. In 1997, the bank's assets rose to GDR2.5 trillion. Interest and fees on loans account for about 75% of revenues.

	DR mil 12/94	12/95	12/96	US$mil 12/96					
Revenues	151,306.7	160,414.1	225,691.3	921.8	P/E Ratio	9.3	Price (6/30/98)		19,150
Net Income	6,644.4	16,705.1	24,117.3	98.5	P/B Ratio	3.0	52 Wk Hi-Low		30,200.0-12,700.0
Book Value	44,135.8	56,466.7	74,710.5	305.1	Yield %	4.2	Market Cap		US$851.9mil

Address	40 Panepistimiou St.	Tel 36-48-311	ADR	--	President	--
	102 10 Athens	Fax 36-22-281	SEDOL	4627018	Chairman	N. Bertsos

Papastratos Cigarette

DJGI Industry: **Tobacco**
Stoxx Sector: **Consumer Non-Cyclical**

Papastratos Cigarette Co. is the largest Greek manufacturer and trader of cigarettes and tobacco products, with a 38% share of the market. Brand names include Assos, Saga, Old Navy, and others. Papastratos recently entered into a cooperation agreement with Philip Morris Co. Ltd. in the United States to manufacture and distribute Marlboro brand cigarettes in Greece. Papastratos has begun expanding into countries such as Albania, the former Yugoslavia, Moldavia, Iraq, the Balkan States, Russia, and Israel. Approximately 50% of Papastratos' turnover is accounted for by exports.

	DR mil 12/95	12/96	12/97	US$mil 12/97					
Sales	84,589.7	90,242.1	94,894.1	334.4	P/E Ratio	18.8	Price (6/30/98)		6,695.00
Net Income	7,743.7	6,785.4	7,567.0	26.7	P/B Ratio	4.5	52 Wk Hi-Low		8,190.0-4,500.0
Book Value	24,658.2	28,273.4	29,646.6	104.5	Yield %	4.9	Market Cap		US$418.9mil

Address	3 Paparrigopoulou St.	Tel 41-20-941	ADR	--	V Chmn Bd Dir	D.P. Iliadis
	105 61 Athens	Fax 41-12-303	SEDOL	4930738	Chmn Bd Dir	A. Averoff

Sidenor

DJGI Industry: **Steel**
Stoxx Sector: **Basic Resources**

Sidenor SA is a leading Greek steel producer, with more than 30 years of experience in the casting and rolling of steel products. The company primarily manufactures a range of specialized steel products, which includes concrete reinforcing steel in bars and coils, merchant bars, wire rod in coils, hot rolled strip, prefabricated wire mesh, and standard wire mesh. In 1997, Sidenor reported 480,000 tonnes of output. Sidenor has a 45% stake in the metal company Sovel Ltd., which has an annual production capacity of 650,000 tonnes.

	DR mil 12/94	12/95	12/96	US$mil 12/96					
Sales	N/A	3,656.2	3,868.9	15.8	P/E Ratio	N/A	Price (6/30/98)		10,200
Net Income	N/A	240.9	538.7	2.2	P/B Ratio	N/A	52 Wk Hi-Low		13,350.0-6,572.7
Book Value	N/A	1,052.5	1,052.5	4.3	Yield %	2.5	Market Cap		US$426.2mil

Address	115 Kifissias Ave.	Tel 53-97-898	ADR	--	President	--
	115 24 Athens	Fax 56-23-952	SEDOL	5294411	Chairman	N. Kapetanakes

Silver & Baryte Ores Mining

DJGI Industry: **Mining - Diversified**
Stoxx Sector: **Basic Resources**

Silver & Baryte Ores Mining Co. mines bentonite, bauxite, natural zeolite, and perlite on the island of Milos. The company is Europe's largest and the world's second largest producer and the world's largest exporter of bentonite, with the EU countries and North America being the largest export markets. In 1996 the company merged with Bauxites Parnasse Mining Co. SA and is now the largest producer of bauxite in the EU, with an annual extraction of 2.2 million tons. Together with its affiliates, the company is also the largest producer of perlite in the world.

	DR mil 12/95	12/96	12/97	US$mil 12/97					
Sales	13,251.7	17,580.8	23,928.9	84.3	P/E Ratio	25.0	Price (6/30/98)		10,965
Net Income	2,108.6	1,620.5	3,803.4	13.4	P/B Ratio	4.8	52 Wk Hi-Low		16,992.0-4,200.0
Book Value	8,630.7	17,689.5	20,451.1	72.1	Yield %	1.1	Market Cap		US$320.6mil

Address	21A Amerikis St.	Tel 36-90-111	ADR	--	V Chairman	E. Voulgaris
	106 72 Athens	Fax 36-01-169	SEDOL	4767947	Chairman Bd Dir	K. Kyriakopoulos

Titan Cement

DJGI Industry: **Building Materials**
Stoxx Sector: **Construction**

Titan Cement Co. is involved in the production and sale of cement and related building materials in Greece and abroad. It controls more than 40 companies, which cover the entire range of construction materials and activities, including aggregates, concrete, ready-mix concrete, quarrying, transport, shipping, trading, and related services. Titan Cement was founded in 1911, and the company joined the Athens Stock Exchange the following year. The company has 1,394 employees, and its headquarters is located in Athens.

	DR mil 12/95	12/96	12/97	US$mil 12/97				
Sales	98,152.8	108,240.4	125,515.6	442.3	P/E Ratio	20.9	Price (6/30/98)	19,905
Net Income	7,660.0	13,195.3	18,197.4	64.1	P/B Ratio	6.2	52 Wk Hi-Low	29,500.0-11,200.0
Book Value	39,452.6	54,000.7	67,341.5	237.3	Yield %	1.6	Market Cap	US$1,242.9mil

Address	22 A Chalkidos St.		Tel 25-91-111	ADR	--	President	--
	111 43 Athens		Fax 21-83-058	SEDOL	4888280	Chairman Bd Dir	A. Canellopoulos

Viohalco

DJGI Industry: **Other Non-Ferrous Metals**
Stoxx Sector: **Basic Resources**

Viohalco SA is involved in the production and processing of copper and aluminum products. The company was founded in 1937 and joined the Athens Stock Exchange in 1947. Viohalco has one factory located in Piraeus, Greece. The two main shareholders in the company are M. Stasinopoulos and E. Moustakas. The company's subsidiaries include Elval, Halcor, and Sidenor, through which Viohalco is involved in the production of steel-based products, including concrete reinforcing bars and wire rods, aluminum sheets and coils, and copper and bronze tubes and rods.

	DR mil 12/94	12/95	12/96	US$mil 12/96				
Sales	N/A	N/A	59,216.6	241.9	P/E Ratio	25.5	Price (6/30/98)	11,000
Net Income	N/A	N/A	8,232.0	33.6	P/B Ratio	7.1	52 Wk Hi-Low	15,100.0-5,010.0
Book Value	N/A	N/A	29,607.7	120.9	Yield %	0.4	Market Cap	US$1,034.9mil

Address	115 Kifissias Ave.		Tel 68-61-111	ADR	--	CFO	M. Diakoyiannis
	115 24 Athens		Fax 68-61-347	SEDOL	4934611	Chairman	M. Stassinopoulos

Ireland

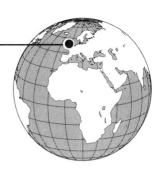

Exchanges:

The Irish Stock Exchange

Ireland

Damien Lynch
Dublin

The foundations for a single European stock market are being laid to coincide with the arrival of the euro in January 1999, and the Irish are determined not to be left behind.

In July 1998, the Irish Stock Exchange confirmed it was looking to European markets, including those in France, Spain, and Scandinavia, for an alliance providing a Europe-wide listing and presence for companies listed in Ireland.

All Irish equities will be traded and settled on the Irish stock exchange in euros beginning January 1, 1999. Although stock brokerages will be able to translate into punts for clients who wish to do business in the local currency, transactions involving securities quoted in any of the 11 euro member states will be executed, recorded, matched, confirmed, and transmitted to settlement in euros. The inter-market settlement process will also be conducted in the new single currency.

Information about prices, turnover, and money raised in the Irish market, which had traditionally been published by the stock exchange in Irish punts, will be published in euros, while historic data will be maintained in punts. Brokers, however, are expected to translate much of the historic information into euros so clients can assess past performance of a company on a comparable basis.

The prospects for Irish equities, especially the leading financial stocks, are considered bright

for 1999. Some onlookers say that if the advent of the euro prompts a narrowing of valuation differentials across markets, a target of above 7,000 for Dublin's ISEQ Overall index before the end of 1999 may be achievable. The ISEQ hit a record high 5461.49 on April 21, 1998, representing a climb of 34% since the start of the year. It ended the first half of the year at 5234.35.

A four-percentage-point cut in the standard rate of Irish corporation tax to 32% that took effect in November 1997 is expected to boost earnings for a large number of companies. Analysts say the most significant benefits are expected in the financial services sector, but companies involved in property, retailing, distribution, housebuilding, and support services may also benefit.

Some analysts see Allied Irish Banks and Bank of Ireland — Ireland's two largest banks — as possible targets for takeover by European

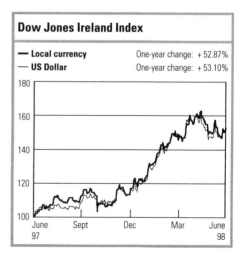

Dow Jones Ireland Index

— **Local currency**   One-year change: + 52.87%
— **US Dollar**   One-year change: + 53.10%

banking rivals trying to enter the thriving Irish economy. The two banks between them account for one-third of the Dublin stock exchange ISEQ index market's overall worth.

Irish bank stocks climbed sharply in the first half of 1998 due to the revaluation of bank stocks worldwide and the record pace of Irish economic growth. Shares in AIB soared 52% in value in the first six months. Bank of Ireland shares climbed 35% over the same period. Bank of Ireland was valued at IEP7.5 billion punts on the Dublin stock exchange on June 30, 1998, and AIB was worth around IEP9 billion.

Led by a record number of U.S.-led investments in the computer, telecommunications, and pharmaceutical industries, the Irish economy has grown by an average rate of 8.4% annually since 1994, when the period of unprecedented gross domestic product (GDP) growth began.

Economists forecast the Irish economy will continue to grow. The Organization for Economic Cooperation and Development (OECD) projected in April that the Irish GDP will grow 8.6% in 1998 and expand a further 6.6% in 1999.

There are, however, a few issues to consider.

Although in theory, turmoil in Asian financial markets should have little impact on the Irish stock market, indirectly it has hit the U.S. stock market, with reduced profits for paper and packaging concern Jefferson Smurfit

---

Country Information

Trading Hours:

   Local: 8:30 am - 4:30 pm

   EST: 3:30 am - 11:30 am

   GMT: 0830 - 1630

Population (6/98):
3,619,480

Unemployment (97):
10.3%

Main Industries:
Food products, brewing, textiles and clothing, chemicals, pharmaceuticals, machinery, transportation equipment, glass and crystal

Gross Domestic Product (97):
US$72.04 billion

GDP per Capita (97):
US$19,822.97

Three-Year Average GDP Growth (94-97):
8.4%

Average Annual CPI Growth (96-97):
+ 1.44%

Monetary Unit:
Irish Punt

Exchange Rate (6/98):
IEP0.72 to US$1.00

and pharmaceutical giant Elan Corp., both of which have strong business ties to the United States.

Irish consumer-price inflation has accelerated in recent months. The consumer price index — up 2.9% in June from a year earlier, compared with a 1.7% annual increase recorded in February — has been moving up in response to a decline in the Irish punt on foreign exchanges in the past 18 months. Most economists forecast Irish CPI will peak at 3% around year-end 1998.

There are also signs of strong wage increases in some sectors, such as public health and safety. If this spreads, it could offset the anticipated positive effects of growth of the economy on corporate profits.

Ireland's stock exchange is located in an historic quarter of Dublin, beside the River Liffey, which bisects the Irish capital. For most of its 200-year history, the Exchange was regulated by the London Stock Exchange. The regulatory connection was broken in 1996, as mandated by the European Union Commission, and the Central Bank of Ireland became the new regulator .

Participants on the stock exchange floor rely mostly on computers and telephones. There are plans to have the stock exchange fully computerized by the end of 1999.

Trades worth an average IEP200 million are executed daily in the 72 company stocks quoted on the main market's list. The total

Ten Largest Capitalized Companies In The Dow Jones Ireland Index
as of 6/30/98

Stock	Market Cap. US$ Thousands
Allied Irish Banks	12,417,174
Bank of Ireland	10,563,378
Elan	6,875,123
CRH	5,463,866
Jefferson Smurfit Group	3,256,296
Irish Life	2,958,592
Kerry Group	2,353,662
Independent Newspapers	1,340,926
Greencore	1,022,186
Waterford Wedgwood	961,266

equity market, involving 86 companies, was worth over IEP47 billion as of June 30, 1998.

The Dublin Exchange trades an average IEP200 million in Irish government bonds daily, and is a regulator of Ireland's debt market. A separate Irish government debt agency, the National Treasury Management Agency, the NTMA, is responsible for daily operations and issuing debt issues to the market.

Most of Dublin's larger equity stocks are also quoted on the London Stock Exchange, and a few are listed on the New York Stock Exchange.

The Dublin Exchange also trades 11 energy exploration companies on a separate exploration-equity list. Falling commodities prices have resulted in a 26% drop in value of Ireland's exploration stocks in the first half of 1998. The natural resource market is capitalized at just over IEP1.33 billion, but the three largest oil stocks — Tullow Oil, Dragon Oil, and Dana Petroleum — account for almost 65% of the total capitalization.

In 1997, seven Northern Ireland-based companies, which are quoted on the London and Dublin Exchanges, were included as constituents in the ISEQ index for the first time.

But Ireland's large computer sector remains barely represented on the Dublin exchange, with many companies in recent years opting for initial public offerings on the Nasdaq exchange in the United States. Indeed, in recent years U.S. investors have actively wooed several companies from the Irish computer and telecommunications industry to list on the Nasdaq.

In early 1997, the Dublin Exchange launched a new Developing Companies Market (DCM) which currently includes just four companies.

State-owned telecommunications company Telecom Eireann may be worth IEP4 billion when it floats on the Dublin stock market in 1999, observers say. It would become one of the largest companies on the market.

Irish-based telecom company Esat Telecom Group raised US$78 million in a public offering on Nasdaq and Easdaq in November 1997; the sum was used to fund the development of its telecommunications network and to compete against Telecom Eireann.

Market Sector Performance In The Dow Jones Ireland Index
1 Year Change Through 6/30/98

Market Sector	Change % (US$)
Financial	84.72
Consumer, Non-Cyclical	39.59
Industrial	36.06
Basic Materials	3.30
Consumer, Cyclical	-3.93

Allied Irish Banks

DJGI Industry: **Banks - Regional (All)**
Stoxx Sector: **Bank**

Allied Irish Banks PLC (AIB) is one of Ireland's two largest banks, with activities in retail and investment banking and related financial services. The bank provides corporate finance, leasing, custodial, unit trust management, and stock brokerage services. The company also offers life insurance and pensions through its Ark Life Assurance subsidiary. Allied Irish Banks owns state-chartered York Bank and Trust and First Maryland Bancorp, both located in the United States. In July 1997, AIB completed the acquisition of Dauphin Deposit Co. for $1.36 billion in cash and shares.

	12/95	12/96	12/97	US$mil 12/97				
Revenues	2,139.4	2,342.4	3,114.0	4,432.8	P/E Ratio	21.6	Price (6/30/98)	8.67
Net Income	239.6	270.9	380.2	541.2	P/B Ratio	5.0	52 Wk Hi-Low	8.67-4.60
Book Value	1,157.0	1,280.8	1,786.3	2,542.8	Yield %	1.7	Market Cap	US$12,417mil

Address	**Bankcentre, Ballsbridge**	Tel **1-660-0311**	ADR	**AIB**	Group CEO	**T.P. Mulcahy**
	Dublin 4	Fax **1-660-9137**	SEDOL	**0019783**	Chairman	**L. Quinn**

In EuroStoxx 50.

Bank of Ireland

DJGI Industry: **Banks - Regional (All)**
Stoxx Sector: **Bank**

Bank of Ireland Group and its subsidiaries offer retail and corporate banking and other financial services. It also operates a private bank and provides treasury and international banking services. The company owns the Irish building society ICS and the life insurance and pensions company Lifetime Assurance Co. Its wholly owned First New Hampshire subsidiaries provide banking services in the United States. In April 1996, the bank announced its intent to buy the United Kingdom's ninth-largest building society, Bristol & West PLC. The deal was completed in July 1997.

	03/96	03/97	03/98	US$mil 03/98				
Revenues	1,744.7	1,584.6	2,515.6	3,419.5	P/E Ratio	20.8	Price (6/30/98)	12.33
Net Income	213.6	266.6	369.8	502.7	P/B Ratio	4.9	52 Wk Hi-Low	13.00-6.62
Book Value	1,211.2	1,395.6	1,404.7	1,909.4	Yield %	1.6	Market Cap	US$10,563mil

Address	**Lower Baggot St.**	Tel **1-661-5933**	ADR	**IRE**	President	**M.A. Keane**
	Dublin 2	Fax **1-661-5671**	SEDOL	**0075600**	Governor	**H.E. Kilroy**

CRH

DJGI Industry: **Building Materials**
Stoxx Sector: **Construction**

CRH PLC manufactures and supplies building materials. Its main products include cement, ready-mixed concrete, aggregates, stone, sand, gravel, and clay. It also makes insulation products, security gates, fencing, and glass products and is active in civil engineering, road surfacing, and construction. CRH, Ireland's biggest building materials company, has operations throughout Europe, North America, and Argentina. In May 1998, it bought privately-owned M.A. Segale Inc. in Seattle for $60 million in cash.

	12/95	12/96	12/97	US$mil 12/97				
Sales	1,910.6	2,427.8	3,213.0	4,573.7	P/E Ratio	20.3	Price (6/30/98)	8.53
Net Income	126.2	148.7	191.8	273.0	P/B Ratio	3.8	52 Wk Hi-Low	9.46-6.03
Book Value	683.8	831.6	1,030.4	1,466.8	Yield %	1.1	Market Cap	US$5,463.9mil

Address	**Belgard Castle, Clondalkin**	Tel **1-404-1000**	ADR	**CRHCY**	CEO	**Don Godson**
	Dublin 22	Fax **1-404-1010**	SEDOL	**0182704**	Chairman	**Anthony D. Barry**

Elan

DJGI Industry: **Pharmaceuticals**
Stoxx Sector: **Pharmaceutical**

Elan Corp. PLC is a diversified healthcare company which develops, manufactures, and distributes pharmaceutical, diagnostic and medical nutrition products. Products include Verelan, Cardizem SR, CD, and the nicotine patch. The company has its own clinical research facility in Athlone, Ireland, which conducts the first phase of human testing and during fiscal 1995 a new research facility located at Trinity College Dublin was opened. Manufacture and distribution of drugs accounted for 55% of 1997 revenues; royalties & fees, 30%; and research revenues, 15%.

	03/95	12/96 *	12/97	US$mil 12/97				
Sales	118.9	182.2	258.5	367.9	P/E Ratio	35.5	Price (6/30/98)	37.00
Net Income	41.7	13.7	119.3	169.8	P/B Ratio	8.5	52 Wk Hi-Low	N/A
Book Value	184.4	279.8	540.8	769.9	Yield %	0.0	Market Cap	US$6,875.1mil

Address	**Lincoln Pl.**	Tel **1-709-4000**	ADR	**ELN**	President & COO	**J. Groom**
	Dublin 2	Fax **1-662-4949**	SEDOL	**0307295**	Chairman & CEO	**D.J. Geaney**

*Irregular period due to fiscal year change.

Fyffes

DJGI Industry: **Food Retailers & Wholesalers**
Stoxx Sector: **Consumer Non-Cyclical**

Fyffes PLC obtains fresh produce and flowers from all over the world and distributes them in the United Kingdom, Ireland, continental Europe, and the United States. The company's wholly owned Vangen Logistics Division provides warehousing and distribution services to retail and catering companies. A string of acquisitions in the last two years has led to double-digit growth in both sales and pretax profit. In July 1997, the company announced the purchase of a 50% stake in the Dutch company Velleman & Tas.

	10/95	10/96	10/97	US$mil 10/97				
Sales	1,120.2	1,290.2	1,318.2	1,978.5	P/E Ratio	15.7	Price (6/30/98)	1.48
Net Income	27.0	27.7	35.3	53.0	P/B Ratio	4.0	52 Wk Hi-Low	1.87-0.81
Book Value	130.6	143.6	120.5	180.8	Yield %	1.4	Market Cap	US$730.5mil

Address	**1 Beresford St.**	Tel **1-873-0200**	ADR	--	CEO	**David V. McCann**
	Dublin 7	Fax **1-873-0546**	SEDOL	**0329523**	Chairman	**Neil V. McCann**

Greencore

DJGI Industry: **Other Food**
Stoxx Sector: **Food & Beverage**

Greencore Group PLC supplies primary foods and related products, food ingredients, and prepared foods to industrial and commercial markets. The company is Ireland's only sugar processor and is a supplier of flour, malt, and packaged foods. Wholly owned subsidiary Interchem is the largest distributor of crop-protection products in Ireland. The company's other subsidiaries are involved in the production of agricultural products, chemicals, machinery, and fertilizers. Agricultural products accounted for 32% of fiscal 1997 revenues; sugar, 29%; and other foods, 39%.

	09/95	09/96	09/97	US$mil 09/97					
Sales	436.9	459.0	466.9	680.3	P/E Ratio		15.9	Price (6/30/98)	3.20
Net Income	38.9	46.2	42.0	61.3	P/B Ratio		2.7	52 Wk Hi-Low	3.80-2.70
Book Value	189.8	238.0	255.8	372.7	Yield %		2.1	Market Cap	US$1,022.2mil

Address	Earlsfort Terrace	Tel 1-605-1000	ADR	--	CEO	David Dilger
	Dublin 2	Fax 1-605-1100	SEDOL	0386410	Chairman	Bernie M. Cahill

Independent Newspapers

DJGI Industry: **Publishing**
Stoxx Sector: **Media**

Independent Newspapers PLC is an international media and communications holding company with interests in newspaper and magazine publishing, outdoor advertising, and electronic media. Its businesses publish in excess of 160 newspapers and magazine's in Ireland, the United Kingdom, France, South Africa, Australia, and New Zealand. The largest publisher of newspapers in Ireland, South Africa, and New Zealand, more than half of the company's sales are generated in Ireland. It has a stake in seven titles in Ireland, accounting for more than 60% of all Irish newspaper sales.

	12/95	12/96	12/97	US$mil 12/97					
Sales	350.4	419.1	579.3	824.7	P/E Ratio		16.8	Price (6/30/98)	3.23
Net Income	30.1	54.2	56.9	80.9	P/B Ratio		1.7	52 Wk Hi-Low	4.08-3.20
Book Value	287.5	395.2	559.8	796.9	Yield %		2.0	Market Cap	US$1,340.9mil

Address	1/2 Upper Hatch St.	Tel 1-475-8432	ADR	--	CEO	L.P. Healy
	Dublin 2	Fax 1-475-2126	SEDOL	0461481	Chairman	Dr. A.J.F. O'Reilly

Irish Life

DJGI Industry: **Insurance - Life & Health**
Stoxx Sector: **Insurance**

Irish Life PLC is Ireland's largest life, pensions, and investment company. It offers investment management and asset financing services to businesses and life insurance, mortgages, savings and personal pension plans to individuals. Irish Life operates in the United Kingdom, the United States, and Europe. In 1996, it bought U.S. Guarantee Reserve Life Insurance Co., which specializes in risk coverage for older-age and lower-to-middle income groups. Premiums earned accounted for 33% of 1997 revenues; investment income, 15%; gain on realization of investments, 20%; and other, 32%.

	12/95	12/96	12/97	US$mil 12/97					
Revenues	1,683.7	1,428.6	2,741.9	3,903.1	P/E Ratio		17.1	Price (6/30/98)	5.60
Net Income	35.4	97.4	122.8	174.8	P/B Ratio		2.4	52 Wk Hi-Low	5.97-2.97
Book Value	78.7	758.0	884.7	1,259.4	Yield %		2.0	Market Cap	US$2,958.6mil

Address	Irish Life Ctr., Lower Abbey St.	Tel 1-704-2000	ADR	--	Managing Director	D. Went
	Dublin 1	Fax 1-704-1900	SEDOL	0459389	Chairman	C. McCarthy

Kerry Group

DJGI Industry: **Other Food**
Stoxx Sector: **Food & Beverage**

Kerry Group PLC is an international food ingredients and consumer foods corporation with operations in Ireland, the United Kingdom, Europe, America, Canada, Mexico, and Australia. The group produces and markets a range of speciality food ingredients, food coatings, bakery mixes, fruit preparations, flavorings, and proteins and manufactures a diverse range of food products spanning the dairy, beef, pork, specialist poultry, savory, and convenience product sectors. Kerry Ingredients accounted for 58% of 1997 revenues; Kerry Foods, 38%; and Kerry Agribusiness, 4%.

	12/95	12/96	12/97	US$mil 12/97					
Sales	1,124.1	1,233.3	1,344.1	1,913.4	P/E Ratio		24.9	Price (6/30/98)	8.20
Net Income	38.1	44.1	-292.7	-416.7	P/B Ratio		18.3	52 Wk Hi-Low	9.57-5.60
Book Value	312.8	349.4	88.1	125.4	Yield %		0.4	Market Cap	US$2,353.7mil

Address	Prince's St.	Tel 66-22433	ADR	--	Managing Director	Denis Brosnan
	Tralee	Fax 66-22747	SEDOL	0490656	Chairman	Michael Hanrahan

Jefferson Smurfit

DJGI Industry: **Paper Products**
Stoxx Sector: **Basic Resources**

Jefferson Smurfit Group PLC is a paper and board manufacturer that makes corrugated cardboard, folding cartons, cigarette packets, paper bags, paper tubes, and containerboard. It also provides printing and waste-reclamation services. The company has operations in the United Kingdom, the Netherlands, Germany, France, Italy, Spain, the United States, Colombia, and Mexico. About 70% of its sales comes from businesses in the United States and neighboring countries. It controls 34% of Smurfit Stone Container Corp. (SSCC), the largest United States linerboard company.

	12/95	12/96	12/97	US$mil 12/97					
Sales	3,032.8	2,594.1	2,570.9	3,659.6	P/E Ratio		22.1	Price (6/30/98)	1.81
Net Income	299.2	133.1	105.1	149.6	P/B Ratio		1.5	52 Wk Hi-Low	2.41-1.56
Book Value	1,362.1	1,419.3	1,565.8	2,228.9	Yield %		0.8	Market Cap	US$3,256.3mil

Address	Beech Hill, Clonskeagh	Tel 1-202-7000	ADR	JS	Finance Director	R.M. Curran
	Dublin 4	Fax 1-269-4481	SEDOL	0819143	Chairman & CEO	Michael W.J. Smurfit

Waterford Wedgwood

DJGI Industry: **Other Home Furnishings**
Stoxx Sector: **Consumer Cyclical**

Waterford Wedgwood PLC is a manufacturer of high quality crystal, china, and ceramics that distributes and retails its products throughout Europe, North and South America, the Middle East, Japan, Australia, and South Africa. The company's main products are Waterford Crystal handcrafted stemware and giftware and Wedgwood bone-china tableware and decorative ware. Additional products include Coalport hand-painted figurines and giftware, Marquis contemporary crystal, and Johnson Brothers earthen tableware. Waterford's products are exported worldwide.

	12/95	12/96	12/97	US$mil 12/97				
Sales	344.5	376.3	417.2	593.9	P/E Ratio		20.0	Price (6/30/98)	0.79
Net Income	24.1	29.0	6.4	9.1	P/B Ratio		3.5	52 Wk Hi-Low	1.06-0.68
Book Value	147.9	171.0	158.7	225.9	Yield %		1.7	Market Cap	US$961.3mil

Address	Kilbarry		Tel	51-73311	ADR	WATFZ	CEO	Redmond O'Donoghue
	Waterford		Fax	51-78539	SEDOL	0942038	Chairman	Anthony O'Reilly

Italy

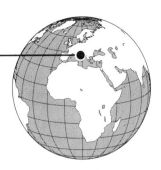

Exchanges:

The Italian Stock Exchange

Italy

Heather O'Brian
Milan

As was the case in many European stock markets, 1998 started with record-breaking peaks in Italian stock trading. Piazza Affari, otherwise known as the Milan Stock Market, saw its key indexes and trading volume reach new highs.

On April 7, the broad-based Mibtel index reached a record of 26,741, up 59% from the start of the year, and the Mib30 recorded a new high of 38,596, up 55%. The record for volume was set on April 3, when some ITL7.898 trillion of shares changed hands. Stock trading occurs on screen-based systems.

Italian investors, accustomed to investing in government bonds, were encouraged to diversify by an environment of ever-lower interest rates.

Some smaller investors were scared off as the year progressed, however, and the market registered its steepest fall ever on April 27, when the broad-based Mibtel dropped 6.4%, mainly because of fears that the U.S. Federal Reserve Bank might raise interest rates.

Still, two weeks into July, the market was up about 50% from the start of the year, with the Mibtel at 25,722 and the Mib30 at 38,473. Some analysts foresaw new records for the second part of the year.

It wouldn't have been a normal year in Milan if political factors and questions about whether the government would succeed in achieving its economic objectives weren't main features of the bourse's backdrop. The

government's far left and sometimes difficult ally, Rifondazione Comunista, in June withheld its support for a parliamentary vote on the expansion of NATO, forcing the government to rely on opposition votes and leading to a more serious rethinking of common policy goals.

It wasn't the first time Rifondazione, which gives the government a majority in the lower house of parliament, had failed to support the center-left government led by Prime Minister Romano Prodi. Rifondazione almost brought the government down in October 1997, before Prodi's government gave in to demands to present legislation for a 35-hour work week.

At the same time, some of the government's economic objectives, particularly for growth, looked increasingly optimistic as the year progressed. The government was sticking to its target of GDP growth of 2.5% in 1998,

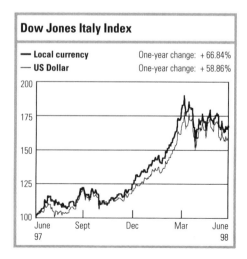

Dow Jones Italy Index

— Local currency   One-year change: + 66.84%
— US Dollar   One-year change: + 58.86%

but many economic observers forecast that a figure closer to 2.2% or 2.3% was more likely.

But the biggest objective was achieved when Italy was admitted into the first wave of economic and monetary union in a special E.U. summit at the beginning of May. Italian interest rates have come down sharply and must come down even further to be in line with the other 10 countries in the single currency plan. With lower rates, Italian stocks became increasingly attractive compared to bonds.

Market capitalization in terms of GDP rose to 42% of GDP in June, from 31.3% at the start of the year. Foreign investors played a strong part in the market's rally and were responsible for almost 50% of all trades in the first months of the year. That percentage has varied between about 40% and 50% since 1996.

Early in the year, the government approved new corporate governance standards designed to make takeover rules fairer and bolster the rights of minority shareholders. Observers said that these changes, although only a first step, should help to serve as an incentive for equity investments.

New corporate governance rules are also designed to align Italy's policies more closely with those of its European Union partners as part of more widespread changes that must be made before the start of economic and monetary union (EMU). Capital gains taxes

Country Information

Trading Hours:
   Local: 10:00 am - 5:00 pm

   EST: 4:00 am - 11:00 am

   GMT: 0900 - 1600

Population (6/98):
56,782,748

Unemployment (97):
12.2%

Main Industries:
Tourism, machinery, iron and steel, chemicals, food processing, textiles, automobiles, clothing and footwear, and ceramics

Gross Domestic Product (97):
US$1,145.37 billion

GDP per Capita (97):
US$19,945.79

Three-Year Average GDP Growth (94-97):
1.6%

Average Annual CPI Growth (96-97):
+ 2.04%

Monetary Unit:
Italian Lira

Exchange Rate (6/98):
ITL1,781.00 to US$1.00

were reintroduced on July 1, after being suspended in 1992 amid a general reworking of the overall tax system. Market participants said that the new standards introduced several advantages, such as the ability to deduct capital losses, that hadn't existed previously.

In an effort to drum up further interest in Milan's medium- and small-capitalization issues, the Milan stock market, in March 1998 introduced futures contracts on the Midex, an index for this category of stocks. Some of Milan's most interesting stocks, such as luxury jeweler Bulgari and airport management company Aeroporti Di Roma, are included in the Midex.

The market also had a number of new additions in 1998, amid initial public offerings for a rash of smaller companies, including industrial-gas producer Sol; tour operator I Grandi Viaggi; chair producer De-Ta; garden machinery companies Emak SpA and Castelgarden; life insurer Bayerische Vita; lighting company Targetti Sankey and security, lighting, and video systems manufacturer Beghelli.

The first soccer club was also quoted on the stock market, as Lazio, one of the top ranking teams in the first division, offered shares in an IPO in May. Its performance on the bourse wasn't as strong as on the playing field, however, with the shares falling below their offer price in their first few months on the market.

Ten Largest Capitalized Companies In The Dow Jones Italy Index
as of 6/30/98

Stock	Market Cap. US$ Thousands
ENI	52,280,004
Telecom Italia	49,033,007
Telecom Italia Mobile	40,485,800
Assicurazioni Generali	33,264,785
Fiat	18,599,616
Credito Italiano	14,920,130
Instituto Nazionale Assicurazioni	11,332,200
Banca Di Roma	11,105,030
Rolo Banca	10,641,736
Banca Commerciale Italiana	10,640,942

The quotation of other soccer clubs is expected to follow, starting with Bologna in the autumn.

Listings of these companies was made easier at the beginning of 1998, when the stock market eliminated a requirement that companies turn a profit three years in a row before being quoted.

The rule had been criticized in the past, particularly since luxury goods producer Gucci turned to listings in Amsterdam and New York a few years back when it was rejected in Milan.

Despite the new offerings, Milan's stock market continues to be dominated by a few big names. Energy giant ENI, which saw the state's stake fall below 40% following the sale of a fourth tranche in June, accounted for more than 10% of the market's overall capitalization.

There was actually a reduction in the number of stocks quoted in the first half of 1998, as some shares disappeared following mergers and other deals. The number of stocks quoted on the official market fell to 294 at the end of June, from 301 at the end of 1997, but the number of companies with shares quoted was steady at 213. (Several companies have more than one class of shares traded on the market.)

A recent study by market regulatory agency Consob identified some 550 Italian companies that could be listed on the market. The listing of new companies, such as those in traditionally strong domestic sectors like fashion, could help to add some variety to the offerings.

Although a planned IPO for Versace has been pushed back to some time in the indefinite future, a small producer of designer jeans and other clothing, Ittierre Holding, began trading on the stock market late in 1997.

In a way, fashion house Valentino is now quoted on the market as it was acquired by holding company Holding di Partecipazioni at the start of 1998. HDP's stated aim of creating a large luxury goods group has led to speculation about possible future acquisition targets.

With the notable exception of ENI, however, Milan's blue-chip stock index is still top-heavy with banks and holding companies. The listing of new companies aside, that could also change amid the rash of mergers and acquisitions striking Milan's overcrowded and largely inefficient banking system, which should further whittle down the number of Italian banks.

At least one bank will disappear from the screens of Milan trading rooms when merchant bank and financial services group Istituto Mobiliare Italiano (IMI) and Istituto Bancario San Paolo Di Torino, both quoted on the market, merge at the end of 1998.

Industry Group Performance In The Dow Jones Italy Index
1 Year Change Through 6/30/98

Industry	Change % (US$)
Best Performing	
Banks (All)	142.80
Financial Services, Diversified	140.10
Banks, Regional	139.13
Heavy Construction	94.01
Insurance, Full Line	83.28
Worst Performing	
Gas Utilities	25.34
Industrial, Diversified	24.55
Oil, Secondary	15.25
Other Oil Equipment & Services (ex. Drilling)	-0.08
Oilfield Equipment & Services (All)	-0.08

Alleanza

DJGI Industry: **Insurance - Life & Health**
Stoxx Sector: **Insurance**

Alleanza Assicurazioni S.p.A. is ranked as one of Italy's top three life insurance companies, and it provides life assurance and fire, theft, accident, health, and title insurance. The company also provides all classes of nonlife insurance, including accident and health. Financial services offered include investment management and annuities. The company is about 65% controlled by Assicurazioni Generali, Italy's largest insurance company. Its wholly owned subsidiaries include Edicom and Crespim, a real estate company.

	lire bil 12/95	12/96	12/97	US$mil 12/97				
Revenues	3,748.4	4,302.1	N/A	N/A	P/E Ratio	52.8	Price (6/30/98)	24,150
Net Income	154.2	246.7	332.7	188.1	P/B Ratio	8.6	52 Wk Hi-Low	29,100.0-13,355.0
Book Value	1,680.0	1,827.1	N/A	N/A	Yield %	0.7	Market Cap	US$8,521.3mil

Address	Viale Luigi Sturzo 35	Tel 02-62961	ADR	--	V Chairman	E. Coppola di Canzano
	20154 Milan	Fax 02-653718	SEDOL	4015970	Chairman	A. Desiata

Autostrade

DJGI Industry: **Heavy Construction**
Stoxx Sector: **Construction**

Autostrade S.p.A. (Concessioni e Costruzioni Autostrade S.p.A.) operates a group of transport-infrastructure businesses that construct, manage, and maintain roadways. It manages these motorways and administers the collection of levies from motorists. The company is controlled by Istituto per la Ricostruzione Industriale through its engineering company Fintecna. The consolidated group consists of 13 companies, of which three are based abroad in the United States, Luxembourg, and the United Kingdom. Toll income accounted for 93% of 1997 revenues.

	lire bil 12/95	12/96	12/97	US$mil 12/97				
Sales	3,051.1	3,225.3	3,384.8	1,913.9	P/E Ratio	32.0	Price (6/30/98)	7,060.00
Net Income	165.4	160.2	267.1	151.1	P/B Ratio	2.6	52 Wk Hi-Low	8,600.0-3,280.0
Book Value	3,102.0	3,137.1	3,294.4	1,862.8	Yield %	2.0	Market Cap	US$2,342.7mil

Address	Via Bergamini 50	Tel 06-43631	ADR	--	Managing Director	P. Ceseri
	00159 Rome	Fax 06-43634090	SEDOL	4065317	Chairman	G. Valori

Banca Commerciale

DJGI Industry: **Banks - Regional (All)**
Stoxx Sector: **Bank**

Established in 1894, Banca Commerciale Italiana S.p.A., known as COMIT in Italy and as BCI internationally, is one of the leading banking groups in Italy. BCI offers extensive corporate and retail banking services, including commercial and merchant banking, short-term and medium-term lending, leasing, securities brokerage, and other financial services, in the domestic and international markets. The bank also offers asset-management, leasing, life insurance, investment banking, and mutual-fund marketing. The company operates more than 1,000 branches in Italy and overseas.

	lire bil 12/95	12/96	12/97	US$mil 12/97				
Revenues	16,314.7	16,063.2	16,740.4	9,465.9	P/E Ratio	46.0	Price (6/30/98)	10,630
Net Income	365.2	377.9	415.1	234.7	P/B Ratio	2.1	52 Wk Hi-Low	10,865.0-3,520.0
Book Value	8,727.7	8,746.3	8,944.9	5,057.9	Yield %	1.6	Market Cap	US$10,641mil

Address	Piazza della Scala 6	Tel 02-88501	ADR	BCIAYP	V Chairman	G. Guitty
	20121 Milan	Fax 02-88503026	SEDOL	4072942	Chairman	L. Fausti

Banca Intesa

DJGI Industry: **Banks - Regional (All)**
Stoxx Sector: **Bank**

Banca Intesa S.p.A. is a multibank holding company that provides commercial and merchant banking services. Through its subsidiaries, the bank also offers services in fund management, investment trust management, leasing, factoring, and property management. The bank has representative offices in several countries worldwide but is based mostly in Italy. Interest and fees on loans accounted for 43% of 1997 revenues; interest income on securities, 18%; interest income on bank deposits, 14%; other interest income, 1%; and noninterest income, 24%.

	lire bil 12/95	12/96	12/97	US$mil 12/97				
Revenues	5,790.3	6,313.5	5,990.7	3,387.5	P/E Ratio	107.2	Price (6/30/98)	9,945.00
Net Income	180.4	189.7	232.7	131.6	P/B Ratio	0.4	52 Wk Hi-Low	10,900.0-2,462.3
Book Value	2,482.1	2,550.3	2,662.2	1,505.4	Yield %	0.6	Market Cap	US$10,267mil

Address	Piazza Paolo Ferrari 10	Tel 02-85941	ADR	--	President	--
	20100 Milan	Fax 02-859473	SEDOL	4076836	Chairman	G. Bazoli

Banca di Roma

DJGI Industry: **Banks - Major International**
Stoxx Sector: **Bank**

Banca di Roma S.p.A. is a multibank holding company that offers retail and merchant banking services. The bank also trades securities and provides life insurance and various other financial services. The group operates through 27 fully consolidated subsidiaries based in Italy, Luxembourg, and France. Interest and fees on loans accounted for 57% of 1997 revenues; interest on securities accounted for 14%, and interest income on bank deposits for 13%. Other interest income contributed only 1% of revenues, whereas noninterest income made up 15%.

	lire bil 12/95	12/96	12/97	US$mil 12/97				
Revenues	18,797.1	18,654.9	15,807.3	8,938.3	P/E Ratio	NMF	Price (6/30/98)	3,700.00
Net Income	85.7	121.4	-3,155.6	-1,784.3	P/B Ratio	1.2	52 Wk Hi-Low	3,985.0-1,240.0
Book Value	10,893.6	10,470.0	9,969.1	5,637.0	Yield %	0.0	Market Cap	US$11,105mil

Address	Via Marco Minghetti 17	Tel 06-67071	ADR	--	President	--
	00187 Rome	Fax 06-678192	SEDOL	4058351	Chairman	C. Geronzi

Benetton

DJGI Industry: **Clothing & Fabrics**
Stoxx Sector: **Consumer Cyclical**

Benetton S.p.A. manufactures and sells woolen, cotton, and woven-fabric fashion apparel and accessories for women, men, and children. Accessories include footwear, spectacle frames, cosmetics, toys, luggage, stationery, household linens, watches, underwear, and leather goods. Manufacturing takes place mostly in Italy, while marketing is done through a worldwide network of over 7,000 specialty stores. In 1997 Benetton acquired Benetton Sportsystem. Benetton products are marketed under the United Colors of Benetton, Sisley, 012, Zerotondo, Di Varese, and 999 brand names.

	lire bil 12/95	12/96	12/97	US$mil 12/97					
Sales	2,939.1	2,871.1	3,636.8	2,056.4	P/E Ratio		23.1	Price (6/30/98)	3,690.00
Net Income	220.3	245.6	290.1	164.1	P/B Ratio		3.3	52 Wk Hi-Low	4,295.0-2,510.0
Book Value	1,657.0	1,820.1	2,030.5	1,148.1	Yield %		1.4	Market Cap	US$3,758.0mil

Address	Via Villa Minelli	Tel **04-224491**	ADR	**BNG**	V Chairman	**G. Benetton**
	31050 Ponzano Veneto	Fax **04-229695**	SEDOL	**5486672**	Chairman	**L. Benetton**

Cartiere Burgo

DJGI Industry: **Paper Products**
Stoxx Sector: **Basic Resources**

Cartiere Burgo S.p.A., Italy's largest paper manufacturer, produces paper, paper pulp, newsprint, and packaging. The group's major output is laminated paper used mainly in magazines and packaging paper used for producing paperboard for boxes. It is controlled by a shareholders' syndicate led by Gemina S.p.A., an investment company controlled by Fiat and merchant bank Mediobanca. The Cartiere Burgo group has subsidiaries in Belgium, Spain, Luxembourg, France, the United Kingdom, and Germany. Paper manufacture accounted for 94% of 1997 revenues.

	lire bil 12/95	12/96	12/97	US$mil 12/97					
Sales	3,366.6	2,607.2	2,759.6	1,560.4	P/E Ratio		12.3	Price (6/30/98)	14,235
Net Income	203.4	100.5	148.1	83.8	P/B Ratio		1.1	52 Wk Hi-Low	16,400.0-9,400.0
Book Value	1,532.3	1,517.6	1,604.5	907.3	Yield %		2.8	Market Cap	US$1,006.9mil

Address	San Mauro Torinese	Tel **011-26071**	ADR	--	CEO	**Giuseppe Lignana**
	10099 Turin	Fax **011-266930**	SEDOL	**4152822**	Chairman	**Lionello Adler**

CIR

DJGI Industry: **Conglomerates**
Stoxx Sector: **Conglomerate**

Compagnie Industriali Riunite S.p.A. (CIR) is the industrial holding company of Italian financier Carlo De Benedetti's group. Its primary interests are in financial services and manufacturing. Its holdings include the computer manufacturer Olivetti; the mechanics company Sasib; the publisher Editoriale L'Espresso; the financial group Cerus; and two companies that produce car components, Valeo and Sogefi. Through its holding in Spanish hotelier Cofir, CIR is also active in tourism and the sale of wine. Instrumental mechanics accounted for 38% of 1997 revenues.

	lire bil 12/95	12/96	12/97	US$mil 12/97					
Sales	12,664.3	3,717.8	3,770.1	2,131.8	P/E Ratio		78.1	Price (6/30/98)	2,250.00
Net Income	-288.3	320.0	24.5	13.8	P/B Ratio		1.5	52 Wk Hi-Low	2,830.0-1,083.0
Book Value	986.2	1,247.8	1,263.1	714.2	Yield %		0.0	Market Cap	US$712.1mil

Address	Via Ciovassino 1	Tel **02-722701**	ADR	--	V Chairman	**V. Ripa di Meana**
	20121 Milan	Fax --	SEDOL	**4162371**	Chairman	**Carlo de Benedetti**

Credito Italiano

DJGI Industry: **Banks - Regional (All)**
Stoxx Sector: **Bank**

Credito Italiano S.p.A., privatized in 1993, is a multibank holding company involved in commercial banking, security brokerage, currency swaps, and other financial services. Credito Italiano also manages mutual funds through its partially owned Gesticredit subsidiary. The bank is controlled by the IRI group. The consolidated group is made up of the parent company, Credito Italiano S.p.A., and 18 other companies, all of which are engaged in financial activities. In 1995, Credito Italiano took over the regional bank Credito Romagnolo. It has 800 offices in Italy and 11 offices abroad.

	lire bil 12/95	12/96	12/97	US$mil 12/97					
Revenues	16,656.7	15,677.2	15,315.0	8,659.9	P/E Ratio		55.7	Price (6/30/98)	9,305.00
Net Income	196.4	281.8	480.8	271.9	P/B Ratio		3.5	52 Wk Hi-Low	10,375.0-3,110.0
Book Value	6,060.6	6,223.2	7,635.3	4,317.4	Yield %		0.9	Market Cap	US$14,920mil

Address	Piazza Cordusio 2	Tel **02-88621**	ADR	**CIAOYP**	V Chairman	**Egidio G. Bruno**
	20123 Milan	Fax **02-288623965**	SEDOL	**4232445**	Chairman	**Lucio Rondelli**

In EuroStoxx 50.

Edison

DJGI Industry: **Electrical Utilities (All)**
Stoxx Sector: **Utility**

Edison S.p.A., Italy's largest private producer of electric energy, heads Montedison Group's energy sector. It operates in three main areas: heat and power generation, oil and gas production, and distribution of refined products. The energy produced is distributed to industrial users and also to Italian state-owned utility Enel. Edison is also involved in the exploration, production, and distribution of natural gas and crude oil. Other activities include the distribution of fuel, GPL, lubricants, bitumen, and logistics systems. It also produces electrical transport and storage systems for automotive.

	lire bil 12/95	12/96	12/97	US$mil 12/97					
Sales	1,173.5	1,762.1	2,523.5	1,426.9	P/E Ratio		22.4	Price (6/30/98)	14,265
Net Income	267.9	369.7	402.5	227.6	P/B Ratio		3.1	52 Wk Hi-Low	18,975.0-7,960.0
Book Value	2,421.4	2,647.6	2,888.1	1,633.1	Yield %		1.5	Market Cap	US$5,074.7mil

Address	Foro Buonaparte 31	Tel **02-62221**	ADR	--	Managing Director	**G. Del Ninno**
	20121 Milan	Fax **02-6222857**	SEDOL	**4764465**	Chairman	**E. Bondi**

ENI

DJGI Industry: **Oil Companies - Secondary**
Stoxx Sector: **Energy**

Ente Nazionale Idrocarburi S.p.A. (ENI) is headquartered in Rome and is Italy's state energy holding company. As Europe's fourth largest distributor of gas, the company distributes hydrocarbons, petroleum fuel, and lubricants. Its main units are AGIP S.p.A., an oil and gas exploration company; AGIP Petroli S.p.A., a refiner; Enichem, a chemicals producer; and Snam, a gas pipeline and distribution company. Energy and related activities accounted for 73% of 1997 revenues; chemicals, 14%; engineering and services, 8%; divesting and other activities, 5%.

	lire bil 12/95	12/96	12/97	US$mil 12/97				
Sales	59,282.0	59,556.0	62,975.0	35,609.3	P/E Ratio	20.0	Price (6/30/98)	11,650
Net Income	4,327.0	4,451.0	5,118.0	2,894.0	P/B Ratio	3.7	52 Wk Hi-Low	13,500.0-9,200.0
Book Value	23,028.0	25,333.0	29,671.0	16,777.5	Yield %	2.4	Market Cap	US$52,280mil

Address	**Piazzale Enrico Mattei 1**	Tel **06-59821**	ADR	**E**	Managing Director	**F. Bernabe**
	00144 Rome	Fax **06-59822141**	SEDOL	**4436399**	Chairman	**G. Moscato**

In DJ Stoxx 50; In EuroStoxx 50.

Fiat

DJGI Industry: **Automobile Manufacturers**
Stoxx Sector: **Automobile**

Fiat S.p.A. is Italy's top-ranked automobile manufacturer and the country's largest private-sector company. It is an international holding company with interests in automobiles, commercial vehicles, agricultural and construction equipment, metallurgic products, automotive components, batteries, production systems, aviation, rolling stock and railway systems, chemicals, fibers, bioengineering, civil engineering, publishing and communications, financial services, and insurance. The group has operations in 58 countries through more than 800 companies.

	lire bil 12/95	12/96	12/97	US$mil 12/97				
Sales	74,765.0	77,458.0	89,058.0	50,357.9	P/E Ratio M	19.3	Price (6/30/98) M	7,780.00
Net Income	2,147.0	2,371.0	2,417.0	1,366.7	P/B Ratio M	1.7	52 Wk Hi-Low M	8,920.0-4,705.0
Book Value	21,437.0	23,075.0	25,323.0	14,318.9	Yield % M	1.5	Market Cap M	US$16,035mil

Address	**Corso Marconi 10**	Tel **011-330311**	ADR	**FIA**	V Chairman	**G. Gabetti**
	10125 Turin	Fax **011-3303260**	SEDOL	**4335601**	Chairman	**C. Romiti**

M=Multiple issues in index; reflects most active; In EuroStoxx 50.

La Fondiaria

DJGI Industry: **Insurance - Full Line**
Stoxx Sector: **Insurance**

La Fondiaria Assicurazioni S.p.A. is a private-sector insurance company. It provides insurance and reinsurance services, including life insurance and all classifications of nonlife insurance, in Italy and abroad. The company's partially owned insurance subsidiaries include La Previdente, Milano, and Dominion Insurance Holdings in London. La Fondiaria is controlled by Ferruzzi Finanziaria, which holds shares both directly and through its majority-owned subsidiary GAIC. In 1997, the company approved the merger of its units Milano Assicurazioni and La Previdente.

	lire bil 12/95	12/96	12/97	US$mil 12/97				
Revenues	7,509.1	7,384.3	N/A	N/A	P/E Ratio	NMF	Price (6/30/98)	10,210
Net Income	53.3	59.3	-350.0	-197.9	P/B Ratio	2.3	52 Wk Hi-Low	13,720.0-7,050.0
Book Value	1,729.8	1,739.5	1,326.0	749.8	Yield %	1.3	Market Cap	US$2,157.7mil

Address	**Piazza Della Liberta, 6**	Tel **055-47941**	ADR	--	CEO	**R. Gavazzi**
	50129 Florence	Fax **055-476026**	SEDOL	**4344771**	Chairman	**A. Pecci**

Generali

DJGI Industry: **Insurance - Full Line**
Stoxx Sector: **Insurance**

Assicurazioni Generali S.p.A., the largest insurance company in Italy in terms of market capitalization, heads a group of insurance companies and other companies that operate in the financial, real estate, and agricultural sectors. The group consists of 109 insurance companies, 216 holding and financial companies, real estate companies, and agricultural companies with operations in over 40 countries. Premiums earned accounted for 69% of 1997 revenues; investment income, 18%; and other income, 13%.

	lire bil 12/95	12/96	12/97	US$mil 12/97				
Revenues	44,752.5	46,531.1	54,340.2	30,726.7	P/E Ratio	53.0	Price (6/30/98)	57,800
Net Income	695.1	1,437.7	1,030.8	582.9	P/B Ratio	4.9	52 Wk Hi-Low	62,000.0-28,843.8
Book Value	9,959.4	10,522.2	1,221.0	690.4	Yield %	0.6	Market Cap	US$33,265mil

Address	**Piazza Duca degli Abruzzi 2**	Tel **040-6711**	ADR	--	Jnt V Chairman	**F. Cingano**
	34132 Trieste	Fax **040-671600**	SEDOL	**4056719**	Chairman	**A. Bernheim**

In DJ Stoxx 50; In EuroStoxx 50.

Holding di Partecipazioni

DJGI Industry: **Clothing & Fabrics**
Stoxx Sector: **Consumer Cyclical**

Holding di Partecipazioni S.p.A. is involved in the design, manufacture, marketing, and distribution of apparel products, as well as in the publishing of newspapers, periodicals, and books. Its subsidiaries include Fila Holdings, Gruppo Finanziario Tessile, and Gruppo RCS Editori. Fila designs, markets, and distributes specialized footwear and clothing, leisurewear, sunglasses, and underwear. Gruppo Finanziario Tessile manufactures, markets, and distributes men's and women's fashions. Gruppo RCS Editori publishes the Il Corriere della Sera and La Gazzetta dello Sport newspapers.

	lire bil 12/95	12/96	12/97	US$mil 12/97				
Sales	N/A	N/A	6,420.6	3,630.5	P/E Ratio	18.1	Price (6/30/98)	1,382.00
Net Income	N/A	N/A	204.6	115.7	P/B Ratio	N/A	52 Wk Hi-Low	1,980.0-780.0
Book Value	N/A	N/A	N/A	N/A	Yield %	1.1	Market Cap	US$2,072.5mil

Address	**Via Filippo Turati 16/18**	Tel **02-62291**	ADR	--	President	**Nicolo Nefri**
	20121 Milan	Fax **02-6379414**	SEDOL	**5144765**	Chairman	--

IFIL

DJGI Industry: **Industrial - Diversified**
Stoxx Sector: **Industrials**

Finanziaria de Partecipazioni S.p.A (IFIL) is the industrial holding company of Fiat. IFIL invests in food, industrial, service, and tourism companies. Its food holdings include the French food manufacturer Danone, Italian cheese and processed-meat company Galbani, and Saint Louis, a holding company that invests in the food and agriculture sectors. IFIL also has exposure to French food, insurance, and financial-services company Worms & Cie. and French hotel operator Accor, and the company has a minority interest in Fiat S.p.A.

	lire bil 12/95	12/96	12/97	US$mil 12/97					
Sales	5,960.0	6,392.4	3,653.4	2,065.8	P/E Ratio	13.9	Price (6/30/98)	8,165.00
Net Income	321.5	338.6	505.5	285.9	P/B Ratio	1.6	52 Wk Hi-Low	11,090.0-5,480.0
Book Value	3,405.8	3,615.5	4,115.3	2,327.0	Yield %	1.7	Market Cap	US$1,998.4mil

Address	**Corso Giacomo Matteotti 36**	Tel **011-55411**	ADR	--	Managing Director	**Gabriele di Genola**
	10121 Turin	Fax **011-547660**	SEDOL	4455736	Chairman	**Umberto Agnelli**

IMI

DJGI Industry: **Banks - Regional (All)**
Stoxx Sector: **Bank**

IMI (Instituto Mobiliare Italiana S.p.A.) is one of Italy's largest banks. It is involved mainly in investment banking, loans, and personal financial services; it also has smaller interests in insurance and leasing through its associated companies. IMI's branches are located primarily in Milan, Rome, and Turin, but it has subsidiaries throughout Europe, the United States, and Mexico. Interest and fees on loans accounted for 60% of 1997 revenues; interest income on bank deposits, 12%; interest on securities, 10%; other interest income, 2%; and noninterest income, 16%.

	lire bil 12/95	12/96	12/97	US$mil 12/97					
Revenues	7,414.3	7,372.8	6,939.1	3,923.7	P/E Ratio	22.6	Price (6/30/98)	28,000
Net Income	551.8	660.5	744.4	420.9	P/B Ratio	2.0	52 Wk Hi-Low	33,550.0-15,140.0
Book Value	7,071.9	7,240.0	7,585.6	4,289.3	Yield %	2.5	Market Cap	US$9,424.8mil

Address	**Viale dell'Arte 25**	Tel **06-59591**	ADR	IMI	Dir General	**F. Barlassina**
	00144 Rome	Fax **06-59593888**	SEDOL	4438113	Chmn & Mng Dir	**G. Pesenti**

INA

DJGI Industry: **Insurance - Full Line**
Stoxx Sector: **Insurance**

Instituto Nazionale delle Assicurazioni (INA) S.p.A. offers life and nonlife insurance in Italy. It also offers health insurance on an indemnity basis. INA has a controlling interest in Fata S.p.A., an insurance company active in the agricultural sector. In May 1996, INA announced a commercial agreement with German insurer Nurnberger Beteiligungs AG. In June 1996, the Treasury announced that it had sold off almost all of its remaining stake in INA through a five-year convertible bond issue. INA's shares are traded on the Milan, London, and New York stock exchanges.

	lire bil 12/95	12/96	12/97	US$mil 12/97					
Revenues	11,545.8	11,788.3	N/A	N/A	P/E Ratio	35.2	Price (6/30/98)	5,050.00
Net Income	411.8	505.0	573.0	324.0	P/B Ratio	1.6	52 Wk Hi-Low	6,285.0-2,370.0
Book Value	11,527.2	11,639.3	12,470.0	7,051.2	Yield %	1.4	Market Cap	US$11,332mil

Address	**Via Sallustiania 51**	Tel **06-47221**	ADR	--	Jnt Mng Dir & Gen	**L. Benassi**
	00187 Rome	Fax **06-472245-23**	SEDOL	4534936	Chairman	**S. Siglienti**

Italcementi

DJGI Industry: **Building Materials**
Stoxx Sector: **Construction**

Italcementi S.p.A. is one of Europe's largest producers of cement. It also produces other building and hydraulic materials and provides engineering design and construction services. Ciments Français, its wholly owned French cement and ready-mix concrete producer, generates nearly 40% of the company's revenues. Italcementi's other holdings include wholly owned Cemensud, 72% of Cementerie Siciliane, and 77% of Cementerie di Sardegna. Cement accounted for 63% of 1997 revenues; concrete and inert materials, 30%; and other activities, 7%.

	lire bil 12/95	12/96	12/97	US$mil 12/97					
Sales	5,469.2	5,142.0	5,574.0	3,151.8	P/E Ratio M	21.1	Price (6/30/98) M	15,980
Net Income	52.9	2.8	78.1	44.2	P/B Ratio M	1.4	52 Wk Hi-Low M	22,400.0-10,600.0
Book Value	2,967.2	2,851.4	2,882.8	1,630.1	Yield % M	0.9	Market Cap M	US$1,526.7mil

Address	**Via Camozzi 124**	Tel **035-396111**	ADR	ILMNY	V Chairman	**P. Barabani**
	24100 Bergamo	Fax **035-244905**	SEDOL	4450076	Chairman	**G. Giavazzi**

M=Multiple issues in index; reflects most active.

Italgas

DJGI Industry: **Gas Utilities**
Stoxx Sector: **Utility**

Società Italiana per il Gas S.p.A., or Italgas, is a utility company that distributes natural gas and water to domestic markets. As the national leader in the distribution of methane gas, Italgas holds full and partial interests in water distribution, sewage management, natural-gas production, and waste water management. Italgas has 14 fully consolidated subsidiaries, two of which are based in Hungary and one in Slovenia. The company also has investments in Spain, Portugal, and Argentina. Natural gas distribution accounted for 93% of 1997 revenues and distribution of drinking water for 5%.

	lire bil 12/95	12/96	12/97	US$mil 12/97					
Sales	3,969.1	4,709.0	5,003.0	2,829.0	P/E Ratio	58.0	Price (6/30/98)	7,240.00
Net Income	97.8	63.0	87.0	49.2	P/B Ratio	2.6	52 Wk Hi-Low	9,645.0-5,260.0
Book Value	1,923.6	1,856.0	1,912.0	1,081.1	Yield %	1.8	Market Cap	US$2,830.1mil

Address	**Via XX Settembre 41**	Tel **011-2394312**	ADR	--	V Chmn & Dir	**A. Mauri**
	10121 Turin	Fax **011-2394795**	SEDOL	4468206	Chmn Bd Dir	**P. Mallardi**

Magneti Marelli

DJGI Industry: **Other Auto Parts**
Stoxx Sector: **Automobile**

Magneti Marelli S.p.A. is one of the largest automotive-components manufacturers in Europe. The company manufactures electronic and electromechanical products for automobiles, including carburetors, instrumentation, engine-control, lighting, and climate-control products. Its customers include Fiat, Ford, BMW, and Toyota. The company is involved in a joint venture with U.S. automotive company Walbro to produce fuel systems in Brazil. The Magneti Marelli Group consists of 45 companies situated in Italy, other European countries, and North and South America.

	lire bil 12/95	12/96	12/97	US$mil 12/97				
Sales	5,862.9	5,802.1	6,686.0	3,780.6	P/E Ratio	15.4	Price (6/30/98)	3,900.00
Net Income	37.6	38.4	127.6	72.2	P/B Ratio	1.4	52 Wk Hi-Low	5,775.4-2,268.7
Book Value	1,340.8	1,315.0	1,438.9	813.6	Yield %	2.0	Market Cap	US$1,207.8mil

Address	Corso Giulio Cesare 300	Tel 011-26831	ADR	--	V Chairman	P. Monferino
	10154 Turin	Fax 011-2422395	SEDOL	4369161	Chairman	C. Camerana

Mediaset

DJGI Industry: **Cable & Broadcasting**
Stoxx Sector: **Media**

Mediaset S.p.A. is Italy's main commercial television group, covering 99% of the territory with three national television channels (Canale 5, Italia 1 and Retequattro). The group has its own facilities for the production of television programs and broadcasts mainly on air, with only one subsidiary, Gruppo Telepiu, operating on cable. In 1997 Mediaset acquired a 25% share in the Telecinco Group, which operates in Spain. Mediaset is also involved in diversifying its core business through its partIcipation in Albacom S.p.A., one of the main national telecommunication operators.

	lire bil 12/95	12/96	12/97	US$mil 12/97				
Sales	2,925.4	3,084.1	3,289.5	1,860.1	P/E Ratio	28.8	Price (6/30/98)	11,345
Net Income	454.6	445.3	462.5	261.5	P/B Ratio	3.7	52 Wk Hi-Low	13,200.0-7,150.0
Book Value	1,863.6	3,372.8	3,593.4	2,031.9	Yield %	2.0	Market Cap	US$7,485.4mil

Address	Via Europa 44	Tel 02-25141	ADR	--	President	
	Cologno Monzese, Milan	Fax 02-514985	SEDOL	5077946	Chairman	F. Confalonieri

Mediobanca

DJGI Industry: **Diversified Financial Services**
Stoxx Sector: **Financial Services**

Mediobanca--Banca di Credito Finanziario S.p.A., a medium- and long-term credit bank, provides loan, depository, and general banking services to industrial enterprises. Clients include companies in the insurance, finance, telecommunications, electricity, and textiles industries. The bank also underwrites and places securities and provides advisory services for mergers and acquisitions. Interest and fees on loans accounted for 65% of fiscal 1997 revenues; interest on securities, 17%; interest income on bank deposits, 5%; other interest income, 6%; and noninterest income, 7%.

	lire bil 06/95	06/96	06/97	US$mil 06/97				
Revenues	2,989.8	3,323.3	3,140.8	1,852.1	P/E Ratio	41.1	Price (6/30/98)	22,550
Net Income	199.6	228.0	289.8	170.9	P/B Ratio	2.7	52 Wk Hi-Low	30,700.0-8,776.5
Book Value	4,047.0	4,176.0	4,440.5	2,618.5	Yield %	0.8	Market Cap	US$7,226.0mil

Address	Via Filodrammatici 10	Tel 02-88291	ADR	--	Deputy Chairman	A. Bernheim
	20121 Milan	Fax 02-8829367	SEDOL	4574813	Chairman	F. Cingano

Mediolanum

DJGI Industry: **Diversified Financial Services**
Stoxx Sector: **Financial Services**

Mediolanum Holding S.p.A is a financial services and life insurance company that has additional interests in fund management and other financial products. The group consists of 10 fully consolidated companies, all of which are based in northern Italy. One of Italy's largest insurance companys, it has over 3,200 agents and financial consultants. The company's primary shareholders are Fininvest S.p.A., which is owned by the Berlusconi family, and CEO Ennio Doris. Premiums earned accounted for 57% of 1997 revenues; investment income, 19%; and other operating income, 24%.

	lire bil 12/95	12/96	12/97	US$mil 12/97				
Revenues	1,582.0	1,900.7	2,404.6	1,359.7	P/E Ratio	70.2	Price (6/30/98)	56,400
Net Income	93.7	104.2	116.4	65.8	P/B Ratio	13.7	52 Wk Hi-Low	64,000.0-19,350.0
Book Value	374.6	536.4	597.8	338.0	Yield %	0.8	Market Cap	US$4,581.5mil

Address	Palazzo Canova	Tel 02-210231	ADR	--	President	
	20090 Segrate, Milan	Fax 02-210252	SEDOL	5060883	Chairman	S. Preda

Montedison

DJGI Industry: **Other Food**
Stoxx Sector: **Food & Beverage**

As Italy's largest private producer of electricity, Montedison S.p.A. is an industrial holding company active in chemical production, agroindustry, and energy production and engineering. A subsidiary of the Ferruzzi group, it is the European leader in the agroindustrial field, where its main products include sugar, oils, starch, and derivatives. Its chemical operations make polymers and fluoride chemicals. Approximately two-thirds of manufacturing facilities are located outside Italy, mainly in the United States and France. Agroindustry accounted for 78% of 1997 revenues.

	lire bil 12/95	12/96	12/97	US$mil 12/97				
Sales	23,393.0	23,206.0	23,445.0	13,257.0	P/E Ratio	8.5	Price (6/30/98)	2,205.00
Net Income	1,070.0	298.0	1,490.0	842.5	P/B Ratio	1.6	52 Wk Hi-Low	2,795.0-1,070.0
Book Value	5,435.0	6,404.0	8,021.0	4,535.5	Yield %	1.8	Market Cap	US$6,160.2mil

Address	Foro Buonaparte 31	Tel 02-62705004	ADR	MNT	CEO	Enrico Bondi
	20121 Milan	Fax 02-63335416	SEDOL	5046924	Chairman	Luigi Lucchini

Olivetti

DJGI Industry: **Communications Technology**
Stoxx Sector: **Technology**

Olivetti S.p.A. is a leading European manufacturer and one of the largest manufacturers of electronic office equipment in the world. It produces information-technology and office products, including typewriters, copiers, calculators, facsimile machines, and cash registers. Most of Olivetti's plants are located in the Italy; however, the main foreign-based plants are located in France and the United Kingdom. The company has a controlling stake in cellular phone company Omnitel-Pronto Italia. In January 1997, Olivetti announced an accord to sell its PC business to a U.S.-based company.

	lire bil 12/95	12/96	12/97	US$mil 12/97				
Sales	9,778.2	8,333.7	6,560.1	3,709.4	P/E Ratio	NMF	Price (6/30/98)	2,645.00
Net Income	-1,597.9	-915.0	16.0	9.0	P/B Ratio	4.0	52 Wk Hi-Low	2,765.0-570.8
Book Value	2,494.9	1,601.9	1,627.4	920.2	Yield %	0.0	Market Cap	US$3,923.2mil

Address	Via Jervis 77	Tel 01-25-522759	ADR	OLVTY	V Chairman	G. Garuzzo
	10015 Ivrea	Fax 01-25-522422	SEDOL	5294228	Chairman & CEO	R. Colaninno

Parmalat Finanziaria

DJGI Industry: **Other Food**
Stoxx Sector: **Food & Beverage**

Parmalat Finanziaria S.p.A. is a dairy and food-products company that produces and distributes consumables, mainly milk and milk-related products. The group has production facilities worldwide, although its primary facilities are in Italy and South America. The group is composed of 42 subsidiaries in Italy and 91 abroad; the great majority of subsidiaries are involved in production, while a smaller number are involved in marketing, financial services, and sporting activities. The company's products are sold under the Parmalat, Santal, Pomi, Pais, KYR, and Mister Day brand names.

	lire bil 12/95	12/96	12/97	US$mil 12/97				
Sales	4,289.7	5,464.7	7,120.8	4,026.4	P/E Ratio	26.5	Price (6/30/98)	3,625.00
Net Income	135.5	190.0	202.6	114.6	P/B Ratio	2.3	52 Wk Hi-Low	4,610.0-2,230.0
Book Value	1,553.0	2,166.3	2,349.1	1,328.3	Yield %	0.4	Market Cap	US$3,013.6mil

Address	Corso Italia 15	Tel 02-72010156	ADR	PARPP	Gen Mngr & Secr	A. Petrucci
	20122 Milan	Fax 02-8693863	SEDOL	4714404	Chmn & Mng Dir	C. Tanzi

Pirelli

DJGI Industry: **Tires & Rubber**
Stoxx Sector: **Automobile**

Pirelli S.p.A., also called Pirellona, manufactures tires for automobiles and cables for the telecommunications, power, and construction industries. Pirelli also produces building and enameled wires, photonic products, and related accessories. The group is involved in ground and submarine turnkey cable installations as well. Pirelli has subsidiaries located throughout Italy, Europe, the United States, Africa, and Asia. Power, telecommunications, and other cables accounted for 51% of 1997 revenues; tires, 48%; and other 1%.

	lire bil 12/95	12/96	12/97	US$mil 12/97				
Sales	10,893.3	10,239.9	11,265.2	6,369.9	P/E Ratio	21.0	Price (6/30/98)	5,550.00
Net Income	257.7	387.3	460.1	260.2	P/B Ratio	2.4	52 Wk Hi-Low	7,000.0-4,125.0
Book Value	3,266.1	3,272.9	4,022.3	2,274.4	Yield %	2.2	Market Cap	US$5,774.4mil

Address	Viale Sarca 222	Tel 02-64421	ADR	PIREY	V Chairman	Alberto Pirelli
	20126 Milan	Fax 02-64423329	SEDOL	4689900	Chm & Man Dir	Tronchetti Provera

RAS

DJGI Industry: **Insurance - Full Line**
Stoxx Sector: **Insurance**

Riunione Adriatica di Sicurta (RAS) S.p.A. is a diversified insurance company that provides a full range of insurance and reinsurance coverage. A large part of its business is automobile insurance, but it also offers life, health, accident, fire, and general-liability coverage. Its life policies and pension schemes are marketed through Banca Popolare di Milano and Banco di Sicilia. Through its subsidiaries, RAS also provides investment and banking services and manages its own property portfolio. Premiums earned accounted for 74% of 1997 revenues.

	lire bil 12/95	12/96	12/97	US$mil 12/97				
Revenues	16,264.5	16,471.7	18,122.8	10,247.6	P/E Ratio	27.0	Price (6/30/98)	23,150
Net Income	391.1	394.8	521.9	295.1	P/B Ratio	2.2	52 Wk Hi-Low	31,500.0-13,450.0
Book Value	5,006.1	4,880.0	6,598.4	3,731.1	Yield %	1.5	Market Cap	US$5,502.1mil

Address	Corso Italia 23	Tel 02-72161	ADR	--	Jnt V Chmn	Giulio Baseggio
	20122 Milan	Fax 02-8900740	SEDOL	4718246	Chmn & Mng Dir	Angelo Marchiò

La Rinascente

DJGI Industry: **Retailers - Broadline**
Stoxx Sector: **Retail**

La Rinascente S.p.A. is a retail and distribution subsidiary of Italy's IFIL group, which owns about 36% of the company. La Rinascente operates department and discount stores and supermarkets. Its sales centers include the Grandi Magazzini Rinascente department stores, UPIM discount stores, Bricocenter hardware stores, SMA-Citta Mercato hypermarkets, and SMA-Supermercati supermarkets. La Rinascente controls 70% of retailer Cedis Migliarini S.p.A. The company is also engaged in the field of financial and real estate services. All its subsidiaries are located in Italy.

	lire bil 12/95	12/96	12/97	US$mil 12/97				
Revenues	5,958.0	6,390.5	7,169.6	4,054.1	P/E Ratio	43.7	Price (6/30/98)	17,700
Net Income	76.2	92.2	100.4	56.8	P/B Ratio	4.4	52 Wk Hi-Low	21,000.0-9,230.0
Book Value	886.7	941.0	1,356.8	767.2	Yield %	1.1	Market Cap	US$2,201.7mil

Address	Palazzo N, Strada 8	Tel 02-57581	ADR	LARCY	Jnt Mng Dir	B.F. Lheureux
	20089 Rozzano, Milan	Fax 02-2364220	SEDOL	4740034	Chairman	L. Arnaudo

Rolo Banca

DJGI Industry: **Banks - Regional (All)**
Stoxx Sector: **Bank**

Rolo Banca 1473 S.p.A. was formed as the result of a merger between Credito Romagnolo S.p.A. and Carimonte Banca S.p.A. in late 1995. The company offers mainly short-term credit, while one subsidiary, Carimonte Fondiario, operates in the medium- and long-term credit sector. The group also offers security trading, leasing, factoring, and real estate services. Rolo Banca operates mainly in northern Italy but has one branch in Luxembourg and representative offices in New York and Hong Kong. Interest and fees on loans accounted for 50% of 1997 revenues.

	lire bil 12/95	12/96	12/97	US$mil 12/97				
Revenues	6,333.1	6,024.9	5,582.6	3,156.7	P/E Ratio	34.6	Price (6/30/98)	43,600
Net Income	166.1	414.5	548.6	310.2	P/B Ratio	4.7	52 Wk Hi-Low	47,300.0-20,150.0
Book Value	3,452.4	3,776.2	4,092.9	2,314.3	Yield %	1.3	Market Cap	US$10,642mil

Address	Via Zamboni 20		Tel 051-6408111		ADR	--	V Chmn Bd Dir	P. Gnudi
	40126 Bologna		Fax 051-584590		SEDOL	4235778	Chmn Bd of Dir	A. Canosani

Saipem

DJGI Industry: **Other Oilfield Equipment & Services**
Stoxx Sector: **Energy**

Saipem S.p.A. is an oil-industry service company that works in pipeline installation and petrochemical plant construction. Its main activities include exploration and drilling for oil, gas, and minerals, land and marine construction, and infrastructure development. The company constructs plants, pipelines, and refineries for the chemical and petrochemical companies. It also provides research services for the oil, gas, and mineral industries. The company is indirectly controlled by state energy-holding company Ente Nazionale Idrocarburi (ENI) through ENI's holdings in Agip and Snam.

	lire bil 12/95	12/96	12/97	US$mil 12/97				
Sales	2,262.1	2,682.0	3,202.0	1,810.6	P/E Ratio	18.3	Price (6/30/98)	9,130.00
Net Income	168.6	175.0	200.0	113.1	P/B Ratio	3.0	52 Wk Hi-Low	11,600.0-8,300.0
Book Value	911.4	1,031.0	1,219.0	689.3	Yield %	1.6	Market Cap	US$2,039.7mil

Address	Via di Cefalonia 67		Tel 02-5201		ADR	--	V Chairman	Francesco Nanotti
	20097 Milan		Fax 02-52033460		SEDOL	4768768	Chairman	F. D'adda

Sasib

DJGI Industry: **Factory Equipment**
Stoxx Sector: **Industrials**

Sasib S.p.A. operates in the diversified precision-engineering sector manufacturing industrial equipment such as signaling, telecommunications, and safety equipment for the railway industry. It also manufactures and installs industrial-process equipment in tobacco, bakery, beverage, and food-packaging plants. It makes automated ovens and measuring, packaging, and pasteurizing machinery. It is 53%-owned by the De Benedetti group through holding company Compagnie Industriali Riunite S.p.A. (CIR). Sasib has subsidiaries in Italy, Europe, the United States, Canada, and China.

	lire bil 12/94	12/95	12/96	US$mil 12/96				
Sales	1,037.7	1,362.2	1,511.4	996.3	P/E Ratio	NMF	Price (6/30/98)	8,000.00
Net Income	51.5	52.5	40.4	26.7	P/B Ratio	1.9	52 Wk Hi-Low	9,610.0-4,410.0
Book Value	631.4	653.4	636.4	419.5	Yield %	2.5	Market Cap	US$376.7mil

Address	Via di Corticella 87/89		Tel 051-360401		ADR	--	V Chmn & Mng Dir	Gian Carlo Vaccari
	40128 Bologna		Fax 051-529419		SEDOL	4776493	Chairman	Vittorio Ripa di Meana

Seat

DJGI Industry: **Other Industrial & Commercial Services**
Stoxx Sector: **Industrials**

Seat S.p.A is an Italian yellow pages publisher that was spun off from the former state telecommunications group Stet S.p.A. in December 1996. It is now controlled by a core shareholder group of eight companies known as Ottobi S.p.A., which holds 61.33% of Seat's shares. In 1998, Seat proposed incorporating Ottobi into a new group to be called Seat-Pagine Gialle S.p.A. The company's clients numbered 528,000, up 47,000 from the previous year. Advertising orders for its telephone directories generated ITL1.375 trillion of 1997 revenues.

	lire bil 12/95	12/96	12/97	US$mil 12/97				
Sales	N/A	N/A	1,714.0	969.2	P/E Ratio	N/A	Price (6/30/98)	1,200.00
Net Income	N/A	N/A	155.0	87.6	P/B Ratio	N/A	52 Wk Hi-Low	1,458.0-535.0
Book Value	N/A	N/A	N/A	N/A	Yield %	0.0	Market Cap	US$2,581.3mil

Address	Via Aurello Saffi		Tel 011-43-51		ADR	--	Managing Director	Lorenzo Pellicioli
	Torino		Fax 011-4354252		SEDOL	5164570	Chairman	Renato Bernini

Sirti

DJGI Industry: **Communications Technology**
Stoxx Sector: **Technology**

Sirti S.p.A. is a telecommunications engineering group whose major shareholder is STET S.p.A., the telecom holding company of state industrial group Istituto per la Ricostruzione Industriale (IRI). Sirti provides telecommunications and signaling systems for the Italian railway, collection systems for motorway tolls, and equipment cables for trunk lines, radio links, and satellite communications. Sirti also offers real estate services. The company's subsidiaries are located in Italy, Central Europe and South America.

	lire bil 12/95	12/96	12/97	US$mil 12/97				
Sales	1,770.0	1,774.3	2,375.8	1,343.4	P/E Ratio	14.5	Price (6/30/98)	9,670.00
Net Income	214.0	157.7	146.7	83.0	P/B Ratio	1.1	52 Wk Hi-Low	12,550.0-9,335.0
Book Value	1,837.8	1,850.5	1,868.7	1,056.6	Yield %	5.4	Market Cap	US$1,193.5mil

Address	Via E. Fermi 2		Tel 02-66771		ADR	--	V Chairman	G. Morchio
	20060 Cassina De		Fax 02-66773333		SEDOL	4811899	Chairman	P.P. Davoli

SNIA BPD

DJGI Industry: **Chemicals - Commodity**
Stoxx Sector: **Chemical**

SNIA BPD S.p.A. is a holding company whose main subsidiaries manufacture fiber, primarily for the apparel industry; chemicals for water-treatment and detergent products; polymers, used primarily for packaging; and bioengineering products. The company is viewed as the European leader of heart surgery products. Its majority-owned SNIA Fibre subsidiary manufactures polyamide filament used in hosiery, woven fabrics, and umbrellas. In March 1997, the SNIA BPD board approved a merger of its SNIA Fibre unit into the parent company.

	lire bil 12/95	12/96	12/97	US$mil 12/97					
Sales	2,943.5	2,965.1	2,844.5	1,608.4	P/E Ratio		16.0	Price (6/30/98)	2,180.00
Net Income	63.5	80.1	107.1	60.5	P/B Ratio		1.3	52 Wk Hi-Low	3,100.0-1,535.0
Book Value	1,262.9	1,277.6	1,351.3	764.1	Yield %		2.8	Market Cap	US$858.6mil

Address	**Via Borgonuovo 14**	Tel **02-6332205**	ADR	--	President	**C. Gatto**
	20121 Milan	Fax **02-6332384**	SEDOL	**4819406**	Chairman	**U. Rosa**

Telecom Italia

DJGI Industry: **Telephone Utilities (All)**
Stoxx Sector: **Telecom**

Telecom Italia S.p.A., Italy's state-controlled telephone company, provides national and international telecommunications services in Italy. It also manufactures telephone equipment, electronic components, and switchboards. Telecom Italia was formed in 1994 by the merger of Italy's five main telecommunications companies. It is controlled by STET, which owns 64.15% of ordinary company stock. Telecommunications services accounted for 83% of 1997 revenues; installation activities, 5%; information technology services, 5%; manufacturing operations 5%; and other activities, 2%.

	lire bil 12/95	12/96	12/97	US$mil 12/97					
Sales	37,373.0	40,522.0	42,816.0	24,210.4	P/E Ratio M		37.2	Price (6/30/98) M	13,085
Net Income	1,459.0	1,732.0	2,609.0	1,475.3	P/B Ratio M		3.2	52 Wk Hi-Low M	N/A
Book Value	17,183.0	17,477.0	29,899.0	16,906.4	Yield % M		1.5	Market Cap M	US$38,576mil

Address	**Corso Italia 41**	Tel **06-85891**	ADR	--	President	**P.G. Jaeger**
	00198 Rome	Fax **06-8589434**	SEDOL	**5297506**	Chairman	**G. Rossignolo**

M=Multiple issues in index; reflects most active; In DJ Stoxx 50; In EuroStoxx 50.

Telecom Italia Mobile

DJGI Industry: **Telephone Utilities (All)**
Stoxx Sector: **Telecom**

Telecom Italia Mobile S.p.A. (TIM) operates mobile phones throughout Italy. It was spun off from the domestic telephone company Telecom Italia S.p.A. in July 1995. Headquartered in Turin, TIM offers telephone services on the TACS (Total Access Communication System) and GSM (Global System for Mobile Communication) networks. The company also offers paging systems, centralized answering systems, and data and fax transmission systems. Mobile phone operations accounted for 88% of 1997 revenues and sales of apparatus accounted for 12%.

	lire bil 12/95	12/96	12/97	US$mil 12/97					
Sales	2,800.5	7,347.5	9,456.3	5,347.1	P/E Ratio		57.4	Price (6/30/98)	10,870
Net Income	350.3	930.2	1,554.5	879.0	P/B Ratio		29.8	52 Wk Hi-Low	11,675.0-5,485.0
Book Value	1,019.2	1,857.1	2,995.3	1,693.7	Yield %		0.8	Market Cap	US$40,486mil

Address	**Via L. Rizzo 22**	Tel **06-39001**	ADR	--	Managing Director	**V. Gamberale**
	00136 Rome	Fax **06-39002111**	SEDOL	**4876746**	Chairman	**V. di Stefano**

Unicem

DJGI Industry: **Building Materials**
Stoxx Sector: **Construction**

Unicem S.p.A., also known as Unione Cementierie Marchino ed Emiliane, is the parent company of businesses that produce cement, ready-mix concrete, premixed plaster, lime, and other building materials. It has interests in plant engineering, clay mining, real estate, and finance. Unicem, Italy's second-largest cement producer, has a production capacity of 10 million tons of cement annually. The company markets its products in Italy and the United States, where it purchased RC Cement in 1995, and it also has investments in Spain and the Netherlands.

	lire bil 12/95	12/96	12/97	US$mil 12/97					
Sales	860.9	864.9	1,047.9	592.5	P/E Ratio		30.2	Price (6/30/98)	17,250
Net Income	14.2	37.8	61.1	34.5	P/B Ratio		2.4	52 Wk Hi-Low	22,650.0-11,870.0
Book Value	689.1	719.2	796.2	450.2	Yield %		1.2	Market Cap	US$632.5mil

Address	**Via Ottavio Marchino 10**	Tel **011-65641**	ADR	--	V Chairman	**V. Marrone**
	15033 Casale Monferrato	Fax **011-6638543**	SEDOL	**4910398**	Chairman	**C. Camerana**

Netherlands

http://www.dowjones.com/indexes/Htmls01/netherla.html

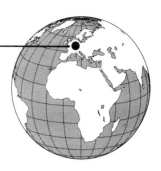

Exchanges:

Amsterdam Stock Exchange (ASE)

Netherlands

Heleen de Graaf
Amsterdam

The euro will land at Amsterdam Exchanges January 4, 1999, the first trading day in the new year, when all share prices on the Amsterdam bourse will be quoted in euros instead of guilders.

The change comes two years after another historic event: the official merger of the Amsterdam Stock Exchange with the Options Exchange into Amsterdam Exchanges.

The bourse has come a long way. Trading of securities in the Netherlands dates back as far as the early 17th century, when the Dutch East Indies Company needed money to fund its far-flung trading voyages.

The 17th century, known in the Netherlands as the "golden century," was a time of great economic prosperity for the country as Dutch ships traveled around the world to trade. Dutch companies have retained their international character, not only because of tradition, but also because of a small domestic market.

This country of almost 16 million people is home to such internationally known names as Royal Philips Electronics, Europe's largest consumer-electronics group; ABN Amro, the Netherlands' largest bank; banking and insurance giant ING Groep; beer-brewer Heineken; and Akzo Nobel, the chemicals concern. The Netherlands also provides a base for Anglo-Dutch giants such as oil-producer Royal Dutch/Shell Group, publisher Reed Elsevier, and the consumer-products group Unilever. Internationally co-owned or not, many of the blue-chips generate a large portion of their profits abroad and often have several listings outside the Netherlands, most notably in New York.

All these international giants are included in the AEX benchmark index. The index is reviewed every year in February, but underwent two extra changes in June 1998, when Vedior and the TNT Post Group were added, bringing the number of stocks in the AEX to 27 from the usual 25.

Vedior, a temporary employment agency, was spun of from retailer Vendex, and TNT Post Group (TPG) split off from telecom group KPN. All shareholders of the old Koninklijke KPN received a share in TPG for every share they held in the Koninklijke PTT Nederland, the name of the company prior to the split.

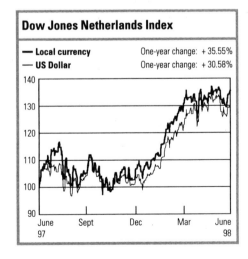

Dow Jones Netherlands Index

— **Local currency** One-year change: + 35.55%
— **US Dollar** One-year change: + 30.58%

The number of companies in the AEX will likely drop again in the course of 1998, when Philips completes the sale of PolyGram, a recording and filmmaking company, to the Canadian spirits concern Seagram.

With an average return of 45% on Dutch stocks in 1997, the Amsterdam bourse outpaced the Morgan Stanley Capital International world average, which rose 36%. It was the sixth consecutive year of outperformance from Amsterdam.

In the first six months of 1998, the AEX index rose 31%, closing at 1197.86 on June 30. Financial and high-tech companies did well, although they also were among the sharp decliners when worries about economic woes in Asia and Russia surfaced from time to time.

Because of the large proportion of international operating companies in the AEX, the index is heavily influenced by factors from abroad, most notably the value of the dollar. Some analysts see the movement of the U.S. currency as the most important indicator for the direction of the AEX index. Also, as many of the blue-chips are listed in New York, what happens on Wall Street has a great impact on the bourse in Amsterdam.

With low interest rates and inflation and healthy, sustainable economic growth, and with the entry of the Netherlands into the economic and monetary union on January 1, 1999, the Dutch market tends to pay more

Country Information

Trading Hours:
  Local: 9:30 am - 4:30 pm

  EST: 3:30 am - 10:30 am

  GMT: 0830 - 1530

Population (6/98):
15,731,112

Unemployment (97):
6.9%

Main Industries:
Agroindustries, metal and engineering products, electrical machinery and equipment, chemicals, petroleum, fishing, construction, and microelectronics

Gross Domestic Product (97):
US$360.47 billion

GDP per Capita (97):
US$23,113.91

Three-Year Average GDP Growth (94-97):
2.7%

Average Annual CPI Growth (96-97):
+ 2.15%

Monetary Unit:
Netherlands Guilder

Exchange Rate (6/98):
NLG2.04 to US$1.00

attention to economic indicators from abroad than to domestic data.

Amsterdam's stock exchange operates with semiautomatic screen-based trading and a modernized clearing system. Trade is carried out with the Trading System Amsterdam (TSA), which was introduced in September 1994. Bourse hours are 9:30 am to 4:30 pm local time.

In 1994, the Exchange introduced the currently used market-maker system to improve liquidity and transparency as well as to narrow price spreads.

Before the end of 1998, the current trading system for the most active stocks will change again: a centralized, anonymous, electronic order book will be used wherever possible. The change is intended to improve the transparency of the market.

Two systems — ASSET and AIDA — will be discontinued and the number of stocks traded in the limit-order book are to be expanded to include all AEX stocks and the Amsterdam Midkap index. ASSET is the Amsterdam securities trading system — a screen used by banks to sell quotes to clients. AIDA is short for an order-driven system called automatic interprofessional dealing system Amsterdam.

Measures taken over the years, such as reviews and updates of the trading systems, have helped Amsterdam regain its share of the market in the trading of Dutch stocks from

Ten Largest Capitalized Companies In The Dow Jones Netherlands Index as of 6/30/98	
Stock	Market Cap. US$ Thousands
Royal Dutch Petroleum	118,660,059
ING Groep	60,078,289
Unilever	50,688,120
Aegon	50,385,101
ABN-AMRO	32,935,689
Philips Electronics	29,081,921
Koninklijke KPN	18,139,915
Ahold Kon.	17,880,045
Akzo Nobel	15,823,012
Heineken	12,291,528

exchanges such as London. Its market share at the end of 1997 stood at 75%, up sharply from around 10% at the beginning of the 1990s.

Amsterdam, in terms of market capitalization, is the ninth largest exchange in the world and the fifth largest in Europe.

In the spring of 1997, the Amsterdam exchanges launched a new market for young, fast-growing companies looking for capital to expand. The new market was set up in conjunction with three similar "new markets" in Paris, Frankfurt, and Brussels, to form the so-called Euro New Markets (Euro NM).

The NMAX, as the new market in Amsterdam is called, aims to provide capital to small companies that don't yet have the track record to apply for a listing on the main market in Amsterdam.

At the end of 1997, the Euro New Markets combined listed 62 companies. There were

651 companies and investment funds listed on the main Amsterdam Exchange.

The planned alliance of the Frankfurt and London stock markets also will bring new challenges for Amsterdam and Exchange president George Moller has said he is interested in joining the partnership.

Industrial companies still generate most of the turnover is shares but the banking and insurance sector is on the rise.

The impact of high-tech stocks is also increasing. Two of these companies, ASML and Baan, were included in the benchmark index less than a year after their listing.

The shares quickly became investors' darlings but, as the financial crisis in Asia continued, rapidly lost fans. The two companies are among the largest movers, both up and down, on many trading days.

Total value of new shares admitted to the stock exchange in 1997, including new issues, secondary placements, exercise of option rights conversions, bonus issues, and stock dividends, rose to NLG51 billion from NLG34 billion in 1996. In the first half of 1998, the value was NLG44.67 billion.

Among the largest new issues were steel group Ispat, detergent manufacturer Benckiser, livestock and fish company Nutreco, temporary employment agency Vedior and investment company Alpinvest.

Market Sector Performance In The Dow Jones Netherlands Index
1 Year Change Through 6/30/98

Market Sector	Change % (US$)
Utilities	57.40
Financial	54.47
Basic Materials	52.45
Consumer, Non-Cyclical	43.06
Technology	19.30
Energy	6.43
Consumer, Cyclical	5.02
Industrial	-11.34

ABN-Amro

DJGI Industry: **Banks - Major International**
Stoxx Sector: **Bank**

ABN-Amro Holding NV is the Netherlands' largest banking group, Europe's fourth and the world's eighth largest bank. It offers a full range of banking services including domestic, international, credit, and investment banking. The bank provides worldwide services to certain customer groups in specific fields such as corporate finance, securities, treasury products and facilities, trade and commodity financing, leasing, and private banking. Interest income accounted for 82% of 1997 revenues; commission, 13%; foreign exchange and trading income, 1%; and other operating income, 4%.

	NLG mil 12/95	12/96	12/97	US$mil 12/97				
Revenues	42,407.0	46,369.0	55,840.0	27,561.7	P/E Ratio	18.0	Price (6/30/98)	47.60
Net Income	2,616.0	3,303.0	3,853.0	1,901.8	P/B Ratio	2.8	52 Wk Hi-Low	55.10-36.60
Book Value	18,337.0	21,128.0	24,022.0	11,856.9	Yield %	2.5	Market Cap	US$32,936mil

Address	Foppingadreef 22	Tel 20-628-9898	ADR	AAN	Chmn Supv Bd	A.A. Loudon
	1102 BS Amsterdam	Fax 20-628-6233	SEDOL	5250769	Chmn Mgt Bd	P.J. Kalff

In DJ Stoxx 50; In EuroStoxx 50.

Aegon

DJGI Industry: **Insurance - Full Line**
Stoxx Sector: **Insurance**

Aegon NV is one of the world's largest insurance companies, offering a full range of life insurance and financial services. The company also is active in accident, health, and general insurance, including some related noninsurance activities. Its American subsidiary Aegon USA is the largest foreign insurance company in the United States. Aegon operates in the banking industry through its subsidiaries FGH Bank, La Bouchère, and Spaarbeleg Bank. Premium income accounted for 66% of 1997 revenues; investment income, 29%; and other operating income, 5%.

	NLG mil 12/95	12/96	12/97	US$mil 12/97				
Revenues	20,159.0	23,552.0	30,177.0	14,894.9	P/E Ratio	41.1	Price (6/30/98)	177.00
Net Income	1,323.0	1,568.0	2,207.0	1,089.3	P/B Ratio	6.9	52 Wk Hi-Low	177.00-68.50
Book Value	7,277.0	8,399.0	14,790.0	7,300.1	Yield %	1.0	Market Cap	US$50,385mil

Address	Mariahoeveplein 50	Tel 70-344-3210	ADR	AEG	Chmn Exec Bd	K. J. Storm
	2501 CE The Hague	Fax 70-347-5238	SEDOL	5462304	Chmn Supv Bd	G. van Schaik

In DJ Stoxx 50; In EuroStoxx 50.

Ahold

DJGI Industry: **Food Retailers & Wholesalers**
Stoxx Sector: **Consumer Non-Cyclical**

Koninklijke Ahold NV, also known as Royal Ahold, is a food producer, retailer, and institutional supplier with operations in Europe and the United States. It operates more than 530 stores in the United States through 5 chains, and in the Netherlands, Ahold owns 6 retail companies and more than 1,500 stores. It also owns Mana supermarkets in the Czech Republic, co-owns Pingo Doce stores in Portugal, and operates health- and beauty-supply stores in Belgium. Retail trade accounted for 91% of 1997 revenues; wholesale trade, 8%; and other sales, 1%.

	NLG mil 12/95	12/96	12/97	US$mil 12/97				
Sales	29,617.3	36,538.1	50,568.5	24,959.8	P/E Ratio	34.8	Price (6/30/98)	65.30
Net Income	456.6	632.4	933.8	460.9	P/B Ratio	12.1	52 Wk Hi-Low	70.00-48.30
Book Value	2,241.9	2,169.3	2,831.4	1,397.6	Yield %	1.1	Market Cap	US$17,880mil

Address	Albert Heijnweg 1	Tel 75-659-9111	ADR	--	Memb Mgt Bd	F.I. Ahlquist
	1507 EH Zaandam	Fax 75-659-8350	SEDOL	5252602	Pres & Mgt Bd	C.H. Van Der Hoeven

In DJ Stoxx 50; In EuroStoxx 50.

Akzo Nobel

DJGI Industry: **Chemicals - Commodity**
Stoxx Sector: **Chemical**

Akzo Nobel NV produces chemicals, fibers, coatings, and pharmaceuticals. Its chemicals are used in oil, plastic, rubber, paper, and detergent. Akzo also provides coatings for aerospace, automotive, industrial, and consumer products. Its fibers are used in clothing, footwear, textiles for home furnishings, carpets, industrial fabrics, and tires. Its pharmaceutical division produces and markets generic drugs, veterinary products, and contraceptive and fertility drugs. Coatings accounted for 35% of 1997 revenues; chemicals, 31%; pharmaceuticals, 19%; and fibers, 15%.

	NLG mil 12/95	12/96	12/97	US$mil 12/97				
Sales	21,488.0	22,438.0	24,052.0	11,871.7	P/E Ratio	19.9	Price (6/30/98)	452.20
Net Income	1,314.0	1,318.0	1,615.0	797.1	P/B Ratio	3.6	52 Wk Hi-Low	452.20-269.00
Book Value	6,605.0	7,703.0	9,035.0	4,459.5	Yield %	7.5	Market Cap	US$15,823mil

Address	Velperweg 76	Tel 85-66-44-33	ADR	AKZOY	Chmn Exec Bd	C. J. van Lede
	6800 SB Arnhem	Fax 85-66-32-50	SEDOL	4011901	Chmn Supv Bd	F.H. Fentener

In EuroStoxx 50.

Baan

DJGI Industry: **Software**
Stoxx Sector: **Technology**

Baan Company NV is a high-technology software company, providing open systems and client/server-based Enterprise Resource Planning software. It develops the Triton family of computer-software products, including its three product lines Triton Applications, Triton OrgWare, and Triton Tools. Baan is active in more than 58 countries worldwide, and it has approximately 2,000 customers. Founded in 1978, Baan maintains dual headquarters in Ede, the Netherlands, and in Menlo Park, California in the United States. The company plans to expand its presence in the Asia-Pacific region.

	NLG mil 12/95	12/96	12/97	US$mil 12/97				
Sales	345.1	655.9	1,329.9	656.4	P/E Ratio	93.4	Price (6/30/98)	73.10
Net Income	24.4	61.4	151.0	74.5	P/B Ratio	24.0	52 Wk Hi-Low	107.80-60.50
Book Value	182.1	271.6	588.8	290.6	Yield %	0.0	Market Cap	US$7,014.5mil

Address	Vanenburgerallee 13	Tel 341-375-555	ADR	BAANF	Managing Director	A.M. Johnson
	3882 RH Putten	Fax --	SEDOL	5380202	President & CEO	T.C. Tinsley

Buhrmann

DJGI Industry: **Paper Products**
Stoxx Sector: **Basic Resources**

Buhrmann NV, formerly known as NV Koninklijke KNP BT, an international group of approximately 150 companies, operates in the sectors of distribution of graphic supplies and office products, production of a variety of packaging material and paper manufaturing and merchanting. The company holds the number one position in the United States, as well as in France for large scale distribution of PC's and office products. Paper merchanting and office product distribution accounted for 69% of 1997 revenues, packaging, 17%; and paper production, 14%.

	NLG mil 12/95	12/96	12/97	US$mil 12/97					
Sales	15,035.0	13,637.0	15,677.0	7,737.9	P/E Ratio		NMF	Price (6/30/98)	52.50
Net Income	470.0	231.0	45.0	22.2	P/B Ratio		2.1	52 Wk Hi-Low	60.50-42.40
Book Value	2,909.7	2,747.7	2,636.7	1,301.4	Yield %		2.1	Market Cap	US$2,677.5mil

Address	Museumplein 9	Tel 20-574-7474	ADR	--	Memb Mgt Bd	F.H.J. Koffrie
	1080 JS	Fax 20-574-7400	SEDOL	5516751	Chmn Mgt Bd	K. De Kluis

Elsevier

DJGI Industry: **Publishing**
Stoxx Sector: **Media**

Elsevier NV co-owns, with Reed International, the publishing and information company Reed Elsevier. Reed Elsevier, in which Elsevier holds a 50% stake, publishes scientific, medical, professional, and consumer books, as well as journals, newspapers, and magazines. Elsevier and Reed International also co-own Elsevier Reed Finance, with Elsevier holding a 54% stake. Elsevier and Reed International amalgamated their operational activities in 1993. Elsevier is listed on both the London Stock Exchange and the Amsterdam Stock Exchanges.

	NLG mil 12/95	12/96	12/97	US$mil 12/97					
Sales	N/A	N/A	N/A	N/A	P/E Ratio		65.3	Price (6/30/98)	30.70
Net Income	701.0	794.0	330.0	162.9	P/B Ratio		8.7	52 Wk Hi-Low	39.10-28.20
Book Value	2,563.0	3,065.0	2,495.0	1,231.5	Yield %		3.1	Market Cap	US$10,045mil

Address	Van Der Sande	Tel 20-515-9341	ADR	ENL	V Chmn Mgt Bd	P.C.F.M. Vlek
	1061 AG	Fax 20-683-2617	SEDOL	4148810	Chmn Mgt Bd	H.J. Bruggink

In EuroStoxx 50.

Fortis

DJGI Industry: **Insurance - Full Line**
Stoxx Sector: **Insurance**

Fortis AMEV NV is a holding company that is, together with the Belgian Fortis AG, the parent company of insurance and banking group Fortis Group, with each holding 50%. Fortis AMEV offers life, accident, health, and general insurance. It offers retail banking and asset management through its Metropolitan, VSB, and ASLK-CGER banking subsidiaries. Its main markets are the Netherlands, Belgium, and the United States. It generates 62% of revenues from insurance and 38% from banking activities. Non-European insurance premiums account for nearly 30% of its revenues.

	NLG mil 12/95	12/96	12/97	US$mil 12/97					
Revenues	695.6	811.0	1,018.9	502.9	P/E Ratio		20.6	Price (6/30/98)	119.10
Net Income	693.2	803.6	1,010.3	498.7	P/B Ratio		2.6	52 Wk Hi-Low	130.50-75.00
Book Value	5,780.6	6,706.1	8,462.8	4,177.1	Yield %		1.9	Market Cap	US$10,762mil

Address	Archimedeslaan 6	Tel 30-257-6576	ADR	FAMVY	V Chmn Mgt Bd	B.J.H.S. Feilzer
	3584 BA Utrecht	Fax 30-257-7835	SEDOL	5014277	Chmn Mgt Bd	J.L.M. Bartelds

Getronics

DJGI Industry: **Communications Technology**
Stoxx Sector: **Technology**

Getronics NV is a group of complementary business units operating in specific areas of information technology and telecommunications. More than 70% of sales are realized in the Netherlands. It is active in areas such as mixed hardware network systems, industrial automation, and information systems consultancy. In June 1998, Getronics said it will acquire Spanish software consultation concern Grupo Control Presupuestario SA. ICT-systems accounted for 53% of 1997 revenues and maintenance, installation, software services, and consultancy accounted for 47%.

	NLG mil 12/95	12/96	12/97	US$mil 12/97					
Sales	1,703.1	2,210.7	2,776.5	1,370.4	P/E Ratio		51.5	Price (6/30/98)	105.50
Net Income	97.5	131.6	180.0	88.9	P/B Ratio		63.8	52 Wk Hi-Low	109.00-58.90
Book Value	259.5	255.2	144.9	71.5	Yield %		0.4	Market Cap	US$4,497.0mil

Address	Donauweg 10	Tel 20-586-1412	ADR	--	V Pres Mgt Bd	P.K. Van Voorst
	1043 AJ Amsterdam	Fax 20-586-1568	SEDOL	5022009	President & CEO	A.H.J. Risseeuw

Heineken

DJGI Industry: **Distillers & Brewers**
Stoxx Sector: **Food & Beverage**

Heineken NV, the world's second largest brewing group, produces and distributes beer, wine, spirits, and soft drinks in more than 170 countries. Its beers include Heineken, Amstel, Amstel Light, and Murphy's Irish Stout. Heineken brews beer in 116 breweries located in 57 countries. Europe and the United States are its main markets, but it also brews and distributes beer in Canada, Africa, and Asia. Beers accounted for 79% of 1997 revenues; soft drinks, 10%; spirits and wine, 7%; merchandise and other trading income and services, 4%.

	NLG mil 12/95	12/96	12/97	US$mil 12/97					
Sales	9,055.9	10,568.1	11,662.6	5,756.5	P/E Ratio		32.9	Price (6/30/98)	79.90
Net Income	664.4	655.4	761.4	375.8	P/B Ratio		4.9	52 Wk Hi-Low	82.33-48.62
Book Value	4,734.1	4,514.0	5,103.2	2,518.8	Yield %		0.7	Market Cap	US$12,292mil

Address	Tweede Weteringplantsoen 21	Tel 20-523-9239	ADR	HINKY	V Chmn Mgt Bd	A. Ruys
	1017 ZD Amsterdam	Fax 20-626-3503	SEDOL	5455821	Chmn Mgt Bd	K. Vuursteen

Hunter Douglas

DJGI Industry: **Other Home Furnishings**
Stoxx Sector: **Consumer Cyclical**

Hunter Douglas NV manufactures window coverings and construction materials. The company is the inventor of the metal venetian blind, which was first introduced in the United States nearly 50 years ago. The company's other activities include trading in metals, particularly aluminum, and producing and marketing precision machinery. Hunter Douglas's products include blinds, shades, and other window coverings. In May 1998, it sold its machine tool unit Laagland to Dutch company Continaf. The group consists of more than 110 companies.

	NLG mil 01/96	01/97	01/98	US$mil 01/98				
Sales	3,467.8	2,234.7	2,626.1	1,273.9	P/E Ratio	19.0	Price (6/30/98)	110.50
Net Income	125.6	158.3	194.3	94.3	P/B Ratio	4.0	52 Wk Hi-Low	113.50-68.90
Book Value	581.8	764.1	1,001.3	485.7	Yield %	1.4	Market Cap	US$1,949.0mil

Address	Piekstraat 2	Tel	10-486-9911	ADR	HDOUY	Exec V President	J.T. Sherwin
	3071 EL Rotterdam	Fax	10-485-0621	SEDOL	5291810	President & CEO	R. Sonnenberg

ING

DJGI Industry: **Diversified Financial Services**
Stoxx Sector: **Financial Services**

ING Groep (Internationale Nederlanden Groep NV) is the largest Dutch insurance/banking group, offering a wide range of banking, insurance, and related financial services. It offers life and general insurance, securities trading, loans, leasing, funds-transfer services, and debt conversion. The company has its own establishments in 47 countries. In 1997, ING acquired Belgium's Bank Brussels Lambert, U.S.-based Furman Selz, and U.S. life insurer Equitable of Iowa. Investment income accounted for 50% of ING's 1997 revenues; premium income, 41%; and other income, 8%.

	NLG mil 12/95	12/96	12/97	US$mil 12/97				
Revenues	52,274.0	59,473.0	74,170.0	36,609.1	P/E Ratio	21.6	Price (6/30/98)	133.20
Net Income	2,649.0	3,321.0	4,105.0	2,026.2	P/B Ratio	2.4	52 Wk Hi-Low	141.20-78.60
Book Value	23,559.0	33,906.0	45,900.0	22,655.5	Yield %	1.7	Market Cap	US$60,078mil

Address	Strawinskylaan 2631	Tel	20-541-5462	ADR	INLGY	V Chmn Mgt Bd	G.J.A. Van Der Lugt
	1000 AV Amsterdam	Fax	20-541-5451	SEDOL	5058877	Chmn Mgt Bd	A.G. Jacobs

In DJ Stoxx 50; In EuroStoxx 50.

KLM

DJGI Industry: **Airlines**
Stoxx Sector: **Consumer Cyclical**

KLM Royal Dutch Airlines, the national airline carrier of the Netherlands, is an international airline that offers scheduled and chartered services for passengers and cargo. It is 25%-owned by the government. The company has interests in computer-reservation systems, helicopter ferrying, forwarding, and trucking. KLM flies to more than 150 destinations on six continents. Along with its wholly owned KLM Cityhopper subsidiary, KLM holds minority interests in Northwest Airlines, Air UK, ALM Antillean Airlines, Martin Air Holland and Koninklijke Frans Maas.

	NLG mil 03/96	03/97	03/98	US$mil 03/98				
Sales	9,536.0	10,358.0	13,364.0	6,420.1	P/E Ratio	2.8	Price (6/30/98)	82.60
Net Income	547.0	236.0	2,203.0	1,058.3	P/B Ratio	1.2	52 Wk Hi-Low	88.90-60.30
Book Value	3,940.0	3,341.2	5,307.2	2,549.6	Yield %	3.6	Market Cap	US$3,005.4mil

Address	Amsterdamseweg 55	Tel	20-649-9123	ADR	KLM	President	L.M. Van Wijk
	1117 ZL Amstelveen	Fax	20-648-8069	SEDOL	4480255	CEO	L.M. Van Wijk

KPN

DJGI Industry: **Telephone Utilities (All)**
Stoxx Sector: **Telecom**

Koninklijke KPN NV (KPN) provides telecommunications services in the Netherlands. In 1998, the company announced a demerger of its postal operations. In addition to its telecommunications activities, the company also distributes a wide range of communications equipment. The company also operates courier services, a cable television network, logistic services, data communication networks, car leasing, safety and security services, and a capital funds venture. Telecommunications activities accounted for 97% of 1997 revenues and other activities for 3%.

	NLG mil 12/95	12/96	12/97	US$mil 12/97				
Sales	19,154.0	20,505.0	15,250.0	7,527.1	P/E Ratio	13.7	Price (6/30/98)	78.30
Net Income	2,257.0	2,462.0	2,690.0	1,327.7	P/B Ratio	2.1	52 Wk Hi-Low	78.30-43.56
Book Value	14,608.0	16,129.0	17,552.0	8,663.4	Yield %	4.0	Market Cap	US$18,140mil

Address	Stationsplein 7	Tel	50-822-822	ADR	--	Chmn Mgt Bd	W. Dik
	9726 AE Groningen	Fax	50-582-2688	SEDOL	5490800	Chmn Supv Bd	J. Groenendijk

In DJ Stoxx 50; In EuroStoxx 50.

Oce van der Grinten

DJGI Industry: **Office Equipment**
Stoxx Sector: **Technology**

Oce van der Grinten NV is the Venlo-based holding company of the Oce Group, which designs, manufactures, and sells products for the reproduction and presentation of information on paper. The product range comprises copier, printer, and plotter systems as well as carrier materials and other imaging supplies for the design, engineering, and office markets. Oce Van is active in some 80 countries, with operating companies in 25 countries. It leases and sells copiers, printers, and printing and reproduction systems through its Office and Engineering Systems divisions.

	NLG mil 11/95	11/96	11/97	US$mil 11/97				
Sales	2,932.5	4,174.2	5,439.6	2,737.7	P/E Ratio	29.0	Price (6/30/98)	86.60
Net Income	108.3	169.5	236.7	119.1	P/B Ratio	4.6	52 Wk Hi-Low	90.20-48.50
Book Value	1,055.4	1,315.5	1,520.8	765.4	Yield %	1.1	Market Cap	US$3,460.5mil

Address	St. Urbanusweg 43	Tel	77-359-2222	ADR	OCENY	Memb Mgt Bd	H.J.A.F. Meertens
	5900 MA Venlo	Fax	77-354-4700	SEDOL	5446751	Chmn Mgt Bd	J.V.H. Pennings

Pakhoed

DJGI Industry: **Marine Transportation**
Stoxx Sector: **Industrials**

Koninklijke Pakhoed NV, also known as Royal Pakhoed NV, provides tank storage, logistics, and support activities to shipping businesses around the world and to the chemical and oil industries. The company is divided into three sectors. The tank storage division provides services for the oil and chemical industries in the Netherlands, North America, Europe, and Asia. The distribution division handles oil and chemical products, mainly in Europe. The third sector, logistics, covers shipping and specialized services. Distribution accounted for 87% of 1997 revenues.

	NLG mil 12/95	12/96	12/97	US$mil 12/97				
Sales	2,069.6	3,594.1	6,218.0	3,069.1	P/E Ratio	11.8	Price (6/30/98)	66.00
Net Income	121.5	75.6	191.0	94.3	P/B Ratio	2.2	52 Wk Hi-Low	78.00-54.00
Book Value	1,010.4	801.7	957.0	472.4	Yield %	3.6	Market Cap	US$1,039.7mil

Address	Blaak 333	Tel 10-400-2911	ADR	--	Mgt Bd	A.H. Spoor
	3011 GB Rotterdam	Fax 10-413-9829	SEDOL	4492067	Chmn Mgt Bd	N.J. Westdijk

Philips Electronics

DJGI Industry: **Diversified Technology**
Stoxx Sector: **Technology**

Philips Electronics NV manufactures electronic products for industrial and consumer use. It is Europe's largest consumer electronics group as well as the world's largest manufacturer of light bulbs. The diversified company also produces televisions, video recorders, multimedia systems, medical systems, and industrial electronics products. Consumer electronics accounted for 31% of 1997 revenues; components and semiconductors, 20%; software and systems, 17%; professional products and systems, 17%; lighting, 13%; and miscellaneous, 2%.

	NLG mil 12/95	12/96	12/97	US$mil 12/97				
Sales	64,462.0	69,195.0	76,453.0	37,735.9	P/E Ratio	10.4	Price (6/30/98)	171.00
Net Income	2,518.0	-590.0	5,733.0	2,829.7	P/B Ratio	3.1	52 Wk Hi-Low	203.70-111.50
Book Value	14,054.9	13,955.9	19,457.0	9,603.6	Yield %	1.2	Market Cap	US$29,082mil

Address	Groenewoudseweg 1	Tel 40-279-1111	ADR	PHG	V President	D.G. Eustace
	5621 BA Eindhoven	Fax 40-278-5486	SEDOL	4685209	Pres & Chmn	C. Boonstra

In DJ Stoxx 50; In EuroStoxx 50.

Randstad

DJGI Industry: **Other Industrial & Commercial Services**
Stoxx Sector: **Industrials**

Randstad Holding NV is a service organization operating in the field of temporary employment. Randstad is also active in cleaning, security, automation, and training services. The company is the market leader in temporary staffing in the Netherlands, Belgium, and Luxembourg, and it ranks among the largest temporary employment organizations worldwide. Temporary staffing accounted for 94% of 1997 revenues; cleaning services, 3%; security services 2%; and other services (automation, training, and technical services), 1%.

	NLG mil 12/95	12/96	12/97	US$mil 12/97				
Sales	4,702.4	5,953.2	7,072.9	7,073.9	P/E Ratio	51.3	Price (6/30/98)	122.50
Net Income	163.3	207.4	257.8	257.8	P/B Ratio	19.6	52 Wk Hi-Low	124.00-68.60
Book Value	405.8	534.9	675.3	675.4	Yield %	0.8	Market Cap	US$6,490.4mil

Address	Diemermere 25	Tel 20-569-5911	ADR	--	President & CEO	F.J.D. Goldschmeding
	1112 TC Diemen	Fax 20-569-5520	SEDOL	5228658	Chairman	J.E. Andriessen

Rodamco

DJGI Industry: **Real Estate**
Stoxx Sector: **Financial Services**

Rodamco NV, partially owned by the Robeco-Groep, operates property-investment businesses worldwide. It has roughly 1.8 million square meters of retail, office, and industrial rental property. Retail property is Rodamco's primary management area. The company holds Australian retail investments with Westfield Trust. Australasian holdings are the focus of the Rodamco Pacific division. North America accounts for more than 40% of Rodamco's property portfolio; continental Europe, 28%; and the United Kingdom, 23%. Rental income accounted for 87% of fiscal 1997 revenues.

	NLG mil 02/96	02/97	02/98	US$mil 02/98				
Sales	882.0	953.0	1,126.0	550.0	P/E Ratio	15.7	Price (6/30/98)	55.80
Net Income	446.0	460.0	590.0	288.3	P/B Ratio	1.0	52 Wk Hi-Low	68.00-53.40
Book Value	8,270.0	8,830.0	8,969.0	4,383.2	Yield %	6.4	Market Cap	US$4,544.1mil

Address	Coolsingel 120	Tel 10-224-2736	ADR	--	V Chmn Mgt Bd	J.A.De Kreij
	3000 AZ	Fax 10-224-2115	SEDOL	4746430	Chmn Mgt Bd	Pieter Korteweg

Royal Dutch Petroleum

DJGI Industry: **Oil Companies - Major**
Stoxx Sector: **Energy**

Royal Dutch Petroleum Co. is the nonoperating holding company of The Royal Dutch/Shell Group of companies. It is one of the world's largest energy concerns. Royal Dutch holds a 60% interest in the Royal Dutch/Shell Group. The group is engaged in the global exploration, production, and marketing of oil and natural gas; it has operating companies in more than 100 countries worldwide. Oil and gas refining and marketing accounted for 80% of 1997 revenues; chemicals, 11%; oil and gas exploration and production, 8%; and other, 1%.

	NLG mil 12/95	12/96	12/97	US$mil 12/97				
Sales	106,062.8	129,451.7	149,509.5	73,795.4	P/E Ratio	27.0	Price (6/30/98)	112.80
Net Income	7,022.6	9,580.9	9,593.3	4,735.1	P/B Ratio	3.3	52 Wk Hi-Low	124.60-99.70
Book Value	56,737.2	65,966.8	73,780.3	36,416.7	Yield %	2.7	Market Cap	US$118,660mil

Address	Carel van Bylandtlaan 30	Tel 70-377-9111	ADR	RD	Memb Mgt Bd	M.A. Van Den Bergh
	2596 HR The Hague	Fax 70-377-3115	SEDOL	5202704	President Mgt Bd	C.A.J. Herkströter

In DJ Stoxx 50; In EuroStoxx 50.

Stork

DJGI Industry: **Factory Equipment**
Stoxx Sector: **Industrials**

Stork NV designs, manufactures, and maintains industrial-process installations. The company has divided its operations into two core divisions: industrial services and industrial systems and components. Industrial services is involved in heavy construction through engineering and contracting. Industrial systems and components develops and manufactures machinery and components for the paper, textiles, food-processing, and packaging industries. Technical services accounted for 39% of 1997 revenues; industrial components, 17%; and engineering and contracting, 17%.

	NLG mil 12/95	12/96	12/97	US$mil 12/97				
Sales	4,121.4	4,915.9	5,504.2	2,716.8	P/E Ratio	11.6	Price (6/30/98)	64.80
Net Income	108.3	136.8	171.6	84.7	P/B Ratio	2.0	52 Wk Hi-Low	91.80-64.80
Book Value	835.4	870.4	997.2	492.2	Yield %	3.5	Market Cap	US$972.7mil

Address	**Amersfoortsestraatweg 7**	Tel **21-695-7411**	ADR	--	V Chairman	**V. Den Boogaard**
	1410 KA Naarden	Fax **21-694-1184**	SEDOL	4925701	Chmn Mgt Bd	**A.W. Veenman**

TNT Post

DJGI Industry: **Consumer Services**
Stoxx Sector: **Consumer Non-Cyclical**

TNT Post Groep NV is a mail, express, and logistics company that is continuing the postal and express activities of Koninklijke PTT Nederland after the demerger of these activities into a separate company in June 1998. The former mother company continues solely as a telecom company under the new name of Koninklijke KPN NV (KPN). The company is based in more than 55 countries and is active in over 200 countries. Mail activities accounted for 47% of the company's fiscal 1997 revenues; express activities, 40%, and logistics for 13%.

	NLG mil 12/95	12/96	12/97	US$mil 12/97				
Sales	N/A	6,577.0	15,100.0	7,453.1	P/E Ratio	35.1	Price (6/30/98)	52.00
Net Income	N/A	636.0	694.0	342.5	P/B Ratio	10.4	52 Wk Hi-Low	N/A
Book Value	N/A	1,732.0	2,369.0	1,169.3	Yield %	0.0	Market Cap	US$12,047mil

Address	**Postbus 13000**	Tel **20-500-1500**	ADR	**TP@**	CFO	**M.P. Bakker**
	1100 KG Amsterdam	Fax **20-500-2500**	SEDOL	5481558	Chairman	**A.J. Scheepsbouwer**

Unilever

DJGI Industry: **Other Food**
Stoxx Sector: **Food & Beverage**

Unilever NV controls 50% of the Unilever group of companies, and United Kingdom-based Unilever NV PLC holds the other 50%. It is one of the world's largest consumer products groups; its products include Country Crock spreads, Wishbone salad dressings, and Ragu sauces. Detergents include Wisk and Dove soap. It makes consumer goods through Elizabeth Arden and Helene Curtis subsidiaries. Foods accounted for 50% of 1997 revenues; home and personal care products, 44%; specialty chemicals (discontinued operations), 4%; and plantations, plant science, and trading operations, 2%.

	NLG mil 12/95	12/96	12/97	US$mil 12/97				
Sales	79,703.0	87,795.0	94,597.0	46,691.5	P/E Ratio	16.6	Price (6/30/98)	161.40
Net Income	3,725.0	4,215.0	10,936.0	5,397.8	P/B Ratio	7.4	52 Wk Hi-Low	169.00-92.10
Book Value	13,724.0	15,085.0	24,469.0	12,077.5	Yield %	1.4	Market Cap	US$50,688mil

Address	**Weena 455**	Tel **10-217-4000**	ADR	**UN**	V Chmn Mgt Bd	**N. Fitzgerald**
	3013 DK Rotterdam	Fax **10-217-4798**	SEDOL	5309746	Chmn & CEO	**M. Tabaksblat**

In DJ Stoxx 50; In EuroStoxx 50.

Wolters Kluwer

DJGI Industry: **Publishing**
Stoxx Sector: **Media**

Wolters Kluwer NV publishes specialized publications, such as legal, scientific, medical, business, educational, and professional training journals and manuals with subsidiaries in Europe and the United States. In addition to publishing books, journals, newsletters, and other printed material, Wolters Kluwer provides computer-based information on diskette publications, on-line services, electronic libraries, and CD-ROMs. In 1998, Wolters said it had acquired U.S.-based Capitol Publishing Group and U.S. tax software publisher Damirus Corp.

	NLG mil 12/95	12/96	12/97	US$mil 12/97				
Sales	2,944.1	4,315.0	5,209.0	2,571.1	P/E Ratio	33.0	Price (6/30/98)	279.20
Net Income	452.3	479.0	579.0	285.8	P/B Ratio	10.5	52 Wk Hi-Low	321.50-230.00
Book Value	733.4	1,193.0	1,814.0	895.4	Yield %	1.1	Market Cap	US$9,381.8mil

Address	**Stadhouderskade 1**	Tel **20-607-0400**	ADR	**WTKWY**	Memb Mgt Bd	**C.H. Van Kempen**
	1000 AV Amsterdam	Fax **20-607-0490**	SEDOL	4977111	Chmn Mgt Bd	**C.J. Brakel**

Norway

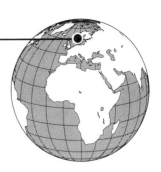

Exchanges:

Oslo Stock Exchange

Norway

Fredrik Tangeraas
Oslo

As a wave of cooperation sweeps European bourses, the Oslo Stock Exchange has so far chosen to go it alone.

The Oslo Exchange, which ranks third in size among the Nordic bourses, has opted to not join the alliance between its nearest neighbors, the Stockholm and Copenhagen bourses, hoping instead to carve out a niche as a big shipping, offshore oil, and oil-services bourse on its own.

Another reason to stay single while other markets are playing the mating game is that the bourse has chosen a trading system different from that of its Scandinavian counterparts. Oslo opted for the Automated Securities Trading System from Computershare Systems Ltd., an Australian company.

Scheduled to start operations in early October 1998, the new system is intended to enhance the Exchange's competitive position and boost liquidity. The Exchange hopes the system will encourage remote membership, boost market turnover substantially, and make trades more transparent.

The Oslo market traces its origins back to the first Stock Exchange Law, which was sanctioned by King Karl Johan in September 1818. Six months later, the bourse in Christiania, as Oslo was know then, opened.

The Exchange's current neoclassical premises weren't completed until 1829. The bourse was the first major institutional building

constructed in Norway after 1814, the year the country's constitution was written, during the early days of Norway's fledgling independence movement. Symbolically, the bourse was the first building ever designed by a Norwegian-educated architect, Christian Heinrich Grosch.

At that time, the Exchange's main purposes were twofold — as a currency exchange and as an auction house for groceries, ships, and ship parts and equipment. But the premises were also used for a range of other purposes, such as bazaars, exhibitions, parties, and even city council meetings, during those early years.

Securities trading finally started in 1881, initiated by two local bankers, N.A. Andersen and S.C. Andersen.

Things got off to a slow start, as only 16 bonds and 23 stocks were listed for trading just once a month. Daily listings of shipping

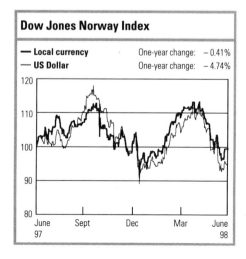

Dow Jones Norway Index

— **Local currency**   One-year change: − 0.41%
— **US Dollar**   One-year change: − 4.74%

and whaling shares were initiated in 1916, whereas daily listings of other stocks didn't start until 1922.

But a lot has happened since then. The number of companies and the industries they operate in have flourished.

As of June 30, 1998, some 228 companies were listed on the Exchange, representing total capitalization of NOK569 billion. Trading in the market's ten biggest companies accounted for 34% of the market's turnover and 49% of the bourse's total value. Market turnover reached NOK186 billion in the first half of the year.

The bourse took a quantum leap to modernity in 1988, when the Exchange's electronic trading system replaced the old auctions. The change permitted continuous trading in all listed shares throughout the day.

Since May 1991, all listed securities have been registered electronically in the Norwegian Registry of Securities, which acts as a central register of ownership.

Derivatives trading began in 1990, following the start of options dealings on the Oslo Bourse. That marked the first time in over 100 years a new trading product was introduced on the Exchange.

The Oslo Stock Exchange has two main indexes and five sector indexes. They are calculated automatically every minute during stock exchange sessions. The key gauge, the

Country Information

Trading Hours:

   Local: 10:00 am - 4:00 pm

   EST: 4:00 am - 10:00 am

   GMT: 0900 - 1500

Population (6/98):
4,419,955

Unemployment (97):
4.2%

Main Industries:
Petroleum and gas, food processing, shipbuilding, pulp and paper products, metals, chemicals, timber, mining, textiles, and fishing

Gross Domestic Product (97):
US$153.40 billion

GDP per Capita (97):
US$34,831.84

Three-Year Average GDP Growth (94-97):
4.2%

Average Annual CPI Growth (96-97):
+ 2.59%

Monetary Unit:
Norwegian Krone

Exchange Rate (6/98):
NOK7.66 to US$1.00

Oslo All-Share Index, includes all the shares on the main list and gives a general overview of movements in the stock market. The OBX index is made up of the 25 most actively traded shares.

All the blue-chip issues appear on the main list, while smaller and medium-sized companies appear on the SMB list, which sets less strict criteria for capitalization and share distribution.

There are generally two kinds of shares, class A and class B shares. Class A shares usually have full voting rights, whereas class B shares usually have limited or no voting rights.

The Oslo Stock Exchange considers itself one the world's biggest shipping exchanges, and that may not be far from the truth, as Norway has traditionally been an important shipping nation.

Shipping companies listed in Oslo include Bergesen d.y., Frontline, and Wilh. Wilhelmsen, as well as the cruise companies NCL Holding and Royal Caribbean Cruises.

The market also has a heavy concentration of oil-related stocks, the result of the country's huge oil and natural gas production. That has not always been to the bourse's advantage. The slump in world oil prices has been an important drag on performance during 1998, knocking down the stocks of oil companies, offshore drilling concerns, and shipping companies. Other recent negatives include rising interest rates.

Ten Largest Capitalized Companies In The Dow Jones Norway Index
as of 6/30/98

Stock	Market Cap. US$ Thousands
Norsk Hydro	10,093,641
Orkla	4,514,070
Den Norske Bank	3,361,595
Petroleum Geo Services	2,644,777
Storebrand As	2,459,021
Christiania Bank	2,309,833
Saga Petroleum	2,083,082
Kvaerner	1,449,493
Bergesen	1,436,670
Netcom	1,276,945

The All-Share index managed to gain only about 3.3% in the first half of 1998, closing at 1297.88 on June 30.

Yet despite the bourse's lackluster performance, some stocks have managed to stand out from the crowd.

For instance, financial sector stocks, such as Den Norske Bank, Christiania Bank, and Storebrand have outpaced the overall Oslo market, buoyed by the wave of consolidation that swept European banks recently and expectations that the trend will finally catch on in Norway, too.

Similarly, shares in mobile phone network operator Netcom have been hoisted higher by rises in European telecommunications stocks.

Throughout its history, Norway has harvested the bulk of its wealth from the sea, either through fishing, whaling, and shipping or, most recently, through offshore oil and natural gas production.

The sea is key to Norway's status as one of the world's richest countries, with per capita income exceeding US$35,000. In the early 1970s, large-scale development of the country's vast crude oil and natural gas reserves off the Norwegian coast got under way, which turned the country into the second largest oil exporter in the world, behind only Saudi Arabia.

The country's economy grew by 5.3% in 1997 and is thought to be growing by 3.5% in 1998, while inflation is seen creeping up to 2.5% in 1998 and 2.75% in 1999.

Even though the Oslo bourse may be going solo for now, it still maintains some international links, having had a long-standing membership in the Féderation Internationale des Bourses de Valeurs, and more recently joining the Federation of European Stock Exchanges, an important forum for coordinating directives and rules for European stock exchanges.

Also, Norway is guaranteed access to Europe's single market through the European Economic Area agreement between the E.U. and the European Free Trade Association. When Norway entered the European Economic Area three years ago, all rules that discriminated against foreign ownership of shares were abolished. Foreign investors are exempt from both turnover and capital gains tax, but must pay a withholding tax on

Market Sector Performance In The Dow Jones Norway Index 1 Year Change Through 6/30/98	
Market Sector	Change % (US$)
Consumer, Non-Cyclical	63.30
Financial	28.20
Consumer, Cyclical	-0.76
Industrial	-7.92
Energy	-13.12
Independent	-13.69
Utilities	-16.48
Basic Materials	-23.43
Technology	-25.81

dividends according to tax agreements between Norway and their respective countries.

For most OECD countries, that rate is 15%, whereas for others it's 25%.

Aker

DJGI Industry: **Conglomerates**
Stoxx Sector: **Conglomerate**

Aker RGI ASA is active mainly in oil and gas technology, cement, and fisheries. One of Norway's leading industrial groups, it was formed when industrial concern Aker and real estate and fisheries conglomerate Resource Group International ASA merged in January 1997. In 1996, Aker and Swedish industrial company Euroc formed a cement and building-materials business, Scancem, in which Aker holds a 33.3% stake. It also holds a 75% stake in Aker Maritime ASA, an oil and gas concern, and a 54.8% stake in fishing concern Norway Seafoods.

	NOK mil 12/95	12/96	12/97	US$mil 12/97				
Sales	15,259.0	11,296.0	25,430.0	3,454.9	P/E Ratio	21.8	Price (6/30/98)	120.50
Net Income	623.0	362.0	590.0	80.2	P/B Ratio	1.6	52 Wk Hi-Low	154.00-112.50
Book Value	4,779.0	4,674.0	5,846.0	794.2	Yield %	3.3	Market Cap	US$874.2mil

Address	Fjordalléen 16	Tel 22-94-64-00	ADR	--	President & CEO	B. Flatgard
	0250 Oslo	Fax 22-94-50-16	SEDOL	4012283	Chairman	K.I. Rokke

Aker Maritime

DJGI Industry: **Other Oilfield Equipment & Services**
Stoxx Sector: **Energy**

Aker Maritime ASA is one of the leading suppliers of advanced technology to the offshore industry. The company's main products include floating production facilities and advanced products, as well as services with high knowledge-based content. Oil platforms accounted for 40% of 1997 revenues; maintenance and modification services, 19%; turnkey projects, systems, and services, 16%; steel substructures for platforms, 15%; and offshore development projects, engineering, and project maintenance, 10%.

	NOK mil 12/95	12/96	12/97	US$mil 12/97				
Sales	N/A	10,825.0	13,778.0	1,871.9	P/E Ratio	30.7	Price (6/30/98)	135.00
Net Income	N/A	229.0	184.0	25.0	P/B Ratio	4.3	52 Wk Hi-Low	180.00-113.00
Book Value	N/A	1,624.0	1,765.0	239.8	Yield %	0.6	Market Cap	US$999.7mil

Address	Box 1884 Vika	Tel 22-94-65-00	ADR	--	President	--
	Oslo 0124	Fax 22-94-65-30	SEDOL	5158023	Chairman	B.R. Gjelsten

Ask

DJGI Industry: **Diversified Technology**
Stoxx Sector: **Technology**

Ask ASA, spun off from Tandberg Data ASA in 1996, manufactures and markets computer/video projectors and overhead panels. The company's projectors are based on amorphous TFT LCD technology. Their LCD overhead panels have VGA, SVGA, XGA, and SXGA resolution. These projectors cover a wide range within the portable and ultraportable market segments, as well as one product in the fixed-installation market. Computer and video projectors accounted for 96% of the company's 1997 revenues, and LCD overhead panels accounted for 4%.

	NOK mil 12/95	12/96	12/97	US$mil 12/97				
Sales	219.2	324.6	604.3	82.1	P/E Ratio	21.6	Price (6/30/98)	59.50
Net Income	21.5	47.3	91.5	12.4	P/B Ratio	7.7	52 Wk Hi-Low	98.00-39.33
Book Value	104.6	104.2	290.2	39.4	Yield %	0.0	Market Cap	US$321.0mil

Address	K.G. Meldahlsvei 9	Tel 69-34-01-55	ADR	--	President	Ole J. Fredriksen
	1602 Fredrikstad	Fax 69-34-06-32	SEDOL	5351844	Chairman	Swein S. Jacobsen

Bergesen

DJGI Industry: **Marine Transportation**
Stoxx Sector: **Industrials**

Bergesen D.Y. ASA is the the largest shipping company listed on the Oslo Stock Exchange. The company, which has interests in the transportation of crude oil and liquefied gases, is one of the world's largest owners and operators of large crude-oil tankers and dry-cargo vessels; the company's fleet consists of 95 ships. Bergesen is also involved in investment and real estate operations. Transportation of liquefied petroleum gas, oil, and dry bulk cargo accounted for 99% of 1997 revenues; rental income and other activities accounted for 1%.

	NOK mil 12/95	12/96	12/97	US$mil 12/97				
Sales	4,359.0	4,511.0	5,575.0	757.4	P/E Ratio M	14.3	Price (6/30/98) M	146.00
Net Income	373.0	1,603.0	636.0	86.4	P/B Ratio M	1.3	52 Wk Hi-Low M	223.00-138.00
Book Value	6,713.0	8,217.0	8,701.0	1,182.1	Yield % M	1.4	Market Cap M	US$1,012.1mil

Address	Drammensveien 106	Tel 22-12-05-05	ADR	BEDAY	V Chairman	P.C.G. Sundt
	0205 Oslo	Fax 22-12-05-00	SEDOL	4100898	Chairman	M.S. Bergesen

M=Multiple issues in index; reflects most active.

Bonheur

DJGI Industry: **Marine Transportation**
Stoxx Sector: **Industrials**

Bonheur ASA is a holding company with operations in passenger and freight shipping services.The company is involved in offshore oil operations in conjunction with associated company Ganger Rolf ASA. Bonheur's fleet consists of 35 vessels and 5 oil rigs. It also has a share in Harland & Wolff, a shipbuilding company, and in DNL, an aviation interest. Bonheur and Ganger Rolf each own 30% of Fred. Olsen Energy ASA and in 1997 transferred all their offshore activities to that company. Shipping operations accounted for 89% of fiscal 1997 revenues and other activities for 11%.

	NOK mil 12/95	12/96	12/97	US$mil 12/97				
Sales	482.6	541.8	411.8	55.9	P/E Ratio	NMF	Price (6/30/98)	300.00
Net Income	16.2	98.4	11.3	1.5	P/B Ratio	1.4	52 Wk Hi-Low	570.00-295.00
Book Value	1,316.2	1,151.2	2,421.4	329.0	Yield %	0.8	Market Cap	US$450.0mil

Address	Box 1159 Sentrum	Tel 22-34-10-00	ADR	--	President	--
	0107 Oslo	Fax 22-41-24-15	SEDOL	4110507	Outside Mgt	F. Olsen & Co.

Christiania Bank og Kreditkasse

DJGI Industry: **Banks - Regional (All)**
Stoxx Sector: **Bank**

Christiania Bank og Kreditkasse ASA provides a comprehensive range of financial services to the retail and corporate markets in Norway and worldwide through branches in the United States, the United Kingdom, and Singapore, offices in Japan, Germany, and Spain, and units in London, New York, Singapore, and Luxembourg. The bank's subsidiaries include life insurance company Norske Liv AS, specialized mortgage company Vestenfjelske Bykreditt AS, fund-management company K-Fondene AS, and finance company K-Finans AS. Interest income accounted for 86% of 1997 revenues.

	NOK mil 12/95	12/96	12/97	US$mil 12/97					
Revenues	10,559.0	12,243.0	12,723.0	1,728.6	P/E Ratio	8.4	Price (6/30/98)		32.10
Net Income	2,776.0	2,154.0	2,209.0	300.1	P/B Ratio	1.6	52 Wk Hi-Low		37.50-24.00
Book Value	7,936.0	9,279.0	10,838.0	1,472.5	Yield %	3.7	Market Cap		US$2,309.8mil

Address	Middelthunsgate 17	Tel 22-48-50-00	ADR	CBKRYP	V Chairman	M. Maeland
	0107 Oslo	Fax 22-48-46-00	SEDOL	4204110	Chairman	H. Arnkvaern

Den Norske Bank

DJGI Industry: **Banks - Regional (All)**
Stoxx Sector: **Bank**

Den Norske Bank ASA is Norway's largest financial group. It is organized into four divisions, including retail, commercial, corporate, and investment banking. Den Norske Bank's services include factoring and leasing, securities trading and management, debt collection services, real estate brokerage, low-risk mortgages, and other financial services. In September 1997, the government said it planned to cut its stake in Den Norske Bank to 33% from about 50%. Interest income accounted for 79% of 1997 revenues; commissions and fees, 13%; and other, 8%.

	NOK mil 12/95	12/96	12/97	US$mil 12/97					
Revenues	14,698.0	14,607.0	15,222.0	2,068.1	P/E Ratio	10.8	Price (6/30/98)		40.20
Net Income	2,657.0	2,702.0	2,590.0	351.9	P/B Ratio	1.7	52 Wk Hi-Low		45.20-28.00
Book Value	12,194.0	13,580.0	15,057.0	2,045.6	Yield %	4.4	Market Cap		US$3,361.6mil

Address	Stranden 21	Tel 22-48-10-50	ADR	--	V Chairman	S. Aaser
	0107 Oslo	Fax 22-48-18-70	SEDOL	4263304	Chairman	G. Heilberg

Det Sondenfjelds-Norsk

DJGI Industry: **Marine Transportation**
Stoxx Sector: **Industrials**

Det Sondenfjelds-Norske Dampskibsselskab ASA (DSND) is a full-service marine contractor. It operates 14 specialized vessels involved in geotechnical investigations, oil well maintenance, diving, and sub-sea contracting. The company's main market area is the North Sea, but it also has operations in the Mediterranean, west Africa, Brazil, and the Gulf of Mexico. Sub-sea contracting and geotechnical surveys accounted for 88% of 1997 revenues; well services, 4%; and other, 8%. In 1998, it entered into a deepwater joint venture in the Gulf of Mexico with partner Horizon Offshore Inc.

	NOK mil 12/95	12/96	12/97	US$mil 12/97					
Sales	95.6	476.6	1,086.4	147.6	P/E Ratio	27.9	Price (6/30/98)		135.00
Net Income	5.2	73.8	139.7	19.0	P/B Ratio	6.1	52 Wk Hi-Low		195.00-87.50
Book Value	164.0	309.1	698.2	94.9	Yield %	0.0	Market Cap		US$560.8mil

Address	Postboks 752 Sentrum	Tel 22-41-21-50	ADR	--	Managing Director	G. Hirsti
	0106 Oslo	Fax 22-41-06-50	SEDOL	5232068	Chairman	K. Siem

Dyno Industrier

DJGI Industry: **Chemicals - Specialty**
Stoxx Sector: **Chemical**

Dyno Industrier ASA is a diversified chemical company that produces explosives, chemicals, and plastic products. Dyno Industrier is a part owner of the methanol producer Methanor. Dyno has more than 100 wholly or partially owned companies in 30 countries world wide. In October 1997, Dyno sold its 36% stake in Austria's Krems Chemie. In June 1997, it bought a 51% stake in TEC Harseim, a Chilean explosives company. The company is one of the world's leading explosives manufacturers. Explosives account for about half of revenues, chemicals for about one-third, and plastics for over 15%.

	NOK mil 12/95	12/96	12/97	US$mil 12/97					
Sales	10,033.0	9,714.0	11,329.0	1,539.2	P/E Ratio	12.6	Price (6/30/98)		137.00
Net Income	343.0	211.0	-62.0	-8.4	P/B Ratio	1.4	52 Wk Hi-Low		213.00-118.00
Book Value	2,658.0	2,718.0	2,538.0	344.8	Yield %	2.2	Market Cap		US$457.6mil

Address	Tollbugaten 22 Sentrum	Tel 22-31-70-00	ADR	--	V Chairman	T. Jemtland
	0106 Oslo	Fax 22-31-78-56	SEDOL	4294274	Chairman	T. Refvem

Elkem

DJGI Industry: **Other Non-Ferrous Metals**
Stoxx Sector: **Basic Resources**

Elkem ASA is one of the world's leading producers of ferroalloys and silicon metal. Its four main areas of operation are manganese and chrome, ferrosilicon, silicon, and aluminum. The company also supplies aluminum, carbon products, and electrode paste for the electrometallurgical industry. Manganese and chrome accounted for 29% of 1997 revenues; carbon and microsilica materials, 23%; ferrosilicon, 21%; aluminum, 16%; and other, 11%. In 1997, Elkem bought a chromium mine in Brazil.

	NOK mil 12/95	12/96	12/97	US$mil 12/97					
Sales	9,320.0	9,334.0	9,594.0	1,303.4	P/E Ratio	4.9	Price (6/30/98)		92.00
Net Income	850.0	736.0	896.0	121.7	P/B Ratio	1.0	52 Wk Hi-Low		156.50-86.00
Book Value	3,206.0	3,700.0	4,356.0	591.8	Yield %	6.5	Market Cap		US$591.9mil

Address	Hoffsveien 65B	Tel 22-45-01-00	ADR	--	President & CEO	O. Enger
	0303 Oslo	Fax 22-45-01-55	SEDOL	4310385	Chairman	F. Jebsen

Fokus Bank

DJGI Industry: **Banks - Regional (All)**
Stoxx Sector: **Bank**

Fokus Bank ASA is the largest publicly owned commercial bank in Norway. The bank was founded in 1987 as a result of the merger of Buskerudbanken A/S, Bondernes Bank A/S, Forretningsbanken A/S, and Vestlandsbanken L/L. As of 1996, Fokus Bank had 77 regional branches. During 1996, the bank accelerated the restructuring program it had undertaken a few years earlier. Interest income accounted for 79% of 1997 revenues; commissions and fees accounted for 10%, trading income for 7%, and other activities for 4%.

	NOK mil 12/95	12/96	12/97	US$mil 12/97				
Revenues	2,803.1	2,949.6	3,034.8	412.3	P/E Ratio	6.3	Price (6/30/98)	59.50
Net Income	427.5	461.7	650.2	88.3	P/B Ratio	1.7	52 Wk Hi-Low	74.88-55.91
Book Value	1,919.2	1,921.1	2,275.8	309.2	Yield %	7.6	Market Cap	US$563.9mil

Address	Vestre Rosten 77	Tel	72-882-011	ADR	--	President	--
	7005 Trondheim	Fax	72-88-20-61	SEDOL	4709251	Chairman	S.H. Annexstad

Fred Olsen Energy

DJGI Industry: **Oil Companies - Secondary**
Stoxx Sector: **Energy**

Fred Olsen Energy ASA, a premier supplier in the offshore industry, provides the oil industry with integrated drilling, floating, production, and fabrication services on a build, own, and operate basis. The company is focusing primarily on the Atlantic Basin; most of its present operations are in the North Sea and West Africa. The company was formed in April 1997 and converted into a joint stock company in September 1997 as a way of consolidating several independent Fred Olsen-related businesses in the offshore industry into an integrated offshore service company.

	NOK mil 12/95	12/96	12/97	US$mil 12/97				
Sales	N/A	N/A	1,072.1	145.7	P/E Ratio	38.1	Price (6/30/98)	102.00
Net Income	N/A	N/A	137.3	18.7	P/B Ratio	1.0	52 Wk Hi-Low	199.00-99.00
Book Value	N/A	N/A	6,015.6	817.3	Yield %	0.0	Market Cap	US$803.0mil

Address	Box 1159	Tel	22-34-10-00	ADR	FRED	CEO & Mng Dir	Helge Haakonsen
	0107 Oslo	Fax	22-41-17-45	SEDOL	5344101	Chairman	Anette S. Olsen

Hafslund

DJGI Industry: **Electrical Utilities (All)**
Stoxx Sector: **Utility**

Hafslund ASA is the result of a demerger of Hafslund Nycomed in May 1996. Hafslund Nycomed's pharmaceutical business was formed into Nycomed ASA, while Hafslund retained the company's energy business. The largest private owner of power plants and transmission networks in Norway, Hafslund's main operations consist of three wholly owned hydroelectricity plants and majority stakes in two others. Generation, marketing, and distribution of hydroelectric power accounted for 62% of 1997 revenues, and distribution of ferroalloys, metals, and minerals for 38%.

	NOK mil 12/95	12/96	12/97	US$mil 12/97				
Sales	9,682.0	1,488.0	2,350.0	319.3	P/E Ratio M	11.1	Price (6/30/98) M	41.50
Net Income	1,357.0	291.0	420.0	57.1	P/B Ratio M	2.1	52 Wk Hi-Low M	47.00-40.00
Book Value	7,322.0	2,138.0	2,320.0	315.2	Yield % M	2.7	Market Cap M	US$370.0mil

Address	Karenslyst Alle 11	Tel	23-01-42-00	ADR	--	President & CEO	H. Hansen
	0212 Oslo	Fax	23-01-42-40	SEDOL	5067550	Chairman	J. Odfjell

M=Multiple issues in index; reflects most active.

Leif Höegh

DJGI Industry: **Marine Transportation**
Stoxx Sector: **Industrials**

Leif Höegh and Co. ASA is one of Norway's leading shipping companies. The company operates a fleet of 120 vessels, of which 49 are owned or partially owned by Leif Höegh. It also operates and manages gas carriers, tankers, liners, open-hatch vessels, reefers, and bulk and car carriers. Leif Höegh transports oil, coal, liquefied natural gas, steel, and other bulk products. Freight by car carriers accounted for 45% of fiscal 1997 revenues; liners, 28%; reefer vessels, 22%; bulk carriers, 3%; gas carriers and others, 2%.

	NOK mil 12/95	12/96	12/97	US$mil 12/97				
Sales	2,943.0	3,471.0	3,475.0	472.1	P/E Ratio	13.3	Price (6/30/98)	112.00
Net Income	303.0	740.0	335.0	45.5	P/B Ratio	1.3	52 Wk Hi-Low	180.00-108.00
Book Value	1,974.0	2,594.0	2,609.0	354.5	Yield %	3.6	Market Cap	US$438.7mil

Address	Wergelandsveien 7	Tel	22-86-97-00	ADR	--	President	Thor J. Guttormsen
	0203 Oslo	Fax	22-20-14-08	SEDOL	4512017	Chairman	Westye Höegh

Kvaerner

DJGI Industry: **Conglomerates**
Stoxx Sector: **Conglomerate**

Kvaerner ASA is Europe's largest shipbuilder and ranks among the five largest in the world. It also has operations in offshore construction, mechanical engineering, and pulping technology. In April 1996, Kvaerner bought Trafalgar House PLC of the United Kingdom for 904 million pounds. Also in 1996, the company sold its fleet of reefer vessels. Kvaerner sold its remaining stake in U.K. group Amec PLC for NOK850 million in 1997. In 1998, the company received a contract from the U.S. Navy to prepare a study for building a $5 billion,1,600-meter offshore runway and troop carrier.

	NOK mil 12/95	12/96	12/97	US$mil 12/97				
Sales	29,620.0	58,214.0	72,962.0	9,912.6	P/E Ratio M	9.2	Price (6/30/98) M	260.00
Net Income	1,772.0	856.0	1,229.0	167.0	P/B Ratio M	1.1	52 Wk Hi-Low M	479.00-260.00
Book Value	9,267.0	9,644.0	10,302.0	1,399.6	Yield % M	2.7	Market Cap M	US$1,150.9mil

Address	Prof. Kohts Vei 15	Tel	67-51-30-00	ADR	KVRAY	President & CEO	S.E. Amundsen
	1324 Lysaker	Fax	67-51-31-00	SEDOL	4502029	Chairman	C. Bjelland

M=Multiple issues in index; reflects most active.

NCL

DJGI Industry: **Other Recreational Products & Services**
Stoxx Sector: **Consumer Cyclical**

NCL Holding ASA (formerly Vard AS) is one of the largest cruise ship operators in the world. In 1996, the company operated nine cruise ships which carried approximately 4 million passengers. The company's fleet was restructured in 1995 and 1996, and now consists of Norwegian Cruise Line Ltd. (NCLL). Royal Cruise Line (RCL) ships were sold or transferred to NCL in 1996. In 1998, the company bought the one-ship Orient Lines in a deal worth $54 million. This addition raised NCL's fleet to 11, and the company has long-term plans for another four new ships.

	NOK mil 12/95	12/96	12/97	US$mil 12/97					
Sales	4,951.0	4,252.6	4,624.2	628.2	P/E Ratio	**NMF**	Price (6/30/98)	37.90
Net Income	-663.8	6.3	-1.8	-0.2	P/B Ratio	4.6	52 Wk Hi-Low	39.40-20.76
Book Value	474.0	1,109.1	2,373.7	322.5	Yield %	0.0	Market Cap	US$1,052.7mil

Address	Ullern Alle 41	Tel 22-51-09-50	ADR	--	CEO	G. Aune
	0311 Oslo	Fax 22-73-11-27	SEDOL	4926931	Chairman	K. Siem

Nera

DJGI Industry: **Communications Technology**
Stoxx Sector: **Technology**

Nera ASA, spun off from ABB Norway, develops, manufactures, and markets telecommunications systems and equipment worldwide. It is one of Norway's leading companies in the field of electronics, with main products being microwave radiolink systems for various types of telecommunications networks together with maritime and land-based mobile satellite communication systems. The company's activities have been extensive in Southeast Asia and it has its own manufacturing facilities in Singapore. In December 1996, Nera applied for listing on the Singapore Stock Exchange.

	NOK mil 12/95	12/96	12/97	US$mil 12/97					
Sales	2,344.3	2,610.0	2,922.5	397.0	P/E Ratio	31.0	Price (6/30/98)	17.70
Net Income	116.7	101.9	78.2	10.6	P/B Ratio	1.5	52 Wk Hi-Low	52.00-17.70
Book Value	682.7	757.0	790.7	107.4	Yield %	2.8	Market Cap	US$152.5mil

Address	Kokstaveien 23, Box 10	Tel 55-22-51-00	ADR	NERAY	President	A. Birkeland
	5061 Kokstad, Bergen	Fax 55-22-52-99	SEDOL	5224678	Chairman & CEO	J.F.R. Odfjell

NetCom

DJGI Industry: **Communications Technology**
Stoxx Sector: **Technology**

NetCom ASA is a private telecommunications operator that offers the Norwegian market a broad range of GSM and other telecommunications products and services. The company had 417,477 subscribers in 1997. Four retail chains comprising a total of 51 stores merged to form KLART SVAR, which had 91 outlets in 1997 and is the largest telecom chain in Norway. Call charges accounted for 76% of 1997 revenues, and connection and subscription fees for 24%. NetCom is listed on the Oslo Stock Exchange and has more than 470 employees.

	NOK mil 12/95	12/96	12/97	US$mil 12/97					
Sales	N/A	884.8	1,669.3	226.8	P/E Ratio	**NMF**	Price (6/30/98)	207.00
Net Income	N/A	-577.4	-186.6	-25.3	P/B Ratio	**NMF**	52 Wk Hi-Low	232.00-75.50
Book Value	N/A	-416.6	-602.4	-81.8	Yield %	0.0	Market Cap	US$1,276.9mil

Address	Box 4444 Torshov	Tel 22-88-80-00	ADR	--	CEO	T. Christoffersen
	140 Sandakerveien	Fax 22-88-80-15	SEDOL	5062469	Chairman	L.F. Onarheim

Norsk Hydro

DJGI Industry: **Conglomerates**
Stoxx Sector: **Conglomerate**

Norsk Hydro ASA, Norway's largest listed industrial company, manufactures products for agriculture and the light-metals, energy, and petrochemical industries. The company produces mineral-based fertilizer and supplies aluminum and magnesium. It also extracts and sells oil and gas, generates electrical power, and produces raw materials for plastics. The Oslo-based company is 51%-owned by the Norwegian state, with the remainder being publicly traded. Agricultural chemicals accounted for 44% of 1997 revenues; light metals, 28%; oil and gas, 18%; petrochemicals, 6%; and other, 4%.

	NOK mil 12/95	12/96	12/97	US$mil 12/97					
Sales	79,732.0	84,840.0	96,169.0	13,065.6	P/E Ratio	16.5	Price (6/30/98)	337.50
Net Income	7,133.0	6,204.0	5,205.0	707.2	P/B Ratio	1.7	52 Wk Hi-Low	434.00-316.00
Book Value	37,154.0	41,547.0	45,717.0	6,211.1	Yield %	2.2	Market Cap	US$10,094mil

Address	Bygdoy Allé 2	Tel 22-43-21-00	ADR	NHY	President & CEO	E. Myklebust
	0240 Oslo	Fax 22-43-27-25	SEDOL	4645805	Chairman	E. Kloster

Norske Skog

DJGI Industry: **Paper Products**
Stoxx Sector: **Basic Resources**

Norske Skogindustrier ASA manufactures and markets newsprint as well as magazine, fluting, and kraft paper, wood-based building materials, and both long- and short-fiber sulphate pulp. The company is one of the world's leading producers of printing paper, and it has paper-producing capacity at mills in Norway, France, and Austria. Norske Skog is also one of the 10 largest sawn-timber suppliers in the Scandinavian countries. In March 1998, Norske Skog bought a 90% stake in South Korea's Shinho Paper Co.'s newsprint plant for $160 million.

	NOK mil 12/95	12/96	12/97	US$mil 12/97					
Sales	12,548.0	13,265.0	13,312.0	1,808.6	P/E Ratio	10.9	Price (6/30/98)	237.00
Net Income	1,699.0	1,317.0	590.0	80.2	P/B Ratio	1.0	52 Wk Hi-Low	296.00-186.50
Book Value	6,545.0	7,635.0	9,064.0	1,231.4	Yield %	3.0	Market Cap	US$891.0mil

Address	Norske Skogindustrier	Tel 74-08-70-00	ADR	--	President & CEO	J.R. Gundersen
	7620 Skogn	Fax 74-08-71-00	SEDOL	4647436	Chairman	L. Westerbo

Ocean Rig

DJGI Industry: **Other Oilfield Equipment & Services**
Stoxx Sector: **Energy**

Ocean Rig ASA is involved in the funding, constructing, marketing, crewing, and operating of a high-risk deepwater rig. In 1998, the company signed a $135 million contract with Friede Goldman International Inc. to outfit a deepwater semisubmersible baredeck hull dulling unit. Completion of the project is planned for 1999 and will cover outfitting of the Bingo 9000-2. In 1998, it acquired Polycrest AS to operate and market the Bingo 9000 rigs in the Norwegian sector of the North Sea. Ocean Rig also entered into a cooperation agreement with French drilling entrepreneur Sedco Forex.

	NOK mil 12/95	12/96	12/97	US$mil 12/97					
Sales	N/A	N/A	N/A	N/A	P/E Ratio	NMF	Price (6/30/98)		5.70
Net Income	N/A	-0.1	8.2	1.1	P/B Ratio	0.7	52 Wk Hi-Low		17.77-5.00
Book Value	N/A	222.7	2,724.5	370.1	Yield %	0.0	Market Cap		US$266.3mil

Address	Box 1537 Vika	Tel 22-04-80-04	ADR	--	Managing Director C. Huseby
	0117 Oslo	Fax 22-04-80-05	SEDOL	5150096	Chairman T.B. Knudsen

Orkla

DJGI Industry: **Conglomerates**
Stoxx Sector: **Conglomerate**

Orkla ASA is one of Norway's largest listed companies and is a main producer of branded consumer goods. It concentrates on the manufacturing, marketing, and distributing of products in its three main areas of operation: branded consumer goods, chemical processing, and financial investments. In February 1997, the company bought the remaining stake in its then 45%-owned brewery unit, Pripps Rignes, from Swedish auto maker Volvo. Orkla is the leading supplier of brand-name consumer goods to grocery markets across the Scandinavian countries.

	NOK mil 12/95	12/96	12/97	US$mil 12/97					
Sales	21,157.0	25,998.0	30,970.0	4,207.6	P/E Ratio M	14.0	Price (6/30/98) M		178.50
Net Income	1,432.0	1,752.0	2,562.0	348.1	P/B Ratio M	2.9	52 Wk Hi-Low M		225.00-132.25
Book Value	8,196.0	9,490.0	11,641.0	1,581.6	Yield % M	1.2	Market Cap M		US$3,681.0mil

Address	Karenlyst Alle 6	Tel 22-54-40-00	ADR	ORKLY	President & CEO	Jens P. Heyerdahl
	0212 Skoyen	Fax 22-54-45-90	SEDOL	5459715	Chairman	Svein Ribe-Anderssen

M=Multiple issues in index; reflects most active.

Petroleum Geo-Services

DJGI Industry: **Other Oilfield Equipment & Services**
Stoxx Sector: **Energy**

Petroleum Geo-Services ASA is a holding company for wholly owned subsidiaries that jointly provide a comprehensive range of petroleum geo-services to the oil industry. The company specializes in three-dimensional seismic acquisition, wellsite surveys and pipeline inspections, and route surveys, and it operates a fleet of 10 advanced three-dimensional and two ocean-bottom seismic crews. Revenues for the first quarter of 1998 surpassed 1997 first quarter revenues by $45.4 million, or 48%. Operating profit increased 35% to $19.8 million.

	NOK mil 12/95	12/96	12/97	US$mil 12/97					
Sales	2,010.8	2,911.2	3,639.9	494.5	P/E Ratio	27.9	Price (6/30/98)		239.00
Net Income	233.2	324.5	379.3	51.5	P/B Ratio	2.9	52 Wk Hi-Low		282.00-176.00
Book Value	2,049.0	3,221.5	5,513.5	749.1	Yield %	0.0	Market Cap		US$2,644.8mil

Address	Box 89, Strandveien 50E	Tel 67-52-66-00	ADR	PGO	COO	B. Bruheim
	1324 Lysaker	Fax 67-53-68-83	SEDOL	4682608	Chairman & CEO	R. Michaelsen

ProSafe

DJGI Industry: **Other Oilfield Equipment & Services**
Stoxx Sector: **Energy**

ProSafe ASA, was established in 1997 after the merger of Safe offshore and Procon Offshore. The company is a leading integrated supplier to the offshore industry with significant activities in the North Sea. Its activities include drilling services, accomodation services (flotel services), engineering and technology, and fabrication. Currently, ProSafe is focusing on markets for platform drilling, lightweight drilling units, and technology and process control. The company has drilling contracts for Gullfaks, Heidrun, Snorre, Troll, Valhall, and Oseberg and Jotun.

	NOK mil 12/95	12/96	12/97	US$mil 12/97					
Sales	592.0	711.9	1,095.2	148.8	P/E Ratio	20.8	Price (6/30/98)		126.00
Net Income	44.3	45.7	98.9	13.4	P/B Ratio	N/A	52 Wk Hi-Low		197.70-96.00
Book Value	147.0	193.1	675.5	91.8	Yield %	N/A	Market Cap		US$422.2mil

Address	Risavika Havnering 224	Tel 51-64-25-00	ADR	--	President & CEO	Reidar Lund
	4056 Tananter	Fax 51-64-25-01	SEDOL	5241893	Chairman	Ole Lund

Rieber & Son

DJGI Industry: **Other Food**
Stoxx Sector: **Food & Beverage**

Rieber & Son ASA is one of the leading Oslo-listed industrial companies. The company manufactures and markets food products, cardboard, corrugated board and PVC film packaging, building materials, and roadbuilding materials. Rieber & Son's food activities are concentrated on dehydrated foods, chilled foods, chocolate and confectionery, and marine foods. The company's main markets are the Nordic region and central and eastern Europe. The food division accounted for 42% of group turnover in 1997; packaging 20%; roads, 30%; and building materials, 8%.

	NOK mil 12/95	12/96	12/97	US$mil 12/97					
Sales	4,631.0	5,211.0	6,672.0	906.5	P/E Ratio	16.2	Price (6/30/98)		75.00
Net Income	289.6	372.1	372.7	50.6	P/B Ratio	3.0	52 Wk Hi-Low		80.00-70.00
Book Value	1,557.7	1,791.0	2,011.5	273.3	Yield %	2.4	Market Cap		US$400.8mil

Address	Nostegaten 58, Box 987	Tel 55-96-70-00	ADR	--	President	--
	5002 Bergen	Fax 55-96-74-96	SEDOL	4738512	Chairman	J.E. Greve

Saga Petroleum

DJGI Industry: **Oil Companies - Secondary**
Stoxx Sector: **Energy**

Saga Petroleum ASA operates primarily in the Norwegian sector of the North Sea. Its main products are oil and liquefied petroleum gas. The company has long-term contracts to supply gas via pipeline to buyers in France, Belgium, Germany, and the Netherlands. The company has interests in 60 production licenses, including 22 operatorships and all major pipeline systems on the Norwegian shelf. Saga produced 70.5 million barrels of oil equivalent in 1997. Petroleum products accounted for 89% of 1997 revenues; pipeline transportation systems, 7%; and other, 4%.

	NOK 12/95	12/96	12/97	US$mil 12/97					
Sales	5,621.0	7,416.0	9,919.0	1,347.6	P/E Ratio M	16.4	Price (6/30/98) M	118.00
Net Income	555.0	786.0	821.0	111.5	P/B Ratio M	2.3	52 Wk Hi-Low M	167.00-113.50
Book Value	5,408.0	5,767.0	7,211.0	979.7	Yield % M	3.0	Market Cap M	US$1,594.4mil

Address	Kjorboveien 16	Tel 67-12-66-00	ADR	SPM.A	V Chairman	L.F. Onarheim
	1301 Sandvika	Fax 67-12-66-66	SEDOL	4768025	Chairman	W. Wilhelmsen

M=Multiple issues in index; reflects most active.

Schibsted

DJGI Industry: **Publishing**
Stoxx Sector: **Media**

Schibsted ASA prints and publishes newspapers, books, and other publications, and it also maintains interests in the film and television industries. The company owns and publishes two of Norway's most popular daily papers, Aftenposten and Verdens Gang, and operates a national TV channel, TV2. It is also involved in film and television production and distribution, studios, film processing, and postproduction activities. Retail sales accounted for 42% of 1997 revenues; advertising income, 36%; subscription sales, 10%; and other, 12%.

	NOK mil 12/95	12/96	12/97	US$mil 12/97					
Sales	3,347.8	4,524.3	5,359.9	728.2	P/E Ratio	18.1	Price (6/30/98)	129.00
Net Income	345.8	401.2	487.9	66.3	P/B Ratio	4.0	52 Wk Hi-Low	150.00-117.00
Book Value	1,599.9	1,890.1	2,252.8	306.1	Yield %	1.4	Market Cap	US$1,166.3mil

Address	Apotekergaten 10	Tel 23-10-66-00	ADR	--	V Chairman	O. Lund
	0107 Oslo	Fax 23-10-66-01	SEDOL	4790534	Chairman	T. Nagell-Erichsen

Smedvig

DJGI Industry: **Oil Drilling**
Stoxx Sector: **Energy**

Smedvig ASA is an integrated offshore company engaged in well construction, mobile production, and reservoir and well technology. It owns and operates mobile drilling units and holds contracts for production drilling, well services, and maintenance on fixed installations in the North Sea. Smedvig is also pursuing projects in Southeast Asia. Platform drilling operations accounted for 28% of 1997 revenues; mobile production units, 26%; operation of mobile units, 20%; operation of tender rigs, 13%; and reservoir and well technology, 13%.

	NOK mil 12/95	12/96	12/97	US$mil 12/97					
Sales	2,019.0	2,451.0	3,084.0	419.0	P/E Ratio	5.9	Price (6/30/98)	93.00
Net Income	205.0	210.0	586.0	79.6	P/B Ratio	1.1	52 Wk Hi-Low	243.00-91.00
Book Value	1,804.0	2,899.0	3,417.0	464.2	Yield %	2.4	Market Cap	US$331.3mil

Address	Box 110, Lokkeveien 103	Tel 51-50-99-00	ADR	SMV	Acting Mng Dir	O. Rod
	4001 Stavanger	Fax 51-53-43-96	SEDOL	4837914	Chairman	P.T. Smedvig

Sparebanken Nor

DJGI Industry: **Banks - Regional (All)**
Stoxx Sector: **Bank**

Sparebanken Nor is Norway's third-largest bank and its largest savings bank. The company provides commercial and investment banking, securities trading and management, real estate, and other financial services. In addition to the main market area in eastern Norway, the bank operates seven district offices and representative offices in Luxembourg, Finland, Denmark, and Sweden. Interest and fees on loans accounted for 78% of 1997 revenues; commissions and fees, 12%; foreign exchange income, 1%; and other, 9%.

	NOK mil 12/95	12/96	12/97	US$mil 12/97					
Revenues	8,654.0	8,779.0	8,956.0	1,216.8	P/E Ratio	8.3	Price (6/30/98)	220.00
Net Income	1,071.0	851.0	868.0	117.9	P/B Ratio	0.9	52 Wk Hi-Low	279.00-185.00
Book Value	5,562.0	6,125.0	6,638.0	901.8	Yield %	6.8	Market Cap	US$748.2mil

Address	Box 1172 Sentrum	Tel 22-31-90-50	ADR	--	President & CEO	K.O. Kran
	Oslo 0107	Fax 22-31-87-64	SEDOL	4848820	Chairman	H. Bo

Storebrand

DJGI Industry: **Insurance - Full Line**
Stoxx Sector: **Insurance**

Storebrand ASA is the largest insurance company in Norway. It provides nonlife insurance, life assurance, and financing. The company was placed under official administration on August 25, 1992, and virtually all of its assets were transferred to a new wholly owned subsidiary, UNI Storebrand Nye AS. The company's shares were relisted on the Oslo Stock Exchange on June 23, 1993. Life assurance premiums accounted for 30% of 1997 revenues; nonlife premiums, 30%; investment income, 24%; securities income, 14%; and other, 2%.

	NOK mil 12/95	12/96	12/97	US$mil 12/97					
Revenues	19,732.3	21,502.7	24,421.3	3,317.9	P/E Ratio	16.7	Price (6/30/98)	68.00
Net Income	1,415.7	1,115.3	1,076.9	146.3	P/B Ratio	3.5	52 Wk Hi-Low	74.50-43.00
Book Value	3,306.3	4,357.2	5,385.9	731.7	Yield %	0.0	Market Cap	US$2,459.0mil

Address	Box 1380 Vika, Ruselokkveien 26	Tel 22-31-50-50	ADR	--	CEO	A. Korsvold
	0114 Oslo	Fax 22-31-53-00	SEDOL	4852832	Chairman	J. Gundersen

Tandberg Data

DJGI Industry: **Computers**
Stoxx Sector: **Technology**

Tandberg Data ASA is a global leader, innovator, and supplier of taped data-storage management solutions to the professional marketplace. The company's product solutions are used for storage of and easy access to digital data, mainly in conjunction with servers, workstations, and minimachines (midrange) and in a wide range of network storage applications. Some of the largest customers include Compaq, IBM, DEC, Sun Microsystems, and Siemens. Over 96% of Tandberg Data's products are exported. Its largest markets are the United States, Europe, and Asia.

	NOK mil 12/95	12/96	12/97	US$mil 12/97				
Sales	1,254.3	828.8	888.8	120.8	P/E Ratio	18.7	Price (6/30/98)	27.80
Net Income	30.3	55.6	51.3	7.0	P/B Ratio	2.3	52 Wk Hi-Low	100.00-21.00
Book Value	236.3	255.8	411.0	55.8	Yield %	0.0	Market Cap	US$140.7mil

Address	Box 134 Kjelsas, Kjelsasveien	Tel 22-18-90-90	ADR	--	President	--
	0411 Oslo	Fax 22-18-95-50	SEDOL	5351907	Chairman	T.E. Holte

Tomra Systems

DJGI Industry: **Pollution Control & Waste Management**
Stoxx Sector: **Industrials**

Tomra Systems ASA is the world's leading supplier of reverse vending machines for beverage containers. The company manufactures, markets, and leases machines for recycling glass, plastic bottles, and various types of beverage containers, and other packaging materials worldwide. The company launched two new machines, TOMRA-600 Ultima, for bottles, and Halton Butler, in 1997. The new MicroLite will be available on the market during the third quarter of 1998. The company's 1997 market share amounted to 95% in Europe and 80% in the United States.

	NOK mil 12/95	12/96	12/97	US$mil 12/97				
Sales	501.0	783.5	1,200.8	163.1	P/E Ratio	65.2	Price (6/30/98)	230.00
Net Income	62.7	102.2	131.3	17.8	P/B Ratio	9.1	52 Wk Hi-Low	255.00-135.00
Book Value	395.4	500.1	1,026.6	139.5	Yield %	0.2	Market Cap	US$1,227.2mil

Address	Box 278, Drengsrudhagen 2	Tel 66-79-91-00	ADR	--	Chairman	J.C. Opsahl
	1371 Asker	Fax 66-79-91-11	SEDOL	4897082	President & CEO	E. Thorsen

Ulstein

DJGI Industry: **Shipbuilding**
Stoxx Sector: **Industrials**

Ulstein Holdings ASA has operations in five business areas: design and ship systems, shipbuilding, engines, propulsion and deck machinery, and steering gear. It develops vessel design, builds ships, and develops and manufactures a wide range of marine equipment and related products through an international service network. Through its subsidiary, Ulstein Maritime Industries Inc., the company entered an agreement in 1998 to purchase U.S company Bird-Johnson Inc., which will make Ulstein one of the world's largest suppliers of equipment for the propulsion and manuevering of ships.

	NOK mil 12/95	12/96	12/97	US$mil 12/97				
Sales	3,000.4	3,271.7	3,870.5	525.8	P/E Ratio	N/A	Price (6/30/98)	156.00
Net Income	75.7	36.8	186.1	25.3	P/B Ratio	N/A	52 Wk Hi-Low	178.00-97.00
Book Value	579.3	741.7	1,152.0	156.5	Yield %	N/A	Market Cap	US$436.0mil

Address	Ulstein Holding	Tel 70-01-40-00	ADR	--	President & CEO	Bard Mikkelsen
	6065 Ulsteinvik	Fax 70-01-40-01	SEDOL	5337758	Chairman	Idar Ulstein

Unitor

DJGI Industry: **Chemicals - Specialty**
Stoxx Sector: **Chemical**

Unitor ASA is the world's leading marine service company. It provides repair, maintenance, welding, and refrigeration services. The company also manufactures and markets marine chemicals, special tools, surface treatments, and fire and safety equipment worldwide. Chemical products include agricultural, industrial, autocare, household, and hygiene products. Repair and maintenance systems accounted for 26% of 1997 revenues; contracts, 23%; marine chemicals, 17%; fire and safety systems, 16%; refrigeration systems, 15%; and other, 3%.

	NOK mil 12/95	12/96	12/97	US$mil 12/97				
Sales	2,846.0	2,690.0	2,497.0	339.2	P/E Ratio	20.2	Price (6/30/98)	113.00
Net Income	85.0	-64.0	90.0	12.2	P/B Ratio	2.4	52 Wk Hi-Low	130.00-85.00
Book Value	995.0	867.0	905.0	123.0	Yield %	3.1	Market Cap	US$288.4mil

Address	Drammensveien 211	Tel 22-13-14-15	ADR	UTORY	V Chairman	E. Astrup
	0212 Oslo	Fax 22-13-45-00	SEDOL	4918347	Chairman	J. Ulltveit-Moe

Portugal

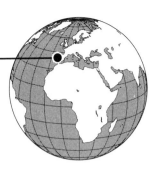

Exchanges:

The Lisbon Stock Exchange

Portugal

Erik T. Burns
Lisbon

The Bolsa de Valores de Lisboa stock exchange inaugurated a shiny new building in 1994, moving the center of trade out of the downtown Praca do Comercio — where an organized market had existed for more than 200 years — to a new site wedged between a Portuguese Communist Party office and a shanty town.

That contrast reflects the market's own position as a thriving outpost of modern capitalism in a country working hard to catch up to European standards as monetary union looms.

The Exchange itself is cutting-edge. Open-outcry ended in the mid-1990s, with a switch to all-electronic trading based on a computer system similar to that used at the Paris bourse.

The BVL's big new trading room stands empty, the digital clocks still flashing the time in key time zones around the world and the old brass bell hanging forlornly in the black and gray marble room. One other souvenir left over from the former site — an ornate marble and iron portal — greets visitors just inside the new glass front door. These days the trading room itself is used only for ceremonial events, like the special sessions to announce the results of the country's many privatizations.

Those privatizations have brought maturity and depth to this peripheral European market. Total capitalization nearly doubled to 7.2 trillion escudos in 1997, from 3.8 trillion escudos in 1996, and trading

volume increased to 1.0 trillion shares from 518 million shares.

The BVL also is the market for government and corporate bonds. Futures contracts are traded in the northern city of Oporto at the Bolsa de Derivados do Porto, which opened in 1996. But bond trading, which used to represent the bulk of Lisbon market activity, has been outpaced by stocks as investment fund rules have been loosened to allow for easier access to equities.

Recent years have also seen the rise of "popular capitalism," as successive governments pursued ambitious privatization programs. The process began by returning banks to private investors, with major companies, including telecommunications company Portugal Telecom SA, utility Electricidade de Portugal SA (EDP), cement company Cimpor SA and pulp producer Portucel SA, all coming to market.

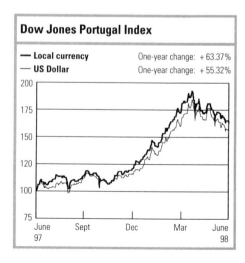

Dow Jones Portugal Index

— Local currency   One-year change: + 63.37%
— US Dollar   One-year change: + 55.32%

That let investors diversify their portfolios away from the financial sector and brought in small savers looking for better returns. The government so far has a good record of attracting heavy demand for its sales, and investors have been rewarded with good aftermarket gains in most of the sold-off shares. The bull market also has attracted private companies. The pace of initial public offerings intensified in 1998. Most are structured like the state sell-offs and also draw strong demand.

The top blue-chip stocks now offer a nice mix: Portugal Telecom is the biggest, followed by Banco Comercial Portugues, EDP, cellular provider Telecel, and retailer Jeronimo Martins. There are six banks in the BVL-30 index and three insurance companies, plus a handful of industrial companies, including a brewer, a cork-products manufacturer, and three construction companies. The index, which is based on market capitalization and liquidity, is revised on a quarterly basis, though the BVL can also make interim changes based on takeovers or the appearance of new stock through a state sale or IPO.

Five of the listed companies also trade in other markets, notably London's SEAQ exchange and the New York Stock Exchange's American Depositary Receipt program, which has heightened foreign interest in Portuguese equities.

In 1997, Dow Jones & Co. added Lisbon to its Global Indexes, a sign of the growing

Country Information

Trading Hours:
　Local: 9:30 am - 4:30 pm

　EST:　4:30 am - 11:30 am

　GMT:　0930 - 1630

Population (6/98):
9,927,556

Unemployment (97):
6.9%

Main Industries:
Textiles and footwear, wood pulp, paper, cork, metalworking, oil refining, chemicals, fish canning, wine, and tourism

Gross Domestic Product (97):
US$97.36 billion

GDP per Capita (97):
US$9,794.45

Three-Year Average GDP Growth (94-97):
2.8%

Average Annual CPI Growth (96-97):
+ 2.16%

Monetary Unit:
Portuguese Escudo

Exchange Rate (6/98):
PTE185.02 to US$1.00

foreign interest and the market's move toward maturity.

Because of falling inflation, lower interest rates and continued infrastructure investment, Portugal's economy has outperformed the European average for the past few years. Portuguese shares have brought extraordinary gains: the benchmark BVL-30 index soared 75% in 1997, after a 35% gain in 1996, and was up around 55% by midyear 1998.

The country enjoys political stability, driven by the continuous — and finally successful — effort to be a starting member of European Monetary Union. The ruling Socialist Party, elected in 1995, has repeatedly stressed its interest in developing the capital markets. With the stream of privatizations, the government has put its assets up for sale, using the receipts to help reduce overall public debt. The sale of state companies brought in a record 800 billion escudos in 1997, and the expectation is the total will top that in 1998.

Finance Minister Antonio Sousa Franco has even said the BVL may eventually be privatized, with the most likely model being a sale directly to the BVL's associated brokers, dealers, and banks. There are currently 11 broker members, nine dealer members, and 29 associated banks. Dealers can manage proprietary portfolios, but brokers are limited to processing client orders.

Ten Largest Capitalized Companies In The Dow Jones Portugal Index
as of 6/30/98

Stock	Market Cap. US$ Thousands
Portugal Telecom	10,053,841
Banco Comercial Portuguese	5,583,918
Electricidade de Portugal (EDP)	4,121,281
Telecel Comunicacoes Pessoais	3,811,606
Banco Espir Santo e Com de Lisboa	3,536,142
Jeronimo Martins	3,341,026
Modelo Continente	2,627,371
BPI	2,511,423
Cimpor Cimentos de Portugal	2,406,382
Sonae Investimentos	2,181,242

Only brokers and dealers can trade directly in the market, though banks remain the main point of contact for small investors, channeling orders through to the market participants. Most brokers and dealers are actually subsidiaries of the major banks, so the chain of command is fairly transparent.

Faced with a new and growing class of investor — the general public — and an increasingly active market, the BVL's administration has worked to keep up. It recently replaced its electronic trading system after repeated technical glitches with the old one, and has come up with a number of additional support services, including a faxed information sheet, a real-time news and price service, an on-line historical database, and a growing Internet website.

The link to Paris, part of the agreement for use of the new trading system, is seen as a first step to deeper cooperation as equity trading in Europe changes with monetary union. With the new system, trades are registered immediately, accounts are debited or credited on a T+3 basis, and by 1999, physical settlement as well will be processed on a T+4 basis through the centralized clearing system at the Bank of Portugal.

Trading costs levied by the Exchange were reduced in 1997. To increase liquidity, the Exchange also decided to eliminate its policy of stopping trade in shares for technical reasons, such as dividend payout periods. Shares were previously halted for up to a week as they went ex-dividend.

The Lisbon Exchange has also been helpful in providing technical support to stock markets being developed in former Portuguese colonies in Africa. The BVL's specialists have consulted on the Mozambican Exchange, and in Cape Verde and Angola. The basis for that assistance is the Exchange's wide experience in handling the sale of state assets.

At home, regulation is undergoing changes as the independent watchdog, the Comissao do Mercado de Valores Mobiliarios, or CMVM, works to update the 1991 Sapateiro Law that covers market activity. New changes include the requirement of timely publication of quarterly earnings by companies listed in the primary market, as well as better transparency on market-sensitive data in general.

Although most market participants see the CMVM as a sluggish bureaucracy, the

Market Sector Performance In The Dow Jones Portugal Index
1 Year Change Through 6/30/98

Market Sector	Change % (US$)
Basic Materials	99.78
Consumer, Cyclical	71.55
Financial	70.20
Consumer, Non-Cyclical	55.97
Utilities	41.95
Industrial	33.51
Independent	30.34

watchdog agency has made some serious efforts to combat fraud, most notably a case in 1996-1997, still under way, that involved allegedly illegal Internet sharedealing from a Lisbon base.

Banco Comercial Portuguese

DJGI Industry: **Banks - Regional (All)**
Stoxx Sector: **Bank**

Banco Comercial Portuguese (BCP) is a private commercial bank that leads a financial group with nearly 40 associates in insurance, mutual funds, portfolio management, merchant banking, factoring, securities brokerage, leasing, venture capital, long-term rental, pension management funds, real estate investments, and tourism. The bank has 742 branches. Banco Comercial owns Banco Portugues de Atlantico. Together, they constitute Portugal's second-largest financial group. In 1997, Banco Comercial planned to open a delegation in the Chinese city of Guangzhou.

	PTE mil 12/95	12/96	12/97	US$mil 12/97				
Revenues	648,701.5	559,577.0	568,436.1	3,091.2	P/E Ratio	24.9	Price (6/30/98)	5,245.00
Net Income	20,273.2	23,268.1	36,134.6	196.5	P/B Ratio	5.7	52 Wk Hi-Low	6,940.0-3,016.9
Book Value	169,541.0	195,620.9	159,353.7	866.6	Yield %	1.6	Market Cap	US$5,583.9mil

Address	Rua Julio Dinis 705/719	Tel 2-696-136	ADR	BPC	President	--
	Porto 4000	Fax 2-699-512	SEDOL	4070269	Chairman	J.M. Goncalves

Banco Espirito Santo

DJGI Industry: **Banks - Regional (All)**
Stoxx Sector: **Bank**

Banco Espirito Santo e Comercial de Lisboa SA (BESCL) is Portugal's third-largest private bank after Banco Comercial Portugues and Banco Totta e Acores. Its main activities are retail and corporate banking, portfolio management, Portuguese and international securities and property investment funds, insurance, mortgage loans, credit cards, and leasing. It provides its banking services through 421 branches in Portugal and in other countries. Banco Espirito Santo is a subsidiary of the Espirito Santo Financial Group SA.

	PTE mil 12/95	12/96	12/97	US$mil 12/97				
Revenues	346,913.0	289,195.0	532,206.0	2,894.2	P/E Ratio	20.2	Price (6/30/98)	5,547.00
Net Income	19,452.0	23,647.0	30,107.0	163.7	P/B Ratio	3.6	52 Wk Hi-Low	8,043.4-3,211.7
Book Value	143,650.0	149,917.0	162,355.0	882.9	Yield %	2.2	Market Cap	US$3,536.1mil

Address	Av. de Liberdade 195	Tel 1-579-005	ADR	--	President	R.S. Salgado
	Lisbon 1250	Fax 1-350-8914	SEDOL	4058061	Chairman	--

BPI Sociedad Gestora

DJGI Industry: **Diversified Financial Services**
Stoxx Sector: **Financial Services**

BPI Sociedad Gestora Participacoes Sociais SA (Banco Portugues de Investimento) is a private investment bank engaged in the handling of capital market operations and financial services and consulting on the management of financial assets. BPI is the nucleus of a financial group that offers extensive services to companies, institutions, and consumers. Main subsidiaries include Banco Borges & Irmaos SA, Banco de Fomento e Exterior SA, BFB Leasing, Gerifirme, Douro Corretora, Banco Fonsecas & Burnay, BPI Pensoes, and Douro Fundos.

	PTE mil 12/95	12/96	12/97	US$mil 12/97				
Revenues	196,980.1	247,019.1	328,166.0	1,784.6	P/E Ratio	24.4	Price (6/30/98)	5,961.00
Net Income	9,662.9	15,107.8	22,216.0	120.8	P/B Ratio	5.8	52 Wk Hi-Low	9,060.0-3,415.0
Book Value	86,167.8	80,520.0	96,260.0	523.5	Yield %	1.7	Market Cap	US$2,511.4mil

Address	Rua Tenente Valadim 284	Tel 2-600-3731	ADR	--	President	--
	Porto 4100	Fax 2-698-787	SEDOL	4072566	Chairman	A.S. Silva

Cimpor-Cimentos de Portugal

DJGI Industry: **Building Materials**
Stoxx Sector: **Construction**

Cimpor-Cimentos de Portugal SA is Portugal's largest producer of cement and concrete. Other activities not directly tied to cement include Cimpor Investments and paper bag production. Formerly state-owned, Cimpor began its privatization process in mid-1994. In January 1997, Cimpor bought three factories in Brazil for PTE 62 billion to increase annual production capacity to 11 million tons from 8 million tons. Cement accounted for 40% of 1997 revenues; ready-mix concrete, 24%; and precast concrete, 2%; other activities accounted for 34%.

	PTE mil 12/95	12/96	12/97	US$mil 12/97				
Sales	118,653.6	128,278.6	167,502.0	910.9	P/E Ratio	27.6	Price (6/30/98)	6,490.00
Net Income	18,396.9	19,745.2	18,113.0	98.5	P/B Ratio	2.8	52 Wk Hi-Low	7,015.0-4,102.0
Book Value	124,625.8	194,114.3	202,590.0	1,101.7	Yield %	1.8	Market Cap	US$2,406.4mil

Address	Rua Alexandre Herculano 35	Tel 1-311-8100	ADR	CTOSYP	President	--
	Lisbon 1250	Fax 1-3522-9936	SEDOL	4175896	Chairman	A.S. Gomes

Electricidade de Portugal

DJGI Industry: **Electrical Utilities (All)**
Stoxx Sector: **Utility**

Electricidade de Portugal SA (EdP), with its subsidiaries (the Group), controls 86% of electricity production and 100% of its distribution in Portugal. The state-owned utility is composed of two sectors: the binding system (binding producers and distributors) and the nonbinding system and other small independent producers (cogeneration, minihydro plants, and new and renewable energies). The government reduced its stake to 51.55% of EDP through three privatization efforts in 1997 and 1998. Early in 1997, EDP formed a consortium to operate in the telecommunications sector.

	PTE mil 12/95	12/96	12/97	US$mil 12/97				
Sales	538,621.0	546,931.2	571,450.7	3,107.6	P/E Ratio	27.7	Price (6/30/98)	4,294.00
Net Income	66,267.8	81,145.2	93,019.5	505.8	P/B Ratio	N/A	52 Wk Hi-Low	5,000.0-2,810.0
Book Value	1,206,731	1,233,122	1,238,516	6,735.1	Yield %	3.3	Market Cap	US$4,121.3mil

Address	Av. Jose Malhoa, Lote A-13	Tel 1-726-3013	ADR	EDP	President	--
	Lisbon 1070	Fax 1-726-5029	SEDOL	5249187	Chairman	A. Almeida

Inparsa

DJGI Industry: **Forest Products**
Stoxx Sector: **Basic Resources**

Inparsa SGPS is a holding company with interests in telecommunications, real estate, tourism, and industry. It was spun off in January 1997 by Sonae Investimentos SGPS in an effort to focus on core retailing business. Inparsa took over Sonae's Pargeste venture capital operations, and it also owns 60% of Sonae Industria, a wood-products company. In 1997, Inparsa, in partnership with utility Electricidade de Portugal (EDP), France Telecom, and Portugese operator Maxitel, was awarded the license for Portugal's third cellular telephone service. Inparsa has a 45% stake in the consortium.

	PTE mil 12/95	12/96	12/97	US$mil 12/97					
Sales	N/A	856.0	1,048.0	5.7	P/E Ratio	N/A	Price (6/30/98)	8,170.00
Net Income	N/A	500.0	630.0	3.4	P/B Ratio	N/A	52 Wk Hi-Low	10,875.0-1,412.4
Book Value	N/A	N/A	N/A	N/A	Yield %	N/A	Market Cap	US$1,291.6mil

Address	Lugar de Espido, Apartado 11	Tel 2-948-7522	ADR	--	President	--
	Maia 4471	Fax --	SEDOL	5195280	Chairman	B.M. de Azevedo

Jeronimo Martins

DJGI Industry: **Retailers - Broadline**
Stoxx Sector: **Retail**

Estabelecimentos Jeronimo Martins e Filho SGPS SA is one of Portugal's largest retailing groups. It is composed of companies whose activities include the manufacturing, distributing, and selling of food-related products and other consumer goods through supermarkets specialized shops. It also has financial and real estate segments. Jeronimo Martins owns three major chains of supermarkets and hypermarkets in Portugal and is part owner of Industrias Lever Portuguesa Lda., Fima Produtos Alimentares, Iglo Industrias de Gelados Lda., and Brazilian supermarket chain SE.

	PTE mil 12/95	12/96	12/97	US$mil 12/97					
Revenues	281,664.8	359,788.9	418,345.5	2,275.0	P/E Ratio	86.9	Price (6/30/98)	8,874.00
Net Income	5,556.0	7,047.4	8,766.4	47.7	P/B Ratio	16.2	52 Wk Hi-Low	12,295.0-4,426.0
Book Value	22,641.0	37,464.4	63,198.1	343.7	Yield %	0.6	Market Cap	US$3,341.0mil

Address	Rua Tierno Galvan Torre 3	Tel 1-381-8400	ADR	--	CEO	J.I. Brito
	Lisbon 1000	Fax 1-388-9822	SEDOL	4477235	Chairman	E.A. Santos

Modelo Continente

DJGI Industry: **Food Retailers & Wholesalers**
Stoxx Sector: **Consumer Non-Cyclical**

Modelo Continente SGPS SA is the main retailing subsidiary of Sonae Investimentos SGPS. Its activities are the retail sale of various foods through supermarkets located throughout Portugal. Modelo also has real estate investments through subsidiary Contimobe-mobiliaria de Castelo de Paiva SA. In 1997, the company opened two new Continente outlets and eight new Modelo stores. Along with expanding activities in Portugal, Modelo is also actively pursuing investment in Brazil through its subsidiary Cia. Real de Distribuicao. Retailing accounts for more than 95% of the company's revenues.

	PTE mil 12/95	12/96	12/97	US$mil 12/97					
Sales	207,036.5	286,286.6	306,693.8	1,667.8	P/E Ratio	58.8	Price (6/30/98)	4,861.00
Net Income	6,964.2	8,007.0	9,436.8	51.3	P/B Ratio	7.5	52 Wk Hi-Low	5,879.0-2,851.0
Book Value	58,002.8	62,970.4	68,808.9	374.2	Yield %	1.0	Market Cap	US$2,627.4mil

Address	Rua Joao de Mendonca 505	Tel 2-953-2678	ADR	--	President	N.M. Jordao
	Matozinhos 4450	Fax 2-952-0950	SEDOL	4599582	Chairman	--

Mundial Confianca

DJGI Industry: **Insurance - Full Line**
Stoxx Sector: **Insurance**

Companhia de Seguros Mundial Confianca SGPS is Portugal's fifth-largest insurer, and it also serves as the holding company for businessman Antonio Champalimaud, reportedly the country's wealthiest individual. It has a network of 843 branches that offer life and nonlife insurance services. The nonlife segment comprises automobile, accident and illness, fire and allied perils, transportation, third-party liabilities, and miscellaneous insurance. Mundial holds majority stakes in Banco Pinto e Sotto Mayor and Banco Totta e Acores, making it Portugal's third-largest financial group.

	PTE mil 12/94	12/95	12/96	US$mil 12/96					
Revenues	N/A	71,312.7	88,029.4	568.3	P/E Ratio	56.0	Price (6/30/98)	4,910.00
Net Income	N/A	3,504.9	4,222.4	27.3	P/B Ratio	3.8	52 Wk Hi-Low	7,150.0-2,563.0
Book Value	N/A	57,246.5	62,035.7	400.5	Yield %	0.0	Market Cap	US$1,289.8mil

Address	Largo do Chiado 8	Tel 1-340-1500	ADR	CTOSYP	President	--
	Lisbon 1200	Fax --	SEDOL	4609135	Chairman	C.J. Ferreira

Portucel Industrial

DJGI Industry: **Paper Products**
Stoxx Sector: **Basic Resources**

Portucel Industrial SA was formed in 1993 as part of the reorganization of state-owned Portucel SA. Through its predecessor companies, Portucel has been producing and selling pulp in western Europe for more than 40 years. It boasts the largest bleached eucalyptus kraft pulp (BEKP) production capacity in Europe and the second largest in the world. Current BEKP capacity is 640,000 tons of pulp and kraft paper per year. European markets absorb most of the company's production, with 93% of the pulp sold there. The state owns more than 56% of Portucel.

	PTE mil 12/95	12/96	12/97	US$mil 12/97					
Sales	70,544.3	46,852.1	55,841.0	303.7	P/E Ratio	NMF	Price (6/30/98)	1,469.00
Net Income	18,137.6	-1,371.1	4,249.9	23.1	P/B Ratio	1.3	52 Wk Hi-Low	1,850.0-1,090.0
Book Value	102,098.1	96,776.5	99,503.9	541.1	Yield %	1.7	Market Cap	US$305.8mil

Address	Rua Joaquim Antonio de Aguiar 3	Tel 1-915-0197	ADR	PICIY	President	--
	Lisbon 1000	Fax 1-530-016	SEDOL	4719078	Chairman	J.O. Godinho

Portugal Telecom

DJGI Industry: **Telephone Utilities (All)**
Stoxx Sector: **Telecom**

Portugal Telecom SA operates in the telecommunications industry. It is the country's principal provider of national and international telephone communications services. Its activities consist of the management of the infrastructure of the public telephone service at the local, regional, and international levels, leased lines, broadcasting services, cable television services, data transmission, and mobile services. Portugal Telecom has also financial holdings in a number of concerns not directly associated with the company's core business.

	PTE mil 12/95	12/96	12/97	US$mil 12/97					
Sales	405,780.6	477,830.6	540,497.6	2,939.2	P/E Ratio	25.7	Price (6/30/98)		9,790.00
Net Income	36,254.3	54,922.2	70,096.6	381.2	P/B Ratio	4.6	52 Wk Hi-Low		11,240.0-6,730.0
Book Value	371,104.3	408,434.9	401,242.8	2,182.0	Yield %	1.8	Market Cap		US$10,054mil

Address	Av. Fontes Pereira de Melo 40	Tel 1-540-020	ADR	PT	President	
	Lisbon 1089	Fax 1-350-4750	SEDOL	4676203	Chairman & CEO	F.I. Nabo

In EuroStoxx 50.

Semapa

DJGI Industry: **Building Materials**
Stoxx Sector: **Construction**

Semapa-Sociedade de Investimentos e Gestao SGPS SA-is engaged primarily in the production and distribution of cement and cement products. Products of the company include ready-mix concrete, hydraulic lime, tile cement, mortar, quarries and aggregates, cement terminals, and wood-cement panels. It is Portugal's second-largest cement company, boasting approximately 40% of market share. Semapa is the holding company for two cement producers, Secil and CMP. The company also sells electric power through its minihydroelectric plants.

	PTE mil 12/94	12/95	12/96	US$mil 12/96					
Sales	N/A	56,851.6	64,643.6	417.3	P/E Ratio	21.3	Price (6/30/98)		4,650.00
Net Income	N/A	1,769.8	3,665.0	23.7	P/B Ratio	4.0	52 Wk Hi-Low		6,120.0-3,926.0
Book Value	N/A	24,648.8	26,681.3	172.2	Yield %	3.4	Market Cap		US$594.8mil

Address	Av. Fontes Pereira de Melo 14-10	Tel 1-314-2630	ADR	--	President	P.M. Pereira
	Lisbon 1050	Fax 1-357-2260	SEDOL	4859598	Chairman	--

Sonae Industria

DJGI Industry: **Forest Products**
Stoxx Sector: **Basic Resources**

Sonae Industria SGPS SA is a wood-processing company. It produces agglomerates, including chipboard and medium-density fiberboard, or MDF. The company has expanded its core wood-processing interests with a major investment in Spanish industrial company Tafisa-Tableros de Madera SA, buying some 45% of the company in 1996. Sonae Industria is currently the fourth largest European group in the wood-based panels sector. In 1997, Sonae Industria was split off from parent company Sonae Investimentos in order to better focus the efforts of both companies.

	PTE mil 12/94	12/95	12/96	US$mil 12/96					
Sales	33,616.0	64,215.9	64,494.8	416.4	P/E Ratio	132.7	Price (6/30/98)		2,900.00
Net Income	-1,185.2	1,092.4	453.2	2.9	P/B Ratio	2.6	52 Wk Hi-Low		3,288.0-1,084.8
Book Value	23,246.3	22,678.9	22,703.2	146.6	Yield %	0.5	Market Cap		US$479.6mil

Address	Lugar do Espido	Tel 2-948-7522	ADR	--	President	C.A.. Silva
	Maia 4470	Fax 2-948-7722	SEDOL	4645753	Chairman	--

Sonae Investimentos

DJGI Industry: **Conglomerates**
Stoxx Sector: **Conglomerate**

Sonae Investimentos SGPS, Portugal's leading privately owned group, is the holding company that oversees Portugal's largest retail and financial group. It has core businesses in retailing, wood-based products, and real estate, as well as a growing presence in communication and information technology. Sonae has been expanding its retail efforts through its holding in Modelo SGPS, a chain of smaller-scale supermarkets. It also has holdings in Brazil, Canada, Spain, and Northern Ireland. In January 1997, it spun off Sonae Industria and launched newly listed Inparsa.

	PTE mil 12/95	12/96	12/97	US$mil 12/97					
Sales	356,697.1	450,951.0	412,342.4	2,242.3	P/E Ratio	19.0	Price (6/30/98)		10,089
Net Income	12,868.8	20,681.6	12,197.4	66.3	P/B Ratio	3.8	52 Wk Hi-Low		11,900.0-6,090.0
Book Value	93,791.7	104,329.6	78,021.8	424.3	Yield %	1.5	Market Cap		US$2,181.2mil

Address	Lugar de Espido, Via Norte	Tel 2-948-7522	ADR	--	President	B.M. Azevedo
	Maia 4471	Fax 2-948-7722	SEDOL	4822686	Chairman	--

Soporcel

DJGI Industry: **Paper Products**
Stoxx Sector: **Basic Resources**

Soporcel-Sociedade Portuguesa de Celulose SA, together with its subsidiaries, form a group comprising five companies whose principal activities are the production of pulp and paper and the exploration of forests to supply raw materials to the paper industry. It is Portugal's second-largest pulp and paper manufacturer. The company's shareholders include the state-owned bank Caixa Geral Depositos SA (CGD), with a 50.4% share, and Arjo Wiggins, with a 43.3% stake. Paper accounted for 70% of 1997 revenues and pulp accounted for 30%.

	PTE mil 12/95	12/96	12/97	US$mil 12/97					
Sales	76,587.9	62,165.9	72,222.0	392.7	P/E Ratio	NMF	Price (6/30/98)		7,600.00
Net Income	11,196.6	277.0	5,217.5	28.4	P/B Ratio	2.9	52 Wk Hi-Low		8,899.0-5,200.0
Book Value	85,103.6	85,382.3	90,599.3	492.7	Yield %	0.0	Market Cap		US$1,317.6mil

Address	Av. Eng. Duarte Pacheco 19-1	Tel 1-387-6406	ADR	--	President	A.R. Barreto
	Lisbon 1000	Fax 1-385-5239	SEDOL	4822095	Chairman	--

Telecel

DJGI Industry: **Telephone Utilities (All)**
Stoxx Sector: **Telecom**

Telecel Comunicacoes Pessoais SA is the country's only privately owned mobile phone operator. Formed in 1990 after the government decided to issue a GSM license to a private operator, it began operating its GSM network in 1992 and floated 39.1% of its shares in an initial public offering. The other main shareholder in Telecel is AirTouch, a U.S. cellular phone company, with a 51% stake. Telecel also owns a paging service called Telechamada. In June 1997, Telepri, made up of Portuguese financial group Espirito Santo and Corticeira Amorim, a cork company, sold its 10% stake in Telecel.

	PTE mil 12/95	12/96	12/97	US$mil 12/97				
Sales	32,399.9	58,831.1	87,664.1	476.7	P/E Ratio	53.1	Price (6/30/98)	32,800
Net Income	2,438.6	7,290.6	13,296.8	72.3	P/B Ratio	31.5	52 Wk Hi-Low	38,500.0-12,960.0
Book Value	14,894.2	22,184.8	35,481.6	193.0	Yield %	0.9	Market Cap	US$3,811.6mil

Address	Rua Tomas da Fonseca Torre A-3	Tel 1-722-5499	ADR	TPORYY	President	A.R. Carrapatoso
	Lisbon 1600	Fax 1-722-5480	SEDOL	5160794	Chairman	--

Unicer

DJGI Industry: **Distillers & Brewers**
Stoxx Sector: **Food & Beverage**

Unicer-Uniao Cervejeira SA is Portugal's largest brewing and beverage group. Its main activities are the production and marketing of beer, soft drinks, and bottled water. The company's products are sold under the brand names Superbock, Carlsburg, Cristal, Tuborg, Nautic, Cheers, Snappy, Frisumo, and Vitalis. Unicer recently introduced an ice-filtered cool beer that has a crisp, light flavor. Beer accounted for 79% of fiscal 1997 revenues; soft drinks, 14%; bottled water, 3%; and malt beverages and other consumable liquids, 3%.

	PTE mil 12/95	12/96	12/97	US$mil 12/97				
Sales	44,211.2	45,731.4	47,443.5	258.0	P/E Ratio	33.8	Price (6/30/98)	4,079.00
Net Income	3,020.1	2,297.6	2,392.8	13.0	P/B Ratio	2.1	52 Wk Hi-Low	4,250.0-2,600.0
Book Value	36,614.3	36,765.4	36,360.0	197.7	Yield %	2.9	Market Cap	US$429.9mil

Address	Via do Norte-Ieca do Balio	Tel 2-619-7570	ADR	--	V President	J.M. da Fonseca
	Porto 4466	Fax 2-901-5510	SEDOL	4911324	Chairman	--

South Africa

Exchanges:

The Johannesburg Stock Exchange

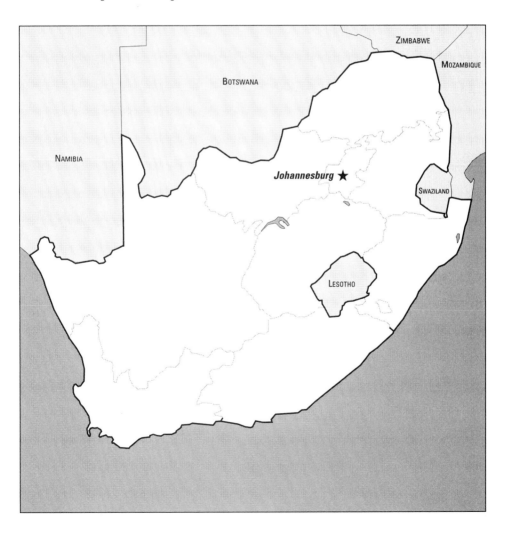

South Africa

Michael Wang
Johannesburg

The Johannesburg Stock Exchange plans to merge its operations with its bond and futures counterparts by the beginning of 1999, adopting a supermarket concept as the future for securities trading

Russell Loubser, president of the JSE, sees the planned amalgamation as a necessity to enable the largest bourse in Africa to better position itself with international investors.

Aside from bread-and-butter equities, the as yet unnamed superexchange also will offer trading in bonds and derivative products, such as options, futures, and warrants. Such an all-under-one-roof bourse follows similar trends in European markets, which are seeking to raise their profile and deal flow.

But it is not that the JSE has been struggling to attract the international investor. For the first half of 1998, foreign net purchases — acquisitions less sales — of South Africa-listed equities totaled 25.87 billion rand (ZAR), almost matching the full-year figure of ZAR26.20 billion of 1997. The half-year tally is a staggering 134% leap from the ZAR11.07 recorded in the first six months of 1997.

What is more remarkable is that foreigners have continued to acquire larger South African equity positions despite a currency crisis that saw the rand plummet more than 24% against the dollar from June 4 to July 6, and 28% since the beginning of 1998. In addition to the discincentive a volatile

currency presents to offshore investors, South Africa also levies a 0.25% tax on the value of each transaction.

The JSE's main indexes were battered by the plunging rand. The All Share Index — the bourse's most comprehensive register of shares — saw a 35% gain from December 31, 1997, to April 21, 1998, erode to just 16% by early July.

The All-Gold Index has been the star performer, jumping 30% between the beginning of 1998 and early July.

Financial services and information technology stocks have been among the most sought after, whereas construction, retail, and media have been weighed down by a South African economy that has averaged growth of less than 0.5% in the three quarters ending March 31, 1998, as measured by gross domestic product.

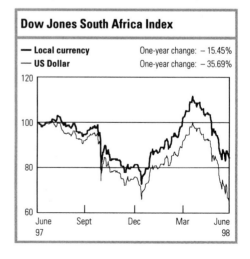

Dow Jones South Africa Index

— Local currency   One-year change: − 15.45%
— US Dollar   One-year change: − 35.69%

Economists predict that with official interest rates near 13-year highs, it will be difficult for economic expansion to improve substantially. Fears of recession are increasing in line with the sharp downturn in Asian economies.

But the JSE is pushing ahead with reforms that will narrow the technological gap between it and major western bourses. Two years ago, the JSE did away with 108 years of traditional open-outcry floor trading, replacing it with electronic screen trading.

In 1998, the JSE shifted its sights to modernizing its archaic, paper-based, scrip settlement system. The bourse plans to license software used by the Swiss Stock Exchange to switch to an electronic back office. That will, among other things, cut settlement time in half, to five business days (T+5). A central depositary for scrip will be created, replacing cumbersome share certificates with electronic entries for the roughly 15,000 transactions conducted daily.

The JSE views reorganization of its back office as essential if it is to be measured alongside the world's major bourses and continue to attract the sophisticated investor.

In addition to merging with the Bond Exchange and the South African Futures Exchange, the JSE is setting its sights on closer ties with equity bourses elsewhere in southern Africa, namely, Zimbabwe, Zambia, Kenya, Mauritius, and Namibia. Mindful of the sovereign pride southern African

Country Information

Trading Hours:
  Local: 9:30 am - 4:00 pm

  EST: 2:30 am - 9:00 am
  (DST) 3:30 am - 10:00 am

  GMT: 0730 - 1400

Population (6/98):
42,834,520

Unemployment (96)*:
29.3%

Main Industries:
  Mining of platinum, gold, chromium, automobile assembly, metalworking, machinery, textile, iron and steel, chemical, fertilizer, and foodstuffs

Gross Domestic Product (97):
US$129.09 billion

GDP per Capita (97):
US$3,370.50

Three-Year Average GDP Growth (94-97):
2.8%

Average Annual CPI Growth (96-97):
+ 8.48%

Monetary Unit:
South African Rand

Exchange Rate (6/98):
ZAR5.96 to US$1.00

*1997 rate not available.

governments attach to their stock exchanges, the JSE is trying to persuade other markets to "piggyback" off its automated trading system, thereby eliminating duplication costs and positioning the region as a more attractive emerging-market destination.

The JSE's reform plans are not without cost. As a result, the bourse is considering abandoning its reliance on fees from its 55 member companies and adopting a corporate structure that would eventually lead to its listing its own shares on the stock exchange.

Perhaps the most eagerly awaited development is the demutualization of Old Mutual and the South African National Life Assurance Co., or Sanlam, the country's two largest insurance and asset management conglomerates. The conversion of millions of policyholders into shareholders is expected to take place between late 1998 and late 1999.

While Old Mutual has let it slip that it is considering the London Stock Exchange as its primary listing, dismaying JSE officials, the local stock exchange debut of Sanlam will be one of the largest listings in recent years. Details of the initial public offering remain sketchy, but it is believed that Sanlam will enter the JSE as one of the top 10 stocks in terms of market capitalization.

South Africa's sole stock exchange continues to evolve from a tightly held network of industrial manufacturing and mining operations dominated by conglomerate Anglo

Ten Largest Capitalized Companies In The Dow Jones South Africa Index
as of 6/30/98

Stock	Market Cap. US$ Thousands
Firstrand	8,313,432
Anglo American Corp. of South Africa	7,928,253
South African Breweries	7,209,711
De Beers Consd/De Beers Centenary	6,741,570
Liberty Life Association of Africa	5,193,025
Standard Bank Investment	5,119,483
Nedcor	4,950,367
ABSA Group	3,944,430
Anglogold	3,912,972
Sasol	3,489,318

American Corp. and four other family and institutional groups.

In the fist six months of 1998, 31 companies made their debut on the JSE. The vast majority are either financial services or information technology companies, taking advantage of a bull run in these sectors. These new listings boosted the total number of companies quoted on the JSE to 651.

One new listing, FirstRand Ltd. — an amalgamation of a commercial banking group and two major insurers — entered the JSE in late May with a market capitalization of more than ZAR53.00 billion, which immediately ranked it as South Africa's largest publicly traded company.

The spate of IPOs has helped boost the JSE's notoriously low liquidity, as measured by equity purchases as a percentage of market capitalization, to almost 24% from less than 17% at the end of 1997.

At the end of May, it ranked 39th of 45 global stock exchanges in terms of liquidity, according to the Paris-based Féderation Internationale des Bourses de Valeurs. In terms of market capitalization, ZAR1.33 trillion at the end of May, the JSE was positioned at 20th, between Taiwan and Rio de Janiero.

The arrival of new equities helped to offset a rise in the number of delistings during 1998 as a result of mergers and acquisitions.

In June, Anglo American delisted seven companies in the merger and listing of Anglogold Ltd., the world's largest gold producer. Rival Gold Fields Ltd. retired three publicly traded gold miners in its multimine amalgamation early in 1998, and London based metals house Billiton PLC said in July that it will buy out the minority holders of its two South African coal mining units — Ingwe Coal Corp. and Trans-Natal Coal Corp. — and delist them at a cash cost of almost ZAR3.00 billion.

The JSE increasingly reflects the country's racial composition. The number of black-controlled companies on the bourse grew to 27 in mid-1998 from 18 a year earlier. The market capitalization of these so-called black chips surged to ZAR57.40 billion, or 4.3% of the JSE's total, from just under 3.0%, or ZAR37.7 billion, in early July 1997.

Moreover, black investors hold influential minority interests in an additional 42 of the

Market Sector Performance In The Dow Jones South Africa Index 1 Year Change Through 6/30/98	
Market Sector	Change % (US$)
Technology	16.01
Financial	-14.17
Consumer, Cyclical	-36.03
Consumer, Non-Cyclical	-37.75
Independent	-44.72
Industrial	-46.09
Basic Materials	-47.20
Energy	-51.61

651 companies listed on the JSE, accounting for a further 5% to 6% of the bourse's market capitalization.

ABSA

DJGI Industry: **Banks - Regional (All)**

ABSA Group Ltd. is one of South Africa's four major commercial banking groups. It has offices in Hong Kong, New York, Shanghai, Singapore, and Sydney. The company was formed in 1991 when United Building Society Holdings Ltd. acquired three other banking concerns, Allied Group Ltd., Volkskas Group Ltd., and Sage Financial Services Ltd., and the merged entity was renamed Amalgamated Banks of South Africa. A year later, the company grew again with the acquisition of Bankorp Holdings Ltd. In late 1997, it was renamed ABSA Group Ltd.

	R mil 03/96	03/97	03/98	US$mil 03/98				
Revenues	N/A	23,794.0	26,995.0	5,363.6	P/E Ratio	14.4	Price (6/30/98)	37.00
Net Income	1,130.0	1,319.0	1,598.0	317.5	P/B Ratio	2.5	52 Wk Hi-Low	50.90-23.95
Book Value	7,211.0	8,092.0	9,839.0	1,954.9	Yield %	0.1	Market Cap	US$3,944.4mil

Address	ABSA Twrs. E., 170 Main St.	Tel 11-350-4000	ADR	ABSA	CEO	Dr. D.C. Cronje
	Johannesburg 2001	Fax 11-350-4928	SEDOL	6910794	Chairman	D.C. Brink

AECI

DJGI Industry: **Chemicals - Specialty**

AECI Ltd., one of South Africa's major industrial groups, is a leading supplier of chemicals and related products to key sectors of the economy. The company also produces explosives, high-quality industrial yarns, plastics, and fertilizers for local and export markets. In May 1998, Sasoil Ltd. launched a takeover of the company. Also in 1998, AECI regained the 51% share of its explosives and accessories business transferred to ICI in 1994. Agricultural products and industrial chemicals accounted for 26% of 1997 revenues; and monomers, polymers, and related products, 18%

	R mil 12/95	12/96	12/97	US$mil 12/97				
Sales	6,705.0	7,506.0	8,275.0	1,701.3	P/E Ratio	9.7	Price (6/30/98)	23.80
Net Income	396.0	427.0	382.0	78.5	P/B Ratio	1.2	52 Wk Hi-Low	28.50-13.05
Book Value	2,566.0	2,854.0	3,107.0	638.8	Yield %	2.6	Market Cap	US$617.6mil

Address	Box 1122	Tel 11-806-8700	ADR	AECLY	Managing Director	M.P. Smith
	Johannesburg 2000	Fax 11-806-8701	SEDOL	6009205	Chairman	L. Boyd

African Oxygen

DJGI Industry: **Chemicals - Specialty**

African Oxygen Ltd. manufactures and markets gases, welding equipment, fluid-handling devices, and other specialized industrial products. The company sells and rents its products through trading outlets under the Handigas brand name. African Oxygen's healthcare division has interests in private hospitals, and the company distributes its products directly to these hospitals. The company is 57% owned by the U.K. company BOC Group PLC, which enables it to have access to advanced technology.

	R mil 09/95	09/96	09/97	US$mil 09/97				
Sales	1,723.2	2,009.7	2,286.5	491.4	P/E Ratio	15.3	Price (6/30/98)	10.00
Net Income	152.8	181.5	200.7	43.1	P/B Ratio	2.7	52 Wk Hi-Low	16.75-10.00
Book Value	921.7	1,117.9	1,138.7	244.7	Yield %	3.7	Market Cap	US$518.5mil

Address	Afrox Hse., 23 Webber St., Selby	Tel 11-490-0400	ADR	--	Secretary	I.M. Matthee
	Johannesburg 2001	Fax 11-493-8828	SEDOL	6000684	Chmn & Mng Dir	R.T. Vice

Alpha

DJGI Industry: **Building Materials**

Alpha Ltd. produces cement, construction materials, ready-mixed concrete, lime, limestone products, industrial minerals, and paper bags. Other activities include the manufacture of fly ash, plastic bags, fertilizer, and explosives. Altur Investments Ltd. holds 54.8% of Alpha Ltd.'s share capital. In May 1998, the company announced plans to sell its non-core lime and industrial minerals operations through a management buyout. Cement accounted for 50% of 1997 revenues; stone and ready mixed concrete, 27%; industrial minerals, 22%; and other, 1%.

	R mil 12/95	12/96	12/97	US$mil 12/97				
Sales	1,453.9	1,727.6	1,967.2	404.4	P/E Ratio	7.8	Price (6/30/98)	45.00
Net Income	175.4	184.4	174.6	35.9	P/B Ratio	1.2	52 Wk Hi-Low	105.00-42.00
Book Value	1,893.7	2,059.5	1,122.8	230.8	Yield %	6.0	Market Cap	US$227.1mil

Address	94 Rivonia Rd.	Tel 11-780-1000	ADR	--	Managing Director	J.G. Pretorius
	Sandton 2196	Fax 11-783-8950	SEDOL	6032201	Chairman	B.E. Hersov

Amalgamated Beverage Industries

DJGI Industry: **Soft Drinks**

Amalgamated Beverage Industries produces and distributes carbonated soft drinks, including brands owned by Coca-Cola Co. and Cadbury Schweppes PLC. Its major products include Coca-Cola, Diet Coke, Fanta, TAB, Sprite, Krest and Schweppes. It produces soft drinks at seven bottling plants: three in Johannesburg, two in Durban, one in Pretoria and another at Midrand between Pretoria and Johannesburg. The company is 68% owned by beverage and leisure company South African Breweries, South Africa's largest brewer.

	R mil 03/95	03/96	03/97	US$mil 03/97				
Sales	1,412.3	1,481.0	1,786.7	404.7	P/E Ratio	40.6	Price (6/30/98)	51.50
Net Income	110.4	117.8	143.2	32.4	P/B Ratio	9.0	52 Wk Hi-Low	59.00-29.80
Book Value	510.1	603.6	651.1	147.5	Yield %	1.5	Market Cap	US$1,262.6mil

Address	14 Pongola Crescent	Tel 11-444-8444	ADR	--	Managing Director	E.T. Odgers
	Sandton 2199	Fax 11-444-8315	SEDOL	6023573	Chairman	H.M. Simms

Anglo American Coal

DJGI Industry: **Coal**

Anglo American Coal Corp. Ltd. is a 52% owned coal-mining subsidiary of South African resources conglomerate Anglo American Corp. Ltd. Anglo American Coal owns a number of collieries in South Africa while its Verref division produces refractories and building products, including ceramic tiles, clay pipes and fittings, and concrete roof tiles. Coal mining and coke production accounted for 90% of 1998 revenues, and refractory and building products contributed 10%. In 1998, sales of coal and coke to Eskom for electricity generation accounted for 66.7% of coal and coke production.

	R mil 03/96	03/97	03/98	US$mil 03/98				
Sales	2,748.3	3,913.8	4,400.2	874.3	P/E Ratio	8.1	Price (6/30/98)	274.80
Net Income	672.6	901.3	918.7	182.5	P/B Ratio	1.8	52 Wk Hi-Low	294.00-185.00
Book Value	2,769.0	3,654.9	4,279.4	850.3	Yield %	5.3	Market Cap	US$1,282.1mil

Address	**44 Main St.**	Tel **11-638-5428**	ADR	**ANAMY**	Managing Director	**A.E. Redman**
	Johannesburg 2001	Fax **11-638-9111**	SEDOL	**6032342**	Chairman	**J.W. Campbell**

Anglo American Corp.

DJGI Industry: **Precious Metals**

Anglo American Corp. of South Africa Ltd., a mining and industrial conglomerate, owns De Beers Consolidated Mines Ltd., the world's largest diamond miner and marketer. It also owns some of the world's largest gold and platinum mines. As the country's largest mining finance group, it invests in gold, coal, platinum, and base-metal production; it has interests in steel, paper, chemicals, motor manufacturing, food processing, real estate, banking, and insurance. In 1997, Anglo merged its gold operations and acquired two major mines creating Anglogold, the world's biggest gold-producing company.

	R mil 03/96	03/97	03/98	US$mil 03/98				
Sales	N/A	N/A	10,783.0	2,142.5	P/E Ratio	5.9	Price (6/30/98)	200.00
Net Income	4,397.0	7,106.0	5,817.0	1,155.8	P/B Ratio	1.2	52 Wk Hi-Low	299.00-159.00
Book Value	25,656.0	34,442.0	40,387.0	8,024.4	Yield %	3.7	Market Cap	US$7,928.3mil

Address	**44 Main St.**	Tel **11-638-9111**	ADR	**ANGLY**	President	**P.A. Armstrong**
	Johannesburg 2001	Fax **11-638-2455**	SEDOL	**6032524**	Chairman	**J. Ogilvie Thompson**

Anglo American Gold

DJGI Industry: **Precious Metals**

Anglo American Gold Investment Co. Ltd. has interests in gold and uranium mines in South Africa, Namibia, and Mali. It also holds a 2.68% interest in Minorco, an international resources company and a 10.2% interest in Gold Fields of South Africa Ltd. The company also participates in gold and uranium prospecting programs worldwide and in the ownership of mineral rights in South Africa. Anglo American Corp., which owns 50.45% of the company's share capital, announced that it will merge its five South African platinum companies into a single entity to be named Amplats.

	R mil 03/96	03/97	03/98	US$mil 03/98				
Sales	529.0	602.0	456.0	90.6	P/E Ratio	11.4	Price (6/30/98)	222.40
Net Income	472.0	543.0	389.0	77.3	P/B Ratio	2.9	52 Wk Hi-Low	273.50-168.20
Book Value	1,526.0	1,711.0	1,824.0	362.4	Yield %	5.1	Market Cap	US$901.0mil

Address	**44 Main St.**	Tel **11-638-9111**	ADR	**AAGIY**	President	--
	Johannesburg 2001	Fax **11-638-2455**	SEDOL	**6032643**	Chairman	**N.F. Oppenheimer**

Anglo American Industrial

DJGI Industry: **Industrial - Diversified**

Anglo American Industrial Corp. Ltd. is a diversified industrial holding company. The group is made up of eight operating subsidiaries, ten principal associated companies, and a portfolio of long-term investments in iron, steel, and engineering; commercial explosives and chemicals; mining and construction equipment; tools and contracting services; pulp, paper, forestry, and timber products; food; electronic and electrical engineering; freight and travel; motor assembly, components and distribution; furniture and appliances; retailing; and building and construction.

	R mil 12/95	12/96	12/97	US$mil 12/97				
Sales	20,522.0	23,717.0	27,880.0	5,731.9	P/E Ratio	6.6	Price (6/30/98)	99.00
Net Income	1,072.0	1,029.0	1,177.0	242.0	P/B Ratio	0.8	52 Wk Hi-Low	211.25-94.00
Book Value	6,841.0	8,711.0	9,688.0	1,991.8	Yield %	3.9	Market Cap	US$1,316.3mil

Address	**44 Main St.**	Tel **11-638-9111**	ADR	--	President	--
	Johannesburg 2001	Fax **11-638-4194**	SEDOL	**6033301**	Chairman	**Leslie Boyd**

Anglo American Investment Trust

DJGI Industry: **Precious Metals**

Anglo American Investment Trust Ltd. is an investment-holding company with interests in diamond-trading concerns. Its major assets are a 25.8% interest in DeBeers Consolidated Mines and a 23.4% interest in DeBeers Centenary. The company's other investments are privately-owned South African diamond companies. The company also has investments in various diamond trading companies. Investment income accounted for 99% of the company's fiscal 1998 revenues, and interest received, 1%.

	R mil 03/96	03/97	03/98	US$mil 03/98				
Sales	471.0	631.0	695.0	138.1	P/E Ratio	5.6	Price (6/30/98)	98.00
Net Income	1,065.0	1,665.0	1,659.0	329.6	P/B Ratio	0.9	52 Wk Hi-Low	176.00-87.00
Book Value	5,796.0	6,842.0	10,915.0	2,168.7	Yield %	6.8	Market Cap	US$1,664.9mil

Address	**44 Main St.**	Tel **11-638-9111**	ADR	**ANGVY**	President	--
	Johannesburg 2001	Fax **11-638-2455**	SEDOL	**6033527**	Chairman	**J. Ogilvie Thompson**

Anglo American Platinum

DJGI Industry: **Precious Metals**

Anglo American Platinum Corp. Ltd. became the holding company and sole listed entity for the restructured Amplats group of companies in September 1997. In conjunction with its wholly owned subsidiary, Amplats Management Services, Anglo American is primarily a platinum-mining house. Its wholly owned subsidiaries are Rustenburg Platinum Holdings Ltd., Potgietersrust Platinums Ltd., and Lebowa Platinum Mines Ltd. Anglo American, together with these three mining companies, is the world's leading producer of platinum and platinum-group metals.

	R mil 06/95	06/96	06/97	US$mil 06/97				
Sales	3,283.5	3,688.8	3,779.7	833.6	P/E Ratio	11.4	Price (6/30/98)	64.50
Net Income	369.0	400.1	278.2	61.4	P/B Ratio	2.5	52 Wk Hi-Low	87.70-50.50
Book Value	2,363.9	2,797.9	2,960.5	653.0	Yield %	2.4	Market Cap	US$2,321.5mil

Address	28 Harrison St.	Tel 11-373-6111	ADR	**AAPTY**	Managing Director	**B.E. Davison**
	Johannesburg 2001	Fax 11-834-2379	SEDOL	6761000	Chairman	**L. Boyd**

Anglo Gold

DJGI Industry: **Precious Metals**

Anglo Gold Ltd. was formed as a result of the merger of Vaal Reefs Exploration & Mining Company Ltd. and other companies in November 1997. Anglo Gold is a global mining and exploration company, involved in the exploration for and mining of gold, uranium oxide, and sulfuric acid. It operates four operating shafts, four gold plant complexes, one uranium plant, and two acid plants. In 1997, the company produced 69.5 tons of gold, approximately 14% of South African total production, and 816 tons of uranium. Gold accounted for 94% of 1997 revenues, and uranium, 6%.

	R mil 12/95	12/96	12/97	US$mil 12/97				
Sales	3,071.2	3,680.7	3,981.9	818.6	P/E Ratio	14.8	Price (6/30/98)	239.00
Net Income	535.3	733.8	651.8	134.0	P/B Ratio	0.8	52 Wk Hi-Low	283.00-151.80
Book Value	4,873.3	5,295.2	5,739.5	1,180.0	Yield %	6.8	Market Cap	US$3,913.0mil

Address	44 Main St.	Tel 11-638-9111	ADR	**ANGDY**	COO	**R.J. Fisher**
	Johannesburg 2001	Fax 11-638-5281	SEDOL	6110129	Chairman & CEO	**R.M. Godsell**

Anglovaal

DJGI Industry: **Mining - Diversified**

Anglovaal Ltd. is a South African financial, industrial, and mining group. It has interests in precious metal and base mineral mining, diamonds, food, cosmetics, packaging, construction and general engineering, electronics communication and information technology, textiles, and other industries. It also has interests in life assurance and financial services. Anglovaal has an indirect stake in South Africa's largest diamond operation, the Venetia mine owned by DeBeers Consolidated Mines Ltd.

	R mil 06/95	06/96	06/97	US$mil 06/97				
Sales	13,900.3	15,510.3	17,170.1	3,787.0	P/E Ratio M	5.0	Price (6/30/98) M	39.20
Net Income	353.8	501.9	495.1	109.2	P/B Ratio M	3.1	52 Wk Hi-Low M	121.00-39.00
Book Value	3,497.9	3,903.7	4,007.4	883.9	Yield % M	0.8	Market Cap M	US$304.0mil

Address	2 Arnold Rd.	Tel 11-283-0000	ADR	**ANVAY**	Finance Director	**D. Barber**
	Johannesburg 2196	Fax 11-283-0007	SEDOL	6041133	Chmn & Mng Dir	**B.E. Hersov**

M=Multiple issues in index; reflects most active.

Anglovaal Industries

DJGI Industry: **Industrial - Diversified**

Anglovaal Industries Ltd. (AVI) is a diversified South African industrial group. The company's interests include construction, electronics, food, cosmetics, packaging, rubber, textile, and engineering-related fields. Anglovaal Industries is a member of the Anglovaal group, owning a 60% interest in its share capital. The company's subsidiaries are AVI Diversified Holdings Ltd., Consol Ltd., Grinaker Holdings Ltd., Irvin and Johnson Ltd., and National Brands Ltd.ñall of which are leading companies in their respective industries.

	R mil 06/95	06/96	06/97	US$mil 06/97				
Sales	12,320.8	13,412.4	12,583.8	2,775.4	P/E Ratio	4.5	Price (6/30/98)	6.50
Net Income	441.2	514.2	472.5	104.2	P/B Ratio	0.5	52 Wk Hi-Low	18.50-6.37
Book Value	3,084.6	3,526.8	4,327.5	954.5	Yield %	4.6	Market Cap	US$367.5mil

Address	2 Arnold Rd., Rosebank	Tel 11-283-0000	ADR	--	President	--
	Johannesburg 2196	Fax 11-283-0007	SEDOL	6040958	Chmn & Mng Dir	**B.E. Hersov**

Barlow

DJGI Industry: **Conglomerates**

Barlow Ltd. is an industrial holding company and parent of a diverse group of manufacturing and distribution businesses focused on infrastructural development. These businesses operate mainly in southern Africa, as well as in the U.K., Europe, the U.S., and Australia. Barlow's interests include cement and lime, earth moving equipment, building materials, paint and protective coatings, steel tube manufacture, and consumer electric durables. In November 1997, the company paid A$72 million for 99% of the share capital in Lanes Ltd., a diversified Australian paint group.

	R mil 09/95	09/96	09/97	US$mil 09/97				
Sales	15,945.6	17,810.7	19,238.9	4,134.7	P/E Ratio	7.0	Price (6/30/98)	31.25
Net Income	528.1	666.9	802.3	172.4	P/B Ratio	1.4	52 Wk Hi-Low	60.75-29.50
Book Value	3,453.7	3,990.1	4,306.4	925.5	Yield %	4.0	Market Cap	US$1,112.4mil

Address	Barlow Pk., Katherine St.	Tel 11-801-2204	ADR	**BRRAY**	Finance Director	**D.C. Arnold**
	Sandton 2146	Fax 11-444-8206	SEDOL	6079123	Chairman	**W. Clewlow**

Bidvest

DJGI Industry: **Other Industrial & Commercial Services**

The Bidvest Group Ltd. is an investment holding company with interests in distribution, service, and trading businesses. Its service subsidiaries offer linen and uniform rental, property and washroom cleaning, and pest-control services. Its trading subsidiaries manufacture and distribute foods, food equipment, and stationery products. Within the past year, the group acquired Waltons Ltd., NCP Yeast, CAARS, Silveray Stationery Company, and Boston Laundries. Bidvest also owns a food-processing and distribution company in Australia called Manettas.

	R mil 06/95	06/96	03/97 *	US$mil 03/97				
Sales	N/A	4,166.7	5,069.9	1,148.3	P/E Ratio	34.8	Price (6/30/98)	45.25
Net Income	N/A	170.4	228.5	51.7	P/B Ratio	4.3	52 Wk Hi-Low	58.40-35.00
Book Value	N/A	785.4	1,998.1	452.6	Yield %	1.0	Market Cap	US$1,875.9mil

Address **Milner Pl., 4 Carse O'Gowrie Rd.** Tel **11-481-4100** ADR **BDVSY** Deputy Chairman **M. Chipkin**
Parktown 2193 Fax **11-643-4517** SEDOL **6100089** Chairman **B. Joffe**
*Irregular period due to fiscal year change.

C.G. Smith

DJGI Industry: **Other Food**

C.G. Smith Ltd. is a diversified South African holding company with interests in the food, fishing, pharmaceuticals, packaging, paper, and textile industries. C.G.S. is one of the largest companies quoted on the Johannesburg Stock Exchange. The company owns about 65% of shares in Nampak, the largest South African packing company. Food and fishing accounted for 58% of fiscal 1997 revenues; packaging and paper, 24%; sugar and related activities, 10%; pharmaceuticals, 6%; and bulk-liquid storage, 2%.

	R mil 09/95	09/96	09/97	US$mil 09/97				
Sales	23,602.2	26,184.4	29,225.8	6,281.1	P/E Ratio	8.7	Price (6/30/98)	16.30
Net Income	604.7	799.8	893.8	192.1	P/B Ratio	1.9	52 Wk Hi-Low	26.80-16.30
Book Value	3,191.2	3,684.1	4,110.7	883.5	Yield %	3.9	Market Cap	US$1,332.9mil

Address **36 Wierda Rd. W.** Tel **11-883-0575** ADR **CGSMY** Finance Director **C.F.H. Vaux**
Sandton 2146 Fax **11-883-3129** SEDOL **6816137** Chairman **D. Cooper**

De Beers Consolidated Mines

DJGI Industry: **Precious Metals**

De Beers Consolidated Mines Ltd. and De Beers Centenary AG represent the South African and Swiss-based diamond mining, trading, and marketing group that dominates the world diamond business. De Beers Consolidated contains its South-African interests; Centenary holds its non-South African mining and trading operations. The London-based Central Selling Organization, through which De Beers markets rough diamonds, reported a year-on-year 41% fall to $1.70 billion in first half 1998 diamond sales.

	R mil 12/95	12/96	12/97	US$mil 12/97				
Sales	2,028.0	2,385.0	2,478.0	509.5	P/E Ratio	9.8	Price (6/30/98)	104.20
Net Income	2,493.0	3,959.0	4,024.0	827.3	P/B Ratio	1.8	52 Wk Hi-Low	178.00-87.00
Book Value	16,192.0	19,344.0	22,437.0	4,612.9	Yield %	10.4	Market Cap	US$6,741.6mil

Address **36 Stockdale St.** Tel **531-839-4111** ADR **DBRSY** Mng Dir **G.M. Ralfe**
Kimberly 8301 Fax **531-839-4210** SEDOL **6259118** Chairman **N.F. Oppenheimer**

Dimension Data

DJGI Industry: **Diversified Technology**

Dimension Data Holdings Ltd. is the second-largest information technology company in South Africa. It recently acquired majority interests in U.K.-based The Merchants Group, a customer management company, and Tac Tech, a desktop networking firm which will expand its range of services. Dimension Data Holdings is structurally organized into four divisions: software, services, communication, and Internet solutions, covering Europe, Australia, New Zealand, and South Africa. The company also increased it's interest in Com Tech Communications from 45% to 70% in 1997.

	R mil 06/95	09/96 *	09/97	US$mil 09/97				
Sales	719.8	1,019.0	1,670.3	359.0	P/E Ratio	95.0	Price (6/30/98)	32.00
Net Income	51.0	84.2	156.9	33.7	P/B Ratio	40.3	52 Wk Hi-Low	40.25-17.40
Book Value	185.2	264.2	376.7	81.0	Yield %	0.0	Market Cap	US$3,045.5mil

Address **1 Meadowbrook Ln.** Tel **11-709-1000** ADR **DIDHY** Grp Fin Dir **M. Rutherford**
Epsom Downs 2125 Fax **11-709-1099** SEDOL **6260035** Chmn & Mng Dir **J.J. Ord**
*Irregular period due to fiscal year change.

Driefontein Consolidated

DJGI Industry: **Precious Metals**

Driefontein Consolidated Ltd., one of South Africa's leading gold mining companies, operates two independently managed mines, the East Driefontein mine and the older West Driefontein mine. The company's capital expenditures were focused on a new subvertical shaft at West Driefontein in which full-scale sinking operations have begun. The company's ore reserves total approximately 40,700 kilograms of gold. Gold Fields of South Africa, a mining-finance group, owns approximately one- third of Driefontein.

	R mil 06/95	06/96	06/97	US$mil 06/97				
Sales	2,541.8	2,361.9	2,483.8	547.8	P/E Ratio	9.3	Price (6/30/98)	30.70
Net Income	857.4	792.7	753.1	166.1	P/B Ratio	1.4	52 Wk Hi-Low	35.85-26.85
Book Value	3,313.0	3,810.0	4,257.1	938.9	Yield %	3.4	Market Cap	US$1,050.7mil

Address **75 Fox St.** Tel **11-639-9111** ADR **DRFNY** Managing Director **K.C. Spencer**
Johannesburg 2001 Fax **11-639-2102** SEDOL **6280215** Chairman **R.I. Robinson**

Edgars Stores

DJGI Industry: **Retailers - Apparel**

Edgars Stores Ltd. manufactures and retails clothing, footwear, accessories, and household textiles through its 702 stores in southern Africa. The company has four factories which manufacture a broad range of family clothing. These factories make denim jeans, men's shirts, and womenswear. South African Breweries holds 64.83% of Edgar's share capital. Retail sales accounted for all of fiscal 1998 revenues. Manufacturing revenues have been treated as inter-company and are cancelled on consolidation.

	R mil 03/96	03/97	03/98	US$mil 03/98				
Revenues	5,325.8	5,888.1	5,641.7	1,120.9	P/E Ratio	12.6	Price (6/30/98)	52.50
Net Income	337.2	320.9	230.5	45.8	P/B Ratio	1.5	52 Wk Hi-Low	136.50-52.00
Book Value	1,484.3	1,800.6	2,002.5	397.9	Yield %	4.7	Market Cap	US$490.9mil

Address	Press Ave., Crown Mines	Tel 11-495-6000	ADR	--	Mng Dir & CEO	D.W. Etheridge
	Johannesburg 2092	Fax 11-837-5019	SEDOL	6304892	Chairman	E.A.G. Mackay

Fedsure

DJGI Industry: **Diversified Financial Services**

Fedsure Holdings Ltd. is a holding company for financial services companies. Its principal subsidiary, Fedsure Life, offers life insurance, group benefit plans, pension programs, and funeral-benefit services. Fedsure Holdings also owns 100% of Fedsure Asset Management, which manages portfolios for corporate and institutional clients, and 65% of Fedgrowth Management Company, which manages mutual funds. In 1997, the company acquired a 25% stake in Msele Financing Holdings, a unit of Thebe Investment Corp.

	R mil 12/95	12/96	12/97	US$mil 12/97				
Revenues	N/A	110.4	163.4	33.6	P/E Ratio	NMF	Price (6/30/98)	72.00
Net Income	N/A	94.8	147.8	30.4	P/B Ratio	N/A	52 Wk Hi-Low	90.00-48.00
Book Value	N/A	734.7	1,642.7	337.7	Yield %	1.0	Market Cap	US$1,921.1mil

Address	Fedlife Hse., 1 de Villiers St.	Tel 11-332-6000	ADR	FSURY	CEO	A.I. Basserabie
	Johannesburg 2001	Fax 11-492-1102	SEDOL	6333971	Chairman	J.A. Barrow

FirstRand

DJGI Industry: **Diversified Financial Services**

FirstRand Ltd., South Africa's largest listed financial services company, is the result of the April 1998 merger of the financial services of Anglo American Corp. and Rand Merchant Bank Holdings (RMBH). Anglo American and RMBH each have a 24% stake in FirstRand. The major business units of the group are First National Bank, Momentum Life, Rand Merchant Bank and Southern Life. The company's range of activities include retail and investment banking, life assurance, annuity insurance, employee benefits, health care, asset management, unit trusts, and property.

	R mil 12/95	12/96	12/97	US$mil 12/97				
Revenues	N/A	N/A	525.5	108.0	P/E Ratio	N/A	Price (6/30/98)	9.10
Net Income	N/A	N/A	210.0	43.2	P/B Ratio	N/A	52 Wk Hi-Low	12.23-5.54
Book Value	N/A	N/A	971.3	199.7	Yield %	0.9	Market Cap	US$8,313.4mil

Address	267B W. Ave.	Tel 12-671-8911	ADR	--	CEO	Laurie Dippenaar
	Centurion 0157	Fax 12-671-8209	SEDOL	6606996	Chairman	Neal Chapman

Foschini

DJGI Industry: **Retailers - Apparel**

Foschini Ltd. operates chains of retail stores that specialize in selling clothing, jewelry, and accessories. The company manages more than 800 stores that operate under the Foschini, Markhams, American Swiss, Pages, and Sterns names. Foschini controls Oceana Investments Corp. PLC, the company's overseas-investment arm, which has a 37% stake in Etam, a clothing retailer with more than 220 stores throughout the United Kingdom. Foschini is ultimately controlled by the Lewis family through a 50% holding by Lewis Foschini Investment Company Ltd.

	R mil 03/96	03/97	03/98	US$mil 03/98				
Revenues	2,183.3	2,256.5	2,399.3	476.7	P/E Ratio	17.3	Price (6/30/98)	12.50
Net Income	227.5	165.1	193.0	38.3	P/B Ratio	2.4	52 Wk Hi-Low	21.36-12.43
Book Value	990.6	1,155.6	1,348.6	268.0	Yield %	0.0	Market Cap	US$466.8mil

Address	9 Riebeek St.	Tel 21-938-1911	ADR	FHNIY	Managing Director	D. Polak
	Cape Town 8001	Fax 21-927-7063	SEDOL	6349688	Chairman	S. Lewis

Gencor

DJGI Industry: **Precious Metals**

Gencor Ltd. is a South African mining conglomerate that produces a wide range of metals, alloys, and mineral products. The company has interests in Gengold, Impala Platinum Holdings, Ingwe Coal, Samancor, Alusaf, and Richards Bay Minerals, all of which are engaged in mining gold, platinum, coal, aluminum, ferro alloys, and titanium. In 1997, Gencor emerged as a precious metals exploration and mining company after selling its other interests to Billington PLC. Sankorp Ltd. holds a 25.73% interest in the share capital of the company.

	R mil 06/95	06/96	06/97	US$mil 06/97				
Sales	6,310.0	8,558.0	14,753.0	3,253.9	P/E Ratio	1.9	Price (6/30/98)	9.15
Net Income	1,003.0	1,803.0	3,098.0	683.3	P/B Ratio	0.2	52 Wk Hi-Low	12.80-6.90
Book Value	8,070.0	10,893.0	17,403.0	3,838.3	Yield %	13.0	Market Cap	US$530.2mil

Address	6 Hollard St.	Tel 11-376-3167	ADR	GNCRY	Secretary	J. Marais
	Johannesburg 2001	Fax 11-838-8860	SEDOL	6014889	Chairman	B.P. Gilbertson

Gold Fields of South Africa

DJGI Industry: **Precious Metals**

Gold Fields of South Africa Ltd. is a mining-finance company with interests in three gold-producing companies: Doornfontein Gold Mining, Driefontein Consolidated, and Kloof Gold Mining. Gold Fields also has a 49% equity stake in Deelkraal Gold Mining, a 65% stake in Northam Platinum, and a 79% stake in Gold Fields Coal. The company's Gold Fields Mining and Development subsidiary finances exploration costs. Investment income accounted for 50% of fiscal 1997 revenues; fees and other sources, 37%; and interest income 13%.

	R mil 06/96	06/97	06/98	US$mil 06/98					
Sales	653.0	694.0	401.0	67.3	P/E Ratio	**NMF**	Price (6/30/98)		68.00
Net Income	394.0	-13.0	990.0	166.1	P/B Ratio	2.4	52 Wk Hi-Low		107.00-60.00
Book Value	2,965.0	2,861.0	4,910.0	823.8	Yield %	3.4	Market Cap		US$1,299.7mil

Address	75 Fox St.	Tel **11-639-9111**	ADR	**GLDFY**	CEO	**A. Wright**
	Johannesburg 2001	Fax **11-639-2101**	SEDOL	**6376266**	Chairman	**R. Plumbridge**

IBM South Africa

DJGI Industry: **Software**

IBM South Africa Ltd., (formerly Information Services Group Ltd.) designs, markets, and distributes IBM and IBM-compatible computer products in South Africa. The company sells mainframes, automated teller machines, systems servers, personal computers, and related equipment. It also provides maintenance, cabling, power-supply installation, and consulting services. In 1997, the company restructured. It acquired full ownership of International Outsourcing Services, disposed of non-core associated companies, and resized and re-aligned its staff resources.

	R mil 12/95	12/96	12/97	US$mil 12/97					
Sales	1,911.3	1,981.6	1,651.8	339.6	P/E Ratio	**NMF**	Price (6/30/98)		11.20
Net Income	101.0	73.8	-43.2	-8.9	P/B Ratio	9.0	52 Wk Hi-Low		11.30-5.20
Book Value	193.0	228.9	198.8	40.9	Yield %	0.0	Market Cap		US$301.5mil

Address	70 Rivonia Rd.	Tel **11-302-9111**	ADR	--	CEO	**B.D. Mehl**
	Sandton 2146	Fax **11-302-9988**	SEDOL	**6879806**	Chairman	**D. Cooper**

Impala Platinum Holdings

DJGI Industry: **Precious Metals**

Impala Platinum Holdings Ltd., through its wholly owned subsidiary Impala Platinum Ltd., is the second-largest producer of platinum in the world. Among the minerals extracted from the company's three primary mines are platinum, palladium, rhodium, iridium, ruthenium, gold, silver, nickel, copper, and cobalt. Consolidated Nominees Ltd. owns 46.5% of its share capital. Implats is re-negotiating royalty payments with the local Bafokeng tribe, who are contesting the legality of its mining operations on the tribe's sovereign land.

	R mil 06/96	06/97	06/98	US$mil 06/98					
Sales	2,316.8	2,633.3	3,380.6	567.2	P/E Ratio	10.8	Price (6/30/98)		50.50
Net Income	175.7	205.3	500.4	84.0	P/B Ratio	0.9	52 Wk Hi-Low		66.80-35.00
Book Value	3,110.5	3,367.5	2,751.6	461.6	Yield %	2.8	Market Cap		US$541.8mil

Address	6 Holland Street	Tel **11-376-2800**	ADR	**IMPAY**	Mng Dir	**S. Kearney**
	Johannesburg 2001	Fax **11-836-5954**	SEDOL	**6457804**	Chairman	**J. M. McMahon**

Imperial Holdings

DJGI Industry: **Other Industrial & Commercial Services**

Imperial Holdings Ltd. is a South African conglomerate with interests in motor vehicle rental and sales, transport, and financial services. Its Imperial Car Rental and Tempest Car Hire subsidiaries operate a fleet of 5,100 cars at its 84 branch offices. Imperial's motor vehicle unit sells passenger and commercial vehicles. Its transport unit maintains a fleet of 2,255 bulk-product and refrigerated vehicles. In March 1997, Imperial acquired a 26% interest in McCarthy Motor Holdings. The company applied for a license to operate as a niche bank.

	R mil 06/95	06/96	06/97	US$mil 06/97					
Sales	N/A	6,421.6	7,238.6	1,596.5	P/E Ratio	48.3	Price (6/30/98)		58.00
Net Income	N/A	246.3	376.1	83.0	P/B Ratio	3.1	52 Wk Hi-Low		70.00-50.00
Book Value	N/A	2,614.3	3,346.4	738.1	Yield %	0.9	Market Cap		US$1,795.5mil

Address	140 Boeing Rd. E., Elma Park	Tel **11-453-0945**	ADR	**IHSAY**	Finance Director	**A.H. Mahomed**
	Edenvale 1609	Fax **11-453-0960**	SEDOL	**6458874**	Exec Chairman	**W.G. Lynch**

Ingwe Coal

DJGI Industry: **Coal**

Ingwe Coal Corp., formerly known as Randcoal Ltd., is one of the world's largest hard coal producers and steam coal exporters. Ingwe was established in 1995 when Trans-Natal Corp. Ltd. and Randcoal Ltd. merged. It operates 14 mines and has interests in 13 collieries in the Mpumalanga and Kwa-Zulu Natal provinces of South Africa. The company produces coal for the industrial market, including the production of coal for the Eskom power stations. Gencor owns a 50% interest in Ingwe, and Rand Mines holds a 46% stake.

	R mil 06/96	06/97	06/98	US$mil 06/98					
Sales	4,681.6	5,816.4	6,430.0	1,078.8	P/E Ratio	5.9	Price (6/30/98)		17.00
Net Income	503.1	711.9	551.7	92.6	P/B Ratio	1.8	52 Wk Hi-Low		29.00-15.70
Book Value	1,610.1	1,909.1	2,398.7	402.4	Yield %	8.8	Market Cap		US$645.9mil

Address	6 Hollard St.	Tel **11-376-9111**	ADR	--	Managing Director	**D.J.K. Murray**
	Johannesburg 2001	Fax **11-838-7190**	SEDOL	**6974488**	Chairman	**M.L. Davis**

Investec

DJGI Industry: **Banks - Regional (All)**

Investec Group Ltd. is involved primarily in private banking and corporate and investment banking. Its private banking division offers a range of lending and investment products, and its investment banking division offers specialist debt finance, corporate finance, and infrastructural development services. The company's South African subsidiaries include Metboard Management, Investec Merchant Bank, and Investec Property Group. It also has two subsidiaries in the United Kingdom, Allied Trust Bank, and Clive Discount, the latter of which is a bond broker.

	R mil 03/96	03/97	03/98	US$mil 03/98				
Revenues	N/A	5,290.0	7,242.0	1,438.9	P/E Ratio	NMF	Price (6/30/98)	230.00
Net Income	N/A	445.0	643.0	127.8	P/B Ratio	6.2	52 Wk Hi-Low	270.00-164.80
Book Value	N/A	3,587.0	6,227.0	1,237.2	Yield %	1.0	Market Cap	US$2,967.3mil

Address	100 Grayston Dr.	Tel 11-286-7003	ADR	IVBOY	CEO	S. Koseff
	Sandown, Santon 2196	Fax --	SEDOL	6465959	Chairman	H.S. Herman

Iscor

DJGI Industry: **Steel**

Iscor Ltd. markets and produces a wide range of iron and steel. The company has mining operations in Vanderbijlpark, Newcastle, Vereeniging, and Kuils River. Iscor mines 8.5 million tons of iron ore a year in Sishen and Thabazimbi and 3.4 million tons of coal a year in Grootegeluk, Durnacol, Hlobane, and Tshikondeni. Iscor also has investments in property-holding, manufacturing, recycling, and service companies. In 1997, the company closed its Pretoria steelmaking facilities. Steel accounted for 75% of 1997 revenues, while mining accounted for 25%.

	R mil 06/96	06/97	06/98	US$mil 06/98				
Sales	11,602.0	12,427.0	13,121.0	2,201.3	P/E Ratio	NMF	Price (6/30/98)	1.12
Net Income	853.0	-633.0	687.0	115.3	P/B Ratio	0.4	52 Wk Hi-Low	3.39-1.10
Book Value	7,853.0	7,207.0	7,724.0	1,295.9	Yield %	7.1	Market Cap	US$481.2mil

Address	Roger Dyason Rd.	Tel 12-307-3000	ADR	ISCRY	Finance Director	M. Macdonald
	Pretoria West 0001	Fax 12-307-3367	SEDOL	6466695	Chairman	H. Smith

JD Group

DJGI Industry: **Retailers - Other Specialty**

JD Group Ltd. is South Africa's leading furniture retailer, with a network of seven major retail chains. It operates Bradlows, Russells, Score, and Montana Harmony furniture stores located throughout South Africa. JD also manages Price 'N Pride discount furniture outlets and Giddys appliance and entertainment-products stores. Its Joshua Doore discount furniture chain includes hyperstores, mid-sized stores, and catalog showrooms. The company also operates 12 distribution centers and has interests in a retailer in Namibia.

	R mil 06/96	06/97	06/98	US$mil 06/98				
Revenues	2,135.6	2,273.0	2,422.0	406.3	P/E Ratio	20.9	Price (6/30/98)	39.90
Net Income	150.1	179.0	221.0	37.1	P/B Ratio	4.1	52 Wk Hi-Low	54.70-28.00
Book Value	784.8	955.0	1,155.0	193.8	Yield %	1.4	Market Cap	US$721.9mil

Address	29 De Beer St.	Tel 11-408-0408	ADR	JDGRY	Managing Director	M. Strauss
	Braamfontein 2001	Fax 11-408-0604	SEDOL	6479648	Chairman	I. David Sussman

Johnnies Industrial

DJGI Industry: **Precious Metals**

Johnnies Industrial Corp. Ltd., (Johnnic), formerly Johannesurg Consolidated Investment Co. Ltd. and one of three companies formed when the Johnnies Group restructured, is a mining and finance company that invests in platinum, gold, chrome, coal, diamonds, base metals, property, media, and consumer-based industries. It invests in such South African companies as Rustenburg Platinum, Randfontein Estates, Consolidated Metallurgical Industries, DeBeers, Free State Development & Investment, and Argus Newspapers.

	R mil 06/95	06/96	06/97	US$mil 06/97				
Sales	200.5	279.2	435.9	96.1	P/E Ratio	10.2	Price (6/30/98)	50.80
Net Income	347.0	489.5	766.7	169.1	P/B Ratio	2.3	52 Wk Hi-Low	73.30-43.50
Book Value	2,081.2	2,586.8	3,318.1	731.8	Yield %	2.0	Market Cap	US$1,332.4mil

Address	28 Harrison St.	Tel 11-373-7111	ADR	JICPY	CEO	V.G. Bray
	Johannesburg 2001	Fax 11-834-5063	SEDOL	6475141	Chairman	M.C. Ramaphosa

Kersaf Investments

DJGI Industry: **Other Recreational Products & Services**

Kersaf Investments Ltd. invests in and takes management responsibility for businesses in the leisure industry in South Africa and overseas. The company has a dominant position in the casino resort industry in South Africa. Its activities also include hotels, cinemas, film and television production and distribution, steakhouse restaurants, fast-food outlets, liquor wholesaling and retailing, and the production of premier wines. Effective July 1, 1997, the group sold its interest in Cinemark and Ster-Kinekor businesses including Ster-Moribo and Home Entertainment.

	R mil 06/95	06/96	06/97	US$mil 06/97				
Sales	2,428.3	2,649.8	2,759.8	608.7	P/E Ratio	2.5	Price (6/30/98)	27.00
Net Income	206.4	344.5	360.6	79.5	P/B Ratio	1.0	52 Wk Hi-Low	41.50-24.00
Book Value	1,284.6	1,421.9	1,620.9	357.5	Yield %	7.4	Market Cap	US$381.5mil

Address	3 Sandown Valley Cr., Sandown	Tel 11-780-7444	ADR	--	Finance Director	D.C. Coutts-Trotter
	Sandton 2031	Fax 11-783-7446	SEDOL	6490694	Chairman	D.A. Hawton

Liberty Holdings

DJGI Industry: **Insurance - Life & Health**

Liberty Holdings Ltd., a South African insurance and investment conglomerate, has major overseas investments held through U.K.-based Liberty International Hldgs. PLC. Liberty is the major shareholder in Standard Bank Investment Corp. Ltd., which South Africa's second-largest banking group. Liberty's subsidiaries include Liberty Life Association of Africa. Its other activities include property construction and development and unit-trust management. Together with U.K.-based Guardian Royal Exchange, it owns Guardian National Insurance Co. of South Africa.

	R mil 12/95	12/96	12/97	US$mil 12/97					
Revenues	13,580.2	12,775.1	27,653.3	5,685.3	P/E Ratio		13.8	Price (6/30/98)	311.00
Net Income	566.6	686.2	1,739.5	357.6	P/B Ratio		1.5	52 Wk Hi-Low	522.00-275.00
Book Value	7,251.5	8,674.7	10,052.5	2,066.7	Yield %		3.6	Market Cap	US$2,568.9mil

Address	1 Ameshoff St., Braamfontein	Tel	11-408-3911	ADR	--	CEO		R. Andersen
	Johannesburg 2001	Fax	11-339-7470	SEDOL	6515058	Chairman		Donald Gordon

Liberty Life Association

DJGI Industry: **Insurance - Life & Health**

Liberty Life Association of Africa Ltd. is the largest proprietary life office and the third-largest life insurer in South Africa. It has 13 associate and affiliate companies with operations in South Africa, the United Kingdom, and France; its subsidiaries offer international insurance and investment-based financial services. Liberty Holdings Ltd. owns 53% of the company. All the company's own operations and those of its 100%-owned subsidiary Chartered Life are based entirely in South Africa. Strategic investments include interests in Standard Bank Investment Ltd. and Premier Group Ltd.

	R mil 12/95	12/96	12/97	US$mil 12/97					
Revenues	10,821.8	12,768.5	26,532.4	5,454.9	P/E Ratio		9.5	Price (6/30/98)	115.60
Net Income	1,204.1	1,538.8	3,081.5	633.5	P/B Ratio		1.8	52 Wk Hi-Low	193.60-104.80
Book Value	12,567.2	14,919.2	17,256.4	3,547.8	Yield %		2.2	Market Cap	US$5,193.0mil

Address	1 Ameshoff St., Braamfontein	Tel	11-408-3911	ADR	LTYLY	CEO		R. Andersen
	Johannesburg 2001	Fax	11-339-7470	SEDOL	6515047	Chairman		D. Gordon

Liberty Life Strategic Investments

DJGI Industry: **Diversified Financial Services**

Liberty Life Strategic Investments Ltd. is a subsidiary of Liberty Life Assocation of South Africa formed for the purpose of holding key strategic investments. These include 26.4% of Standard Bank Investment Corp. Ltd., 29% of Beverage and Consumer Industry Holdings Ltd. (Bevcon), which owns a 33% equity interest in The South African Breweries Ltd. and in which a further 6% interest is held directly by Liberty Life, and 23.6% in the Premier Group Ltd. Liberty Life has joint control of Bevcon and Premier based on an agreement with Johnnies Industrial Corp. Ltd.

	R mil 12/95	12/96	12/97	US$mil 12/97					
Revenues	N/A	235.4	291.9	60.0	P/E Ratio		14.9	Price (6/30/98)	17.45
Net Income	443.5	233.8	736.3	151.4	P/B Ratio		0.9	52 Wk Hi-Low	24.50-14.00
Book Value	10,178.2	11,181.3	11,869.6	2,440.3	Yield %		1.4	Market Cap	US$1,837.0mil

Address	1 Ameshoff St., Braamfontein	Tel	11-408-3911	ADR	--	Deputy Chairman	R. Andersen
	Johannesburg 2001	Fax	11-408-2020	SEDOL	6518897	Chairman	D. Gordon

M Web Holdings

DJGI Industry: **Cable & Broadcasting**

M Web Holdings, formerly MIH Holdings Ltd. is a company based in South Africa specializing in providing pay-television broadcast subscriptions to its customers. In addition to its South African operations, M Web Holdings participates in international activities as well, with operations in Europe, the Middle East, and Africa. The company's holding company is MNH Holdings (Pty) Ltd., a company incorporated in South Africa. The company has a 4% investment in Canal Plus SA, the largest subscription television operation in Europe.

	R mil 03/95	03/96	03/97	US$mil 03/97					
Sales	N/A	1,249.0	1,009.5	228.6	P/E Ratio		2.6	Price (6/30/98)	21.20
Net Income	N/A	-62.8	1,937.8	438.9	P/B Ratio		6.9	52 Wk Hi-Low	29.00-11.57
Book Value	N/A	-432.7	722.9	163.7	Yield %		0.0	Market Cap	US$941.4mil

Address	75 Republic Rd.	Tel	11-889-1911	ADR	--	Managing Director	J.P. Bekker
	Randburg 2194	Fax	11-337-5522	SEDOL	6106797	Chairman	T. Voslo

Malbak

DJGI Industry: **Containers & Packaging**

Malbak Ltd., formerly one of South Africa's biggest industrial conglomerates, restructured its business in 1997 and liquidated its food, retailing, consumer appliances, and healthcare operations. The group will continue as Malbak Ltd. and will henceforth concentrate on the packaging industry. Spun off from former parent mining house Gencor Ltd. in late 1993, the company is 39% owned by Rembrandt. In January 1996, Malbak acquired discount retail chain Clicks Group Ltd. from Premier Group Ltd.

	R mil 08/96	08/97	03/98 *	US$mil 03/98					
Sales	17,649.0	3,156.0	3,189.1	633.6	P/E Ratio		9.4	Price (6/30/98)	4.00
Net Income	615.0	144.0	115.0	22.9	P/B Ratio		1.1	52 Wk Hi-Low	6.02-3.45
Book Value	3,444.0	1,231.0	926.0	184.0	Yield %		1.5	Market Cap	US$226.5mil

Address	4 Pybus Rd.	Tel	11-883-1145	ADR	MLBFF	CEO		R. Bruyns
	Sandton 2196	Fax	11-783-0408	SEDOL	6705871	Chairman		D.C. Brink

*Irregular period due to fiscal year change.

McCarthy Group

DJGI Industry: **Retailers - Other Specialty**

McCarthy Group Ltd. is a holding company that owns 85% of McCarthy Retail's shares and 55% of its convertible debentures. McCarthy Retail sells motor vehicles, furniture, household appliances, electronic equipment, and clothing. Its interests include McCarthy Motor Hldgs., the largest dealership network in South Africa, and Prefcor furniture and clothing retailers. Its motor division is South Africa's sole importer of Yamaha motorcycles, engines, sports equipment, and musical instruments. The company owns 80% of Midas South Africa, which markets and distributes automotive products.

	R mil 06/95	06/96	06/97	US$mil 06/97				
Revenues	38.1	46.9	50.3	11.1	P/E Ratio	3.3	Price (6/30/98)	5.70
Net Income	38.0	47.0	50.6	11.2	P/B Ratio	6.1	52 Wk Hi-Low	20.50-5.70
Book Value	344.2	95.9	96.9	21.4	Yield %	7.8	Market Cap	US$101.3mil

Address	203 N. Ridge Rd.	Tel 31-290222	ADR	--	DeputyChairman	Terry Rosenberg
	Durban 4001	Fax 31-290950	SEDOL	6551245	Chairman	Brian C. McCarthy

Metro Cash & Carry

DJGI Industry: **Food Retailers & Wholesalers**

Metro Cash & Carry Ltd. operates around 200 wholesale distributor outlets throughout South Africa, maintaining a 35% share of the wholesale and distribution market. Internationally, it operates 167 cash-and-carry stores and trade centers in Botswana, Malawi, Zimbabwe, Mozmbique, Kenya, and Israel. The company wholesales groceries, consumer goods, and hardware; it also operates retail consumer-goods stores. In March 1998 the group acquired an additional 5% interest in Davids Ltd., the largest wholesale distributor of food, groceries, and toiletries in Australia.

	R mil 04/96	04/97	04/98	US$mil 04/98				
Sales	7,580.4	8,981.2	10,927.3	2,162.1	P/E Ratio	21.9	Price (6/30/98)	3.75
Net Income	115.8	156.4	200.9	39.8	P/B Ratio	4.8	52 Wk Hi-Low	5.80-3.70
Book Value	734.0	723.3	904.8	179.0	Yield %	2.3	Market Cap	US$594.0mil

Address	Crownwood & Amethyst Rds.	Tel 11-490-2000	ADR	MECREG	CEO	C.S. dos Santos
	Johannesburg 2003	Fax 11-835-2301	SEDOL	6526986	Chairman	D.D.B. Band

Murray & Roberts

DJGI Industry: **Heavy Construction**

Murray & Roberts Holdings Ltd. manufactures construction materials and provides engineering and transport services in Africa. Its products include stainless steel containers, heat exchangers, forklift trucks, automotive components, test and measurement equipment, and cargo transport equipment. Murray & Roberts also develops and manages retail and industrial properties and operates Unitrans, a land-based freight transporter. In May 1998, the company said it was seeking a buyer for its cement, quarrying and ready-mixed materials businesses.

	R mil 06/95	06/96	06/97	US$mil 06/97				
Sales	9,283.3	10,746.5	10,356.7	2,284.2	P/E Ratio	N/A	Price (6/30/98)	6.10
Net Income	408.3	374.5	-498.2	-109.9	P/B Ratio	0.8	52 Wk Hi-Low	13.25-5.40
Book Value	3,018.9	3,326.4	2,692.9	593.9	Yield %	8.0	Market Cap	US$354.1mil

Address	Douglas Roberts Ctr., Skeen Blvd.	Tel 11-455-1410	ADR	--	CEO	Graham Hardy
	Bedfordview 2007	Fax 11-455-2222	SEDOL	6582546	Chairman	Dave Brink

Nampak

DJGI Industry: **Containers & Packaging**

Nampak Ltd. manufactures and markets packaging products. Its packaging division produces beverage and food cans, glass bottles, polycoated cartons, plastic bottles, metal cans and drums, flexible packs, plastic shopping bags, and bread wrappers. Nampak's paper and printing division makes corrugated boxes and partitions, cartons, paper bags, and sanitary products. It also prints business forms and distributes paper and graphics materials. C.G. Smith Limited owns 59.6% of the company's share capital.

	R mil 09/95	09/96	09/97	US$mil 09/97				
Sales	5,896.7	6,572.1	7,070.7	1,519.6	P/E Ratio	12.7	Price (6/30/98)	14.00
Net Income	460.6	526.7	547.2	117.6	P/B Ratio	2.5	52 Wk Hi-Low	23.00-13.55
Book Value	1,984.9	2,331.3	2,663.2	572.4	Yield %	3.0	Market Cap	US$1,193.7mil

Address	Nampak Ctr., 114 Dennis Rd.	Tel 11-444-7418	ADR	NMPKY	Managing Director	Trevor Evans
	Sandton 2196	Fax 11-444-4794	SEDOL	6621397	Chairman	Brian Connellan

Nasional Pers Beperk

DJGI Industry: **Publishing**

Nasional Pers Beperk publishes and distributes both English and Afrikaans newspapers, magazines, and books. The company's consumer magazine titles include Huisgenoot, which has a weekly circulation of more than 500,000, and You, which has a weekly circulation of almost 300,000. Nasional Pers Beperk publishes three daily newspapers, Die Burger, Die Beeld, and Die Volksblad. The company has operations in electronic media, the cellular-telephone industry, and subscription television services.

	R mil 03/96	03/97	03/98	US$mil 03/98				
Sales	1,610.9	1,725.9	1,931.9	383.8	P/E Ratio	6.5	Price (6/30/98)	39.00
Net Income	213.5	674.3	96.2	19.1	P/B Ratio	4.4	52 Wk Hi-Low	55.50-33.00
Book Value	667.1	988.4	1,011.8	201.0	Yield %	0.5	Market Cap	US$731.6mil

Address	40 Heerengracht	Tel 21-406-2121	ADR	--	CEO	F.J. Wiese
	Cape Town 8000	Fax 21-406-2913	SEDOL	6622691	Chairman	T. Vosloo

Nedcor

DJGI Industry: **Banks - Regional (All)**

Nedcor Ltd. is an investment holding company with interests in banking and financial services. Its main banking subsidiaries are Nedcor Bank, UAL Merchant Bank, Syfrets Bank Ltd., and Nedtravel (Pty) Ltd. Its other subsidiaries are active in lending, investment management, mutual funds, and insurance. Nedcor has subsidiaries in 21 African countries. It also has operations in the United States, and its NedFinance Asia subsidiary has an office in Beijing, making it the first African bank to set up operations in China. Nedcor is 53% owned by SA Mutual Life Assurance Society.

	R mil 09/95	09/96	09/97	US$mil 09/97					
Revenues	10,654.0	13,395.0	16,048.0	3,449.0	P/E Ratio	18.2	Price (6/30/98)		128.00
Net Income	782.0	1,082.0	1,426.0	306.5	P/B Ratio	3.9	52 Wk Hi-Low		159.60-90.00
Book Value	4,678.0	5,806.0	6,888.0	1,480.3	Yield %	1.8	Market Cap		US$4,950.4mil

Address	100 Main St.	Tel 11-630-7111	ADR	**NDCRY**	CEO		**R.C.M. Laubscher**
	Johannesburg 2001	Fax 11-630-7558	SEDOL	**6628008**	Chairman		**C.F. Liebenberg**

Omni Media

DJGI Industry: **Publishing**

Omni Media Corp. Ltd., formerly known as Argus Holdings, is an investment holding company with subsidiaries that operate in the publishing and media industries. The company prints and publishes newspapers in the major metropolitan areas of South Africa and, through its subsidiary, CNA Gallo Ltd., operates a chain of specialty retail stores. It also manufactures and distributes compact discs, gramophone records, tapes, video cassettes, music publishing, film exhibition, film and video distribution. Omni also provides telemarketing and related services.

	R mil 03/96	03/97	03/98	US$mil 03/98					
Sales	1,989.6	2,215.8	647.9	128.7	P/E Ratio	20.7	Price (6/30/98)		100.80
Net Income	79.9	273.9	362.9	72.1	P/B Ratio	6.1	52 Wk Hi-Low		103.60-59.00
Book Value	672.0	915.4	1,147.1	227.9	Yield %	0.7	Market Cap		US$1,023.1mil

Address	28 Harrison St.	Tel 11-373-7111	ADR	--	President		--
	Johannesburg 2001	Fax 11-834-9272	SEDOL	**6049494**	Chairman		**V.G. Bray**

Palabora Mining

DJGI Industry: **Other Non-Ferrous Metals**

Palabora Mining Company Ltd., the leading producer of copper in South Africa, extracts copper from one open-pit mine in northeastern Transvaal. The mine, which is expected to remain productive until the year 2000, supplies more than 125,000 tons of copper concentrate annually. Palabora also operates a copper smelter, which produces approximately 105,000 tons of anodes annually and more than 100,000 tons of sulfuric acid. The company also produces zirconia, uranium oxide, and vermiculite as by-products. Palabora provides more than half of the world's supply of vermiculite.

	R mil 12/95	12/96	12/97	US$mil 12/97					
Sales	1,735.6	1,729.4	1,866.1	383.7	P/E Ratio	2.4	Price (6/30/98)		31.50
Net Income	370.2	419.2	368.3	75.7	P/B Ratio	1.2	52 Wk Hi-Low		89.50-26.00
Book Value	351.3	517.3	736.9	151.5	Yield %	4.8	Market Cap		US$149.6mil

Address	Rio Tinto Hse., 122 Pybus Rd.	Tel 11-883-3860	ADR	**PBOMY**	Managing Director	**J.G. Deyzel**
	Sandton 2199	Fax 11-883-2703	SEDOL	**6667904**	Chairman	**F. Fenwick**

Pepkor

DJGI Industry: **Food Retailers & Wholesalers**

Pepkor Ltd. is an investment holding company with interests in retailing operations and in the manufacture of semi-durable goods for use in the retailing operations. It operates more than 2,000 retail outlets, including Pep clothing and semidurables stores, Smart Centre, Ackermans, Poudstretcher, Stuttafords, and Shoprite. Food accounted for 62.3% of Pepkor's fiscal 1997 revenues; clothing for 20.1%; variety stores, 12.4%; and building materials, 5.2%. In 1997, the group disposed of it's holding in Waltons Consolidated Investment Holdings Ltd.

	R mil 02/95	06/96 *	06/97	US$mil 06/97					
Sales	9,684.6	11,949.0	15,029.0	3,314.7	P/E Ratio	11.5	Price (6/30/98)		21.95
Net Income	207.4	194.0	387.5	85.5	P/B Ratio	2.4	52 Wk Hi-Low		37.50-21.80
Book Value	1,026.6	1,357.3	1,731.9	382.0	Yield %	2.3	Market Cap		US$796.1mil

Address	36 Stellenberg Rd.	Tel 21-933-5137	ADR	**PEPKYP**	CEO		**J.F. Le Roux**
	Parow Industria 7490	Fax 21-931-0848	SEDOL	**6681755**	Chairman		**C. Wiese**

*Irregular period due to fiscal year change.

Persetel Q Data

DJGI Industry: **Computers**

Persetel Q Data Holdings Ltd. was formed in October 1997 through the merger of Persetel Holdings and Q Data. It is South Africa's largest and most diversified IT supplier of hardware, software, and services. Persetel Q Data operates principally through two subsidiaries: Persetel Q Data Africa (Pty) Ltd. and Persetel Q Data International (Pty) Ltd., which focus on systems and networks in the corporate information technology market, including the development, marketing, and support of software, hardware, and network systems, software solutions, and the distribution of computers.

	R mil 05/95	05/96	05/97	US$mil 05/97					
Sales	N/A	1,666.3	4,252.0	952.1	P/E Ratio	8.7	Price (6/30/98)		53.00
Net Income	N/A	158.3	1,877.1	420.3	P/B Ratio	8.0	52 Wk Hi-Low		59.90-23.30
Book Value	N/A	874.7	2,121.8	475.1	Yield %	0.4	Market Cap		US$2,944.6mil

Address	1 Charles Crescent	Tel 11-496-2222	ADR	--	Grp Fin Dir	**K.R.M. Evans**
	Sandton 2199	Fax 11-496-1244	SEDOL	**6682844**	Chairman & CEO	**R.J. Marnitz**

Plate Glass & Shatterprufe Industries

DJGI Industry: **Building Materials**

Plate Glass & Shatterprufe Industries Ltd. manufactures glass and board products for the automotive, construction, and furniture industries. Its wholly owned subsidiary Glass SA is one of South Africa's leading exporters of float and automotive glass. Plate Glass consists of four divisions, including Glass South Africa, PG Bison, Belron International, and PG Industries (Zimbabwe). In 1998, the company's operations in the United States were merged with those of a competitor. Plate Glass has also made acquisitions in Canada, New Zealand, and Spain.

	R mil 03/96	03/97	03/98	US$mil 03/98				
Sales	4,528.6	6,564.6	6,744.3	1,340.0	P/E Ratio	10.9	Price (6/30/98)	57.00
Net Income	289.6	279.4	213.9	42.5	P/B Ratio	2.9	52 Wk Hi-Low	147.00-54.00
Book Value	843.5	1,035.4	786.5	156.3	Yield %	5.8	Market Cap	US$397.2mil

Address	20 Baker St., Rosebank	Tel 11-880-4801	ADR	--	Grp Fln Dir	M.W.S. Read
	Johannesburg 2196	Fax 11-788-0665	SEDOL	6692401	Chairman & CEO	Ronnie Lubner

Polifin

DJGI Industry: **Chemicals - Commodity**

Polifin Ltd. is a manufacturer of chemicals and plastics in South Africa. The company was formed in 1995 by a joint venture between rivals Sasol Ltd. and AECI Ltd. When the joint venture was developed, Sasol contributed its ethylene, propylene, and polypropylene operations; and AECI brought its chlor-alkali, plastics, and associated downstream operations to the collaboration. The resulting company, Polifin, is now 40% owned by Sasol, 40% owned by AECI, and 20% owned by private investors.

	R mil 06/96	06/97	06/98	US$mil 06/98				
Sales	N/A	3,644.0	3,770.0	632.5	P/E Ratio	5.3	Price (6/30/98)	5.30
Net Income	N/A	543.0	551.0	92.4	P/B Ratio	1.5	52 Wk Hi-Low	9.94-5.30
Book Value	N/A	1,772.0	2,147.0	360.2	Yield %	6.0	Market Cap	US$489.2mil

Address	156 Hendrik Verwoerd Dr.	Tel 27-329-6111	ADR	--	Managing Director	T.S. Munday
	Randburg 2194	Fax 27-329-6180	SEDOL	6702894	Chairman	P. Du P. Kruger

Power Technologies

DJGI Industry: **Electrical Components & Equipment**

Power Technologies Ltd. is a holding company with interests in energy-control equipment, power and telecommunications cables, lighting products, batteries, and solar energy. In March 1998, the company acquired the Sabat Group, comprising Sabat Battery Co. (Pty) Ltd. and related property-owning companies. In 1997, Power Technologies sold its 53.5% stake in subsidiary General Technologies, ending its involvement in the domestic appliance market and allowing it to concentrate its resources on core business activities in the electrical power industry.

	R mil 02/96	02/97	02/98	US$mil 02/98				
Sales	2,158.3	1,814.2	1,948.9	394.1	P/E Ratio	12.0	Price (6/30/98)	8.06
Net Income	60.9	78.8	112.9	22.8	P/B Ratio	2.3	52 Wk Hi-Low	10.80-6.75
Book Value	469.3	519.4	579.1	117.1	Yield %	2.7	Market Cap	US$231.5mil

Address	20 Georgian Crescent	Tel 11-706-7184	ADR	--	CEO	R.E. Venter
	Bryanston 2152	Fax 11-706-1036	SEDOL	6698023	Chairman	J.B. Maree

Premier Group

DJGI Industry: **Other Food**

Premier Group Ltd. manufactures and distributes food, dairy products, cooking oils and fats, and animal feed. Through its subsidiaries, the company operates maize and wheat mills, manages cotton farms, processes cotton, manufactures pharmaceuticals, and operates wholesale businesses. Premier also retails tools, home-improvement products, videos, and other consumer products. Wholesaling and distribution of groceries and pharmaceuticals accounted for 60% of fiscal 1997 revenues; food, 28%; and retailing, entertainment, and leisure, 12%.

	R mil 04/96	04/97	04/98	US$mil 04/98				
Sales	15,999.1	16,802.5	16,375.0	3,240.0	P/E Ratio	5.0	Price (6/30/98)	1.51
Net Income	553.0	349.4	226.0	44.7	P/B Ratio	0.5	52 Wk Hi-Low	1.51-0.62
Book Value	1,869.7	2,636.2	1,517.0	300.2	Yield %	7.9	Market Cap	US$260.7mil

Address	Rosebank	Tel 11-788-2114	ADR	PRRGY	Finance Director	J. Sturgeon
	Johannesburg 2000	Fax 11-442-5149	SEDOL	6699899	Chairman & CEO	D.D. Band

Pretoria Portland Cement

DJGI Industry: **Building Materials**

Pretoria Portland Cement Co. Ltd. manufactures and distributes cement, lime, and limestone products. Its six factories produce 5.5 million tons of cement each year, accounting for 45% of the market share in South Africa. The company operates a lime plant at Lime Acres in the Northern Cape that produces 2.2 million tons of lime annually. Pretoria also invests in companies that manufacture cement-based products, paper bags, and containers. Cement accounted for 68% of fiscal 1997 revenues; investments, 21%; and lime, 11%. The Barlow Group owns 62.62% of the company.

	R mil 09/95	09/96	09/97	US$mil 09/97				
Sales	1,247.6	1,555.5	1,809.4	388.9	P/E Ratio	9.1	Price (6/30/98)	46.00
Net Income	161.1	193.8	225.6	48.5	P/B Ratio	1.8	52 Wk Hi-Low	85.00-46.00
Book Value	819.3	961.6	1,135.9	244.1	Yield %	6.8	Market Cap	US$363.1mil

Address	Katherine St.	Tel 11-801-9111	ADR	--	Managing Director	J.E. Gomersall
	Johannesburg 2196	Fax 11-444-3643	SEDOL	6701749	Chairman	W.A. Clewlow

PSG Financial Services

DJGI Industry: **Other Recreational Products & Services**

PSG Financial Services Ltd., formerly Servgro International Ltd., invests primarily in the hotel and leisure industries. The company's main interests include an 85% stake in Zeda Holdings, a provider of Avis car-rental services in southern Africa; a 55% stake in Price Forbes Group, an insurance broker and financial consultant; a 48% stake in Fedics Group, a contract caterer and food retailer; a 41% stake in Interleisure, a film and video distributor; and a 43% stake in Interpark, a parking developer. It also has interests in the television rental and repair, cellular communications, and publishing sectors.

	R mil 03/95	03/96	03/97	US$mil 03/97				
Sales	1,139.2	1,352.3	1,680.9	380.7	P/E Ratio	5.5	Price (6/30/98)	7.00
Net Income	74.0	25.3	156.7	35.5	P/B Ratio	1.2	52 Wk Hi-Low	7.45-2.04
Book Value	483.1	489.0	745.3	168.8	Yield %	2.1	Market Cap	US$381.0mil

Address	148 Jan Smuts Ave., Rosebank	Tel	11-442-6320	ADR	SVGRY	President	--
	Johannesburg 2196	Fax	11-442-6335	SEDOL	6796916	Chairman	P.J.J. van der Walt

Rembrandt

DJGI Industry: **Distillers & Brewers**

Rembrandt Group Ltd. is a diversified holding company with main businesses in tobacco, liquor, and mining. The company also has equity stakes in companies that are engaged in banking and financial services, forestry and timber processing, printing and packaging, engineering, medical services, and food, wine, spirits, and various other products that are sold under brand names. The group is 51.1% owned by Rembrandt Controlling Investments Ltd. In 1998, the group sold its interest in Huntcor Ltd. and Usko Ltd.

	R mil 03/96	03/97	03/98	US$mil 03/98				
Sales	N/A	7,036.0	9,368.0	1,861.3	P/E Ratio	8.8	Price (6/30/98)	37.00
Net Income	1,481.0	2,112.0	2,109.0	419.0	P/B Ratio	1.8	52 Wk Hi-Low	48.40-31.25
Book Value	9,023.0	10,774.0	12,870.0	2,557.1	Yield %	2.4	Market Cap	US$3,240.3mil

Address	Coetzier St.	Tel	21-883-2333	ADR	RBDGY	Managing Director	M. Visser
	Stellenbosch 7600	Fax	21-887-1645	SEDOL	6731928	Chairman	J.P. Rupert

Rembrandt Controlling

DJGI Industry: **Conglomerates**

Rembrandt Controlling Investments Ltd. is an investment company with a 51.1% stake in the Rembrandt Group Ltd. Other investments include interests in banking and financial services, forestry and timber processing, printing and packaging, engineering, adhesives, life assurance, medical services, mining, petrochemical products, portfolio investments, tobacco products, food, and wine and spirits. It is a subsidiary of holding company Technical Investment Corp., with the ultimate holding company being Rembrandt Trust (Proprietary) Ltd.

	R mil 03/95	03/96	03/97	US$mil 03/97				
Sales	N/A	N/A	7,036.0	1,593.7	P/E Ratio	7.3	Price (6/30/98)	23.00
Net Income	485.0	756.0	1,125.0	254.8	P/B Ratio	1.5	52 Wk Hi-Low	31.35-19.50
Book Value	3,942.0	4,609.0	5,503.0	1,246.4	Yield %	1.8	Market Cap	US$1,389.1mil

Address	Coetzier St.	Tel	2231-832333	ADR	--	Managing Director	M.H. Visser
	Stellenbosch 7600	Fax	2231-71645	SEDOL	6731940	Chairman	A.E. Rupert

Reunert

DJGI Industry: **Diversified Technology**

Reunert Ltd. is an investment holding company active in the electrical engineering, defense, electronics, and telecommunications industries. Its electrical engineering holdings include wholly owned Circuit Breaker Industries, a maker of circuit breakers and earth leakage-protection products; 41%-owned African Cables, a producer of electrical and communication cables; and 50%-owned GEC Alsthom South Africa, a manufacturer of power-generation equipment. Its other interests include the manufacture of armored vehicles, radar equipment, and fiber-optic cable.

	R mil 09/95	09/96	09/97	US$mil 09/97				
Sales	4,742.6	4,914.9	4,927.4	1,059.0	P/E Ratio	13.6	Price (6/30/98)	6.70
Net Income	182.9	203.0	71.4	15.3	P/B Ratio	1.5	52 Wk Hi-Low	17.00-6.00
Book Value	689.2	849.0	807.8	173.6	Yield %	5.7	Market Cap	US$225.3mil

Address	Woodlands Dr., Woodmead	Tel	11-804-5888	ADR	--	CEO	G. Pretorius
	Sandton 2146	Fax	11-804-5997	SEDOL	6728726	Chairman	C. Parker

Safmarine & Rennies

DJGI Industry: **Marine Transportation**

Safmarine & Rennies Holdings (Safren) offers industrial services in the transport and leisure sectors. Through its three main subsidiaries, wholly-owned Safmarine, Rennies Group, and Kersaf Investments, the company engages in shipping and air transport, travel services, hotel and cinema management, and liquor and mineral water distribution. It is also involved in warehousing, casino operations, and restaurants. Shipping accounted for 52% of fiscal 1997 revenues; hotels and casino resorts, 33%; and cargo services and transportation, 15%.

	R mil 06/95	06/96	06/97	US$mil 06/97				
Sales	5,814.7	6,556.8	8,479.7	1,870.2	P/E Ratio	2.4	Price (6/30/98)	4.50
Net Income	386.1	535.9	589.6	130.0	P/B Ratio	0.7	52 Wk Hi-Low	11.10-4.44
Book Value	2,206.9	2,677.3	3,066.6	676.4	Yield %	9.4	Market Cap	US$386.4mil

Address	Safmarine Hse., 22 Riebeek St.	Tel	21-408-6911	ADR	--	Secretary	C.D.N. Stevens
	Cape Town 8001	Fax	21-419-6844	SEDOL	6766685	Chairman & CEO	D.A. Hawton

Sage

DJGI Industry: **Insurance - Full Line**

Sage Group Ltd. provides life insurance and financial services and develops property throughout South Africa. The company's core business activity is life insurance, but Sage Group also offers a range of financial services, including investment management, mutual-fund management, personal financial planning, and banking. Its property division owns property, develops land, and builds houses. Sage Group's main subsidiaries are Amalgamated Insurance Holdings, Sage Life, Sage Capital Managers, Investor Mutual Funds, and Sage Property Holdings.

	R mil 03/96	03/97	03/98	US$mil 03/98					
Revenues	1,413.1	1,793.3	2,509.6	568.4	P/E Ratio	14.4	Price (6/30/98)		25.00
Net Income	142.9	159.7	211.7	47.9	P/B Ratio	3.6	52 Wk Hi-Low		34.75-20.00
Book Value	786.0	900.6	1,112.6	252.0	Yield %	4.4	Market Cap		US$535.5mil

Address	Sage Ctr., 10 Fraser St.	Tel **11-377-5570**	ADR	**SAGEOT**	President	--
	Johannesburg 2001	Fax **11-834-2107**	SEDOL	**6767321**	Chairman	**H. Louis Shill**

Samancor

DJGI Industry: **Mining - Diversified**

Samancor Ltd. owns and operates two manganese mines, two chrome mines, and nine plants to process the mines' output. Most of its chrome ore is converted into ferrochrome for use in making stainless steel. Samancor is the largest ferrochrome producer in the world. About 80% of the world's high grade manganese reserves occur near Hotazel in the Northern Cape and Samancor holds the rights to a large portion of this deposit. The company also produces dolomite and silica from two mines and two processing plants. Both the Gencor and Anglo American groups are its major shareholders.

	R mil 06/96	06/97	06/98	US$mil 06/98					
Sales	3,791.8	3,702.5	4,082.1	684.9	P/E Ratio	11.7	Price (6/30/98)		25.00
Net Income	675.9	409.2	320.5	53.8	P/B Ratio	1.5	52 Wk Hi-Low		45.50-20.00
Book Value	2,826.3	3,102.6	3,268.8	548.4	Yield %	2.8	Market Cap		US$801.6mil

Address	Samancor Hse., 88 Marshall St.	Tel **11-378-7000**	ADR	**SMNCY**	Managing Director **W.H. Schroeder**
	Johannesburg 2001	Fax **11-378-7368**	SEDOL	**6823052**	Exec Chairman **M. Salamon**

Sappi

DJGI Industry: **Paper Products**

Sappi Ltd. is South Africa's largest forest-products group and one of the world's leading pulp and paper exporters. Its products include timber, specialized mining timber, particle board, pulp, and paper. Sappi owns six fine-paper mills in the United Kingdom and two German mills that produce fine and specialty papers. It has manufacturing facilities on three continents and an international sales network that markets products in more than 70 countries. The group has four regional operating divisions: Sappi Southern Africa, Sappi Europe, Sappi Warren, and Sappi Trading.

	R mil 09/95	09/96	09/97	US$mil 09/97					
Sales	12,549.0	15,271.1	16,216.2	3,485.1	P/E Ratio	7.0	Price (6/30/98)		22.25
Net Income	1,012.7	404.4	346.4	74.4	P/B Ratio	0.4	52 Wk Hi-Low		48.25-18.50
Book Value	6,862.4	7,989.6	8,912.1	1,915.3	Yield %	0.0	Market Cap		US$835.2mil

Address	48 Ameshoff St., Braamfontein	Tel **11-407-8111**	ADR	**SAPIY**	President & CEO **M. Haymon**
	Johannesburg 2001	Fax **11-403-1493**	SEDOL	**6777007**	Exec Chairman **E. van As**

Sasol

DJGI Industry: **Oil Companies - Secondary**

Sasol Ltd. produces and markets liquid fuels, pipeline gas, petrochemicals, fertilizers, and coal. Its synthetic fuels business accounts for roughly 40% of its profits. It also manufactures waxes, alpha olefins, solvents, phenolics, tar products, solvents, and mining explosives. Its subsidiaries include National Petroleum Refiners of South Africa and Tosas, a manufacturer of road-binding materials. Sasol conducts most of its business domestically, but it has petrochemical operations in Europe and the Far East. Export sales accounted for 17.6% of Sasol's turnover in fiscal 1997.

	R mil 06/95	06/96	06/97	US$mil 06/97					
Sales	11,954.8	13,545.0	15,810.0	3,487.0	P/E Ratio	8.5	Price (6/30/98)		34.35
Net Income	1,859.5	2,333.0	2,548.0	562.0	P/B Ratio	1.7	52 Wk Hi-Low		66.25-28.90
Book Value	9,018.1	10,624.0	11,778.0	2,597.7	Yield %	4.3	Market Cap		US$3,489.3mil

Address	1 Sturdee Ave., Rosebank	Tel **11-441-3111**	ADR	**SASOY**	Managing Director **P. Cox**
	Johannesburg 2196	Fax **11-788-5092**	SEDOL	**6777450**	Chairman **J.A. Stegmann**

South African Breweries

DJGI Industry: **Distillers & Brewers**

South African Breweries Ltd. is a brewer of beer and is involved in retailing, hotel operations, and the manufacture of selected consumer goods. Its brewery operations have a virtual monopoly in South Africa. The company sells clothing, textiles, and footwear through its Edgars, Sales House, and Jet retail chains. It owns and operates several hotels in South Africa. Retailing and hotels accounted for 38.5% of fiscal 1997 revenues; beer interests, 30%; manufacturing, 24% and beverages and miscellaneous, 7.5%.

	R mil 03/96	03/97	03/98	US$mil 03/98					
Sales	30,108.0	33,852.1	25,426.2	5,051.9	P/E Ratio	35.1	Price (6/30/98)		122.00
Net Income	1,732.3	2,015.5	1,208.8	240.2	P/B Ratio	5.4	52 Wk Hi-Low		171.00-108.00
Book Value	5,573.3	8,235.0	7,933.6	1,576.3	Yield %	2.7	Market Cap		US$7,209.7mil

Address	2 Jan Smuts Ave.	Tel **11-407-1700**	ADR	**SBWRY**	Managing Director **G. MacKay**
	Johannesburg 2000	Fax **11-339-1830**	SEDOL	**6822101**	Chairman **M.C. Ramaphosa**

Standard Bank Investment

Standard Bank Investment Corp. Ltd. (Stanbic) is the holding company for South Africa's largest banking group in terms of market capitalization and revenue. Standard Bank has operations throughout southern Africa as well as in London, New York, Hong Kong, and Taipei. The company provides commercial banking, merchant banking, leasing, investment advising, insurance brokering, credit card facilities, venture capital, and other bank services. Interest income accounted for 73% of 1997 revenues; commissions and fees, 9% and other income, 18%.

	R mil 12/95	12/96	12/97	US$mil 12/97				
Revenues	14,817.0	18,877.0	22,864.0	4,700.7	P/E Ratio	15.2	Price (6/30/98)	25.30
Net Income	1,215.0	1,547.0	2,003.0	411.8	P/B Ratio	3.0	52 Wk Hi-Low	32.90-18.40
Book Value	6,526.0	8,285.0	10,169.0	2,090.7	Yield %	1.4	Market Cap	US$5,119.5mil

Address	Standard Bank Ctr.,5 Simmonds St	Tel 11-636-9111	ADR	--	CEO	M.H. Vosloo
	Johannesburg 2000	Fax 11-636-5617	SEDOL	6108005	Chairman	C.B. Strauss

Sun International

Sun International (South Africa) Ltd. operates 19 resort hotels and 16 casino licenses that encompass numerous entertainment, recreational, conference, and casino facilities. It was incorporated in May 1977 and listed on the Johannesburg Stock Exchange in November 1985. Sun International is widely acclaimed as the entertainment center of southern Africa, and it stages a variety of international shows, promotions, and sporting events. Gaming accounted for 73% of fiscal 1997 revenues; hotel rooms, 12% ; food and beverages, 11%; and other, 4%.

	R mil 06/96	06/97	06/98	US$mil 06/98				
Sales	2,160.7	2,336.7	2,609.7	437.8	P/E Ratio	3.9	Price (6/30/98)	2.00
Net Income	386.2	390.2	450.9	75.6	P/B Ratio	0.8	52 Wk Hi-Low	3.88-1.70
Book Value	1,928.2	2,004.9	N/A	N/A	Yield %	15.5	Market Cap	US$265.6mil

Address	3 Sandown Valley Crescent	Tel 11-780-7444	ADR	--	Managing Director	P.D. Bacon
	Sandton 2031	Fax 11-783-7446	SEDOL	6769048	Chairman	K. Mthembu

Suncrush

Suncrush Ltd. is a bottler, manufacturer, and distributor of carbonated soft drinks and fruit juices. It has bottling licenses for Coca-Cola of South Africa, Fanta, Sprite, Krest, Schweppes, and Sparletta in KwaZulu-Natal. In January 1997, the company unbundled its investment trusts, Tempora Investments Ltd. and Ettington Investments Ltd. by way of a dividend in specie to its shareholders to provide a separate listing for its bottling operation. At 1997 fiscal year end Dalys Ltd held 45.8% of the shares of the company and was therefore no longer its holding company.

	R mil 06/95	06/96	06/97	US$mil 06/97				
Sales	708.1	770.3	873.3	192.6	P/E Ratio	20.0	Price (6/30/98)	12.50
Net Income	98.8	149.0	98.7	21.8	P/B Ratio	8.2	52 Wk Hi-Low	14.50-10.40
Book Value	491.9	698.9	241.8	53.3	Yield %	1.7	Market Cap	US$451.1mil

Address	491 Ridge Rd.	Tel 31-29-4371	ADR	--	Finance Director	B.S. Allison
	Durban 4001	Fax 11-299125	SEDOL	6806536	Exec Chairman	R.D. Hamilton

Tiger Oats

Tiger Oats Ltd. is an investment holding company operating in the food processing and distribution industries. Operations include milling, baking, food processing, trading, shipping, distributing, and producing confectionery goods and edible oils. The company holds controlling interests in pharmaceutical company Adcock Ingram and food company Oceana Fishing. Food manufacturing, wholesaling, and retailing accounted for 85% of 1997 revenues; pharmaceuticals, 12%; and fishing and cold storage, 3%. Tiger Oats is a 52.4% owned subsidiary of C.G. Smith Foods Ltd.

	R mil 09/95	09/96	09/97	US$mil 09/97				
Sales	11,978.7	13,630.0	15,526.5	3,336.9	P/E Ratio	11.1	Price (6/30/98)	52.50
Net Income	474.9	792.9	709.3	152.4	P/B Ratio	2.1	52 Wk Hi-Low	82.00-52.50
Book Value	2,478.5	3,024.3	3,444.6	740.3	Yield %	3.0	Market Cap	US$1,327.3mil

Address	85 Bute Ln.	Tel 11-320-0111	ADR	TIOAY	Managing Director	N. Dennis
	Sandton 2146	Fax 11-884-2029	SEDOL	6891297	Chairman	R. Williams

Tongaat-Hulett

Tongaat-Hulett Group Ltd. is a holding company with interests in the production of sugar, building materials, consumer foods, aluminum, textiles, starch, and glucose. It also has interests in property. The company operates sugar mills and a sugar refinery. It also operates plants that produce foods such as edible oils, mushrooms, cordials, and dehydrated food. The company's building materials division produces bricks, clay roofing materials, and ceramic tiles. Operations are conducted throughout South Africa. Sugar accounted for 43% of fiscal 1998 revenues.

	R mil 03/96	03/97	03/98	US$mil 03/98				
Sales	4,124.7	4,697.5	4,465.7	887.3	P/E Ratio	7.1	Price (6/30/98)	44.50
Net Income	403.7	547.4	589.3	117.1	P/B Ratio	1.4	52 Wk Hi-Low	81.50-44.00
Book Value	2,615.5	2,919.3	3,447.9	685.1	Yield %	4.7	Market Cap	US$734.5mil

Address	Amanzimnyama Hill, Kwa Zulu	Tel 322-994000	ADR	--	Managing Director	C.M. Savage
	Natal 4400	Fax 322-923333	SEDOL	6443502	Chairman	C.J. Saunders

Trans-Natal Coal

DJGI Industry: **Coal**

Trans-Natal Coal Corp. Ltd. is one of the major South African coal producers that export and supply coal for Eskom as well as other domestic customers. It serves as the investment holding arm for Gencor's mining interests. The company acquires and exploits coal reserves, finances coal mining projects, and markets coal products. Its principal holding is a 51.46% interest in Ingwe Coal, an exporter of steam coal. In fiscal 1995, Trans-Natal Coal merged its assets with those of Ingwe in return for shares. Gencor manages Ingwe through its 45% controlling interest in Trans-Natal Coal.

	R mil 06/95	06/96	06/97	US$mil 06/97					
Sales	3,427.8	4,681.6	5,816.4	1,282.8	P/E Ratio	5.9	Price (6/30/98)		17.90
Net Income	153.5	260.3	367.3	81.0	P/B Ratio	1.8	52 Wk Hi-Low		30.00-16.50
Book Value	701.3	839.9	994.2	219.3	Yield %	8.9	Market Cap		US$328.3mil

Address	6 Hollard St.		Tel 11-376-9111	ADR	**TNCCY**	President	--
	Johannesburg 2001		Fax 11-838-7190	SEDOL	**6901107**	Chairman	**M.L. Davis**

Trencor

DJGI Industry: **Containers & Packaging**

Trencor Ltd. is involved primarily in the manufacture, export, ownership, leasing, and financing the purchase of transport containers in South Africa and abroad. The company also produces truck trailers, road tankers, and trailer components. Its transport division offers cargo shipment, express parcel, and air courier services. The company also has an interest in Forward Corp. Ltd., the listed holding company for a group of industrial and consumer businesses operating in South Africa and abroad.

	R mil 06/95	06/96	06/97	US$mil 06/97					
Sales	1,104.5	1,316.7	1,415.4	312.2	P/E Ratio	12.9	Price (6/30/98)		19.50
Net Income	90.4	263.6	227.1	50.1	P/B Ratio	2.7	52 Wk Hi-Low		27.00-16.00
Book Value	655.6	895.3	1,105.5	243.8	Yield %	2.3	Market Cap		US$500.0mil

Address	Standard Bank Ctr., Heerengracht	Tel 21-21-7310	ADR	--	Secretary	**G.W. Norval**
	Cape Town 8001	Fax 21-419-3692	SEDOL	**6905336**	Chairman	**N.I. Jowell**

Wooltru

DJGI Industry: **Retailers - Broadline**

Wooltru Ltd. operates food, textiles, and general merchandise stores in South Africa and has clothing retail activities in Australia and Zimbabwe. Its subsidiaries include Woolworths Holdings (Pty) Ltd., Select Retail Group Ltd., and Massmart Holdings (Pty) Ltd. in the clothing, food, and other merchandise sectors; Wooltru Properties (Pty) Ltd. in the real-estate management sector; Wooltru Finance (Pty) Ltd., in the financial services sector; and Wooltru Insurance Brokers (Pty) Ltd. in the insurance sector. Department stores accounted for 82% of fiscal 1997 revenues.

	R mil 06/96	06/97	06/98	US$mil 06/98					
Revenues	9,711.3	11,103.3	13,976.0	2,344.8	P/E Ratio M	7.4	Price (6/30/98) M		7.60
Net Income	398.4	432.1	742.3	124.5	P/B Ratio M	1.2	52 Wk Hi-Low M		23.75-7.60
Book Value	1,757.1	2,187.3	N/A	N/A	Yield % M	6.2	Market Cap M		US$320.8mil

Address	93 Longmarket St.		Tel 21-407-9114	ADR	**WLTVY**	Hon. President	**D.R. Susman**
	Cape Town 8001		Fax 21-461-9246	SEDOL	**6979041**	Chairman & CEO	**C.A. Hall**

M=Multiple issues in index; reflects most active.

Spain

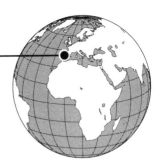

http://www.dowjones.com/indexes/Htmls01/spain.html

Exchanges:

Madrid Stock Exchange

Barcelona Stock Exchange

Valencia Stock Exchange

Bilbao Stock Exchange

Spain

Catherine Valenti
Madrid

The Spanish stock exchange is booming, boosted partly by growing domestic interest. Investing in equities in Spain was once thought of as being within reach of only the nation's wealthiest, but now taxi drivers and cleaning ladies are talking about what the stock market did that day.

Slick television commercials offering shares in the government's latest privatization of a steel company and full-page newspaper ads beckoning people to own stock in one of the nation's largest electricity companies have become familiar sights.

The IBEX-35 index of Spain's most liquid shares grew around 40% in the first half of 1998 to 10,146.40 by June 30, 1998. The index rose 41% in 1997, closing the year at 7255.40. With the average savings account yielding around 1.5%, Spanish families are now looking to the stock market as a way to save for the future.

About 60% of the volume on the Spanish stock exchange was from domestic investors in the first half of 1998, up from around 53% at the end of 1997.

Lower interest rates in Spain and a growth in investment and pension funds are also lifting private investment, along with the government's ongoing program to privatize state-held companies.

In 1998, the government completed the privatization of the country's largest electricity producer, Endesa SA, tobacco

company Tabacalera SA, and Corp. Bancaria de España SA, known as Argentaria. Privatizations have added 1.5 trillion pesetas, or 2.5% of the Exchange's total 62 trillion peseta market capitalization, during the first six months of 1998.

The government is expected to sell stakes in its airline, Iberia SA, and its remaining holdings of Spain's second fixed-line telephone company, Retevision SA, and technology company, Indra Sistemas SA, some time in the coming year.

A large percentage of the offerings is often reserved for foreign investors, another pillar supporting Spanish equities. Sales presentations in major cities, such as London and New York, have become standard practice in Spanish privatizations of recent years.

International investors are attracted by the Spanish market's combination of high

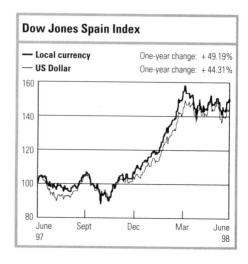

Dow Jones Spain Index

— Local currency   One-year change: + 49.19%
— US Dollar   One-year change: + 44.31%

returns and transparency. The IBEX-35 index's 40% rise in the first six months of 1998 dwarfs the approximately 13% increases in the Dow Jones Industrial Average U.S.'s and the U.K.'s FTSE 100.

Foreigners who invest in Spanish equities are exempt from the 25% withholding tax levied on domestic investors.

The Spanish stock market is actually made up of four stock exchanges — in Barcelona, Bilbao, Madrid, and Valencia — which are all managed under the Sociedad de Bolsas. Not surprisingly, the Madrid stock exchange is the most liquid, representing around 76% of the total trading volume in 1997. Barcelona accounts for about 12% of trading, followed by Bilbao and Valencia, with 9.7% and 2.4%, respectively.

The Sociedad de Bolsas is responsible for the Exchange's electronic trading system, commonly known as SIBE. Electronic trading takes place daily from 10 a.m. until 5 p.m. A small percentage of trading still occurs via the open-outcry method every day, from 10 a.m. to 12 p.m.

An electronic price-setting system was introduced in June 1998 for less liquid shares that are not listed on the IBEX-35. Under the system, bids are placed twice daily, between 9 a.m. and 12 p.m. and between 12 p.m. and 4 p.m., with bids and offers automatically matched at 12 p.m. and 4 p.m.

Country Information

Trading Hours:
  Local: 10:00 am - 5:00 pm

  EST: 4:00 am - 11:00 am

  GMT: 0900 - 1600

Population (6/98):
39,133,996

Unemployment (97):
21.0%

Main Industries:
Textiles and apparel (including footwear), food and beverages, metals and metal manufacturing, chemicals, shipbuilding, automobiles, machine tools, and tourism

Gross Domestic Product (97):
US$531.42 billion

GDP per Capita (97):
US$13,524.60

Three-Year Average GDP Growth (94-97):
2.7%

Average Annual CPI Growth (96-97):
+ 1.97%

Monetary Unit:
Spanish Peseta

Exchange Rate (6/98):
ESP153.08 to US$1.00

But the Spanish stock exchange's volume is dominated by the IBEX-35 index of blue-chip shares. Major industries represented in the index include banking, telecommunications, utilities, construction, real estate, and metals. Telecommunications group Telefonica SA alone represents around 18% of the total capital in the index, and banking shares make up around 39%.

A committee representing Spain's four stock exchanges determines the IBEX-35 listing every six months, based on shares' trading volume, and the index is adjusted on the first days of January and July. The most recent update of the listing, on July 1, 1998, saw restaurant chain Telepizza SA and steelmaker Aceralia Corporacion Siderurgica SA replace utility company Fuerzas Electricas de Cataluna SA and investment group Corporacion Financiera Alba on the IBEX.

Spain's traditional ties with Latin America are reflected in the Spanish stock market. To fund their ambitious to expand plans into the region, many Spanish blue-chips have opted for share offerings.

Capital increases raised the volume on the Spanish stock exchange by 2.5 trillion pesetas in the first half of 1998, to a total of 22.88 trillion pesetas. The largest increase so far this year was Telefonica's giant rights issue, in which the company offered shareholders one new share for every 11 held at the price of 5,000 pesetas a share. Telefonica raised 427.03 billion pesetas in

Ten Largest Capitalized Companies In The Dow Jones Spain Index
as of 6/30/98

Stock	Market Cap. US$ Thousands
Telefónica de España	47,471,247
Banco Bilbao Vizcaya	34,784,571
Banco de Santander	24,572,547
Endesa	22,795,426
Repsol	16,561,155
Iberdrola	14,665,651
Argentaria Corp Bancaria de España	11,012,025
Gas Natural SDG	10,804,208
Banco Central Hispanoamericano	10,317,076
Banco Popular Español	9,465,905

the offer, which it plans to invest in the Brazilian telecommunications market with strategic partners Portugal Telecom, WorldCom Inc., and MCI Communications Corp.

Spanish banks Banco Bilbao Vizcaya SA, Banco Santander SA, Argentaria, and BCH SA have also made or proposed capital increases in 1998.

The day when investors can buy Latin American shares on a European bourse may not be too far off. On the heels of the planned link-up between the London and Frankfurt stock exchanges, the Spanish stock exchange said it is planning to create a new market for Latin America shares by the end of 1998.

The Exchange said it hopes to start off with some 15 of Latin America's leading companies, with the goal of listing up to 50 companies' shares and also futures and options. The new market — like the Spanish stock exchange — would begin trading in euros, Europe's single currency, on January 4, 1999.

Some expect the start of the single currency to bring about a wave of European stock market alliances, with the eventual formation of a pan-European Exchange listing the 11 euro members' blue-chip issues. Low-capital shares would remain on smaller national exchanges. Although the Madrid stock exchange said it hasn't officially requested to be part of the London-Frankfurt stock market alliance, it said it will be closely following further developments in European link-ups.

Meanwhile, Spain has recently seen a wave of smaller issues come to market, with many privately owned companies launching initial public offerings. In the first half of 1998 alone, some 30 companies have listed on the Spanish stock market, compared with 41 companies in all of 1997.

Major initial public offerings expected over the next year include Spain's second cellular phone provider, Airtel, soccer clubs Atletico de Madrid and Real Club Deportivo Espanyol, and electricity distributor Red Electrica de España.

Market Sector Performance In The Dow Jones Spain Index
1 Year Change Through 6/30/98

Market Sector	Change % (US$)
Consumer, Non-Cyclical	70.18
Financial	62.65
Industrial	44.41
Utilities	35.44
Energy	26.56
Consumer, Cyclical	-14.29

Acerinox

DJGI Industry: **Steel**
Stoxx Sector: **Basic Resources**

Acerinox SA is one of Europe's largest stainless-steel manufacturers and exporters. The company sells stainless steel products produced at its hot and cold rolling mills. It's the listed parent company at the heart of Grupo Acerinox, which owns 95% of North American Stainless in Kentucky, with the U.S. company Armco holding the other 5%. In July 1998, Acerinox split its stock 5-for-1. In March 1997, the company agreed to sell most of its 33% participation in the Mexican steel producer Mexinox SA de CV to German company Krupp-Thyssen-Nirosta.

	ptas mil 12/95	12/96	12/97	US$mil 12/97				
Sales	191,244.5	180,891.5	219,100.7	1,438.8	P/E Ratio	12.1	Price (6/30/98)	20,420
Net Income	34,385.0	14,863.9	21,399.3	140.5	P/B Ratio	1.6	52 Wk Hi-Low	29,600.0-19,640.0
Book Value	124,445.2	138,371.6	147,808.6	970.6	Yield %	2.0	Market Cap	US$1,560.3mil

Address	Santiago de Compostela 100	Tel **1-985-174**	ADR	--	President	--
	280351 Madrid	Fax **1-985-195**	SEDOL	4005238	Chairman	**V. Munoz Cava**

Argentaria

DJGI Industry: **Banks - Major International**
Stoxx Sector: **Bank**

Argentaria Corp. Bancaria de Espana SA (Argentaria), is a universal banking group in Spain that is ranked in the top three, by total assets. Its areas of business include corporate, retail, international, and investment banking, as well as mortgage lending, money market trading, fund management, and life insurance. In March 1996, Argentaria concluded the offering of 28.63 million shares, or approximately 23% of its capital, in an initial tranche of the sale of the government's remaining 50% stake in the bank, which lowered the government's stake to 25%.

	ptas mil 12/95	12/96	12/97	US$mil 12/97				
Revenues	1,077,702	1,030,502	891,329.0	5,853.2	P/E Ratio	26.8	Price (6/30/98)	3,440.00
Net Income	74,197.0	31,217.0	63,015.0	413.8	P/B Ratio	3.0	52 Wk Hi-Low	3,587.5-1,892.5
Book Value	581,751.0	566,336.0	569,711.0	3,741.2	Yield %	1.6	Market Cap	US$11,012mil

Address	Paseo de Recoletos 10	Tel **1-537-00-00**	ADR	--	President	--
	28001 Madrid	Fax --	SEDOL	4049720	Chairman	**Francisco González**

Aumar

DJGI Industry: **Heavy Construction**
Stoxx Sector: **Construction**

Autopistas del Mare Nostrum SA (Aumar) builds and operates roads, service roads, and service areas and provides related services under license from the Spanish government. Aumar maintains the operation of toll highways. It also provides road-surfacing and drainage services, renovates service areas, and offers a breakdown service. The company's contract to maintain three tollways, from Tarragona to Valencia, Valencia to Alicante, and Seville to Cádiz, covering 468 kilometers, will expire in 2006. The construction company Dragados y Construcciónes owns 26% of Aumar.

	ptas mil 12/95	12/96	12/97	US$mil 12/97				
Sales	28,577.6	29,915.4	31,658.0	207.9	P/E Ratio	39.7	Price (6/30/98)	3,195.00
Net Income	7,339.7	8,073.7	6,005.0	39.4	P/B Ratio	1.2	52 Wk Hi-Low	3,410.0-2,080.0
Book Value	82,574.9	184,726.0	183,190.0	1,203.0	Yield %	3.5	Market Cap	US$1,392.7mil

Address	Paseo De La Alameda 36	Tel **6-337-20-02**	ADR	--	V Chairman	**E. Duran Lopez-Jamar**
	46023 Valencia	Fax --	SEDOL	4065629	Chmn & Mng Dir	**J.L. Ceron Ayuso**

Autopistas Concesionaria

DJGI Industry: **Heavy Construction**
Stoxx Sector: **Construction**

Autopistas Concesionaria Española SA (Acesa) constructs, manages, and maintains tollways. The company's activities are centered in the northeastern region of Catalonia, where Acesa has maintained and operated the motorway network since 1967. Its tollway concessions include several of Spain's primary tourist roads, such as Laonquera-Barcelona-Tarragona, Zaragoza-Mediterranean, and Montgat-Malgrat, totalling more than 509 kilometers. These concessions will expire in 2016 when Acesa's fixed assets will revert to the Spanish government.

	ptas mil 12/95	12/96	12/97	US$mil 12/97				
Sales	53,539.0	56,600.0	61,946.0	406.8	P/E Ratio	25.3	Price (6/30/98)	2,375.00
Net Income	22,469.0	23,681.0	24,797.0	162.8	P/B Ratio	2.2	52 Wk Hi-Low	2,581.0-1,638.1
Book Value	140,319.0	262,039.0	269,247.0	1,768.1	Yield %	3.0	Market Cap	US$3,729.1mil

Address	Plaza Gala Placídia 1	Tel **3-228-5000**	ADR	--	V Chairman	**E.A. Garcia Irazoqui**
	08006 Barcelona	Fax **3-228-5001**	SEDOL	4065663	Chairman	**J. Vilarasau Salat**

Banco Bilbao Vizcaya

DJGI Industry: **Banks - Major International**
Stoxx Sector: **Bank**

Banco Bilbao Vizcaya SA provides banking, insurance, and other financial services in Spain and Portugal. The bank is represented in 24 countries and has 2,829 branches in Spain and a further 1,520 branches abroad. It services more than 6 million customers, including roughly 3,000 large companies, as well as individuals and small businesses. BBV is the only Spanish financial group that operates in Jersey and the Grand Cayman islands. Interest and fees on loans accounted for 43% of 1997 revenues; other interest income for 38%; and noninterest income for 19%.

	ptas mil 12/95	12/96	12/97	US$mil 12/97				
Revenues	1,406,267	1,607,624	1,857,897	12,200.5	P/E Ratio	38.8	Price (6/30/98)	7,870.00
Net Income	84,013.0	104,260.0	130,848.0	859.3	P/B Ratio	6.9	52 Wk Hi-Low	8,060.0-3,690.0
Book Value	652,161.0	739,440.1	776,665.0	5,100.2	Yield %	1.2	Market Cap	US$34,785mil

Address	Gran Via, 1. 2A Planta	Tel **4-487-55-55**	ADR	BBV	CEO	**P.I. Uriarte Santamarina**
	48001 Bilbao	Fax **4-487-61-61**	SEDOL	5273681	Chairman	**E. Ybarra Churruca**

In DJ Stoxx 50; In EuroStoxx 50.

Banco Central Hispanoamericano

DJGI Industry: **Banks - Major International**
Stoxx Sector: **Bank**

Banco Central Hispanoamericano SA provides retail banking, corporate banking, merchant banking, and insurance services in both the domestic and the international markets. The bank conducts its business activities through 2,561 branches in Spain and 16 operating offices abroad. The bank offers a range of services, including leasing, factoring, asset management, pension plans, and investment funds. Interest and fees on loans accounted for 52% of 1997 revenues; other interest income for 33%; and noninterest income for 15%.

	ptas mil 12/95	12/96	12/97	US$mil 12/97				
Revenues	8,824.6	9,069.4	6,697.3	44.0	P/E Ratio		35.6	Price (6/30/98)	4,820.00
Net Income	100.6	264.0	292.5	1.9	P/B Ratio		3.9	52 Wk Hi-Low	5,190.0-2,495.0
Book Value	3,345.7	3,104.6	2,727.6	17.9	Yield %		1.4	Market Cap	US$10,317mil

Address	Alcalá 49	Tel 1-558-41-00	ADR	BCH	President	--
	28014 Madrid	Fax 1-532-91-21	SEDOL	5316597	Chairman & CEO	José María Amusátegui

Banco Popular Español

DJGI Industry: **Banks - Regional (All)**
Stoxx Sector: **Bank**

Banco Popular Español SA offers commercial-banking services to corporate and private investors, primarily in the Spanish retail market, as well as financial services. The bank consists of five regional banks, France's Banco Popular Comercial, and other financial-services subsidiaries. It has branches throughout Spain, Europe, and South America. Banco Popular Español recently formed Popular Rabobank, a joint-venture agribusiness bank with Dutch Rabobank, and it maintains its joint-venture mortgage bank, Banco Popular Hipotecario, with Germany's Bayerische Hypotheken.

	ptas mil 12/95	12/96	12/97	US$mil 12/97				
Revenues	390,641.0	387,850.0	351,530.0	2,308.4	P/E Ratio		26.9	Price (6/30/98)	13,080
Net Income	57,482.0	61,002.0	65,901.0	432.8	P/B Ratio		4.4	52 Wk Hi-Low	15,240.0-8,110.0
Book Value	318,573.0	341,937.0	328,981.0	2,160.4	Yield %		0.6	Market Cap	US$9,465.9mil

Address	Velázquez 34	Tel 1-520-70-00	ADR	--	Jnt Chairman	L. Valls Taberner
	28001 Madrid	Fax 1-577-92-08	SEDOL	5286140	Jnt Chairman	J. Valls Taberner

Banco de Santander

DJGI Industry: **Banks - Major International**
Stoxx Sector: **Bank**

Banco de Santander SA provides retail banking and financial and investment services in Spain and 30 other countries, including all the leading financial centers. The bank, with 1,320 branches in Spain, has subsidiary banks operating in Portugal, Germany, Chile, and Puerto Rico. In 1994, it purchased of 49% of Banesto. Interest and fees on loans accounted for 38% of 1995 revenues, other interest income for 46%, and noninterest income for 16%. In early 1997, Santander purchased Banco General de Comercio in Brazil and Venezuela's Banco de Venezuela.

	ptas mil 12/95	12/96	12/97	US$mil 12/97				
Revenues	1,632,455	1,887,459	2,209,753	14,511.1	P/E Ratio		33.3	Price (6/30/98)	3,925.00
Net Income	75,394.0	85,598.0	110,627.0	726.5	P/B Ratio		4.5	52 Wk Hi-Low	4,105.0-1,850.0
Book Value	569,801.0	620,093.0	666,325.0	4,375.7	Yield %		1.6	Market Cap	US$24,573mil

Address	Paseo de la Castellana 75	Tel 1-342-48-87	ADR	STD	V Chairman	J. Botín-Sanz
	28046 Madrid	Fax 1-342-48-94	SEDOL	5254783	Chairman	E. Botín-Sanz

Bankinter

DJGI Industry: **Banks - Regional (All)**
Stoxx Sector: **Bank**

Bankinter SA is a private corporation devoted mainly to banking activities. Its subsidiaries are involved in commercial and corporate banking, security investment, and portfolio and pension fund management. The group has 252 branches, all located in Spain. It arranges securities transactions through Mercavalor, a securities company in which it has a 17% interest. Total interest income accounted for 84% of 1996 revenues, noninterest income for 16%. Bankinter, established by Banco Santander and BankAmerica, was known as Banco Intercontinental Español until 1996.

	ptas mil 12/95	12/96	12/97	US$mil 12/97				
Revenues	1,767,048	2,332,750	3,945,532	25,909.7	P/E Ratio		21.4	Price (6/30/98)	9,950.00
Net Income	192,196.0	260,410.0	244,406.0	1,605.0	P/B Ratio		2.9	52 Wk Hi-Low	11,880.0-6,800.0
Book Value	1,007,554	1,252,876	2,555,726	16,783.1	Yield %		2.5	Market Cap	US$2,615.7mil

Address	Paseo de la Castellana 29	Tel 1-319-95-00	ADR	BKISY	Managing Director	Juan Arena
	28046 Madrid	Fax 1-339-76-24	SEDOL	5265956	Chairman	Jaime Botín-Sanz

Centros Comerciales Pryca

DJGI Industry: **Retailers - Broadline**
Stoxx Sector: **Retail**

Centros Comerciales Pryca SA is involved in the commercial operation of retail establishments for the sale to the public of all legally tradable merchandise. The company is the largest hypermarket chain in Spain. Its major shareholders include Banca March SA, the French supermarket chain Carrefour, and the Spanish holding group Corporación Financiera Alba SA. Pryca opened two hypermarkets in October 1996 in Barcelona and Madrid and its first store in La Coruña in Galicia in November 1996. Food retail accounted for 57% of 1997 revenues and nonfood retail, 43%.

	ptas mil 12/95	12/96	12/97	US$mil 12/97				
Revenues	543,374.0	538,619.0	528,690.0	3,471.8	P/E Ratio		26.3	Price (6/30/98)	2,840.00
Net Income	21,743.0	23,951.0	20,422.0	134.1	P/B Ratio		3.5	52 Wk Hi-Low	3,320.0-2,040.0
Book Value	133,487.0	169,379.0	152,333.0	1,000.3	Yield %		2.5	Market Cap	US$3,511.2mil

Address	Calle Campezo 16	Tel 1-301-8900	ADR	--	CEO	G. Plassat
	28022 Madrid	Fax 1-747-46-72	SEDOL	4184267	Chairman	P. Vallbona

CEPSA

DJGI Industry: **Oil Companies - Secondary**
Stoxx Sector: **Energy**

Compañía Española de Petróleos SA (CEPSA), the largest private oil refiner in Spain, by market capitalization, explores for, extracts, and refines oil. It also manufactures and distributes petroleum products such as lubricants, plastics, polymers, and other refined chemicals. Lubricants are marketed under three brand names: Cepsa, Ertoil, and Krafft. CEPSA has 30 industrial plants, including three refineries, and it operates in both the domestic and the international markets. The group operates a network of 1,815 service stations under the name Cepsa Elf throughout Spain and Portugal.

	ptas mil 12/95	12/96	12/97	US$mil 12/97				
Sales	789,522.0	892,536.0	1,042,624	6,846.8	P/E Ratio	17.6	Price (6/30/98)	5,700.00
Net Income	21,853.0	20,850.0	27,779.0	182.4	P/B Ratio	2.2	52 Wk Hi-Low	6,050.0-3,885.0
Book Value	187,907.0	217,024.0	233,954.0	1,536.3	Yield %	2.3	Market Cap	US$3,321.3mil

Address	**Avenida Del Partenon 12**	Tel **1-337-60-00**	ADR	--	Jnt V. Chmn	**A. Jonglez**
	28042 Madrid	Fax **1-725-4116**	SEDOL	**4684121**	Chairman	**C. Olariaga**

Cristalería Española

DJGI Industry: **Building Materials**
Stoxx Sector: **Construction**

Cristalería Española SA manufactures glass, synthetic fibers, insulation, and foundation pipes. The company's main division makes glassware for the construction and auto industries under the Cristanola Plata, Stapid, and Parsol brand names. also sells rock-wool and fiberglass insulation under the Roclaine and Isover brand names. International Saint-Gobain has a controlling share of the company. Flat glass accounted for 37% of 1997 revenues; glass bottles and tableware, 34%; drainage systems, 12%; insulating glass and other material, 9%; and reinforcement fibers, 8%.

	ptas mil 12/95	12/96	12/97	US$mil 12/97				
Sales	144,822.4	147,679.6	156,438.2	1,027.3	P/E Ratio	13.0	Price (6/30/98)	14,980
Net Income	11,891.4	10,976.7	12,153.4	79.8	P/B Ratio	2.2	52 Wk Hi-Low	15,750.0-10,500.0
Book Value	58,196.4	79,764.8	88,088.5	578.5	Yield %	1.9	Market Cap	US$1,283.9mil

Address	**Paseo de la Castellana 77**	Tel **1-397-20-00**	ADR	--	V Chairman	**Philippe Crouzet**
	28046 Madrid	Fax **1-397-2626**	SEDOL	**4234548**	Chairman	**J.L. Leal Maldonado**

Dragados

DJGI Industry: **Heavy Construction**
Stoxx Sector: **Construction**

Dragados y Construcciónes SA is one of Spain's leading construction companies. It engages in activities that include civil engineering and industrial work, building maintenance, infrastructure conservation, and toll road construction and maintenance. In 1997, Dragados won a $50.5 million contract to build electricity substations in Mexico. Civil engineering accounted for 46% of 1997 revenues; building construction accounted for 22%; industrial construction made up 19%, urban services contributed 11%, and property added 2%.

	ptas mil 12/95	12/96	12/97	US$mil 12/97				
Sales	410,222.0	416,507.0	457,149.0	3,002.0	P/E Ratio	29.6	Price (6/30/98)	4,910.00
Net Income	8,744.0	8,875.0	9,565.0	62.8	P/B Ratio	2.2	52 Wk Hi-Low	5,410.0-2,740.0
Book Value	117,841.0	112,232.0	126,439.0	830.3	Yield %	1.8	Market Cap	US$1,842.8mil

Address	**Paseo Alameda de Osuna 50**	Tel **1-583-30-00**	ADR	--	V Chmn & Mng Dir	**Enrique D. López-Jamar**
	28042 Madrid	Fax **1-742-77-53**	SEDOL	**4280143**	Chairman	**Santiago F. Casaus**

ENDESA

DJGI Industry: **Electrical Utilities (All)**
Stoxx Sector: **Utility**

Empresa Nacional de Electricidad SA (ENDESA), Spain's largest utility, is involved in the production, transmission, distribution, and supply of electricity and in the exploration, research, and exploitation of all types of primary energy resources, including coal, gas, nuclear, and hydroelectric. The group is also involved in the mining of black and brown lignite and anthracite, producing 8,200,000 tons of coal during 1996. In 1997, retail sales of electricity accounted for 73% of total sales, wholesale sales for 19%, and other activities for 8%.

	ptas mil 12/95	12/96	12/97	US$mil 12/97				
Sales	861,689.0	1,259,835	1,245,435	8,178.6	P/E Ratio	20.8	Price (6/30/98)	3,355.00
Net Income	149,853.0	165,088.0	166,742.0	1,095.0	P/B Ratio	2.3	52 Wk Hi-Low	4,190.0-2,565.0
Book Value	876,865.0	1,450,841	1,502,895	9,869.3	Yield %	2.3	Market Cap	US$22,795mil

Address	**Príncipe de Vergara 187**	Tel **1-563-09-23**	ADR	**ELE**	CEO	**R. Miranda Robredo**
	28002 Madrid	Fax **1-563-81-81**	SEDOL	**5271782**	Chairman	**R. Martin Villa**

In DJ Stoxx 50; In EuroStoxx 50.

FCC

DJGI Industry: **Heavy Construction**
Stoxx Sector: **Construction**

Fomento de Construcciónes y Contratas SA (FCC) is one of Spain's leading and most diversified construction companies. It has interests in urban services such as waste collection as well as in the cement, property, and financial sectors. FCC's growth strategies have centered on diversifying activities domestically rather than on expanding abroad. In August 1997, FCC took a 16.66% stake in Iniciadora de Infraestructuras, a joint venture with Acesa and four other companies that will analyze motorway projects and bid for contracts offered by the Spanish government.

	ptas mil 12/95	12/96	12/97	US$mil 12/97				
Sales	407,808.0	429,359.0	484,507.0	3,181.7	P/E Ratio	28.2	Price (6/30/98)	7,910.00
Net Income	12,861.0	13,035.0	13,975.0	91.8	P/B Ratio	3.7	52 Wk Hi-Low	8,380.0-4,460.0
Book Value	102,811.0	118,644.0	128,041.0	840.8	Yield %	0.5	Market Cap	US$3,103.2mil

Address	**Iturrama 23**	Tel **3-488-20-38**	ADR	--	Jnt V. Chmn	**E. Koplowitz De Juseu**
	31007 Pamplona	Fax **3-487-97-92**	SEDOL	**5350056**	Chairman	**G. Visedo Navarro**

Financiera Alba

DJGI Industry: **Diversified Financial Services**
Stoxx Sector: **Financial Services**

Corporación Financiera Alba SA is a holding company that operates banks and retail outlets, acquires, develops, and leases real estate, and produces foods, beverages, building materials, and chemicals. Its main holdings include the French cable television station Canal Plus (13%), Spanish builder Gines Navarro (52.5%), and Banco Urquijo (77%). In July 1997, Gines Navarro announced it would merge with OCP to form OCP-Gines, Spain's third largest construction group. Financiera Alba will control 35% of the combined group.

	ptas mil 12/95	12/96	12/97	US$mil 12/97					
Revenues	2,488.0	2,130.0	2,231.0	14.7	P/E Ratio	12.6	Price (6/30/98)	16,850	
Net Income	6,875.0	7,507.0	18,055.0	118.6	P/B Ratio	2.7	52 Wk Hi-Low	22,400.0-14,210.0	
Book Value	96,872.0	87,281.0	91,852.0	603.2	Yield %	0.7	Market Cap	US$1,506.3mil	

Address	Nuñez de Balboa 70	Tel 1-362-61-00	ADR	--	Jnt V. Chmn	J. Prohens Mas
	28006 Madrid	Fax 1-575-67-37	SEDOL	4182432	Chairman	Juan M. Delgado

Gas Natural

DJGI Industry: **Gas Utilities**
Stoxx Sector: **Utility**

Gas Natural SDG SA produces and distributes natural gas to residential, commercial and industrial consumers throughout Spain.. The company is responsible for more than 90% of the natural gas distributed in Spain. Its partially owned subsidiary, Gas Natural BAN, provides gas services to a 15,000-square-kilometer area in Argentina.The company also has a 91% stake in Spanish gas company Enagas. Gas sales accounted for 95% of 1997 revenues; other sales of group gas companies, 4%; and installations and engineering services, 1%.

	ptas mil 12/95	12/96	12/97	US$mil 12/97					
Sales	290,090.0	333,195.0	428,412.0	2,813.3	P/E Ratio	31.2	Price (6/30/98)	11,080	
Net Income	35,838.0	48,444.0	50,627.0	332.5	P/B Ratio	4.4	52 Wk Hi-Low	11,840.0-5,920.0	
Book Value	188,031.0	324,735.0	371,643.0	2,440.5	Yield %	0.7	Market Cap	US$10,804mil	

Address	Avda. Portal de l'Angel 22	Tel 3-402-51-00	ADR	--	CEO	G. Solana Gomez
	08002 Barcelona	Fax 3-402-58-70	SEDOL	5297993	Chairman	A. Brufau Niubo

Grupo Accióna

DJGI Industry: **Heavy Construction**
Stoxx Sector: **Construction**

Grupo Accióna SA is the result of a merger between Cubiertas y Mzov SA and Entrecanales SA, agreed upon in November 1996. Accióna is an almost exclusively domestic construction company specializing in large-scale public-works projects, including civil engineering, construction, and real estate development. Its operations are divided into three segments: urban construction and maintenance, rail and road infrastructure, and maritime works. Nonconstruction businesses account for 11% of revenue. Accióna has a 10.85% stake in Airtel, holder of Spain's second mobile-telephone license.

	ptas mil 12/95	12/96	12/97	US$mil 12/97					
Sales	214,781.0	204,687.0	373,810.0	2,454.8	P/E Ratio	25.5	Price (6/30/98)	36,480	
Net Income	4,029.0	3,405.0	11,433.0	75.1	P/B Ratio	5.1	52 Wk Hi-Low	40,200.0-16,600.0	
Book Value	48,301.0	50,738.0	81,412.0	534.6	Yield %	0.8	Market Cap	US$2,689.5mil	

Address	Avda. Europa 18	Tel 1-663-29-00	ADR	--	V Chairman	A. M. Buxareu
	28100 Alcobendas	Fax 1-663-29-17	SEDOL	4239327	Chairman	J.M. Entrecanales

Iberdrola

DJGI Industry: **Electrical Utilities (All)**
Stoxx Sector: **Utility**

Iberdrola SA, Spain's largest private sector electric utility, is involved in the production, transmission, switching, and distribution of electrical power through hydroelectric production, conventional thermal production, and nuclear production. Serving nearly 8 million customers, the company provides electricity to about 40% of the Spanish market and owns 38% of the country's electricity-generating capacity. Iberdrola also operates a holding company specializing in telecommunications and software, Corporación IBV, together with Banco Bilbao Vizcaya (BBV).

	ptas mil 12/95	12/96	12/97	US$mil 12/97					
Sales	809,177.0	822,390.9	810,167.0	5,320.2	P/E Ratio	21.5	Price (6/30/98)	2,490.00	
Net Income	85,009.0	96,637.0	101,454.0	666.2	P/B Ratio	1.8	52 Wk Hi-Low	2,765.0-1,680.0	
Book Value	947,050.0	1,216,360	1,250,809	8,213.9	Yield %	3.0	Market Cap	US$14,666mil	

Address	Gardoqui 8	Tel 4-415-08-57	ADR	--	V Chairman	José A. Garrido Martínez
	Vizcaya, Bilbao	Fax 4-416-36-78	SEDOL	4424640	Chairman	Iñigo de Oriol Ybarra

Mapfre

DJGI Industry: **Insurance - Full Line**
Stoxx Sector: **Insurance**

Corporación Mapfre operates in the insurance, banking, and real estate sectors. The company offers reinsurance and life and general insurance, including family, fire, homeowners, auto, civil liability, and personal-accident products. Through its wholly owned subsidiary, Mapfre Internacional, the company has interests in insurance companies in 21 countries, with the emphasis on Latin America. Its main activity is in the insurance and reinsurance sector, with premium income accounting for 84% of 1997 revenues and other income accounted for 16%.

	ptas mil 12/95	12/96	12/97	US$mil 12/97					
Revenues	289,284.0	329,541.0	427,928.0	2,810.1	P/E Ratio	31.5	Price (6/30/98)	5,380.00	
Net Income	9,574.0	9,737.0	10,355.0	68.0	P/B Ratio	2.4	52 Wk Hi-Low	6,500.0-3,100.0	
Book Value	99,428.0	125,823.0	138,508.0	909.6	Yield %	1.6	Market Cap	US$2,127.2mil	

Address	Paseo de Recoletos 25	Tel 1-581-11-00	ADR	CRFEY	Managing Director	José M. M. Martínez
	28004 Madrid	Fax 1-581-11-34	SEDOL	5387559	Chairman	Carlos Alvarez Jiménez

Metrovacesa

DJGI Industry: **Real Estate**
Stoxx Sector: **Financial Services**

Metrovacesa SA develops and manages real estate in Spain and Portugal and is Spain's largest property company in terms of rental revenues. It leases residential and office buildings and develops and sells apartment blocks, shopping centers, industrial premises, parking lots, and hotels. Metrovacesa was formed in 1989 as the result of a merger of three companies--Compania Inmobiliaria Metropolitana SA, Compania Urbanizadora Metropolitana SA, and Inmobiliaria Vasco Central SA. It is 25%-owned by Banco Bilbao Vizcaya.

	ptas mil 12/95	12/96	12/97	US$mil 12/97				
Sales	17,322.2	15,873.6	18,769.2	123.3	P/E Ratio	40.2	Price (6/30/98)	4,510.00
Net Income	4,605.6	4,713.0	5,000.3	32.8	P/B Ratio	3.0	52 Wk Hi-Low	5,050.0-2,670.0
Book Value	71,146.2	73,135.4	75,366.4	494.9	Yield %	1.3	Market Cap	US$1,390.6mil

Address	Pza. Carlos Trías Betrán 7	Tel 1-597-43-36	ADR	--	V Chairman	R.E. Valdes
	28020 Madrid	Fax 1-555-21-02	SEDOL	5442685	Chairman	S.A. Usandizaga

Repsol

DJGI Industry: **Oil Companies - Major**
Stoxx Sector: **Energy**

Repsol SA is involved in the exploration, production, refining, distribution, and sale of oil products, petrochemicals, and liquefied petroleum gases, as well as the sale of natural gas. The company holds more than 70% of the Spanish petroleum market, and it is controlled by the Spanish state through the Sociedad Estatal de Participaciónes Industriales (SEPI). The company's oil reserves in the Near and Middle East provide the company with 34% of its global crude-oil production. Repsol has more than 3,000 retail outlets, which operate under the Repsol, Campsa, and Petronor brand names.

	ptas mil 12/95	12/96	12/97	US$mil 12/97				
Sales	1,818,731	2,022,377	2,418,980	15,885.1	P/E Ratio	19.0	Price (6/30/98)	8,450.00
Net Income	117,715.0	119,222.0	126,098.0	828.1	P/B Ratio	2.7	52 Wk Hi-Low	8,600.0-5,920.0
Book Value	658,040.0	847,848.0	924,622.0	6,071.9	Yield %	2.4	Market Cap	US$16,561mil

Address	Paseo de la Castellana 278	Tel 1-348-81-00	ADR	REP	V Chairman	E. De Ybarra Y. Churruca
	28046 Madrid	Fax 1-314-28-21	SEDOL	4733227	Chairman	A. Cortina De Alcocer

In EuroStoxx 50.

Tabacalera

DJGI Industry: **Tobacco**
Stoxx Sector: **Consumer Non-Cyclical**

Tabacalera SA, a state-controlled tobacco company, produces and markets tobacco products and manages food and postage-stamp-distribution businesses. Through its partially owned CETARSA and Compañía de Filipinas subsidiaries, Tabacalera imports and sells tobacco from the United States, Cuba, the Philippines, and Indonesia. In August 1997, the company became the majority shareholder in property developer Inmobiliaria Zabalburu. A privatization of the government's remaining 52% stake in Tabacalera was expected in the first quarter of 1998.

	ptas mil 12/95	12/96	12/97	US$mil 12/97				
Sales	401,327.0	399,801.0	451,146.0	2,962.6	P/E Ratio	40.0	Price (6/30/98)	3,140.00
Net Income	14,031.0	11,727.0	17,340.0	113.9	P/B Ratio	4.7	52 Wk Hi-Low	3,900.0-1,520.0
Book Value	98,132.0	113,040.0	122,988.0	807.6	Yield %	1.6	Market Cap	US$3,776.9mil

Address	Calle del Barquillo 5	Tel 1-532-76-00	ADR	--	President	--
	28000 Madrid	Fax 1-522-75-86	SEDOL	5444012	Chairman	Cesar Alierta

Telefónica de España

DJGI Industry: **Telephone Utilities (All)**
Stoxx Sector: **Telecom**

Telefónica de España is Spain's partially privatized telecommunications company. It operates more than 13 million local telephone lines, 481,600 integrated business-communication lines, and nearly 43,000 public phone booths. Telefónica is building a digital mobile-communication network to which it already has more than 250,000 subscribers. South American subsidiaries include Telefónica de Argentina and Telefónos de Chile. It also owns 80% of Puerto Rico's long-distance service. Telefónica leads a consortium that controls 95% of Peru's telecommunications.

	ptas mil 12/95	12/96	12/97	US$mil 12/97				
Sales	1,740,557	2,006,058	2,363,102	15,518.1	P/E Ratio	35.1	Price (6/30/98)	7,090.00
Net Income	133,214.0	160,282.0	190,063.0	1,248.1	P/B Ratio	3.4	52 Wk Hi-Low	7,510.0-3,790.0
Book Value	1,546,472	1,863,760	1,991,005	13,074.6	Yield %	1.4	Market Cap	US$47,471mil

Address	Gen. Peron 38	Tel 1-231-76-34	ADR	TEF	V Chairman	J.M. Concejo Alvarez
	28020 Madrid	Fax --	SEDOL	4880822	Chairman	Juan Villalonga

In DJ Stoxx 50; In EuroStoxx 50.

Uralita

DJGI Industry: **Building Materials**
Stoxx Sector: **Construction**

Uralita SA is involved in the production of plastics, electrochemical and agrochemical products, fabricated cement products, ceramics, roof tiles, gypsum, and insulation materials. The group operates primarily in the Iberian Penninsula, where it is one of the leading producers of construction materials, but sales to nondomestic customers accounted for 28% of 1997 revenues. Also in 1997, chemicals accounted for 29% of revenues; tubes and plastic, 22%; insulating materials, 11%; tiles, 10%; plaster products, 8%; ceramic products and sanitary ware, 8%; and cement products, 7%.

	ptas mil 12/95	12/96	12/97	US$mil 12/97				
Sales	140,448.0	135,135.0	142,886.0	938.3	P/E Ratio	31.5	Price (6/30/98)	2,185.00
Net Income	6,021.0	2,201.0	3,807.0	25.0	P/B Ratio	2.1	52 Wk Hi-Low	2,225.0-1,430.0
Book Value	50,336.0	53,113.0	52,850.0	347.1	Yield %	1.6	Market Cap	US$725.1mil

Address	Mejía Lequerica 10	Tel 1-448-10-00	ADR	--	V Chmn & Mng Dir	E. Ruiz-Gálvez Priego
	28004 Madrid	Fax 1-447-11-26	SEDOL	4922155	Chairman	Juan A. García Díez

Valenciana de Cementos

DJGI Industry: **Building Materials**
Stoxx Sector: **Construction**

Compañía Valenciana de Cementos Portland SA is principally involved in the production and sale of cement and construction materials. It is also engaged in the production and sale of agricutural products and the acquisition and disposal of securities and investments. The company sells into the domestic market and exports to the United States, Africa, and the Middle East. During 1996, Valenciana de Cementos purchased the North American cement producer Cemex and also took a 67% stake in Corporación Venezolana de Cementos.

	ptas mil 12/95	12/96	12/97	US$mil 12/97					
Sales	107,165.2	118,797.9	279,264.5	1,833.9	P/E Ratio		16.4	Price (6/30/98)	3,910.00
Net Income	13,392.7	12,925.3	32,166.5	211.2	P/B Ratio		4.0	52 Wk Hi-Low	3,910.0-2,375.0
Book Value	75,642.4	96,149.7	132,224.6	868.3	Yield %		0.9	Market Cap	US$3,524.8mil

Address	Hernandex de Tejada 1	Tel 1-377-92-00	ADR	--	V Chairman	J. Domene Zambrano
	28027 Madrid	Fax 1-377-92-03	SEDOL	4923114	Chairman	L.H. Zambrano Trevino

Vallehermoso

DJGI Industry: **Real Estate**
Stoxx Sector: **Financial Services**

Vallehermoso SA is one of the largest real estate companies in Spain. It is engaged in various real estate activities, but primarily in the acquisition of property and subsequent construction work on the property. Construction is primarily contracted to third parties. It operates throughout Spain, notably around Madrid, in the provinces of Andalucia, Cataluna, Levante and in Bilbao, Santander and Zaragoza. The company also has operations in the international market. Sales of buildings accounted for 69% of 1997 revenues; rental income, 17%; property sales, 9%; and services rendered, 5%.

	ptas mil 12/95	12/96	12/97	US$mil 12/97					
Sales	40,148.0	44,136.0	42,981.0	282.2	P/E Ratio		42.1	Price (6/30/98)	5,640.00
Net Income	4,662.0	5,112.0	5,427.0	35.6	P/B Ratio		2.6	52 Wk Hi-Low	6,120.0-3,480.0
Book Value	86,146.0	88,937.0	91,989.0	604.1	Yield %		1.0	Market Cap	US$1,585.2mil

Address	Paseo de la Castellana 83-85	Tel 1-556-10-64	ADR	--	V Chairman	A. A. de la Cierva
	28046 Madrid	Fax 1-597-01-90	SEDOL	4926704	Chairman	M. Eyries

Sweden

http://www.dowjones.com/indexes/Htmls01/sweden.html

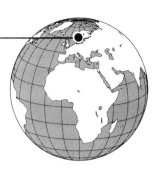

Exchanges:

Stockholm Stock Exchange

Sweden

Carolina Johansson
Stockholm

Faced with intensifying competition from international exchanges, the Stockholm Stock Exchange has been stepping up efforts to attract investors and partners as change sweeps the Nordic region's largest stock exchange.

At the start of 1998, the Exchange merged with the Swedish derivatives trading and clearing group OM Gruppen AB, paving the way for a gradual integration of stock and stock-derivatives trading. In 1997, it signed a cooperation pact with the Copenhagen Stock Exchange that will allow stock brokers to trade Danish and Swedish shares on the same screen.

The so-called NOREX alliance marks the first major step toward creating a stronger Nordic stock exchange structure, and the goal is to bring the Oslo and Helsinki exchanges into the fold too. By mid-1999, the first stock issues will be traded through the NOREX system. Initially, it will handle equity trades only, but plans call for adding bonds and derivatives later.

The launch of NOREX underlines the Stockholm Exchange's ambition to create a northern European financial center to rival those on the continent. Given the globalization of capital and the trend toward increased concentration in a few European financial centers, the Stockholm Exchange has realized that it must get bigger in order to stay competitive.

Although minor from a global perspective, Stockholm would be the natural leader in an eventual pan-Nordic alliance. In terms of market capitalization as well as turnover, it is larger than the Oslo, Copenhagen, and Helsinki exchanges combined.

On its own, Stockholm ranks as Europe's eighth largest exchange, with market capitalization at the end of June 1998 of 2,696 billion kronor, up 25% from 2,164 billion at the start of the year. The aggregate market capitalization of listed shares corresponded to 127% of gross national product, an unusually high share from a global perspective.

The 25% gain in stock prices in the first half of 1998 came after a 24% increase in 1997 and a 38% gain in 1996. The benchmark Stock Exchange General Index stood at 3671.6 on June 30, 1998.

The strong market performance reflects growing corporate profits, favorable capital

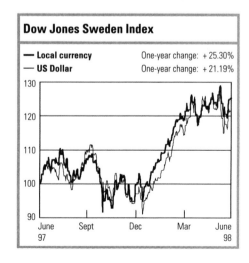

Dow Jones Sweden Index

— Local currency   One-year change: + 25.30%
— US Dollar   One-year change: + 21.19%

flows, and improving macro-economic trends. As inflation fell to around 1% over the past three years, yields on interest-rate instruments dropped to historic lows, causing investors to seek higher returns in the stock market.

At the same time, the government has carried out substantial cutbacks in the traditionally generous Swedish welfare system, spurring fears the system won't be able to fully support future generations. This has increased the need for personal savings, and the past year has seen a boom in pension-fund and mutual-fund investments, resulting in a steady flow of fresh cash to the market.

That trend is expected to continue and even accelerate in the years ahead as pension reform is introduced in 1999, requiring a mandatory amount to be placed in a premium reserve and invested in mutual funds. This will result in an additional flow of capital into the market, estimated at around SEK16 billion annually, a sizable amount considering that the total sum raised through new listings and issues in 1997 totaled SEK17 billion.

Foreign interest in Swedish stocks also has underpinned prices. At the end of 1997, foreign investors owned about 32% of the total market capitalization, and on any given day, about 30% of transactions involve a foreign investor. The main inflow of foreign capital has been from the United States, followed by the United Kingdom.

Other large owners are financial companies, including investment companies and insurers,

Country Information

Trading Hours:

Local: 10:00 am - 5:00 pm

EST: 4:00 am - 11:00 am

GMT: 0900 - 1600

Population (6/98):
8,886,738

Unemployment (97):
8.4%

Main Industries:
Iron and steel, precision equipment (bearings, radio and telephone parts, armaments), wood pulp and paper products, processed foods, and automobiles

Gross Domestic Product (97):
US$227.75 billion

GDP per Capita (97):
US$25,737.53

Three-Year Average GDP Growth (94-97):
2.0%

Average Annual CPI Growth (96-97):
+ 0.51%

Monetary Unit:
Swedish Krona

Exchange Rate (6/98):
SEK7.98 to US$1.00

which own 21% of the market, whereas domestic households own 15%. Domestic stock funds control about 9.5%. State ownership has declined in recent years, but the state still controls about 7.6% of total market capitalization.

New companies are flocking to list on the Exchange. In 1997, a record 54 new companies were listed. Another 11 companies were added in the first half of 1998, bringing the total number of listed companies to 267 by mid-1998.

Despite the influx of new companies, daily trading is still concentrated on a handful of blue-chips. Telecommunications group AB LM Ericsson and pharmaceutical giant Astra AB together represent about 25% of market capitalization, and a dive or rally in one or both of the shares can easily depress or lift the entire market.

In 1997, the two companies accounted for 28% of total trading on the Exchange. The 10 most traded issues accounted for almost two-thirds of the trading volume.

Ericsson and Astra belong to the two largest sectors on the Exchange, engineering and pharmaceuticals. Other large sectors are banks and insurers and the traditional Swedish forestry sector.

Stocks are listed on the Exchange's main A list, or quoted on the OTC (over-the-counter) list or the unofficial O list. The main A list is intended for companies with proven records

Ten Largest Capitalized Companies In The Dow Jones Sweden Index
as of 6/30/98

Stock	Market Cap. US$ Thousands
Ericsson	57,128,549
Astra	33,422,983
ABB	13,217,920
Volvo	13,049,215
Hennes & Mauritz	11,649,806
Investor	11,103,630
ForeningsSparbanken	10,586,085
Svenska Handelsbanken	10,048,439
Skandinaviska Enskilda Banken	9,625,744
Nordbanken Holding	9,333,708

of liquidity in their shares and diversified ownership structures. The OTC list is for smaller companies, and the O list is considered a testing ground, or waiting list, for the main list.

Early in 1998, the Exchange launched the New Market, for trading small company stocks through its automated SAX trading system. The New Market is a direct competitor to the SBI list, an independent market for small company stocks set up in the early 1990s, when the stock exchange lost its monopoly on share trading. About 60 companies, many active in the information-technology sector, are traded on the SBI list.

All stock prices are currently quoted in Swedish kronor, the domestic currency, but once Europe's single currency, the euro, is launched in 1999, the Exchange is likely to list at least the major stocks also in euros. Although Sweden is one of the four European Union countries that won't adopt the euro from the start, the Exchange believes that euro listings will be necessary to prevent stock trading from moving abroad.

Only bourse members are allowed to execute trades via the SAX trading system, and there are currently 48 members, of which 15 are so called remote members, meaning that they are linked to the Exchange and trade electronically but don't have an office in Sweden. Recent years have also seen a rapid growth in discount brokers, many of whom utilize the Internet, and the increased competition has resulted in a drastic drop in fees and commissions.

Trading and registration are fully electronic. Floor trading was abolished in 1990 and computers now match buyers with sellers. As of 1993, the rolling settlement period is set at three banking days.

Sweden has a wide range of stock indexes, including the stock exchange's general index with its various subsector indexes. The index most often quoted by traders is the OMX index, which encompasses 30 large shares.

When trading in Stockholm, foreigners can opt to register their stock holdings through a nominee account, rather than using a direct share account. Foreigners are not affected by domestic tax regulations and don't pay capital gains tax in Sweden. They are, however, subject to withholding tax on dividends, but are normally not taxed more than they would be in their own countries. For Swedish investors, the capital gains tax as well as the dividend tax is 30%.

**Market Sector Performance
In The Dow Jones Sweden Index**
1 Year Change Through 6/30/98

Market Sector	Change % (US$)
Financial	53.90
Technology	43.92
Consumer, Cyclical	27.46
Consumer, Non-Cyclical	10.05
Utilities	7.35
Industrial	-1.34
Basic Materials	-4.46

Trading on the Exchange starts at 10 a.m. local time and ends at 5 p.m. The trading session was extended by one hour in 1996 in order to have more overlap with the U.S. market.

ABB

DJGI Industry: **Electrical Components & Equipment**
Stoxx Sector: **Industrials**

ABB AB is a holding company that owns 50% of the Zurich-based power and industrial company ABB Asea Brown Boveri Ltd.; this is ABB's only principal asset. Swiss holding company BBC Brown Boveri owns the other 50% of ABB Asea. ABB is the world's largest electrical engineering group; it is composed of more than 1,300 companies operating in 140 countries. The company serves customers through electrical power generation, power distribution and control, industrial and building systems, automation products, financial services, and rail transportation.

	SEK mil 12/95	12/96	12/97	US$mil 12/97				
Sales	N/A	N/A	N/A	N/A	P/E Ratio M	48.7	Price (6/30/98) M	113.00
Net Income	4,682.2	4,144.0	2,174.0	273.9	P/B Ratio M	5.0	52 Wk Hi-Low M	131.00-82.00
Book Value	17,655.0	20,413.0	21,053.0	2,652.4	Yield % M	1.9	Market Cap M	US$9,465.0mil

Address	Box 7373, Hamngatan 2	Tel 8-613-65-60	ADR	ABBBY	President	C. Dahlback
	103 91 Stockholm	Fax 8-613-65-65	SEDOL	5212758	Chairman	B. Svedberg

M=Multiple issues in index; reflects most active.

AGA

DJGI Industry: **Chemicals - Specialty**
Stoxx Sector: **Chemical**

AGA AB is one of the world's largest gas companies. It manufactures and markets gases and services to industrial, medical, and specialty gas markets in some 40 countries in Europe, South America, and North America. The company's main products include oxygen, medical, nitrogen, and argon. The fuel gases acetylene and propane, as well as hydrogen and carbon dioxide, are other important products. AGA sells air gases via pipes and in cylinder form to hospitals and to steel, chemical, and engineering companies. In March 1998, AGA sold its California gas operations for $30 million.

	SEK mil 12/95	12/96	12/97	US$mil 12/97				
Sales	13,271.0	12,860.0	14,408.0	1,815.2	P/E Ratio M	25.0	Price (6/30/98) M	125.00
Net Income	2,110.0	2,840.0	1,099.0	138.5	P/B Ratio M	2.5	52 Wk Hi-Low M	132.00-97.00
Book Value	9,398.0	11,755.0	12,275.0	1,546.5	Yield % M	2.4	Market Cap M	US$2,037.7mil

Address	AGA AB	Tel 8-731-10-00	ADR	AGAXY	V Chairman	T. Hedelius
	181 81 Lidingo	Fax 8-767-63-44	SEDOL	4034618	Chairman	Sven Ågrup

M=Multiple issues in index; reflects most active.

AssiDomaen

DJGI Industry: **Paper Products**
Stoxx Sector: **Basic Resources**

AssiDomaen AB is one of Europe's leading forest products companies specializing in packaging paper, packaging, and sawn timber. The company produces unbleached and white-top kraftliner, bleached and unbleached sack, market pulp, plastic-coated paper, cartonboard, and related products in Sweden, Belgium, Denmark, France, Italy, the Netherlands, Switzerland, the United Kingdom, and Germany. Packaging accounted for 42% of 1997 revenues; kraft products, 25%; forestry operations and timber, 18%; plastic-coated paper and cartonboard, 8%; and carton, 7%.

	SEK mil 12/95	12/96	12/97	US$mil 12/97				
Sales	21,016.0	18,548.0	20,725.0	2,611.1	P/E Ratio	32.9	Price (6/30/98)	232.00
Net Income	3,418.0	1,407.0	772.0	97.3	P/B Ratio	1.8	52 Wk Hi-Low	259.00-188.00
Book Value	14,707.0	15,499.0	15,623.0	1,968.3	Yield %	2.4	Market Cap	US$3,442.5mil

Address	Pipers Vag 2, Bergshamra	Tel 8-655-9000	ADR	--	President & CEO	L. Ahlgren
	105 22 Stockholm	Fax 8-655-9401	SEDOL	4051576	Chairman	O. Lund

Astra

DJGI Industry: **Pharmaceuticals**
Stoxx Sector: **Pharmaceutical**

Astra AB, the largest pharmaceuticals company in the Nordic region, manufactures and markets local anesthetics, anti-infective medicines, and medicines for the treatment of intestinal, respiratory, and cardiovascular diseases. Antipeptic ulcer drug Losec, Astra's largest-selling product, and anti-inflammatory inhalation drug Pulmicort are two of the company's brand-name products. In 1994, Astra purchased half of a joint venture with U.S.-based pharmaceuticals group Merck. Pharmaceuticals accounted for 99% of 1997 revenues and medical devices accounted for 1%.

	SEK mil 12/95	12/96	12/97	US$mil 12/97				
Sales	35,800.0	38,988.0	44,904.0	5,657.3	P/E Ratio M	25.5	Price (6/30/98) M	163.00
Net Income	8,764.0	9,449.0	10,201.0	1,285.2	P/B Ratio M	5.8	52 Wk Hi-Low M	173.00-116.50
Book Value	30,679.0	38,279.0	46,015.0	5,797.2	Yield % M	1.1	Market Cap M	US$27,328mil

Address	Astra AB	Tel 8-553-260-00	ADR	AAB	V Chairman	M. Wallenberg
	151 85 Sodertalje	Fax 8-553-290-00	SEDOL	5241503	Chairman	Bo Berggren

M=Multiple issues in index; reflects most active; In DJ Stoxx 50.

Atlas Copco

DJGI Industry: **Industrial - Diversified**
Stoxx Sector: **Industrials**

Atlas Copco AB is an international industrial group that manufactures tools for construction, mining, and compressor- and industrial-technology applications. The company supplies compressors for the manufacture of industrial gases to customers such as French gas producer L'Air Liquide and Danish gas concern Hede Nielsen. Its subsidiaries include U.K. electric-power-tool manufacturer Kango and U.S.-based Robbins, a manufacturer of tunnel-boring machines. The company manufactures products at 58 plants in 14 countries.

	SEK mil 12/95	12/96	12/97	US$mil 12/97				
Sales	24,454.0	25,121.0	30,032.0	3,783.6	P/E Ratio M	17.1	Price (6/30/98) M	217.50
Net Income	1,823.0	1,938.0	2,208.0	278.2	P/B Ratio M	3.0	52 Wk Hi-Low M	265.00-197.50
Book Value	10,474.0	11,851.0	13,453.0	1,694.9	Yield % M	2.0	Market Cap M	US$3,339.8mil

Address	Sicka Industrivag 3	Tel 8-743-8000	ADR	ATLPY	V Chairman	T. Wachtmeister
	105 23 Stockholm	Fax 8-644-9045	SEDOL	4050971	Chairman	A. Scharp

M=Multiple issues in index; reflects most active.

Autoliv

DJGI Industry: **Other Auto Parts**
Stoxx Sector: **Automobile**

Autoliv Inc. is one of the world's leading groups in the production of seat belts, air bags, side impact protection, steering wheels, seat components, and other equipment for passenger safety in automobiles. The company has more than 50 wholly and partly owned units, 17,800 employees, and manufacturing processes in 25 countries. Its customers are the world's auto manufacturing industries. In 1996, Autoliv and U.S.-based Morton International Inc.'s Automotive Safety Products unit merged to form the world's largest automotive safety equipment company.

	$ mil 12/95	12/96	12/97	US$mil 12/97				
Sales	2,739.6	1,734.5	1,432.4	1,432.4	P/E Ratio	NMF	Price (6/30/98)	255.00
Net Income	91.1	113.3	-579.6	-579.6	P/B Ratio	1.9	52 Wk Hi-Low	342.50-231.00
Book Value	N/A	458.5	1,704.0	1,704.0	Yield %	1.0	Market Cap	US$2,336.6mil
Address	Klarabergsviadukt 70		Tel 8-402-06-00		ADR	AUABY	President & CEO	G. Bark
	107 24 Stockholm		Fax 8-244-479		SEDOL	5247374	Chairman	P. Oswald

Avesta Sheffield

DJGI Industry: **Steel**
Stoxx Sector: **Basic Resources**

Avesta Sheffield AB is a world leader in the production and marketing of stainless steel products, including sheet, plate, strip, tube, and fittings. Cold-rolled steel plate accounted for 51% of fiscal 1998 revenues; hot-rolled steel plate, 15%; long steel products, 13%; tubes and pipes, 11%; fittings, 6%; and other operations, 8%. Customers include pulp, paper, offshore, chemicals, energy, construction, food, catering, and transportation industries. The company's main production facilities are located in Sweden, the United Kingdom, and North America.

	SEK mil 03/96	03/97	03/98	US$mil 03/98				
Sales	22,116.0	17,204.0	18,699.0	2,335.6	P/E Ratio	NMF	Price (6/30/98)	39.50
Net Income	2,614.4	-13.0	-33.0	-4.1	P/B Ratio	0.8	52 Wk Hi-Low	93.50-39.50
Book Value	8,513.0	8,348.0	8,305.0	1,037.3	Yield %	2.5	Market Cap	US$782.3mil
Address	Box 16377, Vasagatan 8-10		Tel 8-613-36-00		ADR	--	V Chairman	B. Magnusson
	103 27 Stockholm		Fax 8-208-481		SEDOL	4067283	Chairman	J. McDowall

Electrolux

DJGI Industry: **Other Home Furnishings**
Stoxx Sector: **Consumer Cyclical**

Electrolux AB is the world's largest producer of indoor and outdoor household appliances, owning such brands as AEG of Germany, Frigidaire of the United States, and Zanussi of Italy. The company also manufactures industrial, forestry, and garden products and is involved in the recycling of scrap iron. It operates in Europe, North America, South America, Asia, Africa, and Oceania. In April 1997, Electrolux divested its Husqvarna Sewing Machines unit. Household appliances accounted for 72% of 1997 revenues; outdoor products, 16%; commercial appliances, 10%; and other, 2%.

	SEK mil 12/95	12/96	12/97	US$mil 12/97				
Sales	115,800.0	110,000.0	113,000.0	14,236.4	P/E Ratio	83.5	Price (6/30/98)	137.00
Net Income	2,748.0	1,850.0	352.0	44.3	P/B Ratio	2.4	52 Wk Hi-Low	159.00-103.80
Book Value	21,304.0	22,428.0	20,565.0	2,590.9	Yield %	1.8	Market Cap	US$6,116.7mil
Address	Lilla Essingen		Tel 8-738-60-00		ADR	ELUXY	V Chairman	G. Bystedt
	105 45 Stockholm		Fax 8-656-44-78		SEDOL	5466782	Chairman	R. Andersson

Ericsson

DJGI Industry: **Communications Technology**
Stoxx Sector: **Technology**

Telefonaktiebolaget LM Ericsson is a leading supplier of equipment for telecommunications systems and related terminals worldwide. It manufactures advanced systems and products for wired and mobile telecommunications in public and private networksand is a global leader in mobile telephone systems. Its trademarks include AXE, ETNA, TMOS, Mobitex, EDACS, BusinessPhone, Consono, Eripax, Eripower, MiniLink, Giraffe, EriEye, and Arthur. Mobile telecommunications systems accounted for 43% of 1997 revenues; infocom systems, 29%; mobile phones and terminals, 25%; and other, 3%.

	SEK mil 12/95	12/96	12/97	US$mil 12/97				
Sales	98,780.0	124,266.0	167,740.0	21,132.9	P/E Ratio M	36.9	Price (6/30/98) M	233.00
Net Income	5,439.0	7,110.0	11,941.0	1,504.4	P/B Ratio M	8.6	52 Wk Hi-Low M	238.50-137.00
Book Value	34,263.0	40,456.0	52,624.0	6,629.9	Yield % M	0.8	Market Cap M	US$52,131mil
Address	Telefonplan		Tel 8-719-00-00		ADR	--	President	--
	126 25 Stockholm		Fax 8-719-19-76		SEDOL	4321558	Chairman	L. Ramqvist

M=Multiple issues in index; reflects most active; In DJ Stoxx 50.

ForeningsSparbanken

DJGI Industry: **Banks - Regional (All)**
Stoxx Sector: **Bank**

ForeningsSparbanken AB, formerly Sparbanken Sverige AB, provides savings, loans, and payment services to private individuals, businesses, the agricultural sector, municipalities, nationwide organizations, and county councils in Sweden. It cooperates with about 90 independent savings banks and partly-owned banks. Together, they have the country's largest distribution network for financial services with a total of 1077 branches in 1997. The bank also provides commercial and investment banking, securities brokerage, mortgage financing, and other financial services.

	SEK mil 12/95	12/96	12/97	US$mil 12/97				
Revenues	54,844.0	49,087.0	53,708.0	6,766.4	P/E Ratio	NMF	Price (6/30/98)	240.00
Net Income	3,312.0	3,872.0	342.0	43.1	P/B Ratio	3.1	52 Wk Hi-Low	287.00-166.50
Book Value	20,306.0	20,049.0	27,377.0	3,449.1	Yield %	2.5	Market Cap	US$10,586mil
Address	Brunkebergstorg 8		Tel 8-585-91-00-0		ADR	FGSKY	First V Chmn	B. Dockered
	105 34 Stockholm		Fax 8-796-80-92		SEDOL	4846523	Chairman	G. Collert

Gambro

DJGI Industry: **Advanced Medical Devices**
Stoxx Sector: **Technology**

Gambro AB, formerly known as Incentive AB, began extensive restructuring in 1991. Incentive was an industrial holding company with over 20 subsidiaries and 50-60 different operations. Since completing its transformation, the group changed its name and is now consolidated to a single areaómedical-technology. Gambro provides healthcare products and services for dialysis products, renal care sercices, cardiovascular-surgery products, and blood-component technology. The company has 90 subsidiaries in 26 countries in Europe, Asia, and North and South America.

	SEK mil 12/95	12/96	12/97	US$mil 12/97				
Sales	24,324.0	20,220.0	19,383.0	2,442.0	P/E Ratio	4.3	Price (6/30/98)	145.00
Net Income	2,431.0	2,884.0	11,520.0	1,451.4	P/B Ratio	2.0	52 Wk Hi-Low	161.00-127.00
Book Value	12,246.0	14,581.0	25,385.0	3,198.2	Yield %	1.4	Market Cap	US$4,554.5mil

Address	Hamngatan 2	Tel 8-613-65-00	ADR	--	President & CEO	Mikael Lilius
	103 91 Stockholm	Fax 8-611-28-30	SEDOL	5450031	Chairman	Anders Scharp

Hennes & Mauritz

DJGI Industry: **Retailers - Apparel**
Stoxx Sector: **Retail**

Hennes & Mauritz AB is one of Sweden's largest retail companies. It is involved in the retail and mail-order sale of women's, men's, and children's clothing, fashion accessories, and cosmetics. The company operates 117 stores in Sweden and 374 outside Sweden in Norway, Denmark, Germany, and other European countries, including the United Kingdom. During fiscal 1997, the company opened 56 new stores, the majority of which were in Finland and France. Hennes & Mauritz planspen 75 new stores around Europe in fiscal 1998.

	SEK mil 11/95	11/96	11/97	US$mil 11/97				
Revenues	12,350.3	14,552.8	18,010.9	2,332.1	P/E Ratio	62.3	Price (6/30/98)	509.00
Net Income	973.1	1,331.0	1,690.9	218.9	P/B Ratio	16.3	52 Wk Hi-Low	510.00-272.00
Book Value	4,256.2	5,154.8	6,473.4	838.2	Yield %	0.6	Market Cap	US$11,650mil

Address	Box 1421, Norrlandsgatan	Tel 8-796-55-00	ADR	--	President & CEO	F. Mansson
	111 84 Stockholm	Fax 8-209-919	SEDOL	5195224	Chairman	S. Persson

Investor

DJGI Industry: **Conglomerates**
Stoxx Sector: **Conglomerate**

Investor AB is a large Swedish industrial holding company with a portfolio concentrated in the engineering, pharmaceutical, telecommunications, banking, finance, forest products, media, and service industries. The company owns Saab and 50% of Saab Automobile. In addition to long- and medium-term investments, Investor has an active trading business in stocks, options, currencies, and interest-bearing instruments. Operations also include the development, manufacturing, and marketing of military and commercial aircraft. Investor is based in Stockholm.

	SEK mil 12/95	12/96	12/97	US$mil 12/97				
Sales	43,282.0	13,961.0	20,298.0	2,557.3	P/E Ratio M	22.8	Price (6/30/98) M	465.50
Net Income	3,008.0	9,479.0	3,511.0	442.3	P/B Ratio M	2.3	52 Wk Hi-Low M	466.00-343.00
Book Value	19,753.0	27,855.0	38,017.0	4,789.6	Yield % M	2.1	Market Cap M	US$6,590.8mil

Address	Arsenalsgatan 8C	Tel 8-614-20-00	ADR	--	Jnt V. Chmn	B. Berggren
	103 32 Stockholm	Fax 8-614-21-50	SEDOL	4469630	Chairman	P. Barnevik

M=Multiple issues in index; reflects most active.

Mo Och Domsjo

DJGI Industry: **Forest Products**
Stoxx Sector: **Basic Resources**

Mo Och Domsjo AB is an international company that produces and markets forest-related products, including paper, paperboard, pulp, sacks, and sawn timber. Other operations include wood procurement and management and the wholesale distribution of paper. The company has operations in Sweden, France, the United Kingdom, the Netherlands, Norway, Russia, Belgium, and several other countries. Its products are included under the brand names MoDo Paper, Iggesund Paperboard, MoDo Merchants, Iggesund Timber, and MoDo Skog.

	SEK mil 12/95	12/96	12/97	US$mil 12/97				
Sales	22,319.0	20,115.0	21,878.0	2,756.3	P/E Ratio	12.2	Price (6/30/98)	228.00
Net Income	3,671.0	1,979.0	1,434.0	180.7	P/B Ratio	1.2	52 Wk Hi-Low	298.00-196.00
Book Value	14,471.0	15,670.0	16,375.0	2,063.0	Yield %	3.9	Market Cap	US$1,893.0mil

Address	Box 5407, Strardvagen 1	Tel 8-666-21-00	ADR	--	V Chairman	C. Kempe
	114 84 Stockholm	Fax 8-666-21-35	SEDOL	5036066	Chairman	F. Lundberg

Nordbanken

DJGI Industry: **Banks - Regional (All)**
Stoxx Sector: **Bank**

Nordbanken AB is one of Sweden's largest banks, with a branch network of 360 offices. The bank offers a broad range of banking and financial services to private individuals, small and medium-sized companies, the public sector, and a selection of major Swedish companies. Almost all of its assets and operating income are derived from business in Sweden. In October 1997, Nordbanken announced a proposed merger with Finnish bank group Merita Oy. The new bank, to be called MeritaNordbanken, would be one of the leading financial companies in the Nordic and Baltic region.

	SEK mil 12/95	12/96	12/97	US$mil 12/97				
Revenues	32,826.0	32,580.0	29,616.0	3,731.2	P/E Ratio	13.1	Price (6/30/98)	58.50
Net Income	5,137.0	5,375.0	4,862.0	612.5	P/B Ratio	3.5	52 Wk Hi-Low	61.50-31.43
Book Value	18,643.0	17,409.0	21,530.0	2,712.5	Yield %	2.6	Market Cap	US$9,333.7mil

Address	Smalandsgatan 17	Tel 8-614-70-00	ADR	NBKBY	President & CEO	V. Vainio
	105 71 Stockholm	Fax 8-200-846	SEDOL	5380031	Chairman	J. Palmstierna

Perstorp

DJGI Industry: **Chemicals - Specialty**
Stoxx Sector: **Chemical**

Perstorp AB is a chemical company that produces surfacing materials, acoustics, plastics, specialty chemicals, and biotechnology. The company's surfacing materials include laminate flooring, decorative laminate, and foils, all of which it supplies to the construction industry. It provides noise-control and acoustic-related components for the automotive industry. It also makes instruments used to analyze food and animal feed, and it supplies systems that handle plastics for the materials- and waste-handling industries. Perstorp operates in 17 countries in Europe, Asia and the Americas.

	SEK mil 08/95	08/96	08/97	US$mil 08/97				
Sales	13,004.0	12,690.0	11,357.0	1,440.3	P/E Ratio	23.7	Price (6/30/98)	149.00
Net Income	500.0	449.0	321.0	40.7	P/B Ratio	2.6	52 Wk Hi-Low	174.00-125.00
Book Value	3,603.0	3,722.0	4,045.0	513.0	Yield %	1.8	Market Cap	US$1,177.3mil

Address	Perstorp AB	Tel 435-380-00	ADR	--	V Chairman	C.H. Wendt
	284 80 Perstorp	Fax 435-381-00	SEDOL	4682459	Chairman	G. Wiking

Sandvik

DJGI Industry: **Industrial - Diversified**
Stoxx Sector: **Industrials**

Sandvik AB is a manufacturer of rock-drilling tools, metalworking tools, and engineering components. It is also a leading manufacturer of tube, strip, wire, and bar in stainless and high-alloy steels. Its metalworking-tools division produces tools as well as systems, equipment, and software used to automate steelworking processes. The rock-drilling segment serves the mining and civil engineering industries. Its engineering components division makes production lines for specialized tasks such as parcel sorting. Over 90% of sales are made outside Sweden.

	SEK mil 12/95	12/96	12/97	US$mil 12/97				
Sales	29,700.0	28,265.0	34,119.0	4,298.5	P/E Ratio M	20.6	Price (6/30/98) M	220.50
Net Income	3,727.0	3,114.0	2,725.0	343.3	P/B Ratio M	3.3	52 Wk Hi-Low M	272.00-196.50
Book Value	18,503.0	20,035.0	17,414.0	2,193.9	Yield % M	3.2	Market Cap M	US$5,236.5mil

Address	Storgatana 2	Tel 26-26-00-00	ADR	SAVKY	President & CEO	Clas Åke Hedström
	811 81 Sandviken	Fax 26-26-10-22	SEDOL	4784883	Chairman	Percy Barnevik

M=Multiple issues in index; reflects most active.

SCA

DJGI Industry: **Paper Products**
Stoxx Sector: **Basic Resources**

Svenska Cellulosa AB (SCA) is Sweden's second-largest forestry and packaging group. The company operates through four main divisions: SCA Hygiene Products, which generated 42% of SCA's 1996 revenues, produces toiletries, tissue, and clinical products; SCA Packaging makes corrugated board and container board; SCA Graphic Paper manufactures printing paper, fine paper, and pulp; and SCA Forest Timber transports wood and provides sawn timber. The company owns 1.8 million hectares of forest land and conducts extensive sawmill operations. Europe is its primary market.

	SEK mil 12/95	12/96	12/97	US$mil 12/97				
Sales	65,317.0	55,239.0	58,595.0	7,382.1	P/E Ratio	12.2	Price (6/30/98)	206.50
Net Income	3,464.0	2,117.0	2,759.0	347.6	P/B Ratio	1.7	52 Wk Hi-Low	238.50-158.50
Book Value	22,024.0	22,906.0	24,653.0	3,105.9	Yield %	2.8	Market Cap	US$3,501.1mil

Address	Stureplan 3	Tel 8-788-51-00	ADR	--	President & CEO	Sverker Martin-Löf
	103 97 Stockholm	Fax 8-660-74-30	SEDOL	4865379	Chairman	Bo Rydin

Scania

DJGI Industry: **Land Transportation**
Stoxx Sector: **Industrials**

Scania AB is one of the world's largest heavy-truck manufacturers. It focuses on the development, production, and marketing of heavy trucks and buses; the manufacturing of industrial and marine engines; and operation of an extensive after-sales and service network. It has production plants in seven countries and operations in more than 100 countries. In 1997, Scandia acquired Truck AG and dealerships in Great Britain, Germany and France. Trucks accounted for 60% of 1997 revenues; service related products, 14%; Svenska Volkswagen products, 12%; buses, 8%; and other 6%.

	SEK mil 12/95	12/96	12/97	US$mil 12/97				
Sales	35,528.0	34,428.0	39,719.0	5,004.0	P/E Ratio M	19.6	Price (6/30/98) M	194.00
Net Income	3,280.0	1,981.0	1,985.0	250.1	P/B Ratio M	3.8	52 Wk Hi-Low M	243.00-165.00
Book Value	8,096.0	8,981.0	10,236.0	1,289.6	Yield % M	2.8	Market Cap M	US$2,431.9mil

Address	Scania	Tel 8-553-81-000	ADR	SCVA	President	--
	151 87 Sodertalje	Fax 8-553-81-037	SEDOL	5038932	Chairman	A. Scharp

M=Multiple issues in index; reflects most active.

S-E Banken

DJGI Industry: **Banks - Regional (All)**
Stoxx Sector: **Bank**

S-E Banken AB (Skandinaviska-Enskilda Banken) provides a full range of banking services to its customers and is one of Scandinavia's largest banks. It offers retail, corporate, and investment banking, securities trading and management, insurance, real estate, leasing, factoring, and other financial services in Scandinavia, the rest of Europe, the United States, and Asia through 295 branches. Its Enskilda division provides services for large corporations, banks, and institutions. Its Diligentia division manages the bank's property portfolio. In 1997, it acquired insurance company Trygg-Hansa.

	SEK mil 12/95	12/96	12/97	US$mil 12/97				
Revenues	40,357.0	40,132.0	38,015.0	4,789.4	P/E Ratio	20.8	Price (6/30/98)	136.50
Net Income	2,531.0	4,696.0	2,437.0	307.0	P/B Ratio	2.9	52 Wk Hi-Low	144.00-79.50
Book Value	24,569.0	21,300.0	27,967.0	3,523.4	Yield %	2.2	Market Cap	US$9,625.7mil

Address	Kungsträdgårdsgatan 8	Tel 8-763-80-00	ADR	--	V Chairman	C. Dahlback
	106 40 Stockholm	Fax 8-221-900	SEDOL	4813345	Chairman	J. Wallenberg

Securitas

DJGI Industry: **Other Industrial & Commercial Services**
Stoxx Sector: **Industrials**

Securitas AB is Europe's largest security company. It provides guard services, alarm systems, cash-in-transit services, static guarding, mobile patrol services, and cash processing services and installs and services technical security systems. The company operates in 14 European countries and in the United States. Securitas bought the Estonian secure transport company Inkassaator AS and in 1998, acquired the French Kessler group. Guard services accounted for 59% of 1997 revenues; cash-in-transit services, 23%; alarm systems, 15%; and other, 3%.

	SEK mil 12/95	12/96	12/97	US$mil 12/97				
Sales	7,309.1	9,074.3	10,762.9	1,356.0	P/E Ratio	61.6	Price (6/30/98)	390.50
Net Income	347.0	382.1	445.9	56.2	P/B Ratio	12.1	52 Wk Hi-Low	390.50-174.00
Book Value	1,767.8	2,032.6	2,365.1	298.0	Yield %	0.7	Market Cap	US$3,371.1mil

Address	Box 12307, Lindhagenspian 70	Tel 8-657-74-40	ADR	--	V Chairman	G. Douglas
	102 28 Stockholm	Fax 8-657-70-72	SEDOL	5077883	Chairman	M. Shorling

Skandia

DJGI Industry: **Insurance - Full Line**
Stoxx Sector: **Insurance**

Forsakrings AB Skandia (Skandia Insurance Co. Ltd.) is the Nordic area's largest insurance and financial-services company. Skandia offers pensions, reinsurance, and investment-management services. Its Skandia Norden subsidiary offers life, health, marine, motor, and aviation insurance to individual and commercial customers. Its Skandia International division provides life and general insurance throughout Scandinavia, Europe, and the United States. Its SkandiaBanken subsidiary offers a full range of banking services to its Swedish customers.

	SEK mil 12/95	12/96	12/97	US$mil 12/97				
Revenues	60,992.0	69,852.0	93,312.0	11,756.0	P/E Ratio	17.3	Price (6/30/98)	114.00
Net Income	505.0	1,140.0	3,402.0	428.6	P/B Ratio	3.8	52 Wk Hi-Low	124.50-57.00
Book Value	8,074.0	10,917.0	15,221.0	1,917.6	Yield %	0.7	Market Cap	US$7,313.4mil

Address	Sveavägen 44	Tel 8-788-10-00	ADR	--	V Chairman	B. Braun
	103 50 Stockholm	Fax 8-788-30-80	SEDOL	5461572	Chairman	Sven Söderberg

Skanska

DJGI Industry: **Heavy Construction**
Stoxx Sector: **Construction**

Skanska AB is a construction and real estate company, the largest in the Nordic region. It builds houses, commercial and industrial buildings, roads, railroads, and bridges. The company also supplies products such as prefabricated concrete, steel frames, roofs, and steel and glass doors and windows to the construction industry. The company has operations in 51 countries, including real estate interests in the United Kingdom, the United States, and Germany. Construction accounted for 74% of 1997 revenues; building and installation products and systems, 15%; and real estate operations, 11%.

	SEK mil 12/95	12/96	12/97	US$mil 12/97				
Sales	38,608.0	47,872.0	54,847.0	6,909.9	P/E Ratio	17.4	Price (6/30/98)	358.00
Net Income	1,729.0	4,074.0	7,505.0	945.5	P/B Ratio	2.4	52 Wk Hi-Low	391.00-275.00
Book Value	10,704.0	14,651.0	16,918.0	2,131.4	Yield %	3.1	Market Cap	US$4,700.9mil

Address	Vendevagen 89	Tel 8-753-88-00	ADR	--	V Chairman	B. Rydin
	182 25 Danderyd	Fax 8-755-12-56	SEDOL	4813431	Chairman	M. Schorling

SKF

DJGI Industry: **Industrial - Diversified**
Stoxx Sector: **Industrials**

SKF AB is the world's largest rolling bearing manufacturer. The company specializes in the development, manufacture and marketing of ball and roller bearings, seals, hot-rolled and cold-finished steel products including bars, tubes, rolled rings, forged components, and couplings. Other operations include cutting tools, textile machinery components, aerospace equipment, fastening systems, linear motion equipment, precision gauges, and materials-handling products. SKF AB has factories, sales distribution subsidiaries, and affiliates around the world.

	SEK mil 12/95	12/96	12/97	US$mil 12/97				
Sales	36,700.0	33,589.0	36,922.0	4,651.6	P/E Ratio M	10.8	Price (6/30/98) M	145.00
Net Income	2,026.0	1,692.0	1,558.0	196.3	P/B Ratio M	1.3	52 Wk Hi-Low M	238.50-143.00
Book Value	10,273.0	11,310.0	12,588.0	1,585.9	Yield % M	3.6	Market Cap M	US$1,173.8mil

Address	Goteborg	Tel 31-337-10-00	ADR	--	President & CEO	P. Augustsson
	415 50 Goteborg	Fax 3-337-28-32	SEDOL	4767066	Chairman	A. Scharp

M=Multiple issues in index; reflects most active.

SSAB Svenskt Stal

DJGI Industry: **Steel**
Stoxx Sector: **Basic Resources**

SSAB Svenskt Stal AB is Scandinavia's leading manufacturer of flat products in the commercial steels area. Sheet products include hot- and cold-rolled as well as metal- and organic-coated sheet. The plate products include ordinary commercial steel, high-strength steel, and abrasion-resistant steel. Steel trading accounted for 26% of 1997 revenues; cold-rolled and metal-coated steel sheet, 19%; hot-rolled steel sheet, 18%; heavy steel plate, 16%; organic-coated and profiled steel sheet, 14%; crude steel and slabs, 3%; vehicle components, 2%; by-products and other, 2%.

	SEK mil 12/95	12/96	12/97	US$mil 12/97				
Sales	19,004.0	17,408.0	17,474.0	2,201.5	P/E Ratio	10.6	Price (6/30/98)	123.00
Net Income	2,732.0	1,481.0	1,336.0	168.3	P/B Ratio	1.2	52 Wk Hi-Low	172.00-119.00
Book Value	10,979.0	11,963.0	12,821.0	1,615.3	Yield %	3.7	Market Cap	US$1,441.1mil

Address	Box 26208, Birger Jarisgatan 58	Tel 8-454-57-00	ADR	--	V Chairman	C.E. Feinsilber
	100 40 Stockholm	Fax 8-454-57-25	SEDOL	4847195	Chairman	R. Andersson

Stora

DJGI Industry: **Paper Products**
Stoxx Sector: **Basic Resources**

Stora Kopparbergs Bergslags AB is a forestry company that produces newsprint, fine paper, board and packaging paper, pulp, and sawn timber products. The company also has interests in thermal, hydroelectric, and nuclear power stations. Stora markets its products in Europe and North America. Printing paper accounted for 27% of 1997 revenues; board and packaging paper, 17%; fine paper, 15%; forestry, 11%; wholesale operations, 11%; pulp, 9%; technical office paper, 4%; sawn timber products, 3%; and power, 3%.

	SEK mil 12/95	12/96	12/97	US$mil 12/97					
Sales	57,106.0	45,161.0	44,464.0	5,601.8	P/E Ratio		22.6	Price (6/30/98)	125.50
Net Income	5,367.0	1,560.0	1,582.0	199.3	P/B Ratio		1.4	52 Wk Hi-Low	148.00-92.00
Book Value	29,097.0	29,485.0	29,788.0	3,752.9	Yield %		3.0	Market Cap	US$4,118.6mil

Address	Åsgatan 22	Tel 23-78-00-00	ADR	--	V Chairman	J. Wallenberg
	791 80 Falun	Fax 23-138-58	SEDOL	4810584	Chairman	Bo Berggren

Svedala Industri

DJGI Industry: **Heavy Machinery**
Stoxx Sector: **Industrials**

Svedala Industri AB develops, manufactures, and markets equipment and systems for mineral processing and materials handling for the construction, mining, and minerals-processing industries and for large ports and terminals. The company also manufactures screens, noise-suppression and dust-encapsulation systems, and conveyor belts for the construction industry. It has operations in about 30 countries, with foreign operations accounting for roughly 90% of revenues.In April, 1998, the company acquired Eastern Engineering & Sales Corp., a company with yearly sales of SEK60 million.

	SEK mil 12/95	12/96	12/97	US$mil 12/97					
Sales	10,938.0	11,986.0	13,592.0	1,712.4	P/E Ratio		11.9	Price (6/30/98)	185.00
Net Income	502.0	552.0	676.0	85.2	P/B Ratio		2.3	52 Wk Hi-Low	199.00-120.00
Book Value	2,731.0	3,223.0	3,874.0	488.1	Yield %		2.7	Market Cap	US$1,113.4mil

Address	Box 4004	Tel 40-24-58-00	ADR	--	President & CEO	Thomas Oldér
	203 11 Malmö	Fax 40-24-58-78	SEDOL	4863016	Chairman	Rune Andersson

Swedish Commercial

DJGI Industry: **Banks - Regional (All)**
Stoxx Sector: **Bank**

Swedish Commercial Bank (Svenska Handelsbanken) AB, one of Sweden's largest commercial banks, provides commercial and investment banking, life assurance, pensions, real estate management, leasing, factoring, and other financial services in Scandinavia, the rest of Europe, the United States, Australia, Asia, and Russia. Its wholly owned Handelsbanken Hypotek subsidiary provides mortgages. The company has about 485 branches in Sweden, 30 elsewhere in Europe, several in the Far East, and 1 in the United States. Interest and fees on loans accounted for 67% of 1997 revenues.

	SEK mil 12/95	12/96	12/97	US$mil 12/97					
Revenues	41,613.0	46,974.0	63,690.0	8,024.0	P/E Ratio		13.7	Price (6/30/98)	370.00
Net Income	4,232.0	5,090.0	6,007.0	756.8	P/B Ratio		2.7	52 Wk Hi-Low	372.18-212.88
Book Value	25,744.0	27,335.0	32,140.0	4,049.2	Yield %		1.8	Market Cap	US$10,048mil

Address	Kungsträdgårdsgatan 2	Tel 8-701-10-00	ADR	--	Jnt V. Chmn	B. Rydin
	106 70 Stockholm	Fax --	SEDOL	4868635	Chairman	Tom Hedelius

Sydkraft

DJGI Industry: **Electrical Utilities (All)**
Stoxx Sector: **Utility**

Sydkraft AB is a leading Swedish power producer. It controls 2 nuclear power plants and 112 hydroelectric plants in Sweden, and most of its operations are concentrated in the southern part of the country. The company also distributes and markets energy gases, including natural gas, LPG, and biogas, and it provides district heating and trades in fuel. Additionally, it offers a broad and comprehensive range of consulting, contracting, and technical services in Sweden and Norway. Electricity accounted for 69% of 1997 revenues; heating, 12%; services, 11%; and gas, 8%.

	SEK mil 12/95	12/96	12/97	US$mil 12/97					
Sales	12,155.0	13,572.0	14,513.0	1,828.4	P/E Ratio M		21.8	Price (6/30/98) M	215.00
Net Income	1,760.0	1,818.0	3,463.0	436.3	P/B Ratio M		2.2	52 Wk Hi-Low M	262.00-180.00
Book Value	14,853.0	16,083.0	18,795.0	2,367.9	Yield % M		2.0	Market Cap M	US$2,994.5mil

Address	Carl Gustafs Väg 1	Tel 40-25-50-00	ADR	--	V Chairman	H-D. Harig
	205 09 Malmö	Fax 40-97-60-69	SEDOL	4869337	Chairman	Nils Ynguesson

M=Multiple issues in index; reflects most active.

Trelleborg

DJGI Industry: **Other Non-Ferrous Metals**
Stoxx Sector: **Basic Resources**

Trelleborg AB mines and processes copper, lead, zinc, nickel, silver, and gold and is also involved in the wholesale distribution of plumbing, heating, and electrical products and metals. It also produces rubber/metal anti-vibration products for machinery, engines, cars, trains, and heavy vehicles, brake components and other automotive components, industrial hoses, wheels for trucks and other vehicles, and rubber and bitumen-based sealing products. Trelleborg operates in Scandinavia, the rest of Europe, North America, and other countries.

	SEK mil 12/95	12/96	12/97	US$mil 12/97					
Sales	21,304.0	20,574.0	20,825.0	2,623.7	P/E Ratio		6.0	Price (6/30/98)	105.00
Net Income	2,863.0	1,003.0	2,038.0	256.8	P/B Ratio		1.1	52 Wk Hi-Low	135.00-93.50
Book Value	9,059.0	9,430.0	11,051.0	1,392.3	Yield %		3.3	Market Cap	US$1,386.5mil

Address	Box 153, Nygatan 102	Tel 410-670-00	ADR	--	President & CEO	L. Nilsson
	231 22 Trelleborg	Fax 410-427-63	SEDOL	4902384	Chairman	Rune Andersson

Volvo

DJGI Industry: **Automobile Manufacturers**
Stoxx Sector: **Automobile**

Volvo AB is one of the world's largest manufacturers of trucks, buses, and construction equipment, and it occupies a prominent position as a producer of passenger automobiles. The company also makes marine and aircraft engines. Most of the company's development activities are centered in Sweden, but assembly operations are carried on worldwide. Passenger cars accounted for 52% of 1997 revenues; trucks, 27%; construction equipment, 9%; buses, 6%; military and commercial aircraft engines, 4%; marine and industrial engines and other, 2%.

	SEK mil 12/95	12/96	12/97	US$mil 12/97				
Sales	171,511.0	156,060.0	183,625.0	23,134.1	P/E Ratio M	14.1	Price (6/30/98) M	237.50
Net Income	9,262.0	12,477.0	10,359.0	1,305.1	P/B Ratio M	1.7	52 Wk Hi-Low M	270.50-190.50
Book Value	51,200.0	57,876.0	60,431.0	7,613.5	Yield % M	2.1	Market Cap M	US$9,018.3mil

Address	**Torslandaverken**	Tel	**31-59-00-00**	ADR	**VOLVY**	President & CEO	**L. Johansson**
	405 08Goteborg	Fax	**31-54-49-82**	SEDOL	**4937739**	Chairman	**H. Frisinger**

M=Multiple issues in index; reflects most active.

Switzerland

http://www.dowjones.com/indexes/Html s01/switzerl.html

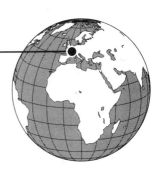

Exchanges:

Swiss Exchange SWX

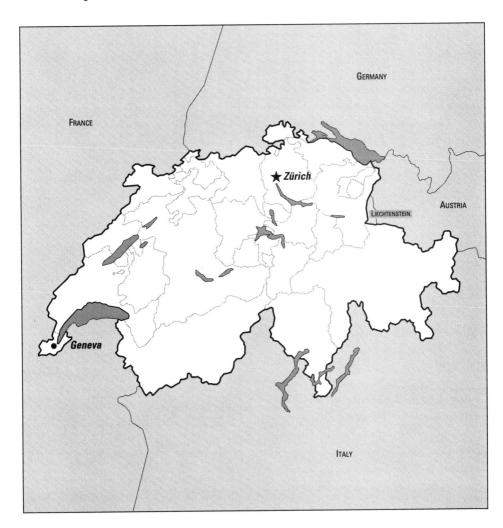

Switzerland

Anita Greil
Zurich

Mergers, new listings, and new ideas continued to push the Swiss stock market higher in 1998. New records were in sight as the Swiss bourse's main SMI index soared to 7822 by midyear, and 8489 on July 21, up 35% from the end of 1997.

The Swiss stock exchange ranks third in Europe, with only London and Frankfurt posting higher turnover. Considering it from a worldwide perspective, Switzerland's bourse comes in sixth.

Interest rates at a record low leave market participants with little alternative to investing in the stock market if they want to hold assets in Swiss francs. The dollar's strength and optimistic outlooks on corporate earnings also contributed to the market's upbeat mood.

A number of extraordinary events helped the financial sector to outperform the rest of the market.

On December 8, 1997, Union Bank of Switzerland and Swiss Bank Corp. announced their plans to merge, starting a wave of mega-bank mergers worldwide that have reshaped the global financial sector. The merger was completed at the end of June 1998.

Meanwhile, Zurich Group, a major Swiss insurance company, completed its merger with U.K.-based B.A.T. Industries' financial services business. The two businesses were combined to form a new company, Zurich Financial Services, headquartered in Zurich. The stock market boom has encouraged new

listings. By midyear 1998, 11 new companies were listed and another 7 were on the waiting list. In all of 1997, 12 companies joined the market.

The new listing catching the bulk of attention in 1998 has been Swisscom's IPO. The first government-owned company to go public, the IPO was scheduled for the third quarter of 1998.

Swisscom AG plans to offer up to a 49.9% stake, while the Swiss federal government will hold the majority of the telecommunications company's share capital. With revenue of around 10 billion Swiss francs and 20,000 employees, Swisscom is the nation's leading telecommunications company. Since January 1, 1998, Swisscom has been a limited company with a special legal status.

A total of 275 different shares are listed on the Swiss Exchange. Twenty-three are included in

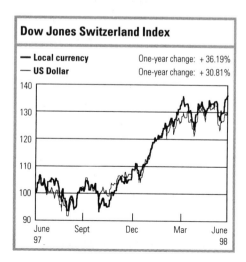

Dow Jones Switzerland Index

— **Local currency**   One-year change: + 36.19%
— **US Dollar**   One-year change: + 30.81%

the Swiss Market Index. The SMI acts as a benchmark for tracking highly capitalized, high-liquidity stocks. By midyear 1998, those 23 companies had a market value of 772.76 billion Swiss francs — around 75% of the market's total capitalization.

A wave of mergers and acquisitions in 1997 and 1998 caused substantial shifts in the market weight of SMI companies, but drugs and chemicals, banks, and insurance stock remained at the forefront. Investors have a varied choice of highly liquid and easily tradable shares in those sectors. By comparison, Nestlé is the only heavyweight in the food sector, representing 16% of SMI capitalization.

The new UBS AG surpassed rival Crédit Suisse Group in terms of market capitalization, making up 14% of the SMI. Credit Suisse itself made a substantial leap forward in market capitalization when it merged with insurer Winterthur, creating Switzerland's first banking and insurance giant. Crédit Suisse has a weighting of 11% on the SMI.

The insurance sector has no such giant on the index. Swiss Reinsurance continues to be the biggest of the four insurers on the SMI, with a weighting of just above 6%. Zurich Group (excluding B.A.T.) is next with a weighting just under 6%, but this should change once Zurich and B.A.T. are fully integrated.

Swiss Life ranks third in the sector with 1.75% of the SMI. In mid-1998, the

Country Information

Trading Hours:
  Local: 10:00 am - 4:30 pm

  EST: 4:00 am - 10:30 am

  GMT: 0900 - 1530

Population (6/98):
7,260,357

Unemployment (97):
4.5%

Main Industries:
  Machinery, chemicals, watches, textiles, and precision instruments

Gross Domestic Product (97):
US$252.10 billion

GDP per Capita (97):
US$35,419.64

Three-Year Average GDP Growth (94-97):
0.0%

Average Annual CPI Growth (96-97):
+ 0.48%

Monetary Unit:
Swiss Franc

Exchange Rate (6/98):
CHF1.52 to US$1.00

company completed its first full year as a joint stock company after being transformed from a cooperatively owned company owned by its policy holders.

The pharmaceutical sector remains the most broadly capitalized, with Roche Holding's dividend rights making up around 13% of the SMI and Novartis's registered shares accounting for 19% of the SMI's total capitalization.

The Swiss Exchange (SWX) has a fully integrated electronic trading and settlement system that completed its first full year of operation in 1997. Electronic trading was readily accepted by participants, with 99% of all stock transactions being executed via the central order book of the SWX in 1997.

Meanwhile, bid-ask spreads for stocks included in the Swiss Market Index have narrowed around 25%, to 0.15%, since electronic trading was introduced in the summer of 1996.

In the summer of 1997, SWX and Deutsche Boerse entered into a strategic alliance to pool their derivatives markets. The Swiss Options and Financial Futures Exchange (SOFFEX) and Deutsche Terminboerse (DTB), its German counterpart, merged under the roof of Eurex, short for European Exchange. The combination allows transnational trading and clearing.

In the first seven months of 1998, Eurex for the first time relegated London's Liffe to

Ten Largest Capitalized Companies In The Dow Jones Switzerland Index
as of 6/30/98

Stock	Market Cap. US$ Thousands
Novartis	102,698,196
Roche Holding	92,382,261
Nestlé	84,074,357
Union Bank of Switzerland	79,452,161
Crédit Suisse Group	59,164,222
Swiss Reinsurance	36,846,084
Zurich Versicherungen-G (Namen)	29,829,182
ABB	12,007,437
Rentenanstalt	9,909,628
Clariant	9,545,853

second place among Europe's futures and options markets in terms of the number of contracts traded, according to Eurex's own account.

From January to the end of July, Eurex traded 126 million contracts, while Liffe managed only 122 million in the same period.

Through Eurex, SWX — renamed Eurex Zurich — and Deutsche Boerse — Eurex Deutschland — are cooperating with France's Société des Bourses Françaises to network the technological platforms of their derivative markets.

The tax treatment of foreign investors remained unchanged in recent years. Non-resident individuals and companies pay a 35% withholding tax on dividends. It is retrievable, but in a lengthy process. A small stamp duty is also levied on share transactions, but this is not regarded as prohibitive.

Foreign investors play an important role in Swiss equity trading. British and U.S. institutional investors, along with the large Swiss pension funds, dominate trading on the Swiss Exchange.

What they like is Switzerland's stable political, social, and economic environment, as well as its strong currency.

By contrast, there is hardly anything like an equity culture among Swiss individuals. Small investors are deterred by the high prices of Swiss stocks, which start at around US$200 a share and rise to several thousand dollars for some top blue-chips.

After numerous delays, the new Federal Stock Exchange Law became effective on January 1, 1998, replacing state legislation in each of Switzerland's 26 cantons. The new law's main goal is to improve the liquidity and transparency of Swiss financial markets. Covering all aspects of securities trading, it focuses heavily on takeover and disclosure procedures.

With the advent of European Economic and Monetary Union, the Swiss Exchange has announced a number of measures in order not to be left behind.

Trading in euro-denominated equities will be possible from the beginning of 1999. Later in the year it will also be possible to use the euro for trading in franc-denominated shares already listed on the Exchange. Parallel trading in Swiss francs

Market Sector Performance In The Dow Jones Switzerland Index
1 Year Change Through 6/30/98

Market Sector	Change % (US$)
Financial	62.64
Independent	55.59
Basic Materials	44.04
Consumer, Cyclical	34.45
Consumer, Non-Cyclical	17.34
Industrial	13.87

and euros will start gradually and increase according to market demand.

Eleven European states are forming the euro-zone, and their currencies will become the euro on January 1, 1999, when their exchange rates will be irrevocably locked at their central parities in Europe's exchange rate mechanism.

ABB

DJGI Industry: **Electrical Components & Equipment**
Stoxx Sector: **Industrials**

ABB AG is a holding company with a 50% stake in the power and industrial company ABB Asea Brown Boveri AG. It develops, manufactures and markets products and systems for power generation, power transmission, local distribution and control of electrical energy, optimization of industrial processes as well as automation services, rail transportation systems and offers a broad range of financial services. In 1997, ABB announced a $866 million restructuring charge to improve its competitiveness in the wake of Southeast Asian currency devaluations.

	SFr mil 12/95	12/96	12/97	US$mil 12/97				
Sales	N/A	N/A	N/A	N/A	P/E Ratio	46.3	Price (6/30/98)	2,240.00
Net Income	822.0	783.0	432.0	295.3	P/B Ratio	5.0	52 Wk Hi-Low	2,575.0-1,633.0
Book Value	3,603.0	4,640.0	4,140.0	2,830.1	Yield %	1.8	Market Cap	US$12,007mil

Address	ABB AG	Tel 56-205-77-00	ADR	ABBGY	CFO	R. Fassbind
	5401 Baden	Fax 56-222-10-26	SEDOL	5273001	Chairman & CEO	G. Lindahl

Adecco

DJGI Industry: **Other Industrial & Commercial Services**
Stoxx Sector: **Industrials**

Adecco SA is a Swiss employment services group with worldwide operations in 40 countries. The company was formed in 1996 through the merger of Adia SA and Ecco SA of France. Working through 2,800 offices in 45 countries, Adecco provides both temporary and permanent personnel placement services on a local, national, and global basis. In 1997, Adecco acquired U.S.-based TAD for $387 million, broadening its international presence, and also added operations in Italy, Finland, India and Uruguay.

	SFr mil 09/95	12/96 *	12/97	US$mil 12/97				
Sales	3,692.6	6,386.2	11,432.1	7,815.0	P/E Ratio	NMF	Price (6/30/98)	684.00
Net Income	78.4	-11.1	-206.0	-140.8	P/B Ratio	5.6	52 Wk Hi-Low	689.00-349.00
Book Value	280.8	2,402.1	2,020.3	1,381.0	Yield %	0.8	Market Cap	US$7,420.3mil

Address	Rue De Langallerie 11	Tel 21-321-66-66	ADR	ADECY	President	F. Weber
	1000 Luasanne	Fax 21-321-66-28	SEDOL	4007029	Chairman & CEO	J.P. Bowmer

*Irregular period due to fiscal year change.

Alusuisse-Lonza

DJGI Industry: **Containers & Packaging**
Stoxx Sector: **Industrials**

Alusuisse-Lonza Holding AG is a diversified holding company with subsidiaries that manufacture chemicals, aluminum and graphite materials, packaging, and automotive components. Its organic chemicals are used in the production of pharmaceuticals, food additives, and fertilizers. It has worldwide subsidiaries. In 1997, A-L announced it would divest some units (packaging segment). Aluminium and aluminium based products accounted for 29% of 1997 revenues; packaging, 21%; chemicals, 16%; pharmaceuticals, 14%; raw material trading, 13%; additives, 6%; and other, 1%.

	SFr mil 12/95	12/96	12/97	US$mil 12/97				
Sales	7,490.0	8,044.0	8,873.0	6,065.6	P/E Ratio	25.6	Price (6/30/98)	1,924.00
Net Income	383.0	413.0	463.0	316.5	P/B Ratio	4.3	52 Wk Hi-Low	1,979.3-1,220.2
Book Value	1,925.0	2,395.0	2,765.0	1,890.2	Yield %	1.3	Market Cap	US$7,903.0mil

Address	Feldeggstr. 4	Tel 1-386-22-22	ADR	--	CEO	Theodor M. Tschopp
	8034 Zurich	Fax 1-386-25-85	SEDOL	4780524	Chairman	Hans K. Jucker

Ciba Specialty Chemicals

DJGI Industry: **Chemicals - Specialty**
Stoxx Sector: **Chemical**

Ciba Specialty Chemicals Holding Inc. is a spin-off from Novartis AG. The spin-off was implemented during the merger of pharmaceutical giants Ciba-Geigy and Sandoz to form Novartis in 1996. The company is a global leader in the development, manufacture, and marketing of specialty chemicals. It has operations in additives, textile dyes, performance polymers, consumer care products, and pigments. Ciba has worldwide subsidiaries. Additives accounted for 30% of 1997 revenues; performance polymers, 21%; textile dyes, 18%; pigments, 16%; and consumer care chemicals, 15%.

	SFr mil 12/95	12/96	12/97	US$mil 12/97				
Sales	6,496.0	6,741.0	7,822.0	5,347.1	P/E Ratio	45.4	Price (6/30/98)	194.75
Net Income	305.0	-516.0	293.0	200.3	P/B Ratio	3.1	52 Wk Hi-Low	214.00-123.50
Book Value	4,886.0	4,389.0	4,336.0	2,964.1	Yield %	1.0	Market Cap	US$8,479.7mil

Address	Klybeckstrasse 141	Tel 61-636-1111	ADR	CSYCY	CEO	H. Vodicka
	4057 Basel	Fax 61-637-8899	SEDOL	5196744	Chmn Mgmt Bd	R.A. Meyer

Clariant

DJGI Industry: **Chemicals - Specialty**
Stoxx Sector: **Chemical**

Clariant AG, established in 1995, is a specialty chemicals group, focusing on textile and chemical dye stuffs. Other activities include paper, pigments, additives and leather. Clariant took over Hoechsts' Speciality Chemical Business in 1997, making the group one of the largest in its sector with six divisions. Process and performance products accounted for 35% of 1997 revenues; pigments and additives, 18%; surfactants, 16%; masterbatches, 11%; fine chemicals, 9%; cellulose ether and polymerisates, 8%; and other, 3%.

	SFr mil 12/95	12/96	12/97	US$mil 12/97				
Sales	2,145.0	2,337.0	6,487.0	4,434.5	P/E Ratio	45.2	Price (6/30/98)	999.00
Net Income	106.0	133.0	319.0	218.1	P/B Ratio	5.4	52 Wk Hi-Low	1,054.0-460.0
Book Value	923.0	1,115.0	2,694.0	1,841.6	Yield %	0.7	Market Cap	US$9,545.9mil

Address	Rothausstrasse 61	Tel 61- 469-6969	ADR	--	President	Dr R.W. Schweizer
	4132 Muttenz	Fax 61-469-6999	SEDOL	5479757	Chairman	Dr R.W. Schweizer

CS Holding

DJGI Industry: **Diversified Financial Services**
Stoxx Sector: **Financial Services**

CS Holding Group is a major diversified banking and financial-services holding company. The company offers full-service banking, investment banking, life insurance, securities trading, asset management, and other nonfinancial services. Its holdings include full-service bank Crédit Suisse, investment bank CS First Boston Group, financial advisory services unit CS Private Banking and CS Asset Management. In 1997, the group acquired Winterthur Insurance and BZW (formerly the European equity and investment banking operation of Barclays).

	SFr mil 12/95	12/96	12/97	US$mil 12/97				
Revenues	29,173.0	34,080.0	70,513.0	48,202.7	P/E Ratio	**NMF**	Price (6/30/98)	337.50
Net Income	1,401.0	-2,589.0	397.0	271.4	P/B Ratio	4.8	52 Wk Hi-Low	341.00-174.00
Book Value	16,177.0	11,562.0	18,803.0	12,853.7	Yield %	1.5	Market Cap	US$59,164mil

Address	**Paradeplatz 8**	Tel **1-212-16-16**	ADR	**CSGKY**	CFO	**R. Thornburgh**
	8070 Zurich	Fax **1-333-25-87**	SEDOL	**4245614**	Chairman & CEO	**L. Muehlemann**

In DJ Stoxx 50.

EMS-Chemie

DJGI Industry: **Chemicals - Commodity**
Stoxx Sector: **Chemical**

EMS-Chemie Holding AG (EMS) produces engineering polymers, adhesives, and protective coatings for a range of industries. The company also makes electric-ignition systems, builds industrial plants specializing in polymer and fiber production, and operates its own power stations. EMS produces 80% of its products in Switzerland, of which it exports more than 90%. In May 1997, EMS and H.B. Fuller Co. agreed to combine their automotive adhesives, sealants, and coatings businesses to form Eftec, a new global, equity-based joint venture company.

	SFr mil 12/95	12/96	12/97	US$mil 12/97				
Sales	923.7	945.2	1,025.9	701.3	P/E Ratio	16.0	Price (6/30/98)	8,800.00
Net Income	204.2	229.1	300.1	205.2	P/B Ratio	5.2	52 Wk Hi-Low	9,000.0-6,485.0
Book Value	951.8	951.2	917.1	627.0	Yield %	0.0	Market Cap	US$2,312.6mil

Address	**Selnaustr. 16**	Tel **1-284-18-80**	ADR	--	CFO	**P. Germann**
	8039 Zurich	Fax **1-284-18-98**	SEDOL	**4295523**	Chairman & CEO	**C. Blocher**

Holderbank

DJGI Industry: **Building Materials**
Stoxx Sector: **Construction**

Holderbank Financière Glaris AG is a holding company with subsidiaries around the world that are active in the production of materials for the construction industry. It provides ready-mix concrete, cement, aggregates, and chemicals used in making concrete. Subsidiaries include French cement producer Cedest, St. Lawrence Cement of Canada, and Holnam of the United States. Cement and clinker accounted for 57% of fiscal1997 revenues; ready-mixed concrete, sand and gravel, 21%; and chemicals for the treatment of concrete/other, 22%.

	SFr mil 12/95	12/96	12/97	US$mil 12/97				
Sales	8,270.0	9,951.0	11,265.0	7,700.8	P/E Ratio M	22.1	Price (6/30/98) M	1,930.00
Net Income	463.0	43.0	618.0	422.5	P/B Ratio M	2.7	52 Wk Hi-Low M	1,965.0-1,093.0
Book Value	4,528.3	4,448.1	5,013.0	3,426.9	Yield % M	1.0	Market Cap M	US$6,512.5mil

Address	**Zürcherstr. 170**	Tel **55-640-34-94**	ADR	**HFGCY**	CFO	**T.H. Schlatter**
	Ch-8750 Glarus	Fax **55-222-86-99**	SEDOL	**4420499**	Chairman & CEO	**T. Schmidheiny**

M=Multiple issues in index; reflects most active.

Nestlé

DJGI Industry: **Other Food**
Stoxx Sector: **Food & Beverage**

Nestlé SA is the world's largest food manufacturer and the market leader in both coffee and mineral water. Operating from 495 factories in 77 countries worldwide, its products include prepared dishes and cooking aids, milk-based products, cereals, instant coffee, pharmaceuticals, pet care products, and baby foods. One of Nestlé's most important acquisitions was French mineral water group Perrier. Dairy products and dietetics accounted for 28% of 1997 revenues; beverages, 27%; prepared dishes and cooking aids, 25%; chocolate and confectionery, 15%; and pharmaceuticals, 5%.

	SFr mil 12/95	12/96	12/97	US$mil 12/97				
Sales	56,484.0	60,490.0	69,998.0	47,850.6	P/E Ratio	31.9	Price (6/30/98)	3,246.00
Net Income	2,918.0	3,401.0	4,005.0	2,737.8	P/B Ratio	5.2	52 Wk Hi-Low	3,288.0-1,730.0
Book Value	17,989.0	21,938.0	24,410.0	16,686.7	Yield %	1.1	Market Cap	US$84,074mil

Address	**Ave. Nestlé 55**	Tel **21-924-21-11**	ADR	**NSRGY**	CFO	**M. Corti**
	1800 Vevey	Fax **21-921-17-20**	SEDOL	**4616696**	Chairman & CEO	**P. Braebeck-letmathe**

In DJ Stoxx 50.

Novartis

DJGI Industry: **Pharmaceuticals**
Stoxx Sector: **Pharmaceutical**

Novartis AG was founded in 1996 by the merger of two of Switzerland's largest pharmaceutical/health-care and chemical companies, Ciba-Geigy AG (founded in 1970) and Sandoz AG (founded in 1886), both located in Basel. With worldwide subsidiaries, Novartis AG focuses on research, manufacturing, and marketing in the fields of health care, agricultural chemicals, industrial chemicals, and nutrition. Healthcare products accounted for 60% of 1997 revenues; agricultural chemicals, 27%; and nutrition products, 13%.

	SFr mil 12/95	12/96	12/97	US$mil 12/97				
Sales	35,943.0	36,233.0	31,180.0	21,314.6	P/E Ratio	33.2	Price (6/30/98)	2,524.00
Net Income	4,216.0	2,304.0	5,211.0	3,562.2	P/B Ratio	6.4	52 Wk Hi-Low	2,749.0-2,070.0
Book Value	25,526.0	27,677.0	26,801.0	18,321.2	Yield %	1.0	Market Cap	US$102,698mil

Address	**Schwarzwaldallee 215**	Tel **61-324-80-00**	ADR	**NVTSY**	CFO	**R. Breu**
	4058 Basel	Fax **61-324-27-44**	SEDOL	**5047831**	Chairman & CEO	**D. Vasella**

In DJ Stoxx 50.

Oerlikon-Bührle

DJGI Industry: **Conglomerates**
Stoxx Sector: **Conglomerate**

Oerlikon-Bührle Holding AG is the Swiss parent of shoes and accessories group Bally, industrial components group Balzers, and military products unit Contraves. It has a variety of other holdings including aircraft maker Pilatus. Its Oerlikon-Contraves subsidiary produces missile systems, ammunition, aircraft, and aircraft parts. Its Kunz and Dietfurt division sells yarns, threads, and grey fabrics. Vacuum and coating systems accounted for 46% of 1997 revenues; shoes (Bally Group), 24%; defense systems, 18%; aircrafts and parts, 8%; and general contracting and other, 4%.

	SFr mil 12/95	12/96	12/97	US$mil 12/97				
Sales	3,611.0	3,435.0	3,735.0	2,553.2	P/E Ratio	46.2	Price (6/30/98)	277.00
Net Income	3.0	62.0	75.0	51.3	P/B Ratio	2.6	52 Wk Hi-Low	310.00-144.00
Book Value	1,092.0	1,213.0	1,292.0	883.2	Yield %	0.5	Market Cap	US$2,238.5mil

Address	Hofwiesenstr. 135	Tel 1-360-96-96	ADR	--	CFO	Hans Widmer
	8021 Zurich	Fax 1-363-72-60	SEDOL	4612757	Chairman	Hans Widmer

Richemont

DJGI Industry: **Tobacco**
Stoxx Sector: **Consumer Non-Cyclical**

Compagnie Financière Richemont AG is a holding company whose main businesses operate in the fields of tobacco and luxury goods. The company also has interests in the retail and electronic-media industries. Richemont holds a 60% interest in tobacco company Rothmans International and a 70% interest in Vendôme Luxury Group, whose products include jewelry, watches, fragrances, menswear, and womens' fashions that are marketed under brand names such as Cartier, Alfred Dunhill, and Karl Lagerfeld. Tobacco products accounted for 69% of fiscal 1997 revenues and luxury goods, 31%.

	SFr mil 03/96	03/97	03/98	US$mil 03/98				
Sales	7,831.3	9,878.2	11,230.7	7,374.1	P/E Ratio	8.6	Price (6/30/98)	1,985.00
Net Income	N/A	1,066.4	793.5	521.0	P/B Ratio	2.1	52 Wk Hi-Low	2,340.0-1,450.0
Book Value	3,499.5	5,402.9	6,194.4	4,067.2	Yield %	1.0	Market Cap	US$6,807.6mil

Address	Rigistr. 2	Tel 41-710-33-22	ADR	--	CFO	J. Du Plessis
	6300 Zug	Fax 41-711-71-02	SEDOL	4738211	Chairman & CEO	J. Ruppert

Rieter Holding

DJGI Industry: **Factory Equipment**
Stoxx Sector: **Industrials**

Rieter Holding AG produces spinning systems and chemical-fiber systems for the textile industry, and noise-control and thermal-insulation products for automobiles. It manufactures machines and integrated installations for staple-fiber spinning and for the manufacture and processing of synthetic fibers. In 1997, the company acquired Ello Ltda (Brazil) and Magee Automotive (USA). The company has production facilities in Europe, North America and Asia. Automotive systems accounted for 55% of 1997 revenues; textile systems, 45%; and other, nominal.

	SFr mil 12/95	12/96	12/97	US$mil 12/97				
Sales	2,007.9	2,200.4	2,636.2	1,802.1	P/E Ratio	18.6	Price (6/30/98)	1,050.00
Net Income	56.2	61.0	123.8	84.6	P/B Ratio	3.2	52 Wk Hi-Low	1,143.0-557.0
Book Value	583.3	685.8	726.1	496.4	Yield %	1.4	Market Cap	US$1,510.8mil

Address	Klosterstr. 20	Tel 52-208-71-71	ADR	--	CFO	H.R. Widmer
	8406 Winterthur	Fax 52-208-70-60	SEDOL	4716154	Chairman & CEO	K. Feller

Roche Holding

DJGI Industry: **Pharmaceuticals**
Stoxx Sector: **Pharmaceutical**

Roche Holding AG is one of Switzerland's largest pharmaceutical and chemical companies. It is active in researching, developing, manufacturing and selling of pharmaceuticals (prescriptive and over the counter products), vitamins and fine chemicals, diagnostic systems and flavourings & fragrances, for both the industrial and the consumer markets. The company has worldwide operations. Pharmaceuticals (prescriptive medicines, OTC products etc.) accounted for 65% of 1997 revenues; vitamins & fine chemicals, 20%; diagnostic systems, 5%; and fragrances and flavours, 10%.

	SFr mil 12/95	12/96	12/97	US$mil 12/97				
Sales	14,722.0	15,966.0	18,767.0	12,829.1	P/E Ratio M	NMF	Price (6/30/98) M	14,895
Net Income	3,372.0	3,899.0	-2,031.0	-1,388.4	P/B Ratio M	7.0	52 Wk Hi-Low M	17,655.0-12,090.0
Book Value	17,554.0	20,780.0	18,250.0	12,475.7	Yield % M	0.6	Market Cap M	US$68,757mil

Address	Postfach	Tel 61-68-88-88	ADR	ROHHY	CFO	H.B. Meier
	Ch-4002 Basel	Fax 61-688-27-75	SEDOL	4745772	CEO	F.B. Humer

M=Multiple issues in index; reflects most active.

SAirGroup

DJGI Industry: **Airlines**
Stoxx Sector: **Consumer Cyclical**

SAirGroup AG is an international airline which transports passengers and freight to some 111 destinations worldwide, via an extensive global air network system with 129 aircraft. The company also operates a catering division and 15 hotels. In 1996, as part of restructuring, the company was divided into four sectors: SAirLines, SAirServices division, SAirLogistics and SAirRelations. Airline operations accounted for 50% of 1997 revenues; catering and retail, 32%; logistics, 11%; and services, 7%.

	SFr mil 12/95	12/96	12/97	US$mil 12/97				
Sales	6,673.0	7,813.0	9,767.0	6,676.7	P/E Ratio	18.2	Price (6/30/98)	499.00
Net Income	-147.0	-497.0	324.0	221.5	P/B Ratio	2.7	52 Wk Hi-Low	499.00-327.20
Book Value	2,702.0	2,095.0	2,225.0	1,521.0	Yield %	0.8	Market Cap	US$3,847.9mil

Address	Hirschengraben 84	Tel 1-812-12-12	ADR	--	CFO	G. Schrorderet
	8001 Zurich	Fax 1-810-80-46	SEDOL	5463471	Chairman & CEO	P. Bruggwisser

Saurer

DJGI Industry: **Factory Equipment**
Stoxx Sector: **Industrials**

Saurer AG is one of the world's largest producers of embroidery and textile machinery and components. The spinning machine business accounts for two-thirds of the group's sales and has been split into separate profit centers. In April 1997, Saurer announced the acquisition of BB Industrie Holding AG, an investment company with a 30% stake in Saurer. Spinning machinery accounted for 64% of 1997 revenues; transmission systems, 16%; embroidery machinery, 11%; surface metallurgy, 8%; and other, 1%.

	SFr mil 12/95	12/96	12/97	US$mil 12/97					
Sales	1,726.5	1,671.1	1,875.5	1,282.1	P/E Ratio	12.9	Price (6/30/98)	1,550.00
Net Income	-75.2	50.8	131.2	89.7	P/B Ratio	3.0	52 Wk Hi-Low	1,710.0-904.0
Book Value	757.6	824.0	762.0	520.9	Yield %	1.6	Market Cap	US$1,571.3mil

Address	Schlossgasse 2	Tel 71-447-52-82	ADR	Z.SAR	CEO	H. Fischer
	9320 Arbon	Fax 71-447-52-88	SEDOL	4829513	President & Chmn	E. Thomke

Schindler

DJGI Industry: **Industrial - Diversified**
Stoxx Sector: **Industrials**

Schindler Holding AG manufactures elevators and escalators and related equipment. It installs its equipment in airports, cruise ships, and large buildings. Its majority-owned ALSO Holding subsidiary distributes computer software and hardware for IBM, Compaq, and Hewlett-Packard. Schindler's other products include moving walkways, passenger-train cars, and remote monitoring systems. Schindler is seeking to achieve a dominant position in the more lucrative servicing and maintenance business, which makes up about 50% of sales in the elevator division.

	SFr mil 12/95	12/96	12/97	US$mil 12/97					
Sales	4,714.9	5,098.4	6,230.0	4,258.8	P/E Ratio M	25.5	Price (6/30/98) M	2,350.00
Net Income	68.2	76.8	120.2	82.2	P/B Ratio M	2.5	52 Wk Hi-Low M	2,695.0-1,510.0
Book Value	1,036.5	1,083.3	1,205.1	823.8	Yield % M	1.3	Market Cap M	US$1,178.0mil

Address	Seestr. 55	Tel 4-632-85-50	ADR	--	President	A. Schindler
	6052 Hergiswil	Fax 4-445-31-34	SEDOL	4778842	Chairman & CEO	A. Schindler

M=Multiple issues in index; reflects most active.

Sulzer

DJGI Industry: **Industrial - Diversified**
Stoxx Sector: **Industrials**

Sulzer AG is an international technology corporation that produces heavy machinery and medical devices. The company's manufacturing products include weaving machinery, reciprocating compressors, air-separation machinery, and boiler plants. Its medical products include pacemakers, artificial joints, and heart valves. Plant and building services accounted for 23% of 1997 revenues; pacemakers and prosthetic products, 23%; pumps and industrial compressors, 22%; process engineering, 17%; weaving machines, 12% and other, 3%.

	SFr mil 12/95	12/96	12/97	US$mil 12/97					
Sales	5,740.0	5,728.0	6,051.0	4,136.5	P/E Ratio	20.3	Price (6/30/98)	1,197.00
Net Income	92.0	82.0	214.0	146.3	P/B Ratio	1.8	52 Wk Hi-Low	1,309.0-879.0
Book Value	2,014.0	1,427.0	2,319.0	1,585.3	Yield %	1.7	Market Cap	US$2,861.0mil

Address	Postfach 414	Tel 52-262-72-72	ADR	SM	CFO	E. Mueller
	8401 Winterthur	Fax 52-262-00-25	SEDOL	4854719	Chairman & CEO	F. Fahrni

Surveillance

DJGI Industry: **Other Industrial & Commercial Services**
Stoxx Sector: **Industrials**

Société Générale de Surveillance Holding SA (SGS) is the world's largest inspection, verification and testing organization. It has a total of 170 subsidiaries, 1170 offices and 309 laboratories in 140 countries which undertake inspection, monitoring and quality assurance services for international trade in agricultural and mineral products, petrochemicals, industrial equipment and consumer goods. Inspection and testing services accounted for 72% of 1997 revenues; services to the insurance industry, 20%; and other services, 8%.

	SFr mil 12/95	12/96	12/97	US$mil 12/97					
Sales	2,627.9	2,953.5	3,270.6	2,235.8	P/E Ratio	13.3	Price (6/30/98)	2,571.00
Net Income	230.4	262.7	229.1	156.6	P/B Ratio	32.7	52 Wk Hi-Low	3,175.0-2,405.0
Book Value	1,154.7	1,254.4	929.6	635.5	Yield %	2.6	Market Cap	US$1,755.0mil

Address	8 rue des Alpes	Tel 22-739-94-98	ADR	--	CFO	P. Lilley
	1211 Geneva	Fax 22-739-98-86	SEDOL	4824767	Chairman	E.S. Amorini

The Swatch Group

DJGI Industry: **Clothing & Fabrics**
Stoxx Sector: **Consumer Cyclical**

The Swatch Group Ltd. is the new name for Swiss Corp. for Microelectronics and Watchmaking Industries Ltd. (SMH). As one of the world's leading clock-and watchmakers, the company believes that the new name will be more easily recognized by consumers. The company produces watches under brand names such as Blancpain; Omega, Rado & Longines; Tissot; Certina; Mido; Hamilton; Pierre Balmain; Endura; Flik Flak and the highly successful Swatch range. The company opened 61 new Swatch stores and 2 Swatch Megastores in 1997 bringing the total to 120 stores.

	SFr mil 12/95	12/96	12/97	US$mil 12/97					
Sales	2,562.0	2,715.0	2,970.0	2,030.3	P/E Ratio M	25.3	Price (6/30/98) M	253.00
Net Income	273.0	280.0	329.0	224.9	P/B Ratio M	3.4	52 Wk Hi-Low M	272.00-174.50
Book Value	2,338.0	2,534.0	2,460.0	1,681.7	Yield % M	0.8	Market Cap M	US$2,498.3mil

Address	Seevorstadt 6	Tel --	ADR	--	President	Nicholas G. Hayek
	Ch-2501 Biel	Fax 32-343-69-11	SEDOL	4762351	Chairman & CEO	Nicholas G. Hayek

M=Multiple issues in index; reflects most active.

Swiss Life

DJGI Industry: **Insurance - Life & Health**
Stoxx Sector: **Insurance**

Swiss Life Insurance and Pension Co., established in 1857, is the leading life insurance company in Switzerland. Premiums are derived from life and non-life business. In 1997, more than 60% of its premiums were from the domestic business. It has subsidiaries in Europe and the United States and sales offices worldwide. The insurer is part of a joint insurance venture, named UBS Swiss Life, with the Union Bank of Switzerland. Premium income accounted for 72% of 1997 revenues, investment income, 22%; and other income, 6%.

	SFr mil 12/95	12/96	12/97	US$mil 12/97				
Revenues	14,930.3	18,485.9	22,572.4	15,430.5	P/E Ratio	96.8	Price (6/30/98)	1,284.00
Net Income	1,305.6	1,508.8	152.5	104.2	P/B Ratio	2.2	52 Wk Hi-Low	1,425.0-565.0
Book Value	4,084.1	5,499.8	6,829.7	4,668.8	Yield %	0.3	Market Cap	US$9,909.6mil

Address	General Guisan-quai 40	Tel 1-284-3311	ADR	--	CEO	A. Donatsch
	8022 Zurich	Fax 1-281-2080	SEDOL	5285868	Chairman	M. Zobl

Swiss Reinsurance

DJGI Industry: **Insurance - Full Line**
Stoxx Sector: **Insurance**

Swiss Reinsurance Co. (Schweizerische Rückversicherungs-Gesellschaft) is one of the world's largest reinsurance companies that provides life, fire, accident, motor, marine, aviation, nuclear energy, and engineering reinsurance. It also offers risk-management services to other companies through its subsidiary International Risk Management. Property insurance accounted for 18% of 1997 revenues; investment income, 15%; life, 14%; motor insurance, 11%; health, 10%; gain/loss on sale of securities, 9%; liability, 8%; engineering, 5%; and other operating income, 10%.

	SFr mil 12/95	12/96	12/97	US$mil 12/97				
Revenues	15,403.0	17,294.0	21,273.0	14,542.2	P/E Ratio	26.4	Price (6/30/98)	3,836.00
Net Income	1,101.0	1,459.0	2,116.0	1,446.5	P/B Ratio	4.9	52 Wk Hi-Low	3,836.0-1,967.0
Book Value	9,105.7	9,875.5	14,182.4	9,695.1	Yield %	1.1	Market Cap	US$36,846mil

Address	Mythenquai 50/60	Tel 1-285-21-21	ADR	SWCEY	Exec Dir	C. Dorschel
	8022 Zurich	Fax 1-285-29-99	SEDOL	4850029	Chairman & CEO	W.B. Kieholz

In DJ Stoxx 50.

UBS Group

DJGI Industry: **Banks - Major International**
Stoxx Sector: **Bank**

UBS Group, Europe's largest bank, is the result of the June 1998 merger between Union Bank of Switzerland and Swiss Bank Corp. With total assets of more than CHF 1 trillion, it is one of the world's leading financial services groups. The new group will concentrate on five core buinesses: private banking, institutional asset management, investment banking, private and corporate clients business, and private equity, which will be operated as a central business area. UBS is a market leader in private equity in Europe and has a strong global franchise.

	SFr mil 12/95	12/96	12/97	US$mil 12/97				
Revenues	N/A	N/A	24,880.0	17,008.0	P/E Ratio	NMF	Price (6/30/98)	546.00
Net Income	N/A	N/A	5,636.0	3,852.8	P/B Ratio	0.7	52 Wk Hi-Low	556.00-285.00
Book Value	N/A	N/A	30,927.0	21,141.7	Yield %	9.2	Market Cap	US$76,916mil

Address	Bahnhofstrasse 45	Tel 1-234-11-11	ADR	UBSUY	CEO	Marcel Ospel
	8021 Zurich	Fax 1-236-51-11	SEDOL	4785110	Chairman	Mathis Cabiallavetta

In DJ Stoxx 50.

Valora

DJGI Industry: **Retailers - Other Specialty**
Stoxx Sector: **Retail**

Valora Holding AG, formerly Merkur Holding AG, is a retailer that operates kiosk and mail-order businesses, restaurants, and vending machines. It also has wholesale trade operations in newspapers and books. In addition, Valora produces and sells beds and mattresses and invests in commercial real estate. Valora's leading interests are represented by market leaders Müller-Imhoof in Switzerland and Epéda and Mérinos in France. Retail trading and restaurants accounted for 63% of 1997 revenues; beds and bedding, 25%; and wholesale trading, 12%.

	SFr mil 12/95	12/96	12/97	US$mil 12/97				
Revenues	2,869.4	2,895.6	2,425.1	1,657.8	P/E Ratio	11.2	Price (6/30/98)	400.00
Net Income	41.2	72.1	146.4	100.1	P/B Ratio	2.2	52 Wk Hi-Low	427.50-275.50
Book Value	557.9	519.5	724.9	495.5	Yield %	1.6	Market Cap	US$1,098.8mil

Address	Fellerstr. 15	Tel 31-990-22-22	ADR	--	V Chmn & CEO	E. Marti
	3027 Bern	Fax 31-992-82-53	SEDOL	4581619	Chairman	R. Hartmann

Zurich Insurance

DJGI Industry: **Insurance - Full Line**
Stoxx Sector: **Insurance**

Zurich Insurance Group is one of Switzerland's largest insurance groups. It is active in life and nonlife insurance, reinsurance, and asset management. It provides life and health, fire and theft, general accident, and public liability insurance coverage throughout Switzerland and other countries worldwide. It recently merged with the financial services unit of B.A.T. Industries PLC and will undergo necessary restructuring. Premiums accounted for 71% of 1997 income; investment income, 19%; gain/loss on sale of securities - pretax, 8%; and other income, 2%.

	SFr mil 12/95	12/96	12/97	US$mil 12/97				
Revenues	31,683.8	37,969.4	38,396.5	26,247.8	P/E Ratio	29.5	Price (6/30/98)	968.00
Net Income	874.1	1,138.2	1,786.4	1,221.2	P/B Ratio	2.2	52 Wk Hi-Low	990.00-540.00
Book Value	10,621.2	13,551.7	20,544.9	14,044.5	Yield %	0.9	Market Cap	US$29,829mil

Address	Mythenquai 2	Tel 1-205-21-21	ADR	ZURRY	CFO	M. Rohrbasser
	8002 Zurich	Fax 1-205-35-55	SEDOL	4995599	Chairman & CEO	R. Hueppi

United Kingdom

http://www.dowjones.com/indexes/Htmls01/uk.html

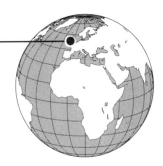

Exchanges:

London Stock Exchange

United Kingdom

David Bentley
London

The London Stock Exchange, a traditionally conservative organization dating back to 17th-century coffee houses, is undergoing an unprecedented period of change.

The past year has witnessed not only radical reform of its decade-old trading system, but an alliance with Frankfurt that could form the core of a pan-European equity market.

All this took place against the backdrop of another period of impressive growth by U.K. shares.

Trailing only the New York and Tokyo bourses in terms of size, London provides a market for around 3,000 companies and more than 12,000 securities, ranging from gilts to warrants to depositary receipts and options.

In July 1998, the Exchange surprised investors by announcing an alliance with its German rival, the Deutsche Boerse. Previously, the Exchange had resisted all suggestions that it join with other markets to cut costs and expand its influence.

The two exchanges plan to develop a joint trading platform, giving investors in both countries a single point of access to the largest companies on both markets by the time the euro is launched in January 1999. The joint exchange expects to offer lower transaction costs, better liquidity, and greater capital efficiencies. Other exchanges are expected to join over time, creating a market of around 300 blue-chip companies quoted in both euros and sterling.

That was the second big change in less than a year to hit the City, as London's trading community is known.

On October 20, 1997, Chancellor of the Exchequer Gordon Brown pushed a button starting the Exchange's electronic order book, known as SETS, and ushered London into the era of electronic trading.

Buy and sell orders placed on the electronic book are displayed for all to see and matched automatically with corresponding requests. Lower costs, greater speed, and narrower spreads were supposed to result.

The new system, however, applies to just 100 or so of the United Kingdom's largest companies, the number growing slowly as the composition of the FTSE 100 index of large-cap shares changes. A quarterly review of FTSE 100 component stocks usually sees two or three poor performers being replaced

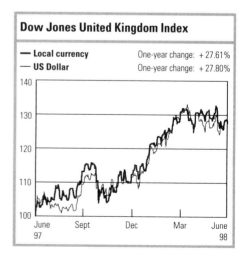

Dow Jones United Kingdom Index

— Local currency   One-year change: + 27.61%
— US Dollar   One-year change: + 27.80%

by the best of the mid-cap stocks. Those issues removed from the FTSE 100 remain on the electronic order book.

And the system was placed alongside the telephone bargaining that had existed since the Exchange's floor was closed in 1986. Market makers still handle much of the dealing in large shares by telephone.

In some cases, low volume on the SETS system has led to unusual price volatility, particularly at the start or close of sessions.

Non-FTSE 100 issues are still traded in the traditional telephone manner, although the Exchange intends to extend the SETS system to these shares once it has had time to mature.

A review of SETS, conducted by the Exchange, outlined the need for greater liquidity and as a result, the market was to open 30 minutes later beginning July 20, 1998, in an effort to concentrate liquidity. There are also plans to align the market's closing hours with Liffe, London's futures and options exchange.

Furthermore, the minimum order size was removed in June in an attempt to attract more business to the electronic order book, and the maximum order size was doubled and plans are afoot to introduce a volume-weighted average closing price before the end of 1998.

The teething troubles of SETS can best be demonstrated by events in March, when a couple of rogue prices got entered during a volatile futures and options expiration period,

Country Information

Trading Hours:

Local: 8:30 am - 4:30 pm

EST: 3:30 am - 11:30 am

GMT: 0830 - 1630

Population (6/98):
58,970,119

Unemployment (97):
7.9%

Main Industries:
Machinery, electric power equipment, automation equipment, railroad equipment, shipbuilding, aircraft, automobiles and parts, electronics and communications equipment, metals, chemicals, coal, petroleum, paper and paper products, food processing, textiles, clothing, and other consumer goods

Gross Domestic Product (97):
US$1,271.71 billion

GDP per Capita (97):
US$21,583.60

Three-Year Average GDP Growth (94-97):
2.6%

Average Annual CPI Growth (96-97):
+ 3.13%

Monetary Unit:
British Pound (Sterling)

Exchange Rate (6/98):
GBP0.60 to US$1.00

triggering a wild 225-point swing in the FTSE 100 over a 15-minute period.

The London Exchange's evolution will doubtless continue in 1999.

Situated amid the European time zones, London is ideally placed between the New York and Tokyo markets, giving it a natural advantage in international trading. Indeed, the London Stock Exchange is noted for the strength of its international markets — with over two-thirds of all trades involving an international client or stock.

The total value of companies listed on the Exchange now stands at over GBP4.4 trillion. Looking at the performance of the blue-chips over the first six months of 1998, two distinct phases emerge.

Initially, the bull run, which began midway through 1996, continued to gather pace. The market's upward path remained intact, despite a sharp lurch downward in November 1997, as the first signs of the Asian financial crisis began to appear. The market's ample liquidity and the extra impetus of megamergers and acquisitions spurred demand again in 1998, as the FTSE 100 breached the 6000 level toward the end of March. Commentators were astounded as the index outstripped many of the most bullish year-end forecasts within the first quarter.

Buoyant economic conditions in the United States, and in the United Kingdom to a lesser extent, with rampant growth and little

Ten Largest Capitalized Companies In The Dow Jones United Kingdom Index
as of 6/30/98

Stock	Market Cap. US$ Thousands
Glaxo Wellcome	107,944,052
British Petroleum	84,896,326
British Telecommunications	79,171,925
Lloyds TSB Group	75,930,679
Shell Transport & Trading	70,006,026
SmithKline Beecham	67,964,393
Barclays	43,531,388
Diageo	42,326,495
Zeneca Group	40,742,900
Vodafone Group	39,154,369

evidence of inflationary pressure prompted a sharp decline in both domestic and global bond yields, which made equities all the more attractive. The FTSE set an all-time record closing high of 6105.8 on April 6.

This seemingly relentless advance then gave way to a period of consolidation and range-trading, as investors adjusted to changing domestic and international conditions. Investors took on a more cautious attitude, as money managers switched investments into cash, fearing a major correction was just around the corner.

Spiraling losses in Asian markets, and the near-collapse of the Japanese banking system demanded a more conservative attitude toward investment, as did higher domestic interest rates, an uptick in inflation and expectations of lower U.K. growth.

Despite nearly a quarter's worth of sideways movement, the FTSE 100 still rose by 13.5%

over the first six months of 1998, and at its peak the index was up 19% from the start of the year.

By contrast, London's second division stocks, which make up the FTSE 250 index, have sometimes managed gains when blue-chips stumbled. Mid-cap stocks moved into vogue in February 1998, as investors grew weary of the major issues. Returns have been pretty impressive as the FTSE 250 climbed 15.3% over the first six months of 1998, outpacing the FTSE 100 index over the same period.

Banking and financial issues have a significant presence in the U.K. market along with oil and pharmaceutical stocks, which also have a major weighting in the FTSE 100 index. Growth in these three sectors has accounted for much of the FTSE's upward drive in recent times. Drug giant Glaxo Wellcome is the United Kingdom's biggest stock in terms of market

capitalization, valued at GBP65.7 billion. As the market's bull run began to fade and investors turned more cautious, defensive stocks such as utilities and food retailers came into play. Telecommunications issues such as Orange and Vodaphone have achieved spectacular growth so far this year, based on projections that their subscriber lists will continue to swell.

On the flip side, sterling's persistent strength has proved a headache for the heavy engineers and exporters, such as British Steel, Rolls Royce, and British Aerospace, as overseas earnings by these companies were eroded by currency translation.

Attracting companies from emerging markets to list on London's Stock Exchange remains a major priority for the 300 or so member companies that jointly own the Exchange.

Officials periodically undertake marketing visits to key centers such as China, South Africa, and India, where they can meet with representatives of the local exchanges.

Investors are usually liable for stamp duty of 0.5% on shares. Dividends are paid with a credit that eliminates much of a domestic shareholder's liability; foreign investors from certain countries can reclaim some of the credit through a tax treaty. Nonresidents do not have to pay capital gains tax when shares are sold.

Industry Group Performance In The Dow Jones United Kingdom Index
1 Year Change Through 6/30/98

Industry	Change % (US$)
Best Performing	
Railroads	109.42
Telephone Utilities (All)	88.62
Diversified Technology	61.07
Advertising	59.57
Insurance, Full Line	55.00
Worst Performing	
Clothing & Fabrics	-22.03
Overseas Trading Companies	-32.41
Mining, Diversified	-35.40
Biotechnology	-82.95
Medical & Biological Technology (All)	-82.95

Abbey National

DJGI Industry: **Banks - Regional (All)**
Stoxx Sector: **Bank**

Abbey National PLC provides retail banking and financial services and invests in treasury assets. The company has interests in real estate and investment companies. Besides extensive domestic operations, it also provides residential mortgages, loans, and real estate services in France, Spain, Italy, and the Channel Islands. Its subsidiaries include Abbey National Treasury Services PLC, Scottish Mutual Assurance PLC, and Abbey National Homes Ltd. In 1996, Abbey National formed a joint venture with Norwich Union Healthcare to enter the private medical insurance sector.

	£ mil 12/95	12/96	12/97	US$mil 12/97				
Revenues	7,016.0	7,177.0	8,706.0	14,394.8	P/E Ratio	16.3	Price (6/30/98)	10.65
Net Income	683.0	767.0	954.0	1,577.4	P/B Ratio	3.3	52 Wk Hi-Low	13.12-7.95
Book Value	3,841.0	4,193.0	4,553.0	7,528.1	Yield %	2.9	Market Cap	US$25,109mil

Address	Abbey Hse., Baker St.	Tel 171-612-4000	ADR	**ABYNY**	CEO	**Peter Birch**
	London NW1 6XL	Fax 171-612-4010	SEDOL	**0004455**	Chairman	**Lord Tugendhat**

Allied Domecq

DJGI Industry: **Distillers & Brewers**
Stoxx Sector: **Food & Beverage**

Allied Domecq PLC is a food and beverage company. It produces, markets, and sells spirits and wine and operates public houses, off-licenses, and franchises. Allied Domecq's brands include Canadian Club, Ballantine's, Courvoisier, Beefeater, and Kahlua. Notable retail interests include Baskin Robbins and Dunkin' Donuts, Victoria Wine liquor stores, and pubs. The company acquired Spanish and Mexican spirits group Pedro Domecq in 1994. Spirits and wine accounted for 57% of fiscal 1997 revenues; retailing, 42%; and food and other, 1%.

	£ mil 08/95	08/96	08/97	US$mil 08/97				
Sales	4,481.6	4,090.0	3,931.0	6,346.5	P/E Ratio	14.0	Price (6/30/98)	5.63
Net Income	274.1	43.0	402.0	649.0	P/B Ratio	2.6	52 Wk Hi-Low	6.34-4.27
Book Value	2,281.0	2,134.0	2,127.0	3,434.0	Yield %	4.4	Market Cap	US$9,807.2mil

Address	24 Portland Pl.	Tel 171-323-9000	ADR	**ALDCY**	CEO	**Anthony J. Hales**
	London W1N 4BB	Fax 171-323-1742	SEDOL	**0018508**	Chairman	**Michael C. Jackaman**

Amvescap

DJGI Industry: **Diversified Financial Services**
Stoxx Sector: **Financial Services**

Amvescap PLC provides global investment management and mutual fund services to institutions and individuals worldwide. The company's European operations are based in London, Paris, and Jersey (Channel Islands) offering a wide range of sterling and U.S. dollar*denominated offshore funds, unit trusts, and SICAV funds. Amvescap's U.S. subsidiaries include Invesco Funds Group, which manages a diverse range of portfolios for pension funds and other institutions. The company also has operating subsidiaries in Japan and Hong Kong.

	£ mil 12/95	12/96	12/97	US$mil 12/97				
Revenues	3,965.8	236.2	530.7	877.4	P/E Ratio	24.4	Price (6/30/98)	5.85
Net Income	36.2	45.0	117.0	193.5	P/B Ratio	NMF	52 Wk Hi-Low	7.43-3.51
Book Value	50.2	47.8	-95.8	-158.4	Yield %	1.2	Market Cap	US$6,346.7mil

Address	11 Devonshire Sq.	Tel 171-626-3434	ADR	**AVZ**	CEO (Europe)	**Norman Riddell**
	London EC2M 4YR	Fax 171-454-3962	SEDOL	**0128269**	Chairman	**Charles Brady**

Anglian Water

DJGI Industry: **Water Utilities**
Stoxx Sector: **Utility**

Anglian Water PLC supplies and distributes water and provides engineering for sewage treatment, disposal, and processing. It also operates under the names Purac and Nordic Water. In terms of area covered, the company is the largest of the 10 regional water companies in England and Wales, providing services to more than 2 million properties. The company's international business has operations in the United States, South America, Europe, Asia, and Australasia. Water supply and sewerage services accounted for 83% of 1998 revenues; international, 15%; and other, 2%.

	£ mil 03/96	03/97	03/98	US$mil 03/98				
Sales	775.7	837.1	850.1	1,422.8	P/E Ratio	20.1	Price (6/30/98)	8.40
Net Income	218.5	184.9	112.9	189.0	P/B Ratio	1.4	52 Wk Hi-Low	9.56-6.52
Book Value	1,477.1	1,579.6	1,582.1	2,647.9	Yield %	4.6	Market Cap	US$3,812.9mil

Address	Anglian Hse., Huntingdon	Tel 148-044-3000	ADR	--	Managing Director	**Alan Smith**
	Cambridgeshire PE18 6NZ	Fax 148-044-3115	SEDOL	**0032412**	Chairman	**Robin Gourlay**

Arcadia Group

DJGI Industry: **Retailers - Apparel**
Stoxx Sector: **Retail**

Arcadia Group PLC was formed out of the demerged Burton Group in 1998. It is a retailer of clothing for men, women, and children, and of cosmetics and miscellaneous home products. The company operates primarily in the United Kingdom. Arcadia operates through a range of multiple stores including Burtons Menswear, Dorothy Perkins, Evans, Top Shop, Top Man, Principles, Racing Green, Hawkshead, and Debenhams. Debenhams is the United Kingdom's leading chain of family department stores. In addition to the traditional stores, the company also provides a home shopping facility.

	£ mil 09/95	08/96 *	08/97	US$mil 08/97				
Revenues	1,878.8	2,006.9	2,231.8	3,603.2	P/E Ratio	7.6	Price (6/30/98)	4.02
Net Income	74.0	110.7	82.6	133.4	P/B Ratio	NMF	52 Wk Hi-Low	5.06-2.95
Book Value	852.8	899.6	914.1	1,475.8	Yield %	5.1	Market Cap	US$1,266.9mil

Address	214 Oxford St.	Tel 171-636-8040	ADR	**BURUY**	CEO & Mng Dir	**John Hoerner**
	London W1N 9DF	Fax 171-927-7806	SEDOL	**0235471**	Chairman	**Adam Broadbent**

*Irregular period due to fiscal year change.

Arjo Wiggins Appleton

DJGI Industry: **Paper Products**
Stoxx Sector: **Basic Resources**

Arjo Wiggins Appleton PLC is an Anglo-French manufacturer and distributor of paper products. The company produces carbonless carbon paper for business forms and credit card receipts, thermal paper for fax machines, stationery, and specialty paper. The company has substantial operations in Europe and North America and interests in other parts of the world. In 1997, the company acquired Arjo Wiggins Qingdao Paper Company Limited and Smoza SRO. Paper manufacturing accounted for 57% of 1997 revenues and paper merchanting accounted for 43%.

	£ mil 12/95	12/96	12/97	US$mil 12/97				
Sales	3,533.2	3,572.4	3,266.6	5,401.1	P/E Ratio	11.2	Price (6/30/98)	2.03
Net Income	18.7	83.6	149.5	247.2	P/B Ratio	1.4	52 Wk Hi-Low	2.55-1.45
Book Value	1,244.0	1,122.8	1,163.2	1,923.3	Yield %	3.9	Market Cap	US$2,842.5mil

Address	Box 88, Gateway House	Tel 125-672-3000	ADR	ARWGY	CEO	Alain Soulas
	Hampshire RG21 4EE	Fax 125-672-3723	SEDOL	0965411	Chairman	Cob Stenham

Associated British Foods

DJGI Industry: **Other Food**
Stoxx Sector: **Food & Beverage**

Associated British Foods PLC processes and manufactures food in the United Kingdom, Australia, the United States, and several European countries. It also retails food and textiles in the United Kingdom and Ireland. Principal trade names in the group's food division include Twinings, Burtons, Allinson, Ryvita, Speedibake, and Kingsmill. Retail stores include Stewart's, Quinnsworth, Crazy Prices, Primark, Penneys, and Lifestyle Sports shops. The group is 50.9%-owned by Wittington Investments Ltd. Manufacturing activities accounted for 94% of fiscal 1997 revenues.

	£ mil 09/95	09/96	09/97	US$mil 09/97				
Sales	4,894.0	5,707.0	4,437.0	7,184.3	P/E Ratio	18.7	Price (6/30/98)	5.66
Net Income	250.0	278.0	681.0	1,102.7	P/B Ratio	1.7	52 Wk Hi-Low	6.65-4.71
Book Value	2,256.0	2,451.0	2,909.0	4,710.2	Yield %	1.8	Market Cap	US$8,487.5mil

Address	Bowater Hse., 68 Knightsbridge	Tel 171-589-6363	ADR	ADBFY	Finance Director	M. Clark
	London SW1X 7LQ	Fax 171-584-8560	SEDOL	0369314	Chairman	G. Weston

Associated British Ports

DJGI Industry: **Marine Transportation**
Stoxx Sector: **Industrials**

Associated British Ports Holdings PLC operates ports and transportation businesses. It also owns investment property and develops and sells property in the United Kingdom. It is the largest ports group in the United Kingdom with 23 ports and two associated companies in the container business. Associated British Ports operates the Red Funnel vehicle- and passenger-ferry service. Ports, transport, and port-related property income accounted for 84% of 1997 revenues; property development, 11%; and property investment, 5%.

	£ mil 12/95	12/96	12/97	US$mil 12/97				
Sales	235.9	247.2	286.9	474.4	P/E Ratio	16.9	Price (6/30/98)	3.34
Net Income	66.6	70.3	76.0	125.7	P/B Ratio	1.3	52 Wk Hi-Low	3.85-2.48
Book Value	849.3	914.4	981.8	1,623.3	Yield %	2.7	Market Cap	US$2,103.3mil

Address	150 Holborn	Tel 171-430-1177	ADR	--	Managing Director	R. Channing
	London EC1N 2LR	Fax 171-430-1384	SEDOL	0056434	Chairman	Sir K. Stuart

BAA

DJGI Industry: **Other Industrial & Commercial Services**
Stoxx Sector: **Industrials**

BAA PLC manages airport facilities in the United Kingdom and overseas. The group owns and operates seven British airports, which account for more than 70% of the United Kingdom's passenger traffic and more than 80% of its cargo transport. Although the company has interests in property investment and development, its main revenue source is airport operations, such as airport landing and takeoff charges, retail and duty-free stores, and car-parking fees. BAA also operates the Pittsburgh, Harrisburg, and Indianapolis airports in the United States.

	£ mil 03/96	03/97	03/98	US$mil 03/98				
Sales	1,253.0	1,373.0	1,679.0	2,810.0	P/E Ratio	47.9	Price (6/30/98)	6.47
Net Income	315.0	296.0	277.0	463.6	P/B Ratio	1.9	52 Wk Hi-Low	7.10-4.51
Book Value	3,167.0	3,461.0	3,739.0	6,257.7	Yield %	2.1	Market Cap	US$11,398mil

Address	130 Wilton Rd.	Tel 171-834-9449	ADR	BAAPY	CEO	Sir John Egan
	London SW1V 1LQ	Fax 171-932-6699	SEDOL	0067340	Chairman	N. Brian Smith

Barclays Bank

DJGI Industry: **Banks - Major International**
Stoxx Sector: **Bank**

Barclays Bank PLC offers personal and investment banking, life insurance, pensions, and mortgage processing. In terms of assets employed, Barclays is one of the largest financial services organizations in the United Kingdom. The bank operates more than 2,000 personal-banking networks in the United Kingdom, as well as offices in Spain, France, and Portugal. Barclays issues the Barclaycard credit card to more than 8 million people. Interest income accounted for 71% of 1997 revenues; commissions and fees, 25%; dealing profits, 3%; and other operating income, 1%.

	£ mil 12/95	12/96	12/97	US$mil 12/97				
Revenues	14,673.0	12,587.0	12,882.0	21,299.6	P/E Ratio	23.2	Price (6/30/98)	17.28
Net Income	1,364.0	1,639.0	1,130.0	1,868.4	P/B Ratio	3.5	52 Wk Hi-Low	19.80-11.92
Book Value	7,026.0	7,266.0	7,576.0	12,526.5	Yield %	2.1	Market Cap	US$43,531mil

Address	54 Lombard St.	Tel 171-699-5000	ADR	BCS	CEO	J. Martin Taylor
	London EC3P 3AH	Fax 171-699-2460	SEDOL	0078201	Chairman	Andrew R. Buxton

Barratt Developments

DJGI Industry: **Home Construction**
Stoxx Sector: **Consumer Cyclical**

Barratt Developments PLC is a builder and developer in the United Kingdom and the United States. Its core activity is building homes; during fiscal 1997 the group completed 7,710 houses in the United Kingdom and 365 in the United States. It is also involved in nonresidential partnership developments with the U.K. government and local authorities. Barratt is active in the southern California housing market. It operates nine leisure resorts in Spain and the United Kingdom that are used by 28,000 time-share owners. Barratt also sells and leases commercial property.

	£ mil 06/95	06/96	06/97	US$mil 06/97					
Sales	579.0	634.3	714.4	1,190.1	P/E Ratio		11.6	Price (6/30/98)	2.65
Net Income	29.2	35.6	45.9	76.5	P/B Ratio		1.7	52 Wk Hi-Low	3.40-2.22
Book Value	221.8	332.0	356.4	593.7	Yield %		3.5	Market Cap	US$1,030.1mil

Address　Wingrove Hse., Ponteland Rd.　Tel **191-286-6811**　ADR　--　CEO　**Frank Eaton**
　　　　　Newcastle-upon-Tyne NE5 3DP　Fax **191-271-2242**　SEDOL　**0081180**　Chairman　**Sir Lawrence Barratt**

Bass

DJGI Industry: **Distillers & Brewers**
Stoxx Sector: **Food & Beverage**

Bass PLC is a leading producer and distributor of beer and soft drinks. It owns, manages, leases, and franchises public houses, hotels, restaurants, bingo clubs, betting shops, and bowling and other amusement centers, and it manufactures, supplies, and operates amusement and gaming machines. Its brands of beer include Bass Ale, Worthington's Best Bitter, Tennent's Lager, and Carling Black Label. In February 1998, Bass acquired Inter-Continental Hotels & Resorts for $2.9 billion. Brewing accounted for 29% of fiscal 1997 gross revenues.

	£ mil 09/95	09/96	09/97	US$mil 09/97					
Sales	3,998.0	4,509.0	5,254.0	8,507.1	P/E Ratio		21.0	Price (6/30/98)	11.23
Net Income	380.0	444.0	250.0	404.8	P/B Ratio		2.2	52 Wk Hi-Low	11.73-7.33
Book Value	3,697.0	3,911.0	3,769.0	6,102.7	Yield %		2.7	Market Cap	US$14,874mil

Address　20 N. Audley St.　　　　Tel **171-409-1919**　ADR　**BAS**　CEO　**Ian M.G. Prosser**
　　　　　London W1Y 1WE　　　　Fax **171-409-8503**　SEDOL　**0243195**　Chairman　**Ian M.G. Prosser**

B.A.T. Industries

DJGI Industry: **Tobacco**
Stoxx Sector: **Consumer Non-Cyclical**

B.A.T. Industries PLC is a diversified conglomerate that manufactures cigarettes and provides financial services. It offers general-insurance products in the United Kingdom through Eagle Star and Allied Dunbar subsidiaries and in the United States through Farmers Insurance Group. The company is an international cigarette manufacturer; major brands include Lucky Strike, Kool, Kent, Benson & Hedges, Capri, Belmont, and Pall Mall. Subsidiaries operated by the company and located in the United States include American Tobacco and Brown & Williamson.

	£ mil 12/95	12/96	12/97	US$mil 12/97					
Sales	12,322.0	12,926.0	13,375.0	22,114.7	P/E Ratio		18.8	Price (6/30/98)	6.00
Net Income	1,472.0	1,506.0	995.0	1,645.2	P/B Ratio		3.9	52 Wk Hi-Low	6.49-5.00
Book Value	5,530.0	5,428.0	4,751.0	7,855.5	Yield %		4.3	Market Cap	US$31,353mil

Address　Windsor Hse., 50 Victoria St.　Tel **171-222-7979**　ADR　**BTI**　CEO　**Martin Broughton**
　　　　　London SW1H 0NL　　　　Fax **171-222-0122**　SEDOL　**0068116**　Chairman　**Earl Cairns**
In DJ Stoxx 50.

BBA Group

DJGI Industry: **Industrial - Diversified**
Stoxx Sector: **Industrials**

BBA Group PLC is an international group of materials technology and aviation businesses. Materials technology products include nonwoven materials, automotive friction materials, aviation hydraulic equipment and landing gear. Aviation services include refueling, cargo handling, catering, cleaning, and maintenance. Among the company's 1997 acquisitions were International Airmotive Holding Company, Korma S.p.A. Monarch Air Services, and Becorit-Gesellschaft Wilhelm Beckmann GmbH & Co. KG. Materials technology accounted for 60% of 1997 revenues.

	£ mil 12/95	12/96	12/97	US$mil 12/97					
Sales	1,033.7	1,080.9	1,101.8	1,821.8	P/E Ratio		18.6	Price (6/30/98)	4.52
Net Income	15.9	92.0	107.2	177.2	P/B Ratio		5.9	52 Wk Hi-Low	5.36-3.18
Book Value	333.5	343.4	320.8	530.4	Yield %		1.8	Market Cap	US$3,193.5mil

Address　70 Fleet St.　　　　　Tel **171-842-4900**　ADR　--　CEO　**Roberto Quarta**
　　　　　London EC4Y 1EU　　　　Fax **171-353-5831**　SEDOL　**0067748**　Chairman　**Vanni Treves**

Beazer Homes

DJGI Industry: **Home Construction**
Stoxx Sector: **Consumer Cyclical**

Beazer Homes Group PLC concentrates on building residences primarily throughout the United Kingdom. In fiscal 1997, Beazer Homes acquired building company Charles Church Group PLC, based in the United Kingdom, from the Royal Bank of Scotland. This acquisition was part of Beazer Homes Group's overall business strategy to establish a separate brand for its exclusive home market. In 1997, the group completed 7,177 houses. Fiscal 1997 turnover was derived entirely within the United Kingdom.

	£ mil 06/95	06/96	06/97	US$mil 06/97					
Sales	413.2	380.2	532.9	887.7	P/E Ratio		10.3	Price (6/30/98)	1.84
Net Income	39.2	33.1	43.9	73.1	P/B Ratio		1.7	52 Wk Hi-Low	2.31-1.56
Book Value	243.7	257.2	282.6	470.8	Yield %		3.7	Market Cap	US$867.2mil

Address　St. James Hse., Lower Bristol R　Tel **122-542-8401**　ADR　--　CEO　**D.M. Webb**
　　　　　Bath, Avon BA2 3SB　　　　Fax **122-533-9279**　SEDOL　**0092104**　Chairman　**V.W. Benjamin**

Berkeley

DJGI Industry: **Home Construction**
Stoxx Sector: **Consumer Cyclical**

Berkeley Group PLC builds and sells upscale homes, mainly in southern, northwestern, and central England. St. George, its wholly owned subsidiary, builds private homes in the London area. The company is also involved in commercial-property development and investment in the United Kingdom. Homes built by Berkeley were sold for an average of more than £152,500. Residential housebuilding accounted for nearly 100% of fiscal 1997 revenues, with commercial property and other activities contributing a nominal amount to revenues.

	£ mil 04/96	04/97	04/98	US$mil 04/98					
Sales	334.3	485.3	599.6	1,002.7	P/E Ratio	10.6	Price (6/30/98)		6.26
Net Income	28.9	49.7	68.7	114.9	P/B Ratio	1.6	52 Wk Hi-Low		7.75-5.82
Book Value	318.7	394.5	578.4	967.2	Yield %	1.5	Market Cap		US$1,296.3mil

Address	19 Portsmouth Rd.	Tel 193-286-8555	ADR	--	CEO	Anthony W. Pidgley
	Codham, Surrey KT11 1JG	Fax 193-286-8667	SEDOL	0094177	Chairman	Graham J. Roper

BG

DJGI Industry: **Pipelines**
Stoxx Sector: **Energy**

BG PLC is involved in the exploration, production, and transportation of natural gas, and it operates an extensive pipeline and gas storage system in the United Kingdom. The company was formed in February 1997 after the breakup of British Gas PLC into two units; the other company formed is Centrica PLC. BG owns the TransCo gas-distribution company. The operation of its pipeline and gas-storage system accounted for 69% of 1997 revenues; exploration and production, 16%; international gas transportation, distribution, and power generation, 6%; and other activities, 5%.

	£ mil 12/95	12/96	12/97	US$mil 12/97					
Sales	8,601.0	4,383.0	4,300.0	7,109.8	P/E Ratio	38.1	Price (6/30/98)		3.47
Net Income	130.0	-571.0	-291.0	-481.2	P/B Ratio	1.6	52 Wk Hi-Low		3.48-2.21
Book Value	18,919.0	17,800.0	8,761.0	14,485.8	Yield %	2.3	Market Cap		US$22,729mil

Address	100 Thames Valley Park Dr.	Tel 118-929-3018	ADR	BRG	CEO	D. Varney
	Berkshire RG6 1PT	Fax 118-929-3184	SEDOL	0154219	Chairman	R.V. Giordano

BICC

DJGI Industry: **Heavy Construction**
Stoxx Sector: **Construction**

BICC PLC manufactures cables, provides engineering and construction services, and develops property. The company has operations in the United Kingdom, the United States, Spain, Italy, and Germany. BICC owns KWO, Germany's third-largest cable company, and has a controlling stake in Grupo Espanol General Cable, Spain's largest cable group. Balfour Beatty, its wholly owned engineering and construction subsidiary, produced about 49% of BICC's 1997 revenues. Cables accounted for another 26%, and metal manufacturing accounted for 13%.

	£ mil 12/95	12/96	12/97	US$mil 12/97					
Sales	4,063.0	4,236.0	4,139.0	6,843.6	P/E Ratio	NMF	Price (6/30/98)		1.31
Net Income	-111.0	3.0	-66.0	-109.1	P/B Ratio	3.0	52 Wk Hi-Low		2.08-1.31
Book Value	423.0	321.0	186.0	307.5	Yield %	6.1	Market Cap		US$917.9mil

Address	Devonshire Hse., Mayfair Pl.	Tel 171-629-6622	ADR	--	CEO	A. Jones
	London W1X 5FH	Fax 171-409-0070	SEDOL	0096162	Chairman	Sir R. Biggam

Blue Circle Industries

DJGI Industry: **Building Materials**
Stoxx Sector: **Construction**

Blue Circle Industries PLC is Britain's cement-market leader, with operations in Europe, North and South America, Asia, and Africa. It has heating and bathroom divisions, and its products include ready-mix concrete, aggregates, bricks, radiators, boilers, gas fires, water heaters, pumps, valves, thermostatic controls, ceramic sanitaryware, baths, and other bathroom fittings. The company acquired St. Marys Cement Corporation of Canada, an Ontario-based cement and building products company. Heavy building products accounted for 66% of 1997 revenues.

	£ mil 12/95	12/96	12/97	US$mil 12/97					
Sales	1,766.0	1,814.8	1,929.7	3,190.6	P/E Ratio	19.9	Price (6/30/98)		3.39
Net Income	142.5	180.8	134.0	221.6	P/B Ratio	2.2	52 Wk Hi-Low		4.49-2.94
Book Value	1,068.0	1,109.9	1,153.8	1,907.7	Yield %	4.3	Market Cap		US$4,281.8mil

Address	84 Eccleston Sq.	Tel 171-828-3456	ADR	BCLEY	CEO	Keith Orrell-Jones
	London SW1V 1PX	Fax 171-245-8272	SEDOL	0105853	Chairman	Lord Tugendhat

BOC Group

DJGI Industry: **Chemicals - Specialty**
Stoxx Sector: **Chemical**

BOC Group PLC produces and markets gases, health-care products, and vacuum technology in Europe, Africa, North and South America, and the Asia/Pacific region. The company supplies compressed gas to the brewing, electronic, food-preservation, and leisure industries, and it provides high-purity gases and delivery systems to the semiconductor industry in Japan and Taiwan. During fiscal 1997, gases and related products accounted for 71% of revenues; health care, 12%; vacuum technology, 9%; and distribution services, 8%.

	£ mil 09/95	09/96	09/97	US$mil 09/97					
Sales	3,543.9	3,752.1	3,677.7	5,954.8	P/E Ratio	14.9	Price (6/30/98)		8.17
Net Income	249.0	278.3	287.6	465.7	P/B Ratio	2.0	52 Wk Hi-Low		11.76-8.00
Book Value	1,632.5	1,793.6	1,866.3	3,021.9	Yield %	2.0	Market Cap		US$6,656.6mil

Address	Chertsey Rd., Windlesham	Tel 127-647-7222	ADR	BOX	CEO	F.D. Rosenkranz
	Surrey GU20 6HJ	Fax 127-647-1333	SEDOL	0108120	Chairman	D.G. John

Boots

DJGI Industry: **Retailers - Drug-Based**
Stoxx Sector: **Retail**

Boots Company PLC develops, produces, and markets health-care and personal-care products. It also operates Boots Opticians stores, A.G. Stanley home-decorating stores, and Halfords automotive-parts stores. Boots also owns Do It All stores. This retail and drugstore group has operations in the United Kingdom, France, and Italy. The chemist division accounted for 72% of fiscal 1998 revenues; retailing of car parts and accessories, 9%; do it yourself activities 7%; health care, 5%; opticians, 4%; contract manufacturing, 2%; and properties, 1%.

	£ mil 03/96	03/97	03/98	US$mil 03/98				
Revenues	4,010.4	4,565.1	4,975.6	8,327.4	P/E Ratio	34.2	Price (6/30/98)	9.93
Net Income	340.6	393.3	264.0	441.8	P/B Ratio	5.5	52 Wk Hi-Low	10.54-7.04
Book Value	2,201.5	1,621.1	1,636.3	2,738.6	Yield %	2.2	Market Cap	US$15,126mil

Address	1 Thane Rd. W.	Tel 115-950-6111	ADR	BOOOY	CEO & Dep Chmn	Lord Blyth of Rowington
	Nottingham NG2 3AA	Fax 115-959-2727	SEDOL	0111441	Chairman	Sir A. Angus

Bowthorpe

DJGI Industry: **Diversified Technology**
Stoxx Sector: **Technology**

Bowthorpe PLC specializes in products and services for electric utilities and electronic products. In a move to restructure the group, its 12 businesses have been focused into three sections: cable management, sensing, and network management and systems, the last of which includes interconnection, telecommunications, data communications, aerospace, and transport systems. In 1996, it closed three underperforming businesses in the data acquisition and environmental sectors. Network systems accounted for 49% of 1997 revenues; cable management, 27%; and sensing, 24%.

	£ mil 12/95	12/96	12/97	US$mil 12/97				
Sales	470.4	517.4	540.6	893.8	P/E Ratio	20.0	Price (6/30/98)	5.24
Net Income	43.3	40.5	51.2	84.6	P/B Ratio	8.1	52 Wk Hi-Low	6.04-2.93
Book Value	163.2	168.3	130.1	215.1	Yield %	2.1	Market Cap	US$1,766.9mil

Address	Gatwick Rd., Crawley	Tel 129-352-8888	ADR	--	CEO	N. Brookes
	W. Sussex RH10 2RZ	Fax 129-354-1905	SEDOL	0116402	Chairman	H.A. Vice

BPB

DJGI Industry: **Building Materials**
Stoxx Sector: **Construction**

BPB PLC is a leading world gypsum group, Europe's largest plasterboard producer, and a major supplier of plasters and plasterboard to the Canadian and South American markets. The group manufactures an extensive range of building materials, plasters, plasterboards, paperboards, and paper and packaging products. BPB operates 80 plants worldwide and distributes over 1,000 products and systems for wall linings, partitions, and ceilings and floors to more than 40 countries. Building materials accounted for 86% of fiscal 1998 revenues and paper and packaging for 14%.

	£ mil 03/96	03/97	03/98	US$mil 03/98				
Sales	1,428.2	1,385.5	1,300.2	2,176.1	P/E Ratio	22.3	Price (6/30/98)	3.63
Net Income	103.0	127.2	83.7	140.1	P/B Ratio	2.3	52 Wk Hi-Low	4.40-2.97
Book Value	792.7	776.3	771.7	1,291.5	Yield %	3.0	Market Cap	US$3,130.3mil

Address	Langley Pk. Hse., Uxbridge Rd.	Tel 175-389-8800	ADR	--	CEO	Jean-Pierre Cuny
	Slough, Berkshire SL3 6DU	Fax 175-389-8888	SEDOL	0068707	Chairman	Alan Turner

British Aerospace

DJGI Industry: **Aerospace & Defense**
Stoxx Sector: **Technology**

British Aerospace PLC is a defense and commercial aerospace company. Its defense work includes the manufacture of military aircraft and electronic systems. The company's commercial aircraft business includes a 20% stake in Airbus Industrie, a regional aircraft joint venture with other European aerospace companies. In November 1996, BAe formed a joint venture with France's Lagardere for guided weapons systems. The new company, Matra-BAe Dynamics, is Europe's largest guided-weapons business. Defense activities accounted for 74% of 1997 revenues.

	£ mil 12/95	12/96	12/97	US$mil 12/97				
Sales	5,741.0	6,464.0	7,267.0	12,015.5	P/E Ratio	57.4	Price (6/30/98)	4.59
Net Income	138.0	309.0	161.0	266.2	P/B Ratio	5.5	52 Wk Hi-Low	5.46-3.27
Book Value	653.0	1,418.0	1,461.0	2,415.7	Yield %	1.0	Market Cap	US$13,404mil

Address	Farnborough Aerospace Ctr.	Tel 125-237-3232	ADR	--	CEO	Richard Evans
	Hampshire GU14 6YU	Fax 125-238-3000	SEDOL	0263494	Chairman	Robert Bauman

British Airways

DJGI Industry: **Airlines**
Stoxx Sector: **Consumer Cyclical**

British Airways PLC is the world's leading international airline, operating international and domestic scheduled and charter air services for the carriage of passengers, freight, and mail and providing ancillary services. The company holds stakes in Deutsche Air, France's TAT European Airlines, Australia's Qantas Airways Ltd., and all of the U.K. regional carrier Dan-Air Services. Scheduled passenger services accounted for 90% of fiscal 1998 revenues; aircraft maintenance, package holidays, and other airline services, 9%; and nonscheduled services, 1%.

	£ mil 03/96	03/97	03/98	US$mil 03/98				
Sales	7,760.0	8,359.0	8,642.0	14,463.6	P/E Ratio	14.5	Price (6/30/98)	6.49
Net Income	473.0	553.0	460.0	769.9	P/B Ratio	2.0	52 Wk Hi-Low	7.03-5.00
Book Value	2,494.0	2,984.0	3,321.0	5,558.2	Yield %	2.6	Market Cap	US$11,246mil

Address	Speedbird Hse., Heathrow	Tel 181-759-5511	ADR	BAB	CEO	Robert Ayling
	Hounslow TW6 2JA	Fax 181-759-9597	SEDOL	0129057	Chairman	Sir Colin Marshall

British Biotech

DJGI Industry: **Biotechnology**
Stoxx Sector: **Technology**

British Biotechnology PLC, a pharmaceutical company, researches and develops pharmaceutical products for cancer, AIDS, bacterial sepsis, cardiac ischemia, pancreatitis, bone marrow dysfunction, chronic asthma, arthritis, and multiple sclerosis. Products include Marimastat, Batimastat, and Lexipafant. The group has signed a three-year agreement with SynPhar Laboratories of Canada to collaborate on the development of cysteine protease inhibitors, a new class of drug designed to combat tissue-destructive diseases like rheumatoid arthritis, osteoarthritis, osteoporosis, and cancer.

	£ mil 04/96	04/97	04/98	US$mil 04/98				
Sales	8.5	10.1	0.5	0.8	P/E Ratio	**NMF**	Price (6/30/98)	**0.37**
Net Income	-25.2	-28.9	-44.9	-75.1	P/B Ratio	1.2	52 Wk Hi-Low	**2.29-0.30**
Book Value	83.0	200.7	157.2	262.8	Yield %	0.0	Market Cap	**US$402.1mil**

Address	**Watlington Rd.**	Tel	**186-574-8747**	ADR	**BBIOY**	CEO	**E. Goldstein**
	Oxford OX4 5LY	Fax	**186-578-1047**	SEDOL	**0129905**	Chairman	**J. Raisman**

British Land

DJGI Industry: **Real Estate**
Stoxx Sector: **Financial Services**

British Land Co. PLC is a property-investment and development company that specializes in long-term income-producing commercial properties, mainly offices and retail outlets. Approximately 84% of the company's holdings are properties to which it owns permanent title, and its investements are located predominantly in the United Kingdom. In March 1998, British Land began an investment portfolio joint venture with U.K. retailer Tesco PLC (TSCDY). Rental income accounted for 81% of fiscal 1998 revenues and property trading accounted for 19%.

	£ mil 03/96	03/97	03/98	US$mil 03/98				
Sales	275.3	332.4	353.3	591.3	P/E Ratio	36.9	Price (6/30/98)	6.16
Net Income	51.0	75.8	107.3	179.6	P/B Ratio	1.1	52 Wk Hi-Low	8.03-5.66
Book Value	1,868.7	2,225.0	2,932.1	4,907.3	Yield %	1.6	Market Cap	US$5,295.8mil

Address	**10 Cornwall Terr.**	Tel	**171-486-4466**	ADR	--	CEO	**John Ritblat**
	London NW1 4QP	Fax	**171-935-5552**	SEDOL	**0136701**	Chairman	**John Ritblat**

British Petroleum

DJGI Industry: **Oil Companies - Major**
Stoxx Sector: **Energy**

British Petroleum Co. PLC is one of the world's largest international petroleum and petrochemical corporations. As the United Kingdom's largest integrated oil company, it explores for, refines, produces, and markets oil and natural gas. It also holds agricultural interests and supplies acrylonitrile and acetic acid to manufacturers worldwide. Its chemicals are used in synthetic fibers, paints, and pharmaceuticals. In 1997, the company made its largest chemicals business buy in 15 years when it acquired Styrenix Kunststoffe from Huls, a unit of Veba.

	£ mil 12/95	12/96	12/97	US$mil 12/97				
Sales	36,106.0	44,731.0	43,460.0	71,858.5	P/E Ratio	20.2	Price (6/30/98)	8.74
Net Income	1,122.0	2,552.0	2,470.0	4,084.0	P/B Ratio	3.6	52 Wk Hi-Low	9.67-7.47
Book Value	11,802.0	12,774.0	13,908.0	22,996.0	Yield %	2.6	Market Cap	US$84,896mil

Address	**Britannic Hse., 1 Finsbury Circus**	Tel	**171-496-4000**	ADR	**BP**	CEO	**John Browne**
	London EC2M 7BA	Fax	**171-496-4516**	SEDOL	**0138495**	Chairman	--

In DJ Stoxx 50.

British Sky Broadcasting

DJGI Industry: **Cable & Broadcasting**
Stoxx Sector: **Media**

British Sky Broadcasting Group PLC (BSkyB), a satellite and broadcasting company, is the leading program provider to the United Kingdom pay-television market. Its pay-TV direct-to-home service has more than 6 million subscribers. Main shareholders are News Corp. with 40%, Pathé SA of France with 17%, and Granada Group PLC with 11%. BSkyB owns and operates 11 channels in the United Kingdom, and has equity stakes in 5 others. Direct-to-home subscribers accounted for 68% of 1997 revevenues. In May 1998, BSkyB confirmed the launch of digital satellite services in June.

	£ mil 06/96	06/96	06/97	US$mil 06/97				
Sales	777.9	1,008.1	1,270.0	2,115.6	P/E Ratio	27.4	Price (6/30/98)	4.31
Net Income	136.5	233.8	288.0	479.8	P/B Ratio	**NMF**	52 Wk Hi-Low	4.85-3.42
Book Value	-767.6	-627.7	-449.9	-749.4	Yield %	1.4	Market Cap	US$12,370mil

Address	**6 Centaurs Business Park**	Tel	**171-705-3000**	ADR	**BSY**	CEO	**S.H. Chrisholm**
	Isleworth, Middlesex TW7 5QD	Fax	**171-705-3030**	SEDOL	**0141192**	Chairman	**G.J. Robinson**

British Steel

DJGI Industry: **Steel**
Stoxx Sector: **Basic Resources**

British Steel PLC manufactures and distributes steel products, steel structural sections for construction, railway tracks, steel sheets for automobiles and domestic appliances, and tin plate for canning. Its U.S.-based Tuscaloosa Steel subsidiary produces coil and cut-plate steel for the construction, transportation, and energy industries. British Steel's automotive customers include Ford, Honda, and Jaguar. The group's operations are carried out in the United Kingdom, Europe, and North America. During 1998, the group acquired Firsteel Group.

	£ mil 03/96	03/97	03/98	US$mil 03/98				
Sales	7,048.0	7,224.0	6,947.0	11,626.8	P/E Ratio	11.6	Price (6/30/98)	1.32
Net Income	777.0	310.0	226.0	378.2	P/B Ratio	0.6	52 Wk Hi-Low	1.90-1.25
Book Value	4,723.0	4,757.0	4,604.0	7,705.4	Yield %	7.6	Market Cap	US$4,355.4mil

Address	**15 Marylebone Rd.**	Tel	**171-735-7654**	ADR	**BST**	CEO	**Brian S. Moffat**
	London NW1 5JD	Fax	**171-587-1142**	SEDOL	**0141147**	Chairman	**Brian S. Moffat**

Bryant

DJGI Industry: **Home Construction**
Stoxx Sector: **Consumer Cyclical**

Bryant Group PLC is one of the United Kingdom's leading quality house builders and also has activities in the construction sector. It primarily builds and refurbishes quality homes and business complexes. During fiscal 1997 the group completed 4,040 homes at an average price of 116,000 pounds sterling. Construction of residential homes accounted for 86% of fiscal 1997 revenues and construction activities, 14%. Its three sectors (homes, construction, and property) are all active in the United Kingdom and Ireland.

	£ mil 05/95	05/96	05/97	US$mil 05/97				
Sales	519.0	453.6	558.4	916.6	P/E Ratio	10.1	Price (6/30/98)	1.10
Net Income	30.7	16.6	26.2	43.0	P/B Ratio	1.2	52 Wk Hi-Low	1.53-1.00
Book Value	244.8	248.2	256.1	420.4	Yield %	5.9	Market Cap	US$525.7mil

Address	Cranmore Blvd., Solihull	Tel **121-711-1212**	ADR	--	CEO	**Andrew MacKenzie**
	West Midlands B90 4SD	Fax **121-712-6453**	SEDOL	**0149408**	Chairman	**Colin Hope**

BT

DJGI Industry: **Telephone Utilities (All)**
Stoxx Sector: **Telecom**

British Telecommunications PLC (BT) supplies inland and international telecommunications services within the United Kingdom and overseas. The company operates more than 120,000 domestic pay phones and has issued more than 3 million charge cards. Its main products and services include local, long-distance, and international calls; telephone lines, equipment, and private circuits for homes and businesses; providing and managing private networks; and supplying mobile communications services. Inland telephone calls accounted for 31% of fiscal 1998 revenues.

	£ mil 03/96	03/97	03/98	US$mil 03/98				
Sales	14,446.0	14,935.0	15,640.0	26,175.7	P/E Ratio	27.7	Price (6/30/98)	7.40
Net Income	1,986.0	2,077.0	1,706.0	2,855.2	P/B Ratio	4.4	52 Wk Hi-Low	7.58-3.57
Book Value	12,678.0	11,116.0	10,785.0	18,050.2	Yield %	2.6	Market Cap	US$79,172mil

Address	81 Newgate St.	Tel **171-356-5000**	ADR	**BTY**	Managing Director	**Michael L. Hepher**
	London EC1A 7AJ	Fax **171-356-5520**	SEDOL	**0140843**	Chairman	**Sir Iain D. Vallance**

In DJ Stoxx 50.

BTR

DJGI Industry: **Conglomerates**
Stoxx Sector: **Conglomerate**

BTR PLC is an industrial manufacturing and engineering company. Its products include automotive systems, power drives, process control, packaging, air-moving devices, generators, and building materials. Two-thirds of the group's sales are exports outside of Europe. In 1998, BTR sold its MBCI metal components manufacturing business to NCI Building Systems Inc. and its global packaging businesses to Owens-Illinois. The company also said it plans to sell all its nonengineering operations to focus on core engineering operations assets.

	£ mil 12/95	12/96	12/97	US$mil 12/97				
Sales	9,010.0	8,413.0	7,435.0	12,293.3	P/E Ratio	6.4	Price (6/30/98)	1.70
Net Income	960.0	431.0	882.0	1,458.3	P/B Ratio	2.6	52 Wk Hi-Low	2.59-1.55
Book Value	2,277.0	2,259.0	2,156.0	3,564.8	Yield %	6.9	Market Cap	US$9,409.8mil

Address	Silvertown Hse., Vincent Sq.	Tel **171-834-3848**	ADR	**BTRUY**	Managing Director	**Alan R. Jackson**
	London SW1P 2PL	Fax **171-834-3879**	SEDOL	**0272133**	Chairman	**Norman C. Ireland**

Bunzl

DJGI Industry: **Paper Products**
Stoxx Sector: **Basic Resources**

Bunzl PLC distributes, converts, and manufactures paper- and plastic-based products in Europe and the United States. The company produces disposable paper and plastic products for supermarkets, fast-food chains, airlines, and hotels. It is a major distributor of fine paper in Europe and manufactures cigarette filters for worldwide sale. Bunzl supplies plastic products to the engineering and oil industries and makes packaging, automotive components, housewares, and gardening products. In February 1997, Bunzl agreed to buy American Filtrona Corp.'s bonded-fibers business.

	£ mil 12/95	12/96	12/97	US$mil 12/97				
Sales	1,758.5	1,579.7	1,704.0	2,817.5	P/E Ratio	15.8	Price (6/30/98)	2.82
Net Income	67.5	72.9	80.2	132.6	P/B Ratio	5.8	52 Wk Hi-Low	3.44-1.89
Book Value	312.4	286.6	221.4	366.1	Yield %	2.4	Market Cap	US$2,131.3mil

Address	110 Park St.	Tel **171-495-4950**	ADR	--	Managing Director	**David Williams**
	London W1Y 3RB	Fax **171-495-4953**	SEDOL	**0154004**	Exec Chairman	**Tony Habgood**

Burmah Castrol

DJGI Industry: **Oil Companies - Secondary**
Stoxx Sector: **Energy**

Burmah Castrol PLC produces and markets lubricants, fuels, and specialty chemicals. The company operates in over 50 countries, manufacturing Castrol GTX motor oil and operating service-station networks in three countries. Burmah Castrol also produces printing inks and metallurgical, construction, and mining chemicals. Lubricants accounted for 67% of 1997 revenues; chemicals, 26%; and fuels, 7%. Lubricants accounted for 74% of pretax income; chemicals, 24%; energy investments, 2%; and fuels, nominal.

	£ mil 12/95	12/96	12/97	US$mil 12/97				
Sales	2,969.0	3,046.8	2,869.1	4,743.9	P/E Ratio	18.4	Price (6/30/98)	10.70
Net Income	135.0	155.1	123.3	203.9	P/B Ratio	3.1	52 Wk Hi-Low	13.28-9.53
Book Value	684.3	737.5	728.9	1,205.2	Yield %	3.8	Market Cap	US$3,802.9mil

Address	Burmah Castrol Hse., Pipers Way	Tel **179-351-1521**	ADR	**BURMY**	CEO	**Jonathan M. Fry**
	Swindon, Wiltshire SN3 1RE	Fax **179-351-3506**	SEDOL	**0155405**	Chairman	**Lawrence M. Urquhart**

Cable & Wireless

DJGI Industry: **Telephone Utilities (All)**
Stoxx Sector: **Telecom**

Cable & Wireless PLC is one of the world's leading international telecommunications groups. With operations in over 50 countries, it provides services including telephone, facsimile, telex, and data transmissions. The company's network includes operations in Russia, Australia, South Africa, Latin America, and the Caribbean. International telephone services accounted for 43% of fiscal 1997 revenues; domestic telephone services, 27%; other telecommunications services, 20%; cableships and contracts, 4%; equipment sales and rental, 3%; and cable television and multimedia services, 3%.

	£ mil 03/96	03/97	03/98	US$mil 03/98					
Sales	5,517.0	6,050.0	7,001.0	11,717.2	P/E Ratio	12.8	Price (6/30/98)		7.28
Net Income	607.0	677.0	1,288.0	2,155.6	P/B Ratio	5.4	52 Wk Hi-Low		7.54-4.32
Book Value	3,259.0	3,749.0	3,088.0	5,168.2	Yield %	1.7	Market Cap		US$27,688mil

Address	124 Theobalds Rd.	Tel 171-315-4000	ADR	CWP	CEO	Richard Brown
	London WC1X 8RX	Fax 171-315-5000	SEDOL	0162557	Chairman	Dr. Brian Smith

Cadbury Schweppes

DJGI Industry: **Other Food**
Stoxx Sector: **Food & Beverage**

Cadbury Schweppes PLC is a beverage and confectionery company that sells its products in 195 countries. Its key product line features soft drinks, sold under the Schweppes, Dr Pepper, Canada Dry, and Crush labels, and chocolate, sold under the Cadbury brand name. Cadbury Schweppes is the third-largest soft-drink maker in the world. In May 1998, Cadbury said it had completed the joint-venture acquisition of Beverage America and Select Beverages for $724 million. Confectionery accounted for 53% of 1997 revenues and beverages accounted for 47%.

	£ mil 12/95	12/96	01/98	US$mil 01/98					
Sales	4,776.0	4,194.0	4,173.0	6,823.1	P/E Ratio	13.5	Price (6/30/98)		9.28
Net Income	309.0	345.0	692.0	1,131.5	P/B Ratio	5.6	52 Wk Hi-Low		9.88-5.32
Book Value	1,229.0	1,200.0	1,669.0	2,728.9	Yield %	1.9	Market Cap		US$15,713mil

Address	25 Berkeley Sq.	Tel 171-409-1313	ADR	CSG	CEO	John Sunderland
	London W1X 6HT	Fax 171-830-5200	SEDOL	0161242	Chairman	Dominic Cadbury

Capital Shopping Centres

DJGI Industry: **Real Estate**
Stoxx Sector: **Financial Services**

Capital Shopping Centres (CSC) PLC owns and manages regional shopping centers in the United Kingdom. The company has a portfolio of shopping centers positioned throughout the country. Capital Shopping currently is developing a GBP250 million, 200-acre shopping center at Braehead, scheduled to be completed in July 1999. The company's ultimate holding company is Liblife Controlling Corporation (Proprietary) Ltd. Rents receivable accounted for 86% of 1997 revenues and service charges and other income, accounted for 14%.

	£ mil 12/95	12/96	12/97	US$mil 12/97					
Sales	103.7	133.0	150.6	249.0	P/E Ratio	26.4	Price (6/30/98)		4.04
Net Income	38.8	44.8	62.4	103.2	P/B Ratio	1.0	52 Wk Hi-Low		4.89-3.82
Book Value	925.1	1,254.9	1,596.2	2,639.2	Yield %	2.3	Market Cap		US$2,747.8mil

Address	40 Broadway	Tel 171-887-4220	ADR	--	Managing Director	Douglas Leslie
	London SW1H 0BU	Fax 171-887-4225	SEDOL	0173418	Chairman	Donald Gordon

Caradon

DJGI Industry: **Building Materials**
Stoxx Sector: **Construction**

Caradon PLC manufactures building products and automobile components in Europe and North America, and it prints securities forms in the United States. The company makes Stelrad radiators, Mira commercial shower systems, and Everest doors and windows. Its Caradon Heating unit is one of Europe's leading makers of radiators, and subsidiary Clarke American is one of the largest printers of financial forms in the United States. Doors and windows accounted for 31% of 1997 revenues; plumbing, 23%; electrical, 19%; structural and engineering, 14%; and security printing, 13%.

	£ mil 12/95	12/96	12/97	US$mil 12/97					
Sales	2,063.2	1,797.8	1,621.6	2,681.2	P/E Ratio	13.4	Price (6/30/98)		1.86
Net Income	67.0	106.3	88.0	145.5	P/B Ratio	4.4	52 Wk Hi-Low		2.22-1.59
Book Value	312.5	423.1	220.7	364.9	Yield %	5.1	Market Cap		US$1,607.2mil

Address	Caradon Hse., 24 Queens Rd.	Tel 193-285-0850	ADR	CRDOY	CEO	Peter J. Jansen
	Weybridge, Surrey KT13 9UX	Fax 193-282-3328	SEDOL	0176268	Chairman	Antony P. Hichens

Carlton Communications

DJGI Industry: **Cable & Broadcasting**
Stoxx Sector: **Media**

Carlton Communications PLC is involved in digital-signal processing, sound mixing, television broadcasting, videocassette manufacturing, and film/TV processing and postproduction. In January 1997 a joint venture of Carlton, Granada Group PLC, and British Digital Broadcasting PLC, won digital-terrestrial television licenses in the United Kingdom. In April 1997, Carlton acquired Rank Film for GBP65 million. Television broadcasting accounted for 45% of fiscal 1997 revenues; video production, 26%; film, 17%; products, 11%; and others, 1%.

	£ mil 09/95	09/96	09/97	US$mil 09/97					
Sales	1,579.6	1,677.5	1,749.7	2,833.1	P/E Ratio	15.6	Price (6/30/98)		5.35
Net Income	165.2	197.6	212.2	343.6	P/B Ratio	14.0	52 Wk Hi-Low		5.58-4.10
Book Value	60.0	129.4	158.1	256.0	Yield %	2.4	Market Cap		US$5,445.3mil

Address	25 Knightsbridge	Tel 171-663-6363	ADR	CCTVY	Managing Director	June F. de Moller
	London SW1X 7RZ	Fax 171-663-6300	SEDOL	0341925	Chairman	Michael P. Green

CGU

DJGI Industry: **Insurance - Full Line**
Stoxx Sector: **Insurance**

CGU PLC was formed out of the 1998 merger of Commercial Union PLC and General Accident PLC. Besides personal lines, the new organization's specialty products include ocean marine, national and global accounts, surety, and national programs. It has subsidiaries, associates, and branches in the United Kingdom, Europe, North America, and other countries worldwide. The group provides a number of financial services related to its core business, including unit trust and investment, management, banking, stockbrokere, private client investment management and personal equity plans.

	£ mil 12/95	12/96	12/97	US$mil 12/97				
Revenues	13,403.0	12,224.0	14,209.0	23,493.7	P/E Ratio	23.7	Price (6/30/98)	11.18
Net Income	444.0	397.0	372.0	615.1	P/B Ratio	2.4	52 Wk Hi-Low	12.72-6.32
Book Value	3,400.0	3,206.0	3,246.0	5,367.1	Yield %	2.9	Market Cap	US$24,055mil

Address	St. Helen's, 1 Undershaft	Tel 171-283-7500	ADR	--	CEO	John G. Carter
	London EC3P 3DQ	Fax 171-283-2068	SEDOL	0216238	Chairman	Nicholas H. Baring

Charter

DJGI Industry: **Building Materials**
Stoxx Sector: **Construction**

Charter PLC is an industrial conglomerate. The company holds subsidiaries that are involved primarily in the manufacture of welding products and rail-track equipment. The company is also involved in air and gas handling and specialized engineering in the United Kingdom, Europe, North America, and other countries worldwide. During 1997, Charter acquired Howden PLC. Welding products accounted for 58% of the conglomerate's 1997 revenues; specialized engineering accounted for 21%; and air and gas handling accounted for 21%.

	£ mil 12/95	12/96	12/97	US$mil 12/97				
Sales	1,097.7	883.4	1,114.2	1,842.3	P/E Ratio	20.4	Price (6/30/98)	6.28
Net Income	58.2	12.0	28.7	47.5	P/B Ratio	NMF	52 Wk Hi-Low	8.65-5.67
Book Value	200.1	217.7	-127.9	-211.5	Yield %	5.0	Market Cap	US$1,007.7mil

Address	7 Holbart Pl.	Tel 171-838-7000	ADR	CTHAY	CEO	Jeffrey Herbert
	London SW1W OHH	Fax 171-239-5112	SEDOL	0188263	Chairman	Jeffrey Herbert

Coats Viyella

DJGI Industry: **Clothing & Fabrics**
Stoxx Sector: **Consumer Cyclical**

Coats Viyella PLC manufactures textile products, such as thread, zippers, and fabric. It sells clothes under the brand names Van Heusen and Berghaus and makes uniforms for British Rail and British Telecom. Coats Viyella also makes precision-engineered aluminum, magnesium, and zinc die-cast components. Operations are carried on worldwide. Thread accounted for 45% of 1997 revenues; contract clothing, 17%; precision engineering, 14%; fashion retail and branded clothing, 11%; home furnishings, 8% and other Indian businesses, 5%.

	£ mil 12/95	12/96	12/97	US$mil 12/97				
Sales	2,339.2	2,455.1	2,304.6	3,810.5	P/E Ratio	NMF	Price (6/30/98)	0.74
Net Income	110.4	56.5	0.7	1.2	P/B Ratio	0.8	52 Wk Hi-Low	1.28-0.74
Book Value	770.7	724.2	665.4	1,100.2	Yield %	6.8	Market Cap	US$868.6mil

Address	28 Savile Row	Tel 171-292-9200	ADR	COAVY	CEO	Neville Bain
	London W1X 2DD	Fax 171-437-2016	SEDOL	0927057	Chairman	Sir David Alliance

Cookson

DJGI Industry: **Industrial - Diversified**
Stoxx Sector: **Industrials**

Cookson Group PLC manufactures specialized materials for industrial use, such as circuit-boards, precision metal castings, fiber optic cables, and ceramics. During 1997 the group acquired Howard H. Sweet & Sons, a subsidiary of Tiffany & Co. of New York, and disposed of Anzon, its antimony products business. In recent years, the company has sold or closed some units to focus on its core businesses. Electronics accounted for 43% of Cookson's 1997 revenues; ceramics, 22%; engineered products, 18%; and plastics, 17%.

	£ mil 12/95	12/96	12/97	US$mil 12/97				
Sales	1,560.2	1,629.2	1,637.1	2,706.8	P/E Ratio	25.8	Price (6/30/98)	2.06
Net Income	104.8	6.7	55.0	90.9	P/B Ratio	2.6	52 Wk Hi-Low	2.77-1.66
Book Value	728.3	516.9	553.1	914.5	Yield %	4.5	Market Cap	US$2,375.3mil

Address	1-11 John Adam St.	Tel 171-766-4500	ADR	--	CEO	Richard Oster
	London WC2N 6HJ	Fax 171-747-6600	SEDOL	0508407	Chairman	Robert Malpas

Courtaulds Textiles

DJGI Industry: **Clothing & Fabrics**
Stoxx Sector: **Consumer Cyclical**

Courtaulds Textiles PLC is a textile, clothing, and fabric company that produces lace, stretch fabric, car upholstery, yarns, and home furnishings. The company has operations in 16 countries in Europe, North America, North Africa, and Asia. Berlei and Gossard bras, Aristoc tights, and Jockey underwear are among its branded clothing operations. It also supplies retailers such as Marks & Spencer with private-label clothing and home furnishings. Courtaulds Textiles is the United Kingdom's largest producer of lingerie and underwear.

	£ mil 12/95	12/96	12/97	US$mil 12/97				
Sales	1,102.5	926.1	909.7	1,504.1	P/E Ratio	11.0	Price (6/30/98)	2.90
Net Income	26.1	-5.2	27.4	45.3	P/B Ratio	1.2	52 Wk Hi-Low	3.73-2.82
Book Value	277.3	244.7	250.0	413.4	Yield %	5.3	Market Cap	US$501.9mil

Address	13/14 Margaret St.	Tel 171-331-4500	ADR	COU	CEO	Colin Dyer
	London W1A 3DA	Fax 171-331-4600	SEDOL	0228794	Chairman	John Eccles

Delta

DJGI Industry: **Electrical Components & Equipment**
Stoxx Sector: **Industrials**

Delta Group PLC is an engineering and industrial-services company that manufactures and distributes electric cables, circuit-protection equipment, and plumbing and engineering products. In Australia, the company distributes electric and electronic products and protective coatings; in Africa, its three associated companies repair motors and transformers, engage in manganese-related production, and manufacture plumbing products. Cables and materials accounted for 28% of 1997 revenues; electrical protection, 25%; plumbing products, 24%; and industrial services, 23%.

	£ mil 12/95	12/96	01/98	US$mil 01/98					
Sales	1,018.5	950.0	839.4	1,372.5	P/E Ratio	**NMF**	Price (6/30/98)		**2.19**
Net Income	30.0	22.8	-43.9	-71.8	P/B Ratio	1.2	52 Wk Hi-Low		3.51-2.02
Book Value	340.5	327.1	282.1	461.2	Yield %	7.3	Market Cap		**US$546.4mil**

Address	1 Kingsway	Tel 171-836-3535	ADR	--	CEO	**Robert Easton**
	London WC2B 6XF	Fax 171-836-4511	SEDOL	0261506	Chairman	**Sir Martin Jacomb**

Diageo

DJGI Industry: **Distillers & Brewers**
Stoxx Sector: **Food & Beverage**

Diageo PLC, formed in 1997 by the merger of Guinness PLC and Grand Metropolitan PLC, is an international food and beverage company. It brews beer and distills gin, rum, brandy, Scotch whisky, liqueur, vodka, and bourbon, and it produces and markets a wide selection of wines, ports, sherries, and vermouths. Guinness brands are now available in 150 countries and are brewed in 50 countries. Brands include Guinness and Harp beers, Dewar's Scotch, and Tanqueray gin. Its United Distillers subsidiary makes Bell's Scotch whisky, Johnnie Walker Scotch, and Gordon's gin.

	£ mil 12/95	12/96	12/97	US$mil 12/97					
Sales	3,486.0	3,562.0	12,280.0	20,304.2	P/E Ratio	30.2	Price (6/30/98)		7.10
Net Income	595.0	685.0	811.0	1,340.9	P/B Ratio	2.8	52 Wk Hi-Low		7.61-5.30
Book Value	4,282.0	4,145.0	6,749.0	11,159.1	Yield %	3.8	Market Cap		**US$42,326mil**

Address	39 Portman Sq.	Tel 171-486-0288	ADR	DEO	Joint Chairman	**G. Bull**
	London W1M 9AG	Fax 171-935-5500	SEDOL	0237400	Joint Chairman	**A. Greener**

In DJ Stoxx 50.

Dixons

DJGI Industry: **Retailers - Other Specialty**
Stoxx Sector: **Retail**

Dixons Group PLC owns a network of retail outlets that feature electronic consumer goods, and it also invests in real estate. Its stores sell such electronics goods as cameras, personal computers, stereo systems, televisions, home-office equipment, and kitchen and laundry appliances. The group sells its products through its retail outlets, mainly Dixons, Currys, PC World, and The Link. Dixons also undertakes property development, mainly in Belgium, Germany, and France. Retailing accounted for 97% of fiscal 1997 revenues and property accounted for 3%.

	£ mil 04/96	05/97	05/98	US$mil 05/98					
Revenues	1,919.7	2,442.5	2,773.8	4,525.0	P/E Ratio	12.6	Price (6/30/98)		4.78
Net Income	70.6	152.7	170.1	277.5	P/B Ratio	5.5	52 Wk Hi-Low		7.20-4.67
Book Value	173.8	324.5	453.9	740.5	Yield %	2.3	Market Cap		**US$3,436.4mil**

Address	Hemel Hempstead	Tel 171-499-3494	ADR	DXNGY	CEO	**John Clare**
	Hertfordshire HP2 7TG	Fax 171-629-1410	SEDOL	0272304	Chairman	**Stanley Kalms**

Electrocomponents

DJGI Industry: **Other Industrial & Commercial Services**
Stoxx Sector: **Industrials**

Electrocomponents PLC is involved in the distribution of electronic, electrical, and mechanical products, supplies, and services to industrial, commercial, and retail customers through its distribution channels in the United Kingdom, continental Europe, and Australasia. Wholly owned subsidiaries RS Components U.K. and RS Components International distribute tools, instruments, and electronic, electrical, and mechanical components in Europe, Australia, New Zealand, India, and Hong Kong. RS Group accounted for 93% of fiscal 1998 revenues and Part International, 7%.

	£ mil 03/96	03/97	03/98	US$mil 03/98					
Sales	559.9	605.8	662.4	1,108.6	P/E Ratio	24.9	Price (6/30/98)		4.70
Net Income	66.7	75.3	80.6	134.9	P/B Ratio	6.4	52 Wk Hi-Low		6.00-4.14
Book Value	246.1	280.5	316.2	529.2	Yield %	1.9	Market Cap		**US$3,359.4mil**

Address	Broadoak, Southgate Park	Tel 173-336-1234	ADR	--	CEO	**Robert Lawson**
	Peterborough PE2 6YS	Fax 173-336-3800	SEDOL	0309644	Chairman	**Roy Cotterill**

EMI

DJGI Industry: **Entertainment**
Stoxx Sector: **Consumer Cyclical**

EMI Group is the world's third-largest record label and the largest publisher of music. Its music-publishing activities include the licensing of songs, lyrics, and melodies for use in film, television, commercials, and radio broadcasts. EMI holds recording rights for groups like The Beatles, and its music labels include Virgin Music, Capital Records, and Chrysalis Records. During 1998, EMI disposed of the HMV Group and acquired Copacabana, CMC Records, AV Music Publishers, Westwood Promotions, Narada Media, and a 50% interest in both Jobete and Priority.

	£ mil 03/96	03/97	03/98	US$mil 03/98					
Sales	5,055.6	3,390.0	2,352.7	3,937.6	P/E Ratio	21.3	Price (6/30/98)		5.24
Net Income	224.7	155.0	228.7	382.8	P/B Ratio	**NMF**	52 Wk Hi-Low		6.15-4.29
Book Value	534.1	-11.2	-672.1	-1,124.9	Yield %	3.1	Market Cap		**US$7,602.2mil**

Address	4 Tenterden St., Hanover Sq.	Tel 171-355-4848	ADR	EMIGY	Finance Director	**S. Duffy**
	London W1A 2Ay	Fax 171-495-1307	SEDOL	0044473	Chairman	**Sir C. Southgate**

Enterprise Oil

Enterprise Oil PLC, one of the world's largest pure-energy exploration groups, explores for and produces oil and natural gas in Europe, Australia, and Southeast Asia, with significant operations in Norway, Italy, and Indonesia. Most of its wells are in the North Sea. The group has interests in 23 producing fields in the United Kingdom and Norwegian sectors and also has an interest in an oil field in Italy. Exports represent nearly two-thirds of revenues. In September 1996, the company announced a strategic alliance with U.S.-based Pennzoil Co. to prospect 102 oil fields in the Gulf of Mexico.

	£ mil 12/95	12/96	12/97	US$mil 12/97				
Sales	762.9	1,012.5	946.9	1,565.6	P/E Ratio	26.0	Price (6/30/98)	5.45
Net Income	101.6	142.5	126.6	209.3	P/B Ratio	3.4	52 Wk Hi-Low	7.30-5.14
Book Value	773.1	808.6	807.1	1,334.5	Yield %	3.2	Market Cap	US$4,526.1mil

Address	Grand Bldgs., Trafalgar Sq.	Tel 171-925-4000	ADR	ETP	CEO	P. Jungels
	London WC2N 5EJ	Fax 171-925-4321	SEDOL	0318866	Chairman	Graham J. Hearne

Eurotherm

Eurotherm PLC manufactures industrial process-control equipment, including products for controlling temperature and atmosphere, instruments for measuring and controlling the thickness of material, and mechanisms for controlling integrated industrial processes. Eurotherm also makes DC and AC drives, which control electric motors, and recorders, which collect and record process parameters. The company has subsidiaries in Europe, the United States, Asia, and Australia. Manufacture of controls and instrumentation accounted for 58% of fiscal 1997 revenues; drives, 36%; and gauging, 6%.

	£ mil 10/95	10/96	10/97	US$mil 10/97				
Sales	195.4	206.5	202.3	338.7	P/E Ratio	18.5	Price (6/30/98)	4.21
Net Income	22.4	24.8	20.6	34.5	P/B Ratio	3.9	52 Wk Hi-Low	4.87-3.05
Book Value	89.1	97.0	97.2	162.8	Yield %	2.4	Market Cap	US$640.7mil

Address	Leonardslee, Lower Beeding	Tel 140-389-2000	ADR	--	CEO	Claes Hultman
	Horsham, W. Sussex RH13 6PP	Fax 140-389-2011	SEDOL	0323116	Chairman	Sir James Hann

FKI

FKI PLC is a group of manufacturing businesses serving the materials-handling, hardware, engineering, and process-control markets. Its hardware operations supply furniture fittings, door and window fasteners, and security products; its engineering businesses make equipment used by the electricity industry. FKI also makes control cables, vehicle lighting systems, and trim components. Its process-control products monitor traffic flows, gas flows, and engine performance. Material handling accounted for 40% of 1998 revenues; engineering, 34%; and hardware, 26%.

	£ mil 03/96	03/97	03/98	US$mil 03/98				
Sales	873.0	1,003.5	1,143.9	1,914.4	P/E Ratio	10.9	Price (6/30/98)	1.75
Net Income	60.7	52.1	90.6	151.7	P/B Ratio	3.1	52 Wk Hi-Low	2.27-1.47
Book Value	383.8	270.3	272.8	456.5	Yield %	4.3	Market Cap	US$1,659.1mil

Address	King Cross Rd.	Tel 142-233-0267	ADR	--	CEO	Robert Beeston
	Halifax HX1 1EB	Fax 142-233-0084	SEDOL	0329459	Chairman	Jeff Whalley

General Electric

General Electric PLC operates within five divisions: electronic systems and defense; power and transportation systems; telecommunications; industrial group-United States; and industrial group. The group is a manufacturer of electronic, electrical, and power generation apparatus and systems operates in a worldwide market. Electronic systems and defense accounted for 48% of fiscal 1997 revenues; industrial group-United States, 19%; telecommunications, 17%; industrial group, 16%; and power and transportation systems, nominal.

	£ mil 03/96	03/97	03/98	US$mil 03/98				
Sales	6,235.0	6,497.0	6,269.0	10,492.1	P/E Ratio	33.8	Price (6/30/98)	5.17
Net Income	623.0	408.0	677.0	1,133.1	P/B Ratio	5.0	52 Wk Hi-Low	5.45-3.44
Book Value	3,112.0	2,687.0	2,594.0	4,341.4	Yield %	2.6	Market Cap	US$23,473mil

Address	1 Stanhope Gate	Tel 171-493-8484	ADR	GNELY	Managing Director	George Simpson
	London W1A 1EH	Fax 171-493-1974	SEDOL	0365334	Chairman	Lord Prior

In DJ Stoxx 50.

GKN

GKN PLC manufactures automotive, agritechnical, aerospace, and military products and vehicles, and it provides industrial and distribution services. The company makes armored fighting vehicles and assorted engineered products in 40 countries. Its products include universal joints, automotive driveline systems, and axles. The group also supplies and supports helicopters, aerospace structures, and waste management. Automotive and agritechnical products accounted for 66% of 1997 revenues; aerospace and special vehicles, 32%; and industrial services, 2%.

	£ mil 12/95	12/96	12/97	US$mil 12/97				
Sales	2,602.8	2,862.6	2,834.0	4,685.8	P/E Ratio	19.5	Price (6/30/98)	7.64
Net Income	187.4	-42.0	276.0	456.3	P/B Ratio	9.9	52 Wk Hi-Low	9.25-4.60
Book Value	926.2	719.8	547.0	904.4	Yield %	1.9	Market Cap	US$9,050.1mil

Address	Box 55, Worcestershire	Tel 152-751-7715	ADR	GKNPY	Managing Director	C.K. Chow
	Redditch B98 0TL	Fax 152-751-7700	SEDOL	0258304	Chairman	Sir D.B. Lees

Glaxo Wellcome

DJGI Industry: **Pharmaceuticals**
Stoxx Sector: **Pharmaceutical**

Glaxo Wellcome PLC is a major international group of companies that research, develop, manufacture, and market pharmaceuticals around the world. The company produces respiratory drugs, systemic antibiotics, migraine treatments, antiemisis drugs, and antiviral compounds including best-selling Zovirax (anti-herpes) and Retrovir (anti-HIV). Glaxo Wellcome has manufacturing facilities in 33 countries and its products are sold in over 150 countries. The company's major markets include the United States, Japan, Germany, France, Italy, and the United Kingdom.

£ mil	12/95	12/96	12/97	US$mil 12/97				
Sales	7,638.0	8,341.0	7,980.0	13,194.4	P/E Ratio	34.6	Price (6/30/98)	17.99
Net Income	717.0	1,997.0	1,850.0	3,058.9	P/B Ratio	35.1	52 Wk Hi-Low	19.85-10.90
Book Value	88.0	1,213.0	1,834.0	3,032.4	Yield %	1.9	Market Cap	US$107,944mil

Address	Glaxo Wellcome Hse., Berkeley	Tel 171-493-4060	ADR	**GLX**	CEO	**Sir Richard Sykes**
	Greenford, Middlesex UB6 0NN	Fax 171-408-0228	SEDOL	0371784	Chairman	**Sir Colin Corness**

In DJ Stoxx 50.

Glynwed

DJGI Industry: **Industrial - Diversified**
Stoxx Sector: **Industrials**

Glynwed International PLC processes specialty metals and plastics, makes finished products for residential and industrial uses, and develops and leases property. Its two divisions are steel/engineering and tubes/fittings. Products include Falcon catering equipment, Aga domestic cookers, gas cookers and fires, and synthetic sinks. It also supplies hot- and cold-rolled metal products. In 1997 the company acquired IPT and Astore. Processing and distribution of metals accounted for almost 55% of 1997 revenues; pipe systems, 33%; and consumer and foodservice products, 14%.

£ mil	12/95	12/96	12/97	US$mil 12/97				
Sales	1,251.7	1,259.5	1,156.1	1,911.5	P/E Ratio	13.2	Price (6/30/98)	2.46
Net Income	56.9	44.0	45.8	75.7	P/B Ratio	2.2	52 Wk Hi-Low	3.23-1.95
Book Value	244.5	249.8	276.2	456.7	Yield %	5.4	Market Cap	US$1,009.1mil

Address	Headland Hse., New Coventry Rd.	Tel 121-742-2366	ADR	--	CEO	**Bruce Ralph**
	Sheldon, Birmingham B26 3AZ	Fax 121-742-0403	SEDOL	0374288	Chairman	**Gareth Davies**

Granada

DJGI Industry: **Restaurants**
Stoxx Sector: **Consumer Cyclical**

Granada Group PLC is a television broadcaster and restaurant and hotel operator, and it also rents consumer electronic goods. In December 1997, the company completed the sale of Société de Gestion de Restaurants-Bars sur les Autoroutes. Granada Group holds the Channel 3 television broadcasting license for the Northwestern, England and the weekend license for London and is a major supplier of programs to the national ITV network. The company also operates satellite, cable, and pay TV services, as well as nightclubs, bowling centers, and hotels.

£ mil	09/95	09/96	09/97	US$mil 09/97				
Sales	2,381.2	3,816.9	4,091.0	6,624.0	P/E Ratio	20.0	Price (6/30/98)	11.02
Net Income	252.6	294.4	471.5	763.4	P/B Ratio	8.8	52 Wk Hi-Low	12.06-7.38
Book Value	566.2	970.3	962.0	1,557.6	Yield %	1.4	Market Cap	US$16,674mil

Address	13 Cleveland Row	Tel 171-537-3939	ADR	--	CEO	**Charles Allen**
	London SW1A 1GG	Fax 171-537-3919	SEDOL	0381125	Chairman	**Gerry Robinson**

Great Universal Stores

DJGI Industry: **Retailers - Other Specialty**
Stoxx Sector: **Retail**

Great Universal Stores PLC sells clothing and accessories through its catalog business and retail outlets. Principal catalogs include Great Universal and Kays, both in the United Kingdom, and Wehkamp in the Netherlands. Its Burberry clothing stores are located throughout Europe and the United States. Its property portfolio includes nearly 1,200 sites. Catalog home shopping and related activities accounted for 69% of fiscal 1997 revenues; finance and other, 15%; Burberrys, 9%; and overseas retailing, 7%. The group acquired Experian Information Solutions Inc. in November 1996.

£ mil	03/96	03/97	03/98	US$mil 03/98				
Revenues	2,757.6	2,855.3	3,362.7	5,627.9	P/E Ratio	18.2	Price (6/30/98)	7.90
Net Income	386.3	378.5	435.3	728.5	P/B Ratio	2.6	52 Wk Hi-Low	9.11-5.90
Book Value	3,758.3	2,859.0	2,310.5	3,866.9	Yield %	2.5	Market Cap	US$13,256mil

Address	Universal Hse., Devonshire St.	Tel 161-273-8282	ADR	**GRUSY**	President	--
	Manchester M60 1XA	Fax 161-277-4056	SEDOL	0384704	Chairman	**Lord Wolfson**

Hammerson

DJGI Industry: **Real Estate**
Stoxx Sector: **Financial Services**

Hammerson PLC is an investment and development company that owns offices and retail assets in the United Kingdom, Europe, and North America. The group has reshaped its property portfolio, reducing the geographic spread through disposals in Australia, the United States, and Canada, and reinvesting the proceeds in the United Kingdom and Europe. The portfolio has also been realigned to increase the percentage of retail and commercial holdings. Worldwide, the company has 700,000 square meters of retail space and over 300,000 square meters of office space.

£ mil	12/95	12/96	12/97	US$mil 12/97				
Sales	168.5	161.6	167.5	277.0	P/E Ratio	30.9	Price (6/30/98)	4.89
Net Income	36.7	53.6	45.0	74.4	P/B Ratio	1.1	52 Wk Hi-Low	5.40-4.31
Book Value	1,064.6	1,101.0	1,252.8	2,071.4	Yield %	2.4	Market Cap	US$2,347.7mil

Address	100 Park Ln.	Tel 171-887-1000	ADR	--	CEO	**Ronald R. Spinney**
	London W1Y 4AR	Fax 171-887-1010	SEDOL	0406501	Chairman	**Geoffrey M. Smith**

Hanson

DJGI Industry: **Industrial - Diversified**
Stoxx Sector: **Industrials**

Hanson PLC, one of the last of the diversified conglomerates, has demerged and is continuing to demerge its divisions into separately quoted companies. The demerger of Millennium Chemicals Inc. and Imperial Tobacco Group PLC was completed in 1996. The Energy Group PLC was spun off in March of 1997. The remaining products of Hanson are bricks, construction lifting equipment, and electrical installation equipment. Cornerstone accounted for 43% of 1997 revenues; ARC, 22%; Grove Worldwide, 22%; Hanson Brick, 9%; property and other activities, 4%.

	£ mil 09/95	10/96	12/97 *	US$mil 12/97					
Sales	9,971.0	6,234.0	2,418.3	3,998.5	P/E Ratio		3.8	Price (6/30/98)	3.64
Net Income	1,015.0	1,419.0	623.0	1,030.0	P/B Ratio		2.7	52 Wk Hi-Low	3.86-2.54
Book Value	3,623.0	2,535.0	876.5	1,449.2	Yield %		2.2	Market Cap	US$3,958.6mil

Address	1 Grosvenor Pl.	Tel 171-245-1245	ADR	HANB	CEO	Derek Bonham
	London SW1X 7JH	Fax 171-235-3455	SEDOL	0408983	Chairman	Lord Hanson

*Irregular period due to fiscal year change.

Hays

DJGI Industry: **Other Industrial & Commercial Services**
Stoxx Sector: **Industrials**

Hays PLC provides business-to-business mail, storage, distribution, and personnel-recruitment services. Its distribution division transports chemicals, foods, and other goods. Wholly owned Britdoc and Data Express subsidiaries deliver mail and parcels for businesses in the United Kingdom. Hays recruits accountants and technical staff in the United Kingdom and Australia. Its subsidiary, Hays Fril, provides transport services in France. Distribution accounted for 51% of fiscal 1997 revenues; personnel, 31%; and commercial, 18%.

	£ mil 06/95	06/96	06/97	US$mil 06/97					
Sales	808.4	966.0	1,129.8	1,882.1	P/E Ratio		35.6	Price (6/30/98)	10.05
Net Income	75.8	91.1	103.3	172.1	P/B Ratio		18.9	52 Wk Hi-Low	11.28-5.63
Book Value	172.5	201.8	172.9	288.0	Yield %		1.0	Market Cap	US$7,108.4mil

Address	Hays Hse., Millmead	Tel 148-330-2203	ADR	--	Managing Director	John A. Napier
	Guildford, Surrey GU2 5HJ	Fax 148-330-0388	SEDOL	0416102	Chairman	Ronnie E. Frost

IMI

DJGI Industry: **Industrial - Diversified**
Stoxx Sector: **Industrials**

IMI PLC makes copper building products, beverage dispensers, food-service equipment, fluid-powered machines, and engineered metal products and has operations in the United Kingdom, Europe, the United States, and the Asia-Pacific countries. Its specialized engineering division makes valves, alloys, casino tokens, and sporting ammunition. Building products include copper tubing, heating and air-conditioning systems, and burner controls. Building products accounted for 36% of 1997 revenues; drink dispensers, 25%; fluid-powered machines, 24%; and special engineering, 15%.

	£ mil 12/95	12/96	12/97	US$mil 12/97					
Sales	1,322.4	1,308.0	1,410.8	2,332.7	P/E Ratio		11.9	Price (6/30/98)	3.72
Net Income	54.3	108.7	108.6	179.6	P/B Ratio		4.0	52 Wk Hi-Low	5.33-2.85
Book Value	464.7	373.9	325.4	538.0	Yield %		3.8	Market Cap	US$2,162.1mil

Address	Box 216, Witton	Tel 121-356-4848	ADR	--	CEO	Gary Allen
	Birmingham B6 7BA	Fax 121-356-0544	SEDOL	0457963	Chairman	Sir Eric Pountain

Imperial Chemical Industries

DJGI Industry: **Chemicals - Specialty**
Stoxx Sector: **Chemical**

Imperial Chemical Industries PLC makes industrial chemicals and materials, paints, and explosives. Its chemical products include titanium-dioxide pigments used in paint, ink, paper, and plastics and acrylics used for coatings, baths, and car components. ICI also produces Glidden and Dulux paints. In 1997, ICI bought the specialty chemicals businesses of Unilever. In March 1998, ICI agreed to buy the European home improvements businesses of Williams PLC. Industrial chemicals accounted for 29% of 1997 revenues; coatings, 28%; specialty products, 24%; and materials, 19%.

	£ mil 12/95	12/96	12/97	US$mil 12/97					
Sales	10,269.0	10,520.0	7,731.0	12,782.7	P/E Ratio		40.6	Price (6/30/98)	9.62
Net Income	535.0	275.0	259.0	428.2	P/B Ratio		47.9	52 Wk Hi-Low	12.42-8.04
Book Value	3,924.0	3,606.0	146.0	241.4	Yield %		3.3	Market Cap	US$11,668mil

Address	9 Millbank	Tel 171-834-4444	ADR	ICI	CEO	Charles Smith
	London SW1P 3JF	Fax 171-834-2042	SEDOL	0459497	Chairman	Sir Ronald Hampel

Imperial Tobacco

DJGI Industry: **Tobacco**
Stoxx Sector: **Consumer Non-Cyclical**

Imperial Tobacco Group PLC was formed as a result of a demerger from Hanson Group PLC in October 1996. It manufactures, markets, and distributes a comprehensive range of cigarettes, rolling tobacco, pipe tobacco, and snuff. It owns four of the United Kingdom's six largest cigarette brands-- Superkings, Lambert & Butler, Embassy, and John Player Special. Its other products include Golden Virginia rolling tobacco. The company generates more than 90% of its sales in the United Kingdom, although it has been expanding internationally, particularly in Asia.

	£ mil 09/95	09/96	09/97	US$mil 09/97					
Sales	N/A	780.0	834.0	1,350.4	P/E Ratio		10.6	Price (6/30/98)	4.42
Net Income	N/A	347.0	212.0	343.3	P/B Ratio		NMF	52 Wk Hi-Low	4.67-3.64
Book Value	N/A	-1,007.0	-1,081.0	-1,750.3	Yield %		4.9	Market Cap	US$3,840.8mil

Address	Box 244, Upton Rd.	Tel 117-963-6636	ADR	IMTBY	CEO	Gareth Davis
	Southville, Bristol BS99 7UJ	Fax 117-966-7859	SEDOL	0454492	Chairman	Derek Bonham

Inchcape

DJGI Industry: **Overseas Trading**
Stoxx Sector: **Conglomerate**

Inchcape PLC, a diversified trading group, operates in five divisions: motors, marketing, bottling, office automation, and shipping. It operates in 72 countries and is the world's largest independent importer and distributor of motor vehicles. Inchcape also provides marketing services for consumer and industrial products and offers insurance, testing, shipping, and buying services. Importation, distribution, and retailing of motor vehicles accounted for 76% of 1997 revenues; marketing of industrial and consumer products, 18%; bottling, 4%; and shipping, 2%.

£ mil	12/95	12/96	12/97	US$mil 12/97				
Sales	6,246.8	5,723.0	5,931.4	9,807.2	P/E Ratio	127.3	Price (6/30/98)	1.91
Net Income	-44.0	22.5	7.8	12.9	P/B Ratio	1.3	52 Wk Hi-Low	2.99-1.36
Book Value	543.0	885.4	788.6	1,303.9	Yield %	5.8	Market Cap	US$1,689.2mil

Address	33 Cavendish Sq.	Tel **171-546-0022**	ADR	--	CEO	**Philip Cushing**
	London W1M 9HF	Fax **171-546-0010**	SEDOL	0460251	Chairman	**Colin Marshall**

Johnson Matthey

DJGI Industry: **Precious Metals**
Stoxx Sector: **Basic Resources**

Johnson Matthey PLC, an advanced materials-technology company, manufactures catalysts, pollution-control systems, electronic materials, specialty chemicals, pharmaceutical compounds, and decorative and specialized materials for the ceramics, plastics, paint, ink, and construction industries. The company controls more than one-third of the world's market for autocatalysts, and it is the world's largest refiner and distributor of precious metals. Precious metals accounted for 70% of fiscal 1998 revenues; electronic materials, 13%; catalytic systems, 12% and ceramic materials, 5%.

£ mil	03/96	03/97	03/98	US$mil 03/98				
Sales	2,528.9	2,423.2	3,133.1	5,243.7	P/E Ratio	11.2	Price (6/30/98)	5.39
Net Income	70.0	77.9	104.6	175.1	P/B Ratio	2.4	52 Wk Hi-Low	6.94-4.74
Book Value	450.6	464.8	493.0	825.1	Yield %	3.3	Market Cap	US$1,956.7mil

Address	2-4 Cockspur St., Trafalgar Sq.	Tel **171-269-8400**	ADR	**JMPTY**	CEO	**David J. Davies**
	London SW1Y 5BQ	Fax **171-269-8433**	SEDOL	0476407	Chairman	**David J. Davies**

Kingfisher

DJGI Industry: **Retailers - Broadline**
Stoxx Sector: **Retail**

Kingfisher PLC is one of the largest retailers in Europe. Its U.K. subsidiaries include Superdrug; B&Q, a home-improvement center; Woolworth's, an established chain of variety stores; and Comet, a home-appliance retailer. The company owns music and video wholesaler Entertainment U.K. and the Music and Video Club. The company also has extensive interests in properties, which are managed by Chartwell Land. Retail sales and services accounted for 99% of fiscal 1998 revenues and property development accounted for 1%.

£ mil	02/96	02/97	01/98	US$mil 01/98				
Revenues	5,280.7	5,814.8	6,409.4	10,479.7	P/E Ratio	16.8	Price (6/30/98)	9.65
Net Income	230.2	277.9	386.9	632.6	P/B Ratio	3.7	52 Wk Hi-Low	11.65-6.56
Book Value	1,271.6	1,415.9	1,757.6	2,873.8	Yield %	2.4	Market Cap	US$10,890mil

Address	119 Marylebone Rd.	Tel **171-724-7749**	ADR	**KGFIY**	CEO	**Geoffrey Mulcahy**
	London NW1 5PX	Fax **171-724-1160**	SEDOL	0981116	Chairman	**John Barham**

Ladbroke

DJGI Industry: **Casinos**
Stoxx Sector: **Consumer Cyclical**

Ladbroke Group PLC operates off-track betting and gaming activities and manages the Hilton International chain of hotels. Currently, Hilton International operates over 160 hotels worldwide. Betting and gaming activities include sports betting, football pools, bingo, slot machine arcades, casinos, and card club management. Ladbroke has businesses in the United Kingdom, the United States, and Europe. In November, it sold its 402-room Hyde Park Plaza Hotel to Regent Corp. for GBP 44 million. Betting and gaming accounted for 75% of 1997 revenues and hotels accounted for 25%.

£ mil	12/95	12/96	12/97	US$mil 12/97				
Sales	3,751.6	3,766.4	3,816.2	6,309.9	P/E Ratio	25.5	Price (6/30/98)	3.29
Net Income	59.9	20.6	151.0	249.7	P/B Ratio	2.3	52 Wk Hi-Low	3.60-2.35
Book Value	1,791.3	1,728.3	1,679.2	2,776.5	Yield %	2.2	Market Cap	US$6,533.5mil

Address	Maple Ct., Watford	Tel **171-856-8221**	ADR	**LDBKY**	CEO	**Peter M. George**
	Hertfordshire WD1 1HZ	Fax **171-856-8483**	SEDOL	0500254	Chairman	**John B. Jackson**

Land Securities

DJGI Industry: **Real Estate**
Stoxx Sector: **Financial Services**

Land Securities PLC is a property-investment and development group. Its commercial properties include offices, shopping centers, supermarkets, and warehouses. Most of its portfolio holdings are based in London. Property, offices, and retail shops make up 83% of the portfolio, and approximately 75% of it is freehold. The company owns more than 3,500 stores, including 100 supermarkets, each of which has more than 10,000 square feet. Rental income accounted for 91% of fiscal 1998 revenues and service charges and other recoveries accounted for 9%.

£ mil	03/96	03/97	03/98	US$mil 03/98				
Sales	462.2	471.0	484.0	810.0	P/E Ratio	25.2	Price (6/30/98)	9.27
Net Income	171.9	178.4	196.7	329.2	P/B Ratio	1.0	52 Wk Hi-Low	11.49-8.48
Book Value	3,524.5	4,037.2	5,001.5	8,370.7	Yield %	3.0	Market Cap	US$8,490.3mil

Address	5 Strand	Tel **171-413-9000**	ADR	--	Managing Director	**Sir Peter J. Hunt**
	London WC2N 5AF	Fax **171-925-0202**	SEDOL	0504502	Chairman	**Sir Peter J. Hunt**

Laporte

DJGI Industry: **Chemicals - Specialty**
Stoxx Sector: **Chemical**

Laporte PLC manufactures and supplies specialty chemicals, absorbents, pigments, compounds, electronic materials, adhesives, sealants, coatings, and hygiene and process chemicals. The company operates in the United Kingdom, North America, Europe, Australasia, and elsewhere. In 1997, Laporte sold its U.S. adhesives and sealants businesses to Sovereign Specialty Chemicals. Compounds and electronic materials accounted for 32% of 1997 revenues; specialty organics, 25%; pigments and additives, 25%; and formulated products, 18%.

	£ mil 12/95	12/96	12/97	US$mil 12/97					
Sales	1,016.1	910.2	732.8	1,211.6	P/E Ratio	38.6	Price (6/30/98)		7.18
Net Income	8.3	40.8	36.1	59.7	P/B Ratio	3.4	52 Wk Hi-Low		8.76-5.95
Book Value	290.6	368.5	414.8	685.8	Yield %	3.6	Market Cap		US$2,330.3mil

Address	103 Wigmore St.	Tel 171-399-2400	ADR	--	Mng Dir & CEO	Jim Leng
	London W1H 9AB	Fax 171-399-2401	SEDOL	0506133	Chairman	George Duncan

Lasmo

DJGI Industry: **Oil Companies - Secondary**
Stoxx Sector: **Energy**

Lasmo PLC is among the largest oil- and gas-exploration and production companies. Its oil and gas fields are concentrated in the United Kingdom and Indonesia, but the company also has fields in Algeria, Libya, Colombia, the North Sea, and Vietnam. Lasmo's substantial liquefied natural gas (LNG) holdings are located primarily in Indonesia. In April 1997, the company said it made a gas discovery in its Kirthar concession in Pakistan. Natural gas accounted for 51% of 1997 revenues; oil and liquid petroleum gas, 47%; and tariff income, 2%.

	£ mil 12/95	12/96	12/97	US$mil 12/97					
Sales	637.0	749.0	722.0	1,193.8	P/E Ratio	64.9	Price (6/30/98)		2.40
Net Income	34.0	67.0	48.0	79.4	P/B Ratio	2.1	52 Wk Hi-Low		2.98-2.32
Book Value	1,079.0	1,082.0	1,097.0	1,813.8	Yield %	1.0	Market Cap		US$3,867.7mil

Address	101 Bishopsgate	Tel 171-892-9000	ADR	LSO	CEO	Joseph Darby
	London EC2M 3XH	Fax 171-892-9292	SEDOL	0531696	Chairman	Rudolph Agnew

Legal & General

DJGI Industry: **Insurance - Life & Health**
Stoxx Sector: **Insurance**

Legal & General Group PLC offers life insurance, pensions, general insurance, and investment-management services. It operates primarily in the United Kingdom, but it has a presence in the United States, Australia, France, and the Netherlands. In January 1998, the company launched a GBP 220 million buyback of convertible bonds. By March, it had acquired 62% of the bonds for GBP 146 million. Premium income accounted for 24% of 1997 revenues; investment income, 18%; gain on investments, 7%; and other technical income, 51%.

	£ mil 12/95	12/96	12/97	US$mil 12/97					
Revenues	9,351.9	10,412.7	12,579.6	20,799.6	P/E Ratio	16.2	Price (6/30/98)		6.40
Net Income	195.2	1,800.5	491.6	812.8	P/B Ratio	3.3	52 Wk Hi-Low		7.60-4.06
Book Value	426.0	2,074.0	2,438.0	4,031.1	Yield %	2.0	Market Cap		US$13,599mil

Address	Temple Ct., 11 Queen Victoria St.	Tel 171-528-6200	ADR	LGGNY	CEO	David Prosser
	London EC4N 4TP	Fax 171-528-6222	SEDOL	0511115	Chairman	Sir Christopher Harding

Liberty International

DJGI Industry: **Diversified Financial Services**
Stoxx Sector: **Financial Services**

Liberty International Holdings PLC is a holding company with two major subsidiaries: Capital Shopping Centres, which specializes in the management and ownership of regional shopping centers, and Capital & Counties, the group's original property business, which engages in commercial and retail property investment, management, and development. The company also has investments in life insurance, pensions, and in other fields relating to the financial services industry. Property investment accounted for 87% of 1997 revenues and property trading accounted for 11%.

	£ mil 12/95	12/96	12/97	US$mil 12/97					
Revenues	182.6	221.1	248.7	411.2	P/E Ratio	18.7	Price (6/30/98)		5.28
Net Income	161.5	70.7	89.6	148.1	P/B Ratio	0.9	52 Wk Hi-Low		6.20-4.67
Book Value	1,124.8	1,327.5	1,652.8	2,732.8	Yield %	3.3	Market Cap		US$2,760.4mil

Address	40 Broadway	Tel 171-222-5496	ADR	--	Managing Director	D. Fischel
	London SW1H 0BT	Fax 171-222-5554	SEDOL	0893772	Chairman	D. Gordon

Lloyds TSB

DJGI Industry: **Banks - Major International**
Stoxx Sector: **Bank**

Lloyds TSB Group PLC is one of the three largest banks in the United Kingdom in terms of market capitalization. It provides retail-banking and insurance services to private and commercial customers. Its retail banking division provides such services as loans, mortgages, banking by phone, and unit-trust sales, and its insurance division provides pensions and several types of life and property insurance. The bank also provides investment services, treasury services, and pension management. Interest income accounted for 75% of 1997 revenues and commissions and fees accounted for 17%.

	£ mil 12/95	12/96	12/97	US$mil 12/97					
Revenues	11,817.0	13,046.0	13,621.0	22,521.5	P/E Ratio	19.2	Price (6/30/98)		8.39
Net Income	961.0	1,575.0	2,335.0	3,860.8	P/B Ratio	7.4	52 Wk Hi-Low		10.70-6.16
Book Value	4,158.0	5,027.0	6,218.0	10,281.1	Yield %	2.1	Market Cap		US$75,931mil

Address	71 Lombard St.	Tel 171-626-1500	ADR	--	CEO	Peter Ellwood
	London EC3P 3BS	Fax 171-929-2901	SEDOL	0870612	Chairman	Sir B. Pitman

In DJ Stoxx 50.

Lonrho

DJGI Industry: **Conglomerates**
Stoxx Sector: **Conglomerate**

Lonrho PLC is an international conglomerate with interests in the mining and refining of natural resources. Other interests include hotels, general trade, textiles, and agriculture. In May 1998, Lonrho spun off its Lonrho Africa, which focused on motors, agribusiness, hotels, distribution, and property and construction, in order to focus solely on mining. The company also plans to sell its Princess Hotel chain. Lonrho's mining division includes Ashanti Goldfields. Mining and refining accounted for 31% of 1997 revenues; motor and equipment distribution accounted for 21%.

	£ mil 09/95	09/96	09/97	US$mil 09/97					
Sales	1,966.0	1,910.0	1,242.0	2,011.0	P/E Ratio	5.5	Price (6/30/98)		2.81
Net Income	79.0	N/A	142.0	229.9	P/B Ratio	0.6	52 Wk Hi-Low		4.53-2.56
Book Value	1,080.0	799.0	975.0	1,578.7	Yield %	6.8	Market Cap		US$931.0mil

Address	4 Grosvenor Pl.	Tel	171-201-6000	ADR	LNROY	CEO	N.J. Morrell
	London SW1X 7DL	Fax	171-201-6100	SEDOL	0256814	Chairman	Sir J. Craven

Lucas Varity

DJGI Industry: **Other Auto Parts**
Stoxx Sector: **Automobile**

Lucas Varity PLC was created in 1996 by the merger of U.K.-based Lucas Industries PLC and U.S.-based Varity Corp. Its product line features braking systems, diesel engines, diesel systems, electrical and electronic systems, and items for the automotive and aerospace industries. Lucas Varity is a leading provider of parts, service, and technical and diagnostic support to vehicle manufacturers and the independent automotive aftermarket. Other automotive accounted for 45% of fiscal 1997 revenues; braking systems, 30%; aerospace, 13%; diesel engines; 11% and corporate/other, 1%.

	£ mil 07/96	01/97 *	01/98	US$mil 01/98					
Sales	2,988.6	3,669.3	4,681.0	7,653.7	P/E Ratio	16.2	Price (6/30/98)		2.38
Net Income	106.3	-138.4	209.0	341.7	P/B Ratio	4.9	52 Wk Hi-Low		2.84-1.82
Book Value	722.6	546.0	458.0	748.9	Yield %	1.9	Market Cap		US$5,596.9mil

Address	46 Park St.	Tel	171-493-6793	ADR	LVA	President	Victor Rice
	London SW1Y 4LB	Fax	171-872-7719	SEDOL	0538686	Chairman	Sir Brian Pearse

*Irregular period due to fiscal year change.

Marks & Spencer

DJGI Industry: **Retailers - Broadline**
Stoxx Sector: **Retail**

Marks & Spencer PLC is an international retailer of clothing, household goods, and food items, most of which appear under the St. Michael and Marks & Spencer trademarks. The company, which is the United.Kingdom's largest retailer, operates stores in the United Kingdom, France, Belgium, Spain, the United States, Japan, Canada, and Hong Kong. M&S also owns Brooks Brothers clothing stores, Kings Supermarkets, and the Marks & Spencer and D'Alliard's chains. Retailing accounted for 97% of fiscal 1998 revenues and financial services for 3%.

	£ mil 03/96	03/97	03/98	US$mil 03/98					
Revenues	7,209.2	7,841.9	8,243.3	13,796.3	P/E Ratio	18.7	Price (6/30/98)		5.46
Net Income	652.6	754.6	828.9	1,387.3	P/B Ratio	3.1	52 Wk Hi-Low		6.65-4.98
Book Value	4,119.6	4,529.3	5,065.8	8,478.3	Yield %	2.6	Market Cap		US$26,036mil

Address	Michael Hse., 37-67 Baker St.	Tel	171-935-4422	ADR	--	President	--
	London W1A 1DN	Fax	171-487-2679	SEDOL	0565402	Chairman	Sir Richard Greenbury

In DJ Stoxx 50.

MEPC

DJGI Industry: **Real Estate**
Stoxx Sector: **Financial Services**

MEPC PLC, the third-largest U.K. office and retail developer, owns, develops, manages, and trades in commercial investment properties. The company operates in the United Kingdom, continental Europe, the United States, and Australia. In March and April 1998, MEPC agreed to sell its U.S. portfolio for $1.315 billion. In February 1998, MEPC agreed to sell most of its Australian portfolio to insurance group Australian Mutual Provident for A$418 million. During fiscal 1997 the group acquired PSIT PLC, FOC Holdings Ltd., and RAM Euro-Centres (Doncaster) Ltd.

	£ mil 09/95	09/96	09/97	US$mil 09/97					
Sales	317.7	321.9	313.3	507.3	P/E Ratio	18.0	Price (6/30/98)		5.27
Net Income	85.4	95.2	55.2	89.4	P/B Ratio	1.0	52 Wk Hi-Low		6.26-4.66
Book Value	1,859.8	1,883.7	2,083.6	3,373.7	Yield %	3.6	Market Cap		US$3,687.0mil

Address	12 St. James's Sq.	Tel	171-911-5300	ADR	--	CEO	James Tuckey
	London SW1Y 4LB	Fax	171-839-2340	SEDOL	0549804	Chairman	Michael Blakenham

Misys

DJGI Industry: **Software**
Stoxx Sector: **Technology**

Misys PLC develops and sells computer systems and ancillary services and has banking and securities operations. It is one of the largest computer services group in the United Kingdom, supplying complete software and hardware solutions to end-users together with support and data services. Its products are used in a wide range of markets that includes insurance broker, construction, frozen and chilled food, clothing, hotels, higher education, health care, and travel services. Banking accounted for 55% of fiscal 1997 revenues; information systems, 32%; and insurance, 13%.

	£ mil 05/96	05/97	05/98	US$mil 05/98					
Sales	279.9	325.5	431.5	703.9	P/E Ratio	56.2	Price (6/30/98)		34.05
Net Income	36.8	45.9	29.3	47.8	P/B Ratio	NMF	52 Wk Hi-Low		36.96-13.63
Book Value	-120.0	-199.0	-351.2	-572.9	Yield %	0.4	Market Cap		US$6,375.5mil

Address	Chapel Oak	Tel	138-687-1373	ADR	--	President	--
	Worcestershire WR11 5SH	Fax	138-687-1045	SEDOL	0596606	Chairman	Kevin Lomax

Morgan Crucible

DJGI Industry: **Industrial - Diversified**
Stoxx Sector: **Industrials**

The Morgan Crucible Co. PLC produces technical-and thermal-ceramics products, carbon materials, electronic components, and chemical products for application in a wide range of industries and services. Morgan operates in 43 countries and sells in over 120 countries. The group is organized into five market-focused divisions: Electrical Carbon, Engineered Carbon, Technical Ceramics, Thermal Ceramics, and Specialty Materials. Thermal ceramics accounted for 34% of 1997 revenues; specialty materials, 21%; electrical carbon, 20%; technical ceramics 17%; and engineered carbon, 8%.

	£ mil 01/96	01/97	01/98	US$mil 01/98				
Sales	847.8	893.1	889.0	1,453.6	P/E Ratio	11.8	Price (6/30/98)	3.89
Net Income	57.6	67.7	77.1	126.1	P/B Ratio	3.6	52 Wk Hi-Low	5.39-3.89
Book Value	263.1	261.5	248.6	406.5	Yield %	2.2	Market Cap	US$1,483.9mil

Address **Morgan Hse., Madeira Walk**   Tel **175-383-7000**   ADR   --   Managing Director **Dr. Edwin Farmer**
Windsor, Berkshire SL4 1EP   Fax **175-385-0872**   SEDOL   **0602729**   Chairman   **Sir James Spooner**

National Power

DJGI Industry: **Electrical Utilities (All)**
Stoxx Sector: **Utility**

National Power PLC is the United Kingdom's largest nonnuclear power generator. The company has coal, oil, and combined-cycle gas-turbine plants and a capacity of 21,000 megawatts. Most of its sales are to regional U.K. electricity companies, but it also owns American National Power, which operates power plants in Virginia, Georgia, New Jersey, and Texas. The company also has stakes in Portuguese power-generator Tejo and power station Pego. In May 1998, National Power said it would invest $250 million in two Chinese power plants.

	£ mil 03/96	03/97	03/98	US$mil 03/98				
Sales	3,948.0	3,535.0	3,354.0	5,613.4	P/E Ratio	21.0	Price (6/30/98)	5.64
Net Income	608.0	584.0	327.0	547.3	P/B Ratio	3.5	52 Wk Hi-Low	6.93-4.80
Book Value	2,666.0	1,935.0	1,951.0	3,265.3	Yield %	4.8	Market Cap	US$11,476mil

Address **Windmill Hill Business Park**   Tel **179-387-7777**   ADR   **NP**   CEO   **Keith Henry**
Swindon, Wiltshire SN5 6PB   Fax **179-389-2525**   SEDOL   **0632016**   Chairman   **John Baker**

NatWest

DJGI Industry: **Banks - Major International**
Stoxx Sector: **Bank**

National Westminster Bank PLC, is a major provider of an extensive range of banking and financial services, both domestic and international. Its international portfolio of businesses provides services to customers ranging from individuals and small businesses to multinational companies. It has several subsidiaries, including Ulster Bank in Northern Ireland and NatWest Markets which operates throughout Europe. Interest income accounted for 71% of 1997 revenues; commissions and fees, 21%; dealing profits, 4%; dividend income and other operating income, 4%.

	£ mil 12/95	12/96	12/97	US$mil 12/97				
Revenues	15,164.0	14,205.0	13,250.0	21,908.1	P/E Ratio	29.3	Price (6/30/98)	10.71
Net Income	1,214.0	439.0	672.0	1,111.1	P/B Ratio	2.5	52 Wk Hi-Low	12.18-7.82
Book Value	6,749.0	7,118.0	7,274.0	12,027.1	Yield %	2.4	Market Cap	US$30,649mil

Address **41 Lothbury**   Tel **171-726-1000**   ADR   **NW**   CEO   **Derek Wanless**
London EC2P 2BP   Fax **171-726-1035**   SEDOL   **0625395**   Chairman   **Lord Alexander**

Next

DJGI Industry: **Retailers - Other Specialty**
Stoxx Sector: **Retail**

Next PLC is a retailer that also provides home shopping and financial services. It retails its goods under its own brand name through approximately 300 stores in the United Kingdom as well as through mail-order catalogs. Next Retail operates the street shops. Next Directory is the mail-order division. Next USA operates retail outlets in the United States. Ventura runs the financial services division. Next retail accounted for 66% of fiscal 1998 revenues; Next Directory, 23%; Ventura, 6%; Next Overseas, 3%; and other activities, 2%.

	£ mil 01/96	02/97	01/98	US$mil 01/98				
Revenues	773.8	946.8	1,176.8	1,924.1	P/E Ratio	14.1	Price (6/30/98)	5.15
Net Income	105.5	118.2	136.6	223.3	P/B Ratio	4.0	52 Wk Hi-Low	8.35-4.78
Book Value	351.5	412.1	480.5	785.6	Yield %	3.5	Market Cap	US$3,216.8mil

Address **Desford Rd., Enderby**   Tel **116-286-6411**   ADR   --   CEO   **David Jones**
Leicester LE9 5AT   Fax **116-284-8998**   SEDOL   **0421861**   Chairman   **Lord Wolfson**

NFC

DJGI Industry: **Other Industrial & Commercial Services**
Stoxx Sector: **Industrials**

National Fertilizer PCL (NFC) offers moving, transport, logistics, and storage services through its subsidiaries and associates. Subsidiaries include Lynx, which provides vehicle and transport services; Allied Pickfords, which is engaged in removal, storage, shipping, and delivery; and Exel Logistics, a warehousing and transport service for the food, media, and apparel industries. Other subsidiaries and associates of the group are engaged in transport and parcels delivery. Logistics accounted for 70% of fiscal 1997 revenues and moving services for 30%.

	£ mil 09/95	09/96	09/97	US$mil 09/97				
Sales	2,200.6	2,462.8	2,290.2	3,708.2	P/E Ratio	28.0	Price (6/30/98)	1.68
Net Income	13.7	61.5	39.3	63.6	P/B Ratio	2.1	52 Wk Hi-Low	2.03-1.28
Book Value	524.8	520.4	525.5	850.9	Yield %	3.9	Market Cap	US$1,957.3mil

Address **66 Chiltern St.**   Tel **171-317-0123**   ADR   **NFC**   CEO   **G. Murphy**
London W1M 2LT   Fax **171-224-2385**   SEDOL   **0618715**   Chairman   **Sir Christopher Bland**

Norwich Union

DJGI Industry: **Insurance - Life & Health**
Stoxx Sector: **Insurance**

Norwich Union PLC provides life insurance, pension, general insurance and health*care services, as well as and other investment activities. The third largest quoted U.K. insurer, principal operations are in the United Kingdom, Ireland, France, Spain, Australia, New Zealand, and Canada, with other businesses in Europe and the Middle East. The group has five million customers worldwide and some GBP49 billion of funds under management. In March 1998, Norwich Union sold its Norwich Union Life Insurance and Norwich Union Investment Management to Royal & Sun Alliance.

	£ mil 12/95	12/96	12/97	US$mil 12/97					
Revenues	7,158.0	8,317.0	5,646.0	9,335.3	P/E Ratio	15.8	Price (6/30/98)		4.35
Net Income	258.0	107.0	268.0	443.1	P/B Ratio	1.6	52 Wk Hi-Low		5.29-3.20
Book Value	N/A	N/A	5,098.0	8,429.2	Yield %	1.8	Market Cap		US$13,887mil

Address	8 Surrey St.	Tel **160-362-2200**	ADR	--	CEO	**Richard Harvey**
	Norwich, Norfolk NR1 3NG	Fax **160-368-3659**	SEDOL	0040932	Chairman	--

Nycomed Amersham

DJGI Industry: **Biotechnology**
Stoxx Sector: **Technology**

Nycomed Amersham PLC is a world leader in the development and supply of invivo diagnostic imaging agents and in the research-based biotechnology supply business. It was formed in 1997 through the merger of Nycomed ASA and Amersham International PLC. Amersham provides complete systems to enable research into genes and proteins and the development and manufacture of drugs based on biological molecules. Pharma is a leader in Scandinavian pharmaceuticals. Imaging accounted for 47% of 1997 revenues; Amersham Pharmacia Biotech, 42%; Pharma, 10%; and other, 1%.

	£ mil 03/95	03/96	12/97 *	US$mil 12/97					
Sales	333.6	351.4	606.6	1,002.9	P/E Ratio	7.6	Price (6/30/98)		4.46
Net Income	29.2	31.0	-44.3	-73.3	P/B Ratio	2.3	52 Wk Hi-Low		25.75-3.90
Book Value	146.1	161.1	116.2	192.1	Yield %	3.6	Market Cap		US$4,692.5mil

Address	Amersham Pl.	Tel **149-454-4000**	ADR	--	CEO	**W.M. Castell**
	Buckinghamshire HP7 9NA	Fax **149-454-2266**	SEDOL	0274753	Chairman	**J.F. Odfjell**

*Irregular period due to fiscal year change.

Ocean

DJGI Industry: **Other Industrial & Commercial Services**
Stoxx Sector: **Industrials**

Ocean Group PLC, a provider of industrial and distribution services, operates in four business sectors: international logistics management, contract logistics, environmental services, and marine services. The group operates in 112 countries worldwide. The group's principal subsidiaries include MSAS Cargo, McGregor Cory, O.I.L., Cory Towage, and Cory Enviromental. In January 1998, Ocean bought a 67% stake in Dutch logistics group Intexo for GBP18.9 million. International logistics management accounted for 79% of 1997 revenues.

	£ mil 12/95	12/96	12/97	US$mil 12/97					
Sales	1,113.2	1,141.5	1,125.0	1,860.1	P/E Ratio	4.8	Price (6/30/98)		7.57
Net Income	16.1	44.0	246.7	407.9	P/B Ratio	2.8	52 Wk Hi-Low		8.15-5.09
Book Value	224.0	241.4	417.4	690.1	Yield %	2.2	Market Cap		US$1,991.2mil

Address	The Ring Bracknell	Tel **134-430-2000**	ADR	--	CEO	**John Allan**
	Berkshire RG12 1AN	Fax **134-471-0031**	SEDOL	0655422	Chairman	**Peter Marshall**

Pearson

DJGI Industry: **Publishing**
Stoxx Sector: **Media**

Pearson PLC publishes books and periodicals, provides electronic information services, and produces television programs. Its book-publishing interests include Penguin Books and Longmans. Its flagship newspaper is the Financial Times; the company also holds a 50% stake in The Economist. Pearson owns the Alton Towers theme park and Madame Tussaud's wax museum and has stakes in broadcasting company BSkyB. In June 1998, Pearson unveiled plans to sell its 40.5% stake in Spain's Port Aventura theme park near Barcelona for a total of GBP40 million.

	£ mil 12/95	12/96	12/97	US$mil 12/97					
Sales	1,830.4	2,048.9	2,293.1	3,791.5	P/E Ratio	163.9	Price (6/30/98)		10.98
Net Income	261.0	240.5	38.3	63.3	P/B Ratio	41.6	52 Wk Hi-Low		11.88-6.65
Book Value	833.2	388.6	152.5	252.1	Yield %	1.8	Market Cap		US$10,593mil

Address	3 Burlington Gardens	Tel **171-411-2000**	ADR	PRSNY	Managing Director	**Frank Barlow**
	London W1X 1LE	Fax **171-411-2390**	SEDOL	0677608	Chairman	**Michael Blakenham**

Peninsular and Oriental Steam

DJGI Industry: **Marine Transportation**
Stoxx Sector: **Industrials**

Peninsular and Oriental Steam Navigation Co. (P&O) is a U.K.-based shipping, construction, and property group that operates cruise, ferry, and marinecargo lines. The company's subsidiaries, in the United Kingdom, P&O Containers and P&O Bulk Shipping, control most of the cargo market in the United Kingdom. P&O operates in the United Kingdom, the United States, China, and Australia. P&O's Bovis Construction Group accounted for 33% of 1997 revenues; P&O Cruises, 18%; P&O Trans European, 14%; P&O Australia, 13%; and P&O Ferries, 12%.

	£ mil 12/95	12/96	12/97	US$mil 12/97					
Sales	6,571.1	7,090.8	5,683.3	9,397.0	P/E Ratio	16.3	Price (6/30/98)		8.63
Net Income	236.0	250.6	333.0	550.6	P/B Ratio	2.0	52 Wk Hi-Low		9.02-6.00
Book Value	2,508.9	2,463.8	2,668.0	4,411.4	Yield %	3.5	Market Cap		US$9,196.3mil

Address	79 Pall Mall	Tel **171-930-4343**	ADR	PIAOT	Managing Director	**Sir Bruce MacPhail**
	London SW1Y 5EJ	Fax **171-930-8572**	SEDOL	0680048	Chairman	**Lord Sterling**

Pentland

DJGI Industry: **Footwear**
Stoxx Sector: **Consumer Cyclical**

Pentland Group PLC is a holding company with interests in footwear, athletic clothing, stationery, and home appliances. Its brand names include Speedo, Mitre, Lacoste, Berghaus, Reusch, Grazia, Kangaroos, and Pony. Holmes, a U.S. subsidiary, manufactures small electrical appliances such as air purifiers. The group operates in the United Kingdom, continental Europe, the United States, the Far East, and elsewhere. Footwear, clothing and sportswear accounted for 80% of 1997 revenues and international trading accounted for 20%.

	£ mil 12/95	12/96	12/97	US$mil 12/97				
Sales	754.9	754.3	653.6	1,080.7	P/E Ratio	15.9	Price (6/30/98)	1.10
Net Income	22.8	-19.0	25.1	41.5	P/B Ratio	1.3	52 Wk Hi-Low	1.29-0.89
Book Value	304.9	283.2	296.0	489.4	Yield %	3.4	Market Cap	US$656.8mil

Address	Lakeside, Squires Ln.	Tel 181-346-2600	ADR	--	President	--
	Finchley, London N3 2QL	Fax 181-346-2700	SEDOL	0094553	Chairman & CEO	R. Stephen Rubin

Persimmon

DJGI Industry: **Home Construction**
Stoxx Sector: **Consumer Cyclical**

Persimmon PLC is a building, development, and residential design company. It operates completely in the United Kingdom. The company builds a broad range of residences, including small townhouses and apartments. Persimmon is also involved in the housing sector. The company completed 6,521 homes last year. The average selling price for a completed property in 1997 was £80,224. Persimmon's most recent acquisitions include Ideal Homes Holdings Ltd. and Comben Group Ltd. As of 1996, Persimmon owned about 17,000 building plots with planning permission.

	£ mil 12/95	12/96	12/97	US$mil 12/97				
Sales	249.4	451.2	525.5	868.8	P/E Ratio	9.4	Price (6/30/98)	2.00
Net Income	16.4	24.8	37.7	62.4	P/B Ratio	1.2	52 Wk Hi-Low	2.60-1.84
Book Value	201.7	269.6	293.4	485.2	Yield %	5.0	Market Cap	US$594.8mil

Address	Persimmon Hse., Fulford	Tel 190-464-2199	ADR	--	CEO	John White
	Yorkshire YO1 4RE	Fax 190-461-0014	SEDOL	0682538	Chairman	Duncan Davidson

Pilkington

DJGI Industry: **Building Materials**
Stoxx Sector: **Construction**

Pilkington PLC is a leading worldwide manufacturer of glass and plastic products used in the automotive, building, transportation, and electronics industries. The group operates in the United Kingdom, Europe, North and South America, and the Asia-Pacific region. The company announced in June 1998 that its restructuring program will cost 7,500 jobs worldwide by March 1999. Flat and safety glass building products accounted for 54% of fiscal 1997 revenues; flat and safety glass automotive products, 46%; and other trading, nominals.

	£ mil 03/96	03/97	03/98	US$mil 03/98				
Sales	2,872.0	2,878.0	2,701.0	4,520.5	P/E Ratio	NMF	Price (6/30/98)	1.11
Net Income	-25.0	2.0	-181.0	-302.9	P/B Ratio	1.9	52 Wk Hi-Low	1.68-1.06
Book Value	971.0	837.0	559.0	935.6	Yield %	4.5	Market Cap	US$2,016.1mil

Address	Prestcot Rd., St. Helens	Tel 174-428-882	ADR	--	CEO	Roger Leverton
	Merseyside WA10 3TT	Fax 174-469-2763	SEDOL	0688462	Chairman	Sir Antony Pilkington

PowerGen

DJGI Industry: **Electrical Utilities (All)**
Stoxx Sector: **Utility**

PowerGen PLC, which was privatized in 1991, generates electricity and markets and trades electricity and gas to regional electric companies, mainly in the United Kingdom. In March 1997, PowerGen took full ownership of Kinetica, a gas marketing and transportation business, for GBP18 million. In September 1996, the Treasury sold its remaining stake in PowerGen. Electricity supply accounted for 65% of fiscal 1998 revenues; direct l sales of electricity to customers, 21%; gas trading and retail, 9%; and other energy and hydrocarbon sales, 5%.

	£ mil 03/96	03/97	03/98	US$mil 03/98				
Sales	2,933.0	2,855.0	2,932.0	4,907.1	P/E Ratio	67.9	Price (6/30/98)	8.28
Net Income	519.0	431.0	-124.0	-207.5	P/B Ratio	3.4	52 Wk Hi-Low	8.90-6.60
Book Value	2,252.0	1,925.0	1,560.0	2,610.9	Yield %	3.5	Market Cap	US$8,903.4mil

Address	53 New Broad St.	Tel 171-826-2826	ADR	PWG	CEO	Edmund Wallis
	London EC2M 1JJ	Fax 171-826-2890	SEDOL	0697822	Chairman	Sir Colin Southgate

Premier Farnell

DJGI Industry: **Other Industrial & Commercial Services**
Stoxx Sector: **Industrials**

Premier Farnell PLC was created in February 1996 when U.K.-based Farnell Electronics acquired U.S.-based Premier. The company operates through four divisions: catalogue distribution, industrial products, appliance spares, and product manufacturing. Its electronic components are distributed mainly to the professional and industrial sectors. Premier Farnell operates in the United Kingdom, North America, and elsewhere. Catalog distribution accounted for 72% of fiscal 1998 revenues; industrial products, 12%; appliance spares, 8%; and product manufacturing, 8%.

	£ mil 01/96	02/97	02/98	US$mil 02/98				
Sales	527.2	637.5	743.6	1,222.2	P/E Ratio	12.1	Price (6/30/98)	3.05
Net Income	78.3	108.5	91.6	150.6	P/B Ratio	NMF	52 Wk Hi-Low	5.60-2.77
Book Value	206.0	-442.5	-400.9	-658.9	Yield %	4.2	Market Cap	US$1,382.0mil

Address	Farnell Hse., Wetherby	Tel 193-758-7241	ADR	PFP	CEO	Howard Poulson
	West Yorkshire LS22 4DH	Fax 193-758-0070	SEDOL	0331841	Chairman	Richard Hanwell

Provident Financial

DJGI Industry: **Diversified Financial Services**
Stoxx Sector: **Financial Services**

Provident Financial PLC is a personal financial-services company that specializes in home credit and insurance. The home credit division consists of over 1.4 million customers borrowing small sums of money for a fixed term, and the insurance division consists of an underwriting and broker operation specializing in motor insurance. The company's operations are located in the United Kingdom and Ireland. It has discontinued its involvement in banking and motor finance. Home collected credit accounted for 79% of 1997 revenues and insurance for 21%.

	£ mil 12/95	12/96	12/97	US$mil 12/97					
Revenues	448.4	429.7	444.2	734.4	P/E Ratio	26.1	Price (6/30/98)	9.40
Net Income	67.8	79.4	93.5	154.6	P/B Ratio	8.8	52 Wk Hi-Low	10.57-5.77
Book Value	232.1	269.5	278.8	461.0	Yield %	2.1	Market Cap	US$4,111.7mil

Address	Sunbridge Rd., Bradford	Tel **127-473-1111**	ADR	--	CEO	**John van Kuffeler**
	West Yorkshire BD1 2LQ	Fax **127-472-7300**	SEDOL	0268596	Chairman	**Antony Warde-Norbury**

Prudential

DJGI Industry: **Insurance - Life & Health**
Stoxx Sector: **Insurance**

Prudential Corp. PLC is the United Kingdom's largest life insurance provider by market capitalization and its largest institutional investor. Its main businesses are life assurance and pensions, life and general reinsurance, general insurance, and investment management. The company serves more than 9 million customers worldwide, with operations in the United Kingdom, Ireland, the Netherlands, Italy, Canada, Australia, New Zealand, Hong Kong, Malaysia, and Singapore. Premiums accounted for 47% of 1997 revenues; investment income, 46%; and other operating income, 7%.

	£ mil 12/95	12/96	12/97	US$mil 12/97					
Revenues	18,244.0	19,197.0	22,459.0	37,134.6	P/E Ratio	18.2	Price (6/30/98)	7.90
Net Income	758.0	1,407.0	837.0	1,383.9	P/B Ratio	5.5	52 Wk Hi-Low	9.57-5.61
Book Value	1,747.0	2,757.0	2,783.0	4,601.5	Yield %	2.4	Market Cap	US$25,574mil

Address	142 Holborn Bars	Tel **171-583-1415**	ADR	PPLCY	CEO	**Peter Davis**
	London EC1N 2NH	Fax **171-548-3725**	SEDOL	0709954	Chairman	**Sir Brian Corby**

In DJ Stoxx 50.

Racal Electronics

DJGI Industry: **Communications Technology**
Stoxx Sector: **Technology**

Racal Electronics PLC manufactures electronic surveillance and intelligence gathering and command information systems for the defense industry. It also provides a broad range of high quality support services to various users in process manufacturing, construction, agriculture, electronics, and shipping. In May 1998, Racal was in the process of divesting its data communications business which accounted for 47% of fiscal 1997 revenues; defense radar and avionics accounted for 19%, radio communications for 12%, and other activities for 22%.

	£ mil 03/96	03/97	03/98	US$mil 03/98					
Sales	1,052.1	1,138.0	920.7	1,540.9	P/E Ratio	40.3	Price (6/30/98)	3.39
Net Income	46.1	31.8	-218.6	-365.9	P/B Ratio	2.2	52 Wk Hi-Low	4.08-2.02
Book Value	424.6	438.9	N/A	N/A	Yield %	1.7	Market Cap	US$1,636.9mil

Address	Western Rd., Bracknell	Tel **134-448-1222**	ADR	RACLY	CEO	**D. Elsbury**
	Berkshire RG121 1RG	Fax **134-454-1190**	SEDOL	0719685	Chairman	**E. Harrison**

Railtrack Group

DJGI Industry: **Railroads**
Stoxx Sector: **Industrials**

Railtrack Group PLC manages the U.K. rail infrastructure. It was created by the Railways Act of 1993, which split up the infrastructure ownership and train operations of British Rail, and was privatized in May 1996. The company provides train operators with access to track, maintains and renews the infrastructure, and undertakes major capital programs. It also oversees timetabling, train planning, and signaling. Passenger franchise revenue accounted for 87% of fiscal 1997 revenues; freight revenue, 7%; property rental income, 5%; and other income, 2%.

	£ mil 03/96	03/97	03/98	US$mil 03/98					
Sales	2,300.0	2,437.0	2,467.0	4,128.9	P/E Ratio	37.3	Price (6/30/98)	14.69
Net Income	269.0	292.0	198.0	331.4	P/B Ratio	2.7	52 Wk Hi-Low	14.69-6.26
Book Value	2,482.0	2,665.0	2,788.0	4,666.1	Yield %	1.6	Market Cap	US$12,365mil

Address	40 Bernard St.	Tel **171-557-8151**	ADR	--	CEO	**J. Edmonds**
	London WCN 1BY	Fax **171-344-7101**	SEDOL	0721293	Chairman	**R. Hortor**

Rank Organisation

DJGI Industry: **Other Recreational Products & Services**
Stoxx Sector: **Consumer Cyclical**

The Rank Organisation PLC is a leisure and entertainment company and an international provider of services to the film industry. The group's activities include gaming, cinemas, nightclubs, themed bars, pub-restaurants, multileisure centers, Hard Rock Cafes, film processing, and video duplicating. Rank has a 50% interest in Universal Studios Inc. in Universal City, Florida, and a theme park and development in Orlando, Florida. The group operates in the United Kingdom, North America, and elsewhere. Leisure-related activities accounted for 32% of 1997 revenues.

	£ mil 12/95	12/96	12/97	US$mil 12/97					
Sales	2,240.6	1,882.0	2,009.0	3,321.8	P/E Ratio	15.5	Price (6/30/98)	3.29
Net Income	450.0	-34.0	193.0	319.1	P/B Ratio	1.9	52 Wk Hi-Low	4.10-2.97
Book Value	1,956.0	1,582.0	1,302.0	2,152.8	Yield %	5.5	Market Cap	US$4,602.0mil

Address	6 Connaught Pl.	Tel **171-706-1111**	ADR	RANKY	CEO	**Andrew Teare**
	London W2 2EZ	Fax **171-262-9886**	SEDOL	0724076	Chairman	**Sir Denys Henderson**

Reckitt & Colman

DJGI Industry: **Household Products (Non-Durable)**
Stoxx Sector: **Consumer Non-Cyclical**

Reckitt & Colman PLC is a network of businesses that creates, manufactures, and distributes household, pharmaceutical, and food products. The group operates in 35 countries and sells its products in over 120 countries. Products are distributed under the brand names Haze, Mop & Glo, Mr. Sheen, Harpic, Dettox, Dettol, Lemsip, and Steradent. In 1996, it bought the international insecticides business of AgrEvo Environmental Health (U. K). Household products accounted for 80% of 1997 revenues and operating income; pharmaceutical products, 12%; and food products, 8%.

	£ mil 12/95	01/97	01/98	US$mil 01/98					
Sales	2,306.1	2,294.7	2,196.6	3,591.6	P/E Ratio		21.5	Price (6/30/98)	11.44
Net Income	325.7	243.9	216.0	353.2	P/B Ratio		5.1	52 Wk Hi-Low	13.00-8.10
Book Value	895.2	772.9	905.6	1,480.7	Yield %		2.1	Market Cap	US$7,779.0mil

Address	1 Burlington Ln.	Tel 181-994-6464	ADR	--	CEO	Vernon Sankey
	London W4 2RW	Fax 181-994-8920	SEDOL	0727871	Chairman	Alan Dalby

Reed International

DJGI Industry: **Publishing**
Stoxx Sector: **Media**

Reed International PLC is a holding company. Its principal investments are its direct 50% share in Reed Elsevier PLC and its 46% share in Elsevier Reed Finance BV. The companies are involved in publishing a wide range of materials and providing electronic information services and financing. The remaining shares are held directly by Elsevier NV and, to compensate for the differences in market capitalization of the two parent companies at the time of the merger, Reed International also has a 5.8% indirect share in Elsevier NV.

	£ mil 12/95	12/96	12/97	US$mil 12/97					
Sales	N/A	N/A	N/A	N/A	P/E Ratio		55.9	Price (6/30/98)	5.42
Net Income	277.0	302.0	90.0	148.8	P/B Ratio		7.8	52 Wk Hi-Low	7.18-5.07
Book Value	1,094.0	1,092.0	786.0	1,299.6	Yield %		2.7	Market Cap	US$10,319mil

Address	Quadrant House	Tel 181-652-3555	ADR	RUK	President	Herman Bruggink
	Sutton SM2 5AS	Fax 181-652-3937	SEDOL	0730835	Co Chairman	Nigel Stapleton

Rentokil

DJGI Industry: **Other Industrial & Commercial Services**
Stoxx Sector: **Industrials**

Rentokil Group PLC is an international service company. The group operates in more than 40 countries, providing pest control, tropical plants care, health-care, medical services, cleaning services, water and ventilation, hospital services, personnel services, office machine maintenance, security, property control, facilities maintenance, and timber preserving. Hygiene and cleaning accounted for 29% of 1997 gross revenues; transport services, 26%; security services, 14%; property services, 12%; personnel services, 12%; and pest control, 7%.

	£ mil 12/95	12/96	12/97	US$mil 12/97					
Sales	842.3	2,269.6	2,812.1	4,649.6	P/E Ratio		41.8	Price (6/30/98)	4.31
Net Income	139.3	219.2	294.6	487.1	P/B Ratio		NMF	52 Wk Hi-Low	4.40-2.07
Book Value	229.7	-130.3	-35.6	-58.9	Yield %		0.7	Market Cap	US$20,574mil

Address	Felcourt, East Grinstead	Tel 134-283-3022	ADR	RTOKY	CEO	Sir Clive M. Thompson
	West Sussex RH19 2JY	Fax 134-232-6229	SEDOL	0732712	Chairman	Henry S. King

Reuters

DJGI Industry: **Publishing**
Stoxx Sector: **Media**

Reuters Group PLC is a global information services company supplying the international business community and news media with a wide range of products including real-time financial data, transaction systems, information management systems, access to numerical and textual historical databases, news, news pictures, and television news. Reuters operates in 90 countries and has a communication network spanning 161 countries. Information products accounted for 64% of 1997 revenues; transaction products, 29%; and media and professional products, 7%

	£ mil 12/95	12/96	12/97	US$mil 12/97					
Sales	2,703.0	2,914.0	2,882.0	4,765.2	P/E Ratio		24.7	Price (6/30/98)	6.85
Net Income	414.0	491.0	390.0	644.8	P/B Ratio		6.0	52 Wk Hi-Low	7.76-5.31
Book Value	921.0	1,232.0	1,622.0	2,681.9	Yield %		2.2	Market Cap	US$16,228mil

Address	85 Fleet St.	Tel 171-250-1122	ADR	RTRSY	Mng Dir & CEO	Peter Job
	London EC4P 4AJ	Fax 171-324-5874	SEDOL	0236913	Chairman	Sir Christopher Hogg

In DJ Stoxx 50.

Rexam

DJGI Industry: **Containers & Packaging**
Stoxx Sector: **Industrials**

Rexam PLC, formerly known as Bowater, is an international printing and packaging company that operates in Europe, Australasia, North America, and South America. Its products include newspapers and directories, aerosol valves, computer stationery, business forms, corrugated packaging, plastic packaging, envelopes, cosmetic packaging, security products, and bulk containers. The group also contains building and engineering businesses. In March 1997, Rexam said its health-care unit had entered into a long-term agreement to supply medical packaging to Allegiance Healthcare Corp.

	£ mil 12/95	12/96	12/97	US$mil 12/97					
Sales	2,391.0	2,205.0	2,002.0	3,310.2	P/E Ratio		11.5	Price (6/30/98)	2.63
Net Income	132.0	-238.0	122.0	201.7	P/B Ratio		2.2	52 Wk Hi-Low	3.50-2.27
Book Value	609.0	563.0	598.0	988.8	Yield %		5.5	Market Cap	US$2,224.3mil

Address	114 Knightsbridge	Tel 171-584-7070	ADR	REXMY	CEO	Rolf Borjesson
	London SW1X 7NN	Fax 171-581-1149	SEDOL	0115971	Chairman	Jeremy Lancaster

RMC

DJGI Industry: **Building Materials**
Stoxx Sector: **Construction**

RMC Group PLC produces and supplies materials for use in the construction industry. Products include ready-mix concrete and aggregates, cement, lime, and concrete products. The group also has business interests in builders' merchanting, do it yourself retailing, waste control, and leisure activities. RMC has subsidiaries in the United Kingdom, United States, and Germany. Ready-mix concrete and aggregates accounted for 62% of 1997 gross revenues; cement, lime and concrete products, 24%; and merchanting, retail, waste control, leisure, and other, 14%.

	£ mil 12/95	12/96	12/97	US$mil 12/97				
Sales	4,116.2	4,081.7	4,007.2	6,625.7	P/E Ratio	14.8	Price (6/30/98)	10.39
Net Income	173.3	175.9	181.3	299.8	P/B Ratio	1.9	52 Wk Hi-Low	13.00-7.60
Book Value	1,369.4	1,425.9	1,446.4	2,391.5	Yield %	2.7	Market Cap	US$4,518.9mil

Address	Coldharbour Ln., Thorpe	Tel 193-256-8833	ADR	--	Managing Director	**Peter Young**
	Egham, Surrey TW20 8TD	Fax 193-256-8933	SEDOL	0726641	Chairman	**James Owen**

Rolls-Royce

DJGI Industry: **Aerospace & Defense**
Stoxx Sector: **Technology**

Rolls-Royce PLC is a world leader in the production of engines and power systems. It provides engineered products and services to world wide markets, including corporate operators, regional airlines, and the military, and to those involved in power generation, marine power, oil and gas, electricity transmission and materials handling. Rolls-Royce operates through its aerospace group, which focuses on gas turbines for civil and military aircraft; and its industrial group. Aerospace activities accounted for 73% of 1997 revenues and industrial activities for 27%.

	£ mil 12/95	12/96	12/97	US$mil 12/97				
Sales	3,597.0	4,045.0	4,216.0	6,970.9	P/E Ratio	16.3	Price (6/30/98)	2.48
Net Income	142.0	-47.0	224.0	370.4	P/B Ratio	2.5	52 Wk Hi-Low	3.00-1.89
Book Value	1,345.0	1,303.0	1,441.0	2,382.6	Yield %	2.4	Market Cap	US$6,180.1mil

Address	65 Buckingham Gate	Tel 171-222-9020	ADR	RYCEY	CEO	**John Rose**
	London SW1E 6AT	Fax 171-233-1733	SEDOL	0747761	Chairman	**Sir Ralph Robins**

Royal Bank of Scotland

DJGI Industry: **Banks - Regional (All)**
Stoxx Sector: **Bank**

Royal Bank of Scotland Group PLC offers retail and corporate banking, insurance, and financial services such as capital-markets and securities investments through hundreds of branches in the United Kingdom. It provides automobile insurance through its subsidiary company Direct Line Insurance, the largest private auto insurance company in the United Kingdom. The group's core market is the United Kingdom but it has interests in the United States through its subsidiary Citizens Financial Group, a leading provider of personal and corporate banking services in New England.

	£ mil 09/95	09/96	09/97	US$mil 09/97				
Revenues	4,528.0	5,033.0	5,862.0	9,491.6	P/E Ratio	16.5	Price (6/30/98)	10.40
Net Income	398.0	496.0	510.0	825.8	P/B Ratio	3.5	52 Wk Hi-Low	11.27-5.60
Book Value	1,538.0	1,871.0	2,308.0	3,737.0	Yield %	2.1	Market Cap	US$15,073mil

Address	42 St. Andrew Sq.	Tel 131-556-8555	ADR	RBSG	CEO	**Dr. G.R. Mathewson**
	Edinburgh EH2 2YE	Fax 131-557-6140	SEDOL	0754783	Chairman	**Lord Younger**

Royal & Sun Alliance Insurance

DJGI Industry: **Insurance - Full Line**
Stoxx Sector: **Insurance**

Royal & Sun Alliance Insurance Group PLC was formed in July 1996 as the result of a merger between Royal Insurance and Sun Alliance. It provides life insurance, general insurance, investment management, property investment, management, and other related financial services. The company has operations in over 120 countries, including Canada, the United States, Europe, Scandinavia, Australia, New Zealand, South Africa, and Latin America. Premiums accounted for 71% of 1997 revenues; investment income, 19%; and gains on securities, 10%.

	£ mil 12/95	12/96	12/97	US$mil 12/97				
Revenues	7,719.2	13,242.0	12,994.0	21,484.8	P/E Ratio	16.8	Price (6/30/98)	6.20
Net Income	402.2	464.0	580.0	959.0	P/B Ratio	1.3	52 Wk Hi-Low	8.13-4.43
Book Value	2,515.2	6,216.0	7,208.0	11,918.0	Yield %	3.4	Market Cap	US$16,119mil

Address	1 Barholomew Lane	Tel 171-583-2345	ADR	--	CEO	**R.A. Gamble**
	London EC2N 2AB	Fax 171-588-1159	SEDOL	0859633	Chairman	**Sir C.J. Benson**

In DJ Stoxx 50.

RTZ

DJGI Industry: **Mining - Diversified**
Stoxx Sector: **Basic Resources**

RTZ Corp. PLC, is a world leader in the exploration and extraction of mineral resources. Metals and minerals mined include copper, gold, iron ore, aluminum, lead, zinc, silver, coal, uranium, borax, titanium dioxide, talc, diamonds, and zircons. The company's operations are located predominantly in North America, Australia, and New Zealand as well as in Europe, South America, Africa, and Indonesia. It has entered into a dual-listed company structure with CRA Ltd. Industrial minerals accounted for 21% of 1997 revenues; aluminum, 19%; copper, 17%.

	£ mil 12/95	12/96	12/97	US$mil 12/97				
Sales	4,881.0	4,530.0	4,711.0	7,789.4	P/E Ratio	12.7	Price (6/30/98)	6.75
Net Income	815.0	701.0	744.0	1,230.2	P/B Ratio	1.6	52 Wk Hi-Low	10.69-6.75
Book Value	4,499.0	4,402.0	4,449.0	7,356.2	Yield %	4.7	Market Cap	US$11,977mil

Address	6 St. James's Sq.	Tel 171-930-2399	ADR	RTZ	CEO	**Robert Wilson**
	London SW1Y 4LD	Fax 171-930-3249	SEDOL	0718875	Chairman	**Sir Derek Birkin**

Rugby

DJGI Industry: **Building Materials**
Stoxx Sector: **Construction**

The Rugby Group PLC is an international concern that manufactures building materials through subsidiaries operating in the United Kingdom, continental Europe, Australia, and the United States. The company is made up of four divisions: U.S. manufacturing and distribution the joinery division, which produces doors, windows, and related products; the cement and lime division; and the metal products division, which manufactures constructional steel products. U. S. activities accounted for 44% of 1997 revenues; joinery, 36%; and cement and lime, 20%.

	£ mil 12/95	12/96	12/97	US$mil 12/97					
Sales	1,143.1	970.5	1,065.3	1,761.4	P/E Ratio	15.2	Price (6/30/98)		1.13
Net Income	28.9	33.8	47.6	78.7	P/B Ratio	1.8	52 Wk Hi-Low		1.43-1.10
Book Value	401.8	415.5	409.2	676.6	Yield %	3.6	Market Cap		US$1,218.2mil

Address	Crown Hse., Rugby	Tel 178-854-2666	ADR	--	CEO	P. Johnson
	Warwickshire CV21 2DT	Fax 178-854-0256	SEDOL	0758707	Chairman	R. Gourlay

Safeway

DJGI Industry: **Food Retailers & Wholesalers**
Stoxx Sector: **Consumer Non-Cyclical**

Safeway PLC is the one of the largest grocery retailers in the United Kingdom, employing over 75,000 people. The flagship Safeway supermarket chain currently represents most of the group's total operating profit. Other outlets include discount supermarket chains Lo-Cost and Presto. The group has expanded its retail interests through a program to open new safeway stores and through a new joint venture progam in Northern Ireland in cooperation with the Fitzwilton Group. Fifteen new stores were opened in 1998.

	£ mil 03/96	03/97	03/98	US$mil 03/98					
Sales	6,069.4	6,589.7	6,978.7	11,679.8	P/E Ratio	17.8	Price (6/30/98)		3.93
Net Income	300.6	294.4	241.0	403.3	P/B Ratio	2.2	52 Wk Hi-Low		4.06-3.18
Book Value	1,932.7	1,877.8	1,972.6	3,301.4	Yield %	3.6	Market Cap		US$7,194.5mil

Address	6 Millington Rd., Hayes	Tel 181-848-8744	ADR	--	CEO	C. Smith
	Middlesex UB3 4AY	Fax 181-573-1865	SEDOL	0049241	Chairman	A. Grant

J. Sainsbury

DJGI Industry: **Food Retailers & Wholesalers**
Stoxx Sector: **Consumer Non-Cyclical**

J. Sainsbury PLC, the United Kingdom's largest supermarket retailer by market capitalization, operates about 460 Sainsbury's grocery stores in the United Kingdom. Its subsidiary stores include Savacentre Department Stores and a do-it-yourself concern called Homebase, both in the United Kingdom. The company also owns Shaw's supermarkets in the United States. Together they serve more than 12 million customers a week. Food retailing accounted for 92% of fiscal 1998 revenues; do-it-yourself retailing, 7%; and other activities, nominal.

	£ mil 03/96	03/97	03/98	US$mil 03/98					
Sales	12,627.0	13,395.0	14,500.0	24,267.8	P/E Ratio	20.5	Price (6/30/98)		5.34
Net Income	488.0	403.0	487.0	815.1	P/B Ratio	2.5	52 Wk Hi-Low		5.61-3.64
Book Value	3,534.0	3,671.0	4,112.0	6,882.0	Yield %	2.6	Market Cap		US$16,960mil

Address	Stamford Hse., Stamford St.	Tel 171-921-6000	ADR	SAINY	Managing Director	D.A. Quarmby
	London SE1 9LL	Fax 171-921-6413	SEDOL	0767640	Chairman	D.J. Sainsbury

Schroders

DJGI Industry: **Securities Brokers**
Stoxx Sector: **Financial Services**

Schroders PLC is an international merchant banking, investment banking, and fund management company. It is the second-largest unit trust in the United Kingdom and is 40%-owned by the founding Schroder family. The company has interests in corporate finance, capital markets, securities, banking, leasing and project finance, treasury and trading, investment management, property asset management, venture capital, and management buy-outs. Schroders owns U.S. investment company Wertheim Schroder. In January 1998, the company shut down its Asian equity business.

	£ mil 12/95	12/96	12/97	US$mil 12/97					
Sales	1,370.7	1,554.7	1,685.8	2,787.4	P/E Ratio	26.5	Price (6/30/98)		15.46
Net Income	139.0	179.2	170.9	282.6	P/B Ratio	4.3	52 Wk Hi-Low		19.99-10.67
Book Value	849.3	941.1	1,046.3	1,730.0	Yield %	1.0	Market Cap		US$5,829.7mil

Address	120 Cheapside	Tel 171-382-6000	ADR	--	President	George W. Mallinckrodt
	London EC2V 6DS	Fax 171-382-3950	SEDOL	0779407	Chairman	Win F. Bischoff

Scottish Power

DJGI Industry: **Electrical Utilities (All)**
Stoxx Sector: **Utility**

Scottish Power PLC is an electric utility with principal operations in Scotland. Aside from the company's core businesses, which involve the generation, transmission, and distribution of electricity, Scottish Power provides electrical-contracting services and sells electric appliances. The company also supplies gas through its Caledonian Gas subsidiary to commercial and industrial customers. In June 1996, the company acquired Southern Water PLC. The supplying of energy accounted for 42% of fiscal 1998 revenues.

	£ mil 03/96	03/97	03/98	US$mil 03/98					
Sales	2,271.5	2,940.7	3,128.2	5,235.5	P/E Ratio	36.5	Price (6/30/98)		5.25
Net Income	296.4	421.1	170.1	284.7	P/B Ratio	4.3	52 Wk Hi-Low		5.84-3.91
Book Value	1,207.7	1,520.5	1,666.2	2,788.6	Yield %	3.9	Market Cap		US$10,492mil

Address	1 Atlantic Quay	Tel 141-248-8200	ADR	SPYAY	CEO	Ian Robinson
	Glasgow G2 8SP	Fax 141-248-8300	SEDOL	0790828	Chairman	Murray Stuart

Securicor

DJGI Industry: **Other Industrial & Commercial Services**
Stoxx Sector: **Industrials**

Securicor PLC is a courier, transport, and security services company. It is engaged in transportation and delivery of express parcels, mail services, and transportation. The company also provides services for the care of cash and valuables, cash processing, and security guards and patrols. Securicor manufactures, sells, and installs communications products, mobile communications, and communications systems networks. Distribution accounted for 48% of fiscal 1997 revenues; security services, 44%; communications, 7%; and insurance and hotels, 1%.

	£ mil 09/95	09/96	09/97	US$mil 09/97				
Sales	1,031.4	1,255.1	1,128.3	1,826.9	P/E Ratio	162.7	Price (6/30/98)	4.88
Net Income	41.4	57.0	16.4	26.6	P/B Ratio	9.4	52 Wk Hi-Low	5.17-2.85
Book Value	200.2	308.2	225.8	365.6	Yield %	0.4	Market Cap	US$4,891.2mil

Address	15 Carshalton Rd.	Tel 181-770-7000	ADR	--	CEO	R. Wiggs
	Sutton, Surrey SM1 4LD	Fax 181-770-1145	SEDOL	0791995	Chairman	Sir N. Macfarlane

Severn Trent

DJGI Industry: **Water Utilities**
Stoxx Sector: **Utility**

Severn Trent PLC provides waste-management services, and it is the United Kingdom's second-largest water company in terms of the area it serves. The company designs and implements advanced disinfection systems for water and sewage treatment and provides water-distribution and waste-management services. In April 1998, Severn Trent bought a chlorine disinfection business, with operations in the United States and Italy, for $16 million. Water and sewerage services accounted for 76% of fiscal 1997 revenues; waste management, 16%; and other, 8%.

	£ mil 03/96	03/97	03/98	US$mil 03/98				
Sales	1,157.5	1,215.3	1,251.3	2,094.2	P/E Ratio	11.2	Price (6/30/98)	10.50
Net Income	327.7	316.7	14.9	24.9	P/B Ratio	1.3	52 Wk Hi-Low	10.72-7.78
Book Value	2,510.8	2,530.2	2,270.4	3,799.8	Yield %	3.4	Market Cap	US$5,955.2mil

Address	2297 Coventry Rd.	Tel 121-722-4000	ADR	--	CEO	Vic Cocker
	Birmingham B26 3PU	Fax 121-722-6150	SEDOL	0054632	Chairman	Richard Ireland

Shanks & McEwan

DJGI Industry: **Pollution Control & Waste Management**
Stoxx Sector: **Industrials**

Shanks & McEwan Group PLC is a waste-management and waste-disposal company that also offers construction services. It operates approximately 40 waste-management sites in the United Kingdom. Its waste-services division manages landfill sites. The company's environmental services division, which is led by the company's wholly owned Rechem subsidiary, specializes in the high-temperature destruction of hazardous waste. Its technical services division develops the company's waste treatment facilities. Waste services accounted for 88% of fiscal 1998 revenues.

	£ mil 03/96	03/97	03/98	US$mil 03/98				
Sales	114.2	144.1	176.7	295.8	P/E Ratio	20.2	Price (6/30/98)	1.80
Net Income	12.1	14.2	16.3	27.4	P/B Ratio	4.0	52 Wk Hi-Low	2.01-1.40
Book Value	69.8	75.2	61.7	103.3	Yield %	2.3	Market Cap	US$599.9mil

Address	Bourne End, Station Rd.	Tel 162-852-4523	ADR	--	CEO	M.C. Averill
	Buckshire SL8 5YP	Fax 162-852-4114	SEDOL	0799524	Chairman	G.H. Waddell

Shell Transport & Trading

DJGI Industry: **Oil Companies - Major**
Stoxx Sector: **Energy**

Shell Transport & Trading Company PLC is a holding company that, in conjunction with the Royal Dutch Petroleum Co., owns investments in the companies constituting the Royal Dutch/Shell Group. Shell Transport & Trading holds a 40% interest in the Royal Dutch/Shell Group. The other 60% is held by Royal Dutch Petroleum. The Royal Dutch/Shell Group is made up of companies that explore for, extract, process, and sell oil, natural gas, chemicals, coal, and metals. Refining accounted for 80% of 1997 revenues; chemicals, 11%; oil and gas exploration and production, 8%.

	£ mil 12/95	12/96	12/97	US$mil 12/97				
Sales	27,838.0	32,831.6	31,289.6	51,735.4	P/E Ratio	23.7	Price (6/30/98)	4.22
Net Income	1,750.0	2,276.4	1,894.4	3,132.3	P/B Ratio	2.9	52 Wk Hi-Low	4.85-3.89
Book Value	15,176.0	14,858.8	14,568.8	24,088.6	Yield %	3.1	Market Cap	US$70,006mil

Address	Shell Ctr.	Tel 171-934-1234	ADR	SC	Managing Director	Mark Moody-Stuart
	London SE1 7NA	Fax 171-934-5252	SEDOL	0803414	Chairman	John S. Jennings

Siebe

DJGI Industry: **Industrial - Diversified**
Stoxx Sector: **Industrials**

Siebe PLC is one of the United Kingdom's largest diversified engineering groups. The company specializes in manufacturing electromechanical and electronic controls for the appliance, automotive, and industrial markets. Its other technical manufactured products include compressed-air and pneumatic equipment; transfer and filtration equipment for gases and liquids; valves; electronics; and safety and life-support products. In 1997, Siebe paid GBP193 million for Cleveland-based Eaton Corp.'s Appliance Control Operations, and plans to divest some, as yet unnamed noncore businesses.

	£ mil 04/96	04/97	04/98	US$mil 04/98				
Sales	2,599.1	3,005.3	3,670.2	6,137.5	P/E Ratio	19.3	Price (6/30/98)	11.97
Net Income	193.0	253.8	309.5	517.6	P/B Ratio	4.6	52 Wk Hi-Low	15.25-9.78
Book Value	1,062.3	1,016.6	910.7	1,522.9	Yield %	1.4	Market Cap	US$10,514mil

Address	2-4 Victoria St., Windsor	Tel 175-385-5411	ADR	SIBEY	CEO	Allen Yurko
	Berkshire SL4 1EN	Fax 175-384-0638	SEDOL	0807041	Chairman	Barrie Stephens

Slough Estates

DJGI Industry: **Real Estate**
Stoxx Sector: **Financial Services**

Slough Estates PLC is a real estate investor specializing in the development of industrial property that is situated in the United Kingdom, Canada, the United States, Belgium, France, and Germany. The company acquires, develops, manages, and owns properties in major business centers throughout the world. It manages about 2.5 million square meters of space, which are occupied by about 2,000 tenants. Other interests include the supply of utility services and property trading. Property investment accounted for 55% of 1997 revenues; utilities, 10%; and property trading, 35%.

£ mil	12/95	12/96	12/97	US$mil 12/97				
Sales	183.4	220.2	263.1	435.0	P/E Ratio	21.9	Price (6/30/98)	3.45
Net Income	55.1	58.7	72.9	120.5	P/B Ratio	1.0	52 Wk Hi-Low	4.13-2.96
Book Value	1,041.1	1,127.2	1,376.5	2,276.0	Yield %	1.8	Market Cap	US$2,270.9mil

Address	234 Bath Rd., Slough	Tel	175-353-7171	ADR	--	CEO	Derick Wilson
	Berkshire SL1 4EE	Fax	175-382-0585	SEDOL	0814104	Chairman	Nigel Mobbs

Smith & Nephew

DJGI Industry: **Medical Supplies**
Stoxx Sector: **Consumer Non-Cyclical**

Smith & Nephew PLC is an internationally active producer of health-care and medical products, including wound dressings, artificial hips and other joints, casting products, eye and ear implants, and arthroscopy equipment. It manufactures consumer health-care goods such as Elastoplast first-aid dressings, Lillets tampons, and Simple skin-care products. Casting and support products accounted for 21% of 1997 revenues; wound management, 18%; consumer products, 17%; endoscopy, 16%; orthopedic implants, 13%; trauma products 9%; and other medical products, 6%.

£ mil	12/95	12/96	12/97	US$mil 12/97				
Sales	996.1	1,068.2	1,031.7	1,705.9	P/E Ratio	14.7	Price (6/30/98)	1.50
Net Income	112.8	120.7	113.7	188.0	P/B Ratio	3.6	52 Wk Hi-Low	1.92-1.45
Book Value	404.4	435.1	461.0	762.2	Yield %	4.1	Market Cap	US$2,773.9mil

Address	2 Temple Pl.	Tel	171-836-7922	ADR	--	CEO	John Robinson
	London WC2R 3BP	Fax	171-240-7088	SEDOL	0816605	Chairman	Eric Kinder

W.H. Smith

DJGI Industry: **Retailers - Other Specialty**
Stoxx Sector: **Retail**

W.H. Smith Group PLC operates retail stores that sell mainly books, stationery, and home entertainment products such as recorded music and videos. It owns and operates about 300 Our Price Music outlets, 35 Our Price Video stores, and 24 Virgin Megastores. Its Do It All hardware-supplies chain is operated as a domestic joint venture with Boots. W.H. Smith owns 82% of U.K. bookselling chain Waterstone's, which has established U.S. branches in Chicago and Boston. It also operates 167 W.H. Smith retail and W.H. Smith music stores in the United States.

£ mil	06/96	05/97	05/98	US$mil 05/98				
Revenues	2,684.4	2,747.0	2,901.0	4,732.5	P/E Ratio	6.7	Price (6/30/98)	5.33
Net Income	-208.1	25.0	50.0	81.6	P/B Ratio	3.6	52 Wk Hi-Low	5.88-3.36
Book Value	393.0	357.8	484.0	789.6	Yield %	3.1	Market Cap	US$2,276.1mil

Address	Audrey House, Ely Pl.	Tel	171-730-1200	ADR	--	CEO	W. Cockburn
	London EC1N 6SN	Fax	171-259-9075	SEDOL	0268530	Chairman	J. Hardie

SmithKline Beecham

DJGI Industry: **Pharmaceuticals**
Stoxx Sector: **Pharmaceutical**

SmithKline Beecham PLC is a producer and distributor of pharmaceuticals for human and animal health-care. The company specializes in the research, development, production, and marketing of pharmaceuticals, over-the-counter medications, and consumer health-care products. Its principal operations are in the United States and the United Kingdom, but it makes considerable sales throughout Europe and Asia and has established facilities there. Pharmaceuticals accounted for 59% of 1997 revenues; consumer health-care, 30%; and clincal laboratories, 11%.

£ mil	12/95	12/96	12/97	US$mil 12/97				
Sales	7,011.0	7,925.0	7,795.0	12,888.6	P/E Ratio	36.9	Price (6/30/98)	7.32
Net Income	994.0	1,072.0	1,127.0	1,863.4	P/B Ratio	23.8	52 Wk Hi-Low	8.46-2.76
Book Value	1,202.0	1,243.0	1,554.0	2,569.4	Yield %	1.4	Market Cap	US$67,964mil

Address	New Horizons Ct., Brentford	Tel	181-975-2000	ADR	SBH	President	J. Leschly
	Middlesex TW8 9EP	Fax	181-847-0830	SEDOL	0135656	Chairman	P. Walters

Smiths Industries

DJGI Industry: **Aerospace & Defense**
Stoxx Sector: **Technology**

Smiths Industries PLC develops commercial and military aerospace electronics, medical systems, and specialized industrial products. It supplies cockpit displays, marine and fighting vehicle systems, data recorders, and navigation systems to the U.S. military and civil aviation industries. The company produces single-use products for anesthesia, respiratory therapy, and intensive-care applications as well as operating tables, medical infusion pumps, and related equipment. The main manufacturing operations are located in the United Kingdom, Europe, and the United States.

£ mil	08/95	08/96	08/97	US$mil 08/97				
Sales	899.3	995.6	1,076.2	1,737.5	P/E Ratio	18.9	Price (6/30/98)	8.30
Net Income	93.9	117.8	131.7	212.6	P/B Ratio	9.1	52 Wk Hi-Low	9.98-7.09
Book Value	225.5	211.8	240.4	388.1	Yield %	2.2	Market Cap	US$4,266.9mil

Address	765 Finchley Rd., Childs Hill	Tel	181-458-3232	ADR	--	CEO	Roger Hurn
	London NW11 8DS	Fax	181-458-4380	SEDOL	0818270	Chairman	Roger Hurn

Tarmac

DJGI Industry: **Heavy Construction**
Stoxx Sector: **Construction**

Tarmac PLC operates construction services and manufactures quarry products and other building materials. The company also contracts to provide building, civil engineering, and mechanical services. Tarmac provides road materials, aggregates, ready-mix concrete, and clay bricks to the construction industry. Although operating primarily in the United Kingdom, the company also operates in Europe, Asia, the United States, Canada, the Caribbean, and the Middle East. Construction services accounted for 57% of 1997 revenues and heavy building materials for 43%.

	£ mil 12/95	12/96	12/97	US$mil 12/97				
Sales	1,958.7	2,637.7	2,773.1	4,585.2	P/E Ratio	13.4	Price (6/30/98)	1.07
Net Income	0.6	3.6	74.9	123.8	P/B Ratio	1.3	52 Wk Hi-Low	1.34-0.95
Book Value	923.1	776.9	797.2	1,318.1	Yield %	5.3	Market Cap	US$1,682.6mil

Address	Hilton Hall, Essington	Tel **190-230-7407**	ADR	--	CEO	**Neville Simms**
	Wolverhampton WV11 2BQ	Fax **190-230-7408**	SEDOL	**0874120**	Chairman	**Sir John Banham**

Tate & Lyle

DJGI Industry: **Other Food**
Stoxx Sector: **Food & Beverage**

Tate & Lyle PLC specializes in sugar refining and processing. It manufactures sugar and cereal sweeteners and processes starch products. Its wholly owned subsidiaries in the United States include cane-sugar producer Domino and beet-sugar producer Western Sugar. The company's cereal-sweetener and starch division includes Amylum, a Belgium-based company; Prignitz-Starke, a German starch producer; and A.E. Staley Manufacturing, a U.S.-based company that makes Stellar fat substitute and Krystar reduced-calorie sweetener.

	£ mil 09/95	09/96	09/97	US$mil 09/97				
Sales	4,509.6	4,879.0	4,352.6	7,047.6	P/E Ratio	15.4	Price (6/30/98)	4.75
Net Income	198.3	174.0	101.7	164.7	P/B Ratio	2.1	52 Wk Hi-Low	5.80-4.01
Book Value	788.1	964.5	971.9	1,573.7	Yield %	3.6	Market Cap	US$3,614.1mil

Address	Sugar Quay, Lower Thames St.	Tel **171-626-6525**	ADR	**TATYY**	CEO	**L.G. Pillard**
	London EC3R 6DQ	Fax **171-623-5213**	SEDOL	**0875413**	Chairman & CEO	**Neil M. Shaw**

Taylor Woodrow

DJGI Industry: **Heavy Construction**
Stoxx Sector: **Construction**

Taylor Woodrow PLC is an international conglomerate involved in construction, housing, property development, and trading. It provides construction consulting to British service companies, but recently the group has focused on its property portfolio. The company's wholly owned Greenham Trading subsidiaries distribute janitorial supplies, video equipment, construction materials, and personal-protection equipment. Contracting accounted for 45% of 1997 revenues; housing, 36%; Greenham Trading, 10%; property investment and development, 7%; and other, 2%.

	£ mil 12/95	12/96	12/97	US$mil 12/97				
Sales	1,154.1	1,189.7	1,295.7	2,142.4	P/E Ratio	14.2	Price (6/30/98)	2.01
Net Income	29.1	46.8	56.2	92.9	P/B Ratio	1.3	52 Wk Hi-Low	2.37-1.64
Book Value	515.6	540.2	612.7	1,013.1	Yield %	2.2	Market Cap	US$1,336.5mil

Address	4 Dunraven St.	Tel **171-629-1201**	ADR	--	CEO	**H. A. Palmer**
	London W1Y 3FG	Fax **171-493-1066**	SEDOL	**0878230**	Chairman	**C J. Parsons**

Tesco

DJGI Industry: **Food Retailers & Wholesalers**
Stoxx Sector: **Consumer Non-Cyclical**

Tesco PLC is a food retailing company that produces Tesco-brand food and operates a chain of 625 stores in England, Scotland, and Wales. Subsidiaries include the William Low grocery chain, French food retailer Catteau, and Hungarian food retailer Global TH. In February 1997, Tesco announced a joint venture with the Royal Bank of Scotland PLC to offer a range of finacial services and a credit card. Tesco also agreed to buy Associated British Foods' Irish food retail business and a business in Poland. Food retailing accounted for 100% of fiscal 1998 revenues.

	£ mil 02/96	02/97	02/98	US$mil 02/98				
Sales	12,094.0	13,887.0	15,915.0	26,158.8	P/E Ratio	25.3	Price (6/30/98)	5.85
Net Income	466.0	520.0	505.0	830.0	P/B Ratio	3.3	52 Wk Hi-Low	6.02-3.70
Book Value	3,588.0	3,890.0	3,876.0	6,370.8	Yield %	2.0	Market Cap	US$21,498mil

Address	Delamare Rd., Cheshunt	Tel **199-263-2222**	ADR	**TESOY**	Managing Director	**David Malpas**
	Hertfordshire EN8 9SL	Fax **199-263-0794**	SEDOL	**0884709**	Chairman	**Sir Ian MacLaurin**

Thames Water

DJGI Industry: **Water Utilities**
Stoxx Sector: **Utility**

Thames Water PLC, the largest of the United Kingdom's privatized water companies, supplies water and sewerage services to customers in London and the surrounding vicinity. The company also carries out a wide range of water services for customers in Africa, Asia, continental Europe, and South America. Other services include sewer surveying, drainage consultancy, and landscaping, as well as insurance and property-development services. The company's subsidiary Thames Water Utilities Limited operates water-supply and sewerage activities.

	£ mil 03/96	03/97	03/98	US$mil 03/98				
Sales	1,193.6	1,287.4	1,383.1	2,314.8	P/E Ratio	33.0	Price (6/30/98)	10.91
Net Income	203.5	320.4	125.7	210.4	P/B Ratio	1.9	52 Wk Hi-Low	10.91-6.94
Book Value	2,170.3	2,165.5	2,147.4	3,594.0	Yield %	3.5	Market Cap	US$6,926.9mil

Address	14 Cavendish Pl.	Tel **171-636-8686**	ADR	--	CEO	**Michael Hoffman**
	London W1M 9DJ	Fax **171-833-6137**	SEDOL	**0886006**	Chairman	**Sir Robert Clarke**

3i Group

DJGI Industry: **Diversified Financial Services**
Stoxx Sector: **Financial Services**

3i Group PLC invests in small and medium-sized businesses that do not have ready access to capital markets. Its investment activities include providing start-up, early-stage, and development capital; providing capital for management buyouts; and acquiring existing holdings. Group investment activities are carried on through offices in the United Kingdom, the Channel Islands, France, Germany, Spain, and Italy. In addition, 3i Group also has interests in joint ventures in Australia, India, and Japan, and it has associated companies in the Netherlands and Portugal.

£ mil 03/96	03/97	03/98	US$mil 03/98					
Revenues	268.0	274.9	314.9	527.0	P/E Ratio	35.8	Price (6/30/98)	6.13
Net Income	70.0	91.3	107.3	179.6	P/B Ratio	1.0	52 Wk Hi-Low	6.71-4.58
Book Value	2,528.8	2,897.4	3,488.9	5,839.2	Yield %	1.7	Market Cap	US$6,077.1mil

Address	91 Waterloo Rd.		Tel 171-928-3131	ADR	--	CEO	B. Larcombe
	London SE1 8XP		Fax 171-928-0058	SEDOL	0888693	Chairman	Sir G. Russell

TI Group

DJGI Industry: **Industrial - Diversified**
Stoxx Sector: **Industrials**

TI Group PLC is an engineering company specializing in engineered seals and sealing systems. It also makes fluid-carrying systems for refrigeration industries as well as aerospace systems and equipment. Its four main business units are John Crane, a producer of engineering seals; Bundy, a producer of specialized tubing for the automotive and refrigeration industries; Dowty, a producer of aerospace turbine engine components; and Messier-Dowty, a producer of landing gear. In 1998, TI bought Finnish sealing and lubricating systems supplier Safematic for GBP17 million.

£ mil 12/95	12/96	12/97	US$mil 12/97					
Sales	1,703.3	1,552.5	1,704.4	2,818.1	P/E Ratio	14.4	Price (6/30/98)	4.55
Net Income	124.3	161.0	150.5	248.8	P/B Ratio	5.6	52 Wk Hi-Low	6.91-4.32
Book Value	400.9	321.9	386.9	639.7	Yield %	3.5	Market Cap	US$3,634.0mil

Address	Lambourn Ct.		Tel 123-555-5570	ADR	TIGUY	CEO	B. Laule
	Abingdon OX14 1UH		Fax 123-555-5818	SEDOL	0868673	Chairman	C. Lewinton

Unigate

DJGI Industry: **Other Food**
Stoxx Sector: **Food & Beverage**

Unigate PLC produces and distributes food and beverages and owns restaurants. Its subsidiaries include Unigate Dairies Ltd., which processes and distributes fresh milk and related products in the United Kingdom; St. Ivel which manufactures a wide range of dairy and fresh food products; and Wincanton Ltd., which is a transportation and distribution business serving major retailers and manufacturers. In 1997, the group disposed of its U.S. Restaurants business. Fresh food products accounted for 54% of fiscal 1997 revenues; dairy products, 27%; and Wincanton logistics, 19%.

£ mil 03/96	03/97	03/98	US$mil 03/98					
Sales	2,094.9	2,364.3	2,310.7	3,867.3	P/E Ratio	14.1	Price (6/30/98)	6.64
Net Income	266.1	88.1	112.6	188.5	P/B Ratio	2.8	52 Wk Hi-Low	7.40-4.79
Book Value	531.9	506.0	566.4	947.9	Yield %	3.3	Market Cap	US$2,656.8mil

Address	Unigate Hse., Wood Ln.		Tel 181-749-8888	ADR	UNGAY	CEO	Ross Buckland
	London W12 7RP		Fax 181-576-6071	SEDOL	0911704	Chairman	Ian Martin

Unilever

DJGI Industry: **Other Food**
Stoxx Sector: **Food & Beverage**

Unilever PLC has a 50% interest in the Unilever group of companies; Netherlands-based Unilever NV controls the other 50%. Its core businesses are the manufacture of specialty food products, beverages, personal products, and detergents. Food products accounted for 52% of 1997 revenue; home and personal care, 45%; and other operations, 3%. Food products include Country Crock spreads, Wishbone dressings, and Ragu sauces; detergents include Wisk and Dove brands; and personal-care products are sold through subsidiaries Elizabeth Arden and Calvin Klein Cosmetics.

£ mil 12/95	12/96	12/97	US$mil 12/97					
Sales	31,516.0	33,522.0	28,473.0	47,078.4	P/E Ratio	13.8	Price (6/30/98)	6.38
Net Income	1,473.0	1,610.0	3,335.0	5,514.2	P/B Ratio	6.5	52 Wk Hi-Low	7.06-4.08
Book Value	5,514.0	5,092.0	7,337.0	12,131.3	Yield %	1.3	Market Cap	US$34,706mil

Address	Box 68, Unilever House		Tel 171-822-5252	ADR	UL	Joint Chairman	M. Tabaksblat
	London EC4P 4BQ		Fax 171-822-5951	SEDOL	0134277	Joint Chairman	N. Fitzgerald

United News & Media

DJGI Industry: **Publishing**
Stoxx Sector: **Media**

United News & Media PLC, which merged with MAI PLC in April 1996, publishes national newspapers and business periodicals and operates as a broadcasting and financial services company. During 1997, the group acquired HTV Group PLC, FPG International Corporation, and Telecom Library and disposed of the regional newspapers division. United News & Media has an agreement with Warner Brothers to build a studio and theme park in West London. The group operates mainly in the United Kingdom, Europe, the United States, the Middle East, and the Pacific.

£ mil 12/95	12/96	12/97	US$mil 12/97					
Sales	1,070.6	1,938.5	2,079.9	3,439.0	P/E Ratio	14.9	Price (6/30/98)	8.38
Net Income	68.7	152.4	277.1	458.2	P/B Ratio	NMF	52 Wk Hi-Low	9.39-6.70
Book Value	224.3	-278.9	-612.3	-1,012.4	Yield %	2.9	Market Cap	US$6,982.3mil

Address	245 Blackfriars Rd.		Tel 171-921-5000	ADR	UNEWY	CEO	Lord Hollick
	London SE1 9UY		Fax 171-928-2728	SEDOL	0916721	Chairman	Lord Stevens

United Utilities

DJGI Industry: **Water Utilities**
Stoxx Sector: **Utility**

United Utilities PLC is a water and electricity company that also has small international and telecommunications operations. It was formed in January 1996 by a merger of North West Water PLC and Norweb PLC. Services include the planning, design, and operations of water and wastewater, electricity distribution, and telecommunications systems, and the supply of electricity and gas. In March 1998, it set up a joint venture with Canada-based Northern Telecom to develop their digital powerline technology, which allows data communications through electrical power networks.

	£ mil 03/96	03/97	03/98	US$mil 03/98					
Sales	1,838.6	2,102.3	2,150.2	3,598.7	P/E Ratio	155.6	Price (6/30/98)		8.72
Net Income	224.4	235.4	30.1	50.4	P/B Ratio	2.4	52 Wk Hi-Low		8.86-6.61
Book Value	1,992.1	2,141.9	2,045.5	3,423.4	Yield %	4.8	Market Cap		US$7,922.9mil

Address	Birchwood Point Business Park	Tel 192-528-5000	ADR	UU	CEO	Brian Staples
	Warrington, Cheshire WA3 7WB	Fax 192-528-5199	SEDOL	0646233	Chairman	Sir Desmond Pitcher

Vodafone

DJGI Industry: **Telephone Utilities (All)**
Stoxx Sector: **Telecom**

Vodafone Group PLC, formed as the result of a demerger from Racal Electronics PLC in September 1991, is a telecommunications company that provides cellular-radio-network, voice-mail, radio-paging, and data-communication services. It also manufactures digital cellular telephones. Nearly all of its sales are generated in the United Kingdom, but the company also operates in Europe, Australia, Hong Kong and Mexico. At the end of its 1996-97 financial year, the company had more than 4 million subscribers on an equity-stakes basis.

	£ mil 03/96	03/97	03/98	US$mil 03/98					
Sales	1,402.2	1,749.0	2,470.8	4,135.2	P/E Ratio	55.9	Price (6/30/98)		7.61
Net Income	309.8	363.8	418.8	700.9	P/B Ratio	22.9	52 Wk Hi-Low		7.77-2.91
Book Value	1,022.1	770.0	282.5	472.8	Yield %	0.7	Market Cap		US$39,154mil

Address	2-4 London Rd., Newbury	Tel 163-533-251	ADR	VOD	CEO	Sir Gerald Whent
	Berkshire RG13 1JL	Fax 163-545-713	SEDOL	0719210	Chairman	Sir Ernest Harrison

William Baird

DJGI Industry: **Clothing & Fabrics**
Stoxx Sector: **Consumer Cyclical**

William Baird PLC primarily produces contract clothing; it also designs, manufactures, and retails branded apparel in the United Kingdom, Europe, and Asia. Name brands include Windsmoor, Planet, and Precis Petites in women's clothing and Dannimac in rainwear. In 1994, the company acquired Morris Cohen, a lingerie producer, and Melka Tenson, a sportswear group. The company disposed of its wholly owned engineering and building-services subsidiary, Darchem Group, in 1996. Operations in the United Kingdom account for 90% of total revenues.

	£ mil 12/95	12/96	12/97	US$mil 12/97					
Sales	671.3	667.3	550.9	910.8	P/E Ratio	10.7	Price (6/30/98)		2.08
Net Income	6.2	-7.8	22.5	37.3	P/B Ratio	1.8	52 Wk Hi-Low		2.87-1.66
Book Value	145.9	127.9	134.4	222.3	Yield %	5.0	Market Cap		US$406.7mil

Address	79 Mount St.	Tel 171-409-1785	ADR	--	CEO	D. Suddens
	London W1Y 5HJ	Fax 171-499-6788	SEDOL	0071114	Chairman	T. Parr

Williams

DJGI Industry: **Building Materials**
Stoxx Sector: **Construction**

Williams PLC is an international manufacturing concern that produces building and security products and fire-protection equipment. Its Kidde and Fenwal Safety Systems subsidiaries specialize in fire-detection, fire-extinguishing, and burner-management products. Building products include paint, electronic appliances, and ventilation equipment; the company also builds garages, conservatories, and kitchens. Its subsidiaries produce door locks, safes, and alarm systems. Security accounted for 42% of 1997 revenues; fire protection, 31%; and home improvement, 27%.

	£ mil 12/95	12/96	12/97	US$mil 12/97					
Sales	1,598.5	1,467.4	2,228.8	3,685.2	P/E Ratio	19.4	Price (6/30/98)		3.85
Net Income	156.0	250.8	165.3	273.3	P/B Ratio	NMF	52 Wk Hi-Low		4.83-3.20
Book Value	197.3	225.8	-389.3	-643.7	Yield %	4.1	Market Cap		US$5,070.8mil

Address	Poyle Rd., Colinbrook Slough	Tel 133-220-2020	ADR	WIHLY	CEO	Roger M. Carr
	Berkshire SL3 OHB	Fax 133-238-4402	SEDOL	0967666	Chairman	Nigel R. Rudd

Wilson Bowden

DJGI Industry: **Home Construction**
Stoxx Sector: **Consumer Cyclical**

Wilson Bowden PLC is a house construction, property development, and property investment group operating entirely within the United Kingdom. David Wilson Homes Ltd. and Wilson Bowden Properties Ltd. are its two main operating companies. Wilson Bowden sold more than 3,000 homes in 1997, up 20% from the previous year, and owned or controlled 12,700 housebuilding plots. Geographical expansion continued with a move into Cheshire. Home building accounted for 76% of 1997 revenues and property development accounted for 24%.

	£ mil 12/95	12/96	12/97	US$mil 12/97					
Sales	228.2	331.9	459.6	759.9	P/E Ratio	13.0	Price (6/30/98)		6.33
Net Income	19.7	27.3	45.6	75.4	P/B Ratio	2.0	52 Wk Hi-Low		7.33-5.00
Book Value	258.8	268.0	302.0	499.3	Yield %	2.0	Market Cap		US$987.9mil

Address	207 Leicester Rd., Ibstock	Tel 153-026-0777	ADR	--	CEO	David W. Wilson
	Leicester LE67 6HP	Fax 153-026-2805	SEDOL	0970073	Chairman	David W. Wilson

George Wimpey

DJGI Industry: **Home Construction**
Stoxx Sector: **Consumer Cyclical**

George Wimpey PLC is the largest private builder of houses in the United Kingdom. The company also has significant land development and property holdings. The group operates principally in the United Kingdom, the United States, and Canada. It also has subsidiaries in the Netherlands, France, Australia, Spain, and the Czech Republic. About 28% of its home completions take place outside the United Kingdom through 34 semiautonomous businesses. McLean homes accounted for 39% of 1997 revenues; Wimpey homes, 37%; and Morrison homes, 15%;

	£ mil 12/95	12/96	12/97	US$mil 12/97				
Sales	634.1	1,116.0	1,223.4	2,022.8	P/E Ratio	9.6	Price (6/30/98)	1.17
Net Income	5.8	21.2	44.0	72.8	P/B Ratio	0.9	52 Wk Hi-Low	1.44-0.93
Book Value	507.6	455.3	475.0	785.4	Yield %	4.9	Market Cap	US$711.4mil

Address	3 Shortlands	Tel 181-748-2000	ADR	--	CEO	Joseph Dwyer
	London W6 8EZ	Fax 181-846-3121	SEDOL	0971344	Chairman	Sir John Quinton

Wolseley

DJGI Industry: **Retailers - Other Specialty**
Stoxx Sector: **Retail**

Wolseley PLC is a marketer of heating and plumbing supplies that also distributes and retails bathroom accessories, pipes, valves, and fittings. The building distribution division in the United Kingdom trades under the name Plumb Center. The company's European outlets include Brossette BTI in France and ÖAG in Austria. Wolseley manufactures pumps, lighting products, electrical accessories, boilers, and burners. Distribution of building products accounted for 89% of fiscal 1997 revenues and manufacturing and other activities accounted for 11%.

	£ mil 07/95	07/96	07/97	US$mil 07/97				
Revenues	3,783.9	4,314.4	4,601.9	7,550.3	P/E Ratio	11.2	Price (6/30/98)	3.52
Net Income	163.6	162.3	176.6	289.7	P/B Ratio	2.2	52 Wk Hi-Low	5.56-3.52
Book Value	635.4	781.5	842.3	1,382.0	Yield %	3.3	Market Cap	US$3,363.0mil

Address	Box 18, Vines Lane	Tel 190-577-7200	ADR	--	CEO	J. Young
	Worcestershire WR9 8ND	Fax 190-577-7219	SEDOL	0976402	Chairman	R. Ireland

Woolwich

DJGI Industry: **Diversified Financial Services**
Stoxx Sector: **Financial Services**

Woolwich PLC, which became public in July 1997, provides banking and financial services in the United Kingdom and in Europe. The group's main activities are lending, investing, and protecting. Lending provides customers with a range of lending products and related services. Investing offers customers a range of investment products and has an offshore deposit-taking bank in Guernsey. Protecting offers a range of life assurance and general insurance products. Interest income accounted for 90% of 1997 revenues; fees and commissions, 8%; and other income, 2%.

	£ mil 12/95	12/96	12/97	US$mil 12/97				
Revenues	N/A	2,135.2	2,423.9	4,007.8	P/E Ratio	21.0	Price (6/30/98)	3.28
Net Income	N/A	238.9	250.1	413.5	P/B Ratio	2.8	52 Wk Hi-Low	3.95-3.15
Book Value	N/A	1,901.2	1,885.3	3,117.2	Yield %	2.9	Market Cap	US$8,768.3mil

Address	Watling St., Bexleyheath	Tel 181-298-5000	ADR	--	CEO	J.M. Stewart
	Kent DA6 7RR	Fax --	SEDOL	0975506	Chairman	B. Jenkins

WPP

DJGI Industry: **Advertising**
Stoxx Sector: **Media**

WPP Group PLC provides advertising, marketing, and public relations services to clients worldwide through its network of 810 offices in 91 countries. It is the world's largest advertising group. Media advertising is conducted primarily through its Ogilvy & Mather Worldwide and J. Walter Thompson subsidiaries. WPP is also active in market and public-opinion research, public relations, nonmedia advertising, direct marketing, and business-to-business marketing. Its clients include more than 300 of the companies included among the Fortune 500.

	£ mil 12/95	12/96	12/97	US$mil 12/97				
Sales	1,554.9	1,691.3	1,746.7	2,888.1	P/E Ratio	25.0	Price (6/30/98)	3.93
Net Income	68.7	100.0	116.0	191.8	P/B Ratio	NMF	52 Wk Hi-Low	4.26-2.38
Book Value	-72.8	5.0	-52.2	-86.3	Yield %	0.5	Market Cap	US$4,811.1mil

Address	27 Farm St.	Tel 171-408-2204	ADR	WPPGY	CEO	Martin S. Sorrell
	London W1X 6RD	Fax 171-493-6819	SEDOL	0974042	Chairman	Gordon K. Stevens

Zeneca

DJGI Industry: **Pharmaceuticals**
Stoxx Sector: **Pharmaceutical**

Zeneca Group PLC is an international bioscience company that develops, produces, and markets prescription pharmaceuticals, agrochemicals, and specialty chemicals. Its prescription pharmaceuticals include Tenormin and Zestril cardiovascular treatments, and Zoladex and Metastron cancer treatments. Its agrichemicals division produces herbicides, insecticides, fungicides, and many other compounds. Zeneca's partners include biotechnology company Xenova Group PLC, Oxford University, and the University of California. Pharmaceuticals accounted for 50% of 1997 revenues.

	£ mil 12/95	12/96	12/97	US$mil 12/97				
Sales	4,898.0	5,363.0	5,194.0	8,588.0	P/E Ratio	33.4	Price (6/30/98)	25.72
Net Income	336.0	643.0	730.0	1,207.0	P/B Ratio	11.3	52 Wk Hi-Low	27.60-17.17
Book Value	1,861.0	2,034.0	2,160.0	3,571.4	Yield %	1.5	Market Cap	US$40,743mil

Address	15 Stanhope Gate	Tel 171-304-5000	ADR	ZEN	CEO	Sir David Barnes
	London W1Y 6LN	Fax 171-304-5151	SEDOL	0989529	Chairman	Sir Sydney Lipworth

Market Sector Codes and Definitions

Basic Materials	**M/BSC**

Producers of raw materials, who may also make finished or semi-finished products from raw materials. Includes:

Chemicals (All)	I/CHM
Chemicals - Commodity	I/CHC
Chemicals - Specialty	I/CHS
Forest Products	I/FOR
Mining - Diversified	I/MNG
Non-Ferrous Metals (All)	I/NFR
Aluminum	I/ALU
Other Non-Ferrous Metals	I/ONF
Paper Products	I/PAP
Precious Metals	I/PCS
Steel	I/STL

Consumer, Cyclical	**M/CYC**

Providers of nonessential goods and services to the retail market, whose profits are strongly affected by changes in consumer spending. Includes:

Advertising	I/ADV
Airlines	I/AIR
Auto Manufacturers	I/AUT
Auto Parts & Equipment (All)	I/AUP
Tires & Rubber	I/TIR
Other Auto Parts	I/OTA
Entertainment & Leisure (All)	I/ENT
Casinos	I/CNO
Recreational Products & Services (All)	I/REC
Entertainment	I/MOV
Toy Manufacturers	I/TMF
Other Recreational Products & Services	I/REQ
Restaurants	I/RES
Home Construction	I/HOM
Home Furnishings & Appliances (All)	I/HMF
Consumer Electronics	I/CSE
Other Furnishings	I/OMF
Lodging	I/LOD
Media (All)	I/MED
Cable & Broadcasting	I/BRD
Publishing	I/PUB
Retailers - Broadline	I/RTB
Retailers - Specialty (All)	I/RTS
Retailers - Apparel	I/SAP
Retailers - Other Specialty	I/OTS
Retailers - Drug-based	I/RTD
Textiles & Apparel (All)	I/TEX
Clothing & Fabrics	I/CLO
Footwear	I/FOT

Consumer, Non-Cyclical	**M/NCY**

Providers of basic goods and services to the retail market whose profits are not strongly affected by changes in consumer spending. Includes:

Beverages (All)	I/BVG
Distillers & Brewers	I/DST
Soft Drinks	I/SFT
Consumer & Household Products & Services (All)	I/HOU
Consumer Services	I/CSV
Household Products (All)	I/HPR
Non-Durable	I/HPN
Durable	I/HPD
Cosmetics & Personal Care	I/COS
Food (All)	I/FOD
Fishing	I/FPR
Other Food	I/OFD
Food Retailers & Wholesalers	I/FDR
Health Care Providers	I/HEA
Medical Supplies	I/MDS
Pharmaceuticals	I/DRG
Tobacco	I/TOB

Energy	**M/ENE**

Liquid, solid or gaseous fossil fuel providers and the companies that service them. Includes:

Coal	I/COA
Oilfield Equipment & Services (All)	I/OIE
Oil Drilling	I/DRL
Other Oilfield Equipment & Services	I/EQS
Oil Companies - Major	I/OIL
Oil Companies - Secondary	I/OIS
Pipelines	I/PIP

Financial	**M/FIN**

Companies whose primary source of profits is the return on financial assets. Includes:

Banks (All)	I/BNK
Banks - Major International	I/BAN
Banks - Regional (All)	I/BAR
Central U.S.	I/BAC
Eastern U.S.	I/BAE
Southern U.S.	I/BAS
Western U.S.	I/BAW
Diversified Financial	I/FIS
Insurance (All)	I/INS
Full Line	I/INF
Life	I/INL
Property & Casualty	I/INP
Real Estate	I/REA
Savings & Loan Associations (U.S. Only)	I/SAL
Securities Brokers	I/SCR

Independent   M/MCG

Very large companies whose activities cut across industries and cannot be classified in any one economic sector. Includes:

Conglomerates	I/CGL
Overseas Trading	I/OVS
Plantations	I/PLN

Industrial   M/IDU

Capital goods manufacturers and companies that provide industrial services. Includes:

Air Freight & Couriers	I/AIF
Building Materials	I/BLD
Containers & Packaging	I/CTR
Electric Components & Equipment	I/ELQ
Factory Equipment	I/FAC
Heavy Construction	I/CON
Heavy Machinery	I/MAC
Industrial & Commercial Services (All)	I/SVC
Other Industrial & Commercial Services	I/ICS
Pollution Control & Waste Management	I/POL
Industrial - Diversified	I/IDD
Marine Transportation	I/MAR
Railroads	I/RAI
Transportation Equipment (All)	I/TRQ
Land Transportation	I/LDT
Shipbuilding	I/SHP
Trucking	I/TRK

Technology   M/TEC

Industries experiencing rapid product changes due primarily to scientific advances. Includes:

Aerospace & Defense	I/ARO
Communications Technology	I/CMT
Computers (All)	I/CPR
Computers - ex. IBM (U.S. Only)	I/CPN
Diversified Technology	I/DTC
Industrial Technology	I/ITC
Medical & Biological Technology (All)	I/MTC
Advanced Medical Devices	I/MDV
Biotechnology	I/BTC
Office Equipment	I/OFF
Semiconductors	I/SEM
Software	I/SOF

Utilities   M/UTI

Electrical, water, natural gas and telephone utilities. Includes:

Electrical Utilities (All)	I/ELC
Central U.S.	I/UEC
Eastern U.S.	I/UEE
Southern U.S.	I/UES
Western U.S.	I/UEW
Gas Utilities	I/GAS
Telephone Utilities (All)	I/TLS
Regional Telephones (U.S. Only)	I/RTL
Long Distance Telephones (U.S. Only)	I/LDS
Mobile Communications (U.S. Only)	I/CTS
Water Utilities	I/WAT

Industry Group Codes and Definitions

Basic Materials M/BSC

Producers of raw materials, who may also make finished or semi-finished products from raw materials.

I/CHM Chemicals (All)

Umbrella group for Commodity (I/CHC) and Specialty (I/CHS) Chemicals. Any company whose business is primarily the production of chemicals, either for other industries or for end users. Producers of plastics and chemical fertilizers are included. Producers of certain specialty chemicals, such as flavors and fragrances, may be placed within the specific industry that uses the products.

I/CHC Chemicals - Commodity

Producers of simple chemical products, including petrochemical feedstocks that are used to formulate more complex chemicals. Also includes plastics.

I/CHS Chemicals - Specialty

Producers of finished chemicals either for other industries or for end users.

I/FOR Forest Products

Producers of wood and lumber products for the building industry (such as plywood, wooden beams, etc.).

I/MNG Mining - Diversified

Companies that mine minerals and metal ores but do not necessarily process the resources into finished products. Gold and coal mining are specifically excluded from this category. Gold is listed under Precious Metals (I/PCS); coal under I/COA.

I/NFR Non-Ferrous Metals (All)

Umbrella group for Aluminum (I/ALU) and Other Non-Ferrous metals (I/ONF), Non-ferrous metals including copper, zinc and nickel.

I/ALU Aluminum

Companies that mine or process bauxite and make semi-finished or finished aluminum products. Aluminum building products such as siding are included under Building Materials (I/BLD).

I/ONF Other Non-Ferrous Metals

Producers of other non-iron metals, such as copper. Precious metals are in their own group (I/PCS).

I/PAP Paper Products

Manufacturers of paper products, both raw and finished. Includes writing paper, envelopes, cardboard and pulp. Paper items like cups, napkins and diapers are included under Non-Durable Household Products (I/HPN).

I/PCS Precious Metals

Producers of gold, silver and other precious metals as well as precious stones such as diamonds.

I/STL Steel

Steel and iron manufacturers. Includes pipes, tubes, wire, rolls and bars made from these metals.

Consumer, Cyclical M/CYC

Providers of nonessential goods and services to the retail market, whose profits are strongly affected by changes in consumer spending.

I/ADV Advertising

Companies providing advertising, public relations and/or marketing services.

I/AIR Airlines

Companies providing primarily passenger air transport.

I/AUT Automobile Manufacturers

Makers of passenger vehicles, including cars and light trucks. Heavy trucks are listed under Land Transportation Equipment (I/LDT); recreational vehicles under Other Recreational Products and Services (I/REQ).

I/AUP Automobile Parts & Equipment (All)

Tire makers and rubber producers. Manufacturers of new and replacement parts for automobiles and trucks. Also, companies that produce accessories for the automobile industry.

I/OTA Other Auto Parts

Manufacturers of new and replacement parts for automobiles and trucks. Also, companies that produce accessories for the automobile industry.

I/TIR Tires & Rubber

Tire makers and rubber producers.

I/ENT Entertainment & Leisure (All)

Umbrella group for Casinos (I/CNO), Recreational Products and Services (I/REC), Restaurants (I/RES), Entertainment (I/MOV), Toy Manufacturers (I/TMF) and Other Recreational Products & Services (I/REQ).

I/CNO Casinos

Casino operators and hotels with gaming rooms. Does not include lottery machines and race tracks, which are listed under Other Recreational Products & Services (I/REQ).

I/REC Recreational Products & Services (All)

Umbrella group for Entertainment (I/MOV), Toys (I/TMF) and Other Recreational Products & Services (I/REQ). Companies that provide leisure-time services or products.

I/MOV Entertainment

Companies engaged in the development, production or distribution of movies, television shows and pre-recorded music. These companies produce and sell entertainment. The television industry is included under Media (I/MED).

I/TMF   Toy Manufacturers
Makers of toys and video/computer games.

I/REQ   Other Recreational Products & Services
Companies that provide leisure-time services such as movie theaters, amusement parks, camera makers, golf courses, cruise ships and products such as records, CDs and blank VCR tapes. Resorts are included in Lodging (I/LOD).

I/RES   Restaurants
Corporations that own and operate restaurants, bars, or fast-food facilities or provide large-scale food catering services.

I/HOM   Home Construction
Residential home builders, mainly specializing in one-to-four family units. Also includes makers of mobile and prefabricated homes that are intended for use in one place.

I/HMF   Home Furnishings & Appliances (All)
Makers of large home appliances, home furniture and carpeting. Includes stereos, VCRs, refrigerators, microwaves, power tools, sewing machines, regular and high-definition televisions (HDTVs).

I/CSE   Consumer Electronics
Makers of consumer electronics products, such as televisions, video recorders and stereo equipment.

I/OMF   Other Furnishings
Makers of home furnishings and carpeting excluding consumer electronics products.

I/LOD   Lodging
Operators of hotels, motels, lodges, resorts, and campgrounds.

I/MED   Media (All)
Umbrella group for Publishing (I/PUB) and Broadcasting (I/BRD). Publishers of newspapers, magazines and books, television and radio broadcasters, and cable TV companies. Also includes greeting cards and collectible cards (e.g., baseball).

I/BRD   Cable & Broadcasting
Television, radio and cable broadcasters and operators.

I/PUB   Publishing
Newspapers, books, magazine publishers and information-service companies that produce original material. Electronic publishers that redistribute news are included under General Services (I/ICS).

I/RTB   Retailers - Broadline
Retail stores that offer a wide spectrum of products, including both soft goods and hard goods. Includes department stores.

I/RTS   Retailers - Specialty (All)
Umbrella group for Apparel (I/SAP), Drug (I/RTD) and Other Specialty Retailers (I/RTS). All retailers that specialize in one or a few lines rather than a wide range of products.

I/SAP   Retailers - Apparel
Retailers specializing mainly in clothing and accessories.

I/OTS   Retailers - Other Specialty
Retailers whose marketing strategy focuses on a limited product line, such as jewelry, automotive parts or close-outs.

I/RTD   Retailers - Drug-based
Operators of pharmacies or drug stores. Wholesalers catering strictly to these retailers are included in the category.

I/TEX   Textiles & Apparel (All)
Umbrella group for Footwear (I/FOT) and Clothing and Fabrics (I/CLO). Makers of textiles, jewelry, finished clothing and leather goods, including shoes and handbags.

I/CLO   Clothing & Fabrics
Manufacturers of apparel, jewelry, fabrics and leather goods, excluding footwear. Luggage included under Housewares (I/HPD).

I/FOT   Footwear
Makers of shoes, boots and other footwear.

Consumer, Non-Cyclical   M/NCY

Providers of basic goods and services to the retail market, whose profits are not strongly affected by changes in consumer spending.

I/BVG   Beverages (All)
Umbrella group for Distillers & Brewers (I/DST) and Soft Drinks (I/SFT).

I/DST   Distillers & Brewers
Makers of alcoholic beverages. Also covers public houses in the United Kingdom. Bars are listed under Restaurants (I/RES).

I/SFT   Soft Drinks
Makers of non-alcoholic beverages, excluding milk and fruit juices, which are included in Food (I/FOD). Bottled water included here.

I/HOU   Consumer & Household Products & Services (All)
Umbrella group for the Consumer & Household Products and Services Industries.

I/CSV   Consumer Services
Providers of consumer services such as lawn maintenance, tax preparation, day care, bus lines, language and training schools and funeral services.

I/HPR   Household Products (All)
Umbrella group for Non-Durable Household Products (I/HPN) and Housewares (I/HPD). Covers soaps, utensils, kitchen and bathroom accessories and paper goods.

I/HPN   Non-Durable
Producers of non-durable household products such as soaps, detergents, batteries and paper goods including napkins, toilet tissue, paper plates and diapers.

I/HPD   Durable
Producers of durable household products such as utensils, non-electric appliances and luggage.

I/COS   Cosmetics & Personal Care
Makers of cosmetics, perfumes and personal-care and hygiene products such as deodorant, contraceptives and feminine hygiene products.

I/FOD   Food (All)
Food manufacturers and processors including farming, fisheries and meat-packers. Milk and fruit juices are products in this industry. Bottled water is listed under Soft Drinks (I/SFT).

I/FPR   Fishing
Fishing companies. This also includes producers of fish products.

I/OFD   Other Food
Food manufacturers and processors, excluding fish products.

I/FDR   Food Retailers & Wholesalers
Operators of supermarkets, food-oriented convenience stores and other food retailers.

I/HEA   Health Care Providers
Operators of hospitals, nursing and convalescent homes, long-term care facilities, in-home health services.

I/MDS   Medical Supplies
Manufacturers of medical supplies used mainly by health-care providers and not generally available at retail. Includes contact lenses, animal drugs and chemicals used to make drugs.

I/DRG   Pharmaceuticals
Makers of prescription drugs and over-the-counter products, such as aspirin, cold remedies and other remedies.

I/TOB   Tobacco
Tobacco products manufacturers.

Energy   M/ENE
Liquid, solid or gaseous fossil fuel providers and the companies that service them.

I/COA   Coal
Coal producers and coal mining. Excludes coal-fired electric plants, which are in Electrical Utilities (I/ELC).

I/OIE   Oilfield Equipment & Services (All)
Umbrella group for Oil Drilling (I/DRL) and Other Oilfield Equipment & Services (I/EQS).

I/DRL   Oil Drilling
Corporations whose major line of business is drilling and exploration for oil, typically under contract for others.

I/EQS   Other Oilfield Equipment & Services
Suppliers of equipment and services for oilfield or platform users.

I/OIL   Oil Companies - Major
Large oil producers whose activities include drilling and refining. Normally, companies in this category conduct substantial amounts of international business.

I/OIS   Oil Companies - Secondary
Smaller oil companies, whose operations are restricted in geography or to certain activities, such as the manufacture of motor oil. Companies in this category usually do the bulk of their business domestically. Also includes gasoline and natural gas.

I/PIP   Pipelines
Operators of pipelines carrying oil, gas or other forms of fuel. Companies that derive the majority of their revenues from direct consumer sales are classified under Gas Utilities (I/GAS).

Financial   M/FIN
Companies whose primary source of profits is the return on financial assets.

I/BNK   Banks (All)
Umbrella group covering the global banking industry. All major and regional banks get this code. Excludes investment banking, which is covered under Securities Industry (I/SCR).

I/BAN   Banks - Major International
Banks with a major presence in more than one country, such as Citicorp and Swiss Bank; money-center banks.

I/BAR   Banks - Regional (All)
Umbrella group for the regional banks. Banks that offer services statewide or cover a particular region. For U.S.

regional banks only, group composed of four geographic regions.

I/BAC   Central U.S.
Banks in Illinois, Indiana, Iowa, Kansas, Michigan, Minnesota, Missouri, Nebraska, North Dakota, Ohio, Oklahoma, South Dakota and Wisconsin.

I/BAE   Eastern U.S.
Banks in Connecticut, District of Columbia, Delaware, Maryland, Maine, Massachusetts, New Hampshire, New Jersey, New York, Pennsylvania, Rhode Island, Vermont and West Virginia.

I/BAS   Southern U.S.
Banks in Alabama, Arkansas, Canal Zone, Florida, Georgia, Kentucky, Louisiana, Mississippi, North Carolina, Puerto Rico, South Carolina, Tennessee, Texas, Virginia and Virgin Islands.

I/BAW   Western U.S.
Banks in Alaska, Arizona, California, Colorado, Guam, Hawaii, Idaho, Montana, Nevada, New Mexico, Oregon, Utah, Washington and Wyoming.

I/FIS   Diversified Financial
Companies involved in two or more industries in the financial market sector or whose products are used in many diverse industries. Includes Fannie Mae, American Express and mutual fund companies.

I/INS   Insurance (All)
Umbrella group for Full Line (I/INF), Life and Health (I/INL), and Property and Casualty Insurance (I/INP).

I/INF   Full Line
Companies that offer a full line of insurance, including life, health, property and casualty.

I/INL   Life
Life and health insurers.

I/INP   Property & Casualty
Property and casualty insurers. Includes auto insurance and re-insurance companies.

I/REA   Real Estate
Companies that invest directly or indirectly in real estate, either through development, management or outright ownership. Also includes Real Estate Investment Trusts (REITs).

I/SAL   Savings & Loan Associations (U.S. Only)
S&Ls, savings banks, thrifts and building associations.

I/SCR   Securities Brokers
Securities brokers and dealers, including investment banks and merchant banks.

Independent   M/MCG
Very large companies whose activities cut across industries and cannot be classified in any one economic sector.

I/CGL   Conglomerates
Very large companies whose activities cut across market sectors and cannot be classified under any single industry or sector.

I/OVS   Overseas Trading
Large, diversified companies engaged in large-scale export trade.

I/PLN   Plantations
Large agricultural companies, typically located in the tropics.

Industrial   M/IDU
Capital goods manufacturers and companies that provide industrial services.

I/AIF   Air Freight & Couriers
Operators of courier services for commercial and consumer users. Includes all types of couriers except Marine Transportation, which is I/MAR.

I/BLD   Building Materials
Makers of basic building materials, such as concrete, wallboard, flooring, tile, lighting, bathroom and kitchen fixtures and home water heaters. Includes paint if it is an end product; if just the pigment, included under Specialty Chemicals (I/CHS). Excludes lumber, which is in Forest Products (I/FOR).

I/CTR   Containers & Packaging
Makers of bags, cans, boxes, jars, drums and glass used for packaging. Manufacturers of small specialty packaging machines are included here. Makers of large packaging equipment are in Factory Equipment (I/FAC).

I/ELQ   Electric Components & Equipment
Makers of electrical parts used in the fabrication of finished products. Includes ceramics and transistors. Also includes finished products such as large-scale heating, ventilation, air conditioning and lighting units. Semiconductors and superconductivity included under Semiconductors (I/SEM).

I/FAC   Factory Equipment
Manufacturers of large machinery designed specifically for the production of products for factories including turbines and machines used on assembly lines. Robotics are included in Industrial Technology (I/ITC).

I/CON   Heavy Construction
Companies engaged in the construction of infrastructures, industrial and commercial buildings and large multi-family residential buildings.

I/MAC   Heavy Machinery
Makers of large machinery not intended for fixed factory use. Machinery in this category normally can be moved to temporary work sites. Includes farm and construction vehicles such as tractors and bulldozers.

I/SVC   Industrial & Commercial Services (All)
Umbrella group for General Services (I/ICS) and Pollution & Waste Control (I/POL).

I/ICS   Other Industrial & Commercial Services
Companies that provide services to other commercial enterprises, such as   commercial cleaning, travel agencies, educational services for business, leasing, temporary service agencies, security agencies, credit services, printing, and management, engineering and other types of consultants. Electronic information providers that do not generate their own information are included here; those that generate their own information are included under Media (I/MED).

I/POL   Pollution Control & Waste Management
Providers of pollution-control services and products.

I/IDD   Industrial - Diversified
Companies that are involved in two or more industries in the Industrial Market Sector and whose products are used in many different industries. A maker of pumps is an example.

I/MAR   Marine Transportation
Corporations that provide on-water transportation commercial and consumer markets. Ports and marine terminals included under General Services (I/ICS). Cruise lines are excluded from this category and are in Other Recreational Products & Services (I/REQ).

I/RAI   Railroads
Providers of railway transportation and railway lines. Not for rail-car manufacturing, which is included in Land Transportation Equipment (I/LDT).

I/TRQ   Transportation Equipment (All)
Umbrella group for Land Transportation Equipment (I/LDT) and Trucking (I/TRK).

I/LDT   Land Transportation
Manufacturers of rail cars, buses and commercial land vehicles, including heavy trucks and truck parts.

I/SHP   Shipbuilding
Companies that build ships and other forms of water transportation. Includes ship parts. Does not include small pleasure craft, which are in Other Recreational Products & Services (I/REQ).

I/TRK   Trucking
Companies that provide commercial trucking. Truck makers included under Land Transportation Equipment (I/LDT).

Technology   M/TEC
Industries experiencing rapid product changes due primarily to scientific advances.

I/ARO   Aerospace & Defense
Makers of air transportation vehicles, major weapons, defense equipment and systems, and radar.

I/CMT   Communications Technology
Makers of high-technology products for communications, including satellites, PBX systems, switching devices, local and wide area networks (LANs and WANs), computer network equipment and connectivity devices for computers.

I/CPR   Computers
Manufacturers of computers, computer hardware and computer sub-systems, such as mass storage drives. Also includes makers of automatic teller machines (ATMs). Data processing included under General Services (I/ICS).

I/DTC   Diversified Technology
High-tech companies that are involved in two or more industries in the technology market sector, or whose products are used in many different industries.

I/ITC   Industrial Technology
Companies whose technology and high-tech products are directed primarily toward industrial production and/or quality control. These include makers of instruments and gauges, lasers, robotics, bar scanners and other high-tech factory equipment.

I/MTC   Medical & Biological Technology (All)
Umbrella group encompassing Biotechnology (I/BTC) and Advanced Technology Medical Devices (I/MDV). Corporations engaged in genetic research and/or the marketing and development of recombinant DNA products. Includes makers of prosthetics, including pacemakers and breast implants. Also includes medical research.

I/MDV   Advanced Medical Devices
Manufacturers of advanced technology medical equipment such as prosthetics, pacemakers and advanced imaging devices. The products are used primarily by health-care providers and not generally available at the retail level.

I/BTC   Biotechnology
Companies engaged in genetic research and/or the marketing and development of recombinant DNA products.

I/OFF   Office Equipment
Makers of office equipment, such as duplicating machines, non computer graphics products, word processors, cash registers, typewriters and fax machines.

I/SEM   Semiconductors
Producers of semiconductors and other integrated chips,
including circuit boards. Includes any other products related to
the semiconductor industry.

I/SOF   Software
Publishers of software for all sizes of computers.

I/RTL   Regional Telephones
Providers of local telephone service.

I/WAT   Water Utilities
Investor-owned water utilities.

Utilities   M/UTI
Electrical, water, natural gas and telephone utilities.

I/ELC   Electrical Utilities (All)
Umbrella code for regional Electric Utilities. Includes fusion,
fission and nuclear power. Cogeneration is included under
Industrial Diversified (I/IDD).

I/UEC   Central U.S.
Providers of electricity in Illinois, Indiana, Iowa, Kansas,
Michigan, Minnesota, Missouri, Nebraska, North Dakota,
Ohio, Oklahoma, South Dakota and Wisconsin.

I/UEE   Eastern U.S.
Providers of electricity in Connecticut, District of Columbia,
Delaware, Maryland, Maine, Massachussets, New
Hampshire, New Jersey, New York, Pennsylvania, Rhode
Island, Vermont and West Virginia.

I/UES   Southern U.S.
Providers of electricity in Alabama, Arkansas, Canal Zone,
Florida, Georgia, Kentucky, Louisiana, Mississippi, North
Carolina, Puerto Rico, South Carolina, Tennessee, Texas,
Virginia and Virgin Islands.

I/UEW   Western U.S.
Providers of electricity in Alaska, Arizona, California, Colorado,
Guam, Hawaii, Idaho, Montana, Nevada, New Mexico,
Oregon, Utah, Washington and Wyoming.

I/GAS   Gas Utilities
Gas utilities and services provided for the utilities. Does not
include natural gas as a commodity, which is included in the
Oil groups (I/OIL or I/OIS).

I/TLS   Telephone Utilities (All)
Umbrella group for Regional (I/RTL), Long Distance (I/LDS) and
Mobile Telephone Systems (I/CTS), including regulated
cellular systems.

I/LDS   Long-Distance Telephones
Providers of long-distance telephone service.

I/CTS   Mobile Communications
Providers of mobile telephone service, including cellular
telephone systems.

Glossary of Dow Jones Indexes

Dow Jones Averages

Dow Jones Industrial Average

This average is often referred to as "the Dow"; it is the best-known and most widely reported indicator of the U.S. stock market's performance. The Dow is a price-weighted average of 30 blue-chip industrial stocks. Their combined value is roughly 20% of the market value of all stocks listed on the New York Stock Exchange.

Dow Jones Transportation Average

This average is a simple price-weighted average of the stocks of 20 U.S. airlines, railroads, and trucking and shipping companies.

Dow Jones Utility Average

This average is a simple price-weighted average of 15 U.S. geographically representative gas, electric, and power utility companies.

Dow Jones Composite Average

This average is a simple price-weighted average of the 65 component stocks of the Industrial, Transportation, and Utility Averages.

Dow Jones Global Indexes

DJ World Stock Index

This index measures the aggregate performance of 34 global stock markets in the Dow Jones Global Indexes. As of June 30, 1998, there were 2,899 component stocks in the index. The three largest markets in the index are the United States with a 51.98% weight, Japan, with 9.45%, and the United Kingdom, with 8.94%. The three smallest markets in the index are the Philippines, with a 0.04% weight, and Thailand and Venezuela, each with a weight of 0.03%.

DJ Americas Stock Index

This measures the aggregate performance of the Brazil, Canada, Chile, Mexico, United States, and Venezuela stock markets. As of June 30, 1998, the 983 component stocks had a total market capitalization of more than US$10 trillion.

DJ Latin America Stock Index

This measures the aggregate performance of the Brazil, Chile, Venezuela, and Mexico stock markets. As of June 30, 1998, there were 122 component stocks.

DJ Latin America (ex. Mexico) Stock Index

This measures the aggregate performance of the Brazil, Chile, and Venezuela stock markets. Using, as of June 30, 1998, 90 component stocks.

DJ Asia/Pacific Stock Index

This measures the aggregate performance of 11 Asia/Pacific stock markets. As of June 30,

1998, the 1,191 component stocks in the index represented 12.89% of the world's investable equity capital, with a total market capitalization of US$2.37 trillion.

DJ Asia/Pacific (ex. Japan) Stock Index

This measures the aggregate performance of 10 Asia/Pacific stock markets. As of June 30, 1998, there were 744 component stocks in the index.

DJ Southeast Asia Stock Index

This measures the aggregate performance of the South Asian stock markets of Singapore, Malaysia, Thailand, Indonesia, Philippines, and Taiwan. As of June 30, 1998, there were 448 component stocks in the index.

DJ Europe/Africa Stock Index

This measures the aggregate performance of 17 stock markets, 16 European markets, plus South Africa. As of June 30, 1998, there were 725 component stocks.

DJ Europe/Africa (ex. Africa) Stock Index

This measures the aggregate performance of 16 European stock markets. As of June 30, 1998, the 649 component stocks in the index represented 31.08% of the world's investable equity capital and had a total market capitalization of US$5.7 trillion.

DJ Europe/Africa (ex. Africa & U.K.) Stock Index

This measures the aggregate performance of the 15 European stock markets excluding South Africa and the United Kingdom. As of June 30, 1998, there were 504 component stocks in the index.

DJ Nordic Stock Index

This measures the aggregate performance of the stock markets in Denmark, Finland, Norway, and Sweden. As of June 30, 1998, there were 147 component stocks in the index.

DJ U.S. Equity Market Index

This index is a benchmark that measures the performance of the U.S. stock market. As of June 30, 1998, the 734 component stocks in the index accounted for 51.88% of the world's investable equity capital and had a total market capitalization of US$9.56 trillion. The base value for the index is set at 100 on June 30, 1982.

DJ Country Indexes

These indexes serve as individual benchmarks for each of 34 countries in Dow Jones Global Indexes. Recent country additions are Brazil, Chile, and Venezuela. Country indexes are calculated in both local currencies and in U.S. dollars.

DJ Sector Indexes

The nine major economic sector indexes are used to compare aggregate sector performance, identify sector shifts, and analyze business cycles. The sectors can be further broken down into any of 122 industry groups.

DJ Industry Group Indexes

These indexes serve as benchmarks for 122 separate industry groups. The industries are classified into the preceding 9 major economic sectors. Industry indexes are typically used to compare market trends and offer opportunities to follow leading and lagging industries.

Basic Materials Sector: This contains producers of raw materials, who may also make finished or semifinished products from raw materials; it includes 11 industry groups.

Consumer, Cyclical Sector: This contains providers of nonessential goods and services to the retail market, whose profits are strongly affected by changes in consumer spending; it includes 29 industry groups.

Consumer, Non-Cyclical Sector: This contains providers of basic goods and services to the retail market, whose profits are not strongly affected by changes in consumer spending; it includes 17 industry groups.

Energy Sector: This contains providers of liquid, solid, or gaseous fossil fuel, and the companies that service them; it includes seven industry groups.

Financial Sector: This contains companies whose primary source of profits is the return on financial assets; it includes 15 industry groups.

Independents Sector: This contains very large companies whose activities cut across industries and cannot be classified in any one economic sector; it includes 3 industry groups.

Industrial Sector: This contains providers of industrial services and capital goods manufacturers; it includes 17 industry groups.

Technology Sector: This contains industries experiencing rapid product changes due primarily to scientific advances; it includes 12 industry groups.

Utility Sector: This contains electrical, water, natural gas, and telephone utilities; it includes 10 industry groups, many of them regional U.S. groupings.

Dow Jones STOXX Indexes

Dow Jones STOXX is an integrated
system of indexes designed for the European
market. It consists of 4 major indexes
and 19 sector indexes, tracking Europe and
the countries in the new EURO Zone.
The 19 sector indexes are: Auto, Bank,
Basic Resources (ex. Chemicals), Chemical,
Conglomerate, Construction, Consumer
Cyclical, Consumer Non-Cyclical, Energy,
Financial Services, Food & Beverage,
Industrial, Insurance, Media, Pharmaceutical,
Retail, Technology, Telecom, and Utility.

Four Major STOXX Indexes:

Dow Jones STOXX

The European broad index is the same as the
DJ Europe index. It measures the aggregate
performance of the 16 European stock
markets. These stocks are grouped into 19
sectors. As of June 30, 1998, there were 649
component stocks in the index.

Dow Jones STOXX 50

This is a blue-chip index of 50 EMU stocks
that are derived from the DJ STOXX broad
index. Components are selected on the basis
of market capitalization, liquidity, and sector
representation.

Dow Jones EURO STOXX

The index measures the aggregate
performance of DJ STOXX, excluding those
countries not in the European Monetary
Union (EMU). As of June 30, 1998, there
were 327 components in the index.

Dow Jones EURO STOXX 50

This is a blue-chip index of 50 stocks derived
from the DJ EURO STOXX index.
Components are selected on the basis of
market capitalization, liquidity, and sector
representation.

Dow Jones REIT Indexes

The Dow Jones REIT Indexes track real estate investment trusts that are traded on the New York and American stock exchanges and Nasdaq. The trusts are grouped into three investment structures: Equity, Hybrid, and Mortgage, which are in turn categorized by property types. Three calculations are performed on each investment structure and property type: capitalization weighting, total return, and dividend yield calculations. As of June 30, 1998, the index comprised 131 issues (119 equity, 4 hybrid and 8 mortgage.)

Other Dow Jones Indexes

Dow Jones AsiaTech Index

The index, which was created specifically for *The Asian Wall Street Journal*, measures the aggregate performance of Asian companies from the technology sector and from the electrical components and equipment, consumer electronics, and telephone systems industries.

Dow Jones EuroTech Index

The index, which was created specifically for *The Europe Wall Street Journal*, measures the aggregate performance of European companies from the technology sector and from the electrical components and equipment, consumer electronics, pharmaceuticals, and telephone systems industries.

Dow Jones China 88 Index

This is a market capitalization-weighted index that measures the aggregate performance of 88 major class A issues from companies trading on the Shanghai and Shenzhen stock exchanges.

Dow Jones Hong Kong Small Cap Index

This index measures the aggregate performance of 100 small capitalization issues that trade on the Hong Kong Stock Exchange.

Dow Jones Shanghai Index

This index measures the aggregate performance of 184 class A issues from companies trading on the Shanghai Stock Exchange.

Dow Jones Shenzhen Index

This index measures the aggregate performance of 182 class A issues from companies trading on the Shenzhen Stock Exchange.

Glossary

52 Week Hi-Low
The high and low share prices from July 1, 1997, to June 30, 1998, based on daily closing prices.

ADR
American Depositary Receipt. This is a mechanism by which U.S. investors can hold ownership interest in shares of a foreign company. Each ADR represents a claim on a specific number of underlying foreign shares. The foreign shares are held by a U.S. sponsor bank on behalf of the ADR owner. The price of an ADR is denominated in U.S. dollars and fluctuates based on the change in share value, as well as on any exchange-rate movements. For companies with American depositary receipts, the ADR trading symbol is listed.

Address
The address, telephone number, and fax number are those of the company's headquarters.

Affiliate
Two companies are affiliated when one owns less than a majority stake of the other or when both are controlled by a third company. Generally, an affiliation is any association between two companies that is short of a parent-subsidiary tie.

Bear Market
When security prices decline 15% or more. Some analysts prefer 20% as the demarcation between a "correction" and a bear market.

Book Value
The difference between a company's assets and its liabilities, usually expressed in per-share terms. Book value is also referred to as stockholders' equity and is calculated by subtracting liabilities from assets and dividing the result by the number of shares outstanding. Comparing book value to share price is one way to gauge whether a company's stock is undervalued or overvalued.

Bull Market
A time period when security prices increase without significant setbacks.

CEO
Chief Executive Officer. In Australia, Hong Kong, Italy, Malaysia, New Zealand, Singapore, Spain, and the United Kingdom, the CEO is sometimes titled Group Managing Director. In Germany, the CEO is also called the Chairman of the Management Board. In China, the CEO is called either the General Manager or the Legal Representative.

Chairman
Chairman of the Board of Directors. In Germany, this refers to the chairman of the supervisory board that oversees the company and the management board.

Common Stock
Represents part ownership of a company. Holders of common stock have voting rights but no guarantee of dividend payments.

Consumer Prices, Consumer Price Index

The CPI is a measure of change in prices of consumer goods and therefore is a key gauge of inflation. In the United States, the figures, released monthly by the Labor Department, are based on a list of specific goods and services as purchased in urban areas. Components include food, housing, apparel, transportation, medical care, and entertainment. The change in consumer prices is usually reported in terms of a percentage increase or decrease. In this guide, aggregates were computed by using weights based on the previous year's consumer expenditure, expressed in private consumption purchasing power parities.

CUSIP

Committee on Uniform Security Identification Procedures. Cusip "numbers" are alphanumeric identifications used by most sectors in the financial industry for classification of various securities for the financial marketplace. They consist of nine characters: the first six numbers uniquely identify the issuer and have been assigned to issuers in alphabetical sequence; the seventh and eighth characters identify the issue; the ninth is based on the other characters and is used to check for accuracy.

Derivative

A complex investment whose value is derived from or linked to an underlying financial asset, such as stocks, bonds, currencies, or mortgages. Derivatives may be listed on exchanges or traded privately over the counter. For example, derivatives may be futures, options, or mortgage-backed securities.

Devaluation

The government's reduction of the value of its currency in relation to the currency of other countries. When a nation devalues its currency, the goods it imports become more expensive, while its exports become less expensive abroad and thus more competitive.

Dividend

The amount paid per share to holders of stock, whether common or preferred. Payouts are generally made in quarterly installments.

Earnings per Share

The figure obtained by dividing the number of common shares outstanding into the net income left after dividends have been paid on any preferred stock. This is also called "primary" earnings per share.

Per-share earnings calculated on a "fully diluted" basis presuppose that all dilutive securities (such as warrants, options, convertible debt, etc.) have been exercised into common shares.

Emerging Markets

Financial markets in nations that are developing market-based economies.

European Currency Unit (ECU)

A monetary unit created in 1979 by nine European nations to promote currency stability in the European Union. It is to be supplanted by the euro in 1999.

European Monetary Union (EMU)

European Monetary Union is a single monetary policy within a single economic market. Only 11 member nations within the European Union will begin using this new currency as of January 1, 1999. These nations are Austria, Belgium, Finland, France, Germany, Ireland, Italy, Luxembourg, the Netherlands, Portugal, and Spain.

European Union (EU)

A supernational and intergovernmental organization of 15 western European nations created under the Maastricht treaty of December 1991 with its own institutional structures and decision-making framework. Before the Maastricht treaty went into effect in November 1993, the organization was known as the European Community or the Common Market. Its members are Austria, Belgium, Denmark, Finland, France, Germany, Greece, Ireland, Italy, Luxembourg, the Netherlands, Portugal, Spain, Sweden, and the United Kingdom. Its council of ministers and the European Commission are based in Brussels, Belgium, and its parliament is based in Strasbourg, France.

Exchange

The primary stock exchange on which the company's shares are listed.

AMEX	American Stock Exchange
NASDAQ	a coined word that was fashioned from National Association of Securities Dealers Automated Quotations system
NYSE	New York Stock Exchange
TSE	Toronto Stock Exchange

Federal Reserve

The central bank of the United States that sets monetary policy. The Federal Reserve oversees money supply, interest rates, and credit, with the goal of keeping the U.S. economy and currency stable. Governed by a seven-member board, the system includes 12 regional Federal Reserve Banks, 25 branches, and all national and state banks that are part of the system. Also called the Fed.

Gross Domestic Product (GDP)

The total value of goods and services produced by a nation inside its borders. It is considered more indicative of a nation's economy than the GNP. GDP per capita is computed by dividing GDP by population. The figures contained throughout this guide were computed by dividing the 1996 GDP by midyear 1997 population statistics. In the United States, the GDP is calculated by the Commerce Department, and it is the main measure of U.S. economic output. It is expressed in current dollars or constant dollars (base date is 1987).

Gross National Product (GNP)

The value of a nation's output of goods and services, usually measured yearly. The value of the final product is taken in consideration, not the sum of its parts. For example, the value of the automobile is counted, not the purchase of the steel used to make it. The three factors that make up the GNP are government spending, consumer purchases, and private investment, which includes investments into foreign economies but not investments from other countries into the home nation's economy.

Group of Seven (G-7)

An organization of the seven major industrialized nations. The countries' leaders meet annually to discuss monetary and fiscal issues that affect the global economy. The G-7 countries are the United States, Canada, Britain, France, Italy, Germany, and Japan. At the 1995 meeting, in Halifax, Canada, G-7 leaders approved a plan — stimulated by the economic problems that followed the devaluation of the Mexican peso in December 1994 — to push International Monetary Fund members to publish timely financial data that would alert financial markets to emerging problems and give them a chance to react before a crisis erupts. However, the meeting ended with the leaders wanting to scale back their annual summit after the 1995 meeting became as much a forum for bilateral squabbles as it was a showcase for international cooperation.

Holding Company

A company whose principal assets are the securities it owns in companies that actually provide goods and services. A holding company is typically formed to enable one corporation to control several diverse companies by holding a majority of their stock.

Index Fund

A mutual fund that seeks to produce the same return that investors would get if they owned all the stocks in a particular stock index, often the Standard and Poor's 500-stock index.

Index Option

An agreement that gives an investor the right but not the obligation to buy or sell the basket of stocks represented by a stock-market index at a specific price on or before a specific date. Index options allow investors to trade in a particular market or industry group without having to buy all the stocks individually.

Indexing

Buying and holding a mix of stocks that match the performance of a broad stock-market barometer such as the Dow Jones Industrial Average.

Industry

Dow Jones classifies each company into one of 122 industry groups. For definitions and codes, see Market Sector Codes and Definitions in the back of this book.

Inflation

A rise in prices. Inflation may be caused by an increase in the money supply; when there are more dollars available to spend, each dollar buys less. It may also be caused by rising manufacturing costs, a decrease in supply of goods, or a combination of such factors.

Initial Public Offering (IPO)

The first offering of stock that a closely held company makes to the public.

International Monetary Fund (IMF)

IMF is a specialized agency of the United Nations that was established in 1945 and that is located in Washington, D.C. Its primary purpose is to develop monetary cooperation among countries and to help countries deal with currency fluctuations, trade expansion, and balance-of-payments difficulties.

Loss

In corporate reports, the excess of expenses over revenue during a company's fiscal period.

Market Cap

Market capitalization. This represents the company's worth based on the market price of its outstanding shares. It is calculated here by multiplying the June 30, 1998, share price by the number of shares outstanding on that day. For a company with multiple classes of shares, the market capitalization is the sum of all shares that are components of the Dow Jones Global Indexes.

Mutual Fund

A fund run by an investment company that provides a way for small investors to pool their money so that together they can afford to hire a professional money manager. Though a fund is owned by its shareholders, it is usually established, managed, and distributed by the fund's investment advisor and its affiliated companies.

Net Income, Profit, Earnings

As they concern an earnings report, these terms refer to the amount of money left after a company pays taxes and all other expenses. A portion may be committed to pay preferred dividends. Some of what remains may, at the company's discretion, be paid in dividends to holders of common stock. The rest may be invested to obtain interest revenue or spent to acquire new buildings, equipment, or other assets to increase the company's ability to make a future profit.

North American Free Trade Agreement (Nafta)

Nafta phases out tariffs among the United States, Canada, and Mexico over 15 years and greatly eases investment across their borders. It was passed by Congress in late 1993 and took effect on January 1, 1994.

Operating Profit/Loss

Net income excluding income derived from sources other than the company's regular activities and before income deductions, including taxes. Also called net operating income/loss.

Options

An agreement allowing an investor to buy or sell something, such as shares of stock, during a specific time for a specific price. Listed options, with standard specifications, such as for expiration, are traded on several exchanges, including the Chicago Board of Options Exchange, the American Stock Exchange, the Philadelphia Stock Exchange, the Pacific Stock Exchange, and the New York Stock Exchange. Options with customized specifications are traded over the counter.

Organization for Economic Cooperation and Development (OECD)

The OECD is an organization of developed nations that was formed in 1961 with a 24-country membership and that is located in

Paris, France. Members are committed to helping developing countries, working toward economic growth, and increasing world trade.

President

In Canada, Sweden, Switzerland, and the United States, this title is usually given to the chief executive of the company.

Price

Share price on June 30, 1998. For companies with multiple share classes, the price of the class with the largest number of shares outstanding is listed.

Price/Book Ratio

A company's share price on June 30, 1998, divided by the book value per share of its most recent fiscal year-end. The P/B ratio is used by investors to gauge how a company is valued by the marketplace in relation to the book value of its assets.

Price/Earnings Ratio

A company's share price on June 30, 1998, divided by the earnings per share of its most recent fiscal year-end. The P/E ratio is a standard measure in examining a company's market valuation in relation to its earnings.

Pro-Forma Earnings

A term that applies to a recently merged company's results. It is the results that the company would have achieved had it been in its combined form throughout the full period covered by a financial report.

Real Estate Investment Trust (REIT)

A trust that invests in a variety of real estate, either through outright ownership of properties or through mortgages or both. REITs are managed by one or more trustees, in the manner of a mutual fund, and trade like a stock. No federal income tax has to be paid by the trust if 75% of the income is real-estate-related and 95% of the income is distributed to investors. Individual investors can be taxed.

Return on Equity (ROE)

A measure of how much a company earns on the investment of its shareholders. It is calculated by dividing a company's net income by its common shareholders' equity.

Revenue

Money earned by business activities.

For banks, revenue includes interest income plus other operating income such as commissions, fees, and foreign-exchange income.

For insurance companies, revenue includes premiums, investment income, and other operating income.

For real estate companies, revenue includes net rental income, property sales, fees, and commissions.

For securities companies, revenue includes investment income and income from asset-management activities, including fees, commissions, and other service charges.

Sales

Net sales of goods and services, or gross sales less returns, discounts, and allowances.

Securities and Exchange Commission

The federal agency that enforces securities laws and sets standards for disclosure about publicly traded securities, including mutual funds. It was created in 1934 and consists of five commissioners appointed by the President and confirmed by the Senate to hold staggered terms. Abbreviated as SEC.

Security

A financial instrument that indicates the holder owns a share or shares of a company (stock) or has loaned money to a company or government organization (bond).

SEDOL

Stock Exchange Daily Official List number. This seven-digit number is an identifier assigned by the International Stock Exchange in London to issues that trade on stock exchanges throughout the world.

Soft Landing

A slowdown in economic growth to a pace that contains inflation without tipping a nation into recession.

Spinoff

The distribution to a company's shareholders of the stock in a division or subsidiary.

Stock-Index Futures

A contract that obliges the holder to buy or sell the cash value of a stock index by a specified date.

Stock-Index Options

An agreement that gives its holder the right, but not the obligation, to buy or sell a specified amount of an underlying investment a stock-index futures contract or the cash value of a stock-index by a given date at a given price.

Stock Option

An agreement allowing an investor to buy or sell shares of stock within a stipulated time and for a certain price. Also, a means of employee compensation that gives workers the right to buy the company's stock during a specified period of time at a stipulated exercise price.

Stock Split

A change in a company's number of shares outstanding that doesn't change a company's total market value, or each shareholder's percentage stake in the company. Additional shares are issued to existing shareholders, at a rate expressed as a ratio. A 2-for-1 stock split, for instance, doubles the number of shares outstanding. The stock price is adjusted accordingly; in a 2-for-1 split, for example, the stock price after the split is half of what it was before. Investors will own two shares after the split for each share they owned before the split, but they will hold the same proportion of the outstanding stock as they did before.

Ticker

The stock-exchange identifier assigned to each issue traded on United States or Canadian stock exchanges.

Ton(s) / Tonne(s)

A ton is 2,000 pounds or 907.18 kilograms, also known as a short ton. A tonne is a metric ton and is equivalent to 2,204.6 pounds. or 1,000 kilograms.

Total Return

A security's total return reflects both the capital appreciation of the security (higher or lower price) and the income that it pays out from interest or dividends. In the case of mutual funds, shareholders must reinvest the income and capital-gains distributions to match the fund's published total return.

United States Bureau of the Census

The Census Bureau is the preeminent collector and provider of the official statistics pertaining to the people and the economy of the United States. This involves the full range of activities required to produce data, including survey and instrument design and data collection, processing, and dissemination. Population data in this guide were provided by the United States Bureau of the Census, International Data Base.

World Bank

An organization created to make loans, primarily in developing countries, with the stipulation that the country's government must guarantee the loan. The full name is International Bank for Reconstruction and Development.

World Trade Organization

An arbitration and oversight body created by the General Agreement on Tariffs and Trade (GATT) to oversee the provisions of that pact. The WTO is the successor to the GATT organization, which was created in 1947 to lower trade barriers. The new organization has a more powerful dispute-resolution system that involves three-person arbitration panels. The panels have to follow strict schedules for rendering decisions, and WTO members can't veto the findings, as was the case under GATT. That's a big plus for United States agriculture, for example, which had won GATT rulings against European Union subsidies of soybeans and other produce, only to have the EU block the decisions. Congress approved the GATT agreement in late 1994.

Yield Percent

The ratio of the most recent full year's dividend per share to share price on June 30, 1998.

Alphabetical Index

Alphabetical Index

Alphabetical Index

Alphabetical Index

Alphabetical Index

Alphabetical Index

Alphabetical Index

Alphabetical Index

Alphabetical Index

Alphabetical Index

Alphabetical Index

Alphabetical Index

Alphabetical Index

Alphabetical Index

Industry Index

Industry Index

Industry Index

Industry Index

Consumer, Cyclical

Beverages (All)

Distillers & Brewers

Soft Drinks

Consumer & Household Products & Svcs (All)

Consumer Services

Household Products (All)

Household Products (Durable)

Household Products (Non-Durable)

Industry Index

Food Retailers & Wholesalers

Health Care Providers

Medical Supplies

Pharmaceuticals

Industry Index

Financial

Industry Index

Industry Index

Savings & Loans (U.S. Only)

Securities Brokers

Industry Index

Containers & Packaging

Electrical Components & Equipment

Industry Index

Industry Index

Industrial - Diversified

Industry Index

Industry Index

To receive additional copies of the 1999 edition of the <u>Dow Jones Guide to the Global Stock Market</u> for $34.95, plus $6.00 shipping and handling (domestically), please fill out the following information:

Name _____

Title _____

Company _____

Address _____

City _____ State _____ Postal Code _____

Telephone _____ E-Mail Address _____

If you are mailing this card from outside of the United States, place it in an envelope and send to:
Dow Jones Indexes, Dow Jones & Company, Inc., P.O. Box 300, Princeton, NJ 08543-0300 USA

To receive the Dow Jones Indexes Newsletter, please fill out the following information:

Name _____

Title _____

Company _____

Address _____

City _____ State _____ Postal Code _____

Telephone _____ E-Mail Address _____

☐ Yes, I'd like to receive the Dow Jones Indexes Newsletter

☐ Yes, I'd like to receive a Dow Jones Indexes Newsletter, plus I want to reserve a copy of the 2000 edition of the <u>Dow Jones Guide to the Global Stock Market</u> at a 25% discount (I expect to be billed)

☐ I'd like to reserve my copy of the 2000 edition at a 25% discount (I expect to be billed)

If you are mailing this card from outside of the United States, place it in an envelope and send to:
Dow Jones Indexes, Dow Jones & Company, Inc., P.O. Box 300, Princeton, NJ 08543-0300 USA

BUSINESS REPLY MAIL

FIRST-CLASS MAIL   PERMIT NO. 136   PRINCETON, NJ

POSTAGE WILL BE PAID BY ADDRESSEE

Dow Jones Global Indexes

Dow Jones & Company, Inc.
P.O. Box 300
Princeton, NJ 08543-9963

BUSINESS REPLY MAIL

FIRST-CLASS MAIL   PERMIT NO. 136   PRINCETON, NJ

POSTAGE WILL BE PAID BY ADDRESSEE

Dow Jones Global Indexes

Dow Jones & Company, Inc.
P.O. Box 300
Princeton, NJ 08543-9963